CHINA

A History of the Laws, Manners
and Customs of the People

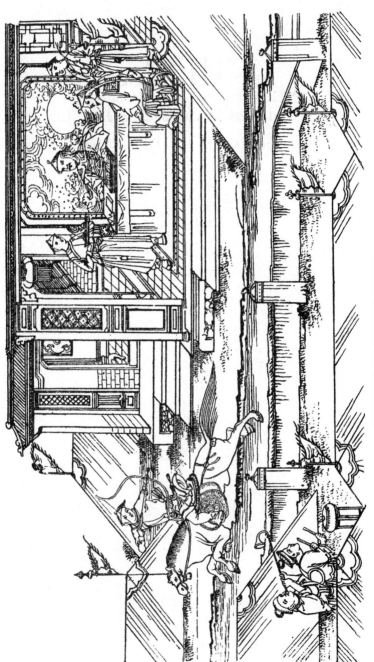

CANDIDATES FOR MILITARY DEGREES.

CHINA

A History of the Laws, Manners and Customs of the People

JOHN HENRY GRAY

Volume I

DOVER PUBLICATIONS, INC.
Mineola, New York

Bibliographical Note

This Dover edition, first published in 2002, is an unabridged reprint in one volume of the two-volume edition published by Macmillan & Co., London, in 1878. Although no plates have been deleted, some have been moved slightly from their original positions and backed up with others to conserve space, while four plates have been moved to more relevant areas of the text.

Library of Congress Cataloging-in-Publication Data

Gray, John Henry, 1828–1890.
    China : a history of the laws, manners and customs of the people / John Henry Gray.
        p. cm.
    Originally published: London : Macmillan, 1878.
    ISBN 0-486-42487-1 (pbk.)
        1. China. I. Title.

DS706 .G69 2002
951—dc21

2002034819

Manufactured in the United States of America
Dover Publications, Inc., 31 East 2nd Street, Mineola, N.Y. 11501

TO

THE RIGHT HONOURABLE

EARL GRANVILLE, K.G.

THESE VOLUMES

WRITTEN DURING A LONG RESIDENCE IN CHINA

ARE MOST RESPECTFULLY INSCRIBED

BY

THE AUTHOR

THE Author of these volumes returned to China in the beginning of last year, and, at his request, I undertook what editorial work seemed necessary in connection with the publication.

W. G. G.

STREATHAM, S.W.
25 *January*, 1878.

CONTENTS.

CHAPTER XIV.

CHAPTER XV.

CHAPTER XVI.

LIST OF ILLUSTRATIONS.

CHINA.

CHAPTER I.

INTRODUCTORY.

In the beginning, so Chinese writers relate, when all was darkness and confusion, there came from a vast mundane egg, which divided itself into two parts, a human being, who is, and has always been known in Chinese annals as Poon-koo Wong. Of the upper portion of the shell, this being formed the heavens, and of the lower part he made the earth. To dispel the darkness by which all was enveloped, he created with his right hand, the sun to rule the day, and with his left hand, the moon to rule the night. He made the stars also. Then he called into existence the five elements of earth, water, fire, metal, and wood.[1] Chinese writers say also that, in order to people the earth, Poon-koo Wong made a cloud of vapour rise from a piece of gold, and a similar cloud from a piece of wood. By breathing on them he gave to the vapour which arose from the gold, a male principle ; and to that which ascended from the wood, a female principle. From the union of these two clouds or spirits, sprang a son and daughter, Ying Yee and Cha-noee ; and the descendants of this pair in due course of time, overspread the whole country. Thus, according to Chinese cosmogony, came into being the land of Han, and its vast population, in other words, the world and its inhabitants. In honour of Poon-koo Wong there are many

---

[1] The five elements denote five innate essences, and the nature of each essence is indicated by its corresponding form of matter.

temples throughout China. The idol of this hero of antiquity is an almost nude figure made of wood or clay. Around the loins is a representation of an apron of leaves. Such, say the Chinese, was his only covering, there being no clothes in those earliest of days.

The *primordia* of all countries are enveloped in much that is obscure and fabulous, and it is extremely difficult for the historian to fix the period when civil history had its beginnings. China is no exception, but there can, I think, be no doubt of the great antiquity of the Chinese Empire. It is not, I believe, rash to say that it has survived a period of four thousand years, without having undergone any great change either in the laws by which it is governed, or in the speech, manners, and customs of its teeming population. It is generally allowed that celestial observations were made at Babylon two thousand two hundred and thirty-four years before the birth of Christ, and such observations are probably the strongest evidence which any nation can produce in support of its claim to antiquity. These were not in any way associated with the history of sublunary events. Those made by the Chinese, on the contrary, have served to mark the events of their national history. They speak of an eclipse calculated in their country two thousand one hundred and fifty-five years before Christ. That this eclipse really took place was proved by the calculations of the missionaries of the order of Jesus, who visited China in the sixteenth century. Gaubil, one of the early Roman Catholic missionaries to China—a man pre-eminently distinguished for his mathematical attainments —examined a series of thirty-six eclipses to which allusion is made in the writings of Confucius. After careful examination he concluded that of these thirty-six eclipses only two were false, and two uncertain. The correctness of the remaining thirty-two, he considered established beyond all reasonable doubt. The chronology of the Chinese, however, extends considerably beyond the first of these eclipses, and is substantiated by satisfactory evidence as far back as the reign of the Emperor Yaou. From the time of this sovereign, the history of China begins to assume the appearance of truth, whereas the account of all preceding reigns is clouded with fable and uncertainty.

To this large and ancient Asiatic Empire, many names are given by its inhabitants. The principal are Tchung Kwock, and Tien Chu. The term Tchung Kwock or Middle Kingdom, was given to the country on the arrogant supposition that it is the grand central kingdom of the globe around which all the other petty states are arranged as so many different satellites. Tien Chu is the term in which the nation sets forth its heavenly origin in contradistinction to the inferior genesis of all other earthly states. By the tribes who dwell between China and the eastern shores of the Caspian Sea, the country is called Cathay, or the Flowery Land ; and as, before the discovery of the Cape of Good Hope, the highway from Europe to China lay through these countries, this was the name Europeans became acquainted with. The word China is said to be derived from the name of an emperor of the short-lived dynasty of Tsin. This emperor, who was named Ching Wong, is said in Chinese annals to have been one of the greatest heroes of whom China, or indeed, any other land can boast. He extended his conquests over the countries immediately contiguous to the western frontier of his kingdom, and he drove the Tartar tribes in the north, back to their mountain fastnesses, and completed the construction of the Great Wall of China to prevent their incursions in future. This monarch is said to have died about two hundred years before Christ, so that the Great Wall of China may be considered to be more than two thousand years old. It can never have been of any great use, except in checking the predatory raids of the nomadic tribes of Tartary. It is fifteen hundred miles long, and so extensive a line could with difficulty be protected at all points. It is now merely regarded as a monument of great labour and antiquity.

China proper lies between 18° and 41° north latitude. It has its eastern extremity, where it borders on the Corea, marked by 124° east longitude, while its western boundary, where it borders on the Burmese Empire and Western Thibet, is cut by 98° east longitude. Thus it may be regarded as the greatest compact country in the world, as it incloses an area of upwards of one million three hundred thousand square miles. Of this vast extent of surface, one side only is entirely washed by the ocean.

The sea-board, however, extends over two thousand five hundred English miles. It includes many bays and estuaries, so studded with islands, that one of the most favourite and appropriate titles of the Emperor, is "the Sovereign of the ten thousand isles." The ocean by which this vast coast is washed, is divided into four sections. The portion of sea between Cochin China and the island of Hainan is called the Tonquin Gulf; that between Hainan and Formosa, is known as the China Sea; that which stretches from the north cape of Formosa along the shores of the respective provinces of Fo-kien, Che-kiang, and Kiang-soo is called the Eastern Sea; and the front section which runs thence to the Corea, the Yellow Sea. As these seas, which form the southern and eastern boundaries of the empire, abound with shoals and banks—the most famous of which are the Pratas and the Paracelles—navigation is attended with no ordinary degree of risk and danger.

Of the oceans or seas of China, what are held to be the north, south, east, and west seas are regarded as objects worthy of adoration. They are worshipped by the officials at each vernal and autumnal equinox, and sacrifices are offered on these occasions. The ceremony of worshipping the eastern sea is performed at Loi-chow, a prefectoral city in the province of Shan-tung; the western ocean is worshipped at Wing-tsi, a country or district city in the province of Shen-si; the southern ocean at Polo, in the province of Kwang-tung; and the northern ocean at Man-chow, in the prefecture of Shing-king, which is beyond the great wall of China.

In 1725, the second year of his reign, the Emperor Yung Ching conferred titles and other honours upon the four dragons, which the Chinese suppose to inhabit these oceans. In honour of Hin Yan, Ching Hung, Shung Tai, and Tchu Ming—to introduce these dragons by their new names—theatrical representations are, I believe, on no account allowed.

The great political divisions of the country are eighteen provinces, viz., Shang-tung, Pe-cheli, Shan-si, and Shen-si in the north; Kwang-tung and Kwang-si in the south; Che-kiang Fo-kien and Kiang-soo in the east; Kan-soo, Sze-chuen, and Yun-nan in the west; and Ngan-hui, Kiang-si, Hoo-nam,

Hoo-peh, Ho-nam, and Kwei-chow, which may be regarded as the midland provinces.

Of these provinces Sze-chuen is the largest, Che-kiang the smallest, and Kwang-tung, from its almost tropical position, one of the most fertile. Each province is sub-divided into poos, districts, or counties, and prefectures or departments. A poo, the capital of which is a market town, consists of a number of towns and villages; a district or county, the capital of which is a walled city, consists of a number of poos; a prefecture or department, the capital of which is also a walled city, consists of a number of districts or counties, and a province, the capital of which is also a walled city, consists of a number of prefectures. The eighteen provinces of China Proper, in their collective capacity, contain upwards of four thousand walled cities, Pekin (which though a royal city, and the seat of the central government, is without exception the dirtiest place I ever entered) being the capital. The cities which rank next to the capital in point of importance, though vastly superior to it in almost every respect, are Nankin, Soo-chow, Hang-chow, and Canton. The market towns and villages of this vast empire are also very numerous.

The walls by which each county, and prefectoral, and provincial capital city is inclosed are from thirty to fifty or sixty feet high. Those by which Pekin is surrounded are in appearance by far the most imposing. In many instances, however, the walls of Chinese cities are undertakings of great magnitude, and are remarkable, both for the extent of their circumference and for their massive appearance, their width affording space sufficient for two carriages travelling abreast.

Thus, for example, those which inclose the city of Nankin are eighteen English miles in circumference. At all events, it took me six hours to walk round them; and I walked, without stopping once, at a rate exceeding three miles per hour. The walls of Chinese cities are castellated, and provided with embrasures for artillery, and loop holes for musketry. At frequent intervals there are watch-towers and barracks for the accommodation of troops. On the top of the ramparts in some places are piled large stones, which in times of

tumult or war are thrown upon the heads of assailants. Such
stones are not by any means despicable missiles. At the commencement of the last war which England, in alliance with
France, waged against China, some soldiers of Her Majesty's
59th Regiment were killed by them in the vicinity of the
Tai-ping gate of Canton. This primitive mode of warfare
belongs rather to the days when, as Plutarch relates, Pyrrhus
was killed at Argos by a tile thrown by a woman, than to
the nineteenth century; or to those still more remote, when
Abimelech, the unworthy son of Gideon, met his death at
Thebez from a fragment of a millstone, which in this case
also a woman's hand had thrown. In consequence of their
great antiquity, the walls of many of the northern cities
are neglected and dilapidated. Those by which the more
important and wealthy cities are inclosed, are in a very
perfect condition, and as a matter of course receive constant
attention. Owing to their great antiquity, however, portions
of them not unfrequently give way with a great crash. The
walls of Canton have to my own knowledge given way
at different points, on two or three occasions. Thus in the
month of June, 1871, a portion of the west wall of the city,
which was very old, and had become saturated with recent
heavy rains, suddenly gave way, and buried in its ruins seven
dwelling-houses. Fortunately the occupants had betaken themselves to other dwelling-houses.

At the north, south, east, and west sides of each Chinese
city, there are large folding gates of great strength. These are
further secured by equally massive inner gates. Each of the
principal outer gates of the city of Nankin is strengthened
by three such inner gates. Of the gates of a Chinese city, the
one which is held in honour above all others is that at
the south. Through the south gate, or gate of honour, which is
especially regarded as the emperor's gate, all officials coming
to the city to hold office enter; and when they vacate office, it
is by the same gate that they depart. No funeral procession
is allowed to pass through this gate, and the same prohibition excludes the bearers of night-soil, or of anything which
is regarded as unclean. The south gate of the capital of the

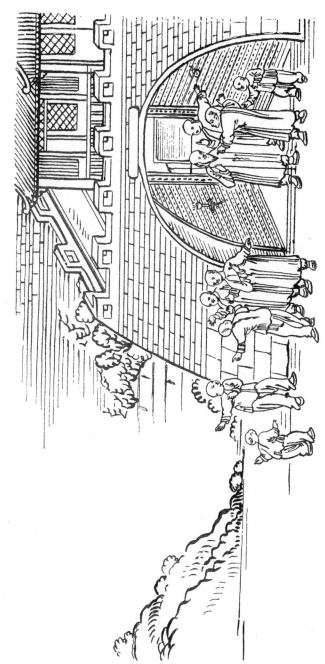

A GOVERNOR LEAVING HIS SHOE AT THE GATE OF A CITY ON HIS DEPARTURE.

empire, is regarded as so sacred, that as a rule, it is kept closed, and only opened when the emperor has occasion to pass that way.

The streets of cities, towns, and villages are generally wider in the northern than in the southern provinces of the empire. Those of Pekin are very broad. Indeed in this respect they equal those of European cities. The narrowness of the streets in the south of China gives them the great advantage of coolness during the summer months. Many of them are so narrow as to shut out in a great measure the rays of a hot tropical sun; and in some instances they are partially covered over during the hot season by the residents, with canvas, matting, or thin planks of timber. Many of the towns, also, in the north of Formosa, are protected in this way. The pathways which run in front of the shops are arched over, and as they are frequently constructed in the form of rude arcades, it is possible to pass from one part of the town to another, without exposing oneself to the sun or rain. Between the footpaths that are covered in this way, there is a thoroughfare for sedan chairs and beasts of burden. It appeared to me, however, that this centre thoroughfare is more generally used as a public dust-bin than as a street. The shopkeepers are in the habit of throwing into it all sorts of refuse, which is not so speedily removed by the scavengers of the town as it ought to be. Manka, which is one of the principal towns in the north of Formosa, is above all others remarkable for the arrangements of its streets after this fashion. At Hoo-chow, a prefectoral city in the province of Che-kiang, I passed through two streets which were constructed in the form of arcades, which are not however so perfect as those of Manka. The streets of Chinese cities are paved with granite slabs, bricks, or paving stones. Those of the city of Canton are paved with granite slabs. The streets of the city of Soo-chow— so long famous for the wealth of its citizens— are in some cases paved with granite slabs, and in others with paving-stones.

Under the streets of Chinese towns there are conduits into which the rain percolates as it falls through the chinks between the granite slabs. Where the streets are paved with paving stones, there are channels or gutters on either side; these,

however, are so narrow as to prove of little or no service, so
that they become pools of filth from which there is a fearful
stench in the summer months.   The streets of Pekin are
macadamised, or supposed to be so.   They are considerably
raised in the centre, so that the rain-water may easily flow
into the conduits on either side.   Road-metal is never laid
on them, however, and in the rainy season they are filthy to
a degree.   In summer, they are so covered with dust as to
render travelling upon them a thing to be avoided.   In the
evening, there is a most intolerable stench ; for the conduits
are then opened, and the stagnant water they contain is scooped
out and scattered broadcast over the streets for the purpose of
laying the dust.   The names which are given to the streets of
Chinese cities are generally very high-sounding.   Thus we have
the Street of Golden Profits ; the Street of Benevolence and
Love ; the Street of Everlasting Love ; the Street of Longevity ;
the Street of One Hundred Grandsons : the Street of One
Thousand Grandsons ; the Street of Saluting Dragons ; the
Street of the Sweeping Dragon ; the Street of the Reposing
Dragon ; the Street of Refreshing Breezes ; the Street of One
Thousand Beatitudes ; the Street of a Thousandfold Peace ; the
Street of Five Happinesses ; the Street of Ten Thousand
Happinesses ; the Street of Ninefold Brightness ; the Street of
Accumulated Goodness.   Other streets are simply numbered, as
First Street, Second Street, Third Street, and so on.

The shops of which the streets of Chinese cities are formed,
and which are built of bricks, are of various sizes.   They are
entirely open in front.   There is, however, no rule without an
exception ; and many of the shops at Pekin are provided with
glass windows.   I saw them also in the banking establishments
in Soo-chow.   These glass windows, however, are remarkably
mean, and they will not bear comparison with the windows which
add so much to the beauty and finish of the shops in the finer
streets of English towns.   At the door of each shop stand two
or more long sign-boards, upon each side of which are painted
in neat, bold letters in gold, vermilion, or other gay colours, the
name of the "hong" and the various commodities which it contains for sale.   The name of the hong or shop consists of two

characters. In some instances a shopkeeper places above the door of his shop a small sign-board resembling in form some particular article which he has for sale. Thus a collarmaker has a sign made in the form of a collar ; a hosier's sign resembles a stocking; a bootmaker's a boot, and a spectaclemaker's a pair of spectacles. In some cases the signs are not shaped to represent the articles, but representations of these, such as hats, fans, and even sticking-plaisters are painted on them. Some shopkeepers not satisfied with having sign-boards suspended from the side-posts of the doors of their shops, seek to make themselves still better known by painting their names and the wares in which they deal in large characters on the outer walls of the cities in which they reside. On the walls of the cities of Tang-yang and Chang-chow, on the banks of the Grand Canal, I observed this to be especially the case. Boards on which are recorded the names of each person residing in the house are also, in compliance with law, placed on the entrance door or outer wall of each dwelling-house. This custom appeared to me to be much more observed in the rural districts than in the cities and towns. Above the entrance-door of each shop hang lanterns ; and, from the roof, lamps of glass or horn upon which are gaily-coloured representations of birds, flowers, gardens, temples. These innumerable, bright-painted sign-boards and lanterns give a Chinese street a most cheerful and animated appearance. The streets of Canton which, in this respect, are most conspicuous, are the Chaong-tan Kai ; the Chong-yune-fong; the Tai-sing Kai ; the Sue-sze-tai Kai ; the Koo-tai Kai ; the Shaong-mun tai ; the Wye-oi Kai ; and the Tai-fat-sze-cheen.

The shops are not distributed indiscriminately throughout Chinese towns, as is the case to a large extent in European cities. They are confined to certain quarters, and even in the streets appropriated to them, they do not occur promiscuously. Each branch of trade has its special place to which it is usually restricted. On each side of a street we should generally find shops of the same kind. Near the entrance of his shop, the master is often seated waiting with much patience for the arrival of customers. No female members of the tradesman's family reside in apartments either above or behind the shop. In the evening, therefore, when the shutters have been put up, the trades-man hastens to his home in the more retired parts of the town, leaving his stock in charge of his assistants and apprentices.

The streets in which the gentry reside, consist generally of well-built houses, which, like the majority of houses in China, are of one story only. They extend, however, a considerable distance to the rear, and are so large and spacious as to be capable of containing a great number of persons. They are approached by large folding-doors. As the walls which front the streets are without windows, they present, in many cases, the appearance of encampments. Detached houses—of which there are many—bear a very striking resemblance to encampments. This is particularly true of the houses of the gentry who reside in the cities of Soo-chow, Yang-chow, Hang-chow, and Hoo-chow ; and it has often struck me in my peregrinations through the provinces of Kiang-si and Kiang-soo. Chinese houses have no fire-places. In the cool season, therefore, the occupants have to keep themselves warm by wearing additional clothing, or by means of portable brass or earthenware vessels in which charcoal embers are kept burning. Owing to the houses and shops which form its streets not being generally of the same height, or arranged in a direct line, a Chinese town or village looks very irregular. This irregularity is due to the fact that the houses are built according to the principles of geomancy, which do not admit of the ridge beams of each house in a street being placed in a direct line. Were they so placed, evils of various kinds would, it is said, be the inevitable result.

In the cities of Pekin, Cheefoo, Nankin, Shanghai, and other northern and midland towns, there are public baths. These in-stitutions are evidently built more for utility than show, and are most unassuming and unprepossessing erections. They are ap-parently, one and all, hot baths, warmed by means of furnaces. The vapour fills the bath-rooms, and gives them not merely the ap-pearance, but the properties of sweating-rooms. In some Chinese towns, so soon as the bath is ready, the proprietor advertises the fact by means of a servant who walks through the streets beating a well-toned gong, which he carries by his side. This plan was,

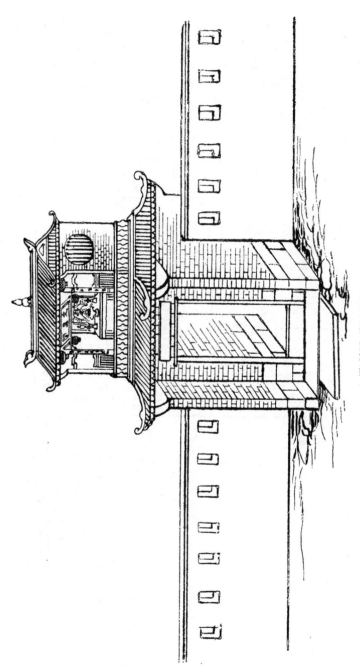

A WALLED VILLAGE.

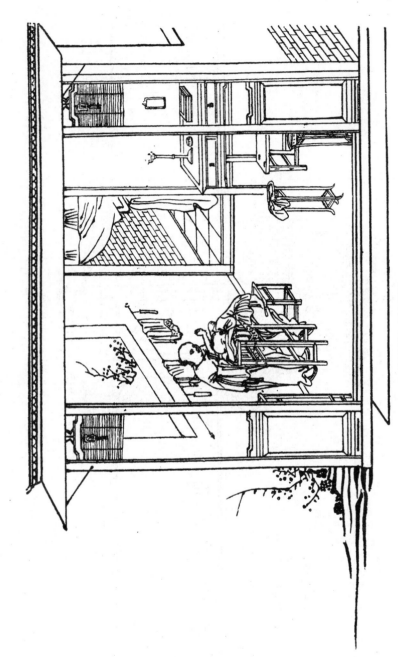

A SHAMPOOER AT WORK.

I noticed, especially practised by bath proprietors in the market town of Cheefoo. To each bathroom is attached an ante-chamber. This is used as an undressing-room, and servants take charge of the clothes of the bathers. On the walls of the ante-chamber of the public baths at Nankin were painted in large Chinese characters several moral sentences very much as follows:—Honesty is the best policy; Do to your neighbour as you would have him do to you, &c., &c.

The streets or squares of Chinese cities are not adorned like the streets and squares of European cities, with stone, marble or bronze statues of the great, the brave, and the learned. In nearly all the principal cities of China there are, however, monumental arches erected in honour of renowned warriors, illustrious statesmen, distinguished citizens, learned scholars, virtuous women, or dutiful sons or daughters. In some instances such monuments are built of brick, in others of marble, in others of old red sandstone, but more generally of granite. A Chinese monument of this nature consists of a triple arch or gateway, that is, a large centre gate, and a smaller gateway on each side. On a large polished slab, which is placed above the middle gateway, are figures done in sculpture, or Chinese characters setting forth the object with which the citizens, by imperial permission, erected the arch.

Some of these monuments are built in the form of pavilions, or domes supported by granite columns. One of the largest monumental arches in China of which I have heard is in the city of Toong-ping Chow, in the province of Shan-tung. It is in honour of a learned scholar named Laong How, who, at the age of eighty-two years, succeeded in taking the very first place on the tripos list at the examination for the Han-lin, or doctor's degree. This arch, which is constructed of granite, and elaborately sculptured, was erected during the Tai-sung dynasty. The inscription on the slab, which is placed above the grand or centre arch, refers to the scholastic attainments, not only of Laong How, but of his son, who, it appears, had, three years prior to the success of his father, obtained precisely similar honours. The city, however, which is apparently conspicuous above all others for ornamental arches is that of Hoo-chow Foo, in the province of

Che-kiang. As the excursionist enters this city by the south gate, an imposing sight, produced by these arches, meets his view. They span a portion of the Tai-naur Kai, or great south street of the city, and are placed in such close proximity to one another as to make this thoroughfare worthy of the name of the street of arches. Each of them is of vast dimensions and richly sculptured. These arches are all in honour of men who were born, and who lived and died in the prefecture of Hoo-chow. Two of them are in honour of a father and his son who had attained high literary honours. On another are recorded the names of thirteen men, natives of Hoo-chow, who, in one and the same year obtained at Pekin almost the highest honours which are offered by the Chinese government to stimulate the *literati* of the country. The only monument I saw in the form of a pavilion or dome, is at Choo-loong-shan, a suburban district of the city of Woo-see Hien, on the banks of the Grand Canal. It is in honour of certain members of the Wha family, who had successfully graduated in honours. Again, the only monumental arch I saw made of earthenware, stands in the vicinity of Yan-chow Foo, on the banks of the Poyang Lake. It was erected, I believe, to perpetuate the memory of a woman conspicuous by her virtue.

To save their cities from destructive fires, the Chinese observe many necessary precautions. In the streets of many of their cities wells are sunk, which are called Taiping-tsieng, or great peace wells. They are large and contain abundant supplies of water, and over the mouth of each a stone slab is placed, which is only removed when any of the neighbouring houses is on fire. It is provided by law, that there shall be placed in various parts of a Chinese city, large tubs to be kept at all times full of water. On the sides of each of these vessels, are written in large Chinese letters the words " peace tubs," or cisterns. On the tops of the houses also it is not unusual for the Chinese to place earthenware jars containing water, so that they may always have at hand sufficient water to enable them to suppress incipient fires. In each large city there are several fire brigades, maintained entirely by contributions on the part of the citizens. The fire engines, water buckets, and lanterns which belong to them, are kept, as a rule, in the different temples of the city; and each brigade is distinguished by a peculiar name. To each guild a fire brigade is attached, and the expenses of the brigade are defrayed by the members of the guild. The officers and men of the brigade are provided with a distinctive uniform or dress, and on their hats are recorded in large Chinese characters the name or number of their brigade, and the words Kow-fo or fire extinguisher.

Besides these provisions by the citizens themselves for the purpose of checking or putting out fires, the members of the local government of each city are called upon to render their assistance. By way of illustration let me take Canton. Each magistrate of the city has in his service several men, whose duty it is, on the occasion of a fire, to prevent robberies. Thus the Kwong-hip, or commandant of the Chinese garrison in Canton, has under him, besides others, eighty men, of whom twenty are to assist in preventing robberies when a fire takes place, and sixty to assist in putting out the fire. Of these men, forty are stationed at the Five Genii gate of the city, and forty in the western suburb. Under the immediate command of the governor there are two hundred men, whose duty in a great measure consists in helping firemen to subdue conflagrations. Throughout the city of Canton there are forty-eight guard houses, and from each of these, in the event of a fire, two men are told off to hasten to the scene. At the close or commencement of each succeeding month throughout the year, the provincial judge and the provincial treasurer, both of whom are very high officials, are supposed to inspect all the government servants whose duty it is to assist in putting out fires. Once more, with the view of making all Chinese officials active in the discharge of these duties, it is enacted that, in the case of eighty houses being destroyed by fire, all the officers of the city in which the conflagration occurred shall be degraded in rank one step; and that in the case of ten houses being destroyed the matter shall be reported to the central government at Pekin. A few days after a conflagration the members of each respective fire brigade which was present on the occasion, receive as an acknowledgment of their good services roast pigs, jars of wine, and small sums of money. The men to whom is assigned the dangerous duty of holding the hoses attached to the engines, receive on such occasions extra rewards. Wounded firemen are remunerated according to the nature of their wounds. The Chinese are, in my opinion, most excellent firemen. They very quickly arrive at the scene of action, and, as a rule, they are most prompt in extinguishing the flames. They are also very daring. During the late war between Great Britain and China, when Canton was set on fire by bomb shells from Sir M. Seymour's guns, I observed from the top of the British factory the various fire brigades steadily persevering in their attempts to subdue the flames, in the face of a constant fire of shot and shell.

Persons who, through carelessness or otherwise, are the cause of fires, are, when caught, severely punished. I remember a large fire occurring in the month of May, 1866, at Honam, a suburb of the city of Canton. The fire originated in consequence of the carelessness of three women, and upon being apprehended they were exposed for several days in cangues or wooden collars at the gates of a temple in honour of the Queen of Heaven. In the month of August, 1871, I saw a respectable druggist named Wong Kwok-hing exposed in a cangue or wooden collar, at the end of the Tung-hing Kai, a street in the south-western suburb of Canton. To the carelessness of this druggist a fire was attributed, which, in the preceding month of March, had destroyed upwards of forty houses. The unfortunate man was daily exposed in this degrading manner for a whole month.

But it is not necessary in these introductory remarks to give a detailed description of the characteristic features and municipal arrangements of Chinese cities and towns. These will frequently come before the reader in the course of this work.

The population of China is now estimated at a very high figure. In 1743 it did not, according to Grosier, exceed two hundred millions of souls. At a census which was taken during the reign of Kien-lung Wong, in the latter half of the sixteenth century, the population, according to the returns which were forwarded by each province to the central government at Pekin, amounted to 307,467,000 souls. According to a census taken by the Chinese in 1813, the population was 360,279,897; and in 1842, according to Sacharoff, it had reached the stupendous figure of 414,686,994. This seems almost incredible. There is no doubt, however, that this vast empire is densely populated in perhaps the majority of its districts. During the rebellion which disturbed the peace of China from 1847 to 1862, there was probably a considerable decrease of the population. Innumerable cities, towns, and villages were then reduced [1] to ruinous heaps, and the inhabitants put to the sword.

Of the moral character of the people, who have multiplied until they are " as the sand which is upon the sea shore," it is very difficult to speak justly. The moral character of the Chinese is a book written in strange letters, which are more complex and difficult for one of another race, religion, and language to decipher than their own singularly compounded word-symbols. In the same individual virtues and vices, apparently incompatible, are placed side by side. Meekness, gentleness, docility, industry, contentment, cheerfulness, obedience to superiors, dutifulness to parents, and reverence for the aged, are in one and the same person, the companions of insincerity, lying, flattery, treachery, cruelty, jealousy, ingratitude, avarice, and distrust of others. The Chinese are a weak and timid people, and in consequence, like all similarly constituted races, they seek a natural refuge in deceit and fraud. But examples of moral inconsistency are by no means confined to the Chinese, and I fear that sometimes too much emphasis is laid on the dark side of their character—to which St. Paul's well-known description of the heathen in his own day is applicable—as if it had no parallel amongst more enlightened nations. Were a native of the empire, with a view of acquiring a thorough knowledge of the English people, to make himself familiar with the records of our police and other law courts, the transactions that take place in what we call the " commercial world," and the scandals of what we term " society," he would probably give his countrymen at home a very one-

---

[1] Of the correctness of this statement I had ample and painful evidence when travelling through the central provinces in 1865-66.

sided and depreciatory account of this nation. Moreover, we must remember that we are in possession of the innumerable blessings of Christianity. Where they do not take refuge in the indifference of atheism, the Chinese are the slaves of grossly superstitious religions; and designing priests, geomancers, fortune-tellers, and others, endeavour by cunning lies and artifices to keep them in a state of darkness worse than Egyptian. Under the political and social conditions of their existence, it is extraordinary what an amount of good is to be found in their national character. Their religion is a mass of superstitions. Their government is, in form, that which of all others is perhaps most liable to abuse—an irresponsible despotism. Their judges are venal; their judicial procedure is radically defective, and has recourse in its weakness to the infliction of torture; their punishments are—many of them—barbarous and revolting; their police are dishonest, and their prisons are dens of cruelty. A considerable mass of the population does not know how to read,[1] and nearly everywhere there is a prejudiced ignorance of all that relates to modern progress. Their social life suffers from the baneful effects of polygamy, and, to a certain extent, of slavery, and their marriage laws and customs hold woman in a state of degrading bondage. This is a grave bill of indictment against the religious, political, civil, and social institutions of any nation; and yet, notwithstanding conditions so little favourable to the development of civil and social virtues, the Chinese may be fairly characterised as a courteous, orderly, industrious, peace-loving, sober, and patriotic people.

I quote from an official report on the Tien-tsin massacre, written in 1871, by Mr. G. F. Seward, then American consul at Shanghai:—

"The prevailing tendency among foreigners in China is to debase the Chinese to a very low place in the scale of nations, to belittle their intellectual capacity, to condemn their morals, to declare them destitute of vitality and energy. Each person who argues the case finds facts ready for his use which seem to him to demonstrate his own view.

"I confess that the case is different with me. Faith in the race is a matter of intuition with me. I find here a steady

[1] This remark applies especially to the Hakkas or wandering people.

adherence to the traditions of the past, a sober devotion to the calls arising in the various relations of life, an absence of shiftlessness, an honest and, at least, somewhat earnest grappling with the necessities and difficulties which beset men in their humbler stages of progress, a capacity to moralize withal, and an enduring sense of right and wrong. These all form what must be considered an essentially satisfactory basis and groundwork of national character. Among the people there is practical sense, among the gentry scholarly instincts, the desire for advancement, the disposition to work for it with earnestness and constancy. Amongst the rulers, a sense of dignity, breadth of view, considering their information, and patriotic feeling. Who will say that such a people have not a future more wonderful even than their past? Why may not the wheels of progress and empire roll on until the countries of Asia witness again their course?"

These views are, in the main, I believe, sound; and, as the wheels of progress and empire may be said to be typified in modern days by the wheels of the locomotive, which has invested man with new powers over time and space, it is not unlikely that the hope which Mr. Seward expresses may be fulfilled at no remote period. The first steam locomotive in China already draws its trains in the vicinity of Shanghai. It is more important that Chinese exclusiveness has perceptibly yielded to the repeated assaults made upon it, certainly not always in a Christian spirit, by the Western nations. This exclusiveness and jealousy of foreigners is by no means to be wondered at. During centuries, which take us back to the beginnings of civil history, the Chinese have developed their civilisation and their thoroughly original type of nationality in a region which Nature herself has rendered difficult of access on its landward sides by barriers of mountain, jungle, and desert, and which for all practical purposes was inaccessible on its southern and eastern seaboard, until science converted the separating seas into the world's highways. Prejudices of race are barriers to intercourse of marvellous strength, and are only to be removed by the constant friction of generations. Up to the present time we have been regarded by the " flowery people " as barbarians; and too often in our intercourse with them we have failed—not to speak of graver shortcomings—in courteous

appreciation.   May the Embassy which, now for the first time
China has sent to our shores, mark the nearer approach of days
when the West will be able to communicate, without let or
hindrance, to this venerable Asiatic empire the multiplied
benefits of a civilisation which, as we are too ready to forget, in
boasting of its triumphs, had its earliest developments in the
East.

POON-KOO WONG.

CHAPTER II.

THE form of government of this vast empire is an absolute monarchy. The emperor regards himself as the interpreter of the decrees of Heaven, and he is recognised by the people over whom he rules as the connecting link between the gods and themselves. He is designated by such titles as the Son of Heaven, the Lord of Ten Thousand Years, the Imperial Supreme; and he is supposed to hold communion with the deities at his pleasure, and to obtain from them the blessings of which he, personally, or the nation may stand in need. This mighty monarch is assisted in the administration of the government by a cabinet council, which consists of four great ministers of state. In addition to this council there are six supreme tribunals for the conduct, in detail, of all governmental business These tribunals, which are designated by the general appellation of Loo-poo, are as follows:—First, that which is termed Lee-poo. This office is divided into four departments. In the first of these, officers are selected to fill the various offices which are deemed necessary for the due administration of the affairs of the respective provinces and districts of the Empire. The second takes cognizance of all such officials. The third affixes the seal to all edicts and proclamations; and the fourth keeps a register of the extraordinary merits and good services of distinguished men. The second board or tribunal is named Hoo-poo, and to it is entrusted the care and keeping of the imperial revenue. The third board is named Lee-poo. To it is entrusted the superintendence of all the ancient usages and religious rites of the people, and the preservation of all temples endowed by the imperial government. The fourth board is named Ping-poo. It has the care of all the naval and military establishments throughout the empire. The fifth is called King-poo. It has the supervision of all criminal proceedings. The sixth and last, which is termed Kung-poo, superintends all public works, such as mines, manufactures, highways, canals, bridges, &c. Over each of these tribunals presides a chief minister, or counsellor, whose duty it is to lay the decisions of his particular board before the cabinet council of four great ministers of state. When the decisions of the boards have been thoroughly discussed by the cabinet, they are submitted with becoming reverence to the notice of his imperial majesty. The power of these ministers, however, is almost nominal, as the emperor regards himself as responsible to none but the gods, whom he is supposed to represent. The people are thus in the hands of the emperor as children in the hands of a parent. But though there is outwardly a contempt manifested by the emperor for any or every suggestion which may be made to him by his ministers, there can be no doubt that, in private, much heed is given by his majesty to the advice of all confidential servants of the State. Very few, indeed, of the sovereigns of China have been sufficiently endued with the wisdom of this world to be able to rule without the counsel or advice of others. The sanction of the emperor to all laws and edicts is conveyed by a seal, and all remarks made by his majesty are recorded in letters of red, by what is styled the vermilion pencil.

Besides the various councils there are two others—the Too-cha-yun, and the Tsung-pin-fow. The former is a board of censors. The censors are supposed to attend the meetings of the board or councils already described, to ascertain whether or not intrigues or plots are being concocted to weaken the stability of the government. Members of this board are not unfrequently sent into the provinces to ascertain how matters of business are being conducted there. Spies are sometimes sent by the

censors to different parts of the Empire for the purpose of scru-
tinizing the public and private conduct of any official or officials
upon whom suspicion may rest. Of these emissaries the local
authorities and principal citizens of all large and influential
cities stand in great awe. His Excellency An, a commissioner
from this board, arrived at Canton in the autumn of the year
1862, and suddenly placed under arrest several unsuspecting
officials and citizens of distinction; and in obedience to his
orders some of them, including the notorious Chong Shun and
Too Pat, were executed in a most summary manner.

In the *Pekin Gazette* of November 12th, 1871, a statement
was published—translated in the *China Mail* of December 23rd,
1871—to the effect that a censor had brought to the imperial
notice a case of triple murder, in which a native of Chekiang
was the complainant. The petitioner stated that his brother
was intercepted on his way from market to purchase peas, and
was surrounded, on account of an old grudge, by a family of
four brothers, with the assistance of two outsiders. Two men
who were carrying the peas were killed on the spot. The
murderers then carried off the petitioner's brother to their house,
where they confined him, and afterwards put him to death by
the sword. The matter was reported to the then district
magistrate Ng, but, in consequence of the Taiping rebellion,
it could not be investigated. Ng's successor in the magistracy,
To by name, had the offenders arrested; but through the
artful device of an underling who had been bribed, they were
set at large. Emboldened by their liberation, the murderers
disentombed the coffins, and mutilated the remains of the
deceased, with a view to the destruction of all means of identification. For this offence another magistrate, Wong, sent out
officers to arrest them, but the police were resisted. The successor of this magistrate ordered the military to assist in
the apprehension of the murderers, but they managed to make
their escape. The matter had been allowed to remain in
abeyance for fourteen years, although three lives were concerned.
The perfect had been petitioned twenty-five times, the inten-
dant of the circuit nine times, the governor once, and the
governor-general once, and yet the complainant had not been

able to obtain redress. Reference had invariably been made
to the magistrate to have the murderers arrested, but they were
allowed to enjoy their ease at home.

The second of these two boards, the Tsung-pin-fow, consists
of six high officials. These keep a register of the births, deaths,
marriages, and relations of the princes of the blood royal, and
report at times upon their conduct. The register in which the
names of the lineal descendants of the imperial family are
recorded is of yellow paper; that in which the names of the
collateral branches are recorded is of red paper. These records
are submitted to the emperor every ten years, on which occasions his majesty confers titles and rewards. These titles are
divided into four classes, the first being hereditary, the second
honorary, the third for services rendered to the State, and the
fourth rewards due to literary attainments. It is imperative
upon the ministers constituting the board of Tsung-pin-fow to
furnish at frequent intervals the various tribunals styled Loo-
poo with reports as to which of the sons of the emperor
possesses in the highest perfection the essential qualifications of
a good sovereign. These reports, like all others, are submitted to
the emperor. The emperor of China has the power of nomin-
ating his successor, whether indeed the person nominated be a
member of the blood-royal family or not. The desire to perpetuate his dynasty scarcely ever admits of the emperor selecting one to fill the throne who is not a member of the reigning
family. As a general rule each emperor is succeeded by his
eldest son. Should the latter be regarded as incapable of administering the affairs of state, the second or third son is called
upon to reign. When the emperor is childless, a selection is
made from a collateral branch of the same dynasty. As in
almost all Chinese families, or clans, the members of the imperial house are very numerous. At one time it was a practice
to give official employment to each of these scions of royalty.
The custom invariably entailed no ordinary degree of trouble
and anxiety on the imperial government by giving rise to con-
spiracies and rebellions, and it was abandoned. Each prince
has now to rest satisfied with the high-sounding, but empty
title of king—a royal rank of which he may be deprived in the

event of any act on his part being deemed beneath the dignity of his family.

The people of China are taught to regard the emperor as the representative of heaven, and the empress as the representative of mother earth. In this position she is supposed to exert an influence over nature, and to possess a transforming power. One of her principal duties is to see that, at stated seasons of the year, worship is duly and reverently paid to the tutelary deity of silkworms. It is also her duty carefully to examine the weaving of the silk stuffs which the ladies of the imperial harem weave and make into garments for certain state idols. The empress is supposed to be profoundly ignorant of all political matters. There are instances on record, however, of empresses of China having manifested the greatest knowledge of these subjects. The present empress-dowager—the mother of the late sovereign, Tung-chee—succeeded, through her curious inquiries into state affairs, in bringing to light a conspiracy of certain members of the cabinet council to depose and murder her son. The principal conspirators were decapitated, whilst others, not so deeply implicated, were sent into perpetual banishment. But besides the empress, the emperor has other wives. These are eight in number, and have the rank and title of queens. These royal ladies are divided into two classes, the first of which consists of three, and the second of five queens. In addition to the wives there are, of course, several concubines.

The choice of an empress, and of queens, turns solely on the personal qualities or attractions of those selected, without any reference whatever to their connections or family reputation. They are selected in the following manner. The empress-dowager with her ladies, or, in her absence, a royal lady who has been invested with authority for the purpose, holds what may not inaptly be termed a "drawing-room," to attend which Tartar ladies and the daughters of bannermen are summoned from various parts of the empire. The lady pronounced to be the *belle* of the assembly is chosen to be in due time raised to the dignity of empress. Those who are placed next in personal attractions are selected for the rank of queens. The daughters of bannermen of the seventh, eighth, and ninth ranks, appear before the empress-dowager, in order that a certain number of them may be appointed to fill the respective offices of "ladies" and women of the bedchamber. This ceremony is, I believe, observed once a year. Queens were chosen for the ancient kings of Persia in a similar manner—to use the words of the book of Esther, in which we find evidence of the practice—" out of the choice of virgins." The young ladies admitted into the imperial *zenana* are, as a rule, daughters of noblemen and gentlemen; but as personal beauty is one of the chief qualifications for the seraglio, the inmates of the palace are, in some instances, women who have been raised from the humbler walks of life. Indeed, a woman of the lower orders of society was, it is said, the mother of the Emperor Hien-fung. She was the keeper of a fruit stall, and being exceedingly fair and beautiful, she on one occasion attracted the attention of the chief minister of state, whilst he was passing in procession through the street in which she resided. Being greatly pleased with her beauty, he obtained for her a home under the imperial roof of Taou-kwang, where in due course she became the mother of the ill-fated sovereign, Hien-fung. I was residing in China when a wife was selected in this way for the late emperor, Tung-chee. The name of their new Empress was made known to the Chinese people by the *Pekin Gazette* of the 11th of March, 1872. The proclamation issued in the names of the two empresses dowager, set forth that a lady named A-lut'ê had been selected to become the kind companion of the emperor, the sharer of his joys, and the partaker of his sorrows. The *Gazette* further informed the people that she was the daughter of Ch'ung Chi, a junior officer in the Hanlin College. His rank, as evidenced by his buttons, corresponded to that of a prefect or ruler of a department. Ch'ung Chi is, as a matter of course, of Mongolian blood. He is also a bannerman of the plain blue banner. He is the son of one Saishanga, an officer of some notoriety in the early part of the previous reign, who lost the favour of his sovereign in 1853, owing to his inability to cope with the Taiping rebellion. In consequence of the defeats which he sustained at the hands of the rebels, he was degraded, and withdrew from public life. In

1861, his private mansion-house in Pekin was confiscated by the government, and converted into the Tsung-li Yamun. He is a man of great learning, having been Chuang-yüan, or first graduate (senior wrangler or senior classic), at the triennial examination for the doctor's degree in 1865. The mother of A-lut'ê is a daughter of the late Tuanhua, Prince of Cheng. This prince was the recognized leader of the anti-foreign party which, towards the close of the reign of Hien-fung, gave so much trouble to the representatives of foreign nations. This party, however, was in the month of November, 1861, most fortunately overthrown by the Prince of Kung, who was upheld by the empress-mother. The leaders of the defeated anti-foreign party were tried and decapitated, and as a mark of imperial favour Tuanhua was permitted to terminate his existence by suicide. In the same issue of the *Pekin Gazette* to which we have alluded was a second decree, appointing three other ladies to be members of his imperial majesty's harem. Of the ladies in question, the first is a daughter of a clerk in the board of punishments ; the second is a daughter of a prefect ; and the third the daughter of Saishanga, the grandfather of A-lut'ê. The ladies of the royal household are under the charge of eunuchs, who are called upon to discharge the usual duties of royal seraglios.

In each of the provinces into which the empire is divided there is a most formidable array of officials, all of whom act directly or indirectly under their respective boards or tribunals. Thus in the province of Kwang-tung,[1] which I venture to select to illustrate the working of the government in each province, there are the following civil mandarins :—viz., a governor-general, a governor, a treasurer, a sub-commissioner, a literary chancellor, a chief justice,—the last four being of equal rank— six *tautais* of equal rank, ten prefects of equal rank, and seventy-two district or county rulers of equal rank. Each of these officials has a council to assist him in the discharge of the duties of his office. Besides these officials, every town and village in the empire has its governing body, so that the number of officials in each province is very great. The various

[1] Kwang-tung has an area computed at more than ninety-seven thousand square miles, and a population estimated at somewhere about nineteen millions.

classes of officers are in regular subordination. Thus, the governing body of a village is subordinate to the ruler of the district or county in which it is situated. The district or county ruler is subject to the prefect of the department of which his district is a part. The prefect is, in turn, subordinate to the *tautai;* the *tautai* to the chief justice or criminal judge, and so on, step by step to the governor-general or viceroy. Each official stands *in loco parentis* to the subordinate immediately below him, while the mandarins are regarded as standing in a paternal relation to the people they rule. The principle pervades all conditions of society down to the humblest subjects of the realm, those who are in the higher walks of life acting the part of parents to those of an inferior grade, while over all is the all-embracing paternity of the emperor.

Chinese officials of certain grades are not allowed to hold office in the provinces of which they are natives, nor are they, without imperial permission, allowed to contract marriages in the provinces in which they have been appointed to hold office. To preclude the possibility of their acquiring too much local influence in the districts, or prefectures, or provinces where they are serving, they are removed, in some instances triennially, and in others sexennially, to other posts of duty. All officers are supposed to be appointed by the emperor on the recommendation of the board of ceremonies, the members of this board being especially regarded as the advisers of his imperial majesty in the bestowal of political patronage. The candidates for office are, or, according to law, ought to be, men who have graduated at the great literary examinations. The members of the board of ceremonies, however, are not at all unwilling, for a consideration, to submit to the notice of his majesty for office the names of men whose literary rank has been bought rather than attained by study. The salaries attached to government offices are very small. This is a system which leads to most scandalous and irregular proceedings. Thus the mandarins of China, though drawing quarterly from the imperial exchequer the smallest possible amount of pay, are enabled, by the accumulated gains of fraud and avarice, to retire from office as men of wealth and substance. They are, and have been for a considerable time past, the very curse of the country, the palmerworm at the root of its prosperity. By their misrule they have plunged this fair land into that deplorable anarchy, confusion, and misery, for which it is now conspicuous amongst nations.

The military mandarins of the province of Kwang-tung are also very numerous. Of this class the Tartar general is of course recognized as the head.

The duties which devolve upon a governor-general, or governor of a province are very arduous. He is responsible to the emperor, who is responsible to the gods, for the general peace and prosperity of his province. It is his duty to take cognizance of all the officials, and to forward triennially to the board of civil appointments at Pekin the name of each officer under his administration, with a short report on his general behaviour. The information is furnished to the viceroy or governor by the immediate superior of each officer. Should the governor-general be accused of any offence, an imperial commission to investigate the charge is at once appointed.

As I shall have occasion to point out more fully afterwards, there are nine marks of distinction by which the rank or position of officials of the Chinese Empire may be readily recognised. A member of the first class, or highest order of rank, wears on the apex of his cap a dark-red coral ball, or button, as it is more generally called. Members of the second class wear a light-red ball or button of the same size. The third class is distinguished by a ball of a light-blue, and the fourth by a ball of a dark-blue colour. An official of the fifth class is recognised by a ball of crystal, whilst a ball of mother-of-pearl is the distinguishing badge of the mandarin of the sixth class. Members of the seventh and eighth classes wear a golden ball, and of the ninth and last class, a silver ball. Each officer may be further distinguished by the decoration of a peacock's feather. This feather is attached to the base of the ball on the apex of his hat, and slopes downward. It is worn at the back. The first of the outer garments worn by an official is a long, loose robe of blue silk, richly embroidered with threads

of gold. It reaches the ankles of the wearer, and is bound round
his waist by a belt. Above this robe is a tunic of violet colour,
which extends a short way below the knees. The sleeves of this
tunic are wide and very long, extending very considerably
over the hands. They are usually folded back over the wrists.
When an official is permitted to approach the imperial presence with the view of conferring with his majesty, or of performing the kow-tow, which in China is the ordinary act of
obeisance, etiquette prescribes that he shall wear the sleeves of
the tunic stretched over his hands. This renders him more
or less helpless. The custom is of ancient origin, and was
adopted to preclude the possibility of any attempt on the life
of the emperor by those whose duties call them occasionally
into his presence. A custom precisely similar prevailed, it
would appear, in the court of Persia. It is thus described by
Mitford in his history of Greece :—

"The court dress of Persia had sleeves so long, that when
unfolded they covered the hand; and the ceremonial required of
those who approached the royal presence to enwrap the hands so
as to render them helpless."

On the breast-plate and back-plate of the tunic of a civil
mandarin there is embroidered in silk, a bird with wings outstretched, standing upon a rock in the midst of a tempestuous
ocean, and gazing at the sun. This bird varies in kind
according to the rank of the wearer. In the chapter on
sumptuary laws, the reader will find a detailed account of the
emblems used to indicate the different ranks of officials. Over
his shoulders each officer wears a short tippet of silk, which is
also richly embroidered, and which, by the device it bears,
indicates the literary rank to which the wearer has attained.
Round his neck there is a long chain of one hundred and eight
balls or beads. It is called the Chu-Chu, and is intended to
remind the wearer of the land of which he is a native. Of the
one hundred and eight beads of which the chain consists,
seventy-two are supposed to represent so many precious stones,
minerals, and metals native to China; and the remaining thirty-
six represent as many constellations or planets which shed their

benign rays on the country. To the left side of this chain are attached two very short strings of smaller beads, supposed to impress upon the mind of the wearer the reverence he owes to his ancestors, and the filial piety at all times due to his parents and guardians. To the right side of the chain is attached a short string of smaller beads, to remind the wearer of the allegiance which he owes to the imperial throne of his country. These robes and decorations of state and office are not confined to officials only. Honorary rank can be purchased, and it is common to see respectable citizens not at all connected with the service of the government attired in costly and magnificent robes, similar in their decorations to those worn by the highest officers of state.

Government residences are provided for all Chinese officials. They are called *yamuns*, and in some cases are very extensive, occupying several acres of land. From the roof of the halls of many of these official residences are suspended richly gilded boards, on which in large Chinese characters are set forth good and excellent words. Some cf these boards are the gifts of succeeding emperors to former occupants who had distinguished themselves by their faithful services. To the *yamuns* are attached public offices for the transaction of business, and to those which are respectively occupied by district rulers, prefects, tautais, chief justices, and revenue commissioners, very extensive prisons are attached.

District rulers, prefects, and chief justices are the officials more particularly appointed to preside in courts for the administration of justice in all cases which may come before them, whether of a civil or criminal nature. Each of these is assisted in the discharge of his duties by a deputy, or deputies. In order, however, to explain fully how justice is administered in China, it is necessary to state that an accused person is first brought before the gentry or elders of his village or district. These punish an offender if his crime be of a minor nature, either by imprisonment in one of the public halls of the village, or by exposing him in a *cangue* for some time at the corner of one of the most frequented thoroughfares of the village, or in the immediate vicinity of the place where the crime was committed. Should the case, however, appear to require the consideration of a higher tribunal, the prisoner, together with the depositions and comments on them, is forwarded by the gentry to the mandarin, or ruler of the poo to which the village belongs. A poo, as I have explained, is a political division of a province, and consists of a number of villages. On the 9th of July, 1873, I was present at an examination of this kind. It was held in the village of Fongchuen, in the county of Pun-yu, and was conducted by the elder of the village. A thief, called Lee Ayune, had been caught the night before in the act of robbing a house. The elders were not satisfied with his confession of that crime, and insisted upon his making a public declaration of all his thefts during the preceding four years. The facts they carefully recorded, and at the close of his examination the prisoner was forwarded, with the depositions, to the ruler of the poo.

Should the mandarin, or ruler of the poo, find that it is within his jurisdiction to punish the prisoner, he does so. Should he decide that the case is one which ought to be submitted to the notice of his superior, he, without delay, sends the prisoner, together with the depositions, and his own comments on them, to the ruler of the district or county of which the poo is a division. The district ruler resides in the county town, which, like all county towns in China, is inclosed by a high castellated wall. Unless the case appears to require the consideration of a higher tribunal, the district ruler deals with it. Otherwise, he sends the prisoner to the prefect of his department. The prefects reside in their respective cities, which are also inclosed by high castellated walls. If the prefect sends the case to a higher tribunal, the prisoner is sent to the provincial capital. Here the provincial or criminal judge, or chief justice as we would term him, has his residence. The chief justice, who only tries those accused of capital offences, submits his decisions to the notice of the governor-general, or governor of the province, as the case may be; and before a sentence of the chief justice can be carried into effect, it is necessary that the criminal should be taken into the presence of the governor-general, or governor, to make an acknowledgment of his guilt.

Until certain questions have been answered by the prisoner in the presence and in the hearing of the governor-general or his deputy, the sentence recorded against his name can neither be ratified nor carried into effect. Should the prisoner stand convicted of treason, or piracy, or highway robbery, the governor-general can order the execution of the prisoner without any reference whatever to the will of the emperor. Should a prisoner, however, be proved guilty either of patricide, or matricide, or fratricide, &c., it is the duty of the governor-general to bring the case under the notice of the members of the board of punishments at Pekin; and the president of this board submits it in turn to the consideration of the members of the cabinet or great council of the nation. In due course it is laid by this august body before the emperor. It is said that his majesty carefully examines the depositions in all such cases before confirming the sentence and ordering the execution. It is also customary for the governor-general or governor to forward to Pekin at the close of each year a register of the names of criminals adjudged worthy of death. These registers are also received by the president of the board of punishments, and forwarded through the cabinet council to the emperor, who inspects each register, and with a vermilion pencil makes a red mark opposite to three or four names on each page. The registers are then returned to the provincial governors in order that the law may take its course with regard to the prisoners against whose names the imperial mark has been placed. On the receipt of the register from the emperor, the execution of these criminal is carried into effect without any loss of time. For the viceroy not to pay peremptory and implicit obedience to the imperial will in all matters would be regarded as highly treasonable. The prisoners whose names have been passed over by the vermilion pencil do not, however, obtain a free pardon. Their names are submitted a second and a third time to the imperial glance. Should they be passed over on the last occasion, the sentence of death is then commuted to transportation for life. In the prefectoral prison at Canton I saw three malefactors whose names had been submitted for the first time to the emperor, and whose good fortune it had been, so far, to escape the extreme penalty of the law. The governor of the prison, who on the occasion was standing by our side, cruelly observed in their hearing that they might not be so fortunate the next time their names were brought under the emperor's notice. One of the malefactors looked thoughtful, but the others, who were evidentl desperadoes, seemed to think it a matter of the most perfect indifference whether they were executed or sent into exile for the period of their natural lives. They would probably have declared themselves in favour of an ignominious death at the hands of the common executioner. Such, however, is not the feeling of Chinese malefactors in general.

I have observed that governors-general or governors of provinces are in certain cases invested with the power of life and death. I may add that before the empire became so disturbed by anarchy and rapine they were the only officials to whom such powers were delegated. Now, however, it is not at all unusual for district rulers to hold commissions by which they are empowered to put to death, without any reference whatever to a higher power, all traitorous and piratical subjects. Thus, when on a visit in 1860 to the district city to Fa-yune, I learned that a few days previous to my arrival not less than thirty rebels had been decapitated under the warrant of the district ruler.

The mode in which trials are conducted in China is startling to all who live in lands where trial by jury is adopted. Trials in Chinese courts of law are conducted by torture. This is carried to such an extent, that people at home can scarcely be expected to give credence to an account of the atrocities of the mandarins in their endeavours to punish vice and to maintain virtue. As in England, however, before the seventeenth century, torture, although actually applied by the administrators of justice, is not the law of the land. The courts in which trials are held are open to the general public ; but the cruelties for which they are notorious have left them deserted by visitors, so that they are now practically courts of justice with closed doors. In former times, moreover, it was usual, on the day of commission, to affix on the outer gates of the *yamun* a calendar or list of the cases to be tried, and of the prisoners' names. This custom has long

JUDICIAL TORTURE.

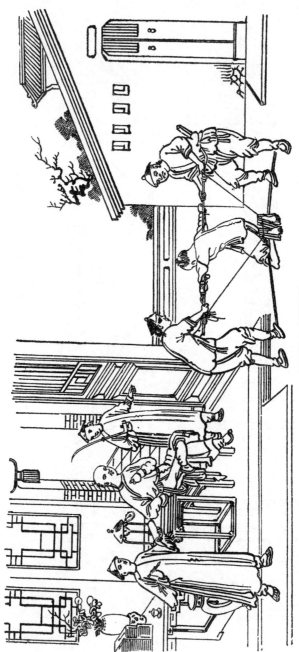

JUDICIAL TORTURE.

been disused, and the calendar is now placed on a pillar in one of the *inner* courts of the yamun, where of course there is no chance of its attracting public attention. The judge when conducting a trial sits behind a large table, which is covered with a red cloth. The prisoner is made to kneel in front of the table as a mark of respect to the court, by whom he is regarded as guilty until he is proved to be innocent. The secretaries, interpreters, and turnkeys stand at each end of the table, no one being allowed to sit but the judge. At the commencement of the trial, the charge is, as in an English court of justice, read aloud in the hearing of the prisoner, who is called upon to plead either guilty or not guilty. As it is a rare thing for Chinese prisoners—mercy being conspicuously absent in the character of their judges—to plead guilty, trials are very numerous. During the course of a trial the prisoner is asked a great many leading questions which have a tendency to criminate him. Should his answers be evasive, torture is at once resorted to as the only remaining expedient.

Let me describe a few of the simplest modes of torture. The upper portion of the body of the culprit having been uncovered, each of his arms—he being in a kneeling posture—is held tightly by a turnkey, while a third beats him most unmercifully, between the shoulders with a double cane. Should he continue to give evasive answers, his jaws are beaten with an instrument made of two thick pieces of leather, sewn together at one end, and in shape not unlike the sole of a slipper. Between these pieces of leather is placed a small tongue of the same material, to give the weapon elasticity. The force with which this implement of torture is applied to the jaws of the accused is in some instances so great as to loosen his teeth, and cause his mouth to swell to such a degree as to deprive him for some time of the powers of mastication. Should he continue to maintain his innocence, a turnkey beats his ankles by means of a piece of hard wood, which resembles a schoolboy's ruler, and is more than a foot long. Torture of this nature not unfrequently results in the ankle bones being broken. Should the prisoner still persist in declaring his innocence, a severer mode of torture is practised. This may be regarded as a species of rack. A large heavy tressel is placed in a perpendicular position, and the prisoner, who is in a kneeling posture, is made to lean against the board of it. His arms are then pushed backwards and stretched under the upper legs of the tressel, from the ends of which they are suspended by cords passing round the thumb of each hand. His legs are also pushed backwards, and are drawn, his knees still resting on the ground, towards the upper legs of the tressel by cords passing round the large toe of each foot. When the prisoner has been thus bound, the questions are again put to him, and should his answers be deemed unsatisfactory, the double cane is applied with great severity to his thighs, which have been previously uncovered. I have known prisoners remain in this position for a considerable time, and the quivering motion of the whole frame, the piteous moans, and the saliva oozing freely from the mouth, afforded the most incontestable evidence of the extremity of the torture. Upon being released from the rack, they are utterly unable to stand. They are therefore placed in baskets and borne by coolies from the court of justice, falsely so-called, to the house of detention on remand. In the course of a few days they are once more dragged out to undergo another examination. Even this torture occasionally fails in extorting a confession of guilt. In all such cases another still crueller torture is enforced. The prisoner is made to kneel under a bar of wood, six English feet in length, and is supported by two upright pillars or posts of the same material. When the back of his neck has been placed immediately under it, his arms are extended along the bar, and made fast by cords. In the hollow at the back of his knee joints is laid a second bar of equal dimensions, and upon this two men place themselves, one at each end, pressing it down by their weight upon the joints of the prisoner's knees, between which and the ground chains are sometimes passed to render the agony less endurable. This bar is occasionally removed from the inner part of the prisoner's knee joints, in order that it may be made to rest on the *tendo Achillis*. When in this latter position, the same amount of pressure is applied to it, with the view of stretching the ankle joints. I have twice witnessed this mode of torturing a culprit, and its severity on both occasions was painfully evident.

But where are the witnesses? exclaims my reader. It would be wrong to say that no witnesses are examined in a Chinese court of justice. It is occasionally possible to see witnesses under examination before these dark tribunals. But as witnesses are also in some instances subjected to torture, it is a matter of no ordinary difficulty for a foreigner who is ignorant of Chinese, to distinguish which of the two unfortunate men kneeling before the judgment seat and receiving castigation is the prisoner, and which is the witness. I remember seeing on one occasion two men kneeling before the tribunal of the ruler of the Namhoi district of Canton. Both of them had chains around their necks, and as they were both occasionally beaten between the shoulders with a double cane, I very naturally concluded at first that they were companions in crime. One of them, however, as it turned out, was suspected of having a perfect knowledge of the guilt of the other, who was upon his trial; and the witness, who was very unwilling to give evidence, received a castigation. In a case of murder which was tried, in 1860, in the same court, two men, father and son, named Kan Wye and Kan Tai-chu, were called upon to bear testimony against the prisoner at the bar. They persistently declared that they were altogether ignorant of the circumstances of the case. This ignorance was regarded by the court as feigned, and they were accordingly beaten and detained in custody. The relatives of these unfortunate witnesses called at my house, and earnestly intreated me to ask the Allied Commissioners, for the city of Canton was then in possession of the English and French troops, to obtain the freedom of Kan Wye and his son. Having heard their statement, I promised to interest myself in the matter. The Allied Commissioners, to whose notice I submitted the case, rendered all the assistance in their power, but without success. The governor-general, to whom they referred the matter, most positively affirmed that it was in the power of the two witnesses to give evidence of a very decided nature in the case. The father and son were frequently examined after this, and on each

occasion they were severely beaten for the tardy manner in which
they gave their evidence. This harsh treatment proved, after a
few months, more than the son could endure, and he died in
the prison. The relatives of the surviving prisoner, who had
attained the ripe age of seventy years, fearing of course that
if his detention in jail were much longer continued he also
would die in prison, urged me to ask the Allied Commissioners
to intercede once more for his liberation. Mr. Commissioner
Pownall was on the occasion of my second appeal most kind,
and requested me to go to the yamun of the magistrate of
Pun-yu in order to confer on the matter with that official in
person. On my arrival at the yamun, I was told that the chief
magistrate had gone from home, and that the hour of his return
was very uncertain. I entered the prison, however, and had an
interview with the old man. Upon approaching him I was not
a little distressed to see that his mouth was much swollen in
consequence of severe blows which had been inflicted on the
preceding day. So swollen were his lips, gums, and tongue,
that it was with great difficulty he held a conversation with the
interpreter who accompanied me. On the following day another
application was made by the Allied Commissioners to the
viceroy for the liberation of the old man. It also was without
success, and in the course of a few weeks from the time of my
interview with him, and a few days after he had received another
severe flogging for declaring that he was unable to give any
evidence, the old man also died in prison.

All foreigners who resided at Canton during the period
that it was in the occupation of the allies, can, I am sure,
bear ample testimony to the praiseworthy manner in which
the Allied Commissioners exerted themselves to put a stop
to the cruelties practised by the mandarins both in their
prisons and courts of law. These establishments were visited
daily by European policemen, whose duty was to report to
the Allied Commissioners whether the mandarins were re-
laxing or not in the severity of their treatment towards the
prisoners under their charge. On one occasion it happened
that the chief magistrate of the district of Pun-yu, who had
been frequently warned to abandon the practice of torture, was

caught by the European inspectors in the very act of inflicting a very severe punishment upon three prisoners, who had attempted to break out of gaol on the preceding day. He was arrested and brought into the presence of the Allied Commissioners, who sentenced him to undergo an imprisonment of forty days. The officials and gentry of Canton, indignant that one of themselves should be degraded and punished by foreign rulers, endeavoured to stir up the people to revolt. The Allied Commissioners hearing of the movement, published without delay the following excellent proclamation :—

"*Proclamation by the Allied Commissioners to the People of Canton.*

"Inhabitants of Canton, one of your magistrates who is charged with the administration of the district Pun-yu, has been arrested, and is now in confinement in the Yamun of the Allied Commissioners, and it would appear from the petitions in his favour which have been presented to the Commissioners, that you are ignorant of the causes which have led to his punishment.

"In this matter the Allies have been guided by that regard for justice which is the ruling principle of their conduct, and as your magistrates are unwilling to inform you themselves of the motive of the punishment inflicted on their colleague, the Commissioners have now no hesitation in doing so, seeing that the vigorous measures to which they have had recourse have been adopted solely in the cause of humanity and in the interests of the people.

"The use of torture in judicial proceedings is revolting to the minds of all civilised people, and is also opposed to the laws of China. As long, therefore, as the present military rule continues in Canton, the allied commanders cannot tolerate practices that are contrary to humanity, on the part of any Chinese officials in carrying out their system of justice, nor can they suffer the people who, for the time, are intrusted to their protection to be subjected under their eyes to useless cruelties of this nature.

"With this view they have constantly prohibited the use of torture in the native tribunals of this city, and they have repeatedly directed the attention of the magistrate of Pun-yu to the formal orders issued on this subject, but only to find that these orders have as frequently been disregarded by that functionary. At last the patience of the Allied Commissioners has been exhausted by a recent act of brutality, consisting of crushing the legs of three prisoners, which has been committed by the Pun-yu, and they accordingly inflict on him a punishment sufficiently exemplary to deter others from following his example.

"Now that you have been made acquainted with the cause of the arrest of the Pun-yu, you should let justice take its course. His suspension need occasion you no anxiety, as other officers have been appointed to perform his functions. Continue, therefore, to attend quietly to your ordinary occupations, without making any attempt to disturb the public tranquillity by foolish demonstrations, which are certain to draw down on the heads of the authors of them the most prompt and severe punishment. Dated Canton, July 17th, 1871."

This proclamation had the desired effect. The district ruler, however, who was so justly shorn of the dignity of his office, refused, at the expiration of his term of imprisonment, to resume his duties, and returned in the course of the following month to Pekin, in search of employment in a portion of the empire where there would be no possibility of his suffering a check at the hands of foreign officials.

The legal process observed in civil cases is not very dissimilar to that in the investigation of criminal cases. Should a dispute arise between two persons with regard to the right to houses or land, it is usual for the disputants to have recourse to arbitration. The persons called upon to arbitrate are, generally, the principal residents or elders of the street or neighbourhood. Should either party be dissatisfied with the decision of the arbitrators, the matter is taken into a court of law, and comes before the district ruler. The person taking the case into court has to incur great expenses in bribing the underlings about the yamun, to allow his petition to be submitted to the notice of this official. The petitioner, having liberally paid these people, is allowed to take up his position at the folding doors of one of the inner courts of the yamun, and, as the district ruler passes in or out, he falls upon his knees immediately in front of the ruler's sedan chair. The magistrate calls upon his chair-bearers to stop, in order that he may ascertain the nature of the suppliant's petition. When the district ruler has read the petition, a day is at once appointed by him for the investigation of it. I have seen at Canton respectable men kneeling in this servile manner at the feet of the chief magistrate of Namhoi. In the hearing of civil cases it is not unusual for the judge to inflict torture. If of very great importance, the cause is appealed to a higher tribunal. It is not, however, to the provincial judge or chief justice that it is in the next instance submitted, but to the provincial treasurer. From his court there is a farther appeal to that of the governor, or governor-general of the province. The decision of the governor or viceroy, however, is not final. An appeal can, in the next instance, be made to the governor or governor-general of the province adjoining that of which the disputants are natives, or in which they are residing. From the verdict of the highest tribunal of the neighbouring province, there is a last appeal to the emperor, through the great council of the nation. In former times it was in the power of persons engaged in law-suits to appeal from the highest tribunal of their respective provinces to the emperor in person. Now, however, it is imperative on those who are engaged in litigation to appeal to the tribunal of the adjoining province, before they can submit their case to the emperor.

In all Chinese courts of law there is bribery and corruption; and the verdicts of the courts are much at the disposal of those who can pay the highest sum for them. There are in Chinese records many instances of officials, who have been bribed, seeking to defeat the ends of justice. One of the most memorable is a case of dispute which took place between two kinsmen, the one belonging to the clan or family Ling, and the other to that of Laong, who were respectively named Ling Kwei-hing, and Laong Tin-loi. In the case in question the corrupt practices and gross injustice of the mandarins were brought before the notice of the emperor, and received his majesty's marked and well-merited condemnation. Ling Kwei-hing the plaintiff, was a man of almost unbounded wealth and influence. Like Ahab, king of Israel, who in the midst of his riches pined so long as the vine-yard of Naboth, the Jezreelite, was withheld from him, so Ling Kwei-hing could not rest until a small estate, the property of his relative Laong Tin-loi, should have become a portion of his already extensive domains. He sought to gratify his covetousness by claiming it as his own. The case was brought into the courts of law at Canton, and the judges of the various courts, who had been largely bribed, gave their verdict in favour of Ling Kwei-hing. Laong Tin-loi, knowing that justice was altogether on his side, and that the courts of law in which the case had been successively heard had been influenced against him through the plaintiff's wealth, resolved to set out on a journey to Pekin with the view of seeking redress at the hands of His Imperial Majesty, Yung-ching. This emperor, who, it is said, was remarkable for his love of justice, truth, and mercy, graciously received the suppliant. So fully satisfied was the emperor that Laong Tin-loi had suffered wrong at the hands of the mandarins, that he at once despatched an imperial commissioner named Hung Tai-pang to re-investigate the matter. The examination terminated in favour of Laong Tin-loi. Ling Kwei-hing, with every member of his family, one male excepted, was put to death. All the mandarins before whose respective tribunals the case had been brought, were deprived of rank and dismissed from the Imperial service. It would appear that Laong Tin-loi, previous to leaving Canton *en route* to Pekin, went to the temple in honour of Pak-Tai, situated in the Yoong-kwong street, or the western suburb of Canton to seek the blessing and guiding care of the god. On his return, he placed on the walls of the temple—where it remains to this day—a votive tablet expressive of his gratitude. The house in which Laong Tin-loi resided, and in which several members of his family were put to death by Ling Kwei-hing, stands in the centre of the village of Tam-chune, and is sometimes visited as a place of interest by native sight-seers and holiday-makers. The subject of the foregoing narrative is the burden of a popular Chinese play which, to the great gratification of the masses, is often performed on the stage of the Chinese theatre.

With the view of encouraging officials in the efficient discharge of their duties, honours of various kinds and grades are held out to them; and the viceroys, and governors, and other high officers of state have special instructions to submit to the notice of His

Imperial Majesty the names of all officers, civil and military, serving under them and worthy of such honours. These are bestowed not only upon the living, but also upon the meritorious dead. They are much sought after. Dresses of honour, in texture, colour, and shape, similar to those worn by the emperor and the other members of the imperial family, are occasionally conferred upon officials, both civil and military, for distinguished services ; and to receive from the emperor the imperial yellow jacket is considered one of the highest honours. Marks of approbation similar to this were, it would appear from the book of Esther (vi. 8), occasionally bestowed by the ancient kings of Persia upon their subjects. Such a distinction was conferred by Ahasuerus upon Mordecai the Jew; for he said, " Let the royal apparel be brought which the king useth to wear . . . . and let this apparel . . . . be delivered to the hand of the king's most noble princes, that they may array the man withal whom the king delighteth to honour." We gather from the book of Genesis (xli. 42) that this custom prevailed also in Egypt. Nor were the Jews strangers to it, if I rightly interpret a certain episode in the friendship of David and Jonathan (I Samuel xviii. 4.)

As I have already stated, conspicuous merits are in some instances recognized by posthumous honours. Thus the *Pekin Gazette* of November 11th, 1871, contained the following memorial : [1] —

" Tseng-Kho-Fan, Viceroy of the two Kiangs, and Chang-Chih-Man, Governor of Kiang-Soo, in a joint memorial humbly report to the throne the extraordinarily meritorious conduct of the late Chun-Choong-Yuen, Prefect of Kat-On, Prefecture in Kiang-Si, during the time the city was attacked by the Taiping rebels, eighteen years ago, in sacrificing his life to the cause of the government. When the city was besieged by the enemy, who numbered between 50,000 and 60,000, the mandarin in question defended it with a garrison of only 1800 men strong ; yet frequent sorties were made, in which the rebels were slaughtered in great numbers beyond calculation. One day a breach in the wall had been made, but the deceased took active measures to have it mended, and while personally superintending its reconstruction, he missed his footing, and fell from the wall, injuring his legs badly. On

[1] The translation here given was published in the Hong-Kong *China Mail* of December 23rd of the same year.

the eighth day of the twelfth moon in that year he went out again to attack the enemy, but was wounded in several places so that blood trickled down to his ancles. Famine raged within the city, and the people had to live on the flesh of dogs, and to use fuel in lieu of candles ; yet in this time of extreme difficulty and misery he most indefatigably maintained his position until the beginning of next year, when the rebels stormed the city from all sides, having previously laid powder mines underground to destroy the walls. Having effected an entrance at the west gate, the rebels were bravely met by the deceased official and his eldest son, when they were both killed, and their heads cut off for exposure at the east gate. Of all the precedents on record none could equal with the present in point of merit. The memorialists therefore pray that authority be granted for a memorial temple to be erected to the dedication of the deceased official, who bravely defended an isolated city with a handful of men against a formidable enemy, numbering several tens of thousands strong; with no prospect of any relief from outside, and no food for the sufferers within. The son, moreover, shared the fate of the father, and this was an act of loyalty as well as filial piety, which should not be compared with an ordinary case of self-sacrifice. Therefore a temple should be erected to their memory and to that of their followers in the noble cause."

As another example of posthumous honours I may cite the case of one of the memorialists themselves. When the news of the death of Tseng Kwo-fan from apoplexy, in March, 1872, reached the ears of the emperor, an edict was immediately issued, bestowing upon that departed worthy the posthumous title of Tai-Foo (vice-tutor to the emperor), with the epitaph Wen-Chen (correct principles of literature). This title is seldom conferred, and during the past thousand years it has been bestowed upon seven persons only. A public funeral was also granted to the remains of this great man, and to defray the expense of it a sum of three thousand taels was drawn from the imperial exchequer. A public sacrifice, at the expense of the government, was offered to the manes of the departed viceroy. By the command of the emperor, this ceremony was conducted by Muk Tang-foo, the Tartar general of Kiang-soo. Imperial commands were also given that tablets bearing the names and titles of the deceased should be placed, one in the temple in honour of " Illustrious

Faithful Servants," and another in that which is dedicated to "Perfect and Virtuous Ministers of State." The decree gave permission for the erection of temples in his honour at Honan, the province in which he was born, and in Kiang-soo, the province which, at the time of his death, he was so successfully governing. The edict further gave orders that the hereditary title of Marquis should at once be conferred upon his eldest son, and that his successor in office be commanded to report to the central government the names of all his surviving children, with a view of their being appointed to posts of honour. It added that any entry standing against his name in the official register must at once be erased. This last provision may require explanation. In China governmental registers are kept in which are recorded, in some the merits, and in others the demerits of the various civil and military officials of the empire. This custom, which is of great antiquity, was also practised by other nations. In the respective books of Ezra, Nehemiah, and Esther there are several passages which afford evidence of the diligence shown in early ages by the Persian government, in keeping a record of the services of its officers; and in several Greek writers there are also allusions to this practice.

With the view of deterring officials, civil and military, from the commission of vice, it is also in the power of rulers of provinces to memorialise the throne for the punishment of all such delinquents. In a copy of the *Pekin Gazette* which was published on 12th of November, 1871, I observed an imperial edict in reply to a memorial on the part of one Lee Hung-chang, requesting the degradation and dismissal of mandarins for misconduct and a manifest incapacity to arrest offenders. The edict ordered that the magistrate of Toong-ping Heen, in the province of Chili, who had most signally failed in capturing the perpetrators of a daring robbery, should at once be deprived of his button, and that, should he fail within a given time to arrest the offenders, he should be placed under arrest for examination and punishment. It contained the imperial commands for the immediate dismissal of one named Pui Fook-tak from the magistracy of Nam-woh Heen. He was represented as a man of ordinary abilities, and, although the offence preferred against him had not been substantiated, yet it was clear that he had called into his service men of evil reputation, and had in consequence lowered the dignity of his office. But promotion and honour on the one hand, and degradation and disgrace on the other, fail in a very lamentable manner to make the officials of China honest men.

Although Chinese officials are perhaps as a class the most corrupt state servants in the world, there are amongst them men of high integrity and honour. These exceptional men are held in much esteem by the people, who avail themselves of every opportunity of doing them honour. During my long residence at Canton I only met with one such worthy. He was named Acheong, and for two years as governor ruled over the vast province of Kwang-tung. So many and great were the blessings which he conferred upon the people by his excellent administration, that they actually adored him; and when he left Canton they rose *en masse* to do him honour. I had an opportunity of witnessing his departure, and the ovation which he received from the citizens, who thronged the streets, was most impressive. In the imposing procession which escorted him to the place of embarkation, and which took at least twenty minutes to pass a given point, were carried the silk umbrellas which had been presented to him by the people, and the red boards—of which there were probably more than three hundred—upon which high-sounding titles had been inscribed in honour of the faithful minister. The route was spanned at frequent intervals by arches. From these banners were suspended which bore in large letters, painted or embroidered, such sentences as "The Friend of the People;" "the Father of the People;" "the Father and Mother of the People;" "the Bright Star of the Province;" "the Benefactor of the Age." Deputations awaited his arrival at various temples, and he alighted from his chair to exchange farewell compliments with them, and to partake of the refreshment provided for the occasion. But the formal arrangements could not speak so clearly to his popularity as the enthusiasm of the people. The silence generally observed when a Chinese ruler passes through the streets was again and again broken by hearty exclamations of "When will your Excellency

THE CANGUE.

come back to us ?" At many points the crowd was so great as
to interrupt the line of march, and the state chair was frequently
in danger of being upset. It was evident that the mottoes which
were inscribed on the banners hung out on the route of this
virtuous servant of the state, faithfully interpreted the public
feeling.

CHAPTER III.

IN this chapter I propose to give a description of Chinese prisons, respecting the cruelties practised in which so much was said and written in the early part of 1858—the year in which Canton was assaulted and captured by the allied armies of Great Britain and France. When I have described these " habitations of cruelty," I shall proceed to give an account of the various degrees of punishment which are meted out to those who have been convicted of breaking the laws of their country. Many of these punishments are barbarous and cruel in the extreme. For example, in the gaol of the city of Chin-kiang I saw a poor wretch who for three days and three nights had not been allowed to sit down. His wrists were bound together by a long chain, the end of which was made fast to one of the rafters of the roof of his cell. In some instances prisoners are tied up by ropes which are made fast under their arms, their feet not being allowed to touch the ground. Some of the modes of capital punishment in China may justly be described as examples of abominable and revolting cruelty. I need not, however, anticipate details which it will be my unpleasant duty to narrate in the course of this chapter; and the facts which I have to bring before the reader will speak for themselves.

The prisons of China consist, according to their class, of a certain number of wards each. Thus, for example, the prisons of the respective counties of Namhoi and Pun-yu, in the province of Kwang-tung, which are first-class county prisons, consist, besides cells in which prisoners on remand are confined, of six large wards, in each of which are four large cells, making in all twenty-four cells. The same arrangements may be said to prevail in all county prisons. The walls of the various wards abut one upon another, and form a parallelogram. Round the outer wall of this parallelogram a paved pathway runs, upon which the gates of the various wards open. This pathway is flanked by a large outer wall, which constitutes the boundary wall of the prison. The cells are of considerable dimensions. In each ward the four cells are arranged two on a side, so as to form the two sides of a square, and resemble cattle-sheds, the front of each being inclosed by a strong palisading of wood, which extends from the ground to the roof. They are paved with granite, and each is furnished with a raised wooden dais, on which the prisoners sit by day and sleep by night. They are polluted with vermin and filth of almost every kind, and the prisoners seldom or never have an opportunity afforded them of washing their bodies, or even of dressing their hair, water in Chinese prisons being a scarce commodity, and hair-combs articles almost unknown. In each cell are placed large tubs for the use of the prisoners; and it is difficult to conceive how human beings can breathe the stench—for the air seems nothing else—which arises from these tubs, more particularly during the hot season. In the centre of each ward is a small shrine in which stands an idol of a deity called Hong-koong-chu-shou. This god, who receives the homage of the prisoners, is supposed to possess the power of melting into tenderness and contrition the hard and stubborn hearts of the wayward and wicked. The natal anniversary of this most suggestive and melancholy mockery of deity is celebrated by the prisoners with an attempt at feasting. The expense of the repast which is provided on such occasions is defrayed by the governor of the gaol. This Cerberus, however, takes very good care to repay himself by appropriating, at intervals, portions of the small sums of money doled out daily for the maintenance of his unwilling guests.

The approach to the prison is by a narrow passage, at the entrance of which there is an ordinary sized door. Above this entrance door is painted a tiger's head with large staring eyes and widely-extended jaws. Upon entering, the visitor finds an altar on which stands the figure of a tiger hewn in granite. This image is regarded as the tutelary deity of the prison gates. The turnkeys, with the view of propitiating it, and securing its watchfulness, worship it morning and evening, gaolers in China being held responsible for the safe custody of the miserable beings who are intrusted to their care. On a visit which I paid to the prison of the Namhoi magistrate at Canton, I saw one of the turnkeys presenting offerings of fat pork to this stone tiger, before which he was also burning incense and making genuflexions. At the base of the large wall which I have described as forming the prison boundary, there are several hovels—for by no other name can they be designated—in some of which all the female felons are lodged, and in others whole families, who have been seized and detained as hostages by the mandarins. There is a law which admits of the seizure and detention as hostages of families, members of which, having broken the laws of the empire, have fled from justice. Such hostages are not liberated until the offending relatives have been secured, and consequently they are not unfrequently imprisoned during a period of five, ten, or twenty years. Indeed, many of them pass the period of their natural lives in captivity. Thus the mother, or aunt, of Hung Sow-tsuen, the leader of the Taiping rebellion, died, after an imprisonment of several years, in the prison of the Namhoi magistrate at Canton. During her captivity I frequently visited the unoffending old woman, and grievously indeed did she feel her imprisonment for no crime or offence of her own. Should the crime of the fugitive be a very aggravated and heinous one, such, for example, as an attempt upon the life of the sovereign of the empire, it is not unusual to put the immediate, although perfectly innocent, relations of the offender to death, whilst those who are not so nearly related to him are sent into exile. In 1803 an attempt was made to assassinate the emperor Ka-hing. The assassin was no sooner apprehended than he was sentenced to be put to death by torture; and his sons, who were in the happy days of childhood, were put to death by strangling.

The mortality in Chinese prisons is so great that a dead-house is regarded as a very necessary adjunct. The bodies of all who die in prison are thrown into the dead-house, and remain there until the necessary preliminaries, which are of a very simple kind, have been arranged for their interment. In the course of my repeated visits to the prisons of Canton [1] during a period extending from 1858 to 1861 inclusive, I frequently saw these receptacles full of corpses, presenting the most revolting and disgusting appearance. Some of the unhappy men had evidently died from the effects of severe and often repeated floggings. Others, it was clear, had fallen victims to one or other of the various diseases which not unfrequently prevail in Chinese prisons, and which such dens are only too well fitted to create and foster. In the month of March, 1859, I saw in the dead-house attached to the prison of the Pun-yu magistrate at Canton, five dead bodies, all with the appearance of death from starvation—a capital punishment which Chinese rulers not unfrequently inflict upon kidnappers and other grave offenders. The opinion which I have expressed with regard to the cause of the death of these five men was fully supported by three or four gentlemen who were with me, and of whom one was, by profession, a medical practitioner. Immediately in front of the door of the dead-house, and at the base of the outer boundary wall of the prison, there is a small door of sufficient size to admit of a corpse being passed through. Through the aperture the corpses of all who die in prison are passed into the adjoining street to be carried away for burial. It would be paying too much reverence to the remains of a deceased prisoner to allow them to be carried through the gates of the yamun to which the prison is attached. Besides, if this were done, the Chinese authorities would consider the gates of the yamun polluted. I may remark in passing that according to the Latin

---

[1] Besides the two county prisons in the city of Canton there is in the Chā-Fan street a gaol in which prisoners from the more distant parts of the province are confined. There are also prisons in the streets called Shu-Yin-Lee and Koo-Wa-Lee. The former of these prisons was built in the eighth year of the reign of the Emperor Taou-kwang ; and the latter, at an expense of six thousand three hundred taels, was erected in the fifty-first year of the reign of Keen-lung-Wong. In the prison of the district magistrate of Namhoi from four hundred to six hundred prisoners, and in that of the district magistrate of Pun-yu, from two hundred to three hundred prisoners, are generally confined at one time.

historian Livy, the corpses of all prisoners who died in the prisons of ancient Rome were, in a similarly ignominious manner, cast into the adjoining street.

In point of appearance the unfortunate inmates of Chinese prisons are, perhaps, of all men, the most abject and miserable. Their death-like countenances, emaciated forms, and long, coarse, black hair, which according to prison rules they are not allowed to shave, give them the appearance rather of demons than of men, and strike the mind of the beholder with impressions of gloom and sorrow that are not easily forgotten. All prisoners in each ward, with only one exception, wear fetters. The exception is the prisoner who is supposed to be more respectable, and who conducts himself better than any of his fellows in crime. He is allowed the full freedom of his limbs, and upon him, as a mark of confidence and trust, devolves the privilege of acting as an overseer over his fellow-prisoners in the same ward. A custom similar to this prevailed in ancient Egypt; for we read that the keeper of a prison in that country committed to the charge of Joseph all the prisoners who were in the same ward with him.

The dress worn by Chinese prisoners consists of a coat and trowsers of a coarse, red fabric. On the back of the coat is written in large characters the name of the prison in which its wearer is confined, so that should he escape from durance he would at once be recognised as a runaway or prison-breaker, and his recapture would in all probability be as speedily effected.

The imperial clemency is occasionally extended to prisoners, especially on the accession of an emperor, or on the occasion of his marriage, or on the completion of any of the decades of his age or reign. Thus, an amnesty edict was published in the *Pekin Gazette* of February 12th, 1872. It began by stating that the late emperors of China were ever merciful and kind, and that, in respect to his love for his subjects, their successor was not one whit behind them. " The four last Manchu emperors," said the edict, "had each issued a special amnesty on entering the eleventh year of their reigns. The present emperor wishes to emulate this merciful example, and requests the Board of Punishments to devise a scheme for commuting the offence of

all prisoners throughout the empire, except those of the worst
character. In the meantime let all prisoners who are suffering
for petty offences be at once liberated." For the promotion of
the comfort of prisoners, humane persons sometimes give or
bequeath sums of money. For instance, in the tenth year of
Taou-kwang, a provincial treasurer in the province of Kwang-
tung, named Ow, gave ten thousand dollars to the salt monopoly,
the interest from which sum was to be expended annually in providing the prisoners in the principal gaol of the city of Canton
with a few creature comforts. Many of the high officials of the
province, in imitation of Treasurer Ow's example, invested other
sums, the interest of which was to be employed in providing
medicine, and fans in summer, and warm underclothing in
winter, for all the prisoners in the large gaols in the city.

Each prison is presided over by a governor, who has under
him a considerable number of turnkeys. Thus, each large prison
in Canton has a governor, twenty-four turnkeys, thirty-seven
watchmen, and fifteen spearmen. In a barrack beyond the doors
or gates of each prison is a resident force of ten soldiers. There
are also, according to law, a physician, five clerks, and six bearers
of firewood and water; but whether these latter officials are
usually found in Chinese prisons I am unable to say. The
turnkeys, watchmen, spearmen, &c., from the great amount of
misery which they daily witness, must, I apprehend, be more
casehardened than the most incorrigible of the criminals. The
policemen who are attached to the yamun are also men of vile
character, and it is unfortunately too common for them to share
the booty with the thief, and hoodwink or satisfy the magistrate.

The governor of a Chinese prison purchases his appointment
from the local government. He receives no salary from the
state although he does this. He is compelled, therefore, to re-
coup himself by exacting money from such relatives or friends
of prisoners as are in good circumstances, and anxious, naturally, that their unhappy friends should experience as little
as possible of the sad deprivations and cruelties for which Chinese prisons are so justly and so universally notorious. It was,
if I mistake not, customary at one time for governors of gaols
in Great Britain to purchase their appointments, and for services

rendered to receive from the imperial exchequer no salaries. Like the governors of Chinese gaols to-day, they enriched themselves by exacting from the relatives or friends of prisoners sums varying, I suppose, according to their means or standing. Prisoners, of course, who were without influential friends, or who had none at all, like thousands of criminals in Chinese prisons to-day, remained neglected and forgotten, or died from sheer inability to obtain even the commonest necessaries of life. These days were brought to a close by the indefatigable labours of the great philanthropist, John Howard, and it would, indeed, be an unspeakable mercy to Chinese prisoners were a Chinese Howard to appear. To each prison a granary is attached, in which rice of the cheapest and coarsest kind is stored by the governor. This rice is one of his perquisites, and he retails it to the prisoners at a most remunerative price. Vegetables and firewood for culinary purposes, both of which are daily offered for sale to the prisoners, are supplied by him. As the government allowance to each prisoner *per diem* does not exceed twenty-five *cash*, the reader does not require to be told that prisoners who are without friends are not often able to buy even vegetables and firewood. In the prison of the Namhoi magistrate at Canton, I once saw a prisoner who, unable to purchase firewood, was endeavouring to satiate the cravings of hunger by eating unboiled rice.

The law provides that once a month each prison shall be inspected by a government official. It is his duty to ascertain how many prisoners have died in prison during the month, and to make inquiries respecting the conduct of the various turnkeys, watchmen, and spearmen employed. After each inspection this officer is supposed to forward his report to the viceroy or governor. Should it appear that, owing to the neglect of the officers of the prison, two per cent. of the men under confinement have died during the course of the month, an entry, not only against the name of the governor of the prison, but against that of the deputy magistrate under whose jurisdiction the prison is placed, is made in the book of faults. Should three per cent. have died, two entries are made in this book; and in the case of the mortality reaching four per cent., both the governor and the deputy magistrate are dismissed from office. In the event of six or seven per cent. of the prisoners dying, the ruler of the country or district to which the prison belongs is degraded one step. Corresponding to the book of faults there is a book of merits, in which, if the results of the inspections are satisfactory, entries are made which secure proportionate rewards for the officials concerned.

Besides the prisons in which convicts are confined there are also within the precincts of the yamun houses of detention. These are neither so large nor·so strongly inclosed as the common gaols. There is, generally, in such houses of detention a tolerably large chamber. This is set apart for the reception of prisoners on remand who have friends able and willing to satisfy the demands of the governor. By this arrangement such prisoners avoid the misery of being shut up in the same ward with men, in many instances, of the vilest character, and often covered with filth, or suffering from various kinds of cutaneous diseases. The arrangement is a great advantage to the governor of the gaol, and to all prisoners who can afford to pay for it, but a great disadvantage to the other prisoners. The space required for the convenience of prisoners who have friends to look after their wants leaves very little room, indeed, for the reception of the great majority of the poor prisoners. They are huddled together in a common ward, sometimes so crowded that its inmates find it difficult to lie down in it. In the streets adjoining the yamuns, there are other houses of detention, at all events in the city of Canton. In not a few cases I have seen these houses so densely crowded as to remind me of the heartrending history of the Black Hole of Calcutta. I had an opportunity of inspecting one of these "lock-ups" in the hot month of August, 1861. It was crowded to excess ; and— certainly not to my astonishment, for the heat was intense—all the prisoners were in a state of complete nudity. Had as many Europeans been incarcerated in so small a cell, they must all have inevitably perished. The confinement of prisoners on remand in such places is often much protracted, the administration of justice in China being attended with long delays.

I visited a great many Chinese prisons and lock-ups, and

found them all very like each other, both as to their construction and management. Of all the prisons, however, which I have visited, that which inspired me with the most melancholy interest was the prefectoral prison at Tai-wan Foo, the metropolis of Formosa. No fewer than one hundred and ninety-seven souls, the crew of H.B.M.'s hired transport ship *Narbuddha*, were, during the first war which Great Britain waged with China, confined in this prison; and from it they were all, with one exception only, eventually led forth to execution. In the cells which these unfortunate men are said to have occupied, I found many Chinese prisoners who were endeavouring to interrupt the dull monotony of their life by making fans, and I bought specimens of their labour. On withdrawing I visited the plot of ground—the common execution-ground—on which the officers and crew of the *Narbuddha* were decapitated. Several skulls were bleaching in the sun, and one of them, from the very high frontal bone, appeared to be the skull of a European.

From the prisons of China let us now turn to the various degrees of the other punishments to which Chinese convicts are subjected. Cases of petty larceny are generally dealt with by flogging. The culprit is handcuffed, and, with the identical article which he stole, or one similar, suspended from his neck, is marched through the streets of the neighbourhood in which the theft was committed. He is preceded by a man beating a gong, and, at each beat of the gong, an officer who walks behind gives him a severe blow with a double rattan across the shoulders, exclaiming, "This is the punishment due to a thief." As the culprit has to pass through three or four streets, his punishment, though regarded by the Chinese as one of the minor ones, is certainly not lacking in severity. The flow of blood is often very great. I remember the case of a thief who had stolen a watch from one of his countrymen, and whom I saw flogged through the Honam suburb of Canton, where I was then residing. The officer appointed to flog him was very corpulent, and, from his great earnestness in the discharge of his duty, became quite breathless before the various streets along which the culprit was sentenced to pass had been fully traversed. The person from whom the watch had been stolen, seeing that

FLOGGING A THIEF THROUGH THE STREETS.

the thief might escape the full severity of his penalty, snatched the double rattan from the hand of the exhausted officer, and applied it himself most unmercifully to the thief's back. Women who are convicted of thieving, are, in some instances, punished in this way, Occasionally a long bamboo is used in cases of petty larceny. When this is the case, however, the culprit receives his flogging in court in front of the tribunal. He is at once denuded of his trousers, and the number of blows varies according to the nature of the larceny from ten to three hundred. I saw a punishment of this kind inflicted on an aged man, who at each blow groaned piteously. His sufferings awakened no sympathy in court. It was apparently a source of delight to the judge and his officers, and the face of each official was expanded by a broad grin. The cangue, or wooden collar, is another mode by which petty offenders in China are punished. The form of the cangue is represented in the annexed illustration. Cangues vary in weight, some being considerably larger and heavier than others. The period for which an offender is sentenced to wear the cangue varies from a fortnight to three months. During the whole of this time the cangue is not removed from the neck of the prisoner either by day or by night. Its form prevents the prisoner stretching himself on the ground at full length, and, to judge from the attenuated appearance of prisoners who have undergone it, the punishment must be severe to a degree. The name of the prisoner and the nature of his offence are written on the cangue in large letters, " pour encourager les autres." The authorities often make the offender stand from sunrise to sunset at one of the principal gates, or in front of one of the chief temples, or public halls of the city, and he is regarded as an object of universal scorn and contempt. On one occasion at Canton I saw three salt merchants treated in this way for attempting to smuggle salt. They were, evidently, persons in a respectable position amongst their fellows, and they apparently felt their painful and humiliating position very keenly. Passing, in January, 1866, through the streets of the city of Chun-tso-sheng, in the province of Kiang-soo, I observed twelve farmers of apparent respectability wearing the

cangue at the gates of the temple in honour of Shing-Wong.
It was the day on which the fair, or great market, was being
held, and the farmers were surrounded by a number of inquisitive spectators. Their offence was either unwillingness or inability
to pay their land taxes. At the city of Woo-chang I saw three
farmers who were being punished in this way for a similar
offence.

At Soo-chow I saw an old farmer who had a cangue round
his neck, and who was bound by a chain to a stone pillar at the
entrance gate of the monastery called Pow-on Sze. He also was
suffering for a similar offence. On the same day, and in the
same city, I saw two men wearing cangues, and bound to a
stone pillar at the grand entrance to the temple of Shing Wong.
From the inscription on their cangues I learned that they had
been fighting with each other. There was a snow storm, and the
fettered pugilists, who were most thinly clad, suffered severely
from the inclemency of the weather. The old farmer, however,
had wisely provided himself with thick winter clothing, and
seemed, under the circumstances, tolerably happy. Of all the
wretched creatures whom I ever saw undergoing this sentence,
perhaps the most miserable was a Chinese youth, who had been
made to sit, for stand he could not, in one of the principal
streets of Manka, a small commercial town in the north of the
island of Formosa. Very emaciated and begrimed with dirt,
he had the appearance of one *in articulo mortis*. Prisoners undergoing this punishment are, in some instances, made to beg
their daily bread from door to door, in order that they may not
be a burden upon the state. At Chinkiang I saw a wretched-
looking man asking alms of all whom he met. His success as
a beggar was by no means great, for all that he received during
the time I was in the same street with him, was a cup of tea
and a boiled land crab, which he received with apparent gratitude from a sympathising shopkeeper. At Soo-chow I saw
another miserable-looking being to whose neck a cangue was
fastened, begging in the streets for what his keepers refused to
give him, namely, the common necessaries of life. At Chan-
chee-kow, a city situated at the base of the great wall of China,

THE CANGUE.

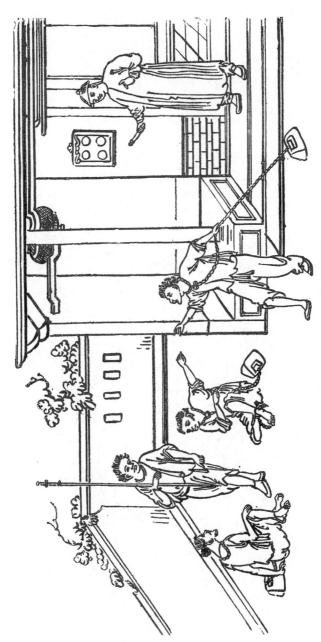

PRISONERS EXPOSED OUTSIDE A YAMUN.

I saw a prisoner begging for his bread from door to door. He had a large chain round his neck, and the end of it was fastened to a strong wooden fetter, encircling the calf of his left leg. He was, without exception, the most villanous-looking man I ever saw. As he asked and received alms at the hands of the members of the Mohammedan guild in the city, he was probably an unworthy follower of the prophet of Mecca. These prisoners are obliged to return every night to their respective prisons. I noticed in my travels through the central provinces that cangues were placed at the gates of cities, and at the doors of yamuns or public offices, as a warning to evil-doers.

The next mode of punishing a criminal is that of confining him in a cage. The cages are of different forms. One is too short to allow the prisoner to place himself in a recumbent position, and too low to admit of his standing. Another is a narrow cage, not high enough to admit of the offender standing altogether upright. To the top is attached a wooden collar or cangue, by which the neck of the criminal, which it is made to fit, is firmly held. Another cage resembles the former in all respects but one. The difference consists in its being longer than its occupant, so that whilst his neck is held fast by the wooden collar attached to the top of the cage, the tips of his toes barely touch the floor. Indeed, the floor, which is only a few inches from the ground, is sometimes removed, so that the prisoner may be suspended by the neck. This punishment almost invariably proves fatal. In 1860, a man was exposed in this manner in front of the outer gates of the yamun of the district city of Shun-tuk or Tai-laong. He had been convicted of plundering a tomb. At the close of the third day, after extreme sufferings, he breathed his last. I saw several of these cages in the prefectoral prison at Canton. It appeared to me that this cruel punishment was much more practised in district and prefectoral cities than in provincial capitals. The victims are, as a rule, thieves and robbers. They are often punished by being bound to stones by means of long chains passed round their necks. The stones are not large, but sufficiently heavy to inconvenience them as they walk to and from the prison to the entrance gates of the yamun in front of which they are daily exposed. These stones are their inseparable companions by night and by day, throughout the whole period of their incarceration. In some instances they are bound to long bars of iron, and are daily exposed to the scorn of all the passers by. At Manka I saw six or seven men who were being punished in this manner.

In all cases of conspiracy and rebellion the laws of China are especially severe. It is, however, not unusual, as a mark of imperial clemency, to punish persons who have been seduced into rebellion by others, by cutting off their ears rather than their heads, and setting them at liberty. In a tea saloon at Tat-leng-shee, a village near Canton, at which I used to halt, I was several times served with tea and cakes by a waiter one of whose ears had been cut off. This young man, I learned, had been induced to join the rebels who, during the years 1853–54, so greatly disturbed the peace of Kwangtung, and of the adjoining province of Kwangsi. Having been taken in one of the many unsuccessful assaults which the rebels made on Canton he was cast into prison, where he lay for several months. On his trial it appeared that he was a simple unwary fellow, and he was merely dismissed from the judgment-seat minus an ear. When travelling on one occasion from Ki-lung in the island of Formosa to the coal districts in the vicinity of that town, I observed that one of the sedan-chair bearers was without an ear. Like the waiter in the tea saloon, he had been convicted of sedi-tious practices. It would, however, be a mistake to suppose that all one-eared persons in China have been guilty of sedition. I lived on the most friendly terms with an iron merchant of the clan or family, Foong, or Fung, who was minus his right ear. It was a source of great sorrow to him, as strangers were disposed to conclude from it that he had at one time been guilty of sedition The very contrary was the case, for the rebels had cut off the ear of the loyal old man. They captured him at the head of a regiment of braves whom he was leading against them. For-tunately he prevailed upon them to spare his life.

During this rebellion the imperialist forces who had driven the rebels from several villages in the vicinity of Canton, pro-ceeded to cut off the ears of many of the innocent and unoffend-ing villagers, asserting that they ought not to have allowed the

rebels to enter. In one of these villages which I visited I saw
not only men, but boys of ten or twelve years of age who had
been treated in this brutal manner. I had my attention also
directed to a very aged man who had been cruelly scalped;
and, upon leaving the village, a man who was following me took
me to a place beyond its precincts, where three headless human
bodies were lying. They were peasants who, for no offence
whatever, had been decapitated by the brutal soldiers. The
women were all bitterly lamenting the calamities with which
their unoffending village had been visited. Again, when the
city of Canton was recaptured in 1854, several of the insurgents
were punished for their sedition in a very singular manner.
The infuriated royalists, with the view of marking their prisoners
of war for life, cut the principal sinew of the neck of each, so
that his head inclined towards the shoulder.[1]

For capital and other offences of a serious nature there are
six classes of punishments. The first class is called Ling-chee.
It is inflicted upon traitors, parricides, matricides, fratricides,
and murderers of husbands, uncles, and tutors. The criminal is
bound to a cross, and cut either into one hundred and twenty, or
seventy-two, or thirty-six, or twenty-four pieces. Should there
be extenuating circumstances, his body, as a mark of imperial
clemency, is divided into eight portions only. The punishment
of twenty-four cuts is inflicted as follows: the first and second
cuts remove the eye-brows; the third and fourth, the shoulders;
the fifth and sixth, the breasts; the seventh and eighth, the

---

[1] The cruel custom of maiming the bodies of prisoners of war was evidently
practised by the ancient Egyptians. Dr. Richardson describes the picture of a
battle-field which, it would appear, is painted on the walls of the temple of
Medinet Habou, in the following terms :—" The south, and part of the east wall
is covered with a battle scene, and the cruel punishment of the vanquished,
by cutting off their hands and maiming their bodies, is performed in the
presence of the chief, who has seated himself in repose on the back part of his
chariot to witness the execution of his horrid sentence. Three heaps of amputated
hands are counted over before him, and an equal number of scribes with scrolls
in their hands are minuting down the account. As many rows of prisoners stand
behind to undergo a similar mutilation in their turn, their hands tied behind
their backs or lashed over their heads or thrust into eye-shaped manacles; some
of their heads are twisted completely round; some of them are turned back to
back and their arms lashed together round the elbows; and thus they are marched
up to punishment."

parts between each hand and elbow; the ninth and tenth, the parts between each elbow and shoulder; the eleventh and twelfth, the flesh of each thigh; the thirteenth and fourteenth, the calf of each leg; the fifteenth pierces the heart; the sixteenth severs the head from the body; the seventeenth and eighteenth cut off the hands; the nineteenth and twentieth, the arms; the twenty-first and twenty-second, the feet; the twenty-third and twenty-fourth, the legs. That of eight cuts is inflicted as follows: the first and second cuts remove the eye-brows; the third and fourth, the shoulders; the fifth and sixth, the breasts; the seventh pierces the heart; the eighth severs the head from the body. A great many political offenders underwent executions of the first class at Canton during the vice-royalty of His Excellency Yeh. On the 14th day of December, 1864, the famous Hakka rebel leader, Tai Chee-kwei by name, was put to death at Canton in this manner. I most inadvertently visited the execution-ground five minutes after the criminal had been thus put to death by torture, and I saw the fragments of his remains scattered over a portion of this renowned *Aceldama*. His hands and feet were amongst the most conspicuous portions of his remains.

All leaders of sedition, however, are not punished in this cruel and unmerciful way. For example, in 1872, a man named Soo Ying-chee, who came from the southern parts of the province of Kwang-tung, and who for several years had proved a source of great trouble to the government at Canton, was simply decapitated. Soo Kee-chaong, the adopted son of Soo Ying-chee, and a partaker of his crimes, was put to death at the same time in a similar manner. In all probability the imperial clemency—shown to them in regard to the mode of their execution—was owing to the fact that they were taken prisoners by an act of deception, the Viceroy having assured Soo Ying-chee and his son by adoption, that he would, upon their laying down their arms, promote them to great honour. There is nothing surprising in the fact that Soo Ying-chee at once listened to this proposal, as it is very common not only for the various provincial governments, but for the central government of the country, to enlist on their side powerful

THE CANGUE.

THE CANGUE.

leaders of treasonable and seditious parties by offering them rank, titles, money, and a free pardon. To this policy the reader will remember the ancient Jews, also, had recourse. Thus David, in order to secure the services of Abner, who was upholding the cause of Ish-bosheth, the son of Saul, promised that on the downfall of Ish-bosheth and the amalgamation of the two kingdoms Abner should be appointed to the command of the great army of the nation.

To resume the subject of Chinese executions. On the nineteenth day of the first month of the seventh year of Tung-chee (February 12th, 1868), a woman named Lau Laam-shi was cut into twenty-four pieces on the common execution ground of Canton for having poisoned her husband. She was a native of Yung-yuen, a district or county in the prefecture of Wei-chow. Being enamoured of a rich neighbour named Chan Asze, whose second wife or concubine she hoped to become if she could get rid of her husband, who was a peasant, she resolved to remove the obstacle in the way of what she regarded as her advancement in life by poison. At the time of her execution she was slightly inebriated. When being bound to the cross upon which she was to suffer, she begged the executioner to despatch her with haste. He first, very roughly, blindfolded her with a piece of rope. She received in all twenty-four cuts, the fifteenth of which pierced her heart. The ropes by which her arms and neck were bound to the cross were then cut, and the upper part of the body fell forward, the lower part remaining tightly bound to the perpendicular beam of the cross. As the upper part fell forward, an assistant executioner pulled the head forward by the hair to enable the executioner to sever it from the trunk. This unfortunate woman had been two years in prison, having committed the crime for which she suffered in the fifth year of Tung-chee, or A.D. 1866. On the ninth day of the eleventh month of the eighth year of the same Emperor's reign, that is, on the 11th December, 1869, a woman named Mok Yu-shee was similarly punished for murdering her husband. In her crime she was assisted by her paramour, Lou San-koo, who was also brought to justice. At her execution her guilty paramour, so soon as she had been bound to the cross upon which she was to be cut into pieces, was made to kneel before her, and his head was then at one blow severed from his body.

The second class of capital punishment, which is called Chan or decapitation, is the penalty due to murderers, rebels, pirates burglars, ravishers of women, &c., &c. Prisoners who are sentenced to decapitation are kept in ignorance of the hour fixed for their execution until the preceding day. Sometimes they have only a few hours'—in some instances, only a few minutes' warning. On the 26th of September, 1872, I was present in the gaol of the Namhoi magistrate at Canton a few minutes previous to twenty-two malefactors being made ready for execution. When I entered the ward in which the majority of these men were confined, they were in perfect ignorance of the ignominious death which they were to undergo in the course of an hour. Nor did they know until a few minutes before being pinioned. My Chinese servant who accompanied me very nearly revealed to them the fact that in a few minutes they would be led forth to execution. The foolish fellow, who had been cautioned before we went in not to refer to the fate awaiting the criminals, at once asked the turnkey in a rather loud tone to point out the men who were that day to suffer. The prisoners, who had gathered round us, were much startled, and the turnkey pacified them by assuring them that no such event was at hand.

When the time has arrived for making the condemned men ready for execution, an officer in full costume, carrying in his hand a board on which is pasted a list of the names of the prisoners who are that day to atone for their crimes, enters the prison, and, in the hearing of all the prisoners in the ward assembled, reads aloud the list of the condemned. Each prisoner whose name is called at once answers to it, and he is then made to sit in a basket to be carried once more into the presence of a judge. As he is carried through the outer gate of the prison, he is interrogated through an interpreter, by an official who acts on the occasion as the Viceroy's representative. The questions put to each prisoner, are very much like the following:—What is your name? What is your family or clan name? Of what district are you a native? How long have you been con-

fined in this prison ?   Of what crime have you been convicted ?
When and where was your crime committed ?   Had you any
accomplices, and if so what are their names ?   Are you guilty ?
The representative of the viceroy, who has a list before him of
the name, surname, native place, &c., of each prisoner, compares
the answers which he receives with his list, and finding that
they agree, he orders him to be carried to execution.   As the
prisoners pass the outer gate of the gaol which admits them
into the courtyard of the yamun, they encounter the gaze of an
idle crowd, who have come to see the procession of the condemned.   As a rule on these occasions they seem quite uncon-
cerned.   Noticeably, they are very quiet.   Sometimes, however,
they make a parade of their indifference.   On one occasion—it
was in the year 1870—I was in the courtyard of the chief
magistrate of Namhoi when thirty-five men were brought out of
prison to be made ready for execution ; and three or four of
these, upon seeing so many people assembled, laughed outright,
while one, who was evidently a wag, jocosely remarked that he
had at last attained to a position of gentility, having two servants
to carry him in a basket.   When the prisoners who are to be
executed, arrive in the courtyard of the yamun to which the
prison is attached, their friends generally provide them either
with a few cakes, or a little soup, or with pieces of betel nut to
chew, or with wine, and a small dish of fat pork.   What is most
generally given to these men by their friends, or in the absence
of their friends, by friendly turnkeys, is betel nut.   The effect is
that of a narcotic.   It gives the countenance a very flushed
appearance, which has led many foreigners to suppose that
Chinese malefactors are made more or less drunk by opium or
wine, before they are carried to execution.   Fat pork and wine,
however, are preferred on such occasions to betel nut ; but it is
not every prisoner who has friends to procure these luxuries
for him.

It is surprising to witness the nonchalance with which many
of these prisoners partake of these viands.   Others of them
may be seen smoking cigarettes with perfect calmness.   Some,
however, weep in anticipation of the dreadful fate which is
immediately before them.   But there is very little time either

for reflection or refreshment. The process of pinioning takes
place in the courtyard of the yamun, and whilst the prisoners are
still sitting in their baskets, and is entered upon without much
delay. Indeed the custom of giving condemned men something
to eat prior to their execution is, in some cases, observed when
the prisoners are on the way to execution. In December, 1866,
I saw three Tartar soldiers being fed with fat pork and wine by
their respective relatives on their way to the execution-ground. As
the prisoners were pinioned, the food prepared for them had, as a
matter of necessity, to be put into their mouths by their friends.

The process of pinioning the malefactors having been accomplished they are conveyed through the right or eastern arch of
the three-arched gateway, into the presence of the magistrate
whose judgment-seat has been removed from the court and
placed in the porch of the inner approach to his official residence. His last duty to these men consists in summoning each
into his presence, in order that a strip of bamboo, on which a
piece of paper bearing the criminal's name has been previously
pasted, may be bound to his head. This is done that when
they are conveyed through the streets of the city to the execution-ground, the citizens may note what criminals have been
led forth to execution. In March, 1860, I witnessed an execution of the second class at Canton. There were only three criminals ; one was a military mandarin, named Poon Fat-yune. He
had held a commission as colonel in the imperial army of China,
and had been accused and convicted of cowardice. While he
was commandant of the forces at Kwei-chow Foo, the city had
been assaulted and captured by rebels, and as the latter were entering by the north gate, Poon Fat-yune, it appeared, was taking
his departure by the south gate. The other two were pirates,
and from their emaciated appearance it was evident that they
had suffered great privations in prison. The mandarin was executed under an imperial warrant, the pirates under that of the
viceroy of the province. The latter were carried to the common
execution-ground, which is beyond the city walls, in the open
baskets which are ordinarily used for this purpose at Canton.[1]

---

[1] At Foo-chow malefactors are conveyed to the place of execution in cages, and
at Pekin in carts.

The colonel, seated in a sedan chair, the blinds of which were closely drawn, was borne to the same place by four well-dressed bearers. The procession was headed by a company of spearmen; the two pirates came next, followed by the colonel; and behind the prisoners, marched another company of soldiers, armed, some with spears, some with swords, and others with matchlocks. These were followed by three equerries who preceded a large sedan chair of state, in which was seated the Wye-Yune or deputy ruler of the county Namhoi, in whose presence, as sheriff, the execution was to take place. After three equerries who rode behind this chair, was carried another sedan chair of state, in which was seated an official whose duty it was to pay adoration to the Five Genii on the occasion. In close proximity to the place of execution, there is a small temple in honour of these gods, and they are regarded as having the power of preventing the spirits of decapitated criminals being hurried by revengeful feelings into inflicting injuries on the judge, magistrates, and others who have administered the law. .In the rear of these state chairs a herald on horseback carries in his right hand a small yellow banner bearing two Chinese characters implying "By Imperial decree." Without this banner the Wye-Yune or sheriff dare not authorize the executioner to strike the fatal blow. On arriving at the ground, where the executioner was conspicuous by the bright blade he carried, the spearmen filed off and arranged themselves on each side of a table covered with red cloth. The Wye-Yune took his seat in a chair, also covered with red cloth, in front of the table. The pirates were unceremoniously ejected from their baskets upon the mud with which a night of rain had covered the ground. A large mat was spread for the more delicate knees of the colonel, and he was supported by two of his servants wearing Chinese livery. This last attention of his servants was rendered necessary by the fact that the colonel was in a state of inebriety. A large basin of intoxicating wine called sam-chu, together with a dish of fat pork, had been administered to him before he quitted the precincts of the yamun. When an assistant executioner had placed the prisoners in a kneeling position, with their heads bent forward

—for in China they do not use the block—the Wye-Yune, who was still seated at the table, ordered the executioner, through a herald, to deal the fatal strokes. In less than twelve seconds the unhappy men were standing in the presence of that God of whose might, majesty, holiness, justice, and mercy, they had lived and died in a state of ignorance. One of the servants of the colonel immediately placed lighted tapers on the ground near the feet of the headless corpse of his master, whilst the other burned gold and silver paper, supposed to represent money, to supply the wants of the departed soul in the world of spirits. At the close of these religious ceremonies, they proceeded to wrap the headless trunk in the large mat upon which he had knelt to receive the fatal blow. A coffin was then brought, in which his remains were conveyed to the residence of his family.[1] The headless corpses of the pirates lay, uncared for, where they fell. The two bodies were eventually pressed into one shell, and removed by the Ng-Sock, members of a pariah class, for interment in the cemetery of malefactors. This cemetery is termed the pit for the bones of ten thousand men. The weapon of the executioner was shaped like a scimitar, and must have had an exceedingly sharp edge, for the malefactors fell before it like blades of grass before the scythe of the mower.

As a rule, malefactors are very patient and submissive when being placed in line for execution. When a large number, say thirty, are executed together, they are ranged in rows of four or five, and several executioners are employed. Sometimes the prisoners are violent and abusive. A scene occurred in 1865, (23rd January), in which a prisoner—one of fifteen who were being executed at Canton—addressed the executioner as follows: —" A man who is beheaded can only come to earth again to fill the lowest and vilest office, namely, that of an executioner. And an executioner cannot fail to die an ignominious death. You may therefore expect my return to earth again, and in about eighteen years' time I shall probably not only fill your contemptible office, but at the same time cut off your head." A curious scene

[1] For the privilege of removing the body the friends of the colonel would probably have to pay a sum of money to the executioners. A case came under my notice in which the friends of a Chinese Mohammedan who was executed for theft paid the executioners ten dollars for this privilege.

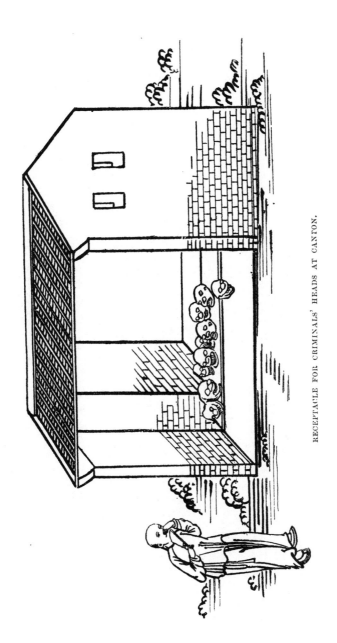

RECEPTACLE FOR CRIMINALS' HEADS AT CANTON.

occurred in the following year, 1866 (June 8th), when sixteen men were executed. One of them had a very fierce altercation with a deputy executioner, in the course of which some very strong Chinese expletives were freely exchanged. The cause of this quarrel was because the malefactor would not bend his neck. He said that his neck was long, and that it presented a target which no skilful swordsman could possibly miss. The chief executioner endeavoured to persuade the obstinate malefactor that he was not an enemy, but a friend; and that it was not by his decree, but by that of the emperor that he was in his present painful position. He added that he was desirous of inflicting as little pain as possible, and that, if the criminal would only consent to bend his neck, his head would be severed from his body by a single blow. These arguments had their weight, and the malefactor consented to do as he was bid.

The late M. A. Correa, Esq., who was the Canton correspondent of the Hongkong *China Mail*, describes an extraordinary scene which took place in 1869, when twenty-eight criminals were executed at Canton. They commenced shouting at the top of their voices, "Preserve life! preserve life!" and—"two of them, in the last line, who were already kneeling to receive their fate, suddenly sprang to their feet, and though they were manacled, the strength of four or five soldiers—in attendance with others upon the presiding magistrate—failed to place them in their former position. The executioner becoming somewhat excited, and evidently thinking there was no time to lose, gave them the *coup de grâce* while they were standing. No sooner was this bloody act brought to a close, than the sheriff with sword and mace-bearers, and a lot of ragged attendants, left the scene. At this moment, a number of the populace came upon the ground, and gazed on the headless bodies of their countrymen with the most perfect apathy and indifference."

It is not unusual to expose the heads of malefactors as a warning to others. On the public execution-ground at Canton, there was formerly a receptacle for this purpose. It was removed several years ago, and the heads are now cast into coarse earthenware tubs containing quicklime. It is very common to expose those of burglars and pirates in the immediate

vicinity of the scenes of their crimes, and I have seen the
heads of pirates exposed in cages, attached to the tops of long
poles, by the sea-shore at Macao; and in many of the towns and
villages in the neighbourhood of Canton, I have seen the.heads
of burglars bleaching under the burning rays of a tropical sun.
At the town of Chung-lok-tam, which is in the province of
Kwang-tung, at a distance of thirty English miles from its
capital, I saw, in 1861, upwards of thirty heads of burglars,
which were hanging in cages in close proximity to the market-
place.   On the banks of the Toon-ting lake, and at Eching, a
city on the river Yang-tsze, I saw heads exposed in this way.
On the banks of the Grand Canal I saw a head suspended from
a monumental arch, and another, for want of a better elevation,
placed on a tomb.   On entering the city of Nankin, I noticed
the head of a man suspended by the tail from the branch of a
tree.   This criminal had murdered a woman.   When travelling
on the plains of Inner Mongolia in 1865, similar sights met my
eye on three or four occasions.

I have stated that all traitors, parricides, matricides, fratricides,
murderers, burglars, pirates, highway robbers, &c, &c., suffer
either the first or the second class of punishment.   An exception is made in favour of criminals who are upwards of
eighty, and of those under sixteen years of age.   At present, for
example, in the prison of the chief magistrate of the Namhoi
district, at Canton, there is a youth named Chu Chan-mang,
who, in 1861, poisoned his schoolmaster in the neighbouring town of Fat-shan.   A lingering death would certainly have
been his fate, had he not been under sixteen years of age.
The probability is that he will have to spend his days in
a Chinese prison.

The third class of punishment is called Nam-kow, or death
by strangulation.   This is inflicted on kidnappers, and all
thieves who, with violence, steal articles the value of which
amounts to five hundred dollars and upwards.   The manner
in which this form of capital punishment is inflicted, is as
follows:—A cross is erected in the centre of the execution
ground, at the foot of which a stone is placed, and upon this
the prisoner stands.   His body is made fast to the perpendicular

HEAD OF A MALEFACTOR, EXPOSED AT NANKIN.

SHACKLED AND MANACLED.

beam of the cross by a band passing round the waist, whilst his arms are bound to the transverse beam. The executioner then places round the neck of the prisoner a thin but strong piece of twine, which he tightens to the greatest extent and ties in a firm knot round the upper part of the perpendicular beam. Death by this cruel process is very slow, and is apparently attended with extreme agony. The body remains on the cross during a period of twenty-four hours, the sheriff, before leaving the execution ground, taking care to attach his seal to the knot of the twine which passes round the neck of the malefactor. In the years 1866-67, many persons convicted of kidnapping coolies were put to death at Canton by strangulation. In the month of December of the former year, I saw a group of three kidnappers who were suspended in this way from crosses. The crosses were placed in a row, at a distance of a few feet only from one another. At the top of each cross, and immediately above the head of the malefactor, was a strip of paper setting forth his name and offence.

The fourth class of punishment is called Man-kwan, or transportation for life. The criminals who are thus punished, are embezzlers, forgers, &c., &c. The places of banishment in the north of China and Tartary are named respectively Hack-loong-kong, Elee, Ning-koo-tap, and Oloo-muk-tsze. To one of these places all convicts from the midland and southern provinces are sent. The labour of the unhappy men varies in a great measure according to their former outward circumstances of life. Those who are of a robust nature and who have been accustomed to agri-cultural pursuits, are daily occupied in reclaiming and cultivating waste lands. Others, more especially those who have been sent from the southern provinces, where the heat in summer is almost tropical, are in consequence of the severity of the cold which prevails in northern latitudes, made to work in government iron foundries. The aged, and those who have not been accustomed to manual labour, are daily employed in sweep-ing the state temples and other public buildings. One of the old hong merchants of Canton, who had been transported to one of these northern settlements for bankruptcy—probably fraudulent—was, in consideration of his age and former position, set to sweep the courtyards of a state temple. Convicts who have held official rank have to labour, some in the imperial gardens and others in the imperial stables, which are at the respective northern cities of Jehole and Yit-hoi. Certain convicts have their names and crimes tattooed on their cheeks, not only in the language of China, but in that also of Mantchuria. In some instances a convict from China proper is conveyed beyond the Great Wall of China and discharged, with an assurance that his life will be forfeit should he ever return. When travelling in Mongolia, I met a Chinese youth who asked alms of me in the Canton dialect. A native of the district city of Sam-sui, which is situated at a distance of thirty English miles from the city of Canton, he had been transported for some offence into the wilds of Mongolia, and his sorrowful condition made me wish that I could have taken him back to Canton as one of my attendants. In some portions of the empire convicts are sent out from prison each morning to beg their daily bread. At the small market town of Yim-poo, which is in the vicinity of Canton, a convict from Nankin used to find employment either as a porter, or a sedan-chair bearer, or as a farm labourer. Every night he returned to the yamun, where he was a prisoner; and in this way, he told me, he had spent twenty years of his life. He was very anxious to be permitted to return to Nankin to die there, so as to receive the sacred rites of ancestral worship from his posterity. If these day ticket-of-leave men are found to abuse their partial liberty by extorting money from shopkeepers, stealing, and other lawless acts, they are sent back into confinement.

The fifth class of punishment is termed Man-low, or transportation for ten or fifteen years. The criminals of this class are petty burglars, persons who harbour those who have broken the laws, &c., &c. Such offenders are generally sent to the midland provinces of the empire, where the arrangements for convict labour are similar to those of the penal settlements of the north. Convicts of this class, who are natives of the midland provinces, are sent either to the eastern, or western, or southern provinces of the empire. The barbarous practice of tattooing the cheeks is also resorted to with these. I have seen many so tattooed in the prisons of Canton. The sixth class is called Man-tow, or transportation for three years. A punishment of this nature is the portion of whoremongers, gamblers, salt smugglers, &c., &c. A convict of this class is transported to one of the provinces immediately bordering upon that of which he is a native, or in which his crime was committed.

Convicts are removed to the penal settlements in large numbers at a time. They are made to travel sixteen English miles *per diem.* The journey when possible is performed by water, otherwise the convicts are generally obliged to walk. When on the march, the convicts are bound together in companies varying from two to five each. The chains or ropes by which they are bound, pass round their necks. Their feet are also fettered, and their arms bound in various ways. The ancient Egyptians were accustomed to bind their prisoners in a similar manner. In the illustrations which may be traced in the ancient sculptures of that country, we occasionally see long trains of prisoners being conducted in procession. In some instances they are represented as bound together in companies of two, or three, or four, or five each. To the custom of shackling prisoners we find many references in the sacred scriptures. Such a practice is, at all events, clearly set forth in the following passages—2 Chron. xxxiii. 11; Ps. ii. 3; Ps. cxlix. 8. In some instances they are conveyed to their destination in waggons. When leaving Jehole in Inner Mongolia, I observed a large tilted waggon, full of convicts, entering the city. When the journey is performed on foot, many, especially of the aged and infirm, die by the way in consequence, I suppose, of bad nourishment and over-fatigue. Female convicts in particular are unable to stand these journeys, especially such as have small or contracted feet.

Before closing this chapter, it remains for me to notice a mode of summary execution sometimes resorted to by the elders of a district. It consists in casting an offender, bound hand and foot, into the nearest river or pond. It is only legal when the death warrant under which the prisoner suffers, bears the signatures, if not of all, at least of a certain number of the elders of his village. The crimes which evoke such speedy justice are

various. Thus on a Sunday morning in the year 1859, whilst
on my way to church, I observed a large and excited crowd
approaching the banks of the Canton river. They were taking
two men to the river to drown them. They cast them into the
current bound hand and foot. These wretched men, I afterwards learned, had either kidnapped or decoyed several of their
fellow-countrymen on board a foreign vessel, by which they
were conveyed as bondmen to the colonial possession of a
European kingdom. Again, in the afternoon of the 1st of
August, 1868, two men, who were also accused and convicted of
kidnapping their countrymen, were, at the command of the elders,
bound hand and foot together, and cast into the creek which
skirts, on the north side, the foreign settlement of Shameen. There
can, I think be no doubt that the drowning of these men was
carried out in the immediate vicinity of the foreign settlement
and in presence of two or three members of the foreign community, to point out to foreigners the inevitable fate of all
Chinese engaged by them to kidnap coolies for bond-ser-
vice either in the West Indian possessions of Great Britain, or
in the countries of North and South America. The drowning
of these men was, I may add, at no very great distance from
the doors of the private residence of the British West Indian
Emigration Agent.

During the Canton rebellion of 1854–55, many of the rebels
were put to death in this way by the elders of the villages to
which they respectively belonged. Indeed, on one occasion, in
the year 1854, not less than fifteen men were drowned at
Honam, Canton. These men were flung one morning at eight
o'clock into that portion of the Canton river which flows past
the plot of ground where the English and other foreign residences then stood. In some instances, however, rebels were not
put to death by drowning, but were permitted by the elders—
their own clansmen in many instances—to choose such forms
of death as were least obnoxious to them. Thus at Si-chu, in
the district of Namhoi, and at various villages in the neighbouring district of Shun-tuk many seditious persons terminated
their lives, some by opium, some by a cup of poison which the
Chinese call Tai-soee-yok, others by a poison called Woo-mun-

IN THE STOCKS.

kaong; some by strangulation. These unfortunate offenders preferred capital punishment at the hands of the elders of their respective villages, and in the presence of their families, to falling into the hands of the mandarins by whom they would have been first tortured, and then decapitated. In one instance which came under my own notice a woman named Mak Shee, who resided in the village of Laong-hoo, which is in the vicinity of the market-town of Sinnam, so reviled the elders of the village in question for putting her husband, whom they had found guilty of sedition, to death—calling upon them, now that they had taken away the support of her life, to supply her and her children with bread—that eventually they ordered her to be bound hand and foot and cast into the waters of a neighbouring river. When visiting the silk districts of Kwang-tung in 1862, I learned on reaching the market-town of Koon-shan, that, only a few days before, the gentry and elders had ordered twenty-one men who had attacked and captured two large cargo boats heavily laden with silk, to be put to death by drowning. These unfortunate wretches were, it appeared, all bound together before they were plunged into the stream.

Although the penal code of China is extremely severe, especially in cases which touch the safety and stability of the throne, or the peace of the empire, it has many very humane traits. Thus it is in accordance with the tenor of the laws for a judge to grant a free pardon to an only son who has been sentenced to undergo transportation for a definite or indefinite period of time. This pardon is, of course, granted to the delinquent for the sake of his parents. Again, should three brothers, the only sons of their parents, combine in committing a crime deserving of decapitation or transportation, the two youngest would on conviction be punished according to law, whilst the first-born would be pardoned, though equally guilty. Should a father be transported, the law allows his son to accompany him into exile. Wives, also, whose husbands are convicts, are, by the same merciful consideration, allowed to sojourn with their husbands in the penal settlements. The imperial clemency is also extended to all offenders who are idiots, or who have mutilated or crippled bodies, and are thereby rendered unequal to labour. Further, the law does not admit of convicts being sent into banishment during the first month of the year, which is regarded as a month of rest and indulgence to all; nor yet during the sixth month, as the heat of summer is then supposed to have reached its height, and travelling is in consequence attended with much personal risk and inconvenience.

In this and the preceding chapter I have described much that must have filled the reader with pain and indignation. No one can read unmoved, of courts of justice where iniquity and reckless cruelty prevail—of officials whose venality is a pit in which many an innocent family has perished—of gaols in which human beings are penned in dens of noisome filth and squalor, with, in too many instances, barely such necessaries as suffice to keep life in their emaciated bodies—of barbarous punishments which recall the darkest pages of European history. It is a very obvious reflection, but I cannot close without remarking how profoundly grateful we ought to be that our heritage has fallen to us in a land whose judges are incorrupt, and whose laws are imbued with the spirit of that Word which teaches rulers and people alike " to do justly, and to love mercy, and to walk humbly with their God."

CHAPTER IV.

FROM various passages in the writings which the Chinese regard as canonical, it may be gathered that they were at one time favoured with a knowledge of that Being whom to know spiritually is life eternal, and that in Him, whom they worship as Wang-Teen, and whom they speak of as Shang-Te, they worshipped God. The Shoo-King and the She-King ascribe to this Being the attributes of omniscience, omnipotence, and immutability; and the worship once rendered to Teen seems to have been in many respects similar to that of the patriarchs under the Old Testament dispensation. At the earliest period when we have any account of it, this primitive religion was associated with an idolatrous worship of the spirits of departed ancestors, and of spirits supposed to preside over the various operations of Nature. In this corrupt development the Chinese almost entirely lost sight of that God whom they had acknowledged as the Creator of the universe and its Supreme Ruler. With this religion, which still holds its place as the national or established religion of the land, the name of Confucius is associated. It is to him as the compiler and editor of what have been termed the canonical books of the Chinese, and the most illustrious and influential teacher of morality they have produced, that its permanence as a distinct system and its supremacy in the state over the religions by which it is surrounded are mainly due.

Confucius flourished in the latter half of the sixth century before Christ—a century remarkable in the East for its spiritual and intellectual activity. Among his own countrymen, Laou-tsze the founder of Taouism, and among the Greeks, Pythagoras, were propounding philosophical systems which in some points bear a curious resemblance to each other. In India Buddha was successfully promulgating his new doctrines. The birth of Confucius took place in the year 551 B.C. in Tsow, a district now of the province of Shan-tung. The Chinese never permit a sage to be born without such accompaniments, and it is said to have been signalized by supernatural events. The more modest account of his genealogy—for one narrative places at the head of his pedigree the Emperor Hwang-te, who flourished more than two thousand years before the Christian era—proves him to have been a scion of a ducal house, and traces his descent from a brother of Chow, the last sovereign of the Yin dynasty. Many of his ancestors were certainly ministers and soldiers of distinction, and one of them especially was remarkable for his humility and his devotion to literature. His father, Shuh Leang-heih, was a soldier of great bravery, and Confucius was the child of his second marriage, when he was upwards of seventy years of age. A story of his early years represents him as indicating the bias of his mind in his play, in which he often imitated the arrangement of sacrificial vessels, and went through ceremonial postures. At the age of fifteen he was, he tells us, devoted to learning. When he was nineteen he married. Shortly after he seems to have held his first political appointment as keeper of the stores of grain in his native principality of Loo. In the following year he was put in charge of the public fields and lands. His reputation soon spread among the states into which the kingdom was divided, and subsequently during a public career which extended over fifty years, he received invitations from various courts to hold offices, which his self-respect—a feature not less conspicuous in his character than his genuine humility —often induced him to decline. Notwithstanding the love of pleasure in princes, and the machinations of the courtiers by whom he was opposed, he rendered substantial services in his various offices; but his official influence was entirely subordinate to that which he exercised as the recognized authority upon all questions relating to the early history of the empire, and as the

eloquent expounder of those great moral principles which his
historical studies had convinced him should form the basis of
legislation. He had begun early in life—in his twenty-second
year—to labour as a public teacher, and he succeeded in making
himself the centre of a very large circle of disciples, whose
devotion is a proof of his extraordinary force of character, and
of the moral excellence of his life. His reputation was such
that he is said to have had three thousand disciples. From
these he selected seventy-two, whom he divided into four classes.
He set apart the first for the study of morals; the second was
required to devote itself to the art of reasoning; the third to
devising the best forms of government; and the fourth to
exercising the power of public teaching.

In his constant endeavour to promote in the mind of the
nation a reverent regard for those principles by which the great
emperors Yaou and Shun had been directed nearly two thousand
years before, Confucius devoted himself to reducing the traditions and rough records of antiquity into a perfect form, and he
succeeded before his death in compiling and editing what have
been termed the Five Canonical Books of the Chinese, that is,
the five " King " which they reverence as embodying the truth
upon the highest subjects from those whom they venerate as
holy and wise men. These books consist of:—

I. The Yih-King, or Book of Changes, a cosmological and
ethical treatise, the crude beginnings of which are ascribed to
Fuh-he, the reputed founder of Chinese civilization.

II. The Shoo-King, or Book of Historical Documents, in
which we have an account of the reigns of Yaou and Shun, and
of the dynasties of Hea and Shang, as also of many of the
sovereigns of Chow. The narrative frequently assumes the
form of a dialogue, and contains much of a didactic nature.

III. The She-King, or Book of Poetry, a collection of poems
to which Confucius attached great value as a means of moulding
the national character.

IV. The Le-ke, or Record of Rites. This is a national ceremonial, and the Chinese consider the observance of its ceremonies and usages to be essential to the maintenance of social
order and the promotion of virtue.

V. Ch'un Ts'ew, or Spring and Autumn, a history of his time, and of several reigns immediately preceding it, the title being derived from the events of every year being arranged under the names of the seasons, two of which are named by synecdoche for the whole four.

The first four, "King," are said to have been compiled and edited by Confucius. In the fourth, however, there is said to be much from later hands. Only the fifth, "Spring and Autumn," is an original work by the sage himself.

The four *Shoos*, or writings rank next to these books in the estimation of the Chinese. In three of these, the Lun-Yu, or Digested Conversations between Confucius and his disciples; the Ta Hëo, or Great Learning; and the Chung Yung, or Doctrine of the Mean, we have a record of his doctrines and sayings, by his disciples. The fourth of the *Shoos* consists of the works of Mencius, a celebrated writer of the Confucian school, who died B.C. 317.

When death was removing him from the scene of his labours Confucius must have felt that his efforts for his country had been crowned with but scanty success. He died at the age of seventy-four, leaving the land for which he had lived more than ever the prey of the evils which he had vainly endeavoured to extirpate. "The kings," he said on his death-bed, "will not hearken to my doctrines. I am no longer, therefore, of service upon earth, and it is time for me to quit it." After his death his name was, as to the present day it continues to be, held in the highest veneration by all classes of society.[1] The tenets of other ancient philosophical schools have been super-

---

[1] To this statement there was one notable exception. When, towards the close of the third century, Che Hwangte—a man of inordinate ambition—had succeeded in establishing the supremacy of the Tsin dynasty, he ordered the sacred books which Confucius had written to be destroyed, in order that they might not suggest an unfavourable comparison between his own and former reigns. This order was tremblingly obeyed—the Yih-King alone being exempted from the general destruction, as it was not a historical work. It was then customary, as it is now, for the literati to commit to memory the writings of their favourite philosophers, and as they naturally showed themselves hostile to his rule, this Vandal completed his infamous scheme by putting more than four hundred of them to death. Under succeeding sovereigns, however, and especially under the auspices of the Emperor Han-ou-te, these lost works were successfully recovered or restored.

seded, but those which came from the lips of Confucius are to-day read, admired, and embraced by a large portion of the great human family. Throughout the empire his works are regarded as the standard of religious, moral, and political wisdom. It is only by a knowledge of them that literary and political distinction can be won; and filial piety, which after the death of parents assumes the form of ancestral worship, must be considered the central doctrine of his system, and regarded at this hour as the national religion of the Chinese.

Although Confucius has sometimes been ranked with founders of religion like Buddha and Mohammed, this is rather owing to his labours on the "King," and to his extraordinary reputation as a moral teacher, than to any claim which he has to be considered as a distinctively religious teacher. There are certainly no grounds for supposing that he added any new doctrine either to the metaphysical speculations or the religious system of these books. In his recorded sayings, there is no information as to his views, either on the subject of man's creation, or of the future which awaits him beyond the grave. On the contrary, we learn in the three *Shoos*—in which his disciples have done for the Chinese sage what Boswell did for Dr. Johnson—that his talk was not about religious questions, but about history, poetry, and the rules of propriety, and above all about whatever concerned the growth of social virtue in the individual or the state. The providential government of an overruling Providence was recognized by Confucius. He taught that in this world the good are rewarded and the bad punished. On one occasion, when in danger from the fury of the people of K'wang, who mistook him for an old enemy of theirs—a tax-gather—he made the memorable declaration:—" After the death of King Wan, was not the cause of truth lodged here in me ? Had Heaven wished to let this cause perish, I, a future mortal, could not have got such a relation to that cause. So long as Heaven does not let the cause of truth perish, what can the people of K'wang do to me ? "

Confucius evidently attached great importance to the solemn public worship of Shang-Te, by the head of the state in person assisted by his ministers. " By the ceremonies of the sacrifices to heaven and earth," we find him saying to his disciples, when he is speaking of the wisdom of the ancients, " they served God : and by the ceremonies of the ancestral temple they sacrificed to their ancestors. He who understands the ceremonies of the sacrifices to heaven and earth, and the meaning of the several sacrifices to ancestors, would find the government of a kingdom as easy as to look into his palm." It has been sometimes represented that in their worship of heaven and earth, the Chinese adore as two separate divinities, the physical firmament and the solid globe. There is sufficient evidence, however, in their literature that this gross view of their religion is erroneous ; and the passage which I have just quoted shows that in the mind of Confucius, the object of their adoration in the worship of heaven and earth, is the Supreme Being. Indeed in the year 1700— after the idolatrous elements of their religion had been at work for nearly four thousand years—the monotheism of the Chinese was the subject of official affirmation by the Emperor Kanghe to Pope Alexander VII. In the edict which he then issued, he made the singular statement that the " religious customs of China are political." In the passage which we quoted from the Doctrine of the Mean, Confucius looks at the great religious ceremonies of the nation from a political point of view. It is doubtless to the fact that he fell so far short of realising man's position here as a fallen spiritual being, whose relations are directly with a personal God, and have their issues in eternity, that the marked absence of religious sentiment among the Chinese at the present day is in a large measure owing. His dim and imperfect knowledge on a subject of such vital importance, cannot be a matter of surprise to us when we reflect that, like Socrates and Plato, he was unenlightened by that Divine Revelation which has disclosed to man the great end of his creation, and enabled him to look forward to death, not merely with submission, but with joyful anticipation and hope.

Identifying himself with all that belonged to the intellectual condition of his age, Confucius virtually constituted himself the interpreter of the national religion, but his work lay essentially in the social and political world. His mind was intensely

practical. His attitude towards religion was that of one who
held it folly to waste, in vain attempts to light up the obscurity
in which the future of man is veiled, those energies which ought
to be strenuously devoted to discharging the duties of life. The
saint of Confucius is neither the absorbed ascetic of Buddha,
nor the contemplative recluse of Laou-tsze. He is the dignified
head of the well-ordered family; the dutiful and patriotic
citizen who seeks after righteousness in his doings and propriety in his conduct, distinguished by reverence towards his
parents and towards the emperor, both of whom virtually stand
between him and God. But the "superior man" of Confucius
is not conspicuous merely for his dutifulness and reverence,
He must be possessed of sincerity, knowledge, magnanimity
and energy ; and with all his reverence for authority, Confucius
held that a sovereign's claim to the allegiance of his subjects
might become void through his wickedness, so that his people
might be justified in dethroning him.

Although his moral system is founded on self-culture, it was
clearly from a social and political standpoint that he dealt with
man. He spent his life in promoting a reverent recognition by those
who ruled and those who were ruled, of the duties which belong
to the several relations of society. Without seeking to revolu-
tionize existing institutions, he endeavoured to open the eyes or
his countrymen to their moral significance. "There is government," as he once put it, "when the prince is prince and the
minister is minister, when the father is father and the son is
son." He held it to be especially incumbent upon rulers that
they should be virtuous, for the effect of their example upon the
people is as that of wind upon the grass, which it bends in the
direction in which it blows. But he sought to hedge up the
path of each official, and indeed of every man in the state by a
variety of forms and ceremonies of a nature to remind him of
the duties of his position, and to strengthen in him a sense
of propriety—which in his view was of the greatest importance.

The doctrine most prominent in his system is that of filial
piety. In the family he found the prototype of the state; and
to this day the Chinese government is only to be understood

through the relation which exists between a father and his son. In recognition of the sanctity of fatherhood, the child reverences the parent; the parent the magistrate; and the magistrate the emperor.[1] The "superior man," Confucius taught, "bends his attention to what is radical. That being established, all right practical courses naturally grow up. Filial piety and paternal submission!—are they not the root of all benevolent actions?"[2] In his scholarly and exhaustive prolegomena to his translations of the Chinese classics, Dr. Legge relates an incident which illustrates the strong vein of practical common sense which distinguished the philosopher. About the year 500 B.C., while Confucius occupied the post of Minister of Crime at the court of Loo, a father against whom his son had been guilty of some offence, asked for the punishment of the latter at the hands of the law. Exercising his discretion, however, the new Minister of Crime, from whom no doubt such a decision was little expected, gave orders that not only the son, but the father also, should be put in prison. The head of the Ke is said to have remonstrated. "You are playing with me, Sir Minister of Crime. Formerly you told me that in a state, or a family, filial duty was the first thing to be insisted upon. What hinders you now from putting to death this unfilial son, as an example to all the people?" Whereupon Confucius replied with a sigh, "When superiors fail in their duty, and then proceed to put their inferiors to death, it is not right. This father has not taught his son to be filial; to grant his prayer would be to murder the innocent. The manners of the age have long been in a melancholy condition; we cannot expect the people not to be transgressing the laws."

As one of the fruits of the teaching of Confucius, we find that singular prominence is still given to the doctrine of filial piety. No one I believe can have resided in China

---

[1] To teach the people their duties to their parents and their rulers it is provided that the magistrates of cities and towns and the elders of villages shall, on the first and fifteenth days of each month, read aloud in the public halls, with which cities, towns, and even villages are provided, certain portions of the Book of Sacred Instructions.

[2] *The Chinese Classics, translated into English.* By James Legge, D.D. *Confucian Analects,* b. i. ch. ii. 2.

without noting the marked respect which children pay to their parents and guardians. Their filial piety manifests itself not only in the ordinary duties, but in signal instances of self-denial. It is quite usual for sons to go to prison, and into banishment, for offences committed by their parents. In 1862, I found in the district city of Tsung-fa, a youth suffering incarceration in the stead of his grandfather, who had been committed to prison for bankruptcy. Availing itself of this sentiment, the government seizes the parents of offenders when it is unable to effect the capture of the offenders themselves. I may mention the case of a Chinese assistant or overseer on board a foreign store-ship at Kum-sing-moon, who hastened at once to surrender, when he heard that his parents had been imprisoned at Canton because he was suspected of having taken part with the rebels in 1854. Of course the parents were liberated, but the son was decapitated within forty-eight hours after his surrender. One of the most striking acts of Chinese filial devotion is cutting a piece of flesh from the thigh or arm, in order that it may be prepared with other ingredients as a restorative for a parent in extreme cases of sickness. Such acts of piety are not very unusual. At Pit-kong in the county of Shun-tuk, I was acquainted with a youth who had cut a large piece of flesh from his arm out of devotion to his mother, who was supposed to be suffering from an incurable disease. He was evidently proud of the scar which remained. At the silk town of Yung-ak in the same district there was living, in the year 1864, an old woman of the clan or family Ho, whose recovery from a sickness which threatened to prove fatal was attributed to her daughter-in-law, who had cut a piece of flesh from her arm to supply the restorative. That such acts are encouraged by the government is evident from this extract which we quote from the *Pekin Gazette* of July 5, 1870 :—

" Mā-Hsin-Yi, the Governor-General of the two Kiangs (Kiang-man and Kiang-si), memorializes the throne to the effect that a young girl of Kiang-ning Fu cut off two joints of one of her fingers, and put the flesh thereof into the medicine which her mother was taking for a disease which the physicians had pronounced incurable. The traditional and orthodox Chinese custom, for which (as the memorial says) there are numerous precedents even in recent years, is to cut off a portion of the flesh of the thigh. This the young girl, aged only fifteen, at first actually attempted to do, but had not either strength or courage to complete the operation. The governor-general indulges in boundless laudations of this act of filial piety, which had of course its reward in the immediate recovery of the mother. He begs that the emperor will bestow some exemplary reward on the child, such as the erection of a triumphal arch in the neighbourhood to commemorate the act. By this means," he says, "filial piety all over the world will receive encouragement."

It is no exaggeration to say that to the tenacious hold which the teaching of Confucius has enabled this doctrine—which is the foundation of order in the state—to take upon the mind of this people is due to a large extent its wonderful national longevity. It is impossible not to ask how China has contrived to outlive the nations of antiquity with which she was contemporary, the ruined masses or scattered fragments of whose "Eternal Babylon," "Eternal Nineveh," and "Eternal Thebes," are all that remain to us of their vanished grandeur. It would seem as if in their keeping of the fifth commandment the Chinese had found the blessing which God has attached to its fulfilment. To this people by whom God himself has been very much forgotten, but by whom this law written in their hearts, and preached with such power by one so essentially their representative man, has been exalted and honoured, He has granted length of days in the land which He has given them.

Upon the broad basis of this doctrine of filial piety, Confucius may be said to have re-established the superstructure of ancestral worship—a form of worship which more than any other feature of the ancient religion of the Chinese, or of the religions which now flourish by its side, has taken hold of the national mind. Through the length and breadth of the land there is not a dwelling which does not contain a shrine or altar before which, morning and evening, adoration is paid to departed ancestors; and at stated seasons of the year the people may be found making pilgrimages to the tops of high hills, and to distant and secluded vales, where, before the tombs of their ancestors, they prostrate themselves in awe and reverence. The worship thus paid is regarded as the continuation of the homage and reverence shown them upon earth, rather than as worship rendered to a god; for they do not seem to consider these spirits to be invested with attributes which render them greatly superior to the conditions of being under which they existed in the flesh. They believe that the happiness of these spirits depends in a great measure on the worship and offerings of posterity, and that those who are careful to render it to them secure the favour of the gods. Sometimes they ascribe to the spirits of their ancestors the power of exercising a providential care over them, and of punishing them should they neglect to discharge their religious duties. On several occasions, and at all seasons of the year, I have seen Chinese at the tombs of their ancestors seeking to obtain oracular information. The state worship which is rendered in the Temple of Imperial Ancestors is celebrated with the greatest solemnity and splendour, and it can only be offered, like that which is paid to Teen, by the Emperor himself and his principal mandarins.

The worship of ancestors had its natural development in the canonization and worship of the spirits of great sages, heroes, benefactors of mankind, such as the ancient patrons of agriculture and silk-weaving, eminent statesmen, philanthropists, distinguished physicians, and martyrs to virtue. Conspicuous among the multitude of canonized worthies who fill the Pantheon of China are Kwan-te, the god of war, Confucius himself, "the most holy teacher of ancient times," Man-chang, a god of learning, Teen-how, the Queen of Heaven, and others of whom the reader will find some account in the chapter of mythological sketches.

Parallel with their worship of the spirits of ancestors and of deified mortals is that which they render to the *Shin* or spirits whom they suppose to preside over Nature in her different departments or operations. To sun, moon, and stars, to the elements, to the seasons, to fertile land and waving grain, to every high hill, to streams and rivers, to clouds, rain, wind, and thunder, to the four seas and to the passing year, they assign

tutelary spirits whom they worship. For them the encircling
air is peopled with such beings, both good and bad. "How vast
is the influence of the Kwei-shin!" is the language in which
Confucius speaks of them. "If you look for them you cannot
see them; if you listen you cannot hear them; they embody all
things; without them things cannot be. When we are commanded to fast, purify, and dress ourselves, in order to sacrifice
to them, all things appear full of them." Conspicuous amongst
these are the gods of the land and of the grain, of the sun, moon,
and stars, and Lung-Wong, the Dragon King, or Neptune of the
Chinese. The belief of the Chinese in such beings reminds one
of the ministry of angels and genii in which the ancient Persians
—from whom the Jews are said to have borrowed much of their
angel lore—had such implicit faith.

During the four thousand years over which their history
extends, the Chinese have never disgraced their religion with
the stories of illicit love which are conspicuous in the Greek
and Roman mythologies; and they have never fashioned an
image of that Being whom they recognize as Supreme. But
the essential monotheism of their religion has suffered from
a perpetual eclipse; and, as if the one pure element in it were
not already sufficiently obscured by creature worship, the people
have been virtually driven into idolatry by the jealousy with
which the worship of Wang-Teen has been confined to the
emperor and his court. In the present day no very sharp lines
are drawn between the national gods of the Chinese and those
of Taouism and Buddhism, and the people are often guided in
their superstition simply by the reputation which an idol enjoys,
or the supposed efficacy of certain rites.

Another cause of the uncertainty of their monotheism is to
be found in the materialistic speculations of the school of
Confucianists who flourished in the Soong dynasty A.D. 960-
1271. These philosophers—the most prominent of whom was
Choo-foo-tsze, who died A.D. 1200—fixing upon the crude speculations of the Yih-King as their point of departure, endeavoured
to explain the creation of the universe. Without explaining his
meaning, Confucius had said that the *Tae-Keih* or Great Extreme was at the beginning of all things, and into this, as an

ultimate principle, they resolved the personal God of the Shoo-King and She-King. I need not attempt to discuss their precise position among philosophers. It is sufficient to state that the practical effect of their speculations was to pervert the body of the *literati* to materialism or atheism.

In the midst of conflicting views and systems, the Chinese are unanimous in the reverence with which they continue to regard Confucius ; and, as their religion is rather a body of ceremonies than a system of doctrine, we may gather a clearer idea of it from the worship which is paid to this deified philosopher. Services are held in his honour twice a month. He is worshipped with great solemnity by all the mandarins, civil and military, throughout the empire, in the middle months of spring and autumn of each year. At Pekin the worship is led by the emperor in person, and in a provincial capital by the governor-general. For the two days preceding the ceremony the mandarins are supposed to fast. On the eve of the solemnity, a bullock, and several sheep and pigs, are conducted in procession with banners and bands of music to the temple of Confucius by an official attired in court costume. There the animals are paraded before the altar, on which incense is kept burning in honour of the occasion. When the butcher, kneeling knife in hand before the altar, has received the command to rise and slay the victims, they are conducted to an adjoining slaughter-house. Their carcasses, shorn of hair and wool,[1] are afterwards conveyed to the temple, and arranged on the high altar as expiatory sacrifices, if we may use the expression, in honour of the great heathen philosopher. Thank-offerings, consisting of flowers, fruits, and wines, in three different kinds respectively, together with nine different kinds of silk fabrics—all in white—are laid upon the same altar. On the succeeding day, the emperor or the governor-general who is to act as Pontifex Maximus—Shing-Si-Koon is the term used by the Chinese—proceeds to the temple. He is first called upon to wash his hands. When he has done so, and when the civil and military officers of the district, who on such occasions wear court costume, have arranged themselves in solemn order with their faces

---

[1] The blood, hair, and wool of the victims are buried in the earth.

turned towards the altar of the sage—the civil officers on the
east, and the military officers on the west, side of the grand
quadrangle of the temple—a master of ceremonies calls aloud
" Ying-shan," or, " Receive the Spirit." When he has called a
second time to those assembled—this time in the words " Kŭ-
ying-shan-sok "—the vocalists and musicians,[1] who are supposed
to be seventy-four in number, sing and play a hymn which is
termed Chu-ping-chaong. This hymn consists of seven verses,
each of which is formed of eight lines, each line having four
characters. This portion of the service having been brought to
a close, a herald calls aloud " Shaong-haong "—" Let the incense
arise." The governor-general then approaches by the eastern
staircase, the shrine in which the altar stands, and takes up his
position straight in front. Almost immediately behind him
stand thirty-six boys in neat uniforms, each bearing in his hand
a plume of the feathers of the Argus pheasant. There are four
other boys, two of whom bear standards, and two long rods or
wands. A herald again cries " Ying-shan " or " Receive the
Spirit," upon which his excellency kneels down and performs
the Kow-tow. On rising to his feet he is presented with a
burning incense stick by an attendant who stands on the east
side of him. This he raises with both hands above his head
with the same movement which a Roman Catholic priest uses
in elevating the host. An attendant who stands on his left side
now receives the burning incense stick, and places it in a large
incense burner standing on the altar. The governor-general
again kneels before the altar and performs the Kow-tow. He
is then escorted from the shrine, by the western staircase to his
position at the head of the officials who line the sides of the
quadrangle. As soon as he has taken up this position, all the
mandarins, together with his excellency, kneel down at the
command of a master of ceremonies, and perform the Kow-tow.

---

[1] Although the musical part of the service devolves principally upon the
vocalists, who chant hymns of praise in honour of the sage, an orchestra is
arranged on one side of the altar, consisting of musicians attired for the occasion
in robes of state. In the hands of many of these, it is usual to place various
kinds of ancient musical instruments, but, as the use of these is unknown to
the Chinese musicians of the present day, the choral part of the service is especially
prominent;

During the rendering of this act of obeisance the minstrels chant in honour of Confucius the hymn called "Chuk-sze." In the number of its verses and metre, this hymn is precisely the same as that called "Chu-ping-chaong." In the performance of the various duties which devolve upon him in the course of the ceremonial, the governor-general, escorted by two bedells, has to proceed into the immediate presence of the altar, which groans under expiatory and eucharistic offerings, no fewer than nine times, and on each occasion he presents to the tablet or idol a certain number of the offerings. He raises each offering as it is presented above his head. In the case of the animals such an elevation is of course impossible, and portions only of their flesh are elevated. At the close of the ceremony, and whilst the governor-general is standing before the altar, a letter or prayer to Confucius, copied by a caligraphist on a sheet of yellow paper, is read aloud by a herald in the hearing of all present. It is then conveyed to the spirit of the departed sage by being cast into a sacred furnace. Offerings, both expiatory and eucharistic, are presented on these occasions in the presence of the tablets of the ancestors of Confucius, and of those also of his disciples.

I have said that the mandarins wear, as a mark of reverence, their court costume. This includes the official cap. The wearing of a cap or bonnet is universal among the people, both in the worship of their gods and in ancestral worship. It was the custom observed by the ancient Jews, and also by the Romans. Virgil makes more than one allusion to it in the *Æneid*. To quote one reference only—

> "Quin, ubi transmissæ steterint trans æquora classes,
> Et positis aris jam vota in littore solves;
> Purpureo velare comas adopertus amictu:
> Ne qua inter sanctos ignes in honore deorum
> Hostilis facies occurrat, et omnia turbet."
>   ÆNEID, iii. 1, 432.

The reader will have noticed that the officiating mandarin is called upon to wash his hands before entering into the presence of the object of his adoration. The circumstance reminds one of the lustrations of the Levitical priesthood, who were commanded on pain of death to wash their hands in the brazen laver of the temple before they drew near to the altar of the Most High. I cannot but add how much impressed I was on finding that the Chinese, a people who for so many centuries have been essentially exclusive, are accustomed to offer expiatory sacrifices. I am, of course, aware that frequent references are made to such sacrifices by Pagan writers both of ancient Greece and ancient Rome; and—to quote one reference only—the language of the poet has no doubt been the heartfelt sentiment of many a worshipper—

> " Cor, pro corde, precor, pro fibra sumite fibras ;
> Hanc animam vobis pro meliore damus."
>
> OVID, *Fasti*, 6, 161.

The possibility, however, of my being a spectator of such sacrificial rites never occurred to me until I entered upon my duties in the midst of this singular people, who, from generation to generation, have preserved with remarkable fidelity the customs of a remote past. And when I found myself actually present on an occasion of solemn state worship in which expiatory sacrifices were offered up, it brought vividly before my mind scenes with which the pages of the Old Testament abound. I can only regard the idea of such sacrificial rites among the Chinese as a heritage—through what channels transmitted in this case, as in the case of other pagan nations, I am at a loss to say—of the teaching of Noah, who introduced to the post-diluvian world a knowledge and practice of religious ceremony which he had inherited in the first instance from his God-fearing forefathers.

In honour of Confucius there is a temple in every provincial, prefectoral, and district city throughout the empire. In architectural design these temples are all precisely similar. Each is approached by a large entrance consisting of a centre and two side gates. At either side of this triple gateway there is a pillar bearing an inscription to remind the *literati* that it is a reverential duty, becoming their station in life, to alight from their sedan-chairs, or horses, and to walk into the courtyard of a building so hallowed. Upon entering, the visitor finds facing him, an artificial crescent-shaped pond spanned by a neat stone bridge of three arches. The water is supposed to be pure, an

EXTERIOR OF A CONFUCIAN TEMPLE.

emblem of the purity of the sage and of his doctrines. At the end of the courtyard is a covered triple gateway in red colour, through which the votary passes into the first quadrangle. Facing the gates at the opposite end of the quadrangle stands the altar in honour of Confucius; and above it is a large red tablet with the name of the sage in gilded letters. In some of the temples an idol takes the place of the tablet. In my travels through China I discovered this to be the case in several instances; and the practice, I apprehend, is not a very recent one. In 1856 an idol of Confucius was placed by the *literati* in the temple which stands in the Namhoi district of Canton. This step met with strong opposition from many who believed that, as Confucius was very much opposed to idols, great calamities would befall the city. This prediction of the iconoclasts received its fulfilment, for in September of the same year a quarrel arose between the British consular authorities at Canton and the Viceroy Yeh, which led to the bombardment of the city, and to a war of three or four years' duration. During the bombardment by the British, a shot struck and greatly damaged the pedestal on which the figure of Confucius stands.

In close proximity to this altar are others in honour of Mencius, Tsang-tsze, and other renowned authors. On the right and left of the quadrangle there are cloisters containing shrines, above the altars of which are the monumental tablets of the seventy-two disciples, as well as tablets, of others who, since the days of Confucius, have rendered themselves famous as expounders of his doctrines. In the second quadrangle of the temple stands a shrine in honour of the parents and grandparents of the sage, who receive a share of the veneration of the people whose moral condition their gifted descendant so zealously endeavoured to improve. To each Confucian temple are attached the following shrines, namely, the How-tai-Tsze, a hall in which tablets are placed bearing the names of officials conspicuous for their fidelity, and of men renowned for their filial piety as sons and grandsons; the Ming-wan-Tsze, a hall containing tablets bearing the names of officials who have proved great benefactors to the districts over which they have ruled; the Haong-yin-Tsze, or hall with tablets bearing the names of

native sages ; and the Tsit-how-Tsze, or hall with tablets bearing the names of virtuous women, natives of the district.
There is a hall in the prefectoral Confucian temple at Canton
termed Yee-fow-Tsze, which was built by Keying, the well-
known Chinese commissioner to Canton. It contains a tablet
with the name of one Ho Yow-shu, a man of great wealth, who
succeeded in taking the Chun-tsze degree at Pekin. The tablet
of Ho Yow-shu, however, was not placed in its present position
on account either of his wealth or his learning, but in consequence of his having after the death of his wife steadfastly
remained a widower. He died far advanced in years. His wife
died shortly after her marriage, being then, like her husband,
very young. I may mention an incident which may serve to
illustrate the care with which the *literati* confine the honour of
a place in the hall of native sages to those only who have really
been distinguished for their mental attainments. In the hall of
a temple had been placed the tablet of one Loo Man-kum.
This man had been distinguished as chief of the Hong merchants rather than for his learning, and his tablet was an eye-
sore to the *literati*. After several years they petitioned the
officials of the city to remove it. They refused, and the matter
was eventually referred to the central government at Pekin, who
despatched a commissioner to Canton. This official agreeing with
the *literati* that the tablet was unworthy of its position, orders
were given for its removal. A cord was tied round it, and it
was dragged from the altar beyond the precincts of the temple.

The temples in honour of Confucius are often imposing. The
temple at Foo-chow and that also at Yang-chow are very noteworthy. In the latter I was shown a large inner chamber containing a great number of blocks on which, the attendant informed me, were engraven the writings of Confucius, which are
here printed and published. At Noo-chang there is a temple
remarkable for the fact that it stands not within, as is invariably
the case elsewhere, but without the walls of the city. The inhabitants say that within the walls there was not, according
to the opinion of the geomancers, a site sufficiently propitious
to be used for the erection of a temple in honour of one so
renowned as the immortal sage of China.

Of all the Confucian temples, however, that which stands in the city of Pekin is by far the most interesting. The vaulted roof is painted blue, and is elaborately decorated; the floor is covered with a carpet made, I believe, of camels' hair. In the court-yard of the temple are rows of cedar trees, which, having been planted prior to the Ming dynasty, are now upwards of five hundred years old. There are also ten stones shaped like drums, upon each of which are engraven stanzas of poetry. These stone drums are said to have been in existence since the days of Yaou and Shun, who flourished, the former B.C. 2357, and the latter B.C. 2255. In a classic written a little later than the days of Confucius, a reference is made to these stones. In consequence of the reverence in which they are held, they have always been kept in the royal cities in which the Emperors of China have resided. At one time they were lodged in the city of Sie-nan Foo, and while they were in the keeping of this city, some of them were lost. One of the missing stones, however, was found after the lapse of many years in a farmyard, where, having been converted into a trough, it was used for the purpose of watering cattle. It is, of course, defaced. As I looked at these stones with their worn record of sacred tenets, said to have been graven upon them more than four thousand years ago, I could not help feeling much impressed, and there came into my mind that portion of the inspired Word in which we read of "the two tables of the testimony," which "were written on both their sides," and "were the work of God, and the writing was the writing of God, graven upon the tables." The custom of recording on stone was very generally practised in the earliest ages of the world. It was on tables of stone, for example, that Thoth engraved, not only the theology of Egypt, but the annals of the earliest ages of that most ancient country. In Crete, there stood at one time very ancient tables of stone, on which were engraven descriptions of the religious ceremonies of the Corybantes. At Athens there was formerly a column on which was engraven what was said to have been a law of Theseus, the great legendary hero of Attica. Osiris, Sesostris, Hercules, and other heroes of antiquity are also said to have resorted to this expedient as a means of perpetuating their deeds.

There are no fewer than three temples to Confucius in Canton, namely, the one in the Namhoi district, to which I have already referred; one in the Pun-yu district, and one in the prefecture, of which the two districts are integral portions. In point of architecture and extent, they are all precisely the same. In the grounds of the prefectoral temple there is a *mons sacer*, or sacred mount, upon the summit of which stands an arbour. In this arbour is placed a broad, smooth, black marble slab, on which is engraven a representation of "the most perfect sage." There is a portrait also of Ngan-tsze, a great upholder of the doctrines of Confucius, whose custom it was to study on this sacred mount. The arbour is called Kow-sze, or the nine duties. It was built in the third year, A.D. 1129, of the Emperor Kin-too.

Confucian temples are occasionally used as colleges, and as halls in which to hold ordinary public examinations. In each temple two officials, called Kow-Koon, are lodged in chambers on the right and left of the principal quadrangle. All bachelors of arts of the district in which the temple stands are under the direction of these officials; without whose sanction they cannot be arrested. When a bachelor of arts stands at the bar of a magistrates' court, it is usual for the Kow-Koon to occupy a seat on the bench. In every school and college of the empire there are tablets bearing the name of Confucius, before which daily worship is offered by the members.

TAOUISM.

CONFUCIANISM fails lamentably in this respect—it does not provide for the spiritual wants or desires of man's nature. In the writings of Confucius and in the traditions of his teaching the Chinese found a powerful incentive to national well-doing, but there was no sustenance for that part of man's complex nature which impels even the most barbarous races to adopt a religion. Hence, side by side with Confucianism, which in point of origin it slightly preceded, flourished Taouism, a system which, while giving a speculative account of God and of the universe, presented several points to which the religious feelings of men attached themselves with greater readiness:

Buddhism was introduced from India much later, in the first century of the Christian era, and it found the people still unsatisfied and ready to welcome it.

Although the doctrine of Taou had been recognized by philosophers before Laou-tsze developed it as the central dogma of his system, he is justly regarded as the founder of the sect which derives its name from it. Born about the beginning of the sixth century B.C., he lived to see Confucius, who visited him at the court of Chow, actively engaged in his career as a public teacher. His parents were probably very poor, his father being according to one account a peasant who, after remaining unmarried up to his seventieth year, married a peasant woman of forty. Through his learning and abilities Laou-tsze succeeded in obtaining office at the court of Chow. It is impossible to say how many years he retained this appointment, and what was its precise nature. It is clear, however, that his duties were in connection with the keeping of the archives and other historical treasures of the State. Eventually, finding that they interfered with his devotion to philosophy, and influenced largely, no doubt, by the troubled and threatening aspect of the times, Laou-tsze sought retirement amongst the hills near his native village, on the eastern borders of Honan, and devoted his whole time and energies to philosophic research. In this retirement he enjoyed leisure for the quiet reflection which is considered by the sect as essential to advancement in moral excellence, and produced his celebrated work, Taou-tih-King.

The ethical doctrines of this book, which exalt virtue as the *summum bonum*, are based upon its metaphysical speculations. It is by stillness and contemplation, and by union with Taou, that virtue is to be achieved. The word Taou means, in the first place, a way, and then, a principle. Hence its use to signify the ἀρχή, or Supreme Principle of the universe. What we are to understand by this principle is a question involved in great obscurity, owing, firstly, to the difficulty in deciding whether Laou-tsze regarded Taou in the light of a personal Being, or of a principle antecedent to the personal deity; and, secondly, because it is not quite clear whether he considered Taou to be a creative power distinct from the universe, or whether he regarded the latter as merely a pantheistic manifestation. If, as is probable, Laou-tsze was a pantheist, he certainly held that higher form of pantheism which, while necessarily confounding to some extent the universe with its principle, assigns to the latter "a superiority over the mass which it pervades." Taou is immaterial and eternal, and the universe—an emanation from this transcendent source—exists in the silent, yet ceaselessly active omnipresence of Taou, and everywhere bears the impress of plastic Reason. The masterpiece of creation is the holy sage who, when he dies, returns to the bosom of Eternal Reason to enjoy endless rest, while the wicked are condemned to prolong a miserable existence on earth in successive lives, dying only to be born again in some new form. The fundamental idea in the system of Laou-tsze seems to have been unity. Carrying this principle into the region of morals, he made virtue consist in losing sight of self in the universe. Man, he taught, should go through life as if nothing which he possesses were his own, and should love all his fellow creatures, not excepting his enemies. He urged that nothing could be compared to the happiness enjoyed by him who had once attained to virtue, and that he, and only he, could regard with indifference health or sickness, joy or sorrow, wealth or indigence.

In the existing Taouism of China it is difficult to recognise the metaphysical speculations and ethical doctrines of this remarkable philosopher. The former are disguised in gross superstition. For the latter we have indolent indifferentism. Laou-tsze himself, the frugal and plain-living thinker, is hardly to be recognised amid the false splendours of his apotheosis. He is now the third of a trinity of persons in whom Taou has assumed personality, called in the writings of the sect "Shang-Tes of mysterious nothingness," and worshipped as "The Three Pure Ones." The Taouists assert that he left Heaven in order to become incarnate in the sage of Chow, and they have invented many marvels to support this statement. It appears that Laou-tsze was eighty-one years in the womb of his mother; that during her pregnancy she was fed daily by food from heaven, which descended in the form of a red cloud. At his birth he had long flowing white locks, as well as inscriptions on

his hands and feet. So soon as he was born, he mounted nine
paces in the air, and exclaimed, pointing with his left hand
to heaven, and his right hand to earth, " Heaven above—earth
beneath—only Taou is honourable."

According to a very interesting article on this subject, which
appeared in the fourth number of the *China Review*, from the
pen of the Rev. John Chalmers, Taouism passed through four
stages of development. Starting as a *speculative* system, it wandered further and further from the confines of reality. The
representatives of the *dreamy* stage of Taouism are Chwang-tsze
and Leeh-tsze, both of whom, as might be expected, were very
hostile to the practical school of Confucianism. At this stage
the spirit of self-abnegation which Laou-tsze inculcated, was less
insisted on than the vanity of human pursuits and beliefs.
Taouism had now become wedded to fable, and spiritual beings
and their histories had come to occupy a larger place than
the doctrines they were intended to illustrate. The transition
into the *adventurous* stage was easy. With the regions where
the Queen of the Fairies or the Western Royal Mother lived,
Taouists were quite familiar in the pages of their philosophers.
Tidings had reached them of the whereabouts of the Eastern
Royal Father, and it only remained to realise these dreams.

Even Confucianists yielded to the fashionable mania, and
escorted the great hero of the day, Chi Hwang-ti—the despot
who attempted to destroy the sacred books—to mountain tops
and plains where they hoped by solemn rites to establish
communications with the immortals.

When the Confucians failed, the Taouists "had a more hopeful
scheme of reaching Fairyland by sea. An expedition was fitted
out, which was to consist of some thousands of virgins and as
many young men, headed by a Taouist magician, Sü-fuh. It
was supposed that the sight of so many human beings of virgin
purity would so charm and propitiate the immortals that their
accustomed shyness would be overcome, and they would readily
come and ally themselves to the mighty potentate of China.
Sü-fuh returned from this expedition, if in reality he ever started
on it, reporting that he had seen Fairyland in the distance, but
could not reach it on account of adverse winds.

"The scheme was not to be abandoned, however. Sü-Fuh and

others had actually seen and conversed with genii, and individuals had been known to attain to immortality by eating certain medicinal herbs. Tsin-chi Hwang-ti was therefore resolved to try every means to obtain an interview with some of these immortals, and to procure the medicine, whatever might be the expense. He roamed about the country, sometimes incognito, and sometimes in state, hoping to meet with genii. At Chi-foo and other points on the coast he looked out on the ocean, wondering, it would seem, why Fairyland did not come floating on its bosom, to do honour to him. Thousands of people were compelled to throw themselves into the sea or into rivers, in order to bring the spirits. But it was all in vain. At last, after twelve years of cruel tyranny over men, and of fruitless search for genii and immortal medicine, he was persuaded once more to go to Chi-foo in person, to shoot sharks, which, he was told, were in fact a sort of malignant spirits that had all along prevented the good ones from coming to him. With much trouble a big fish was brought within bowshot of the Emperor, and he killed it with many arrows. But before he reached home again he was taken ill and died. Two years more, during which the son outdid the father in cruelty and extravagance (but not in the quest for genii), completed this Everlasting Dynasty. . . . . In the following dynasty (the Han) more hopeful enterprises were entered on than the search for Fairyland in the Gulf of Shang-tung. But the fifth Emperor of the Han dynasty seventy years after, took up the work of Chi Hwang-ti, and allowed himself to be duped in a similar way for fifty years. He was even bolder, or else more condescending, for he actually committed himself to the perilous deep and remained afloat for more than ten days. There was a heavy sea on, and he returned a sadder and a wiser man. In the last two years of his reign, in his old age, he bitterly bemoaned his mis-spent life."

When adventurous quests had ceased to be the order of the day, Taouism betook itself to alchemy, and sought to transmute the baser metals into gold and silver, and to discover the elixir of immortality. We hear of spiritual medicine, gemmy food, and fountains of nectar, as well as less euphonious substances, cinnabar, orpiment, sulphur, ochre, the spleen of the five viscera, the five elements, the " raven in the sun," and the " hare in the moon." The metaphysical system of Laou-tsze, which had taken hold of men by the power of its ethical doctrine, and the union of the speculative and practical, became a harbour of refuge for every kind of superstition. Not to be outdone by their rivals, the Buddhists, who could point to Shâkyamuni as deity incarnate, the Taouist priests deified Laou-tsze, and the two sects rivalled each other in providing gods of every kind for the wants of the people. Whenever popular sentiment seemed to indicate that it was ripe for such a step, a new god was provided, either by the deification of a hero, or the personification of a principle, or social element, such as wealth, war, and longevity.

The highest regions of the heavens are supposed to be the residences of the three persons of the Taouist trinity, who are styled in the authorised writings of the sect ' Shang-tes of mysterious nothingness," or " of empty nothingness ; " and the central regions are supposed to form the abode of the gods whose origin I have described. At the head of the deities in this central kingdom are Yuh-hwang and Pih-te, who, in contradistinction to the three Shang-tes of mysterious non-existence, are called " Shang-tes of mysterious existence." To Yuh-hwang is entrusted the superintendence of the world, the inhabitants of which he instructs and punishes. Pih-te, in whose composition there are Buddhist and Confucian as well as Taouist elements, is a very popular deity, and some account of him will be found in the chapter on Chinese mythologies.

The priests of the sect of Taou are very numerous, and appear to constitute the whole of its professed disciples, They may be recognised by their loose, flowing robes, and by the singular manner in which they tire their long black hair. This is gathered and bound together on the crown of the head, by a wooden comb, the shape of which bears a striking resemblance to the back of a tortoise. Celibacy is not imperatively necessary. Many priests, however, eschew matrimony and spend their days in the seclusion of monasteries. The most famous of these are the Sam-yune-koong and the Ying-yune-koong-Koon-Yam-Shan. Other priests resort to the mountains, especially to those of the Low-fow Shan range, and lead the lives of hermits with the hope of attaining a place amongst the genii, when called upon to quit this sublunary scene. In some of these monasteries I found the priests engaged in the study of the philosophical writings of Laou-tsze. As a rule, however, very few of them are able to understand these writings, or to give expression to the philosophical tenets contained in them. Instead they have had recourse to works on astrology and alchemy, and profess to hold communication with the spirits of the departed. These they are credited with the power of summoning, and the manner is this :—Upon entering the house where his services are required, the priest asks the day, the hour, and the year of the birth and death of the deceased person with whom he is to communicate. He then places on an altar a basin of uncooked rice, two tapers, and one uncooked egg, and rests his head on the altar, whilst the person employing him waves burning paper over his head. When the priest has cried, or made a howling noise, for the space of one hour, the spirit is supposed to be present at his summons. Sometimes Taouist women perform these incantations.

Besides the idols of Laou-tsze, Chwang-tsze and other gods, the Taouists worship the sun, and moon, and stars, supposing them to exercise a controlling power over the destinies of men. They pander in every possible way to the superstitions of the people, and, creeping into their houses, especially " lead captive silly women." The Chinese are profound believers in ghosts, and the priests of Taou reap a rich harvest by being frequently called upon to eject these unearthly visitants from haunted houses. They usually erect an altar in such a house, and place on it offerings of rice and fowl. After a few adjurations to the spirit, calling upon it to quit the house, they break in pieces a square tile of clay upon which a mystic scroll has been inscribed. Of the efficacy of this ceremony the people appear to entertain no doubt. As the Chinese believe that when disease does not yield to medical treatment, the vitals of the invalid are being preyed upon by an evil spirit, the physician is often discarded, and the exorcising powers of the priests of Taou called into requisition. It is scarcely possible to pass along the streets of a Chinese city at night, without finding these priests at work. An altar is erected in the dwelling house, upon which are placed offerings of pork, fowl, and rice. The priests, three in number, stand round the altar, and address a number of prayers to the noxious spirit calling upon it to vacate the body of the sufferer, and to satiate its inordinate appetite by partaking of the pork, fowl, and rice served for it upon the altar.   The prayers are intoned, and accompanied by the discordant notes of the shrill pipe, the noisy drum, and the clanging cymbals. Should the spirit be disinclined to attend, intimidation is resorted to as a more effectual means. The priests threaten to despatch a letter to the gods of the infernal regions, calling upon them to recall the spirit to the miseries of hell.   Should this fail, eating fire and walking on hot embers are tried as a last resource.

The reader may be disposed to think that the ignorant only can be guilty of such absurdities.   They are, however, I regret to say, indulged in also by the learned and wealthy.   When passing along the streets of Canton on one occasion, I observed in one of the principal dwellings, the large doors of which were thrown open, a Chinese gentleman and his son, kneeling in front of an altar which was surrounded by Taouist priests engaged in chanting prayers.   Having been informed that foreigners were standing in the vestibule of the house, the gentleman withdrew his attention, for a moment, from the religious ceremony, to ascertain who we were. He was a Chinese merchant of great wealth and influence with whom I was acquainted ; and he proceeded to inform me that he was seeking, by the prayers of the priest, the expulsion of an evil spirit from the body of his sick child. My astonishment was considerable, upon finding that a man of great shrewdness and intelligence in the ordinary transactions of life should allow himself to become such a dupe.

Similar scenes of gross extravagance may be witnessed in their temples as well as in the dwelling-houses of the people. Whilst I was visiting one of these temples, a father brought his son to the priests who were lodged in it, saying that the child was possessed of a devil. Having consulted the idol, the priests informed him that there were no fewer than five devils in the body of his son, but that they were prepared to expel them all on the payment of a certain sum. The father agreed. The child was then placed in front of the altar, and on the ground near his feet were placed five eggs, into which the priests adjured the devils to go. As soon as they were supposed to have entered the eggs, the chief of the priests covered them over with an earthenware vase, and at the same time sounded a loud blast upon a horn. When the vase was removed, the eggs by a trick of legerdemain were found no longer on the ground, but in the vase. The priest then proceeded to uncover his arm, and made an incision with a lancet in the fleshy part. The blood which flowed from the wound was allowed to mingle with a small quantity of water in a cup. The seal of the temple, the impression of which was the name of the idol, was then dipped into the blood and stamped upon the wrists, neck, back, and forehead of the poor heathen child, who was suffering from an attack of fever and ague. In several of these places of pagan worship are to be found men who, prostrating themselves before images of wood and stone, seek to obtain a knowledge of the future awaiting them. The oracular information thus sought, is conveyed by the deity in a very singular way. Having knelt before the idol and made known his desire, the votary proceeds to a priest who is standing in front of a table covered with sand in one of the aisles of the temple. The priest supports with the tips of his fingers one end of a long pencil, which is made to run along the sand-covered table, describing in its course a variety of characters, intelligible only to the priests' sect. Near this table another is seated who translates the mystical language into Chinese. In the autumn of 1861, I observed a very respectable Chinese gentleman with whom I was acquainted, entering one of the temples of Taou. Upon inquiring for what purpose he had come there, I was told by him that he was about to set out on a voyage to one of the more westerly provinces of the empire, and that he was desirous of receiving information from the idol, whether the voyage which he meditated would be exempt from disaster. I followed him into the temple and saw him kneel down in front of the idol. Having continued for some time in prayer without uttering an audible word, he rose to his feet and appealed to the priest, who was standing at a table similar to the one I have just described, to inform him of the idol's reply. The answer given was to the effect that his intended voyage would be free from all harm and loss. It certainly did not seem to me possible that the priest could have derived his information as to the nature of the gentleman's appeal, from anything that the latter said or did while he was in the temple.

Candidates for the Taouist priesthood have to devote five years to study. At the termination of their collegiate career, they are initiated into the priesthood by a simple ceremony. This consists of a fast of three days duration ; bathing the body in water scented with the leaves of the orange tree; then going into the presence of the idol of Tai-Shang-Laou-keun or Laou-tsze, to seek the blessing of that deity. The priests receive a license to perform the duties of their office from mandarins appointed for that purpose. There are two mandarins of this class in Canton, one living in a yamun in T'say-yan-lee street of the new city and holding office under the prefect, and the other residing in a yamun in the street called Choong-hom-lan, also of the new city, and holding office under the Nam-hoi magistrate. For this license they are obliged to pay four dollars. The priests are presided over by abbots called Sze-Sze, who are numerous in each province. The abbots in turn are subject to an arch-abbot, who lives in great style at his princely residence on the Dragon and Tiger mountains in the province of Kiang-si. The power of this dignitary is enormous, and is acknowledged by all the priests of the sect throughout the empire. Like the Lama of Thibet, he appears to hold a position subordinate only to that of the Emperor. I believe he is admitted into the presence of the Emperor once in each period of three years. The office is confined to one family or clan called Chaong, as it has been for several centuries. On the demise of the arch-abbot, the Chinese are credulous enough to believe that his successor is chosen in the following singular manner. All the male members of the clan are cited to appear at the official residence. The names of each, having been engraved in lead, are deposited in a large earthenware vase filled with water, and round this are stationed priests who invoke the three persons of the Taouist trinity, to cause the piece of lead bearing the name of the person on whom the choice of the gods has fallen to come to the surface of the water. The headquarters of Taouism in the province of Kwang-tung, are on the Low-fow Shan or Tiger mountains, where there are numerous monasteries, nunneries, and hermitages constructed with much taste. These abodes of retirement from the cares of life are beautifully situated amidst varied scenery, and overlook the most lovely landscapes. It is sad to think that scenes so fair should form the headquarters of one of the grossest systems of superstition that ever extended a vast network of lies to entangle foolish and depraved hearts; and that the cloisters which stud these hills should be occupied by devotees who—ignorant of the Triune Jehovah, and following the instructions of the fallible founder of their sect, and the absurd traditions which have been superadded to them—present one of the most melancholy of the many examples which earth affords of the blind led by the blind.

A few words may not be out of place here on the Taouist nunneries. Taouist nuns do not shave their heads, like the nuns of the sect of Buddha—of whom I shall have occasion to speak later—but tire their hair upon the top of the head like their priests. In Canton and its suburbs, there are many nunneries, some containing only a few inmates. At Choo-loong-Shan, near the district city of Woo-see Hien, I visited a celebrated Taouist nunnery, and was introduced to several of its inmates, some of whom were by no means devoid of personal attractions. They were unlike Buddhist nuns in respect of their feet, which were contracted. The institution appears to have been once renowned for the beauty of its devotees; and it is recorded that when the Emperor Keen-lung Wong lodged near it, in the course of a tour through the northern and central portions of his kingdom, he became enamoured of one of the nuns, and made her an inmate of his harem. A gentleman of wealth, of the clan or family Koo, who followed the Emperor's example, succeeded, it is said, in making a most happy selection; for the son whom his wife bore him, on becoming a candidate for the Hon-Lum degree at Pekin, took the first honours. I heard afterwards that these *religieuses* had a bad reputation; and however reluctant to entertain evil reports of either monks or nuns of any sect, I was disposed on this occasion to give credence to the rumour. In 1871, a Taouist nunnery was temporarily suppressed at

Canton, under somewhat extraordinary circumstances. A number of operatives in the Poon-loong-lee ward of the western suburb, in which the monastery stood, on asking the nuns to contribute towards the Dragon Festival fund, met with a refusal. Enraged at this, the artisans accused the inmates of being guilty of grossly immoral conduct, and called upon the elders of the district to give their sanction to the suppression of the nunnery, which they declared to be a sink of iniquity. This was granted, and a number of men armed with sticks and stones assailed the door of the establishment, and effecting an entrance drove the poor women from their cloisters. Upon the payment, however, some days later, of a few taels of silver to their ruffianly assailants, the nuns were permitted to resume the occupation of their desolated home.

Taouist nuns not unfrequently subject themselves to severe mortifications. On the occasion of my visit to Pekin, I saw a devotee who had caused herself to be inclosed in a brick tower, having resolved to remain in this solitary confinement until she had obtained funds sufficient to enable her to rebuild the temple in the courtyard of which her temporary prison stood. The tower was provided with a small aperture through which she received her food, and could see all persons passing that way. As they approached, she was able to command their attention by means of a long rope attached to the clapper of a bell which was hung in the centre of the gateway. To my knowledge, she solicited alms in this tower during a period of three weeks.

BUDDHISM.

WE proceed to consider the religion of Buddha, which was brought from India to China in the first century of the Christian era. As early as 250 B.C. Buddhist missionaries had begun to make China the scene of their labours, and in the second year before Christ a number of sacred books of their sect were presented to the Emperor of China by an ambassador of the Tochari Tartars. But Buddhism can only be said to have taken root in the empire after its official recognition and introduction by the Emperor Mingti, of the Han dynasty. It is related in Chinese history that in the year of our Lord 61, this emperor saw in a dream the image of a foreign god entering his palace. Greatly impressed with the vision and the splendour of the image, Mingti consulted a younger brother, a great patron of the Taouists, and he was led to regard the dream as a supernatural intimation that he should adopt the religion of Buddha. Ambassadors were accordingly despatched to India, who returned with an idol of this god, and a number of priests of the sect. The Taouists have borrowed from the Buddhists the doctrine of a trinity of persons, and a variety of forms and ceremonies, and have always taken part with the Buddhists against Confucianism, on the side of popular superstition. Others maintain that an embassy was set on foot in consequence of a prophetic saying attributed to Confucius, that the most holy sage would be found in the west. There can be no doubt that an anticipation of the coming of the Messiah was entertained by many Asiatic nations; but it has never been clearly established that it had penetrated beyond the frontiers of China. There is nothing very improbable, it has been remarked, in supposing that Mingti had a dream in which an idol was the prominent figure, as it is on record, that a gigantic figure of Buddha, which the Chinese armies captured in the course of their campaigns in Central Asia, was brought with other trophies to the Chinese court in the year 121 B.C.

On arriving at the Imperial Court, the Indian priests were received with much favour, and urged without delay to commence the work of propagating their religion. The labours of these pagan missionaries, and of those who came after them, were so successful that in a short time temples of the sect were erected in almost every part of the empire. Long after it had taken firm root in the land, the progress of Buddhism continued to be marked by many fluctuations. Some of the emperors were disposed to look upon it as a foreign innovation, and—instigated by the Confucianists—they made its followers the victims of several severe persecutions. Towards the end of the thirteenth century, according to a census of the Buddhist temples and monks in China taken by Imperial command, there were 42,318 of the former, and 213,148 of the latter. This powerful superstition seems to have seen its best days. At present the prosperity of the sect is evidently on the decline, and, especially in some portions of the empire, it appears to have waned before the iconoclastic elements of the Taiping rebellion.

The conjectures of writers with regard to the founder of Buddhism have been very various. Some have supposed Buddha to be identical with Noah, others with Moses. Not a few have contended that he was no other than Siphoas, the thirty-fifth monarch of Egypt. The Hindoos regard him as the ninth incarnation of Vishnu. According to the account now generally agreed upon by European scholars, Shâk-yamuni Gâutama Buddha was a religious reformer who lived in the latter half of the seventh and the first half of the sixth century before the Christian era, the year 543 B.C. being fixed as that in which his death took place. He was born in Kapilavastu, on the borders of Nepaul, and claimed to be of royal descent. Buddhist tradition asserts that the bitter experiences of polygamy induced him to abandon his prospects as a prince, and to seek in the solitude of a wilderness, and in a life of austere asceticism, that peace of mind which he was unable to find in his home. Behind this lay a profound sense of the miseries to which mankind is subject. As he brooded on them, life became empty of significance and value. To escape from misery, he argued, man must virtually escape from existence, and he placed his heaven in Nirvâna, which has been interpreted by some to mean " a complete extinction of the soul at death," and by others a more or less unconscious state of existence. To attain Nirvâna or rest, there must be a complete extinction not merely of sinful dispositions and desires, but of the desire for life itself. These conclusions derived their force from the doctrine of metempsychosis, or transmigration, then held by all classes of Indian society. Rejecting Brahmanism, and ignoring the doctrine of a Supreme Being, Buddha still retained in a modified form [1] this feature

---

[1] Strictly speaking, Buddhism denies the existence of the soul, and bridges over the chasm which it thus creates between each successive life by the mystery of *Karma*. As Mr. Rhys Davids puts it in a very interesting article which appeared in the *Contemporary Review* for January 1877 :—" When a sentient being (man, angel, or animal) dies, a new being is instantly produced in a more or less painful and material state of existence, according to the Karma, the

of the elder religion; and whatever we are to understand by it precisely, Nirvâna involved at least a cessation from the continuity of restless and miserable existence in successive lives. In that sinful condition which he termed *Trishnā*, thirst, or Upādāna, grasping, life must, he taught, go on reproducing itself in numberless births, the more or less painful condition of each life being exactly determined by the *Karma*, or desert of the being who has died.

"This dogma of the soul's pilgrimage through nature," remarks the Rev. E. J. Eitel in the second of his *Three Lectures on Buddhism*, "is a mighty weapon in the hands of an eloquent preacher. There is nothing so very frightful to us descendants of western nations in the idea of transmigration. There may be rather something attractive in it for many. For life is to us the highest blessing, and death we hate. Many would therefore submit to a thousand deaths if they were to live again a thousand times, and they would not care much how their lives might be, for life is precious to us in itself. But a different thing altogether it is with the sons of hot climates, with the lazy indolent Hindoo, with the sedentary Chinaman. To him life itself has no particular fascination. He counts death—if he may rest after that—a blessing."

But Buddhism recognizes the fundamental moral principle, that there is no rest for the wicked. The weight of his guilt carries the sinner down in that graduated scale of existence which, culminating in the highest heaven, ends in the lowest hell. Condemned first to torture in one of the infernal kingdoms, he is released only to reappear as a hard-worked animal, or an unclean cur, or a poverty-stricken mortal. Until the soul, awakened to its higher life by a knowledge of the doctrines of this system, has entered upon the "noble path," and after numberless births has been weaned from its attachment to the things of time and sense, the haven of rest cannot be reached.

---

*D*esert—merit or demerit—of the being who has died." To the question, What becomes of consciousness of identity? Buddhism is, of course, not able to give a satisfactory reply; but its reply, such as it is, is sufficient to establish a connection in the minds of the people between this doctrine and the doctrine of metempsychosis.—ED.

So soon as Buddha had solved, as he thought, the problem of salvation, he began a course of open-air preaching, and by his eloquence succeeded everywhere in making converts. One of the great sources of his power over the masses was the idea that myriads of ages before he came to them as Buddha, he had become a *rahat* (*i.e.*, had reached the final state of perfection which entitled him to enter Nirvāna), and that he had voluntarily flung himself once more into the stream of existence, and endured its miseries in numberless births, in order that he might thereby become the deliverer of mankind. Preaching the complete insignificance of caste and property, and the vanity of all earthly good, he taught his followers to lead lives of voluntary poverty and celibacy. He urged them to sustain the body upon a strictly vegetable diet, and utterly condemned the slaughter of cattle, or of any living creature—on which principle he was also strenuously opposed to war.

Like the speculative system of which Laou-tsze was the founder, Buddhism quickly developed into an idolatry, under which every kind of superstition sheltered itself; and of this idolatry the founder of the sect is the central object. Buddha, as worshipped by the Chinese, is represented in the form of a triune deity, the three persons of which are popularly known as Buddha Past, Buddha Present, and Buddha Future. Buddha Past, which is Shakyamuni himself, represents a state—Nirvāna—in which the soul, which is regarded as an igneous aerial particle when separated from the body, is reunited with the substance of the heavens, and so exists in that trance-like state which the Buddhists regard as the highest felicity. Into this state, however, the Chinese are taught that no soul can enter who has not previously passed through the state of Buddha Present. The duties which devolve upon this person of the Buddhist trinity, consist in imparting instruction to, and seeking to promote the salvation of, men in answer to prayer. Only those, however, who have attained a higher state of intelligence, can understand and appreciate the exalted wisdom of this second person of the Buddhist trinity. As soon as the duties of the votary have been fully discharged, he enters upon the state of Buddha Past, where the soul is supposed to be reunited to the substance of the heavens. Buddha Future is so-called because he is the recognized successor of Buddha Present, whose place as Buddha Present become Buddha Past is always being filled up by what was Buddha Future. Buddha Future is as it were at once the servant of Buddha Present and the coming Messiah of Buddhism. He is supposed to enter more fully into the wants and requirements of men. He is regarded as the guide and guardian of mankind in their endeavours to attain that degree of wisdom and holy abstraction from the things of time and sense which is requisite to qualify them to pass into Nirvāna. As Buddha Future is thus the connecting link between sinful man and Buddha Present, it is customary for him to be more invoked than the latter. The path, however, which leads to the supreme holiness and felicity of Buddha Past is not an easy one, and only those who are gifted with pre-eminent wisdom and self-denial can hope to be successful. The majority of votaries seek, by the far less exacting worship of Amitâbha, to obtain entrance into a Paradise in "the pure land of the western heaven." This is the Nirvāna of the common people. In this land of delights, however, they do not secure an eternity of bliss, but the blissful revolutions of centuries of thousands and of millions of years.

Some devotees, more earnest or confident of their powers, resort to the mountains and solitudes, to gain the holiness that may secure them absorption in Buddha Past. In the Lin-fa Shan hills, near the Bogue Forts, I found a priest who had for this purpose taken up his abode in a cave. He appeared to think that he would in all probability be called upon to pass through various states of existence before he reached the goal towards which he was pressing. I could not help feeling how sad it was that the earnestness of this devotee, whom Satan had placed under strong delusions to believe a lie, had not for its object that gracious Being who, when upon earth, as God manifested in the flesh, said to all sin-convinced souls, "Come unto me all ye that labour and are heavy laden, and I will give you rest." Other devotees shut themselves up in the cells of monasteries, and for years refuse to hold communication with their brethren. During this time they allow their hair and nails to grow to a prodigious length.   In 1865, I saw a priest who for the space of a year had not reclined in his cell.   He was confined in it more like a wild beast than a human being, his food being passed to him through a trap-door.   Many Buddhist devotees seek to subdue the flesh, by inflicting painful severities on their bodies.   I remember meeting with a company of priests, one of whom pulling up the sleeve of his coat and uncovering an arm without a hand, begged for alms, assuring me that he had, by a slow process, burned his hand to the stump, as an atonement for his sins, and as a recommendation for his promotion at some future time to the state of Buddha Past.   At Pekin, when visiting a monastery of this sect, I saw a priest who had shut himself up for several days and nights in a large sedan chair, the interior of which was thickly studded with sharp nails of great length, so that he could not move in any direction.   He informed me and others who stood round his penitential chair, that the nails acquired a heavenly virtue in proportion to the misery which they caused him, and that he was prepared to sell them for a few candareens each, as antidotes against evil.   He assured us that he had resolved to remain in the sedan chair, until every nail had been sold.   At Tien-tsin I saw a priest who had passed through his cheeks a sharp skewer, to the end of which he had attached a chain.   To relieve him of its weight, some little boys were holding up the chain—an act which was of course regarded as very meritorious.   Sometimes these devotees perform pilgrimages of penance to distant shrines, travelling hundreds of miles on foot.   It is remarkable that the Buddhists should subject themselves to such self-torture, as Buddha himself on one occasion preached a most powerful sermon against such follies.   They seem, however, only to be following the tendency which is in man to invest his vain gods with the attributes of cruelty.   The religions of heathendom consist in a great measure of what we may term ceremonies of depreciation, and in the self-mutilation of the Buddhists, we see the same spirit at work which led the priests of Baal to cut themselves with knives.

"Agreeably to the inference which all this furnishes," says Dr. Doran in writing on this subject, "we find Tacitus declare

(Hist. i. 4), 'Non esse curæ dies securitatem nostram, sed
ultionem.' In fact it was a current opinion amongst the ancient
heathen that the gods were jealous of human happiness." [1]

Many of these devotees join the order of mendicant friars, and
beg from door to door for their daily bread, as a way of redemp-
tion from sin and its consequences. Not a few members of the
order travel over a vast extent of country, in search of funds
for the restoration of decayed monasteries. These begging friars
are lodged in monasteries; in the absence of these retreats,
they seek asylum by night in the cottages of the people, never
failing to impress upon the minds of their hosts that it is a good
deed to entertain the wandering friar, and that the doers will
have their reward in another world. The mendicant friars
generally travel in companies of three, two beating small gongs
to announce their approach, whilst the third carries on a stand
a small idol of Buddha to induce those whom they meet to contribute to the fund which they have established for the restoration of decayed monasteries. In the busy streets of Canton, I
once saw a Chinese shoemaker forcibly eject three such begging
intruders from his shop. The friars evidently regarded the son

[1] A curious illustration of this morbid sentiment is afforded in a device to
which Chinese parents occasionally have recourse in the case of a sickly, or puny,
or only son. They procure the adoption of such a lad into other families, in
order that the boy's chances of long life and good health may be increased. Of
this singular practice, the Rev. Justus Doolittle writes in his *Social Life of the
Chinese* (vol. ii. p. 229) :—" His real parents imagine that the gods will let him
live, if his parents think so little of him as to allow him to be adopted into
another family, on the principle that he is a worthless or ·indifferent lad. Some
believe that certain gods or evil spirits are desirous of ruining the health of
bright children, or children of particular promise. Now the parents of the
beloved lad, or the only son, though they really almost idolise him, hope to be
able to cheat and delude such gods into the belief that their child is of no
particular consequence, by having him adopted into the family of some friend.
They, in fact, desire that he should live to grow up as one of the greatest boons
they can possibly hope for in this world. Influenced by the same secret reasons
parents sometimes shave off, for the space of several years, all the hair from the
head of their only son just as a priest of the Buddhist sect has the hair all
shaved from his head ; they call him *little priest*, and pretend to treat him as a
worthless child, and of no more consequence in the affairs of the world than is
the despised priest. For the same reason they designate him by very derogatory
names or epithets, hoping to delude the maliciously-disposed gods into the idea
that they care little or nothing about the lad's health or life."—ED.

of St. Crispin as an infidel, for whom the next world reserved
its sternest penalties.

In the north of China, the priests do not traverse the country
in company, but singly.   Their manners are very sanctimonious.
In some cases a priest will halt to pray at every fifty paces.
Some of them never raise their eyes from the ground.   In Chi-li
one finds them stationed at frequent intervals along the highways, each priest provided with a gong, which he sounds on
the approach of a wayfarer.   They stimulate almsgiving by
promising to pray for blessings on the donors.   As I passed
them, they invariably promised that they would pray for rain
if I gave them alms, a drought at that time prevailing in
Chi-li.

The great majority of the priests reside in monasteries.   In
all these establishments stand colossal figures of the Buddhist
trinity, before which the priests pray, morning and evening.
Like those of the heathen in the time of our Lord, these prayers
are but " vain repetitions."   Indeed the language in which their
liturgical services are written, and which is called after the
birthplace of Buddha, is not only unintelligible to the Chinese
generally, but to the priests themselves.   The chanting of the
prayers is sometimes accompanied by the music of flutes or fifes,
and the Chinese clarionet.   All the Buddhist temples are
collegiate as well as monastic institutions, and numbers of young
candidates for the priesthood are generally engaged, under the
superintendence of the senior priests, in the study of their
sacred writings.   When their collegiate course is completed, the
young men are called upon to present themselves for dedication.
On their part the ceremony consists in prayer.   They are also
called upon to take certain vows—generally nine in number.
In the monasteries of the province of Kiang-si, the priests
usually take twelve vows ; and in those of Soo-chow and Hang-
chow there are priests who have taken one hundred and eight
vows.   That they may be always duly reminded of these vows,
it is customary to make an impression for each vow on the
fleshy part of the arm, with a sharp-pointed iron rod heated red
hot.   Some priests have these marks imprinted on the forehead.
The custom of placing these marks on the forehead is more

popular with the priests of the province of Kiang-si than with those in the more southerly parts of China.

The nine vows which the priests take at the time of their dedication are as follows :—That they will neither kill, nor steal, nor commit adultery; that they will neither slander, nor revile, nor lie; that they will not indulge in feelings of jealousy, or hatred, or folly. In the case of those who take twelve vows, the three following are added, namely : that they will not give vent to feelings of anger, nor foster infidel notions, nor listen to profane conversation. Though many are trained in the temples from boyhood, men who have passed the middle age of life desirous of escaping from the cares of the world, are often permitted to assume the sacerdotal character. As the priests of Buddha are all celibates, it is necessary for such persons, if married, to put away their wives. In the event of the monastic life proving irksome, they are at liberty to throw aside the priestly character with all its obligations, and return to more congenial pursuits.

The monks seldom attain to a great age. This is owing, I believe, in a great measure to the fact that they are all addicted to opium-smoking. Their idle life too must have a tendency to shorten their days, for nothing is so conducive to longevity as agreeable studies and vigorous outdoor exercise. To all rules, however, there are exceptions, and in Buddhist monasteries I have occasionally met with very aged men. The most venerable by far of all the bonzes I met resided in a monastery near Koo-pee-ko. He was eighty-five years of age, and had spent eighty years of this period in the monastery where I found him, having gone thither as a pupil on the completion of his fifth year.

Every large monastery is presided over by an abbot, who holds office during a period of three years. The senior priests meet in council the day before the election of this dignitary, and name two persons as eligible for the office. On the day of the election, one of these is chosen by the votes of the senior priests. A day is then set apart for the consecration of the abbot elect. It is held as a gala day, not only by the priests of the monastery, but by the respectable people of the district. In 1861, I attended the consecration of an abbot at the famous temple of Honam, and as the ceremony was appointed to take place at half-past one o'clock in the the morning, it was necessary to proceed to the temple before the gates were closed on the preceding night. Upon my arrival, I inquired if I might be permitted to spend the night there. The priests, with all of whom I was well acquainted, gave me a hearty welcome, and escorted me at once to the quarters of the abbot, who ordered a chamber to be set apart for my especial use. After some time I returned to the reception-room of the abbot elect, where I found him engaged in entertaining a select party of friends at supper. Of this repast I was invited to partake. The viands consisted of roast pork, boiled fowl, fish, rice, and vegetables ; and as the diet of the priests, according to the teaching of Buddha, ought to be of a vegetable nature only, I could not but regard the abbot elect as guilty of an infringement of the rules of the monastery, and of a direct violation of a doctrine which it was his duty to observe and promulgate. Supper being ended, the abbot together with his cousin, who was one of the guests, retired to an opium couch in the same apartment, and enjoyed four or five pipes of the obnoxious drug. The pipe was filled and presented to the abbot on each occasion by his cousin. Having satiated his appetite, and as it was now ten o'clock, the abbot and the majority of his guests retired to their chambers. After a short conversation with the abbot's cousin, who informed me that he was a proprietor of passenger boats plying between Hongkong and Macao, I also retired. Sleep was out of the question, for the lay brothers, who, as watch-men, patrol the courts of monasteries by night, kept me awake by the prayers which they repeated in a dull monotone as they paced from court to court, calling upon Buddha to grant sweet repose to the holy fathers. At two o'clock in the morning I was summoned to witness the ceremony of conse-cration. Upon entering the reception room of the abbot, I found it crowded with monks, all attired in full costume. After friendly salutations and expressions of attachment had been exchanged between the abbot and the monks, a proces-sion was formed for the purpose of escorting him to the principal

shrine of the monastery containing the colossal idols of the three
Buddhas.   The procession was headed by several musicians who
were in robes of scarlet silk with gold facings, and carried
clarionets, flutes, gongs, and cymbals.   The morning being very
dark, the passages of the monastery along which the procession
had to pass were illuminated by several Chinese lanterns,
bearing curious designs.   Immediately behind the musicians
followed two priests, the one carrying a small tray covered
with odoriferous flowers, and the other a copy of the liturgical services of the sect of Buddha.   Next came the abbot
arrayed in purple.   He was followed by two priests, the one
bearing the rod of office, and the other the abbot's crosier.
Then followed upwards of one hundred monks walking two
abreast.   When the abbot had come into the presence of the
idols, he intoned a prayer of dedication from the copy of the
liturgy which had been placed on the altar by the priest who
carried it in the procession.   The prayer of dedication ended,
the abbot performed the kow-tow in front of the three Buddhas,
amidst a salvo of fire-crackers, and the discordant notes of
drums and cymbals.   He was then escorted to the various
shrines within the precincts of the monastery, and before each
of these a similar ceremony was gone through, the only difference
in each case being in the prayers.   When the shrines had been
visited, the procession returned in the same order to the throne
room, where the abbot prostrated himself at the feet of an idol
of the abbot who, several centuries before, had established the
monastery.   Upon rising to his feet, he advanced towards the
throne, and after various genuflections ascended the high dais
upon which it stood.   At this moment a priest advanced from
the crowd who were standing around in solemn silence, and
performed the kow-tow in front of the throne.   When this
act of homage had been fully rendered, the abbot took his seat,
his train-bearers spreading the skirts of his garments over the
low back of the chair.   Having made certain declarations with
reference to the property, and the efficient discharge of the
duties of office, he received a switch made of horse-hair, which
he waved gracefully about his person.   This act was indicative
of his desire to remove from himself everything polluted.

At this part of the ceremony the abbot was invested with the rod of office and crosier, which were placed on either side of the throne in stands ready to receive them. He then vacated the throne, and as he paused at the foot, the monks in attendance all performed the kow-tow in his presence. Upon his return to the reception-room he held a levée, at which he received the congratulations of the monks. The last presentation was a young priest who had been instructed by the abbot, and who showed his regard and reverence by throwing himself at his feet. The monks having retired to their cells, the abbot, with his lantern-bearers, hastened to pay his respects to each in return, a ceremony which did not terminate until the sun had made considerable process in his daily march.

At ten o'clock the temple was crowded by monks from the various monasteries in Canton and its neighbourhood. They were received and presented to the abbot by a master of ceremonies. As they attempted to perform the kow-tow, they were interrupted by the abbot, who sought to impress upon the mind of each his wish to dispense with the ceremony. The mandarins, however, several of whom attended in their court dresses, were permitted to proceed with the kow-tow. I could not help thinking that priestly arrogance was a feature of this idolatrous religion. A large banquet at which upwards of two hundred priests were present, was given at noon in the refectory of the monastery. The abbot was seated in state at a high table, round which twelve priests stood to serve him. He was escorted to and from the banqueting hall by bands of music, and during the procession was the object of much popular interest, the courtyards of the monastery being crowded almost to suffocation.

The duties of an abbot consist chiefly in receiving and disbursing the revenues of the monastery, which arise from endowments in lands and houses; in seeing that the services of the sanctuary are duly performed; in attending to the morals of the priests who are subject to his authority; and in expounding the doctrines of the sect in the hearing of the assembled brethren. Now-a-days, if not altogether abandoned, the latter duty is very much neglected, as the abbots of the various monasteries appear to consider their office as public preachers fully and efficiently discharged when they have read aloud the Book of the Law in the hearing of the priests—a ceremony which it is their custom to observe on the first and fifteenth days of each month.

The priesthood is supplied by men from all classes of society. The great majority of the priests are from the lower orders of the people. Few, very few, indeed, of the wealthier classes ever think of abandoning their home comforts for the gloom and solitude of a Buddhist cloister. It is not unusual for poor parents, with sickly children, to seek admission for them into monasteries, that they may be educated for the priesthood, and may obtain without exertion the common necessaries of life. There is a law, however, which prohibits all the male members of a family becoming priests. If there are but two sons in a family, one only, the younger son, is permitted.

Although education is popular in China, no great pains are bestowed upon the youthful candidates for the priesthood. This explains the low degree of intelligence of the monks as a body. The majority are sadly wanting in earnestness in the discharge of religious exercises. No doubt this is one of the chief reasons why Buddhism no longer has the power over the minds of the people which it had in the Middle Ages, when imperial zeal and popular favour combined to render it paramount throughout the land. To this reason for the evident decay of Buddhism in China may be added the still more urgent one, that the priests as a body are not at all an exemplary class of men. Among the professors of every religon there are, of course, good and bad; but in Christian lands, a minister who is a defaulter is an exception to the general rule. In heathen China—I am not now confining my remarks to Buddhists—the majority of the priests are notorious for their violation of monastic rules, and their utter disregard of the tenets which they profess to hold, and the morality to which they are bound. In almost every cell there is an opium couch, upon which its frocked possessor may be seen stretched at length in the full enjoyment of the noxious drug. A former abbot of the Honam temple, named Chip Hong, complained bitterly to me of the degeneracy of the priests of the present day, and attributed it to the system which allows of men becoming priests at an advanced period of life, and, as is often the case, for the purpose of escaping from impending justice.   In some instances Buddhist temples are regarded as inviolable sanctuaries for transgressors of the law.   The abbot added that the priests who had been brought up in monasteries from boyhood were the best ; although even they, he said with a sigh, are in some instances unfortunately contaminated by the bad example of those admitted into the priesthood in later life.   In the monastery over which he formally presided, I once saw a person who had joined the order with a view of escaping from justice.   He had taken part with the rebels who infested Kwang-tung in 1854, 55, and had exposed himself to the extreme penalty of the law.   As he had a little property, he was admitted without difficulty, his funds having been appropriated for the further endowment of the monastery. Under such circumstances, the monks are always ready to become securities for the future good conduct of a newly-acquired brother.   In a monastery near the prefectoral city of Shu-hing, I found a monk who had not only been a rebel, but the proprietor of several houses containing no fewer than two hundred women ; and in one of the monasteries on the White Cloud Mountains I found one who had taken his vows to escape the penalty of having killed a man in a drunken brawl. In Canton a Buddhist priest and his concubine were flogged through the streets in 1864 ; and in 1869, in the same city, the case became public of a priest from the White Cloud Mountains having been found in a house of ill-fame, robbed of his clothes and money, and bound hand and foot.   In 1861, a young monk who was in charge of a small temple at Canton, called Hoi-foksze, and who had been trained from his early boyhood for the priesthood in an adjoining temple, committed a most diabolical murder.   A collector of taxes called to ask payment of a tax for the rice grounds with which the temple was endowed.   Having come a long distance and being much fatigued with his journey, he was compelled to spend the night in the temple.   The young monk was addicted to gambling, and finding that the tax-gatherer had about his person a large sum of money, resolved, if possible, to obtain it. At the dead hour of night, therefore, the priest entered the apartment in which the tax-gatherer lay, and stabbed him to the heart. Having rifled the pockets of his victim, he cut the murdered body into pieces, so as to carry it with greater ease to a place of conceal-ment. The mangled remains were eventually put into a box, and conveyed on that night and the following night by the priest and his servant, who, for a portion of the stolen money, had become *particeps criminis*, to the banks of the Canton river, and thrown into its waters. The servant ultimately betrayed his master, who was speedily apprehended. I frequently visited this unfortunate monk. He was confined with several other prisoners in a large ward, where, as there were no boards, he was obliged to sleep on the damp ground. He was soon after seized with a low typhoid fever, which rescued him from a disgraceful death. The commission of such a deed by a Buddhist priest is of course very exceptional; but the fact remains that many of them occupy the same dangerous border-land of careless and immoral living from which this man so easily slipped into the abyss of crime. One of the duties of the abbot consists in attending to the morals of his priests; and in each monastery there is a tribunal, before which priests are occasionally arraigned for offences, such as drunkenness, profane swearing, whoredom, thieving, &c. The punishment is a flogging, administered with hearty goodwill by one of the lay brothers, on the naked back of the offender. The priest who has been thus punished is further degraded by being made to beg his bread from temple to temple. In the city of Canton, priests who have been arraigned before the abbot for any of these offences and flogged have to spend the thirty days of each calendar month throughout the course of the year thus:—five days at the monastery of Honam; five at that which is called the Flowery Forest Monastery; five at the monastery of the Great Buddha; five at the temple of Lon-gevity, and five at the monastery of the Sleeping Buddha. The apartments allotted to these degraded priests are the worst which the monasteries contain, and the rice doled out to them is coarse in quality and scanty in measure. So illiberal is the hand which supplies their necessities, that the pangs of hunger not unfrequently compel them to traverse the streets with wallets on their backs, begging food from door to door. I remember seeing a young priest bastinadoed and degraded in the monastery of Honam for having stolen some articles of wearing apparel belonging to a brother monk. I had known him for several years. When I first saw him, he was not more than ten years of age. When he arrived at years of discretion, however, it was discovered that he was addicted to opium-smoking and gambling ; and that to obtain the funds requisite he was obliged to steal. His tutor, who was an incorrigible opium-smoker, had trained up his pupil in the ways of vice. He called me on one occasion to admonish the young man, in whom he still professed to feel an interest, and he was both surprised and indignant when I informed him that I thought the evil work of demoralization, which he was so desirous of checking, had had its commencement during the time the youth was under his care. I could adduce many more instances which came under my notice during my long residence in China, of the depravity of the Buddhist priesthood. The examples already given are sufficient to indicate that my statement as to the low morality of the order is not exaggerated. The priests do not appear to attain to a good old age ; and those among them who have reached fifty years seem very infirm and decrepit.

It is customary to burn the dead bodies of Buddhist priests, and the ceremony of cremation invariably takes place twelve hours after death. One afternoon in March, 1856, I witnessed it in the monastery at Honam. As I entered the inner gates my attention was directed to an apartment, the doors of which were crowded by a number of priests arrayed in sackcloth, and wearing white bandages round their foreheads. Drawing near I learned that the priests were preparing to convey to the funeral pile the mortal remains of a departed brother. The corpse, attired in a cowl and with the hands fixed in the attitude of prayer, was placed in a bamboo chair in a sitting posture, and carried to the pyre by six secular monks. All the monks were in attendance, and walked two abreast, immediately behind the remains of the departed friar. As the long procession advanced, the walls of the monastery echoed with the chanting of prayers and the tinkling of cymbals. When the bearers reached the pyre, they placed the chair containing the corpse upon it, and the fagots were then kindled by the chief priest. Whilst the body was enveloped in flames, the mourners prostrated themselves upon the ground in obeisance to the ashes of one with whom they had been accustomed to join in prayer and praise. When the fire had burned itself out, the attendants collected the charred bones and placed them in a cinerary urn, which was then deposited in a small shrine within the precincts of the monastery. The cinerary urns remain in this shrine until the ninth day of the ninth month, when the ashes which they contain are emptied into bags of red cloth, which are then sewn up and thrown into a large ossuary, or species of monastery mausoleum. These edifices, built of granite, are called by the Chinese Poo-toong-tap, and are upon an extensive scale. That belonging to the monastery of Honam is a noble piece of masonry, and is divided into two compartments, one being for the ashes of monks, and the other for those of nuns. The bags of red cloth with their contents are consigned to these receptacles through small apertures just sufficiently large for their admission. At the monastery called Wallam-sze, or Flowery Forest, the remains of the monks are burned in a temple set apart for the purpose. It is some distance beyond the north-east gate of Canton, and the bodies of the dead priests are carried to it in large sedan chairs which are inclosed on all sides. The ashes of the monks of this monastery are conveyed to a mausoleum beautifully situated on the banks of a small rivulet called King-ti-hang, which flows at the foot of the White Cloud Mountains. The remains of monks are not, however, always disposed of by cremation—occasionally they are interred. In June, 1871, the remains of Hang Sun, one of the most distinguished of the monks of the Honam monastery, were conveyed for interment to the cemetery at Tai-kum-chung. A newspaper correspondent in writing of the ceremony thus described it :—

" Previous to the removal of the corpse, bonzes, to the number of 200, assembled to assist in discharging the last rites. Around a temporary altar, which was erected in the hall where the dead man lay in state, many of the monks arranged themselves in order, and engaged in a mass for the repose of the soul of their departed brother. At the close of this ceremony, an aged priest, clad in purple vestments, came forward, and presented to the portrait of the deceased, which was suspended above the temporary altar to which I have referred, the insignia of the high office which, it appears, the departed friar had at one time held. A conductor of ceremonies then gave commands for the removal of the corpse —a command which was quickly obeyed. The priests now arranged themselves in long rows on each side of the avenue by which the monastery is approached, and, as the coffin was borne past, they followed it, two abreast, to its last resting-place. At the outer gate of the monastery two monks were stationed, whose duty consisted in giving to each respectable person present a small piece of silver money. Each gift of this nature was inclosed in a white paper envelope, upon which Chinese cha-racters, implying 'lucky money,' were written. A great many gentlemen from the city and its environs, who were friends of the deceased, joined this sombre cavalcade. Each of them, as well as each of the monks, wore on the occasion a broad white sash round his waist."

As regards architecture and internal arrangement, all the large monasteries are precisely alike. As the visitor enters the gates his attention is arrested by two large figures. These are called Chun-Kee and Mā-Sic, and the gates are supposed to be in their charge. Under a second gateway there are four figures called Mo-li-Hang, Mo-li-Shon, Mo-li-Hoi, and Mo-li-Ching, of equal size with the former, and placed two on each side. They are described as the representatives of the North, South, East, and West of China, and are supposed to give effect with alacrity to the will of Buddha. Beyond the second gateway is the principal hall of the temple, in which are placed the three idols known as Buddha Past, Present, and Future. In the rear of this principal hall are two others, the one of which contains a dagoba,[1] under

[1] Many of these dagobas are made of white marble, and are very grand and imposing. The dagoba in the Hoi-Tong-sze, or Ocean Banner Monastery, is magnificent, but it is surpassed by one in a large Lama temple at the north side of the city of Pekin. On the sides of this dagoba there are representations of

which there is a relic of Buddha, and the other an idol of the goddess of Mercy. There are also several other smaller shrines of Kwan-te, Vishnu, and other deities of less note. One of these contains an idol of the first abbot of the monastery. Before it is placed a board on which are recorded the names of all the departed abbots of the cloister. On each side of the large courtyards in which the principal halls of the temple are erected, are rows of cells for the monks, a visitors' hall, a refectory, and, sometimes, a printing-office, where the liturgical services used by the priests, new works on the tenets of Buddha, and tracts for general distribution are printed. The visitors' hall consists of two chambers, between which there is a courtyard. On entering this hall the visitor goes to what is termed the lowest chamber, where he remains until he is bidden by the priest whose duty it is to receive the guests, to a more honourable apartment. The refectories are very large, and the priests, who are regarded as guests, are so disposed at table as to enable the abbot, who is *ex officio* their host, to see their countenances. Tables are arranged on each side of the hall, and only a single row of monks is seated at each table, their faces, of course, being turned inwards, while the abbot presides on a *daïs* placed at the upper end between the rows. In a country where people are so much addicted to form and ceremony, the observance of this custom is looked upon as the essence of politeness. The priests are summoned to breakfast and dinner by a gong, and are obliged to appear on such occasions attired in their cowls. When they are all assembled and seated, a master of ceremonies makes his appearance, and, at a sign from him, they all rise from their seats, and, placing their hands in the attitude of prayer, repeat a grace. A portion of the food thus blessed is then placed on a stand at the door of the refectory, as an offering to the fowls of the air—an observance which is much appreciated by a large

Buddha's birth ; his early training for the priesthood ; his narrow escape from the hands of wild barbarians, who plotted his destruction ; his merciful preservation by the interposition of a sacred flower, which is ever attending upon him ; his death and deification. Under the dagoba, a dress of Buddha is said to have been deposited. Dagobas, in some instances, are of a pagoda-shape, as in the Flowery Forest Monastery in the city of Canton, and in the Mā-cha Monastery in the vicinity of the same city.

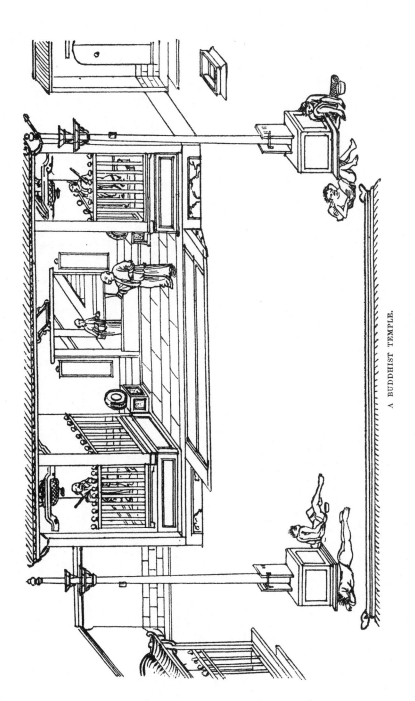

A BUDDHIST TEMPLE.

company of sparrows, who present themselves with polite regularity at the hours of breakfast and dinner. The food served in the refectory is of a vegetable nature only. As such a diet, however, although prescribed by the rules of the order, is distasteful to the priests, all who have incomes sufficiently large have private messes, consisting of six or eight members, at which roast pork, boiled fowl, and salt fish are eaten with great relish, and occasionally washed down by potations of strong spirituous liquor. While at dinner in the refectory, the priests are supposed to maintain strict silence, although there is no Reader, as in many Christian monasteries, to occupy their attention. The walls of the dining-room, however, are covered with boards, upon some of which are painted in very legible characters quotations from various moral writers, warning the priests of the impropriety of eating too hastily or impatiently, and urging the importance of the rules of the dining-room. Upon others are recorded the rules of the monastery, and the vows of the monks.

In some of the temples the idols are very numerous, and in Yang-chow Foo I visited one in which there are said to be no fewer than ten thousand. The idols, which are very diminutive, are contained in one large hall, and in their fanciful but orderly arrangement present a very singular appearance. In the centre of the hall stands a pavilion of wood, most elaborately carved, under which is placed a large idol of Buddha. The pavilion within and without is literally studded with small idols which are, I believe, different representations of the same deity. On each of the four sides of the hall are small brackets supporting idols of Buddha; and a still larger number of these are placed on the beams and pillars of the vaulted roof. Two are full-sized figures of the sleeping Buddha. At Pekin and Canton there are halls precisely similar. The hall of ten thousand idols at Canton is, like the monastery of which it forms a part, in a most ruinous state, and the majority of the idols with which its walls were at one time adorned have disappeared.

Idols[1] are usually made of wood, but clay is also frequently

[1] In a monastery at Hae-loong-tang, in the province of Chi-li, I saw, on an altar, figures in copper of human beings, males and females, which somewhat

used. In the prefecture of Shu-hing, where marble quarries abound, they are in many cases made of that material. At Pun-new-chan, a market town on the banks of the Grand Canal, I saw in a ruined monastery three large iron idols representing the Past, Present, and Future Buddhas. I have also seen in certain temples stone, earthenware, and porcelain figures. The three large idols in the Tai-fat monastery at Canton, are said to be made of copper, and many of the small idols of Buddha are also said to be made of the same material. Buddha is represented in a variety of postures, and some of the figures have smiling, whilst others have sorrowful, countenances.

Buddhist temples are more frequented by female than by male votaries, in search of such blessings as wealth, offspring, longevity, or literary distinction. To prevail upon the deity to grant the gift prayed for, the votary repairs to the pagoda in the large hall of the temple, and there, in presence of the various figures of Buddha, prefers his petition, and offers a vow to preserve the life of some living creature—such a vow being regarded most favourably by Buddha. The animal, very often a fowl, is then presented in front of the pagoda, and solemnly dedicated to the deity, after which it is consigned to the especial care and blessing of the priests, ample provision for its maintenance having been previously made. In the monastery of Honam, Canton, there is a large pig-sty containing ten or twelve sacred pigs of very ample dimensions, for which provision has thus been made. Of all the sacred pigs which I saw, by far the largest was in the Pow-toong monastery, in the vicinity of Wu-chang. It was perfectly black, and had been presented to the temple in the year 1855, by a rich Chinese merchant. At the former monastery, in addition to its well-stocked pig-sty, there is a poultry-yard well filled with fowls, ducks, and geese, and a pen containing a few sheep and goats. In some of the temples

surprised me. Such figures are, I believe, not at all uncommon in the monastic establishments of North China. Some of them tend to remind the beholder of the mythological story of Jupiter and Europa. The essence of this corrupt worship, which the Buddhists borrowed from an Indian religion, consists, I suppose, in a reverence for the male and female principles of the universe.

one may find several head of hornèd cattle placed there by anxious suppliants. In one monastery near Hoo-shee-woo, in the province of Chili, I saw a number of sacred horses and mules; and of all the *equidæ* I saw in China, these were the best groomed. All animals thus consecrated to Buddha are, as a rule, carefully tended by the monks; and when they die, their remains are consigned to the earth with no ordinary degree of tenderness. In the grounds attached to many of the temples are ponds into which fishes of all kinds, rescued by worshippers of Buddha from the troughs in which they lay exposed for sale at the fishmonger's stall, are thrown as votive offerings. On the banks of such ponds generally stands a pillar of stone, upon which the words, "Preserve life," are inscribed in large characters. In the temple at Honam I once saw a person offering to Buddha ten or twelve large carp which were disporting themselves in a tub of water placed in front of the altar, and which were eventually put into the pond. In the temple of the Flowery Forest monastery, or Temple of the Five Hundred Genii, as it is not unfrequently called, there is a pond in the rear of the visitors' hall, the waters of which are alive with tortoises placed there by votaries desirous of rescuing them from the table of the epicure —an act considered so highly meritorious as to procure from the beneficent Buddha temporal blessings. Another mode of propitiating Buddha, is to set at liberty a number of sparrows or pigeons. At the temple to which I have just referred, I once saw a lady making a vow before its beautiful marble pagoda to preserve the lives of several tens of sparrows. When the vow had been made, the cage containing the birds was carried by the priest in attendance into an adjoining corridor, where the lady, opening the door of their prison, set them free. As sparrows are so frequently made the subject of a vow, large numbers of them are in consequence exposed for sale at the shops of poulterers. The birdcatcher has rather a singular method of taking these birds. He besmears the end of a long rod with birdlime, and so soon as he espies a number of sparrows clustering together on the ground or among the long coarse grass, he thrusts the point of his rod amongst them with such dexterity as generally to bring away one or two on the end of it. The captured birds are then lodged in a cage which he carries on his back. In several Buddhist temples there are cages resembling hen-coops, containing pigeons which have been bought and placed there by the monks themselves. On the doors of the cages are written the words, "Preserve life;" and on a visitor to the temple dropping a piece of money—the value of a pigeon—into a cage, a feathered inmate is set at liberty by a monk in attendance. Sometimes the vows which are made at the shrines of Buddha are not fulfilled until the blessing which the votary seeks has been bestowed. Upon receiving the blessing, he seldom fails to return to the temple and fulfil it, lest he should be visited for his unfaithfulness. One of the vows sometimes made by votaries of both sexes, is that of abstinence from animal food for a definite period of time. I have known many instances where this vow has been openly violated. With the view of making atonement for sins some expend large sums of money in paving highways. Thus one of the flights of granite steps by which the White Cloud Mountains are ascended was erected at the expense of a widow by way of atoning for the sins of her husband.

Many of the Buddhist monasteries have been built on the sides of hills and mountains, and command extensive and magnificent views. The most beautiful I have seen in the south of China, in point of situation, is that called the Ting-hoo-Shan on the banks of the western branch of the Canton river, and near the entrance to the Shu-hing pass. On all sides of this monastery lie scenes of rich variety and beauty. Here spread wide plains adorned with waving grain; there hills covered with trees of luxuriant foliage, rise in gentle slopes, down which rivulets hasten to lose themselves amongst the stately trees that surround the monastery. In the distance, the mountains forming the Shu-hing pass raise their summits towards the clouds, while between their rugged sides the western branch of the Canton river rolls with apparently resistless impetuosity, till widening beyond into a smooth expanse, it presents the appearance of a lake at the base of the mountains. At this monastery there is a pagoda shrine which is regarded as very sacred ; and which no

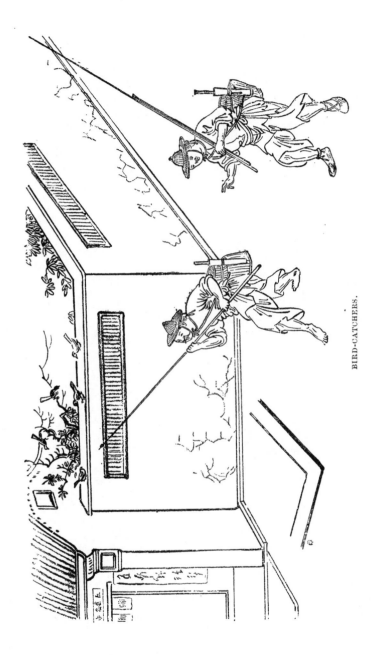

BIRD-CATCHERS.

one is allowed to enter who has not first washed his body in holy water. Jars filled with holy water are also kept at this temple for the purposes of sale, and while I was there, three nuns arrived who had come to purchase a supply of the sacred element. The monastery suffered much during the rebellion of 1855. It is now, however, rebuilt.

Near the Kum-Shan or Golden Hills, and about twenty miles in a westerly direction from Canton, stands another monastery, which in point of beauty of situation, is entitled to rank next to the Ting-hoo-Shan Monastery. It is so situated on the banks of the Canton river, that during the summer season, when the river is very full in consequence of heavy rains, it is entirely surrounded by water. On its west side, forming a bend of the river, are the Kum-Shan or Golden Hills, from the summit of which there is a charming view of the surrounding country. Near this point the banks are adorned with groves, amongst the trees of which nestle neat-looking villages. This monastery was founded upwards of eight hundred years ago, and in consequence of its great antiquity, and the want of funds for repairs, it is now in a very dilapidated state. Its antiquity, however, and the beauty of its situation have caused it to be regarded by the Chinese as one of the seven wonders of the province of Kwang-tung.

Of the monasteries I visited in the midland provinces, by far the most beautiful is that of Teen-tung-Sze, in the province of Tche-kiang. It is distant thirty English miles from the city of Ning-po, at the head of a beautiful valley. The immediate approach is through an avenue of lofty cedars, and the hills which inclose it are covered with trees from base to summit. I was disappointed with the buildings of the Khan-loo or Sweet Dew Monastery, which is situate at Chin-kiang. It is delightfully placed on a high hill, and commands a most pleasing and extensive view. Its name is said to have been given to it by one Chong-Fee, who was either the friend or brother of Lou-Yuen-Tak or Lou-pee, one of the Chinese emperors. Before ascending the throne, he is said to have visited this cloister, and to have written the sentence now recorded on a tablet—*Tsin-San-Tae-Yeh-Kiang-Shan*, or "The largest river and most

important hill of which the empire can boast." This statement
is certainly true of the river, for the stream which rolls so
majestically past the base of the hill is the Yang-tsze.

The most beautiful of the monasteries which I saw in the
north of China was the Ta-chia Sze. It lies at a distance of
twenty-three English miles to the north-west of Pekin. In
the grounds there is an ornamental pond containing a great
number of goldfish ; and a spring of singular purity, into
which visitors throw copper cash to enable the priests to buy
birds from the poulterer in order to set them free. There is
also a graceful pagoda used as an ossuary for the ashes of
priests. Occasionally the grounds and courtyards of temples
are ornamented in the most fanciful way. The monastery of
Chow-chong-Sze, however, at Chow-loong-shan, a city on the
banks of the Grand Canal, bears the palm in this respect;
and of those remarkable for their rockeries the Longevity
Monastery in the western suburb of Canton may be
mentioned.

In China there are no rock-cut temples. India, it would
appear, is the only country famous for such singular structures.
My attention was directed to some very diminutive shrines and
idols of Buddha, carved on the sides of old red sandstone
rocks. The most singular of these bas reliefs were those
which I saw in the vicinity of Hang-chow.

The friars have very singular legends to tell. My attention
was directed by one of the priests of the Kum-Shan Monastery, to a tablet upon which were inscribed a few verses of
poetry, said to have been composed several centuries ago by a
mandarin who passed a night there on his way from Canton
to Pekin. The stanzas referred to a dream which the mandarin is said to have had under the hospitable roof of the
friars, and in which he saw a priest worshipping him, and
presenting him with cakes of rice-flour. Next morning, as he
was preparing to resume his journey, a priest came towards
him, bearing in his hand a tray covered with cakes of rice-
flour. He was at once reminded of his dream, and he asked
the priest to whom he was going to present the cakes. The
latter replied that he was on his way to place them upon the

altar in honour of a monk who flourished two hundred years before, and was canonized after death. The mandarin having summoned the friars into his presence related his dream, and asked the interpretation of it. It was not far to seek. Strong believers in the doctrine of metempsychosis, the priests at once concluded that the mandarin was no other than the famous monk, who had returned to earth as a political ruler of the people.

Of the Jade Stone Flower Monastery, which is in the city of Yang-chow Foo, in the province of Kiangsoo, I was told a singular legend. About thirteen hundred years ago, a very extraordinary flower—so the story runs—bloomed in the garden of a house in Yang-chow; and the Emperor Yung-kwang hearing of the marvel, proceeded to the city to inspect it. The journey was rather long, and when his majesty travelled by water, his barge was drawn by men and women in fine clothing ; and, when he rode, the team of his carriage consisted of human beings not less imposingly arrayed. The house was fitted up as a temporary palace for his convenience, and attracted by the singular beauty of the flower, which he daily inspected, the emperor resided for some time at Yang-chow. Eventually, however, feeling that his health was declining, he set out for Lok-yang, his capital—a city in the province of Honan. He died en route, and the palace was converted into a monastery, and called Koong-wah-koon, or Jade Stone Flower Monastery, Although it was in a very ruined state when I visited it, I was kindly received by a few Buddhist monks, who informed me that the flower had long since passed to the Western Paradise, there to bloom in the vigour of immortal youth.

The Buddhist nunneries in China are very numerous. The small nunneries contain from ten to twenty inmates, while in others there are upwards of eighty nuns. They are supported by funds arising from endowments of houses or lands. Aspirants are received into the nunneries at the early age of ten, and their novitiate continues until they have attained their sixteenth year. At this period the female mind is considered as mature, and they are called upon " to take the veil." The ceremony consists in the candidate making a declaration in the presence of the idol of Koon-Yam, the Goddess of Mercy, that she will maintain a state of perpetual virginity, that she will neither eat fish, nor flesh, nor fowl, that she will drink no wine, and that she will endeavour to obey and carry out in her daily life the tenets embodied in the religion of Buddha. This declaration having been made in the presence of the idol of Koon-Yam, and in the hearing of witnesses, the head of the young lady, which has been kept partially shaved since the day she entered the nunnery, is entirely shaved by a female attendant, and she is attired in robes bearing a striking resemblance to those worn by the monks of the sect. The costume of a nun resembles that of a monk so closely, that a foreigner experiences no small difficulty in distinguishing the one from the other. Although it is usual for candidates for the sisterhood to enter the convents at ten, there are many who have recourse to this life of retirement at much more advanced periods of life. The great majority of the women are from the lower ranks. All classes of society, however, are represented in the cloister. Female members of wealthy families are occasionally induced to go there to avoid unwelcome matrimonial alliances. Each nunnery is presided over by a lady abbess, who is called in Chinese Sze-Foo. The office is held for life. The duties of the nuns consist principally in offering up prayers and masses to Koon-Yam, in behalf of the spirits of deceased women. For this purpose they go generally in a party of nine to the house of the deceased, and having taken up their position before the altar prepared for the occasion, and behind which is a small idol of Koon-Yam, they chant prayers all day long. In the absence of all such engagements, they spend their time at the nunneries in a most indolent way, lounging about as if utterly devoid of energy. This at all events is my conclusion after visiting several such establishments. The observation applies with greater force to the senior nuns, as the younger and poorer sisters embroider silk, in order to enable them to command more of the common necessaries of life, than the small portion of the endowment fund allotted to them places at their disposal. At the celebration of the Chinese New Year festivals in 1860, I saw a party of nuns at a pic-nic in the pleasure grounds attached to

BUDDHIST NUNS.

one of the principal temples at Canton, and the zeal with which they entered into a little recreation could not have been surpassed by a bevy of school-girls holiday-making in the green fields of merry England.

The Buddhist nunneries have not escaped from the grave charges to which I referred when treating of Taouist institutions of this kind. In proof this I may make an extract from the columns of the Hong-kong *Daily Press* of Friday, September 13th, 1872.

"It seems," says the correspondent from whose letter I quote, "that the Buddhist and Tauist nunneries in China are no purer than their sister institutions in Europe. Those in Wu-chang, at any rate, have been accused of corrupting the morals of the people, and a virtuous (?) mandarin hearing what was going on, has pounced upon the nuns, and nearly put an end to their order.

"The news at first created great commotion in the temples, and many of the inmates escaped—especially those of the Tauist sect who had only to undo their hair, change their dress, put on ear-rings, and the disguise was complete. It was not so easy, however, for the Buddhist nun, with her shaven head, to elude the search of the yamen runners, probably having, also, too little money to offer as a bribe. Some twenty of them, with a few notorious Tauist ladies, were taken into custody. They were nearly all young, their ages ranging between eight and twenty-six. This mandarin afterwards issued a proclamation, stating in a general way that the bad repute of the nunneries had necessitated his taking this decided step, and calling upon the relatives of those whose names were appended to come and take the girls home ; otherwise they would be handed over to any eligible parties who might wish to have a wife."

LAMAISM.

About 350 years after Buddhism was officially recognized in China, it was introduced into Thibet, and thence, in course of time, spread to Mongolia and Mantchuria, where it still flourishes under the name of Lamaism. The lamas or priests acknowledge as their spiritual head the Grand Lama of Thibet, who is to them what the Pope of Rome is to the priests of the Latin Church. This pope of Lamaism is the political as well as spiritual ruler of Thibet, and is subordinate to the Emperor of

China only. The present ruler has invariably and decidedly opposed all European travellers entering his kingdom ; and, during my stay at Pekin in the spring of 1865, he sent a despatch to the Emperor of China, requesting his imperial majesty on no account to sanction the departure of Europeans from China *en route* to Thibet, and assigning as a reason that on the last occasion the crops had failed, cattle had become barren, and women had turned aside from the paths of virtue.

The lamas are chosen from all classes in society, and in Mongolia each family in which there are two or more sons is obliged to dedicate one to the service of Lamaism. Like their *confrères* in China, each lama is a celibate, and shaves his head. His dress consists of a long yellow robe. This is bound round the waist by a girdle to which is attached a fan case, and, sometimes a case containing a spoon, a knife, a pair of chop sticks, and a brazen wine cup. When conducting the public services of their temples, the lamas wear cloaks and caps of the same colour as their robes, the cap somewhat resembling the helmet conspicuous in our representations of Britannia. Upon entering the temples to celebrate public worship, the lamas are received at the door by the chief priests. During prayer they sit in Turkish fashion, with their legs tucked under them, upon long low ottomans arranged on each side of the hall by which the high altar is approached. Their prayers invoke the blessing of the idols of the sect upon the emperor, the priesthood, and the state. They are intoned, and, in some cases, are so well rendered as to remind Europeans of the cathedral services daily celebrated in Christian lands. In some instances, this is done to the blowing of horns and shells, and the clapping of hands. A very singular musical instrument is also used, consisting of a human thigh bone hollowed out and converted into a musical pipe. Whilst the lamas are engaged in public prayers, the chief priests, who on such occasions wear dark purple robes, pass along the lines of praying priests, and cense each worshipper. When I was at Lama-miou, a market-town in Mongolia, I witnessed in one of the temples a curious incident. The lamas who were present, after praying for twenty minutes, were each, whilst in a sitting posture—the attitude of prayer—presented with a cup of brick-tea, served up with butter, and of the consistency of soup. Before they partook of this beverage, one of the chief priests, standing in the centre of the temple, informed them in a loud voice that the tea had been graciously provided for them by the last will and testament of a good Mongolian prince, recently deceased, and that they were in duty bound to pray for the repose of his soul. Having drunk the tea, the ecclesiastics resumed their prayers in good earnest for the space of twenty minutes. At the close, each lama was presented with a large cake, also provided by the will of the deceased prince.

Being celibates, the lamas reside in monasteries. In the Ta-fo cloister which I visited at Pekin, I found no fewer than one thousand inmates. In the town of Lama-miou there are no fewer than ten thousand monks, and at Ye-hole they are equally numerous. By way of penance, they not unfrequently leave their monastic retreats on toilsome pilgrimages to distant shrines. Such journeys occupy long periods of time, as the pilgrims not only walk at a very slow pace, but at the end of every three steps prostrate themselves and perform the Kowtow. In 1865, a friend of ours met a lama who had left his home on a pilgrimage to the Woo-tai Shan monastery in the province of Shen-si, and who informed him that twelve months would elapse before he reached his journey's end. Many of the lamas, however, do not reside in monasteries, but lead a nomadic life on the vast plains of Mongolia, acting not only as priests in their respective encampments, but as shepherds. They often suggested to my mind shepherds who, of old, watched their flocks and herds in the valleys of Judæa. Thus Moses kept the flock of Jethro, his father-in-law, a priest of Midian. The twelve patriarchs were also shepherds, and David was called from leading his father's sheep to contend with the formidable giant of Gath. In some cases, I observed the ladies of Mongolian families tending the flocks, and there are several passages in Holy Writ,[1] which indicate that in ancient Palestine work of this kind not unfrequently devolved on the daughters of emirs or chieftains. I looked in vain, however, amid so much that

[1] The passages I allude to are Gen. xxiv. 17, 20 ; xxix. 9 ; Exodus ii. 16.

reminded me of what I had read of patriarchal times, for " towers of the flock," as those structures from which the approach of an enemy might be discovered, are termed in Scripture. Once, indeed, I saw at a considerable distance what appeared to be a tower of this kind, but on advancing a couple of miles towards it, I discovered it to be a lama temple.

Lama temples are, as a rule, very imposing. Amongst the most noticeable are those which were built at Ye-hole, by the Emperor Kien-lung Wong. One of these has a copper dome, which, being highly burnished, is of dazzling brightness when the sun shines upon it, and has the appearance of gold. When I visited the temple of Lama-miou, and while standing in the principal shrine, inspecting more especially the eight or ten large, yellow satin umbrellas, and banners of the same material upon which were representations of Buddha, I was accosted by one of the priests. In the course of an interesting conversation he informed me that there resided in the town, a lama able to predict with perfect accuracy every event which was destined to occur throughout the course of the ensuing five hundred years. It was also in the power of this prophetic lama to call to mind every event of the past five hundred years. I was most anxious for an interview, but his engagements were so numerous as to preclude the possibility. In the Ta-fo temple at Pekin, there is an idol—said to have been brought from Siam—which is seventy feet high; and, as a rule, the idols in lama temples are larger than those in the Buddhist temples throughout the empire. On the altar of this colossal idol are placed incense burners, candlesticks, and stands for flowers. Such vessels are made of zinc or copper, or of marble. In addition, a singular vessel which consists of the upper portion of a human skull, lined with gold, or silver, or copper, and filled with precious articles, may be sometimes seen upon altars. The skull is either that of one who has been distinguished for his abilities, or of a youth who has died in his eighteenth or nineteenth year—an age which is regarded with peculiar reverence by the Mongolians. At the gates of many of the temples are prayer wheels. On each wheel a prayer is recorded, and the votary who is passing by, or who is unable to remain in the temple until the service is concluded, repeats once the prayer which he is about to set in motion, and then turns the wheel and goes his way. The wheel is supposed to waft the prayer to heaven and the petition is considered to be repeated, as often as it revolves. Another feature of the courtyards of monasteries is the prayer-pillars. These consist of stone pillars upon which are engraven prayers to Buddha. They are placed in the court-yards of the monasteries, so that monks may be induced as they walk to and fro, to pause and engage in devotion. They are often elaborately carved.

It has often been remarked that Buddhism—especially Lamaism—has many external points of resemblance to Roman Catholicism. The many Christian forms and ceremonies which were pressed into the service of paganism by the priests of Thibet, were probably derived from Nestorian and Roman Catholic missionaries who laboured in Central Asia. Indeed, the whole system of Lamaism seems to have been re-organized on that of the Roman Catholic Church, and this pagan worship is said not only to have its pope, its cardinals, and its bishops, but infant baptism, confirmation, litanies, processions, services with double choirs, masses for the living and the dead, the worship of saints, exorcisms, and fast days ; in addition to which may be men-tioned the use of the cross, the mitre, the dalmatica, the cope, chaplets and rosaries, holy water, flower-stands on the altar, and so forth. I am unable to speak with certainty on *all* these points, but it has been asserted that they are to be found in the Buddhist church of Thibet. From Thibet many of these cere-monies found their way into China, but they are much less numerous in the *cultus* of the Buddhist priests of the Empire, than in that of the lamas of Thibet, Mongolia, and Mantchuria.

MOHAMMEDANISM.

Confucianism, Taouism, and Buddhism are not the only re-ligions of human origin which have obtained a *locus standi* in the empire. Within six hundred years after the religion of Buddha had been established in China by the Emperor Mingti, an Arab, called Wos-Kassin—supposed to have been a maternal

uncle of Mohammed—introduced into the "central flowery
land" the faith of Islam. This apostle of Mohammedanism,
together with a chosen band of followers, arrived in China in
the seventh century, and proceeded to disseminate that strange
system of falsity to which its founder gave such vitality, by constituting himself the relentless antagonist of idolatry, and the un-
compromising promulgator of the doctrine of the unapproachable
supremacy and perfect oneness of God. Its converts—who are
not drawn from the ranks of the poorer classes only, but include
a great number of the wealthy and respectable—are to be found
especially in the northern, southern, and western provinces of
the empire. In the northern and western provinces they are
very numerous, whole villages being occupied by them alone.
During the campaign in the North in 1860, the Moslem soldiers
in the Indian regiments which were sent to China found many
warm friends among their Chinese co-religionists, between
whom and themselves there was the powerful bond of hostility
to idolaters. The Chinese Mohammedans are by no means disobedient to the injunctions of their prophet, which impress
upon them the sacred duty of warring against the enemies of
the faith. They are perpetually at war with the government of
the country. In 1863, the Mohammedans living in the North
of China were in a state of open revolt, and spread ruin
and devastation on every side. So formidable did they prove
that the Governor-General of Canton, Lew Tchang-yu, who,
as Governor of Kwang-si, had acquired a reputation for great
military genius, was summoned to Pekin to take command of
the army, which had hitherto proved unsuccessful against the
Moslem rebels. In the same year a commissioner, named Salin,
arrived at Canton to obtain funds for the maintenance of an
army engaged in suppressing a similar uprising by the Mohammedans in the western province of Yunnan.

Although the Chinese Mohammedans have for centuries been
separated from their co-religionists of other climes, they hold
with much tenacity the doctrines which Mahomet taught.
They invariably represent God as the Supreme Eternal Being,
before all worlds, neither begotten nor made, and maintain that
there is none like Him. They acknowledge their belief in the

existence of angels, and describe them as beings of absolute purity, variously occupied in the service of their Creator. Four of the angelic host who serve God day and night, they hold in especial reverence, namely, Gabriel, the minister of revelations; Michael, the guardian angel of God's ancient people Israel; Azrael, the messenger of death; and Israfael, to whom it has been deputed to summon all men, the quick and the dead alike, that, in the presence of God, they may give an account of the deeds done in the body. Two angels are supposed by them to accompany every man in the journey of life, to note his various actions, and report them fully to the Supreme Being. They are taught by the Koran to look upon the Paradise of God as a region within which provision will be made for the indulgence of those "fleshly lusts, which war against the soul;" and in speaking with Mussulmans of a future state of rest, it is easy to discover that the notions which they entertain with regard to it are of a very sensual nature. They hold, of course, that Mohammed is the chief of all the prophets whom God has sent; and the number of these is not less than 224,000.

In the practice of the duties enjoined by their religion, the Mohammedans of China appear to be quite as strict as those whom I have seen in Egypt and other countries. They pray five times a day—a duty which is not considered obligatory by all Mohammedans, many of whom only pray thrice a day. They worship with their face toward the holy city of Mecca, with the usual genuflections. When they are going to read the Koran, they wash their hands before they presume to handle the sacred book. Every Friday—the Mohammedan Sabbath—they resort in large numbers to the mosques. When engaged in the worship of the sanctuary they wear a long white robe, and a turban of the same colour. Before entering the mosque they take their shoes off, but they do not, like the Arabs, carry them into the temple, holding them in the left hand, sole to sole. Women and youths are excluded from their congregations, and the men maintain the utmost gravity of demeanour during the service. So soon as prayers are over, they return to their ordinary occupations. On one occasion finding myself on a Friday in Chan-chu-kow—an influential town

situated at the base of the Great Wall of China—I went to
see its mosque, a spacious and not inelegant building, which
commands an extensive view of the city. In its courtyard was
a very well-dressed, handsome youth of fourteen or fifteen years
of age, who, in answer to my question why he waited outside
instead of joining the worshippers, informed me that he was
under the prescribed age. The mosque inside was literally
crowded with votaries, the best-dressed Chinese I ever saw.
The Koran was preached by a priest, leaning, as is the custom
upon the top of his staff—as Jacob " worshipped, leaning on
the top of his staff."

The stated seasons for fasting, are observed by Chinese Mussulmans with apparent strictness. During the Ramadan, which
is the ninth month, they appear to spend the greater portion
of the time within the walls of their mosques ; and the attenuated appearance of many of them is a very good proof that
their abstinence has been genuine. The duties of almsgiving,
and of abstinence from all intoxicating wines, and from swine's
flesh, are strictly observed by them at other times also. A Chinese
author, noticing this abstinence from wines and certain meats,
and also Moslem alms-deeds and kindnesses to dumb animals,
accuses the followers of Mohammed of having borrowed these
features of their religion from Buddhism—an accusation which
Mohammedans indignantly repel. Of alms they give apparently
very liberally every Friday. As a rule, however, their alms are
bestowed only upon the poor of their own sect. When at Chan-
chu-kow I observed several Mohammedan gentlemen dispensing
alms to the poor and indigent followers of the prophet at one of
the halls or guilds of the sect. The names of the poor pensioners
were recorded on a large board on the walls of the guild, and as
each was called by a secretary, he responded, and received his
usual portion. The rite of circumcision is scrupulously observed,
nor are they forgetful of a duty said to be incumbent upon every
good Moslem—the performance of a pilgrimage to Mecca to
touch the black stone of the Kaaba, to obtain the pardon of their
sins and an entrance into Paradise. The pilgrimage to Mecca is
naturally easier to the Mohammedans of the western provinces of
the empire, than to those in the northern and southern provinces.

They possess numerous mosques throughout the empire. These edifices bear a great resemblance to other Chinese temples. In Canton there are no fewer than four mosques, two of which were built by Wos-Kassin. A very ancient tomb in a mosque situated beyond the great North Gate, contains the remains of this zealous propagator of Mohammedan tenets, who, after a residence of fifteen years in the land of his adoption, died in the full assurance of entering that Paradise which Mohammed had devised. The mosque, which is situated in the old city of Canton, is distinguished by a tower, which was built in order that the *muezzins* might summon the Moslem population to prayers. The doorway of the tower is now blocked up by soil, which has been allowed to accumulate around the entire base. When the city was in the occupation of the allied armies of England and France, some of the British officers made an aperture in the wall, and finding a spiral staircase, they succeeded in reaching the top. From the worn appearance of the steps it was concluded that the *muezzins* must have been very regular in the discharge of their duties.

In one or two of the mosques of this city there are apartments in which are lodged stranger Mohammedans who have found their way to the busy marts of Canton. In the mosque near the Taiping Gate, which is best adapted for the reception of visitors, I have met with Moslem merchants from the provinces of Sze-chuen, Yunnan, and Kwang-si. I found these Mohammedans more intelligent than those of Canton, and evidently much more earnest in their devotion to the precepts of Mohammed.

Some of the mosques present a very imposing appearance. That which stands in the city of Chin-kiang is, perhaps, particularly noteworthy. It is supported by arches, and resembles very much the crypt of a Christian church. This structure, together with a schoolroom, is inclosed by a high wall, and in consequence looks somewhat like an encampment. The mosque in the city of Hang-chow is very grand and imposing, and the entrance-doors resemble a Cairene gate. In each mosque there is placed a tablet on which is written in large characters of gold, "May the emperor reign ten thousand years!" In each

Buddhist or Taouist monastery a similar tablet is placed upon the high altar. The emperor is evidently determined that the people shall learn that to him, the son of heaven, as well as to the gods, allegiance and homage are due. To each of the principal mosques a school is attached, in which the children are taught to read the Koran in the original tongue.

北帝

PIH-TE.

CHAPTER V.

POPULAR GODS AND GODDESSES.

ANY exposition of the religious systems of the Chinese which did not give some account of the gods and goddesses whom the people delight to honour, would be extremely incomplete. If the Chinese do not trouble themselves much about religious doctrines, they are very much interested in the canonized mortals and imaginary beings whom they suppose to dispense the blessings and the ills of life. Their religion is essentially a *cultus*. The worshipper who kneels at the shrine of Confucius will also worship the Taouistical Pak-te; and, on special occasions, Taouist and Buddhist priests may be seen praying in the same national temple. "Like master, like man," is a proverb which is capable of being applied to a nation and its gods, and this chapter about the gods and goddesses of the Chinese may help the reader to understand the people.

In China the military and the learned classes divide between them the honours and emoluments of the state, and Kwan-te, the god of war, and Man-chang, the god of learning, have their votaries everywhere. Kwan-te, a distinguished general in the third year of the Christian era, was not canonized until nearly eight hundred years after his death. Now he has a state temple in every provincial, prefectoral, and district city of the empire; and, morning and evening, in almost every house, adoration is paid before the representation of him which stands on the ancestral altar. He is regarded as the protector of the peace of the empire, and of its multitudinous families. The immediate occasion of his being canonized is said to have been the drying up of the large and numerous salt-wells in the province of Shansi. This calamity was a cause of great perplexity and distress. The ministers of the Emperor Chin-tsung, like the magicians whom Pharaoh summoned to read his dreams, were helpless, and in his perplexity Chin-tsung turned to the Arch-Abbot of the Taouists, who declared that the wells had been dried up by an evil spirit. An appeal must therefore be made to Kwan-te, who now reigned as a king in the world of spirits. The emperor straightway wrote a despatch to Kwan-te on the subject of his conversation with the Arch-Abbot, and the Imperial communication was conveyed to the departed warrior in the flames of a sacred fire. An hour had scarcely elapsed, when Kwan-te appeared in mid-heaven riding on his red-coloured charger. The god declared that until a temple had been erected in his honour, the petition of the emperor could not be attended to. A temple was accordingly erected with much haste, and so soon as the top-stone had been placed, the salt wells again yielded their supplies. It is said that Kwan-te appeared in 1855 to the generalissimo of the Imperial forces, whom he enabled to defeat the rebels near Nankin. For this interposition, the Emperor Hien-fung placed him on a footing with Confucius, who had been regarded till then as the principal deity in the national Pantheon. In the porch of the state temple of Kwan-te, at Canton—one of the finest temples in the city—is a figure of the red horse of the god, beside which stands the figure of a stalwart armour-bearer, as if waiting to receive the commands of his master. Even armour-bearer and horse have their votaries; and in the large town of Cum-lee-hoi in the silk districts of Kwang-tung, I saw women worshipping these images, and binding small bags or purses to the bridle rein of the charger.

Man-chang is especially worshipped by collegians and school-boys. He is supposed to record their names in a book of remembrance, and to inscribe opposite each name the character of the individual. In front of his idols there is generally an angel bearing this book of remembrance in his hand. He was famous for his great literary attainments, and his love of virtue. It is

recorded of him, as of many other Chinese sages, that his
parents were very old when he was born ; and one of his grandfathers was the emperor who invented the bow and arrow.
While a mere boy Man-chang mastered the most profound works
without the aid of a teacher; and when he died, the gods in
conclave called upon him to be the tutelary deity of aspirants
to literary distinction. In all the principal cities of the empire
there are state temples [1] in honour of this god. In Canton there
are no fewer than ten. The offerings presented to Man-chang
are bundles of onions, and sometimes his altars are covered with
bunches of these too odorous bulbs. His votaries are not confined to students, and I have seen persons of both sexes, and of
all ranks of life among them. On one occasion I ventured to
ask a man who with his wife had been engaged in earnest
prayer to this god, what blessings he sought. He replied that he
and his wife were desirous that their children should become
well versed in classical literature, and so be qualified to hold
high political positions. His most important temple is at Chu-
toong-yune, the principal city of the district in which Man-
chang was born. On one of the beams which support the roof
is a brazen eagle, from the bill of which a long cord hangs in
front of the altar. Attached to the cord is a pencil with which
the deity is supposed to write mystic scrolls on a table covered
with sand, or, as others say, upon sheets of paper placed on the
table. These written oracles, the productions of a crafty priesthood, are generally announcements of impending calamities, and
are forwarded to the authorities in order that they may adopt
precautionary measures. In 1853, when Kwang-tung was overrun with rebels, a communication of this nature was forwarded
to the governor-general of the province. It called upon the
people to eschew rebellion as one of the greatest crimes, and
Yeh, who was then governor-general, embodied the oracle in a
proclamation, which was posted in the crowded thoroughfares of
Canton and its suburbs.

As might be expected, where so much depends on the recurrence of rain, one of the most prominent of the deities who

---

[1] These temples, like those in honour of Kwan-te, are reserved for the worship
of government officials.

preside over nature in her various functions, is Lung Wong, the
Dragon King, in whose keeping are the "fountains of the deep."
Formerly he was only worshipped in seasons of drought, but, in
consequence of mercies vouchsafed to the Cantonese, he is now
included in the list of those who are worshipped at the vernal
equinox and the winter solstice.[1] In seasons of drought, the
intercessory service generally extends over three days. When
the god fails to hear the district ruler, the prefect supplicates
him. A proclamation is issued, calling upon the people to eat
neither fish, flesh, nor fowl, until a favourable answer has come.
The proclamation is supplemented by an edict forbidding fishmongers, butchers, and poulterers to sell to the people. As the
drought is not a matter of immediate consequence to them, the
fishmongers, butchers, and poulterers, show their respect for the
edict by bribing the petty mandarins and police. If Lung Wong
will not hear the prefect, the governor-general beseeches him.
In this case, the ceremony is invested with unusual solemnity.
Having attired himself in sackcloth, and bound his neck with
chains, and his ankles with fetters, in sign of deep humility and
penitence, the governor-general proceeds to the temple, accompanied by a long train of sorrowing citizens. Four small banners
of yellow silk upon which are inscribed respectively the Chinese
characters for Wind, Rain, Thunder, and Lightning, are borne
at the head of the procession, and then placed in an incense
burner upon the altar, surrounded by a number of lighted
tapers. After a variety of genuflections, the governor-general
consigns a written prayer, addressed to Lung Wong, to the flames
of a sacred fire. This ceremony is followed by a salvo of fire
crackers, the beating of gongs, and the clanging of cymbals,
amidst the din of which the governor-general retires, and is
escorted by the citizens to the gates of his palace. Should refreshing showers fail to follow these appeals, the people conclude
that the god is asleep, and to rouse him from his slumbers, they
remove him from his throne, and expose him for a time to the
burning rays of the sun. It is also usual for the emperor to
command the Arch-Abbot of Taouism, whose residence is in the

---

[1] Lung Wong is worshipped as well on the first and fifteenth day of each lunar
month, when sacrifices of a sheep, a pig, and fowls are offered to him.

Dragon and Tiger mountains of Kiangsi, to pray for rain. Should the prayer prove ineffectual, the Arch-Abbot's salary, which is paid out of the Imperial treasury, is generally withheld.

The amount of misdirected energy which the Chinese officially spend upon this Dragon King is something wonderful; and a very singular illustration of the melancholy absurdities and extravagances in which idolatry delights, was afforded in Canton on the occasion of a drought upwards of thirty years ago. The governor-general of the province, having in vain observed the prescribed forms of prayer and fasting, issued a proclamation, calling upon the wise men of the province to devise some means by which the deity might be made propitious, promising a large pecuniary reward to the person whose scheme should prove successful. Strange to say, none of the geomancers and fortune-tellers came forward. One of the priests of the sect of Taou, however, offered his services. He was supported by his *confrères*, and the invocation of Lung Wong was begun in front of an altar erected in the open air. The priests interceded for four days in succession; but, alas! the deity still continued inexorable. Finding his efforts of no avail, the priest decamped by night and, it is said, eventually died from the effects of fever brought on by exposure to the sun during his four days of prayer. Meanwhile the drought continued, and the price of grain rose to an unprecedented figure. At this crisis a geomancer came forward, and obtained the sanction of the Viceroy to the following ridiculous arrangements for propitiating the Dragon King. After having closed the south gate of the city—a device usually resorted to in such emergencies—he placed under it several water tubs, filled to the brim, and containing frogs. A number of boys were then ordered by the soothsayer to tease the frogs so as to make them croak. In a few days rain is said to have followed this extraordinary exhibition of human folly.

On the 7th of May, 1871, I saw the Viceroy Sue Tai-yan walk in procession to the temple of this god in Canton, accompanied by the officials and leading gentry of the city. Each person wore undress robes, and carried an incense stick in his

hand. This he placed on the altar, afterwards performing the
kow-tow. At the close of the observances in which the Viceroy
and other members of the procession took part, a number of
Buddhist and Taouist priests, the former on the right, and the
latter on the left, side of the temple, began to pray with great
earnestness.

The temple to which the emperor resorts on such occasions
is situated at Hae-loong-tang. It is by far the most imposing of the temples in honour of the Dragon King which I
visited, and contains apartments for the reception of the emperor. I found in it a number of elders, farmers, and peasants,
who had come from the neighbouring villages, and had marched
to the temple in procession. They sought to prevail upon the
god to grant a few copious showers. Each wore a wreath of
the leaves of the weeping willow round his head, and some of
them carried branches of this tree in their hands.

In seasons of drought appeal is sometimes made to Yuh
Hwangte, or the Pearly Emperor, who holds higher rank than
Lung Wong. I once saw a singular procession on an occasion of
this kind, in the neighbourhood of Yan-chan Foo, on the banks
of the Poyang lake. To show the god the parched state of the
earth, and to drive away the spirits which caused the drought,
they carried his idol in an open state chair to the banks of the
lake. In the crowd which followed were two men denuded of
the greater portion of their clothing, and armed with swords.
Sometimes they cut the air with their weapons, as if executing
the vengeance of the god on the evil spirits; sometimes they
bounded three or four feet from the ground. On the lake was
a boat in which sat the elders of the city, in their best attire,
and holding branches of the weeping willow. Yuh Hwangte
is the canonized son of one of the kings of the Kwong-Yim-
Mew-Lok, and his natal anniversary is one of great rejoicing not
only on the part of the priests of the sect of Taou, but on the
part of the people generally.

Another popular state deity is Shing Wong, or the Protector
of Walled Cities. Formerly the rank of this god was inferior
to that of a governor-general, an anomaly which curiously illustrates the light in which the Chinese regard their gods. At

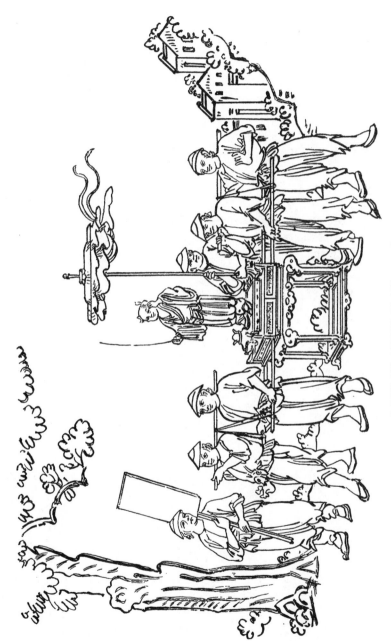

A RAIN-GOD CARRIED IN PROCESSION.

Canton this disparity of rank was marked by the gate of the temple of Shing Wong being closed, whenever his excellency the governor-general passed in procession. This ridiculous custom was abolished by the Emperor Kien-lung, who raised Shing Wong in the scale of deities; and now it is incumbent upon all governors-general to worship him annually on the second day of the year. His great festival, however, is on his natal anniversary, namely, the twenty-fourth day of the seventh month, when the prefect presents a new suit of silk garments to him in the name of the government. He also washes the face of the idol, and with his own hands attires it in the new garments. Sometimes members of wealthy families seek to recommend themselves to the god by asking to be allowed to provide these garments. In such a case the donor sends the suit of clothes to the temple in a gilded chair, a few days before the anniversary. Numerous attendants accompany the chair in procession. The worship rendered to Shing Wong at the celebration of his anniversary takes place at a very early hour of the morning, and at Canton so anxious are the numerous worshippers to be present at the ceremony that those who reside beyond the walls of the city take up their quarters in the temple on the preceding evening. It is a harvest time for pickpockets, who practise their art on the sleeping votaries. So soon as the prefect arrives, generally a little after midnight, the sleepers are aroused by the beating of gongs. A scene of great bustle and confusion ensues. The prefect brings with him the jadestone seal of the god, which is always under his care, and is only produced at this anniversary. Another seal with which the god is invested, and which is made of copper, always remains in the temple. Persons who have sick relatives now hasten into the presence of the god to invoke his blessing, and to have an impression made by his jadestone seal on the garments of the sick which they have brought with them. For this impression they pay a larger sum of money than for one from the copper seal. The garments so stamped are conveyed to their sick owners, who are attired in them, in order that they may be cured of their maladies. Other votaries may be seen crowding around the altar to buy sheets of yellow paper

on which a few mystic scrolls, also stamped with this seal, have
been written. These sheets are carried away to be placed in
dwelling-houses, which they are said to keep free from all
evil. Others present petitions, calling upon the god to send
some of his spiritual retainers to their houses, to remove evil
spirits from the bodies of sick relatives. In some of the
temples of Shing Wong may be seen implements of torture
by which he is supposed to punish evil spirits. During the
day a portable idol of the god is escorted by the prefect and
his guards through the principal streets of the city. The procession, which is of great length, is headed by banners and
bands of music, and it occupies so much time in traversing
the numerous narrow streets that business is almost entirely
suspended for the day.

In every temple of this deity there are representations of the
judgments inflicted on the wicked in the ten kingdoms of the
Buddhist hell. The judicial proceedings are represented as
conducted after the manner of criminal trials in Chinese courts
of justice. In each kingdom is a king seated on the throne
of justice, and round him are the officers of the court, with
the ministering attendants. As the punishments which are
represented as being inflicted on the wicked in these ten kingdoms at least throw some light on the workings of the oriental
imagination, I venture to give a *résumé* of them.

The first of the kingdoms is presided over by Tsung-kwong
Wong, and the spirits who are punished before his tribunal are
those of persons who have committed suicide ; of priests and
nuns who, having received money for saying masses, have
neglected to do so, and of those who have been guilty of
numberless offences. The spirits of the last-named are made to
ascend a lofty tower from which they gaze into a large mirror
suspended as it were in mid heaven. In this they see the forms
of the loathsome beasts, reptiles, and insects which they are
destined to animate when they return to earth. Homicides are
punished like Tantalus, and, in the midst of water, are unable
to quench their thirst. The priests and nuns are confined in a
gloomy chamber named Poo-king-shan. Here by the light of a
dimly-burning lamp, pendent from the roof, they are condemned

to read aloud the neglected masses printed in very small type. Suicides are the prey of insatiable hunger and unquenchable thirst, and, twice during each month, they are supposed to experience the same agony which attended their acts of self-destruction. The worship, moreover, which their children pay to the *manes* of these wretched beings is intercepted. After an imprisonment of two years, the spirit of a suicide returns to the place where the act of self-destruction was committed, in order that it may repent. Should it bring plagues upon the people in the neighbourhood instead of repenting, it is recalled to undergo the horrors of a long imprisonment. A spirit which repents during this incarceration, returns again to the earth in human form. The spirits of those who have expended sums in the purchase of obscene publications to secure their destruction; or of those who have appreciated so highly the blessing of a written language as to have traversed the streets, or employed others to do so, to gather from the pavements and the walls of dwellings scraps of written paper, so as to prevent any portion of their written language being trodden under foot of men, come to this kingdom to receive rewards. Tsung-kwong's natal anniversary is celebrated on the first day of the second month, and as the Chinese believe that all who worship him on that day will be forgiven, its recurrence generally sends many votaries to prostrate themselves before his mercy-seat.

The second kingdom is supposed to be situated under the south sea, and is said to be presided over by Cho-kong Wong. The offenders sent here for punishment, are priests who have decoyed children from their homes for the purpose of making monks of them; husbands who have put away their wives under false pretences; persons who have feloniously disposed of property intrusted to their care; men who have injured or maimed their fellow-creatures by a careless use of firearms or other weapons; ignorant physicians who have persisted in prescribing for the sick; householders who have refused to manumit their slaves, when the latter were in a position to purchase manumission, and mandarins who have oppressed the people. The priests are represented as being thrown into an ice-pond. The fraudulent trustees are carried into dark clouds, and suffocated by the sand with which these are impregnated. Mandarins who oppress the people are confined in cages in which the sufferer cannot stand upright. After having been tormented in hell for centuries, the wicked spirits return to the world in the bodies of reptiles or other loathsome animals. The virtuous who here receive their rewards, are those who have expended money in purchasing medicine for the sick poor; who have given rice to the indigent and needy; who have instructed the young and ignorant; and who have avoided posting placards on walls, lest they should fall down, and the characters written or printed on them be trodden under foot. These virtuous spirits are then forwarded to the tenth kingdom, whence they return to earth in bodies of human form to enjoy riches and honours.

The third kingdom, which is supposed to be underneath the eastern ocean, is ruled by Sung-ti Wong. This king punishes ministers of state who have been guilty of ingratitude towards the emperor; wives who have been ungrateful to their husbands; undutiful sons; disobedient slaves; rebellious soldiers; malefactors who have escaped from prison; merchants who have acted fraudulently towards their partners in trade; men who have involved their sureties; geomancers who have given false opinions with regard to ground selected for houses or tombs; ploughmen who have turned up coffins, and have neglected to give them sepulture in other ground; men who have refused to worship the tombs of their ancestors; those who have published pasquinades in which they have held up their neighbours to contempt; scribes who have not properly represented the ideas of the illiterate who have engaged their services; forgers, perjurers, &c., &c.

The punishments of these offenders vary in degree and intensity. The bodies of some, are fed upon by tigers, and like the liver of Prometheus, they are never diminished, though perpetually devoured. Some are being incessantly pierced with sharp-pointed arrows; some are being continually disembowelled, whilst others are bound to red-hot funnels of brass. These wretched men return to the earth as monsters. Persons who have at their own expense erected bridges over rivulets, or paved highways, are the virtuous who come to this kingdom. These are rewarded, and sent to the tenth kingdom in order that they may again return to earth in important positions.

The fourth kingdom is also said to be under the eastern sea. It is ruled over by Oon-koon Wong. Those come to it who have not paid their taxes, or their house rents. Physicians who have administered medicines of an inferior quality to their patients; silk mercers who have sold bad silk; persons who have not given place to the aged or blind in the streets or public assemblies; men who have wilfully destroyed grain crops, or who have removed their neighbour's land-marks; priests who have violated monastic rules; and libidinous persons, drunkards, whoremongers, busybodies, fornicators, gamblers, and brawlers are also consigned to this place of torment. Some are thrown into large ponds of blood; not a few are pounded in mortars; and others are suspended from beams supporting the roof of the hall of torture, by hooks passing through the fleshy parts of the body. The virtuous are those who have provided coffins at their own expense for the decent interment of the poor. The souls of the wicked eventually return to the world to animate beasts, reptiles, and insects, whilst the virtuous return to their fellow-men to enjoy riches, happiness, and honour.

The fifth kingdom is presided over by Yim-lo Wong, who is said to be inexorable in his dealings with all transgressors. Those who in the first kingdom were condemned to gaze upon a vast mirror which revealed the loathsome animals into which they were to pass, are here compelled to ascend a pagoda, from the lofty summit of which they behold at one view the scenes of their birthplace, and all the past delights which arose from intercourse with their nearest relatives, and with their dearest friends. With their misery intensified by this view of the irrevocable past, they descend to the judgment hall to experience torture in a variety of forms, and when this succession of agonies has been passed through, they again ascend the pagoda to view once more the scenes of the past which make their present intolerable. Besides these, there are in this region unbelievers in the doctrines of Buddha, backbiters, slanderers, revilers of good and virtuous men, and incendiaries. Some are sawn asunder, others are metamorphosed into animals

or birds. Persons who have been renowned upon earth for their
alms-deeds are forwarded by Yim-lo Wong to the tenth kingdom, where they are highly honoured. As the anniversary of
this king's birth is on the eighth day of the first month,
numerous votaries prostrate themselves before his idol and
make solemn vows that they will amend their ways. A vow
made on this day, is regarded as a sure means of obtaining a
full pardon of all past offences at the hands of Yim-lo Wong.

The sixth kingdom is supposed to be under that portion of
the sea which washes the northern coast of China. It is ruled
over by Pin-shing Wong, who deals out punishment to men who
are always complaining of the seasons; to sacrilegious thieves
who scrape the gold from idols ; to those who do not respect the
writings of Confucius; to those who place filth in the vicinity
of temples; to those who worship the gods, without having first
cleansed the body ; to readers of obscene books; to those who
paint upon chinaware or embroider in silk representations of
the gods or angels, or of the sun, moon, and stars ; to those
who destroy good books, and to those who wantonly waste rice.
The thieves who have scraped the gold from idols, are hanged up
by the hands, and disembowelled ; the destroyers of good books
are hanged up by the feet, and flayed alive ; those who have never
been satisfied with the seasons are sawn asunder, whilst other
offenders are made to kneel, with their knees uncovered, upon
sharp-pointed particles of iron. The virtuous are recompensed
who have contributed of their substance to funds established
for the erection and endowment of temples.

The seventh kingdom, which is said to be situated under the
north-western ocean, is governed by Ti-shan Wong. Forgers;
aged men who suck the breasts of women (a custom practised
to some extent in China); physicians who make medicine of
human bones, which are found scattered about in large numbers
in Chinese graveyards; robbers of tombs ; women who endeavour
to procure abortion; schoolmasters who neglect their pupils;
masters who maltreat their slaves ; oppressors of the poor and
of their neighbours, and those who seek to curry favour with
the wealthy and great, are arraigned before Ti-shan Wong. The
robbers of tombs he commands to be thrown into volcanoes

The practitioners who haste to be rich by carrying off the scattered bones of graveyards, are boiled in oil, whilst others are placed in the cangue. It is supposed, however, that persons who have been guilty of any of these offences can atone for them in this life, by purchasing birds exposed for sale at a poulterer's shop, and giving them their freedom; or by providing coffins for the decent interment of paupers, who, in the absence of poor-houses, are occasionally found dying or dead at the corners of the streets of Chinese cities. The good whom this king recompenses, are those who have let blood from their arms or legs, in order that they may save a sick parent, whose only chance of recovery the physician has declared to lie in a medicine of which this forms the principal ingredient.

The eighth kingdom is ruled over by Ping-ting Wong, before whom those appear who have neglected to support their parents, or to comfort them when sick, or to celebrate their funeral obsequies. Men who have proved ungrateful to their bene-factors, or who have indulged in obscene conversation, are also judged by him. Punishment is inflicted here upon women who have hung clothes out to dry upon the house-tops—a proceeding which the Chinese regard as highly displeasing to departed spirits, with whose flight through the air it is supposed to inter-fere. Undutiful sons are metamorphosed into animals or trampled under the hoofs of horses. Men who have been guilty of ingratitude, are cut asunder; the obscene are bound to stakes and deprived of their tongues; and housewives who have cared more for the drying of their "linen" than the comfort of departed spirits, are plunged into a lake of blood. Persons who have contributed to the wants of mendicant Buddhist friars are rewarded here.

In the ninth kingdom, the sceptre of which is swayed by Too-shu Wong, the transgressors are persons who have been guilty of arson; artists who have prostituted their talents by painting obscene pictures; priests who have misspent funds given to them for the benefit of their monasteries; monks who have sold to those visiting their monasteries religious tracts which they ought to have distributed gratuitously; men who have killed birds, fishes, fowls, pigs, &c.; men who have sown discord between husbands and wives, or between parents and children; and those also who have administered aphrodisiacs to women. The offending priests and monks are thrown upon sharp spikes; the destroyers of fowls, pigs, and fishes are devoured by such creatures; those who have sown discord between husbands and wives, are speared with tridents; those who have set parents and children at variance, are devoured by wild beasts; and those who have given drugs for base purposes, are gored by sows. The benevolent who have supplied the poor with hot tea in the cold months of winter, and with cold tea in the heat of summer, and provided medicine for the afflicted in times of pestilence, and watermen who have given free passage in their ferry-boats to the poor, are here rewarded.

The tenth kingdom is that to which all those to whom in the other kingdoms punishments or rewards have been meted out, are eventually conveyed in order that they may again return to earth—the virtuous as men of honour and distinction, and the wicked as beasts, birds, insects, or reptiles.

With the view of impressing upon the minds of the people the fearful punishments which await the wicked in these ten kingdoms, symbolical processions are got up in the fourth month of the year, in many of the towns. In 1865, I saw a large procession of this kind at Tien-tsin. It consisted of men, boys, and girls, attired in prison dress, who were led along the streets by others representing the imps by whom the punishments of Hades are inflicted. These executioners were dressed in the most absurd garments, and their faces were concealed by masks of the most hideous aspect.

Hung-sing Wong, the god of the southern ocean, is another of the deities receiving state worship who deserves to be mentioned. At the great annual celebration of his worship, the temple in his honour near the mouth of the Canton river, a few miles below Whampoa, is thronged with votaries. The grounds in front of it are covered with booths, provided with soups and viands of all kinds for the crowds of pilgrims who come from all parts of the province, and the proceedings extend over three days and three nights. A temple in his honour which once stood at a place called Ngan-kong-hoy, in the Namhoi district, was destroyed by order of the Emperor Kien-lung; and the curious story attached to its destruction is so characteristically Chinese, that I venture to relate it. It so happened that in one of the apartments of the temple, a teacher, of the clan Ho, kept a school. It chanced that in an adjoining room he had placed a basket in which were a few grains of rice. A cock, having found its way into the room, perched upon the edge of the basket, which fell over and covered it. Very much perplexed by the sudden and mysterious disappearance of the bird, the owner called upon the god to inform him as to its whereabouts. The oracular response—so the story goes—was to the effect that the cock was in the temple, and eventually it was found in the basket. The owner at once concluded that the man to whom the basket belonged had been trying to steal the bird, and publicly accused the schoolmaster of being a thief. Naturally, the false accusation greatly excited the master's anger. In the course of a few years, it came to pass that he succeeded in obtaining high literary honours at Pekin, and this achievement enabled him to have an interview with the Emperor Kien-lung, who ascended the throne in 1736. In the course of a conversation which took place between the sovereign and his subject, the latter complained of the grave accusation which had been brought against him, and begged his majesty to punish those at whose hands he had suffered the indignity. The request was granted, and the emperor forthwith ordered that the temple in which Ho's misfortune had occurred, should be destroyed.

Upon the destruction of this temple the inhabitants of the six neighbouring villages, thinking it a disgrace that the idol should be without a temple, resolved to shelter it in turn in their respective ancestral halls. Accordingly, on the sixteenth day of the eighth month of each year, the idol is now taken to Ngan-kong-hoy by the villagers whose year of guardianship has expired, and it is there met and borne away amidst great rejoicings by the villagers in whose ancestral hall it is to be sheltered during the coming year. Among the villagers whose turn it is to be so favoured, a different person is selected for every day of the year; and it is the duty of each person so selected to present offerings of fowls, pork, wine, tea, &c. The expense of these daily offerings is defrayed by the money which, on the day of changing the residence of the god and on the two succeeding days, is received from those who attend the dramatic representations given for the gratification of the holiday-makers.

The most popular of those deities which do not receive official worship, is Pih-te or Pak-tai, to use the Cantonese form of the word, the great god of the north, concerning whom Chinese mythology has much to say. Existing before the world, Pak-tai became a chief or supreme director of its destinies. His most remarkable incarnation happened on this wise : Pak-tai, into whose heart had entered the spirit of the sun, visited the ancient nation of Tsing-lok-kwok, and upon the queen of this people coming into his presence she was overshadowed by the spirit of the sun, and at the end of the fourteenth month she gave birth to an avatar or incarnation of Pak-tai. He was passed from the womb through an incision made under the left ribs of his mother. At the time of his birth, a cloud of rich and variegated colours hung over the whole nation ; the air was impregnated with the most fragrant odours, and earth spontaneously yielded rare and precious stones. Shortly after his birth, the child gave proofs of great strength of intellect and marvellous purity of soul. At the age of seven, he was well versed in various branches of literature. At fifteen, he left his home, despite the entreaties of his parents, and became a wanderer on the mountains. There a heavenly teacher appeared to him named Yuk-Tsing-Shing-Tsu, by whom he was instructed in sacred tenets and doctrines. After five hundred years' probation he ascended into heaven, seated in a chariot of nine different colours, and attended by a company of angels and a cavalcade of fair women. He then assumed the name of Pak-tai.

After this, in consequence of the extreme wickedness of its inhabitants, the earth was, according to Chinese annals, destroyed by a deluge in the reign of Yaou, B.C. 2357. This date nearly corresponds with that at which, according to our chronology, the Noachian deluge took place, and many have come to the conclusion that it is identical with the deluge referred to in the Hebrew Scriptures. When the waters, which had risen until they covered the tops of the highest mountains, had abated, Pak-tai reappeared on earth for the purpose of eradicating from the hearts of those whom the gods had saved, and of their descendants the evil which had called down so fearful a judgment, and of imparting to them that knowledge of agriculture, and of the arts and sciences which had been lost. Again, during the Shang dynasty—which ruled over China from B.C. 1766 to B.C. 1122—the people once more became wicked, and Pak-tai returned to reform them. His first measure was to dethrone the reigning house of Shang, and to establish in its place the dynasty of Chan. He next waged war against the evil spirit, whose legions are said to have been assisted by a turtle and a snake, each of great size and of prodigious strength.

Pak-tai is regarded by the Chinese as one of the most beneficent of deities, and his temples are generally crowded with votaries. It is usual for all persons embarking in trade to seek his blessing, and, should their undertaking prove successful, they place upon the walls of his temple a gilded tablet containing four Chinese characters expressive of gratitude. On a visit to one of the principal temples, in 1862, I was much struck by seeing one of the most intelligent of the Chinese merchants with whom foreigners are connected, seeking oracular information from his idol. He told me he was about to enter upon a large business transaction with an English merchant, and that he was praying for the directing care of Pak-tai. It is usual for partners in trade to draw up at the close of the year, a declaration in vermilion characters on yellow paper to the effect, that in all business transactions they have been faithful to one another. This declaration they take to one of the temples of this god, and, after reading it aloud in the presence of the idol, they burn it in order that it may be conveyed to the god and registered. Masters and servants also ratify their agreements there, and his temple is resorted to for the purpose of taking oaths or making solemn declarations. This is general in the case of men who are accused of theft, and wish to declare their

innocence. In 1862, I saw in the temple of Pak-tai at Canton
a venerable man who had been brought there by a young man
to make such a declaration. When they had offered prayers
and burned incense, the latter asked his companion—"Dare you
declare in the presence of the idol that you are not guilty of
stealing my clothes ? " The old man solemnly declared himself
to be quite innocent of the charge, and his accuser appeared
perfectly satisfied with the answer.

Amongst the deities worshipped by the Chinese the Five
Genii also hold a conspicuous place. They preside over what
are regarded as five elemental substances—namely, Fire, Earth,
Water, Metal, and Wood. In the fourth month of each year
they are honoured with sumptuous banquets. Votaries repair
in large numbers to their temples at this season, to thank
these deities for having restored them to health. They appear
in red dresses similar to the dresses of Chinese convicts or
prisoners, with chains round their necks, fetters on their ancles,
and handcuffs on their wrists, in sign of their humility and
unworthiness. These deities are said by the Taouist priests
to heal the sick, as the body of man is composed of the elements over which they preside. Health or sickness depends
on the just or unjust proportions of the five elements in the
body.

Upon a large altar at the feet of the Five Genii in their
temple in the " Great Market Street" of Canton, are five stones
supposed to be the petrified remains of five rams upon which
these gods rode into the city, each bearing in his hand an ear of
corn. The first is said to have been dressed in white, the
second in yellow, the third in black, the fourth in green, and the
fifth in red. On passing through one of the principal markets
the Genii said, May famine never visit the markets of this
place, and winged their flight through the air. On the plot
where the rams stood were found five stones, which were at
once identified with the rams. In consequence of the supposed visit of the Genii, the city of Canton is sometimes called
the City of Rams, the City of Genii or Angels, and the City
of Grain.

The " Great Bell-Tower" of the temple contains the largest

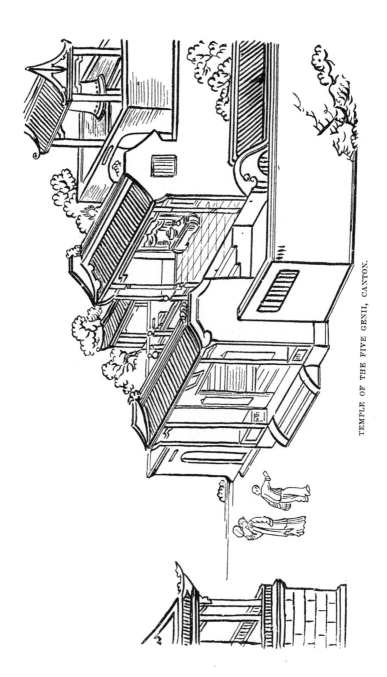

TEMPLE OF THE FIVE GENII, CANTON.

bell, I believe, in the south of China.[1] It is, however, never sounded, as both Tartars and Chinese—the Tartars especially—believe that upon its being sounded evil will betide the city. Almost all Chinese bells are without a clapper. In 1865, whilst Admiral Sir Michael Seymour was bombarding Canton, the bell was sounded by a shot from one of the guns of H.M.S. *Encounter*. To this, of course, the Chinese attributed the subsequent capture of the city by the allied armies of Great Britain and France.

Among the goddesses whom the Chinese worship Tien-How, the Queen of Heaven, occupies a very conspicuous place. This canonized saint was a native of the province of Fokien, and a member of the clan Lum. Her future greatness was indicated by supernatural events, and before she was a year old she displayed remarkable precocity. When eleven years old she expressed a wish to enter a Taouist nunnery; but the opposition of her parents induced her to continue under their roof. Her brothers, four in number, were merchants. On one occasion when they were absent on a trading voyage, she fell into a deep trance, from which she was roused by the loud lamentations of her parents, who supposed her dead. On recovering she informed them that she had seen her brothers at sea in the midst of a violent storm. Shortly after, the youngest son returned home and reported that his eldest brother had been lost at sea. He stated that during the storm a lady appeared in mid-heaven, and by means of a rope dragged the ship into a safe position. While he was relating this, his sister entered the room, and at once congratulated him on his escape. She said that she had hastened to the rescue of her elder brother, but while in the very act of saving him, she was awakened from her vision by the cries of her sorrowing parents.

---

[1] The largest bell I saw in China was one in a small monastery not far from Pekin. It is perhaps one of the largest in the world, and on it in *basso relievo* appear several thousands of Chinese characters, constituting, I believe, a Buddhist classic which priests when they retire into seclusion for three years commit to memory. With the view of rendering bells lucky, it is customary to smear them with the blood of some animal—a quadruped, generally a goat, being offered in sacrifice.

After her death, which took place when she was twenty, her relatives declared that her spirit returned to the house once a month. They concluded, therefore, that she had become a goddess, and erected a temple to her. Her fame soon spread, and native annals contain various instances of her saving tempest-tossed crews. So recently as the eighteenth century she interposed to save an ambassador of the empire; and she is also credited with having done so during the Sung dynasty, some seven hundred years before. Her temples, therefore, are now to be found in all the provinces, and the more honourable designation of Tien-te-How was bestowed upon her by Taou-kwang. This goddess is worshipped at all times by numerous votaries, and especially by fishermen and sailors. The twenty-third day of the third month, is honoured as her natal anniversary; and state worship is paid to her at the celebration of the New Year's festivities, and at the equinoxes.

Koon-Yam, the goddess of Mercy, is worshipped with great pomp on the nineteenth day of the second month, which is the anniversary of her birth, and also on the anniversaries of her death, and canonization. The story of the career of this canonized Buddhist nun is full of marvels; and it is scarcely possible to enter her temples without finding women and children in them. On her anniversaries, women resort to them in large numbers, and light incense sticks at the sacred lamp above the altar. They carry the burning incense to their homes, as the smoke is supposed to possess a purifying effect. Other votaries who have sick relatives, expose tea to the smoke which rises in clouds from the incense burning on the altar. On their return home they administer the tea to the sick. Koon-Yam is also much worshipped during the Tsing-Hing or Wor-shipping of Graves, as she is supposed to extend her protecting care over the souls of departed ones. Paper clothes, even houses, servants, and sedan-chairs fashioned of the same material, are at such a season burnt in front of her altars. The goddess is supposed to convey these offerings to the depart d spirits for whom they are intended. The ceremony is usually performed at midnight. At this season, also, ladies resort to her temples to pray for afflicted husbands or children. The form of worship observed on such occasions, is conducted by Buddhist priests. Two tables are placed about six feet apart in front of the idol, and fruits and flowers are arranged upon them as offerings. The ladies sit or kneel near the tables, and the priests march round them to slow music. The music quickens, and at last the priests are found careering round the tables. This absurd service is brought to a close by the priests rushing wildly towards the ladies, and tendering them their congratulations.

The temples in honour of the goddess of Mercy are very numerous throughout the empire. In the most important of these at Canton were at one time several ornaments of great value which had been presented to the goddess by the emperor Taou-kwang, in return for blessings which she was supposed to have conferred on the southern portion of the empire. One of these was a jadestone ornament of great value, which was presented in acknowledgment of a victory which the goddess was supposed to have given to the Chinese troops over the British barbarians in 1841.

Another goddess who is popular with Chinese wives is Kum-Fa, the tutelary goddess of women and children. A native of Canton, she flourished during the reign of Ching-hwa who ascended the throne A.D. 1465. When a girl of tender years, she was a constant and regular visitor to all the temples in her immediate neighbourhood. She is said to have had the power of communing with the spirits of the departed. Becoming at length tired of the world, she committed suicide by drowning. In course of time her body rose to the surface of the water, and when it was taken out the air became impregnated with sweet-smelling odours. It was placed in a coffin, and a sandal-wood statue or idol of Kum-Fa rose apparently from the bed of the river, and remained stationary. A temple was erected for the image, but an iconoclast deliberately destroyed it by fire, and it is now replaced by a clay figure. Her principal temple stands in the Honam suburb of Canton. Her votaries are mostly wives who desire to become mothers. She is the Venus Genitrix of the Chinese. The list of the duties which her ministering attendants divide among them, is a perfect *résumé* of the art of rearing children. One is considered to be the guardian of children suffering from small-pox. The second presides over the ablutions of infants. The third superintends the feeding of new-born babes and young children. The fourth is the especial patroness of male infants. The fifth attends to the careful preparation of infants' food. The sixth watches over women labouring with child. It is in the power of the seventh to bestow upon women who have conceived, male or female children in answer to their prayers. The eighth can bless women with male offspring. The ninth makes children merry and joyful. The tenth superintends the cutting of the umbilical cord. The eleventh causes women to conceive. It is the privilege of the twelfth to make children smile. The thirteenth has the care of infants until they are able to walk. The fourteenth teaches them to do so. It is the calling of the fifteenth to teach them how to suck. The sixteenth watches over unborn babes. On the seventeenth it devolves to see that their bodies are, immediately before birth, free from sores or ulcers. The eighteenth is regarded as the special patroness of female infants. To impart strength to infants, is the duty of the nineteenth; and the twentieth of the attendants of Kum-Fa is named Fo-shee-fa-fu-yan.

Such of these attendants as have idols are represented as holding children in their arms, and are not unfrequently worshipped by barren women. The votaries bind string round the necks of the infants in the arms of these figures. Packages of tea are exposed for sale in the temples of Kum-Fa, and are bought by mothers for their sick children. The mother first presents the tea to the goddess, and then mingles with it the ashes of the incense sticks which are burning on the altar.

The natal anniversary of Kum-Fa is celebrated with great rejoicing. In the north of China, this goddess appears to be more popular than she is in the south.

Chinese idolatry reaches the acme of its absurdity, if not also of its sinfulness, in the worship which is paid to a canonized monkey, on whom has been conferred the sounding title of the " Great Sage of the whole Heavens." Hatched from a boulder, this animal proclaimed himself the king of the monkeys, and eventually, learning the language and manners of men, and

THE THREE PURE ONES.

finding himself possessed of supernatural powers, he obtained a place amongst the gods, notwithstanding their unwillingness to receive him, and compelled Yuh Hwangte to bestow this title upon him. An idol of this animal with outstretched hands, as if in the act of conferring a blessing, stands in the temple of the Five Genii. It is annually provided with a cap and a silk suit. Among those who worship it, women who are *enceinte* and gamblers are frequently found. Chinese mothers sometimes actually dedicate their children to its service.

Among their other important deities may be mentioned the Shay Tseih, to whom, as God of the Land and of the Grain, state worship is paid twice annually; and Fung-Fo-Shan, or the Wind and Fire Gods, who also receive state worship. It may be added, that in every walled city there are temples called Chung-lee Sze. These are in honour of Faithful Ministers, and in them are placed the tablets of those who have distinguished themselves in the service of the state.

CHAPTER VI.

LITERARY distinctions form the avenue to all posts of honour and importance in China, and there is perhaps no country in which education—up to a certain point—is more generally diffused among the male population. The system of competitive examination, and the fact that literary attainments are necessary qualifications for the highest political appointments, prove an immense stimulus to national education. Thus there is little or no difficulty experienced in prevailing upon Chinese parents to send their children to school; and, as schools are very numerous, and the wants of schoolmasters in general of a very simple nature, the poorest of the people are able to procure for their children an education which may enable them some day to rise to eminence. But although the state does so much in this way to encourage learning, I do not think there is any class of the community educated at its expense, except the sons of high officers of state, and Mantchurians of noble birth, who resort to a national institution established for them at Pekin. They receive instruction in the Chinese, Mongolian, and Mantchurian languages; and when their education is complete, they are despatched to various parts of the empire to serve as *attachés*, until more important offices become vacant for them. Distinguished students among them are instructed for the astronomical board, the chief duties of which are to inform the emperor when an eclipse of the sun or moon is likely to take place.

Education is not confined in China, as is sometimes supposed, to the stronger sex. On the contrary, in the south of China, at least, the seminaries for the board and education of young ladies, presided over by tutors or governesses, are exceedingly numerous; and it is not unusual to find private tutors giving instruction to young ladies in their homes. Some may be disposed to imagine that the education of females in China is a novelty; but this is so far from being the case that it is common to find in Chinese libraries, books containing biographical notices of women who, under former dynasties, were renowned for their great literary attainments. There can be no doubt, however, that education is not nearly so generally diffused among women as it is among men. Amongst the poorer classes they are ignorant to a degree, and in the northern provinces female education, to judge from an interesting letter which I received on the subject, seems to be almost entirely neglected. Mrs. Collins writes to me regarding the neglect of female education in the northern provinces as follows:—

"During my stay at Pi-yuen-sze this spring—1855—I was visited by more than three hundred and twenty women of various grades in society. Amongst them came a princess of the imperial family, married to a mandarin of the highest rank —a coral button; accompanied by her four daughters—fine-looking, interesting girls from sixteen to twenty-three years of age—two-daughters-in-law, a young son, and a number of female attendants. I inquired if the lady could read, but received a negative answer, and on asking the same question of the younger ladies, was met by the usual reply, 'Girls are not taught in these northern parts.' The mother was a fine, dignified woman of about fifty years of age, a perfect lady according to Chinese ideas, with that air of quiet command which distinguishes Tartar ladies of rank. Amongst all my visitors, only two women, and those not of high rank, could read. Last year, out of two hundred and ninety women, the proportion was somewhat larger. Three Tartar ladies and two Chinese women of lower rank, were readers. The little daughter of the district magistrate came to see me, and told me that she read every day with a teacher, who instructed at the same time two boys of other families."

As in England, Chinese schools are of two kinds—day-schools and boarding-schools. The day-schools are chiefly held in the *atria* of temples which are not much frequented, and in the spare chambers of guilds. Each boy is provided with a desk and chair, and the desks are arranged so as to prevent the pupils talking in school hours. In order that the master may know that the pupils are attending to their studies, they are made, when committing their lessons to memory, to read aloud. Thus the din which arises from a Chinese schoolroom appears to a foreigner more characteristic of a bedlam than a place of study. There are, also, schools of a superior class, which are attended by young men of eighteen years of age and upwards. In these each pupil is provided with a separate apartment, and there is a common hall, in which the principal delivers lectures on the Chinese classics. Youths attending schools of this class are supposed to be preparing for the B.A. examination; and until they have taken this degree, they are not entitled to become members of a university. Other students seek the seclusion of the country, choosing scenes of romantic beauty for their pursuit of learning. Students in the south of China frequently resort to the Sichu mountains, where hermitages, pagodas, and temples, constructed with great taste, and embosomed in trees of rich foliage, afford them comfortable retreats.[1]

Parents send their children to school at the early age of six, and show great care in the choice of a master. A good teacher must excel in virtue, as well as in learning and aptitude for teaching. The anxiety of a Christian parent to have his children

---

[1] The most eligible of these retreats is at the head of a ravine which abuts on the banks of the Po-yang Lake. It is called the White Deer Grotto, because the learned sage Choo-foo-tsze, so long ago as the twelfth century, lived in a grotto near it, with a white deer as his constant companion. Tradition says he used to send this animal, with a basket tied to its antlers, to the neighbouring village for provisions. The college has accommodation for two hundred students, but I did not find more than six or seven in it. The mantle of the learned Choo had evidently not fallen on the courteous principal, and the few pupils he had, did not seem to me to be men of promise. Attached to the college is a temple in honour of Confucius, in which, I was told, the students daily worshipped. Instead of the usual tablet this temple had an idol of Confucius, although it is known that he was opposed to idols, and the sage is represented as having a black face. There were also idols of his distinguished disciples. The retreat is at the base of a mountain two thousand feet high, and many of the neighbouring hills are covered with fir trees. A mountain torrent, flowing through the ravine, adds to the romantic beauty of the scene.

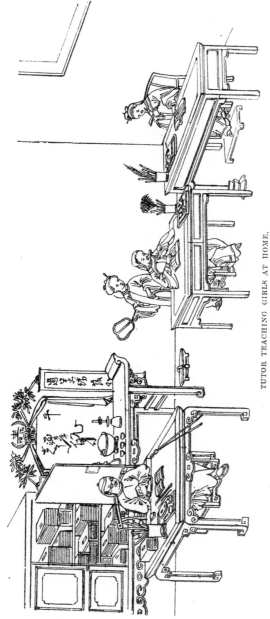

TUTOR TEACHING GIRLS AT HOME.

made acquainted with the truths of revelation, can scarcely be greater than the earnest desire of a Chinese to have his offspring thoroughly instructed in the doctrines of the ancient sages When choice has been made of a teacher, a mutual friend generally arranges, in behalf of the parents, the terms of his remuneration; and a written agreement is drawn up. A dinner is given to the schoolmaster by parents of all classes on the occasion of their sons becoming pupils; and in the houses of the wealthy, theatrical entertainments are given when a schoolmaster or tutor has been selected for the education of a son. The boy makes his appearance at school for the first time on a lucky day,[1] selected by a fortune-teller, and he bears a present of money for his teacher. He is also provided with what is termed a scholar's visiting card. On entering the school, he first turns to the shrine of Confucius, with which every school is provided, and worships the great philosopher. He then salutes his teacher, and presents his gift and visiting card; and when he has been exhorted by the latter as to his duties, is conducted to his desk. The vacations take place at the New Year, and during the autumn. Schoolboys are, however, frequently called upon to return home to observe certain religious festivals, such as worshipping the tombs and the tablets of ancestors, and the celebration of the birthdays of parents and grandparents. The boys are very active and full of fun, and in this respect remind one strongly of English schoolboys. The masters are usually men who have taken the B.A. degree, but who have failed in obtaining higher literary distinction. I have, however, met with men holding the degree of Doctor, who evidently preferred teaching to a government berth. The Chinese schoolmaster stands *in loco parentis* to his pupils, and is a great believer in the truth of the saying, "Spare the rod, spoil the child." In every school which I visited, and I have visited a great many, I found the cane; and both boys and girls are unsparingly punished for any offence against the rules of propriety or the regulations of the school. On one of these visits, a friend of

---

[1] No schoolboy goes to school for the first time on the anniversaries of the death and burial of Confucius; or on the anniversaries of the death and burial of Tsong-Kit, the inventor of letters.

mine, a captain in the Royal Navy, was with me, and so soon as the pupils saw his uniform, they rushed from the schoolroom by a back-door, in a panic. They thought that a detachment of blue-jackets was at hand to march them off; and the school-master evidently could not help sharing their alarm.

In all schools in the south of China pupils begin with the trimetrical classic, from which they are advanced to the thousand character classic, and the young pupil's book of poetry. The sentences of the first book consist of three characters each, and are such as may be easily understood and committed to memory. Although the style is exceedingly simple, the contents are considered of great importance; and when the pupil is able to explain the references which they contain to history, literature, biography, and zoology, he is considered to have made a great step in advance. In schools of other provinces, children sometimes begin by committing surnames to memory. The thousand character classic is formed of a thousand different characters, those of the same class being grouped together. Each sentence consists of four characters, and every two sentences form a rhyming couplet, which makes it easy for the pupil to commit them to memory. In the book of odes for the young, each sentence is composed of five characters. The design of this book is to stimulate pupils to diligence in their studies, in order that they may secure that passport to power, wealth, and fame —a great literary reputation. The mind of the pupil is indoctrinated with a profound admiration for the wise men of ancient times, who devoted themselves to leading men to the knowledge and practice of universal goodness; and thus taught from their youth to regard the works of their great sages as immeasurably superior to anything that later ages can produce, the *literati* of China have themselves originated nothing.

When the pupil has mastered this course of instruction, he enters upon the study of the four Shoos. I have already referred to these in the preceding chapter. The education of the Chinese may be said to consist principally in the study of moral philosophy, and the fundamental aim of these works may perhaps be summed up in a few words. It is to teach men to be virtuous that they may discharge honourably and successfully the

political and social duties of life. The metaphysical speculations which they contain, like those of the Shoo-King, are
exceedingly crude. The Great Learning and the Doctrine of the
Mean—or the Golden Medium, as Collie has rendered the title
—were composed respectively by Tsang-foo-tsze and Tsze-sze,
devoted disciples of Confucius, the latter being his grandson.
The fourth of the shoos consists of the works of Mencius, a
vigorous and original thinker, who lived about one hundred
years after Confucius. The government stipulates that at the
various examinations for degrees, the themes or texts for the
candidates' essays shall be taken from the four Shoos; and the
students commit them to memory and attend lectures upon
them. The lecturers at the universities are promoted according
to the success with which their instructions are attended, and
the desire of promotion proves an incentive to exertion. I
have occasionally visited the upper schools and colleges when
the lecturers have been expounding the doctrines of the sages.
The silence which reigned on these occasions was so great, that
in this respect I might have fancied myself in a Christian
church. Even the servants seemed to suspend their labours for
the time, lest they should disturb the lecturer ; and it is only as
a special favour that any one is permitted to go near the hall
when a lecture is going on. When the student has mastered
the four Shoos, he studies the classic on Filial Piety. This work
is attributed to Confucius, and it is said that he informed the
gods of its completion, and that they showed their approval of
it by causing a large rainbow to span the sky, and gradually to
descend towards the earth in the shape of a huge pearl. The
student next enters upon the study of the five King, the
contents of which I have briefly described in the preceding
chapter. This course is followed by the study of History and
General Literature ; and in order to master the rules of composition, the student familiarizes himself with the essays of
eminent writers. At this stage he is often called upon to discuss the merits of what he has been reading, with his tutor.
The tutor attacks the reasoning of an essay, and the pupil is
expected to defend it. At the end of this course, he is supposed
to be ready to pass his B.A. examination.

For the B.A., or first degree, examinations are held throughout
the empire twice in every three years, and for the second, or
M.A. degree, examinations are held once in every three years.
The former take place in the prefectoral cities of each province.
They are held in large halls like the Theatre at Oxford, or
the Senate House at Cambridge. The examiners in each province are the district rulers, the prefects, and the Literary
Chancellor. Before going up for their examination, the candidates repair to their respective district cities, and deposit at the
office of the district ruler a document signed by one or more of
the gentry of the district. This document sets forth that they
are qualified to attend the examination for the degree of B.A., as
free-born subjects of the realm, and that they do not fall within the
prohibitions which exclude the children of playactors, watermen,
policemen, &c. It also states the candidate's age, and his place
of birth. All taxes due to the government must be paid by
the fathers of the young men, before the latter are admitted as
candidates. On the day of examination, the candidate repairs
at an early hour to the examination-hall of his prefectoral city.
He carries a small basket of a singular shape, containing his pens,
inkstand, and ink, and he purchases from an official the paper
upon which his essays are to be written. The paper is sold to
the students at a greatly increased price, and as in one province
alone the candidates sometimes number eight thousand, this
arrangement must bring a considerable sum to the imperial
exchequer. At a certain hour a cannon is fired, and the porter
closes the gates of the hall. No one can now enter or leave the
hall until the examination is over. When the students, who
only occupy one side of the long tables, which are arranged in
parallel lines, have seated themselves, the themes for the essays
are given out. These, as I have stated, are taken from the four
shoos. When the candidate has written the two essays required
of him, he proceeds to compose a poem of twelve lines, each line
containing five characters. Each candidate then recites, or writes
from memory, a portion of the sacred edict, and at the close of
the day a gun is again fired, and the students are permitted to
retire. Any of the students, however, who are slow writers, are
furnished with lamps to enable them to finish their papers.

The essays are perused by the examiners on the following day, and the names of the candidates are classified according to merit. Two or three days after, the list of successful candidates is posted on the walls of the hall. Those candidates whose names do not appear in the list do not attend any of the succeeding trials, of which there are six or seven. At the second examination, which is conducted by the prefect and held in an inner hall of his yamun, only one of the themes is selected from the four Shoos; the other is chosen from the five classics. The successful candidates attend a third examination, conducted by the literary chancellor. The essay on this occasion is on a phrase from one of the four Shoos. A poem of twelve lines is also required, as well as a disquisition on the principles, or light of Nature. The literary chancellor also conducts the remaining four examinations, in which, as in the previous ones, the candidates write essays and poems. Out of the six or seven thousand candidates, probably not more than a hundred remain for the final competition, and of this number not more than sixty are admitted to the degree of B.A. It is sometimes supposed that because so few candidates are successful, the standard of literary attainments proposed by government is very high. This, however, is an error, for whatever number may come forward, the literary chancellor is not allowed to approve more than sixty candidates. Those approved present themselves at the yamun of the literary chancellor, in order to be invested with an order of merit. This badge is a golden flower which is placed on the apex of the cap or hat, and is regarded as the gift of the emperor. A richly-embroidered tippet or collar, corresponding to the hood worn by graduates of English universities, is also placed on the shoulders. When this ceremony, called Kum-Fa, is over, the happy candidates are invited to dine with the literary chancellor.

So soon as the list containing the names of the favoured sixty is published, the rivers and creeks in the vicinity present a most animated appearance. Boats of light construction may be seen urged forward in every direction by crews of four or six men, in order to carry to anxious parents the tidings of their sons' successes. Men also traverse the streets of towns, informing the public in stentorian voices, that they have correct lists of the successful candidates for sale. On reaching his home, the newly-made graduate finds his first few days occupied in paying visits of ceremony. Notably, he must go to worship at the ancestral hall of his clan, and the schoolmaster has to be visited. The graduate rides in a sedan-chair borne by four men, and is escorted by several of his relatives and friends, also in chairs. The procession is lengthened by gilded canopies, under which are offerings of pork, cakes, fruits, and flowers. Each canopy is borne by four bearers. Musicians and banner-men lead the way, and when such a procession passes through the streets of a town, the young graduate is the hero of the hour.

The Bachelors of Arts now become members of universities, of which there seems to be one in every walled city. At these they prepare themselves for the M.A. examination. The examinations for this degree are held in provincial capitals only.[1] The candidates not unfrequently exceed seven or eight thousand, being all the Bachelors of Arts in the province who may be disposed to present themselves. The examination is held in a large hall divided into rows of cells. It is called the Kung-yuen, and there is one in every provincial capital. Each student enters a cell, in which he remains by night, as well as by day, until the examination is over. The rows are distinguished by different names and the cells are numbered, so that there is no difficulty in summoning a candidate, should the examiners call for him. In a square formed by the rows there is a large building in which the examiners are lodged. These are a body appointed by the emperor, and two of them are sent from Pekin to each province. They are men conspicuous by their literary attainments, and the provincial officials receive them with every mark of honour and respect. On the morning of the sixth day of the eighth month of every third year, the examiners are escorted by all the mandarins to the Kung-yuen. The governor-general on this occasion rides in an open chair borne on the shoulders of

---

[1] There is one exception to this rule. Candidates residing in the island of Formosa do not require to cross the channel to Foochow, the capital of the province of which Formosa is a political division. They are examined at the prefectural city of Tai-wan.

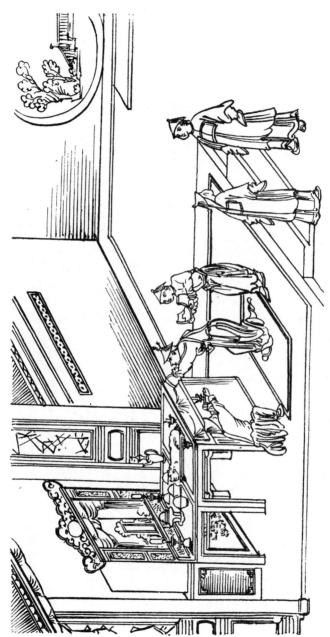

A B.A. WORSHIPPING HIS ANCESTRAL TABLETS, AFTER TAKING HIS DEGREE.

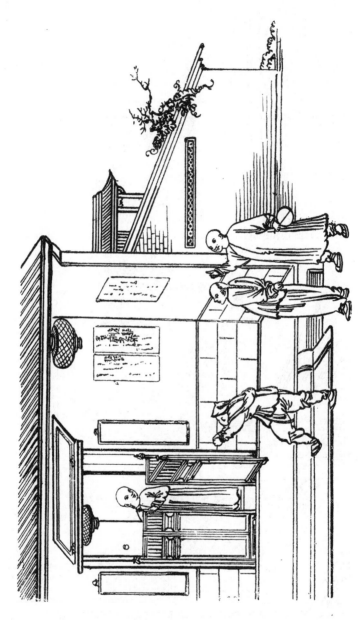

A VISIT OF CONGRATULATION TO A SUCCESSFUL LITERARY COMPETITOR.

sixteen men. Two days after, the examination is held, and the students having purchased their paper, go to their cells as their names are called out by the *futai* or governor. Before they are allowed to enter their cells they are searched for books of reference. The first examination lasts two days, during which three essays are written on quotations from the four Shoos; and a poem of twelve lines of five feet each. During the second trial, also lasting two days, five essays are written on themes from the five classics. At the third trial, five essays are written on any subjects which the examiners may think fit to propose. The candidates give their papers to the officers appointed to receive them. These deliver them to officers who superintend the copying of them in red ink. Other officials carefully compare the copies which have been made, with the originals, and paste a sheet of paper over the name of the candidate, which is written on a blank page. The essays are then distributed among ten examiners, whose duty it is to decide whether or not the grammar is correct, and the course of reasoning sound and logical. Those which they approve, are submitted to the examiners from Pekin. When the final scrutiny is over, the names of the successful candidates are unsealed and published in the order of merit. The student whose name heads the list, receives the title of Kai-yuen. The new Masters of Arts are decorated in the governor-general's yamun with a golden flower, and a tippet or collar more richly-embroidered than that which is worn by the B.A. graduates. The ceremony is followed by a banquet, at which they meet all the important officials of the city and neighbourhood. The excitement is, of course, much greater than on the occasion of a B.A. examination. The success of the graduate is a matter of rejoicing not only to his family, but to his clan; and on the walls of an ancestral hall are suspended boards containing the names of those of the clan who have taken this degree. The letter in which the examiners inform the head of a family of the success of one of its members, is posted on the walls of his house. Visits of ceremony and rejoicings, of course, await the graduate of the second degree on his return home; and he is escorted by friends and relatives, attended by bannermen and musicians, to the ancestral hall of his clan, in order that he may render homage to the departed ancestors whose surname he bears. When these proceedings are over, he begins to make the necessary preparations for a journey to Pekin, in order to pass the third or Tsin-sze degree. The examination for this invariably takes place on the sixth day of the third month of the following year, and is presided over by the prime minister and one of the royal princes, with three other examiners. The proceedings are similar to those of the other examinations. The successful candidates—the first of whom is styled Hwuy-yuen—do not return to their respective provinces, but remain at Pekin in order to attend the examination for the fourth degree, the Han-lin or LL.D. Their names, however, are forwarded by the government to the governors of their provinces, and by them to the rulers of their districts. The district rulers order tablets bearing the names in gilt letters to be carried in state chairs, with offerings of various kinds, to the happy parents of the graduates. The district rulers are generally well rewarded for sending the welcome intelligence ; and I remember the parents of a graduate being so delighted with their son's success that they made a present of four hundred dollars to one of these officials.

The examination for the degree of Han-lin or LL.D. is conducted in the Imperial Palace at Pekin by the emperor himself. The test is a written answer to any question which the emperor may propose. The successful candidates are divided into four classes. Those of the first class have the degree conferred on them, and are reserved for important vacancies. Graduates of the second class become members of the inner council ; those of the third class obtain situations in the six boards, and those of the fourth become district rulers. The newly-made Han-lin are entertained at dinner by the emperor, and, as a mark of great honour, each guest sits at a separate table, upon which the most *recherché* viands are spread. The graduate at the head of the list is called Chwang-yuen, and his reputation extends to all parts of the empire. Wandering heralds carry his name to remote villages as well as populous towns, and both high and low make a point of becoming acquainted with some particulars of his family and early training. When he travels, the keepers of

the various hostelries at which he lodges consider themselves
highly honoured by the presence of so distinguished a visitor.
In 1872, Canton had the honour of Chwang-yuen, and the
most distinguished of the Han-lins for that year entered
the city in state. The Han-lin Hall, in which the degree
of Doctor of Laws is conferred, is in the form of a parallelogram, and on each of the four sides there is a cloister
Against the walls of the cloisters are placed marble slabs
on which are inscribed the original text of Confucius. In
the centre, under a pavilion, is the throne on which the emperor sits when called upon, in the discharge of his imperial
duties, to explain the doctrines of Confucius to his ministers.
When the degree of Doctor of Laws is conferred, the approved
candidates arrange themselves round the throne, and as the name
of each candidate is called, the emperor makes a mark against it
with his vermilion pencil in a list which he has before him.

The essays which are written by the candidates for the various
degrees must contain at least three hundred and sixty characters,
and not more than seven hundred and twenty. Marginal notes or
corrections may be made to the number of one hundred characters. The Chinese recognize no fewer than six modes of writing
their characters, and as the essayists are instructed to pay
marked attention to caligraphy, they adopt the Kiai-shoo, which
is the most elegant form of character. The other styles of
writing are the Chuen-shoo, which is "the ancient mode of
writing, and is derived immediately from hieroglyphics, and is
either a caricature or a stiff and imperfectly written character;"
the Le-shoo, which is "used by officials' attendants, and is
written with greater freedom than that employed in books;"
the Hing-shoo, which is "the regular running hand in which
anything which requires despatch is written;" the Tsaou-tsze,
"a hasty and abbreviate" style, used in ordinary transactions
and correspondence; and the Sung-ti, "the regular form of
the character used in printing." The respect which the
Chinese pay to their written language, amounts almost to worship. They never lose sight of the fact that it is the medium
through which they have become possessed of the wisdom of the
ancients. The *literati* employ men to traverse the streets of towns

and villages, to collect waste paper from dwelling-houses
and shops, lest fragments bearing Chinese characters should be
trodden under foot. Each man is provided with two baskets,
and at his cry, " Sow-suee-chu," or " spare the printed paper," the
people rush to the doors and empty their waste-paper baskets
into his. When his baskets are full, he takes them to a temple
or guild provided with a furnace for the purpose of consuming
such collections. In many instances, the ashes of this paper are
put into earthenware vases, and flung into a tidal stream that
they may be borne out to sea.

Besides the classics which I have mentioned, the Chinese
have, of course, a numerous array of historical, political, and
philosophical works, and of novels, and romances, and miscel-
laneous writings. But though they have been a literary nation
from a period long anterior to the Christian era, they have no
public libraries, unless this name can be given to libraries[1] reserved for the especial use of government officials. Although
there are no public libraries for the use of the people, they cannot complain of the want of public lecturers. In many of the
towns and cities there are men known as *Kong-Koo*, who take up
their quarters in the halls of temples, and deliver lectures on
the ancient history of China, and the writings of the sages.
Each auditor pays a small sum of money to the lecturer, and a
Chinese attending a course of these lectures, acquires a pretty
fair knowledge of the history of his country. As the honora-
rium which the lecturer receives is very small, he seeks to add
to his gains by driving a trade in fruit and cigars ; and the table
at which he is seated is covered with them. It is not unusual to
see a person advance when the lecturer is discoursing, and remove an orange or a cigar, having first laid the price of it on
the table.

There is no important country in the world in which the
liberty of the press is so little recognized as in China. The
ignorance in which the people are kept with regard to passing

---

[1] The libraries of private gentlemen, it may be mentioned, are on a much
smaller scale in China than in our own country. The famous Emperor Kien-lung
Wong left a library of 168,000 volumes, but this appears small in comparison
with European imperial libraries.

A PUBLIC READER.

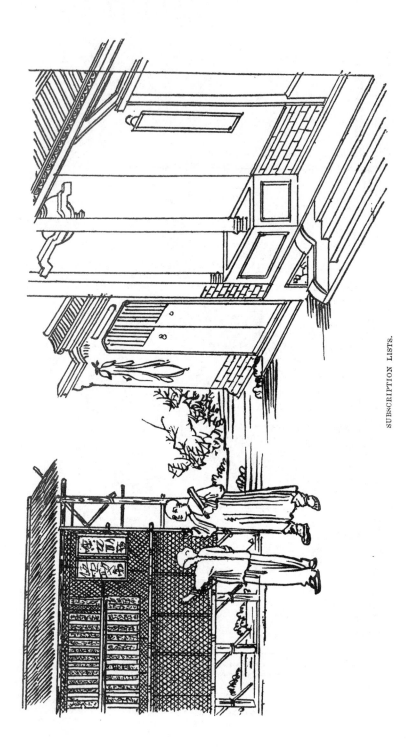

SUBSCRIPTION LISTS.

events, whether of a trifling or a serious character, is surprising. Until quite recently there was nothing in the shape of a Chinese newspaper throughout the length and breadth of the land, except the *Peking Gazette*,—now published daily— which is the official organ of a corrupt government. It is, I suppose, the oldest newspaper in the world, and is said to have been in existence long before printing was invented in Europe ; and it is a singular proof of the stationary character of the Chinese, that it should so long have continued the sole newspaper of the empire. The intelligence which it contains, is generally of a meagre nature, and has reference to governmental details. Little reliance can be placed on the veracity of its communications, and, notably, serious defeats sustained by the Imperial troops are turned on its pages into glorious victories. A copy of the Gazette is forwarded to each provincial capital, and republished there under the strict surveillance of the local government. Should the publisher in his re-issue add or take away from the original, he is liable to a punishment of one hundred blows, and to a banishment of three years. In each provincial capital a court circular is published daily, containing the names of the visitors, official and non-official, who have called at the Viceroy's palace on the preceding day. It also announces the birthdays of the members of the Imperial family, and of the local officials of high rank.

The people derive a great deal of their information as to recent events from newsletters. These are sold in the streets. They abound so much in the marvellous as to be altogether unworthy of credit, and the barefaced mendacity with which they recorded the overthrow of the British and French troops by the Imperial forces has probably never been surpassed. The following is an extract from one of the newsletters sold in Canton during the late war :—

" Hearing that Prince Tseng had fallen back to Tung Chow, the English and French divided their forces. The majority advanced to Tung Chow, and the English ordered a thousand cavalry to commence action. Prince Tseng also ordered his Tartar cavalry to give battle, and seven hundred English cavalry were killed by the discharge of gingalls. The infantry then advanced, and shooting and slaying commenced on both sides, while the roar of cannon continued without intermission throughout the day. The fight lasted from seven in the morning until three or four in the afternoon, when the English and French were thoroughly routed—out of every ten men, eight or nine were killed. Therefore the officer Parkes, and the officers who were taken in company with him by Prince Tseng were all put to death at Tung Chow, while of the defeated troops who returned to Takoo, there remained scarcely five thousand.

" On the occasion when the English and French advanced to attack Tung Chow, their design was to insult Pekin. Afterwards when Prince Tseng saw that the turbulent barbarians after their defeat dare not attempt to come up to Tung Chow to fight, though still intending to attack Pekin, he sent a despatch to the emperor to the effect that he had heard the turbulent barbarians intended to take Pekin, and that they ought to be allowed to enter the city, when they could all be hemmed in and taken alive: so the gates of the city ought not to be closed. Therefore, accordingly, the four gates of Pekin were opened wide; neither the dogs, nor the chickens were alarmed. Then upwards of twenty thousand English and French, having left the Takoo Forts, advanced straight to Pekin, and marched seven or eight days, without meeting hindrance from anyone, until they arrived at Yuen-ming-yuen, which is 100 lee from Pekin. This palace is of vast extent, and contains wonderful flowers, and strange fruits, besides curiosities in number beyond the power of computation. It is, indeed, the greatest palace in all the eighteen provinces of the Central Flowery Empire. The English troops entered the Palace and lived there for some days; and the general of the land forces with five hundred officers came to look at Pekin, to find out the true state of affairs. They saw all the walls armed with swords and guns and warlike weapons in thorough readiness—very unlike the city of Canton! Moreover, they saw the Tartar soldiers with arched eye-brows and glaring eyes, bracing their muscles and grinding their teeth, rubbing their fists and smoothing their palms, burning to spring down from the walls to seize their enemies. Yet as Prince Tseng had not given the word of command, they did not break their ranks.

" The English soldiers, seeing this, returned to Yuen-ming-yuen, and then Prince Tseng hearing that the turbulent barbarians had entered the palace was greatly rejoiced; and issued orders to the garrison of Pekin to attack the English and French, and to kill them all, not leaving so much as a single shred. The Tartar troops on receiving this order were greatly delighted, one and all ; and one hundred thousand men rushed forward to the fight. They beleaguered the palace, and slew for a day and a night.

The English and French were thoroughly defeated. Fifteen thousand were slain. Five thousand escaped with their lives and tried to get back to Takoo. Midway, however, they again encountered Prince Tseng's army, and in the battle which followed four thousand were killed! One thousand and upwards were taken alive, and brought before Prince Tseng for his orders. The Prince put out the eyes of 200 of the most able-bodied, or else cut off their noses, and then let them go back to Takoo. Two hundred beaten soldiers at last got back to Takoo, and saw the English and French admirals, who were greatly wroth when they saw the disgrace of these men, and their gall and liver were thoroughly disturbed. They wished to retreat with the English soldiers to Shanghai; but as the frost had set in, and they moreover feared the ridicule of the barbarians of all countries, they were greatly perplexed, and they are now holding the Takoo Forts.

"It is reported that all the barbarian newspapers say that Pekin has been taken, and that His Majesty the Emperor and his ministers have fled; but these are all falsehoods, and must not be believed.

"I also send you a picture which will explain everything.

"There were also more than thirty ships of war belonging to the Americans, Spaniards, Dutch, and Russians, who saw all the fighting at Takoo."

In the absence of a public press, advertisements of public auctions, tenements to let, &c., &c., appear in the form of placards. The subscription lists of benevolent funds are published in the same way; and when a temple or a public hall has been erected by voluntary contributions, the treasurer usually has a placard pasted on the walls of the building to show how the funds have been laid out. Placards are also resorted to as a means of ventilating grievances of all sorts; and an oppressive official, or a citizen who has made himself obnoxious, may awake some morning to find the bitter complaint of one whom he has injured, or the plain-spoken opinion of an anonymous critic, posted on his door. Poor people oppressed by opulent neighbours, and unable to obtain an audience of a magistrate because they cannot fee his underlings, have recourse to them to make known their grievances. Those who cannot even afford to pay for the printing of a placard often seat themselves near the doors of those who have injured them, and proclaim their grievances to passers-by. I once came upon an old woman sitting near the door of a house, and loudly accusing the occupant of having kidnapped her daughter.

In a country in which the fourth estate exists in so rudimentary a form, where there are no railroads and telegraphs, and which has no properly organized postal arrangements,[1] public opinion is essentially local in its tone. It is almost entirely the creation of a middle class known as the " literary and gentry," who stand midway between a vast body of interested officials on the one hand, and the mass of the people on the other. This middle class consists of those who have been admitted to a government examination, but who have not succeeded in being of the select number to whom degrees are granted. They exercise a salutary and, within limits, a powerful influence.

" They act," writes Mr. Low from the United States Legation, at Pekin, in an official letter[2] to his government, " as advisers to the lower classes, and their good offices are sought by the governing class in the management of local concerns. By their superior intelligence they are enabled to control most of the property, and yet few acquire such wealth as would enable them to oppress the people, were they so disposed.

" This class create the public opinion of the country, which exercises a controlling influence over the officials, and is usually powerful enough to thwart the intentions and nullify the action of the officers, from the emperor down, whenever popular rights are in danger of being invaded or the people unduly oppressed. So powerful is the influence of the *literati* that all officials endeavour to conform their action to the popular will, and in this view the government of China is essentially democratic in practice."

[1] There is no postal system under the direction of the government. In a large city, like Canton, there are houses where letters addressed to persons residing at distant ports are received and forwarded. At their destination the letters are delivered by agents, who collect the postage on delivery. As a rule, such letters are intrusted to the captains of passenger boats. In such cases, the letter is sometimes prepaid, the sender writing on the envelope the amount he has paid. In some instances, the postage is paid on receipt, the sender recording on the envelope the amount which it is necessary for the receiver to pay, and prepaying the postage of the reply. The Chinese are tolerable adepts at letter-writing, and it is customary for them to correspond with relatives or friends at a distance. Persons who cannot write have letters written for them by fortune-tellers, who are scribes as well.

[2] The letter is under date Jan. 10, 1871.

CHAPTER VII.

MARRIAGE.

PROBABLY no other nation sets such store by the maxim that "in the multitude of a people is the King's honour, but in the want of people is the destruction of the prince;" and from the earliest times the institution of marriage has occupied an important place in the polity of the Chinese. Young men and maidens are made to feel that it is their duty to become the founders of small communities of rational creatures, from whom in turn other communities are to spring. The more children—especially male children—a Chinese has, the more he is reverenced, a large family of sons being regarded as a mark of the divine favour. Indeed, the desire for male offspring seems to have as strong a hold upon this people as it had upon the ancient Jews, although the motives which actuated Hebrew parents in praying that sons might be given to them are wanting to the Chinese. In their case also, however, the desire is one which has its root in religious belief. It is a natural outcome of the doctrine that the spirits of the departed are rendered happy by homage received at the hands of their male posterity. I remember being much impressed by the great grief with which an old lady with whom I was acquainted deplored the death of her son, who was upwards of sixty years of age, she herself being eighty-two years old. When I spoke to her grandsons, however, on the depth of their grandmother's sorrow, they explained to me that she especially grieved because death had removed the being whose homage she had looked forward to as the great source of her happiness in the world of spirits. To take a case which bears more directly on the subject of marriage : an aged Chinese refused to enter into an engagement with an American missionary lady, to allow his granddaughter to remain for a period of seven years at the missionary school. His granddaughter, who was then fifteen years of age, ought, he said, to present him with great-grandsons long before the expiration of the seven years.

The marriage relation has at all times been regarded by the Chinese as a personal one. But although this involves the doctrine that monogamy is the rule prescribed by morality, polygamy, in some parts of the empire at all events, is very much practised. In some of the northern provinces, and more particularly in that of Shantung, however, the great majority of the inhabitants are monogamists in the strictest sense of the term. Various causes have contributed to the prevalence of polygamy amongst the Chinese, notwithstanding their theoretical monogamy. Prominent among them is the strong desire for offspring to which I have referred. In the earliest ages, childlessness was held to justify the taking of a second or third wife in addition to the first, but apparently as an exception only, and as the privilege of the wealthy classes. At the present day, a second or third wife is regarded rather as a female servant than as a wife, until she has borne children. Another cause may be found in the fact that parents choose wives for their sons—a custom which prevailed also in ancient times amongst the Jews.[1] In many cases the wives thus selected prove most unsuitable ; and as a young man is at liberty to select a second or third wife for himself, he often avails himself of an early opportunity of doing so. The law which compels gentlemen and tradesmen to give their female slaves in marriage also operates in favour of polygamy. Any one failing to do so, is liable to be summoned before the tribunal of the town or village in which he resides, and to receive a severe flogging for his neglect.[2]

---

[1] See, for example, Gen. xxi. 21, and xxxviii. 6 ; and Deut. xxii. 16.

[2] Where this law is evaded slaves are either bribed or compelled by their masters to appear before a magistrate, and declare that they remain unmarried in consequence of their repugnance to marriage.

Another fact tends to promote polygamy amongst this singular people. A husband is not expected to cohabit with his wife after she has conceived, nor after the child is born, during the whole period that it is being nourished at the mother's breast. Any violation of the rule, is supposed not only to cause the child to become sickly, but to provoke the displeasure of the ancestors, and bring misfortune upon all the members of the family. Wealthy Chinese are generally very careful in the practice of such abstinence. I remember a young gentleman, who resided in the southern suburb of Canton, being severely chastised by his parents for a violation of it.

These reasons may in some measure account for the practice of polygamy on the part of the Chinese. Let me add a few words as to its evil effects. These are illustrated in the private history of almost every Chinese family in which it is practised. Many indeed are the heart-rending scenes which I have witnessed in such homes. It has a tendency to promote licentiousness, and leads to infidelity on the part of husbands. It introduces envy, hatred, malice, and all uncharitableness into households, and in not a few cases drives jealous wives to commit suicide. I have often known it to result in a husband expelling from his house, or selling, one of his wives, upon the false accusation of a rival. Naturally, therefore, many Chinese ladies are opposed to matrimony. In one street alone—the Shap-pat-kan street in the Honam suburb of Canton—I knew four families in which there were ladies who positively refused to marry, upon the ground that, should their husbands become polygamists, there would remain for them a life of unhappiness. To avoid marriage some become Buddhist or Taouist nuns; and others prefer death itself to marriage. During the reign of Taou-kwang, fifteen virgins whom their parents had affianced, met together upon learning the fact, and resolved to commit suicide. They flung themselves into a tributary stream of the Canton river, in the vicinity of the village where they lived. The tomb in which the corpses were interred is near Fo-chune, and is called the Tomb of the Virgins. At a village near Whampoa called Siu-tong-ki, in

July, 1873, eight young girls, who had been affianced, drowned themselves in order to avoid marriage. They clothed themselves in their best attire, and at eleven o'clock, in the darkness of night, the eight maidens, who had bound themselves together, threw themselves into a tributary stream of the Canton river.

Almost all Chinese, robust or infirm, well-formed or deformed, are called upon by their parents to marry so soon as they have attained the age of puberty. Were a grown-up son or daughter to die unmarried, the parents would regard it as most deplorable. Chinese parents who are apprehensive that, owing to a weak constitution, the last hours of their son or daughter are not far distant, often make immediate arrangements for the marriage. A young man of marriageable age, whom consumption or any other lingering disease had marked for its own, would be called upon by his parents or guardians to marry at once. I may quote the case of a delicate youth with whom I was acquainted. He was a member of the family or clan " Eng "—probably at the time one of the most influential and powerful families in the city of Canton. His parents having been informed by the family physician that their son's sickness would soon terminate fatally, determined that without loss of time he should fulfil an engagement of marriage into which he had entered. On the day selected, the bride elect of the dying youth was brought to his residence with all the pomp and parade which attend a Chinese wedding. The ceremony was no sooner ended than the bridegroom was reconducted to his sick chamber, where, in a few days, he breathed his last.

In China, as in Christian countries, there are prohibitory degrees of marriage. A man, for example, is not allowed to marry a woman who bears the same family or clan name as himself. The punishment for doing so is sixty blows, and the marriage is declared null and void. Neither may a man marry his cousin on his mother's side, nor his stepdaughter, nor his aunt, the sister of his mother. Offenders, if dealt with according to the strict letter of the law, would be put to death by strangulation. The principal mandarins are not allowed to marry women who reside in the provinces, prefectures, or counties, over which they bear rule. This law was framed to prevent nepotism, and to check the exercise of an undue influence on the part of one family over other families in the same district. No lady may marry until she is fourteen years of age; while not to marry 'after becoming affianced, unless for urgent private reasons, until she is upwards of twenty-three years of age, is regarded as very wrong. The latter of these rules of life is, I believe, borrowed from the writings of Confucius. Playactors, policemen, boatmen, or slaves, are not allowed to marry women of any other class than that to which they respectively belong. A marriage may not be solemnized when either of the parties is in mourning.

Marriages take place at all times of the year. The principal season, however, is from the fifteenth day of the eighth month to the fourth month of the year following. During the ninth month, however, which is regarded as very unpropitious, no marriages take place, except, as will afterwards be shown, in cases of extreme urgency. At the commencement of the marriage season, books containing songs in honour of wedlock are exposed for sale at the various bookstalls. With regard to the hour of the day at which marriages are solemnized there is no restriction. In some of the districts round Canton they are always celebrated at night, not so much on account of the heat of the day, as because, although the bridal processions may not be so grand as they ought to be, they pass unremarked, the darkness concealing all defects. At such marriages, lanterns and torches are absolutely necessary. Lanterns, however, are always a feature in the procession, either by day or by night. This custom appears to prevail throughout the East, as it has done for ages past. That the Jews used lanterns and torches is very clear from the opening verses of the twenty-fifth chapter of St. Matthew's Gospel; and the writings of the most famous poets of Greece and Rome contain numerous references to it.[1]

Marriages, as I have said, do not take place during the ninth month of the year, unless in cases of urgency. Only the anticipated death of one of the parents of either of the affianced

[1] See, for example, *Iliad* vi. 492; *Eurip. Phœniss.* 346; *Medea,* 1027; *Virg. Eclog.* viii. 29.

parties, would render such a step imperative. Where a
father, for example, supposes his own dissolution to be
imminent, he will command the immediate solemnization of
the marriage of his affianced son or daughter, so great is the
anxiety of Chinese parents to witness the consummation of an
event which they consider of paramount importance. Such marriages, of course, take place in haste. I was present at one on
the 27th of July, 1870, in a street of the Honam suburb of
Canton, called On-wing-lee. The wedding was solemnized in
the residence of a gentleman named Chu Ayune, who desired to
see his son married before his own death, which was imminent.
The youth, who was named Atchue, was in his fifteenth year,
and the young lady was of the same age. It was touching to
see the bridal pair doing obeisance to the dying father, who
was scarcely able to give them his blessing; and to witness the
tenderness with which the youthful bride presented to him the
customary cup of tea and bowl of rice. At the close of the
ceremony, the bride was reconducted to the home of her parents,
to remain there until she was of a riper age. My friend Chu
Ayune breathed his last two days after.

On the 3rd of December, 1871, I was present at a similar
wedding between a man named Pang Wing and a woman
named Ho-asing, both in the humbler walks of life. The
marriage was solemnized at the house of the bridegroom's
mother, in the Ma-choo-pow street of the western suburb of
the city of Canton. The mother of the bridegroom, who was a
very aged woman, was *in articulo mortis*. She lay upon a bed
in the *atrium* of the house, with her feet towards the door, in
order that her soul upon leaving the body might have free exit
on its way to Elysium. The ceremony was entered upon
without delay, and duly and properly gone through. What a
scene ensued! When the wedding garment, which with its
wide folds enveloped the whole body and arms of the bride,
was removed, it was discovered that she was a leper! When
the fact was disclosed, a number of the female relatives of the
bridegroom, gave vent to their feelings of indignation and anger
in howls which made the welkin ring. They then turned, as
if actuated by a common impulse, towards the bride, whose

appearance was now ghastly, to pour upon the unfortunate woman a torrent of the keenest invectives and most sweeping vituperation. The poor woman at last looked towards me for pity ; and evidently fearing that more serious evils might befall her, she earnestly begged that she might be extricated from the embarrassing situation. She was at once divorced, and returned to her mother, who positively refused, however, to refund to the bridegroom the dowry which had been paid by him for what he justly considered a very bad bargain. A part of the sum was eventually returned. During the scene, the bridegroom's aged mother, who "lay a-dying," never once moved. Indeed, so motionless was she, that it appeared as if she had passed away for ever. She lingered till the following morning, having witnessed on her death-bed, in one brief hour, the marriage of her only son, and its singular sequel, the immediate divorce of the bride whom he had unwittingly espoused.

It may be asked, and the question is naturally suggested by this episode, how are matrimonial alliances brought about in China ? Throughout the length and breadth of the land there is a class of people called go-betweens, or match-makers, who obtain a livelihood by selecting wives for those who desire to become husbands, and husbands for those who wish to become wives. These go-betweens or match-makers are generally females, or aged men. Parents who seek to affiance their children, usually make application to one of this class, and the go-between consults the list, which she always carries about with her, of the names of eligible ladies and gentlemen. The age at which young people are affianced is from seven to fourteen years. In some parts of the empire, however, more especially in the districts occupied by the Hakkas, children are affianced in infancy. This custom is condemned by many Chinese, on the ground that the children on coming to mature age may show that they have been tainted with leprosy, or lunacy, or some disease which would render it necessary to cancel the engagement. I have already stated that in cases of lunacy, matrimonial engagements are broken off. The rule, however, is not invariable, as will appear from the following account of the marriage of a youth with whom I was acquainted.

Leong Aman, a young man residing in Lin-chee-tong, a village in the vicinity of the market town of Sai-nam, who had for some time been betrothed to a young lady, was called upon to leave home *en route* for Shu-hing Foo, where he had business to transact. During his stay he became insane, and whilst in this condition frequently expressed his conviction that a young woman was constantly following him, with the view of eventually becoming his wife. Upon his return home, he still laboured under this hallucination. His parents consulted a fortune-teller, and were informed that he was being pursued by the soul of a female who had died a virgin, and who was anxious, even in the world of shades, to obtain a husband. They resolved to defeat the project of their son's ghostly persecutor, by marrying him forthwith to the girl to whom he was already affianced. As in duty bound, however, they first proposed to the parents of the girl that the engagement between the young couple should be set aside on the ground of their son's lunacy. This proposition, strange to say, did not meet the views of the girl's parents. They argued that if the marriage did not take place, the soul of the deranged youth would become, in turn, a ghostly persecutor of their daughter, and would, in all probability, entail upon her a similar melancholy malady ! Accordingly, this singular marriage was solemnized at the village of Lin-chee-tong, on the 10th of December, 1871.

As in Mesopotamia and other countries of the East, it is customary for the Chinese to marry their children according to seniority.[1] Parents, when engaging the services of a go-between to assist them in selecting a wife for their son, are supposed to impress upon the mind of the agent their anxiety that the maiden chosen should be more remarkable for her virtue than her beauty, upon the ground, probably, that a virtuous woman is a crown to her husband. On the other hand, the young lady's parents are supposed to prefer that their daughter should be given in marriage to a young man more renowned for his wisdom than his wealth, upon the score that the father of a fool has no joy, and that fools and their money are soon parted. The go-between is also supposed to select as husbands and

[1] See Genesis, chap. 29, v. 26, and the Book of Tobit, chap. viii. v. 1.

wives those who are in all respects likely to suit one another. It is her duty also to ascertain that the families of the contracting parties are respectable, the members being free from leprosy, lunacy, and crime, and not being either playactors, slaves, or boat-people.

This system of Chinese parents selecting wives for their children, and making these binding engagements in their name, has a tendency not only to render breaches of promise impossible, but to prevent elopements. Of course, it does not put such enterprises out of the question. Occasionally, though rarely, Chinese gentlemen elope with young ladies who have been affianced to others. When elopements do take place in China, the offending parties are, as a rule, unmarried young folks, whose parents occupy, or have occupied, neighbouring dwelling-houses. I remember a young woman named Chan Achan, who was betrothed to a young man she had never seen, eloping with the son of the next-door neighbour. The fugitive lovers were eventually apprehended and put into the prison of the Poon-yu magistrate at Canton, for breach of promise and for disobedience to parents. The misconduct of the gentleman was aggravated by the crime of abduction. I frequently visited this couple during their imprisonment. In the spring of 1874, a Taouist priest named Lob-hung, eloped with a young lady, who was a member of the Fung family. The young couple in this case also lived as neighbours, both residing in the Paak-sha street of the western suburb of Canton. They had betaken themselves for concealment to Poon-tong, one of the largest and most populous suburban districts of the city, but they were eventually discovered and made to return to their homes. The parents of the young lady, who moved in a higher sphere than those of the priest, were naturally grieved, but they wisely concluded that their only course was to give her to him in marriage.

To return to the ceremonies connected with marriage in China. When a go-between, who has been employed by parents in their son's interest, has succeeded in selecting a suitable young lady, the ceremony called Man-Ming takes place between the fathers. The order of procedure in this ceremony is some-

what tedious, but it shows the care and deliberation with which
the Chinese proceed in what they naturally consider a matter of
the utmost importance. The father of the young man furnishes
the father of the young lady with a document which sets forth
the hour, the day, the month, and the year of his son's birth,
and the number and maiden name of the wife who is his son's
mother. He receives a similar document from the young lady's
father. The parents next consult their departed ancestors, and
for this purpose each places the document he has received on
his ancestral altar. When the ancestors are supposed to have
given their blessing, the parents, or persons appointed by them,
have recourse to an astrologer, who casts the horoscopes of the
youthful pair. Should the result be favourable, an engagement
is entered into. It is effected by the parents, for, till the day of
the solemnization of their marriage, the young people are not
allowed to see each other. The father of the youth writes a
letter to the father of the young lady, stating that he has a
desire to receive her as a wife for his son. This letter is delivered by " the friend of the bridegroom " on a lucky day
selected for the purpose. The writer of the letter, before placing
it in the hand of the friend of the bridegroom, stands in front
of his ancestral altar, and, looking towards the west, kneels
down and performs the kow-tow, taking care to knock his
head six times upon the ground. Rising from his knees, he
gives the letter to the friend of the bridegroom, and bids him
bear it with all haste to the young lady's father. When he
arrives on this mission, the bridegroom's friend is received at
the door by a person appointed for that purpose. The young
lady's father having been informed of his arrival, goes to
the door to meet him, and conducts him to the ancestral hall,
where he takes his appointed place on the east side, the west
side being reserved for the host. At the command of the conductor of the ceremonies they approach the ancestral altar, and
make a profound obeisance to the ancestral tablets. The host
then moves to the east side of the hall and stands with his face
towards the west, while the friend of the bridegroom takes up
his position on the west side, facing the east. He then addresses
a few respectful words to the host, and presents the letter. This

is placed unopened upon the ancestral altar. The friend of the bridegroom next presents to the host, in the name of the bridegroom elect, several boxes of cakes and a live pig. In some parts of the empire a wild goose and gander are amongst the gifts. These birds are regarded by the Chinese as emblems of faithfulness in wedlock, and it is said that the same goose and gander always pair, and that should either the one or the other die, the survivor spends its remaining life in single blessedness. Where wild geese cannot be procured, tame geese are often substituted. In some few instances, wooden or tin figures of wild geese are preferred to live tame geese. The cakes are conveyed to the house in large red boxes, which are borne by men wearing red tunics. To the lid of each box a broad strip of red paper is affixed, upon which are written the Chinese characters Shaong and Hee, which mean twice glad, or twofold gladness. On this occasion also a dowry, which varies according to the position of the family, is given by the father of the suitor. A similar custom was practised by the ancient Jews. According to the law of Moses, the dowry given by the father of a Jewish suitor was, in an ordinary case, from thirty to fifty shekels.[1] Amongst the ancient Greeks this custom must also have prevailed, as Pausanias regards it as singular that a man should give his daughter in marriage without receiving a dowry in return, and gives a reason for the exception made in a particular case (Lacon iii. 12-2). When the cakes have been arranged on the ancestral altar, the host kneels before the tablets and twice performs the kow-tow, upon which the friend of the bridegroom is conducted to the visitors' hall and invited to take tea. The host, who remains behind, removes the letter from the box in which it is contained, reads it aloud in presence of the tablets, kneels before them, performs the kow-tow thrice, and proceeds to write his reply. This letter, duly addressed and sealed, is placed in a small box. At the same time the boxes in which the cakes were brought, are refilled with cakes by the host's servants. Before leaving, the friend of the bridegroom is again conducted into the ancestral hall, where the host, placing him on the left side of the hall, presents with both hands the

---

[1] *Vide* Exod. xxii. 16 ; Deut. xxii. 29 ; 1 Sam. xviii. 25 ; and Hosea iii. 2.

box containing the reply. The host now kneels once more before the ancestral tablets, and twice performs the kow-tow. Upon rising he invites his guest to partake of a repast, an invitation which is only accepted at the third time of its repetition. They enter the dining hall and, after bowing to one another, take their seats, the guest on the east side of the table, and the host on the west. As this is a meal of ceremony only, the host and his guest content themselves with taking wine with each other three times, although the table is covered with various viands. The friend of the bridegroom now takes leave of his host, and, followed by the bearers of the boxes of cakes, hastens to return with the reply to the house of his friend's father. On his arrival he is conducted to the ancestral hall, where similar ceremonies are duly observed. In both cases the cakes, after remaining some time on the ancestral altar, are divided amongst the relatives or friends of the contracting parties.

As it may interest my readers to be made acquainted with the tenor of the letters which are exchanged on such occasions, I give a translation of two such documents which fell into my hands. The translation of the first, which is from the father of the bridegroom elect, is as follows :—

" The sun has long since risen, and the brightness of his rays illumines the house wherein resides the fair. At this hour, too, she, like the sun, has left her couch and attired herself in a costume becoming the hour of the day, and her rank and station in life. Her face has gazed upon the mirror, which has reflected back upon her the beautiful features of which it is possessed. Indeed, all nature has now assumed a beautiful aspect, and all creatures, as it is designed by nature, are now pairing. I write this as an evidence of my respect and devotion. Permit me, therefore, respectfully to congratulate you, my venerable relative, whose honourable family has resided for so many ages in Seng-Moon, or Yut Hoee, where its respected members have ever been distinguished for their literary attainments, their essays being written in a style almost unparalleled. Further, the essay of your son in particular has obtained for him high literary honours ; but no wonder, as your ancestors were one and all men of distinction, and your descendants, therefore, cannot be otherwise than men of renown.[1] Your own rank is also great, and your son will prove a worthy successor of the same. I, for my part, have been from boyhood slothful and indigent. I wander through the world as one without any fixed purpose, and the rank which I hold is of a degree more honourable than I deserve. Your daughter is gentle and virtuous, and as for my son he is so weak in intellect as to be unworthy of her. But, as you, upon hearing the words of the match-maker or go-between, thought him worthy and at once consented to the engagement, it is only right that the union should take place. There will be unbroken friendship between me and you after the celebration of the marriage rites of our children. This is the day appointed for me to give, and for you to receive the customary presents. I therefore beg to forward them herewith. They are, however, of a very ordinary kind and of no value. Indeed, I only forward to you, together with a few simple things, a wooden hair-pin, and I am in truth ashamed that I have no jewels, precious stones, and silk fabrics to present. You will, I am sure, readily excuse me. When these, the preliminary ceremonies, have been observed, we shall anxiously await the wedding day."

The translation of the reply received from the father of the bride elect is as follows:—

"Winter sets in, and the wild geese now fly about in large flocks. The Pheng-Tye buds, and ere long its branches will be thickly covered with flowers. This day the second quarter of winter commences, and your presents were on the occasion accepted with warm thanks. I beg most respectfully to congratulate you, my venerable relative, whose honourable family at one period resided in the province of Fokien, but is now settled in the provincial capital of Kwang-tung. Your illustrious name was famous in Kougha, and your many virtues were highly commended by the learned men of In-pheng. I have, therefore, at all times regarded your incomparable good conduct as ranging as high above that of your fellow men as the crane flies high above the earth. Your manners, too, are without a parallel, being as gentle as the vapour compared with the tempestuous winds. I am so poor as to be unable to maintain

---

[1] From this it would appear that the Chinese have a strong belief in the doctrine that "like begets like."

"Nec imbellem feroces
Progenerant aquilae columbam."

myself, neither can I find means to escape from the numerous troubles by which I am beset. The disposition of your son is benevolent. His mind, which is highly cultivated, is as lofty as the heaven is high above earth. My daughter, who was born in a poor cottage and is uneducated, rejoiced much on hearing the words of the match-maker to the effect that you were anxious that I should agree to give her in marriage to your son. Thus your son and my daughter are bound by this marriage contract. The presents which you sent me are like the Tenga Ha and Yee of Shang-hoo (two valuable curiosities) and I am very sorry that I could not in return present you with a similar compliment. These ceremonies are the signs of increasing generations. When your son and my daughter are united in marriage, there will be unbounded affection between them."

The next ceremony connected with betrothal is called Nap-Pie, or presentation of silks. This was in ancient times called Nap-Ching. A court dress, with other gifts, is sent to the bride elect by the parents of the lover. It is followed by a banquet at his residence. The court dress is sent to the young lady on a lucky day, accompanied by a letter, and is made to correspond with the rank of the youth whose wife she is about to become. The same observance of rank is shown with respect to the other gifts. If the youth be of the first, second, third, or fourth rank, sixteen pieces of silk, ear-rings, bracelets, hair-pins (cf. Genesis xxiv. 22), and ten boxes of cakes are also presented to the lady. Sometimes one hundred boxes of cakes are presented instead of ten. Such munificence, however, is not sanctioned by law. Should the gentleman be of the fifth, sixth, or seventh rank, he sends, together with the court dress, twelve pieces of silk, ear-rings, bracelets, hair-pins, and eight boxes of cakes. The ceremonies which are observed on the giving and receiving of these gifts, are precisely similar to those which are performed at the celebration of Nap-Tsoy. The *menu* of the grand dinner which follows at the residence of the bridegroom elect, is also regulated by his rank. If the youth, or his father, be of the first rank, the banquet consists of six different kinds of meats, together with many other viands; if of the second rank, it consists of four kinds of meats, and if of the third, of three kinds. On the tables of those of the fourth, fifth, sixth, seventh, eighth, and ninth ranks, only two kinds of meat, with other viands, are served up.

When the contract has been ratified in this manner, that is, by the giving and receiving of cakes and other presents, nothing save an attack of leprosy, lunacy, or any other serious malady on the part of either of the betrothed couple, or unfaithfulness on the part of the woman, can render it null and void. So sacred is such an engagement considered, that, should the lady prove unfaithful during the period preceding her marriage, she would be regarded as guilty of violating her marriage vows. Such contracts were, it is clear, regarded in this light by the ancient Jews.[1] But the reader cannot realize the extent to which a betrothal is considered sacred and binding by the Chinese, until he has learned the most exacting of all its conditions. In the event of a bridegroom elect dying before the solemnization of his marriage, the young lady to whom he was affianced is called upon to live in the house of his parents in a state of perpetual virginity. A lucky day is selected for her proceeding thither, and the first duty which she performs on her arrival, is that of kneeling before a wooden tablet bearing the name of the departed youth, and bewailing his premature death. I once met at the residence of one of the principal families of Canton, a young lady, certainly not more than seventeen years of age, who was the victim of this cruel system. She was regarded as the widow of the deceased, and, doubtless, received at the hands of her new connections all the attentions due to her station. When a lady of this class attains the sixty-first year of her age, she is much honoured by all her connections and friends. As a mark of their appreciation of what they consider an act of great virtue, it is usual to erect a monumental arch. The government generally contributes to the fund established for this purpose. These arches are commonly built of brick, or granite, and, in some parts of the empire, of marble. In the vicinity of Wo-chan Foo, on the banks of the Po-yang lake, I remarked one made of porcelain. Should a lady who has been affianced die before the solemnization of her marriage, it is an

---

[1] This appears not merely from the history of Joseph and Mary, but from certain passages of the Pentateuch, as, for example, Deut. xxii. 25—28.

almost invariable rule—at all events it is observed among
genteel families—for the youth to whom she was betrothed, to
go through a ceremony by which he is supposed to become the
husband of his departed *fiancée*. On a lucky day chosen for the
occasion, the gentleman, attired in the dress of a bridegroom,
awaits at his residence the arrival of the tablet on which her
name is recorded. This tablet is conveyed to his house in a
bridal chair, in which are placed a fan and a pocket-handker-
chief. The chair is preceded by a musician playing on a wind
instrument, which he holds in his right hand, while with his left
he beats a tom-tom or small drum, suspended from his waist-
belt. The bridal-chair is received at the residence of the bridegroom with ceremonies not unlike those with which a bride is
for the first time ushered into the presence of her lord. The
tablet is placed on the ancestral altar of the bridegroom's family,
and his younger brothers and sisters, and nephews and nieces
perform the kow-tow before it. From the top of the tablet is
suspended a silver coin or medal, upon which are engraven the
name, and the dates of the birth and death of the deceased. A
number of Taouist priests are also in attendance to offer up
prayers or masses for the repose of the spiritual bride, whom
they call upon to promote the happiness of her new family,
and especially to prosper in all things her lord and husband.
Weddings of this nature take place by night only, the day-time
not being regarded as congenial to spirits. When a lady who
is affianced dies, it is the duty of her parents to forward intelligence of her death to the parents of the youth to whom she was
engaged. These reply by sending a pig's head, four cakes of
dough, candles, a shroud, and a broken hair-comb. The pig's head,
cakes, and candles are presented as offerings to the deceased;
the comb is placed in her coffin. These ceremonies and the
funeral obsequies having been duly observed, arrangements for
the marriage are at once entered upon. At a ceremony of this
nature which I witnessed, the bridegroom, whose name was
Lo Kow-chee, jocularly observed to me that he had become the
husband of a piece of wood, alluding to the tablet which bore
in letters of gold the name of his departed *fiancée*.

After the Nap-Pie or presentation of silks, the next cere-

mony is the Tseng-Kee or selection of a lucky day for the
marriage. The day of the selection is one of great rejoicing.
In the Tseng-Kee it is customary either to consult an astrologer, or to refer the matter to the oracle of a deity. In an
event of such importance as the marriage of the emperor, the
selection of a propitious day is referred to the board of
astronomy. I remember seeing in the *Pekin Gazette* of March
12th, 1872, the decree, issued in the name of the two empresses
dowager, which directed this board to choose in the ninth
month, October of the same year, a propitious day on which to
solemnize the marriage of the late sovereign Tung-chee. By
the same decree the princes of Kung and Paoyun were appointed to make all the necessary ceremonial arrangements.
In ordinary cases where the mysterious lore of the astrologer
is not called into requisition, an appeal is frequently made to
the god Chaong-Wong-Yae. It is usual, therefore, to find persons
anxiously bent on this mission at the temple in honour of this
deity at Si-chune, or at the still grander temple in honour of
the same deity at Shek-tseng. The goddess Loong-Moo, or
Dragon's Mother, is occasionally referred to on a matter of such
importance. In her temple in the vicinity of Hwang-chu-kee,
I have frequently seen ladies seeking information as to lucky
days on which to solemnize the marriages of their children.
When the information has been obtained, it is customary for
the father of the bridegroom elect to send a congratulatory
letter to the father of the bride elect, and if he be of the first,
second, or third rank, he sends at the same time two sheep and
four pots of wine. The wine is termed "glad wine." If
however, the sender be of the fourth, fifth, sixth, seventh, eighth,
or ninth rank, two geese and four pots of wine are forwarded
with the congratulatory letter. "The friend of the bridegroom"
is deputed to convey the letter and gifts. On his arrival at the
residence of the father of the *fiancée*, he asks that gentleman
to name a day for the marriage. The latter replies, "Let the
father of the youth to whom my daughter is affianced name the
day." Upon this the friend of the bridegroom makes a profound
bow, and presents the letter in which the day is named.
A reply is sent approving of the day in question. For ten

or fifteen days, or in some cases for thirty days preceding
the wedding day, the bride elect, together with her sisters,
female friends, and attendants, bewails and laments her intended
removal from the home of her fathers. During this season of
lamentation, the sorrowing virgin declares at frequent intervals,
and apparently with much feeling, that to be removed from her
father and mother will prove to her worse than death itself.
Mention is, I apprehend, made of a custom similar to this in the
thirteenth verse of the twenty-first chapter of Deuteronomy.
The passage runs as follows:—

" And she shall put the raiment of her captivity from off her,
and shall remain in thine house, and bewail her father and her
mother a full month."

The night immediately preceding the wedding day is wholly
set apart for weeping and wailing, not so much by the bride
elect as by her attendants. This lamentation is termed Hoi-
Tan-Tsing, or to give vent to feelings of sorrow. When, in
consequence of the destruction of the British and other foreign
residences by the Cantonese, I lived in a Chinese dwelling-
house at Honam, I was on one occasion disturbed for several
nights by loud lamentations issuing from one of the neighbouring houses. Upon making inquiries, I was told that the
daughter of a neighbouring gentleman was about to be married,
and that her sisters and female relatives and friends were
bewailing her intended departure from the home of her fathers.
On the day immediately preceding the wedding day, or on a
lucky day, even if it precede the wedding day by eight or ten
days, it is customary for her parents to send the trousseau of
the bride and all kinds of furniture, bedding, &c., to the residence
of her future lord. These are carried by men wearing red tunics ;
and in order that the people in the neighbourhood may be made
aware of the liberality of the father, the men appointed to carry
these various packages and boxes have to walk in procession
with their burdens through all the streets adjoining that in
which he resides. On the morning of the marriage day a large
breakfast is made ready at the house of the bridegroom. The
tables are arranged on the east and west sides of the dining-hall.

Near the entrance-door stands a table, upon which are placed four wine-cups. These cups are usually made of gourds, and are called the Hop-Kun, or uniting cups. In the court-yard, and at the foot of the steps by which the hall is approached, there is another table, upon which are set viands for the special use of the bridegroom, who is now called to attire himself. Should he have no rank so-called, he is at liberty, if his father or grand-father be of the third rank, to wear a dress of the fifth rank. If, however, his father be of the fourth or fifth rank, he wears a dress'of the seventh rank, and if his father be of the sixth rank, he wears a dress of the eighth rank. Thus attired he enters the visitors' hall, where he is awaited by his father, to whom he does obeisance by kneeling down and knocking his head six times upon the ground. Whilst kneeling, he is presented with a cup of wine, and requested to send for the bride elect. Formerly it was customary for the bridegroom to go for his bride, except when he was indisposed, when the duty devolved upon " the friend of the bridegroom." Even now the bridegroom occasionally, though very rarely indeed, goes for the bride. In 1867, a young gentleman came from one of the midland provinces to Canton for the purpose of marrying a daughter of Acheong, who at that time was governor of the province of Kwang-tung; and, in 1869, a young Tartar came all the way from Pekin to marry the daughter of H. E. Suee Lun, the viceroy of the two Kwangs. The bridegroom nowadays, however, unless the circumstances are somewhat exceptional, sends a large bridal chair, which is richly carved and gilded, or, if not gilt, covered with the enamel of kingfishers' feathers, for the bride's conveyance. The sons and daughters of high officials or men of rank, are borne in a large state chair, covered with red cloth and adorned with fringes. Such a chair reminds one of the " litter of red cloth adorned with pearls and jewels," which, we read in the *Arabian Nights*, King Zahi-Shah made ready for the journey of his fair daughter. In almost all the country districts in the vicinity of Canton, a rude sedan chair made of wood and painted red, is invariably used. Above the door of the bridal chair, a strip of red paper is suspended, upon which is written either " Kee-Lun-

Tsoy-Tsze," or " Kee-Lun-Choy-Chu," implying that the influence or presence of the Kee-lun is here. Sometimes, however, the strip bears a portrait of the god Chaong-Wong-Yae,
or an impression of his seal. The bridal chair is carried last
in the marriage procession, preceded by many richly-carved
and gilded pavilions of wood, under which are sweetmeats
and ornaments. Among the processional emblems is a small
orange-tree heavily laden with fruit, and with strings of "cash"
hanging from its branches. The prolific orange-tree, with its
strings of cash, is emblematical of the numerous offspring, and the
increased wealth expected to result from the happy union. A
canopy or pavilion under which there is a representation of
the Kee-lun, is also borne by the bridal retinue. The Kee-lun,
to which I have already referred, is a fabulous quadruped, which,
the Chinese say, never fails to appear when a sage is born into
the world. A wild goose and gander—which it will be remem-
bered are the Chinese emblems of faithfulness in wedlock—
or in their absence their tame representatives, are included in
the varied list of bridal signs. The train is not complete
without an effigy or figure of a dolphin, emblematical of rank
and wealth. Red boards, on which are carved in letters of gold
the titles of the respective ancestors of the bridegroom and his
bride, are carried by men clad in red tunics. Large lanterns
elaborately carved and gilded, and in each of which there is
a large red candle, are conspicuous on the shoulders of the
bearers. Bannermen and musicians in richly embroidered
dresses, umbrella-bearers, fan-bearers, and equerries, in number
proportionate to the rank of the bridegroom, swell the bridal
following, and add to the picturesque symbolism of the procession, in the front of which it is not unusual to lead a goat,
with its horns gilt, and its head decorated with a wreath of red
paper.

When the procession, which of course is not complete until
the bride has joined it with her attendants, leaves the bridegroom's house, the conductor is told to direct its course through
all the adjacent streets, so that the friends and neighbours may
have an opportunity of seeing it. Should any one attempt to
impede its progress there are lictors at hand, armed with whips

and chains, ready to bind and flog all refractory obstructors. Its near approach to the bride's house is announced by men who beat gongs for this purpose at almost every step. "The friend of the bridegroom," who accompanies it, bears a letter, written on red paper tinged with gold, and addressed to the bride, calling upon her to avail herself of the bridal chair, and to embrace the earliest opportunity of setting out to her new home, where an affectionate welcome awaits her. This letter is carefully preserved by the bride. It is regarded much as marriage lines are in England, and should she be so unfortunate as to be divorced, it must be returned by her. Letters of this kind are all very like each other, and I subjoin a translation of one which was addressed by a Chinese friend of mine, named Chong Chee-wo, to the father of the lady to whom his son was affianced. The translation runs as follows :—

"On urgent business. In ancient times it was customary for a bridegroom to go to the house of his bride elect for the purpose of escorting her to her new home. Now, however, it is usual for the father of the bridegroom to address a letter to the father of the bride, begging of him to send the bride with all haste to the house of her future lord. As this latter custom is one of much greater convenience, allow me, I pray you, to put it in force on this occasion. Moreover, a bridegroom, to discharge with effect the ceremonies which devolve upon an escort, must have a perfect knowledge of bridal etiquette—a knowledge this in which my son, as is the case with other bridegrooms, is lamentably deficient. Sending a letter, therefore, is surely more satisfactory to both parties. My son now waits in the hall of ceremonies to receive your daughter. Bid her come, as all things are now ready. May you have peace for a hundred years, and prosper for five generations. This communication comes to you with greeting."

On the arrival of the procession, the bride, who wears a costume corresponding to the rank of her future husband, enters the visitors' hall, where her father and mother, the former standing on the east side of the hall, and the latter on the west, are waiting to receive her. When she has performed the kow-tow, and while she is still kneeling, a female attendant gives her a cup of wine, and her father delivers a short address on the

the duties of husbands and wives. The mother, in her turn, dwells briefly upon similar subjects. The bride then expresses a hope that her parents and brothers may obtain the blessings of wealth, rank, and progeny, and retires to her chamber in order once more to lament the near approach of the hour in which she is to depart from the home of her youth. The father now goes to the door, and making a profound bow to "the friend of the bridegroom," begs him to enter. The latter does so holding a goose in each hand, and they proceed to the visitors' hall, where the father, taking his place on the east side, calls upon "the friend of the bridegroom" to stand on the west side. Having here delivered the geese to a servant, who places them on a table, the bridegroom's deputy is requested to take up a position in the centre of the hall, where, looking towards the north, he twice performs the kow-tow. It is now time for the bride to make her appearance. Before she leaves her chamber, a large fold of red silk is thrown over her head and face by a female attendant, for the purpose of concealing her features. Thus veiled she is brought into the visitors' hall by two female attendants, who direct her to bow to "the friend of the bridegroom," who duly acknowledges the salutation. Escorted by her two female attendants, one on each side, she enters the bridal chair. A few well-dressed female attendants, corresponding in some measure to our bridesmaids, having placed themselves in front of it, the conductor of ceremonies is ordered to lead the procession to the bridegroom's house, and the bridal chair is borne forward amidst the clang of gongs, and the discordant notes of rude musical instruments. Immediately behind it, four men bear an ordinary sedan chair, in which is seated the youngest brother of the bride, on whom, it would thus seem, devolves the duty of giving his sister away in marriage. The procession is joined by the attendants in red tunics, bearing red boards, with the titles of the bride's ancestors.

On arriving at the house of the bridegroom's father, the bridal chair, passing between the ranks of the bannermen, musicians, lantern-bearers, and others, who have fallen into line on each side of the principal entrance, is carried into the porch and placed upon the ground. The bridegroom now approaches and knocks with his fan at the door of the chair. This is opened by the bridesmaids, and the bride alights. Her features still remain concealed by the veil of red silk. She is placed on the back of a female servant, and carried over a slow charcoal fire, on each side of which are arranged the shoes which were borne in the procession as a gift to her future husband. Above her head, as she is conveyed over the charcoal fire, another female servant raises a tray containing several pairs of chop-sticks, some rice, and betel-nuts. By this time the bridegroom has taken his place on a high stool, on which he stands to receive the bride, who prostrates herself at the foot, and does obeisance to her lord. This high stool is intended to indicate the great superiority of the husband over the wife; for, in China more than in any other country of the habitable globe, woman is regarded as the weaker vessel. Descending from his elevated position, the bridegroom removes the veil of red silk. Now for the first time he catches a glimpse of his wife's face. It is still, however, more or less hidden by the strings of pearls which hang from her bridal coronet. The bridal pair are conducted to the ancestral hall, where they prostrate themselves before the altar on which the ancestral tablets are arranged. Heaven and Earth, and the gods of the principal doors of the house, and the parents of the bride are the next objects of their worship. A further act of homage, which consists in pouring out drink-offerings to the ancestors of the family, having been duly performed by the bridegroom only, the happy couple are escorted to the bridal chamber, where they find the orange-tree with its strings of cash, emblems of fruitfulness and wealth, and the burning tapers, which formed a part of the procession, placed on the nuptial couch. From the top of the bed are suspended three long strips of red paper. On the first of these are written the characters, On-Chong-Tai-Kat, or "from this bed much good fortune will arise;" on the second, Pak-Mow-Kum-Kee, which imply that in a hundred matters or affairs of a bad nature there will be no need for alarm; and on the third, Pak-Tsze-Tchin-Sun, or "a hundred sons and a thousand grandsons be your portion." The bridegroom having now saluted the bride, they sit down and partake of tea and cake. During this interval the strings of

pearls which hang from her coronet are drawn aside by the maids
in attendance, in order that the bridegroom may have an opportunity of seeing the features of his bride, who, that he may
receive a correct impression of them, has carefully omitted the
use of rouge in her toilet operations. Chinese ladies or matrons
freely indulge in cosmetics ; but on the day of their marriage
and during seasons of mourning these are prohibited. While the
bridal pair are thus engaged, many of the relatives and friends
assembled to celebrate the wedding, enter the chamber, and
freely remark on the personal appearance of the bride. Although
these remarks are passed with singular freedom, and are less
complimentary than truthful, they are not made in a subdued
tone of voice, but spoken so that every one may hear them. The
blessing of a numerous offspring is invoked upon the bride by
her new relatives and friends. The bridegroom soon rejoins
the guests, with whom he enters into conversation on the
ordinary topics of the day. At seven o'clock in the evening a
banquet in honour of her parents-in-law is prepared by the bride.
When all things are ready the parents enter the banqueting-hall,
where the bride, after bringing the principal dish or *caput cœnum*
from the kitchen and placing it on the table with her own hands,
assumes the position of a waiting-maid. Filling the cup of her
father-in-law with wine, she presents it to him with both hands,
and whilst he is drinking the contents, she kneels at his feet and
twice knocks her head upon the ground. To her mother-in-law,
whose cups she now fills, she is equally reverential. The
banquet over, and the parents-in-law having washed their hands,
the bride is called upon to partake of a repast. On a table
which her father-in-law orders the servants to place at the top
of the steps by which the dining-hall is approached, various
viands are set, and she is invited to occupy a chair on the east
side of the table. Her mother-in-law fills a cup of wine and
presents it to her. Before receiving it, however, she rises from
her chair, and kneeling at the feet of her mother-in-law, does
obeisance by twice knocking her head upon the ground. At the
conclusion of this repast the parents-in-law leave the hall by
the west, and the bride by the east staircase. In some parts of
the empire it is customary for the bridal pair to retire to their

private chamber to dine. Here the bride does not partake of food provided by her husband, but of viands which she has brought from her father's house. This singular custom is regarded as an evidence of modesty on her part and is carefully observed by her for three days. On such occasions four very intimate friends of the family are present, whose duty it is when each cup of wine is pledged, to address the bridal pair on the respective duties of husbands and wives towards each other. At the conclusion of this banquet, the bridal pair are greeted with a discharge of fire crackers. When the smoke has made its escape, a female attendant enters, bearing a tray, which, kneeling, she holds towards the bridegroom with a request that he will remove a small linen sheet which is placed upon it.[1] The bridegroom having spread the sheet upon the nuptial couch, again seats himself, when the female attendant, having taken her master's boots off, withdraws, leaving him alone with his bride. The bridegroom now removes from her waist a girdle, which with its strings of cash is regarded as emblematical of good fortune.

In some of the districts round Canton it is not unusual for the bride to be kept up during the greater part of the night, answering riddles. These are generally proposed to her by the bridegroom's relatives and friends. Should she fail in giving a correct answer to a riddle, she has to pay a forfeit of cakes to the person by whom it was put. The observance of this singular custom is attended with much drinking on the part of the gentlemen, and angry quarrels not unfrequently result. At the village of Pa-chow, near Whampoa, an old gentlemen of the clan or family Chaong, whilst engaged in celebrating his son's marriage, was killed by his nephew on an occasion of this sort. The youth, who was intoxicated, upon being rebuked by his uncle for setting riddles of an improper nature, flew into a violent passion, which was not appeased until he had imbrued his hands in the old man's blood.

In many districts of the province of Canton, the bride and bridegroom separate at once after the marriage ceremony has

---

[1] On the following morning this sheet is presented to the bridegroom's parents. A custom similar to this was observed by the ancient Jews.

been performed. So soon as the festivities are brought to a close, the bride returns to her father's house, there to await the completion of the period of time—generally three years—which it is thought should elapse before the bridal pair are permitted to live together. If the residence of the bride's father be within easy distance of that of the father of the bridegroom, she is allowed to visit her husband's parents for a few days once every month. Otherwise, such visits take place twice or thrice only, throughout the year. The dragon festival and other joyous occasions of the kind, are generally selected for them. The bridegroom has at such times opportunities of conversing with his bride ; but these visits of ceremony are, I believe, very distasteful to Chinese brides. I may narrate the sad sequel of the marriage of a youth with whom I was well acquainted. This youth, Ng Acheong by name, a native of a village situate at the base of the Lin-fa Hills, in the vicinity of the Bogue Forts, where this custom is strictly practised, was called upon during the month immediately following his marriage to leave the provincial capital where his duties were, on a short visit of ceremony to his parents, who were expecting to be honoured by the presence of his bride, their daughter-in-law. The bride was the first to arrive. On the morning following her arrival, however, it was discovered that during the night she had committed suicide by taking poison. It appeared she had carefully concealed the poison—which was a root called Woo-Mun-Kaong by the Chinese—in her clothing previous to the departure from her father's house. A few hours after this discovery the bridegroom arrived, only to receive the intelligence of the suicide of his bride. This singular and foolish custom also prevails in the county of Shun-tuk, which is one of the political divisions of the province of Kwang-tung. With the view of suppressing it, the magistrates of the district in question not unfrequently issue proclamations calling upon parents to compel their daughters to reside at once with their husbands.

At an early hour on the morning of the third day after the marriage, the bride is escorted to the ancestral hall to worship the ancestors of the bridegroom. The ancestral tablets are removed from the altar, and placed on a table which stands in the centre of the hall. On the east side of the hall stands a table, covered with viands. The bridegroom takes up his position in front of this, while the bride places herself before a similar table on the west side. In the centre of the floor of the peristyle, or courtyard, of the ancestral hall, is placed a large cushion, upon which the father of the bridegroom kneels, and looking towards the ancestral tablets, does obeisance by performing the kow-tow. Having also poured out libations of wine, he reads to the spirits of his ancestors a letter, the tenor of which is much as follows :—" My son has married, and all the ceremonies attendant upon such an occasion having been duly observed, I now, therefore, give command to him and his wife to render you homage, in the hope of propitiating you and prevailing upon you to grant them many blessings." When this address has been read, the bridal pair kneel before the ancestral tablets and thrice perform the kow-tow. The parents, uncles, and aunts of the bridegroom next receive the homage of the happy couple, after which the parents present the bridal pair with pieces of money wrapped in red paper. If the bride's parents reside at no great distance, it is her further duty on the third day after her marriage to pay a visit of ceremony to them at noon, remaining with them for at least a few hours. Should the distance be great, a more convenient day is selected. On this visit she is accompanied by a number of servants, bearing numerous boxes of cakes and fruits together with roasted pigs, fowls, &c. These presents are in acknowledgment of their daughter's chastity. The head and hind quarters of one of the pigs are returned to the donors, for the sake of luck. In some instances the bride is accompanied by a master of ceremonies, whose duty it is to present to the parents a letter which plainly expresses what the gifts are intended to acknowledge. This letter is carefully preserved. The custom is not very dissimilar to one which was observed by the ancient Jews (Deut. xxii. 13—17).

A bride who is found to be unchaste is not unfrequently divorced, and sent to her parents on the morning after the marriage. Sometimes a husband hesitates to make his wife a public example. He therefore rests satisfied with allowing

her to return on the third morning after marriage to the house
of her parents, without the customary presents of roast pigs,
fowls, &c. My attention was once called to an instance. The
family of the bride manifested great indignation against the
bridegroom, declaring that the accusation brought against the
daughter was false, and insisting on the customary presents.
These the bridegroom, persistent in his declaration, declined
to give.   An investigation ensued, which terminated in the
bride acknowledging her guilt.[1]

The bridegroom also pays a visit of ceremony to her parents on
the same day as the bride. He is received at the door by his father-
in-law, and they enter the ancestral hall, where the bridegroom
places upon the altar several gifts. Looking to the north, he
then kneels at the feet of his father-in-law, and twice performs
the kow-tow.   This act of obeisance the latter cheerfully
acknowledges by looking towards the west and performing the
kow-tow.   This, it may be observed, is the only occasion on
which the father-in-law kneels in the presence of his son-in-law.
The bridegroom now expresses a desire to pay his respects to
his mother-in-law, who to afford him an opportunity stands at
the door of her apartment. A repast is now made ready, of
which he is invited to partake; and after drinking three cups
of wine at the request of his father-in-law, he returns home.
The visit of the bride on this occasion may extend to six, or
even eight hours. In the evening she must be present in her
new home to entertain the wedding guests.

On the evening of the fourth day following the marriage, it
is the duty of the bridal pair to entertain at dinner the friends
of their respective families.   The invitation cards which are
issued on such occasions are stereotyped, and read very much
as follows :—

"On the eighth day of the present moon your younger
brother is to receive his bride; on the seventh day the
wine cups will be cleaned and prepared; on the tenth day
wine will be poured out, when he will presume to draw your
carriage to his lowly abode, that your conversation may be enjoyed; and when, in the arrangement of the ceremony, your

---

[1] It appeared she had secretly lived in incest with her brother.

assistance will be expected.   To attend the ceremony your brilliant presence is entreated.   To what an elevation of splendour will your presence assist us to rise !

> " To the Eminent in Literature,
>> " Venerable First-Born,
>>> " At His Table of Study.

" From Ho Kow, born in the evening, and who bows his head to the ground and worships."

In 1856, I had the pleasure of being present together with four or five English ladies, and as many gentlemen, at a banquet of this kind.   When we arrived at the outer gate of the house, we were very politely requested by the porter to wait a few moments, in order that our arrival might be formally announced. Whilst we were waiting, several Chinese musicians who were seated within the porch, played a wedding tune.   On entering, we found the bride and bridegroom stationed, the one on the right, and the other on the left side of the door, in order to receive and welcome us.   We were escorted by them to the visitors' hall, where we remained in conversation for some time. The English ladies were then invited to enter the part of the dwelling-house set apart for the use of the female members of the family.   During their absence, we had the opportunity of seeing several interesting ceremonies.   Amongst other native visitors, Ngow-qua and several other wealthy Chinese gentlemen called to congratulate the bridal pair.   On each occasion the bride came into the outer hall, where gentlemen visitors are entertained, to receive the congratulations of these friends. Each visitor prostrated himself at the feet of the bride, and knocked his head upon the ground, saying at the same time, " I congratulate you !   I congratulate you ! " whilst the bride, also upon her knees and knocking her head upon the ground replied, " I thank you !   I thank you ! "   This congratulatory ceremony was brought to a close by the lady presenting each visitor with a cup of tea.   At the banquet, which was served at seven o'clock in the ancestral hall immediately in front of the altar, there were present no fewer than thirty elegantly dressed Chinese ladies, some of whom were tolerably good-looking. The Chinese and English ladies did not, as in England, occupy places at table among the gentlemen, but sat by themselves. The bride and bridegroom did not dine with us, but assumed the character of waiting servants. When with her attendants the former had placed on the table the last course, consisting of boiled rice, she observed that we had been most inhospitably entertained. If the dwelling-house of a gentleman be deemed too small to entertain all who are invited to assist in the celebration of the marriage of his son, it is not unusual for him to erect a large mat shed, or tent. This plan is frequently resorted to in Chinese villages. At the village of Ha-long, near Canton, I was present, in 1864, at a marriage, which was celebrated by the friends and relatives of the bridal pair, in a large mat tent put up for the purpose. Two hundred guests had room enough and to spare in it. Sometimes the large mat tea-saloons which are erected for the benefit of travellers by the sides of the high-roads, are rented by Chinese parents on these occasions.

A Chinese is at liberty to take to himself as many wives as he can afford to maintain. The second and third wives are generally women of large feet and low origin, the first wives being almost invariably, excepting of course in the case of Tartar ladies, women of small feet. The first wife is invested with a certain amount of power over the others, and assigns to them their various domestic duties. Indeed it is not usual for second or third wives to sit in her presence, without having first obtained her permission to do so.[1] Upon the first wife of a Chinese gentleman of rank is bestowed a title which corresponds to that of her husband, as is the case with the wives of peers and baronets among ourselves. It is customary for such ladies, when paying visits, to be escorted through the streets of a city by a retinue of equerries, swordsmen, lictors, and other attendants, equal in number to that to which their husbands are entitled. On such occasions it is a rule with ladies of rank not to close the blinds of their sedan chairs, as do other ladies. They permit themselves to be seen by the public, as if proud

---

[1] In a family, however, where the second or third wife succeeds in usurping the affections of the husband, the authority of the first wife is ignored.

of the equipage and attention which mark their rank. In the
case of the demise of a first wife, the second does not succeed
to her position. She remains in her former station, which, as
has already been stated, is, in the event of her having borne no
children, that of a servant rather than of a wife. Nor are
the tablets of the wives who die without issue placed upon the
principal altar of the ancestral hall, but usually upon shelves
put up for the purpose in an adjoining chamber. When dying,
second or third wives who have not borne children are
removed from the dwelling-house to an humbler abode. They
are not entitled to die in the dwelling-house of their master!
I remember an instance of this which occurred in 1862. The
fourth wife of a wealthy Chinese gentleman, named Eng Sze-tai,
who resided at Honam, a suburb of the city of Canton, was in a
dying state; and at the command of her husband, this woman,
whose last hour was seen to be approaching, was removed to an
out-house which was occupied by one of the men-servants.

I have observed that second and third wives are in many
instances women of low origin; and this remark is true to an
extent which the English reader could not realise, unless I added
that they are not unfrequently public women, known previously
to the Chinese husband, who as a rule is unfaithful to his wife.
Even in the upper ten it is not unusual to meet with wives of
this rank. In the Eng, or Howqua family, there are many such
ladies. Nor are other instances far to seek. A gentleman of
rank named Hoiee Chaong-kwong, who resided in the Koo-tai-
Kai street of Canton, and who was for many years Chief Justice
of the province of Kwang-si, was renowned throughout the city
and its neighbourhood not so much for his legal acumen, as for
being the husband of a second wife whose personal charms, say
the Chinese, were without a parallel. This lady was selected
by Hoiee Chaong-kwong as his second wife, and so great was
his affection for her that, upon the death of his first wife, he
memorialized the Emperor Taou-kwang to confer upon her the
title and dignity of a first wife. The second or third wife of
Chaong Yik-lai, the famous governor of Kwang-tung, was for
some time a prostitute at Canton. It ought, however, to be
stated that women are occasionally found in houses of ill-fame

who are the daughters of respectable parents, and who, during times of rebellion, have been seized by shameless villains and sold to the proprietors of such establishments. In some cases, female slaves are chosen to be the second or third wives of Chinese gentlemen. To a gentleman who is in search of a second or third wife, a go-between or match-maker can always furnish the name of a householder who, having three or four good-looking female slaves in his establishment, is willing to give them in marriage. The gentleman inspects the slaves at their owner's house. This interview takes place in the principal hall, and the girls, attired for the occasion in the habits of ladies, are brought in for inspection, one at a time, by the match-maker. In 1864, I saw a transaction of this sort in the house of a Chinese gentleman at Canton. The intending purchaser narrowly scanned the figure of the blushing maiden; who was made to uncover her arms from the wrists to the shoulders, and her legs from the ankles to the knees. In order to prove that she was not halt, she had to walk from one end of the hall to the other; and that it might be clearly shown that she had no impediment in her speech, she had to speak for several seconds in a loud tone. Whilst he was examining the young woman as a cattle-dealer would examine a brute beast, he was encouraged, or discouraged, by remarks passed on her personal appearance by two gentlemen who accompanied him. On the floor was a red lacquer-ware box containing sweet cakes, which were intended as a present to the girl. My presence evidently had a tendency to interrupt the sale and transfer, and I withdrew. No purchase, however, was effected, as I saw the poor girl in the house of her master on several subsequent occasions. Where a gentleman succeeds in selling his slave girl as a second or third wife, it is usual for him to give a small dowry. This is given on the day preceding her marriage, and consists of one summer and one winter dress, a pair of richly-embroidered shoes, a bed coverlet and bed curtain, a dressing-case, an umbrella, and a trunk. Although the marriage of a second or third wife is not attended with that degree of pomp and ceremony which marks the marriage of a first wife, the religious rites are precisely the same in both cases. At the close of the religious observances, the second wife is taken into the presence of the first, before whom she kneels and performs the kow-tow. At such marriages it is usual to call into requisition the services of an aged man, who is one of a class called Fā-Koong. Upon him devolves the duty of exhorting the newly-married couple to live together in the bonds of affection. The bride is also exhorted to love, honour, and obey the first wife of her husband. The man selected for this office must have attained the ripe age of seventy years, and preference is given to a married man, whose wife has been his partner from his early manhood, and is of the same age as himself. I have already had occasion to state that polygamists are, in many cases, frequenters of houses of ill-fame. It remains for me to add that in cities and towns there are Chinese who, independent of the many wives which they have, keep mistresses, although I cannot say that such cases are numerous.

It is considered very improper for a widow to contract a second marriage; and in genteel families such an event rarely, if ever, occurs. Indeed, if I do not mistake, a lady of rank by contracting a second marriage exposes herself to a penalty of eighty blows. Amongst the lower orders, however, such marriages occur, poverty being generally alleged as an excuse. It is not unusual, indeed, for parents-in-law, if poor, to compel their widowed daughters-in-law to contract second marriages. Where cases of this kind come to the knowledge of the magistrate, the parents-in-law, having received in the first instance a punishment of eighty blows, are transported to one of the neighbouring provinces for three years. Many poor widows do not hesitate to commit suicide, in order to avoid compliance with these demands; and proclamations are sometimes issued by the mandarins, calling upon parents not to force their widowed daughters-in-law to contract second marriages. In a large city like Canton, there are houses where poor widows from the country take up their abode, in the hope of obtaining husbands. Such establishments are presided over by match-makers, or go-betweens, and, in some instances, by aged men. On the occasion of a widow marrying, it is not unusual for the brother of the deceased husband to take the children of her first marriage from her, and to regard them, in future, as his own; while the children, if any, of the second marriage are not unfrequently looked upon as the offspring of a wanton. A Chinese gentleman with whom I was well acquainted, paid me a visit on one occasion, accompanied by two of his personal friends; and upon introducing them to me he observed—speaking in English, of which his companions were ignorant—that they did not belong to the *élite*, inasmuch as they were the issue of a second marriage which their mother had contracted. He wished me to understand that he regarded his companions as the sons of a woman who, by polite society, was considered as not strictly virtuous.

Whilst on the subject of marriage, I may state that a singular custom, called the "double marriage," is observed in Chinese families, the members of which for three generations are still living, and the senior male members of which have obtained rank. The "double marriage" cannot take place until the grandparents have each reached the age of sixty years, and it is then celebrated in the following manner :—The grandmother returns to her native place, in order that her husband may have an opportunity afforded him of seeking her hand once more in marriage. When the necessary preliminaries have been arranged, and a lucky day has been selected for a renewal of the marriage tie, the bridal chair, attended by bannermen and musicians, is sent by the grandfather to the house where his aged spouse has taken up her abode. The procession is headed by a master of ceremonies, who presents the old lady with a letter, in which her husband begs of her to seat herself in the bridal chair, which he has sent for her conveyance, and to return to her home, in order that he may have the honour of renewing his nuptial vows. A number of relatives and friends assemble at the house, in order to greet the happy old lady on her return; and the ceremony is brought to a close by much feasting and merriment.

One other marriage custom, as absurd as it is wicked, remains to be noted. In China, not merely the living are married, but the dead also. Thus the spirits of all males who die in infancy or in boyhood, are in due course of time married to the spirits of females who have been cut off at a like early age. If a youth of twelve years dies, it is customary when he has been dead six or seven years, for his parents to seek to unite his spirit in wedlock with that of a girl whose birth and death corresponded in point of time with those of their son. For this purpose application is made to a go-between, and when a selection has been made from this functionary's list of deceased maidens, an astrologer is consulted. When the astrologer, having cast the horoscopes of the two departed spirits, has pronounced the selection judicious, a lucky night is set apart for the solemnization of the marriage. On that night, a paper figure representing a bridegroom in full marriage costume, is placed in the ceremonial hall of his parents' house; and at nine o'clock, or in some instances later, a bridal chair, which is sometimes made of a rattan-frame covered with paper, is despatched in the name of the spirit of the youth to the house of the parents of the deceased girl, with a request that they will be so good as to allow the spirit of their daughter to seat itself therein for the purpose of being conveyed to her new home. As one of the three souls of which the body of a Chinese is supposed to be possessed, is said after death to remain with the ancestral tablet, the tablet bearing the name of the girl is removed from the ancestral altar and placed in the bridal chair, where it is supplemented by a paper figure intended to represent the bride. The bridal procession is headed by two musicians, one of whom plays upon a lute and the other upon a tom-tom, and sometimes the wearing apparel which belonged to the deceased girl, and which for the future is to be in the keeping of the parents of the departed youth, is carried in it. On the arrival of the procession, the tablet and the effigy are removed from the bridal chair, and placed, the former on the ancestral altar, and the latter on a chair close to that occupied by the effigy of the bridegroom. A table covered with various kinds of viands is placed before the effigies, whilst five or six priests of Taou are engaged in chanting prayers to the spirits, calling upon them to receive one another as husband and wife, and to partake of the wedding repast. At the close of this ceremony the effigies are burned, together with a great quantity of paper clothes, paper money, paper man-servants and maid-servants, fans, tobacco-pipes, and sedan chairs. I was once present at such a ceremony. It took place at the house of a Chinese friend named Cha Kum-hoi, who resided in the Kwong-ga-lee street of the western suburb of Canton. The immediate occasion of this marriage was, it so happened, the illness of this gentleman's wife, which was attributed by the geomancer or fortune-teller to the angry spirit of her son, who was importunate to be married. A matrimonial engagement was therefore immediately entered into on behalf of the deceased son, and was duly solemnized as I have described it.

WIFE AND CHILDREN OF AN OPIUM-SMOKER.

CHAPTER VIII.

DIVORCE.

THE law of divorce in China has, apparently, from time imme-memorial, afforded great facilities to men in all ranks and conditions of life for putting away their wives. On the other hand, as was the case amongst the ancient Jews, a wife cannot cite her husband, however culpable his conduct may be, before any of the civil tribunals with the view of obtaining a dissolution of marriage. The grounds upon which a husband can obtain a divorce from his wife are the following:—Incompatibility of temper, drunkenness,[1] theft, desertion, disobedience, lewdness, undutifulness towards himself or towards his parents, a discovery of her unchastity on the first night of marriage, and unfaithfulness.

The facility which so comprehensive a list gives to Chinese husbands for putting away their wives, is not lessened by the very simple mode of procedure through which a divorce is obtained. The husband seeking a divorce, invites his father and other male relatives and kinsmen to meet in the ancestral hall of the clan or family, for the purpose of hearing and investigating the charge, or charges, which he is prepared to prove against his wife. To each one invited, a betel nut

[1] Drunkenness probably includes opium-smoking. Thus, in 1871, a physician, named Lum Hok-hin, who resided in the Honam suburb of Canton, put away his wife upon discovering that she was an opium-smoker. She had only been married to him for a few weeks, when she was sent back by the disappointed husband to her native village.

wrapped up in green leaves is respectfully presented by the aggrieved husband. In some of the rural districts the husband convenes a meeting of this kind by beating a gong, and "crying" his invitation to his male relatives and kinsmen through the village. The proceedings in the ancestral hall begin with worship being rendered to the ancestral tablets. In the presence and in the hearing of his wife, the aggrieved husband then states his case, and supports it by all the evidence he can bring forward. When the merits of the case have been fully discussed by the relatives, they give a decision supposed to be founded on the evidence. If the charge be established, a bill of divorcement is immediately given by the petitioner to the respondent. This bill, which is not written in the dwelling-house of the petitioner, but outside, is usually signed by both the parties concerned. Each signature consists of an impression made in ink by the tip of the forefinger of the right hand. It ought to be added that a Chinese husband cannot put away his wife for any of the minor offences which make divorce possible, should he be in mourning for a parent at the time when the offence was committed.

But what, it may be asked, becomes of the wives who have been divorced? A first wife when divorced is, as a rule, permitted to return to the home of her parents, or, in the absence of parents, to the home of a near relative. Should she, however, be so unfortunate as to have neither father, nor mother, nor near relative, she is usually sold by the husband who has divorced her to a "go-between." In this case she may, if no worse fate befall her, become the wife of another man. A second, or third wife, when divorced, generally meets with a very sad fate. If sold to a go-between, and if she be at all good-looking, she is at once re-sold to the proprietress of a public brothel, who for a female of prepossessing appearance is always prepared to give a high price. In August, 1861, I met with a very sad illustration of the melancholy fate which in this way frequently befalls a divorced wife of inferior rank. A female of prepossessing appearance, and evidently in deep distress, was being forced by a procuress and her attendants along the principal streets of Canton. I learned

TRIAL OF AN ADULTERESS IN AN ANCESTRAL HALL.

FLOGGING AN ADULTERER.

that, in consequence of a minor fault on her part, she had been divorced and sold. Sometimes, it occurs that a second or third wife, when divorced, is cruelly turned into the open streets by the person who a few minutes before called himself her husband. In such a case she is, of course, driven to have recourse to a life of beggary, or, what is infinitely worse, a life of prostitution. I have not unfrequently seen women who have been divorced from their husbands, begging in the streets of Canton. On one occasion I was induced to make some inquiries into the history of one of these women, and learned that she had been dismissed for ever from the bed and board of her husband in consequence of her violent temper. I asked a Chinese merchant to make inquiries in this case for me. Shortly afterwards the woman disappeared from the street in which it had been her custom to beg ; and I next saw her near the door of the merchant, no longer in the tattered robes of poverty, but in the fashionable dress of a Chinese lady. Probably, as her appearance was prepossessing, he had made her an inmate of his harem.

Many Chinese gentlemen, however, seek to save their divorced wives from beggary and prostitution. In such cases the woman receives a sum of money sufficiently large to supply her with all the common necessaries of existence, if not for life, at all events for many years to come. An illustration of this will be found in the following translation of a bill of divorcement which was given by a gentleman named Kwan Hang, who resided in a street of Canton called Kat-chong-fong, to a woman named Wong Aheong, who was his second wife. The bill of divorcement ran as follows :—

" My second wife, Kwan Wong-shee, having been most negligent in the discharge of all her domestic duties, and having been repeatedly warned by me of her shortcomings in this respect, and no signs of amendment on her part having been observed by me, I, Kwan Hang, having referred the case to the elders, now find that it is my painful duty in consequence of her undutifulness to put her away. She is, therefore, from this time at liberty to become the wife of another. Should she, however, after the pecuniary provision which I have made for her, resort for a livelihood either to a public brothel, or become the kept mistress of any one, it is still in my power to seize her person and have her arraigned before one of the city tribunals with a view to her being committed to prison. Further, let it be clearly understood that, should misfortunes of any kind befall this woman Wong Aheong, her parents and guardians have no claim upon me.

"In proof of which I write this bill of divorcement and place it in the hands of Wong Aheong.

"Sixteenth day of sixth month of sixth year of Toong-chee."

Desertion on the part of the wife constitutes a much more serious offence against the laws of marriage than either un-dutifulness or an ungovernable temper. A woman who deserts her husband, may not only be divorced, but may be brought before one of the tribunals of the city in which she lives, in order to undergo a punishment of one hundred blows. Were she on deserting her husband to become the wife of another, the added crime of bigamy would bring her within the reach of the law's ultimate penalty, death by strangulation. Many Chinese husbands, however, are anxious to recapture their runaway wives, not because they wish them to be punished, but because of the affection which they entertain towards them. I have occasionally seen amongst other placards on the walls of Chinese cities and towns, bills offering rewards on the part of such husbands—who are generally not of the lower ranks of life—for the capture of their runaway wives.

If a husband desert his wife in a season of distress, the wife, on the expiration of the third year of his absence, may become the wife of another. Before doing so, however, she is obliged to prove the desertion on the part of her husband three years before, to the satisfaction of the magistrate of her district. Neglect to do so, would subject her on conviction to a punishment of one hundred blows, and her marriage with a second husband would be declared null and void. Again, if, at the time she lodges her declaration of desertion with a view to a second marriage, any of the relatives of the absent husband come forward and express their readiness and ability to support her during the prolonged absence of her husband, the magistrate refuses permission for her to marry again. The absence of a husband for a period of twenty or thirty years on business of an official or commercial nature, does not disannul his marriage; and were the wife of such an one in his absence to become the wife of another, she would in the event of his return be put to death by strangulation. It may here be mentioned that, should husband and wife be mutually dissatisfied with each other, they are quite at liberty to sign a deed of separation.

Another of the offences for which a wife may be punished as well as divorced, is that of beating or striking either of her parents-in-law. Should this offence, for which as in the other instances she is tried in the ancestral hall by the husband's relatives, be proved against her, she is severely flogged through the principal streets of the town or village in, or near which is the home from which she is expelled. This punishment may appear very severe for the offence in question. But such certainly is the chastisement inflicted upon all offenders of this kind in Si-chu, Si-nam, and other rural districts in Kwang-tung. The hands of the woman are bound behind her back, and as she walks through the streets, she is preceded by a man beating a gong. At each sound of the gongs the husband from whom she has been divorced, gives her a severe blow across the shoulders with a rattan. Should the husband be absent, the corporal punishment is inflicted by a brother, or a cousin, or an uncle of the absentee. An offender of this class is, also, in some districts occasionally exposed as a gazing stock in the market-place of the town to which she belongs.

In the preceding chapter, I have already given some account of the consequences attendant on the discovery of a bride's unchastity. The most serious charge, however, upon which a Chinese husband can obtain a divorce from his wife is that of unfaithfulness. Even a suspicion of this exposes her, however innocent she may be, to much harsh treatment at his hands. I remember an instance, which occurred in 1861, of a gentleman named Foong Kām-sām, beating his wife to death on the bare suspicion that she had been unfaithful to him. This monster of cruelty resided in a street of the western suburb of Canton, named Shāt-sām-poo. It appeared from inquiries which I made on the spot, that the poor woman had gone from home for two or three hours during the evening in question, to witness a religious festival. On her return her husband accused her of unfaithfulness, and, binding her hand and foot, deliberately flogged her to death. When I entered the house on the following day, I found the almost naked corpse of the poor woman stretched on the floor. It presented a very sad spectacle, the whole body, more especially the head, face, and shoulders, being very much lacerated. The mother of the murdered lady had stationed herself outside, on the opposite quarter of the street; and, in a state of frenzy, she continued to speak to the passers-by of the brutal conduct of her son-in-law for several hours. The murderer was taken to prison, but not so much, I apprehend, in the character of a prisoner, as of one from whom the authorities were simply anxious to obtain an explanation of the circumstances attendant on the violent death of his wife. I was present at the police court when the wretch was undergoing his examination, and was not a little astonished when his discharge from further confinement was ordered by the magistrate.

Where a wife is taken by her husband in the act of adultery, the law authorizes him then and there to put the adulterer and adulteress to death. The law, however, is also very positive in directing that, if he shed blood, he must kill both of the offending parties. If, while putting one of the guilty couple to death, he were to show mercy to the other, the deed would not be distinguishable from murder, and he would be tried for this crime before the head tribunal of his native district. For should he kill the adulteress only, her nearest friends and relatives would decline to receive his bare assertion as valid evidence regarding the occasion of her death, and would demand his execution as a murderer. Were he, on the other hand, to kill the adulterer only, the relatives and friends of the latter would become his prosecutors.

A further condition is, that the husband shall receive no assistance in putting the guilty couple to death. Were he to do so, the person or persons assisting him would thereby render themselves liable to a charge of murder. There can be little doubt, however, that in nearly all such cases the event is premeditated, and friends of the husband are in ambush with the view of rendering assistance if necessary. The manner in which a tea merchant in Canton avenged himself upon his second wife and her paramour, presents a case in point. The merchant, whose name was Suen Lu, had reason to suspect that there was a *liaison* between Achaong, his second wife, a young woman of great beauty, and his adopted son, a young man called Wong ā-Wan. On one occasion, therefore, Suen Lu took leave of his family, setting forth that it was his intention to proceed on a journey to the neighbouring province of Kwang-si, of which he was a native. Before leaving, however, he entered into an arrangement with two servants—whom he could trust—that, should the *ruse* deceive the guilty couple, they should place a long stick of burning incense at the front door. The signal was given, and the aggrieved husband, rushing into the chamber, slew with his own hands, it was declared, both Achaong and her paramour. On the occasion, however, of a visit to the residence of the merchant, I was distinctly told by a member of the family that the deed of blood was not effected by Suen Lu himself, but by the two servants. Suen Lu was taken before the magistrates in order that he might give an explanation of his conduct, and receive, not a sentence of death, but, as is usual on such occasions, the present of a roll of red cloth together with 20,000 cash. At the same time a nominal punishment of twenty blows was inflicted upon him to expel the murderous spirit from his breast. During my residence at Canton, two or three cases of a similar nature came under my notice.

This summary vengeance—slaying the guilty with their "crimes broad blown"—is not confined to the southern province of Kwangtung. The *Chinese Recorder and Missionary Journal* for July 1860 records a case which occurred in that year at Tientsin. In the course of the article the following remarks are made with respect to the point we have just been discussing:—

"It is affirmed that the husband did not avenge himself unassisted. According to some, his son, aged fifteen or sixteen years, urged him, and even assisted him, to put to death the guilty persons. It is said the lad himself killed his own mother, and then told his father to cut off her head. Others believe that the husband's brothers aided him in his revenge. All agree in stating that nowadays the magistrate never thoroughly investigates the circumstances of a case of adultery and deaths, but, in order to save himself trouble, readily believes the assertions of the aggrieved husband who presents himself with two heads for his inspection.[1] Many years ago a man, who brought two heads to the magistrate's office, and affirmed them to be those of his wife and her lover, in reply to the question whether he had any one to aid him in killing and beheading the parties, frankly admitted that he did receive assistance. Thereupon the individual who he said aided him, was arrested and prosecuted. After that, the husband, in every similar case in this place, has promptly denied having any assistance. It simplifies matters very much to believe undoubtedly everything that the wronged husband affirms in regard to the killing and beheading. While every one believes that one man could not slaughter two persons there is no official recognition of such an impossibility, and the investigation of the circumstances is just as superficial as the public form, or method of procedure, will allow. The husband is regarded in law and in public sentiment as only having done his duty in putting to death the guilty. His character is above reproachful comment."

But Chinese husbands do not always resort in such cases to so vindictive a course. The aggrieved husband is frequently content to summon his servants, and keep the criminal pair prisoners in the chamber in which they have been taken until he has received payment on the part of the adulterer of a heavy fine. Should the latter not have the required sum at hand, a communication is forwarded either to his parents or guardians, or to his agents, requesting them to provide the amount in question without loss of time. If the money is not forthcoming on so short a notice, they are not unfrequently called upon to hand over the title-deeds of their own, or of the offender's property, as security for the payment of the fine imposed. The husband who exacts a fine is, I believe, expected to condone the offence of his wife, although doubtless she only

---

[1] The sword is the weapon which Chinese husbands generally use on such occasions. Among the boat population of Canton the guilty couple are sometimes, I believe, bound together and flung into the river.

remains in the family in the position of a domestic servant. If the adulterer be a poor man, the husband deprives him of his tail, and orders him to be severely flogged through the principal streets of the town or village in or near which the criminal act was committed. The offender is then banished from his native place, without even the permission to return at stated periods of the year to worship in the ancestral hall of his family, or at the tombs of his ancestors. The adulteress is sold to a "go-between," who eventually disposes of her by sale either to a slave-dealer, or a keeper of prostitutes, or, it may be, to a poor labourer who is in search of a wife. Should the husband not put her away, the adulterer cannot be compelled to leave his home and his friends. In 1870, I saw a young man, apparently not more than twenty-one years of age, and his paramour flogged through the streets of one of the suburbs of Canton in a most unmerciful manner. His arms were bound behind his back, and the upper part of his body was naked. Immediately behind him came the woman, apparently about thirty years of age. Her arms were also bound behind her back, and she was receiving quite as severe a castigation. They had been seized by the woman's husband—a playactor—and two of his friends, and handed over to the elders of the district. At a meeting of this body which took place at noon on the following day, some were of opinion that the guilty pair ought to be bound hand and foot and cast into the Canton river. But the majority resolved that they should be flogged through the principal streets of the suburb. When the flogging was over the youth, whose name was Laong-ā-Ying, was permitted to return to the house of his widowed mother. The adulteress was sold by her husband for the sum of one hundred dollars to the proprietor of a public brothel. I visited the youth on the day following that on which he was flogged, and I was shocked when I saw how fearfully lacerated his back and shoulders were.

It may be remarked here that the punishment of an adulterer by beating him severely with rods, which has always been practised by the Chinese, was, it would appear from Diod. Sic. I. 89, 90, also usual with Egyptians; while, in

Rome under Justinian, adulteresses, as in some instances in the present day in China, were scourged.

Before passing from the subject of this chapter, which I do with a sense of relief, I must not omit to add that the crime of adultery is regarded by the Chinese as more heinous when it is committed between persons who bear the same surname.

CHAPTER IX.

PARENTS AND CHILDREN.

THE birth of a child, like every other important social event in China, sets a long train of observances in motion. So soon as the midwife's care begins—for the Chinese consider that the obstetric art ought only to be practised by females[1]—some of the members of the family engage in the worship of Kum-Fa. In cases of severe labour, a Taouist priest is called in, who repeats certain prayers, and traces a mystic character with a new pen upon a piece of yellow paper. The scroll is burned, and the ashes of it are given to the patient in a cup of water. So soon as the child is born, the exact hour is noted, to enable the fortune-teller to cast its horoscope. The midwife puts the umbilical cord[2] into an urn containing charcoal ashes, which is carefully sealed and kept. At the end of ten years, it is usually thrown away; but in some cases it is kept during the lifetime, and interred with the remains. Parents believe that if they were to commit any portion of the body to the ground, the interment of the child would soon follow. Should the child die shortly after birth, it is customary to expose the urn on a neighbouring hill, or in a cemetery. I have occasionally stumbled upon such urns in my walks near Canton.

[1] There are a few *accoucheurs* in China, men who have resorted to this means of livelihood in their old age ; but, as a rule, midwives are employed.

[2] Sometimes the umbilical cord is baked, and given in the form of a powder to the infant as an antidote against small-pox. Several years ago a physician in Szechuen wrote a treatise recommending its use in this way.

The child is at once washed with water, in which a herb called by the Chinese Kum-Ngan-Fa, or the gold and silver flower plant, the rind of green ginger, and the leaves of the whampu and pomeloe trees have been boiled. A custom like this is referred to in the book of Ezekiel (xvi. 4). The child is then wrapped in swaddling clothes, also an ancient Jewish custom. These are simply bands that closely confine the limbs. On the third day the infant is again washed in aromatic water. On this occasion the near relatives are invited to attend, and when "baby" has been washed they sit down to a repast, the especial feature of which is pork-patties, and balls of flour with sugar in the centre. The food of the patient consists chiefly of fowls, fine rice, and ginger-wine. Duck's eggs also form an item of her diet. These are also given, together with jars of ginger-wine, as birth-gifts to her relatives and friends. On her recovery the lady receives in return presents of silk embroidered work.

Amongst the upper classes, it is not usual for the husband to have an interview with his wife until a month after the birth of the child; and no visitor can be received at the house during this time. A large bunch of evergreens is suspended above the principal entrance of the house to intimate this; and visitors upon seeing it do not stop even to leave their cards. All persons residing in the house are regarded as unclean until the month has expired. The same rule applies to persons entering the house during the period in question. The members of such a family are, of course, not allowed to enter any of the public temples. At the close of the month, the mother washes her body, as a rite of purification, with water in which leaves of the pomeloe tree have been boiled. The father having worshipped the tablets of his ancestors, repairs, together with one of his wife's handmaidens, to a temple—the Temple of Longevity is frequently selected—with the view of thanking the gods for having given him a son. Until one hundred days have expired, the mother is required to remain at home. This custom reminds one of the Hebrew mother, who, by the law of Moses, was required to stay at home for about forty days after the birth of a male child, and about seventy days after the birth of a female child.[1] With the Chinese, as was the case among the Hebrews, the ground of the restriction lies in the mother being regarded as unclean. At the close of this period, she repairs with her child to a temple. Very often the temple is one in honour of Kum-Fa, and the child is dedicated to the goddess. If the mother has previously prayed for offspring to Koon-Yam, or to Tien-How, she repairs, of course, to the temple where her prayers were offered. When the child is one month old, he receives an infantile name. His head is then shaved for the first time, and the ceremony, which is called Mun-Yut is, in the case of wealthy families, attended with much rejoicing. All the male and female members of the family are present in their holiday robes, and the infant makes his appearance in a dress of a bright red colour. The barber who operates is generally an old man, the Chinese regarding it as auspicious that he should have reached a patriarchal age. He is dressed specially for the occasion, and receives more than his usual fee. In many cases, however, the mother or grandmother of the child prefer to do the shaving themselves. The hair is wrapped up in paper, and carefully preserved. When the barber has done his work, an aged man, hired for the office, next advances, and placing his hand on the head of the little one, exclaims, " May long life be thy portion." Those present then sit down to a liberal repast, and the little hero of the party is made to taste a very small piece of a rice flour cake presented by his grandmother. All who have bestowed gifts upon the child are invited to this banquet. Such presents consist of wearing apparel, bracelets, anklets, &c., &c. The infant receives on the occasion a red bedstead, a red chair, and a cap, on which are small golden, or silver, or copper figures of Buddha, or eight figures representing the eight angels. For the figures in question, letters representing old age or wealth, are occasionally substituted. The child is not permitted to rest on the bedstead until the father has consulted the calendar, and selected a lucky day for the purpose. A coat of many colours [2] is presented to a favourite child by its parents.

[1] See Lev. xii. 2-5.

[2] That the Jews had a similar custom is, of course, apparent from the narrative of the life of Joseph. " A garment of divers colours " was also the dress of " king's daughters that were virgins."

It is supposed to protect the infant from evil spirits, by diverting their attention from the wearer. The almanac is also consulted to ascertain what things must be kept out of the child's sight. It sometimes sets forth that it is unlucky for infants to touch or see articles made of bamboo during a certain month. Sometimes the prohibited articles are of iron or copper. Whatever the almanac proscribes is either removed or covered up.

The first visit the child pays is to its grandmother; and the day after the Mun-Yut is often selected for this. The aged dame bestows upon her little grandchild a gift consisting of four chickens, four onions, sticks of sugar-cane, two cabbages, and a quantity of rice-husks. The vegetables enumerated being very quick in attaining maturity, imply her desire for the rapid growth of the little one. The rice-husks signify her wish that the mind of her grandchild may readily receive instruction, and that education may result in scholarship. When the child is one or two years of age, or at the time when it first begins to walk, it is presented with a pair of shoes called Mow-Yee-Kai, or kitten shoes. They resemble a cat's face at the toes, and are supposed to render the child as surefooted as a cat.

The female children of Chinese parents are, in some instances, put to death. Many reasons are assigned for a practice so wicked and unnatural. Poor people plead their poverty as an excuse. They contend that it is better to put their infant daughters to death than be obliged, as is, alas, the case with many, to sell them as slaves, or for the base purposes of prostitution. Infanticide, however, is not invariably confined to the poor, as the reader will learn from what I have said in another chapter on the subject of Chinese foundling hospitals. But though it is more or less practised by the nation, some Chinese regard the crime as one of a most diabolical nature. Let us take a case to illustrate the phases of national feeling with regard to it. In the spring of the year 1872, a woman who resided in the western suburb of Canton was seen by a neighbour to drown her adopted female child in the Wong-sha creek. The neighbour informed the elders of the district of the murder, and the accused was immediately seized, and imprisoned in the back room of a neighbouring temple. On the

A CHILD'S FIRST VISIT TO ITS GODMOTHER.

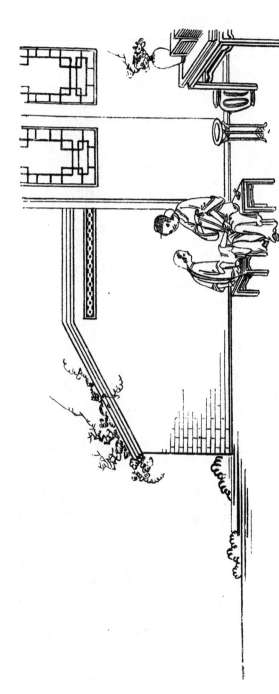

BANDAGING THE FEET.

following day she was arraigned before the elders, and excused herself on the ground that the child was sickly. On the entreaties of her husband, who, in the most importunate manner, begged for her pardon, they liberated the murderess, for by no other name can she be designated. The elders were thus lenient, although a governor-general, who some twenty years before had ruled over the united provinces of Kwangtung and Kwangsi, had issued an edict declaring that all mothers found guilty of a crime so unnatural and so diabolical as infanticide, would be severely punished. In 1848, the chief-justice or criminal judge of Kwang-tung issued an edict, in which he condemned it in very strong terms. In this edict the attention of the people was directed to the teaching of Nature, with the view of reproaching them for such acts of barbarity. "You should," he said, "consider that insects, fish, birds, and beasts, all love what they produce. On leaving the womb they are as weak as a hair, and can you endure instantly to compass your offspring's death?"

The custom of compressing the feet of female children is much practised. Many reasons have been given for the observance of this foolish custom. Some regard it as originating in a desire to mark the characteristic which eminently distinguishes the Chinese from the Tartars and Hakkas. The latter from the earliest times have been nomadic. The Chinese have always been children of the soil—naturally *adscripti glebæ*. In the northern provinces I noticed that nearly all the women had contracted feet; and the same may be said of the island of Formosa. In some other portions of the empire the custom does not prevail to the same extent. The process of binding the feet, generally done with bandages of cloth, is commenced when the child is five or six years old. It is at first very painful, and the child cries bitterly for days. In some instances the feet are compressed to such an extent as to render walking almost impossible. It is not unusual to see women with small feet riding along the high roads on the backs of their female attendants. When houses are on fire, the female inmates who have small feet often perish from sheer helplessness.

There is apparently no law to restrict parents in the exercise of authority over their children. They can even sell them; and in some cases sons are taken as bondsmen by creditors, for debts which have been contracted by their fathers. Sometimes, with the view of relieving their parents from pecuniary embarrassments, children voluntarily sell themselves as bondsmen or slaves. The similarity which exists· in this respect between the ancient Jews and the Chinese of to-day is very striking. Amongst the Jews children were often taken as bondsmen for debts contracted by their parents (2 Kings iv. 1, Isaiah l. 1, Neh. v. 5); and a father had unlimited power over his children, even when they had attained manhood (Gen. xxi. 21, Exod. xxi. 9, 10, 11, Judges xiv. 2). The power of a Chinese father over his daughter is still greater than that which he can exercise over his sons; and here again the history of the Jews furnishes us with a parallel. A Jewish father could set aside a sacred vow made by his daughter, whereas he had no power to do so in the case of a son (Numbers xxx. 4). Chinese parents are evidently great believers in the maxim that to spare the rod is to spoil the child. Thus, though they may sometimes be seen showing much love towards their children, at other times they may be observed chastising them very severely. I have frequently seen Chinese mothers beating their children with great severity. Should a child die under chastisement, the parents are not called upon to answer for their conduct before any tribunal. Among the boat population on the Canton river, I have seen mothers when very angry with their children, deliberately throw them into the river, and when the children on rising to the surface clung to the sides of the boats, sometimes the infuriated mothers pushed them off into the current again. I once witnessed a very alarming scene of this nature. A youth belonging to a ferry boat which plied on the Canton river, had gone ashore to gamble at a fruit-stall, and lost more than he could afford to pay. The keeper of the fruit-stall threatened to settle the matter by taking a portion of his wearing apparel. The youth strongly objected to this, and requested that his parents might be sent for. When his mother came she paid the debt, but dragged the offender on board her boat, and then immediately cast him headlong into the stream. The youth when he rose to the surface of the water clung to the sides of the boat, and most earnestly begged for mercy. The enraged mother, paying no heed to his entreaties, again and again pushed him back, till at last I felt compelled to interfere, lest the lad should perish. There were several other boats near at the time, and their crews evidently thought that the offender was only getting what he deserved. Amongst the lower orders, chastisement is sometimes inflicted upon adults. Parents punish their sons long after they have reached manhood, and aged mothers beat married daughters of thirty years of age and upwards. I remember seeing in Hang-chow a mother of sixty beating her son, a man who had reached the age of thirty. The young man, I learned, was a drunkard, and in order to gratify his love of drink, was in the habit of pilfering the earnings of his mother, who owned a large silk-weaving factory. On the occasion in question, he was returning from a carousal, and when the old lady saw him, she uttered a loud shriek, and rushed upon him with the fury of a tiger. Seizing him by the queue with one hand, she belaboured him most unmercifully with the other. A crowd instantly thronged the entrance-door of the house, but no one interfered. The erring son received his castigation with meek submission.

The Chinese regard the infliction of punishment on children, when it is called for, as an important duty on the part of parents. One may sometimes find in the residence of a Chinese gentleman one of his sons walking with fetters on his ankles. Such a punishment is inflicted for gambling, or other vicious propensities. I saw a youth so shackled in a house in Canton. Though evidently a source of much trouble and anxiety to his parents, he did not appear at all ashamed of himself. Besides such punishments, the offending youth is sometimes not allowed to receive the customary present of pork which is annually given to each member of a Chinese clan or family on his return from worshipping at the tombs of his ancestors. These presents are bought by funds arising from the ancestral altars, and they are regarded as the gifts of the ancestors. To be deprived of them is, therefore, considered a most grievous punishment. Sometimes a son who is a source of much trouble to his parents is expelled from his home. I was acquainted with a family which consisted of the parents and two sons. The

elder son, who was a source of great grief to his parents, was
driven by them from his home, and I saw this youth, who was
only fourteen years old, asking alms in the streets of Canton.
He ran away on first seeing me. I saw him twice afterwards
begging in the same street. The parents assured me that they
had been obliged to drive him away in consequence of his
vicious habits. Eventually they received him back on his promising to amend his ways. Again, a military officer who resided
in Canton, and with whose friends I was acquainted, had an
adopted son, whom he turned adrift on account of the lad's
gambling propensities. The youth used to pawn the clothes off
his back, and steal any articles of value within his reach. He
also was received back on condition of amendment, but at once
took to his evil ways again. The father then ordered him to be
bound, and in order to make him remember how much pain and
sorrow others had suffered from his conduct, inflicted a severe
sabre cut on his thigh. The wound was besmeared with salt,
and the lad was once more driven from what might have been a
happy home. He eventually became a Buddhist monk. Sometimes parents cast their disobedient children into a public prison.
Prisoners of this class are commonly bound by chains to large
stones, and exposed daily, together with other offenders, at the
principal gates of the prison. In the prison of the Pun-yu
magistrate at Canton, I found a young gentleman incarcerated
for having, in a state of intoxication, threatened to stab his
uncle, who stood to him *in loco parentis*, his parents being dead.
When I first saw him in prison, the youth was dressed in silk
robes. Before he had been many months in prison, he became
as filthy and repulsive in appearance as his fellow-prisoners. I
frequently visited him, and he earnestly begged me to intercede
for him with his aunt, who, he assured me, was the only person
who would take pity on him. I was requested to pay no attention to his entreaties. I saw him again on board the British
barque *Red Riding Hood* (then at Canton) when I was preaching
to her European crew. I was in the act of going over the side
of the ship, when in a Chinese who, dressed as an ordinary
coolie, came forward in a most graceful manner and saluted me,
I recognized the unfortunate youth. He informed me that his

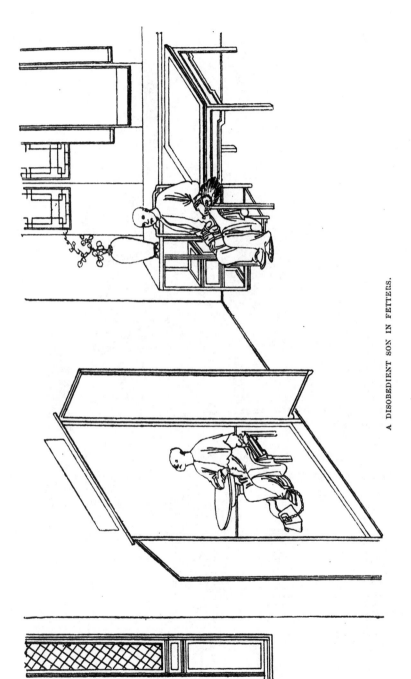

A DISOBEDIENT SON IN FETTERS.

A SON BEING PUT INTO A CANGUE BY HIS FATHER.

aunt had removed him from prison, on his promising to go as a coolie to the British West Indies. A somewhat similar case was that of a very respectable tradesman of the western suburb of Canton, who cast his second son into the prison of the Namhoi magistrate, where the wayward young man lay in chains for four months. On the intercession of his mother, he was released only to be sent, however, to the neighbouring kingdom of Cochin China.

Over such sons Chinese mothers, as do Christian mothers, weep, and daily intercede for their pardon. I remember the case of a mother who had such a son to deplore. His father, a very wealthy gentleman, had put him in prison because he gambled, smoked opium, and was of a quarrelsome disposition. The mother was very urgent in her intercession with her husband, and spent days and nights in grief for her son. She used to pray for him to the spirits of her ancestors, and at the close of each day she suspended above her door a lighted lantern or lamp, thinking thereby to hasten the prisoner's return. The punishments inflicted upon sons or daughters who beat their parents are in some instances of a far more severe nature than any I have as yet recorded. In a case of which I read, where a son, aided by his wife, had beaten his mother, both offenders were decapitated.[1] The mother of the son's wife was, at the same time, severely flogged, and then sent into exile. The students of the district in which the crime occurred were not allowed, during a period of three years, to attend the literary examinations. The magistrates were, one and all, deprived of their offices and banished; and the house in which the offender lived was razed to the ground. This is said to have taken place during the reign of Ka-hing. Since then an offence of this kind has been visited with a punishment of almost incredible severity. In 1865, a man named Chaong An-ching, aided by his wife Chaong Wong-shee, flogged his mother. Upon the circumstances being made known to Tung-chee, in whose reign the crime was perpetrated, an imperial order was issued, to the effect that the offenders

---

[1] This reminds one of the Mosaic law, which decreed that children convicted of cursing or assaulting their parents should be put to death. (Exod. xxi. 15, 17; Lev. xx. 9.)

should be flayed alive, that their bodies should then be cast into a furnace, and their bones, gathered from the ashes and reduced to a powder, should be scattered to the winds. The order further directed that the head of the clan to which the two offenders belonged, should be put to death by strangulation; that the neighbours living on the right and left of the offenders should, for their silence and non-interference, each receive a flogging of eighty blows, and be sent into exile; that the head or representative of the graduates of the first degree (or B.A.), among whom the male offender ranked, should receive a flogging of eighty blows and be exiled to a place one thousand li distant from his home; that the granduncle of the male offender should be beheaded; that his uncle and his two elder brothers should be put to death by strangulation; that the prefect and the ruler of the district in which the offenders resided, should for a time be deprived of their rank; that on the face of the mother of the female offender four Chinese characters expressive of neglect of duty towards her daughter should be tattooed, and that she should be exiled to a province, the seventh in point of distance from that in which she was born; that the father of the female offender, a bachelor of arts, should not be allowed to take any higher literary degrees, that he should receive a flogging of eighty blows, and be exiled to a place three thousand li from that in which he was born; that the mother of the male offender should be made to witness the flaying of her son, but be allowed to receive daily for her sustenance a measure of rice from the provincial treasurer; that the son of the offenders (a child) should be placed under the care of the district ruler, and receive another name; and, lastly, that the lands of the offender should for a time remain fallow. An account of this event was published by the provincial treasurer of Hupeh—the province in which the crime was committed—and ordered to be circulated throughout the empire.

Parricide is regarded as one of the most heinous offences of which a man can be found guilty, and is punished by a lingering death. Indeed, so great is the abhorrence in which this crime is held, that there is a law which expressly declares that not only shall the offender be subjected to a lingering death, but that the schoolmaster who instructed him in his youth shall be decapitated, and that the bones of his grandfathers shall be exhumed and scattered to the winds. It is also customary to close the ancestral hall of the clan to which the parricide belongs, that the spirits of his ancestors may be deprived of the homage of their posterity. The crime of parricide, however, is one of very rare occurrence in China. If the Chinese can lay claim to any virtue more than another, it is that of filial piety.

When parents die, the eldest son stands *in loco parentis* to his younger brothers, and much respect is paid to him by them. He rebukes them when they are wayward, and encourages them in well-doing. In a case in which a younger brother had struck his elder brother's wife, it was decided by the elders of the village to which the parties belonged, that the elder brother should be permitted to flog the younger brother. This was done before them, and to make the punishment more degrading, the implement used was a broomstick. The Chinese say that a person who has been flogged with a broomstick will be for ever unlucky.

In concluding this chapter, I may observe that it has always appeared to me that the children of Chinese in the upper walks of life are not, as a rule, robust. This circumstance is, I suppose, to be attributed in a great measure to the practice of polygamy ; for among the lower orders of society, whom poverty compels to be monogamists, the children are vigorous and active.

CHAPTER X.

SERVANTS AND SLAVES.

IN all Chinese families of respectability—to use the word in a limited sense—there is a numerous array of domestic servants. The male servants in the family of an ordinary Chinese gentleman, include, as a rule, a porter, two or three waiting men or footmen, three or four sedan bearers, and others who are engaged in keeping the house in a state of general neatness and cleanliness. They are sometimes hired from month to month, and, in other instances, for a period of six months at wages ranging from three to four or five dollars a man per month. Board and lodging are of course included in the arrangement. In some cases, masters add to this clothing, and a sum of money for the purchase of tobacco and other minor " creature comforts." Testimonials as to past good conduct and general ability are, of course, required from such servants seeking an engagement. Cooks, and waiting servants in families of a lower grade in society, hire themselves for a period of twelve months at least, as do also agricultural labourers. For these servants there are what in England are termed statute hirings, which are held by the appointment of the local authorities in squares or other suitable places. At Canton the statute hirings take place from the first to the fifteenth day of the first month of the year, and are held in the quadrangle before the temple of Longevity The square is on such occasions densely crowded with both masters and servants, and is enlivened by peep-shows and exhibitions of various kinds on a small scale. On one side may be found a cage which is concealed from view by an inclosure of matting, and contains a tiger or a panther. At another point a large basket containing a fretful porcupine, or a pig with six legs, or a duck with four feet attracts the curious ; there are also soup, meat, tea, cake, and fruit stalls at which the hungry and faint are invited to regale themselves at the trifling expense of a few *cash*. There are always plenty of gambling booths at such gatherings, and many of the servants lose portions, if not the whole, of their small and hard-earned wages for the past year.

It may be mentioned here that hiring in the open street is a matter of daily occurrence in Canton and in other large cities in Kwang-tung. In the Gow-chow-ka street of the Honam suburb of Canton, a large concourse of day labourers assemble every morning at five o'clock for the purpose of being hired. They remain in the street if unhired until noon is far advanced. In the courtyards of the temples, also, it is not unusual to see men standing idle at all hours of the day, because "no man hath hired them." In the Tai-ping-Kai, or Ta-tung-Kai street of the same suburb, journeymen carpenters and bricklayers may be seen waiting to be hired from five o'clock till nine A.M. The carpenters form a line on one side of the street, the bricklayers on the other. They are as a rule hired by public contractors. The wages which they receive are very small, being not more than a quarter of a dollar and three meals *per diem* to each man. The workmen, also, stipulate that at the time of the new, and again at the full moon, and also on the ninth and twenty-third days of each lunar month, extra food, or its equivalent in money shall be given to them.

To return to the position of domestic servants in China. In the families of Chinese gentlemen, female servants generally, and male servants in some instances, are the property of their masters by purchase. In the houses of wealthy citizens, it is not unusual to find from twenty to thirty slaves attending upon a family. Even citizens in the humbler walks of life deem it necessary to have each a slave or two. The price of a slave varies, of course, according to age, health, strength, and general personal appearance. The average price is from fifty to one hundred dollars, but in time of war, or revolution, poor parents, on the verge of starvation, offer their sons and daughters for sale at remarkably low prices. I remember instances of parents, rendered destitute by the marauding bands who infested the two southern *Kwangs* in 1854-55, offering to sell their daughters in Canton for five dollars apiece. The ranks of slaves are also recruited from the families of gamblers, whose losses not unfrequently compel them to sell their children. Amongst the many Chinese friends and acquaintances I made during my residence at Canton, one, an old man named Lum Chi-kee, was what may be termed a slave-broker; and I remember two bright-looking youths being sold to him by their profligate father, who had gambled his means away. The eldest lad fetched fifty dollars, and the younger forty. The old slave-broker offered one of the youths to me at the advanced price of 350 dollars. The usual price of an ordinary able-bodied male slave is about 100 dollars. Persons when sold as slaves generally fall first of all into the hands of brokers or go-betweens. Such characters are either aged men or women. Before buying slaves, a dealer keeps them for a month on trial. Should he discover that they talk in their sleep, or afford any indications of a weakness of system, he either offers a small sum for them, or declines to complete the purchase. This precaution is necessary, as in re-selling a slave the broker is often required to give a warranty of sound-ness. A slave is carefully examined by an intending purchaser especially as to any signs of leprosy, a disease which prevails amongst the Chinese, and of which they naturally have a great horror. The broker is made to take the slave into a dark room, and a blue light is burned. Should the face of the slave assume a greenish hue in this light, a favourable opinion is entertained. Should it show a reddish colour it is concluded that the blood is tainted by this loathsome disease.

The slavery to which these unfortunate persons are subject, is perpetual and hereditary, and they have no parental authority over their offspring. The great-grandsons of slaves, however, can, if they have sufficient means, purchase their freedom. Slaves are designated as "noo" and "pee," the former being applied to male, and the latter to female slaves. These terms clearly indicate, if I mistake not, that those to whom they are applied are members of the families of their respective masters. Formerly slaves assumed the surname of their masters ; but the custom is now obsolete. Slaves although regarded as members of the family, are not recognised as members of the general community. They cannot, for example, sue in courts of laws. In short, they are outside the pale of citizenship, and within the reach of the avarice, or hatred, or lust of their masters. Masters can sell female slaves either to other gentlemen as concubines or to the proprietors of brothels as public prostitutes ; or they can, I apprehend, use them for the gratification of their own lusts. Occasionally a master marries one of his slaves. Should he do so, he must give notice of the event to his friends and neighbours, who come to the wedding to make merry. The marriage is not proposed to the slave by her master, but by his wife, her mistress. Indeed it is not unusual for a barren spouse, if she have an amiable and good-looking slave, to suggest to her husband that he should take the girl as a second wife. This custom reminds one of the familiar episode in Scripture history, in which Sarah, finding herself growing old, induced her lord to marry her bondmaid, Hagar, in the hope that the Divine promise of offspring, which was apparently void, so far as she herself was concerned, might not fail of fulfilment. Such marriages take place also on other grounds. Thus a lady named Tung Lou-shee, who resided in the western suburb of Canton, proposed that her husband should marry a young and prepossessing slave, although she herself had borne several children to him. She did so on the ground of her own growing infirmities, and stipulated that the husband and his youthful bride should reside in a neighbouring house. The husband accordingly took the slave as a second wife.

Masters seem to have the same uncontrolled power over their slaves that parents have over their children. Thus a master is not called to account for the death of a slave, although it is the result of punishment inflicted by him. In 1853, I saw in the Shap-sam-poo street, of the western suburb of Canton, the corpse of a female slave who had been beaten to death by her mistress. When the slave was supposed to be in *articulo mortis*, her mistress had given orders to have her removed to the Beggar's

Square, as foreigners call it, which is in front of the Mee-chow temple, in order that she might die there. The policemen, wishing to extort money from this monster of cruelty, ordered the dying slave to be taken back and placed at the doorstep of the house. Finding that her house was daily attracting crowds of inquisitive onlookers, the mistress gave the policemen the sum they demanded, and the corpse—for the girl died within a few minutes after she had been placed at the door—was removed for interment to an adjoining cemetery. Again, in 1869, a gentleman of the family Ho, who resided in the Honam suburb of Canton, upon convicting his slave, a little boy of the tender age of fourteen, of a theft, immediately bound the little fellow hand and foot, and cast him headlong into the Canton river. The agonizing shrieks of the lad attracted the attention of the officer in command of one of H.M.'s gunboats, which was at anchor in the river in question. He fortunately suc-ceeded in saving the lad, who was eventually forwarded to the allied commissioners—the city being at the time in the occupation of the allied armies of Great Britain and France. Orders were at once issued for the apprehension of Ho, and the prisoner was handed over to the Chinese authorities, who treated the matter with perfect indifference. They were disposed to let him go free, on the ground that he had violated no law. At the command of the allied commissioners, however, he was detained in the prison of the Namhoi magistrate. I saw this man several times in the prison, where, of course, he was obliged to associate with criminals of the very worst kind. In a case which is reported in the British Consular Trade Reports for 1869-70, an old woman who had been guilty of almost in-credible cruelty to a young girl, one of the inmates of her brothel, pleaded that she could do what she liked with her slave. Vice-Consul Forrest, who reports the case, insisted upon pun-ishment being inflicted, and the accused had her ears pierced with arrows, and was carried through the streets accompanied by a crier to proclaim her enormities. She was flogged at in-tervals, and eventually died from the torture. This woman, if she can be called a woman, had ploughed away the elbow and knee-joints of the girl with a pair of Chinese scissors, because she had refused to receive the advances of a Chinese coolie. Other portions of her body had been similarly treated and the girl died almost immediately after leaving the court. The police had much trouble in preventing the neighbours from lynching the woman.

The work which devolves upon female slaves in China is that of attending upon the ladies of the household. They make excellent ladies'-maids, and in that capacity require to be adepts in the art of hairdressing and applying cosmetics. Not unfrequently, also, a female slave is employed to carry her mistress on her back, when a lady is possessed of very small feet; and it is surprising to find in country districts what distances female slaves will carry their small-footed mistresses, at a jog-trot. As nursemaids they are, as a rule, very careful of their charges, and show great affection for them.

Although masters hold their slaves so entirely at their disposal, and sometimes lamentably abuse their power, I believe that in all respectable Chinese families slaves are treated with great consideration. I cannot, however, say the same with respect to female slaves who reside as maids-of-all-work in the houses of persons who are not in what are termed easy circumstances. The slaves of such families not unfrequently run away, in consequence of harsh treatment and hard work. Of the truth of this statement I have evidence in the shape of a collection which I made of Chinese placards. In the absence of public newspapers these are the great medium for the communication of general information. Such as are notices of the desertion of slaves contain a full and particular description of the general appearance of the runaways, and state the rewards to be paid on their recapture. In one of them the advertiser, in describing the features of his fugitive slave, observes that her face is very similar to that of a cat. I have frequently heard bellmen in the streets of large Chinese cities describing in general terms the personal appearances of certain runaway slaves, and offering, at the same time, sums of money for their recapture. I ought, however, to explain that a bellman in China does not use a bell, but a gong. This is suspended from a pole carried between himself and an assistant. Attached to the gong is a small paper banner upon which the particulars of the case are written in very legible characters.

When female slaves run away it is not unusual for their mistresses to attach a garment belonging to the fugitive to a hand mill-stone, which they then turn round, mentioning at the same time in an audible tone of voice the name of the runaway. Should this ridiculous ceremony prove ineffectual, mistresses resort to the temple of Sin-Foong or leader of the army. The votary asks his help, and ties to the leg of the idol's horse, a piece of string to bind the slave with.

As might be expected, slavery gives rise to a great deal of kidnapping. Female children, in particular, are seized and taken to a distance from their homes in order that, when they have grown up, they may be sold as slaves, or, in some instances, to the proprietors of brothels. Kidnappers of children are severely dealt with. Women taking female children are sometimes flogged through the streets. Boys as well as girls are kidnapped and sold as slaves in the north of China. Men convicted of kidnapping boys are, in certain cases which I need not specify, punished with death. The chief of the band is decapitated, the second put to death by strangulation, and the others, who are regarded as guilty in a lesser degree, are transported for life. In the northern provinces, and especially at Tientsin, which seems to be the very Sodom of the empire, the stringent laws which are enacted with regard to the nefarious purposes for which they are kidnapped are evidently of no great force.

In the royal palace at Pekin eunuchs are regularly employed. Their duties are connected with the imperial zenana. The head eunuch, who is appointed by the emperor, and who is generally an aged man, and one in whom much confidence may be placed, is designated as the Tsong-Koon, or superintendent of the seraglio. It is the privilege of this functionary to receive all necessary commands from the empress in person. He stands, to all intents and purposes, in the same position to the Chinese empress as that in which we learn from the book that bears her name Hatach stood to Queen Esther; while the other eunuchs, of whom there are a great many, occupy a subordinate position corresponndig to that held by the chamberlains alluded

OPIUM-SMOKERS.

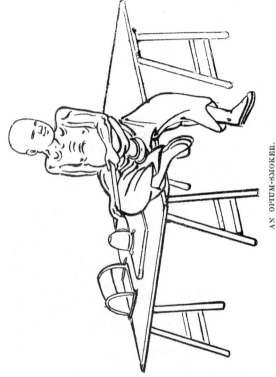

AN OPIUM-SMOKER.

to in the same book (iv. 4).   When the emperor resorts to the
temples to worship, his eunuchs are in attendance, and assist
him in kneeling before the altars.

The privilege of entering the imperial harem affords these
functionaries opportunities of conferring with the sovereign, and
by ingratiating themselves into his good graces they sometimes
rise to positions of eminence.   In the year 1868, one of this
miserable class came in this way to exercise a very mischievous
ascendency.[1] Like better men before him, however, he suddenly
fell, and at last died at the hands of the common executioner.

In all Chinese families of "the upper ten thousand," an inti-
macy exists between masters and men-servants on the one hand,
and mistresses and female servants on the other.   Servants not
unfrequently make suggestions in reference to the well-being of
the family, and in many instances, domestic matters of a grave
nature are discussed before them.   My first experience in this
respect surprised me.   On the occasion of one of many visits
which I paid to the district city of Fa-yune, the principal
magistrate of the place having been informed that one of my
companions was an English physician, invited us to call at his
residence, stating that he was anxious to consult the foreign
medical practitioner with regard to the health of his son-in-law.
On going to his house we were at once conducted to the visitors'
hall, where he invited us to sit down and partake of his hospitality.   We had scarcely taken our seats, when the son-in-law, an
emaciated looking man of twenty-six years of age, came in, and—
to our astonishment—apparently all the servants of the family.
I concluded that they had come to see the foreign visitors.
But when the chief magistrate proceeded to call the attention of
our companion to the state of his son-in-law's health,—the young
man was an opium-smoker—grave suggestions were, at frequent
intervals, made by many of the principal servants and slaves.
Further experience taught me that such scenes in Chinese families are by no means uncommon.   Such freedom of intercourse

[1] That eunuchs held posts of honour and distinction under Hebrew sovereigns
is clear from the following passages of Holy Writ :—1 Kings xxii. 9 ; 2 Kings
viii. 6 ; 2 Kings ix. 32, 33 ; 2 Kings xx. 18 ; 2 Kings xxiii. 11 ; Jer. xxxviii. 7 ;
Jer. xxxix. 16 ; and Jer. xli. 16.

between masters and servants has always been characteristic of
Oriental life. When King David, on hearing of the death of his
child, ceased to fast and weep, his servants were ready with the
question, "What thing is this thou hast done?" The little
Israelitish captive not only suggested to her Syrian mistress that
Naaman should ask "the prophet that is in Samaria" to cure
him of his leprosy, but when he despised the instructions he
received from the prophet, she expostulated with the distinguished general. Ulysses when he returned after an absence
of several years to his home was kissed by all his slaves.

Slavery may be said to exist in a limited form in China if we
compare it with what was once practised in the British West
Indies and the United States; but it cannot be too soon numbered among the abuses of the past. No one can dwell in a
country in which slavery, even in a mild form, is practised, without discovering its degrading and debasing effects upon the mind.
Homer did not put it too strongly when he said that a slave is
only half a man.

CHAPTER XI.

FESTIVALS.

PUBLIC festivals in China are as a rule in honour of the deities, and the occasions of this kind, as well as others of a private nature, which are observed as holidays, are so numerous that, although the Chinese have no Sabbath, or weekly day of rest, I am disposed to think few nations, if any, have more days of recreation in the course of the year. It opens with the San-Lin, or New Year's festival, the Bacchanalia of the Chinese. As the Chinese year commences from the new moon nearest to 15° of Aquarius, into which sign the sun passes in the month of January, the festival takes place towards the end of this month. It usually extends over a period of from one to three weeks, and may be regarded as commencing several days before the close of the Old Year. During these days everybody who can devotes himself to pleasure, and the mandarins only attend to business of a very pressing character. With others it is a time of bustle and excitement, which increases as the last day of the year approaches. " Merchants and shopmen hurry to and fro closing accounts and collecting debts; and wretched is thought the plight of the man who cannot close his annual term with a satisfactory balance on the favourable side. The retail houses overflow with customers, as it is an object with sellers to clear off their goods as quickly as possible, and with purchasers to supply their wants at an unusually moderate rate. The quantity of money that circulates in consequence as the year wanes must be enormous, and in many cases shops

are kept open until late on the closing day, and the occupants
may be observed in a feverish state of excitement receiving
money and taking rapid account of their transactions, fearful
lest the new year should dawn upon them ere their books are
properly balanced." In private houses, servants devote themselves to " cleaning." When the floors have been washed, they
are covered with carpets. Old scrolls and charms are taken
down to be replaced by fresh ones. The tables, and the antique
wooden chairs which one finds in a Chinese house, are covered
with red cloth embroidered with flowers. The ancestral hall is
decorated with flags and flowers. On the last day of the year,
strips of red paper,[1] with characters implying good fortune,
wealth, happiness, and so on, are posted on each side of the
outer doors of the house; and on the doors themselves are hung
large pictures of two Chinese generals, who, it seems, were of
signal service to an Emperor who reigned more than three
thousand years ago. This Emperor could not sleep, because he
had dreamt that evil spirits entered the palace in the night, and
his minister's protestations to the contrary failed to reassure
him. He ordered these generals to keep watch at the gates
during the " witching " hours, and his slumbers were once more
undisturbed. They are now regarded, accordingly, as the gods
of the portals, and their portraits are always placed on the doors
at the New Year. Poor people who are unable to purchase the
portraits fix placards with the names of the generals to the
doors.

A few days before the New Year, generally on the 28th or
29th of the twelfth month, what is called the Tuen-Nin, or
Wa-shun, takes place. This ceremony, which is observed by
all classes of society, consists in giving thanks to the tutelary
deity of the house for his preservation of the dwelling and its
inmates during the year. At the close of worship, a dinner is
given at which all the inmates are present. In wealthy families,
this banquet is on a larger scale, beginning on the 27th and

---

[1] The scrolls are written by calligraphists, generally decayed or unsuccessful
scholars, who, at this season especially, are to be found seated at their little
tables, in the courtyards of temples, public squares, tea-gardens, and by the
roadside. A family in which a death has occurred within the year uses strips of
blue paper with inscriptions expressive of mourning.

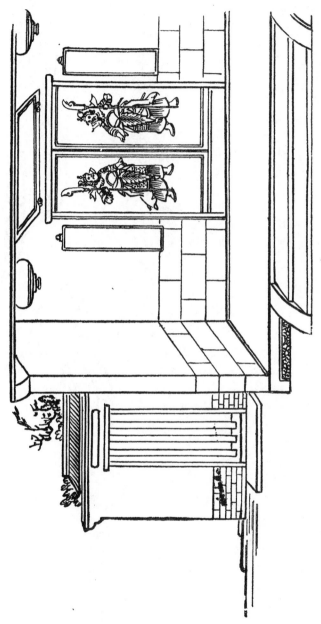

DOORS OF A CHINESE GENTLEMAN'S HOUSE.

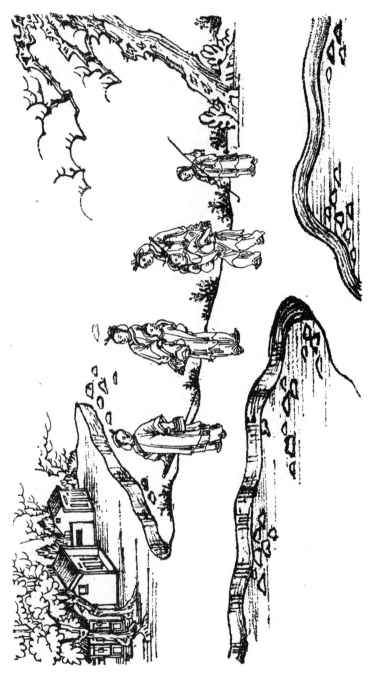

LADIES BEING CARRIED BY THEIR SLAVES.

extending to the last night of the year. On that night, from six until nine o'clock, boys from eight to thirteen or fourteen years of age, traverse the streets calling out "Mi-sow," or, I sell my folly, or I sell my lazy habits to another, in order that next year I may be wiser. This custom is very common in Canton, in the provinces of Hoonam and Hoopeh. From eight o'clock until nine, respectable people observe a superstition called Keng-Ting, which means learning by the mirror. The person seeking a sign, places a sieve upon an empty stove, and upon the sieve a basin of water and a looking-glass. He then silently steals out, and listens attentively to what the first passers-by are saying. Should the words be of good import, he concludes that good success awaits him throughout the coming year Amongst the lower orders, the superstition is known as Chong-Kwa-Tow, to meet the fortunate head.

Throughout the course of the last day of the year, the members of a family frequently prostrate themselves before the ancestral altars of the house, and the night is specially devoted to religious observances. Lamps are placed in front of the altars, and the servants replenish them with oil, that they may be found burning on the dawn of the first day of the year. At night, the male members of the family proceed to one or more of the temples in the neighbourhood to worship the gods. The elders also are present attired in their rich robes of silk, and at midnight they worship on behalf of the people. The temples are well lighted, and as each votary pours out his libation and presents his prayers and offerings of food and paper money, three or four minstrels stationed at the door discourse strains of discordant music. These offerings are attended with a salvo of fire-crackers, the temples are filled with smoke, and the smell of gunpowder renders it difficult for one to continue a spectator of the proceedings.

On stepping into the streets, however, the visitor finds the same stifling odour, as people after worshipping their *Lares* and *Penates,* or household gods, rush to the doors of their houses, and discharge fire-crackers to terrify evil spirits. On such occasions, the inhabitants of a large city like Canton seem to vie with one another as to which of them will let off most fire-crackers, and make the greatest noise. This goes on until sunrise; and many Chinese have an idea that keeping awake during the last night of the old and watching the first sunrise of the new year, for ten or twelve years in succession, insures long life. Beggars are very active on this night. Wretched and forlorn, they may be seen traversing the wards in which they dwell, carrying baskets containing small placards on which are written the Chinese characters, Hai-moon-tai-kat. These imply, "May great good fortune flow into the house on the opening of the door," and a placard is affixed to the door of each house. In the morning they call at the houses they have placarded and demand alms. On New Year's Day, the streets, thronged during the night, are comparatively deserted. All the offices, shops, and warehouses are closed, as many of their then occupants are gone to their homes in the country to congratulate their relatives and friends. Those who remain may be seen running to and fro in holiday dresses. Sedan-chairs, with well-dressed gentlemen, or richly-attired ladies, pass along the streets in quick succession. To the poles of the ladies' chairs long sticks of sugar-cane are attached. These are lucky presents for the ladies to whom visits are being paid. As a rule, however, they are not removed from the poles, the will to give them away being taken for the deed. This is an economical way of making *etrennes*, or New Year's gifts, and one which, I venture to say, is quite in keeping with the character of the Chinese. Amongst wealthy people, however, presents[1] are exchanged at this great annual festival.

When visitors are received on New Year's Day, kowtows and congratulatory wishes are exchanged; and should they be relatives of the family, they are escorted to the ancestral altar, where they worship their departed forefathers. The tables in the reception rooms are covered with sweetmeats of all kinds, and each guest is served with a cup of tea, in which an almond or an olive has been placed as an emblem of good fortune. The young people of a family take their part in the cere-

---

[1] It is also usual for the heads of families to make small presents of money and wearing apparel to their domestic servants. Shopkeepers forward small presents to their regular customers in grateful acknowledgment of their patronage.

monies of the day, and after worshipping at the ancestral altar, are received by their parents, and elder brothers, to whom they pay marked homage. Afterwards they go to the houses of their schoolmasters and tutors, to whom their homage is not less reverential.

On New Year's Day, civil and military mandarins of all grades pay congratulatory visits to the governors-general of their respective provinces. At Pekin, the princes and principal officers of state repair to the imperial palace to make obeisance to the Emperor, who, seated on his Dragon Throne, receives them with more than ordinary urbanity. According to the letter of the law, all officers of state throughout the empire ought to be present. As this is impracticable, they resort, at four o'clock in the morning, to temples called Man-Chaong-Koon, or emperor's temples, of which one is usually to be found in every walled city. In each of these there is a throne, said to be an exact model of the Dragon Throne at Pekin. It is approached by nine steps, and on it is a tablet [1] bearing an inscription to the following effect—"May the reigning sovereign rule over the land ten thousand years, and ten times ten thousand years." The mandarins, as a mark of reverence, perform the kowtow at a considerable distance from the throne. This ceremony was observed on a grand scale at Canton, in 1861. The mandarins then appeared in their court dresses, which they had not worn since 1857, owing to the empire being at war with England and France. A law prohibits officials appearing in full dress when the country is at war with another power. At the conclusion of the ceremony, the mandarins take off the appendages to their dress which etiquette requires them to wear in the imperial presence, and repair to worship at the respective temples of Confucius, Man-chaong, and Kwan-te.

On the second day of the year, also at a very early hour of the morning, the officials proceed to the temples of Lung Wong, the Dragon King; Fung-Fo-Shin, the Wind and Fire gods; Tien-How, the Queen of Heaven; and Shing Wong the Protector of Walled Cities. On this day, banquets are held by the

---

[1] Similar tablets are placed in all Taouist and Buddhist temples, and Mohammedan mosques.

Chinese at which a fish called Lee-yu is the principal dainty, and cockles are served up as a lucky dish.

During the first week of the year it is customary to send presents of cakes made in the form of balls, and fried in oil. Oranges, wine, and cocoa fried in oil, are also sent as gifts to friends. The gifts are borne by women ; who for the nonce are called either tea-carrying women, or bearers of New Year's tea. In the course of a walk from Whampoa to Canton, I met once, several hundreds of these women carrying presents. From the fourth to the seventh day all spinsters and married women worship Apo, the presiding goddess of the marriage-bed. Sour ginger, and eggs dyed red, are offered to the goddess; and in the case of wealthy persons, roast pork, boiled fowls, and a water vegetable called by the Chinese Tsze-Koo.[1] The seventh day is especially a ladies' holiday, and on it they resort in large numbers to public gardens. In the country, it is usual to meet with troops of them on their way to such places of resort. Some toddle along on their little feet, supported by female attendants ; others are carried on the backs of their servants. With the Cantonese, the public gardens at Fa-tee are very popular at these times, and as the approach is by water, the creeks and streams that surround them are gay with flower-boats filled with richly dressed ladies, who have, as usual, been unsparing in their use of cosmetics. Great anxiety is manifested by all classes respecting the state of the weather during the first ten days of the year. Should it be propitious, men, horses, cows, dogs, pigs, goats, fowls, cereal crops, fruits, and vegetables will flourish and abound. I need scarcely add that soothsayers and fortune-tellers reap a rich harvest during the first month of the year.

In Canton, and the province of which it is the capital, lantern markets are held from the first to the fifteenth day of the month. The public squares are chosen for the purpose, and the lanterns, which seem actually to crowd them, are of all kinds of fantastic shapes, resembling beasts, fishes, flowers, and fruits. Amongst the lantern buyers are men to whom children have been born during the year, and who suspend their purchases as votive offerings in temples near their homes. Men desirous of

---

[1] This is supposed to be efficacious when married women desire female children.

offspring affix their names and addresses to these lanterns, which are forwarded to them at the end of the month, having been first lighted at the ever-burning lamps before the altars. The messenger who conveys such a lantern is accompanied by minstrels, and presents with it a lettuce in the centre of which is placed a burning candle with two onions at the base. A dinner is given on the occasion of this ceremony, and the lantern is suspended in front of the ancestral altar. At the lantern markets, wax figures of men, which are called Sam-Sing, are also sold. These are clothed in silk, and are known respectively as Fok, or happiness; Lok, or rank; and Sow, or Longevity. The Sam-Sing are generally placed by those who purchase them, above the ancestral altar, or above that which has been erected to the god of wealth.

On the evening of the fifteenth day it is customary in some parts of the empire for members of a clan to dine together. On this occasion a large lantern which has been placed, on New Year's Day, in front of the clan's ancestral altar, is sold by auction, sometimes at a high price, to the highest bidder. These lanterns are procured in shops, and paid for out of lands or houses with which ancestral altars are endowed. In some parts of Kwang-tung, a tree with many branches—expressive of the hope that the clan may never lack representatives—is placed in front of the altar in the common ancestral hall. Clan dinners are given in these halls, from the first to the fifteenth day, by those who have been successful in business during the past year, or those to whom children have been born. Either on the seventh or on the fifteenth day of the month, dinners are given in each district to the poor by such of their neighbours as have had male children born to them, or have just come to reside in the district for the first time. Such banquets consist of rice, fish pork, fowls, vegetables, and wine, and are held in the hall of the principal temple of the district. A short time before the hour fixed for the feast, messengers are sent through the streets to summon the guests, either by beating gongs, or by going quickly from from door to door. This method of invitation seems to be of venerable antiquity, for we read in St. Luke, " that a certain man made a great supper, and bade many : and sent his servant at supper time to say to them that were bidden, Come, for all things are now ready." Morier, in his account of his second journey into Persia, describes a similar custom. Speaking of a feast to be given by the second vizier, he says, that "on the day appointed, as is usual in Persia, a messenger came about five o'clock in the evening to bid us to the feast."

Throughout the first month, large processions, representing scenes of ancient history, traverse the streets by night. The processionists, who are in dramatic costumes, are preceded by the representation of a large dragon, which, like the monsters of a pantomime, is carried by men, the upper part of whose bodies are concealed in it. Boys follow, bearing lanterns of various shapes on long poles. Statute hirings are another feature of the season. These are held during the first half of the month, in the large squares in front of the principal temples of cities and towns. I have already alluded to these fairs, but I may here describe a peculiar mode of gambling practised at them, which I omitted to notice. A large fish, all alive—in some instances a large piece of pork—is placed on the top of a pole, and hungry-looking fellows may be seen staking a week's earnings on the guess they have made as to its weight. When each speculator has declared his opinion, and handed in his stake, the fish, or pork, is taken down and weighed, and the winner declared.

One other custom by which the first month of the year is signalized in the southern provinces remains to be noted. The peasants of neighbouring villages meet in the open plains, form sides, and attack each other with stones. These encounters are sometimes very serious affairs. In one which I saw on the island of Honam, so many peasants were injured that the elders requested the police to prevent its renewal next day. Next morning the police accordingly seized one of the ringleaders, and bound him to a tree. The peasants, however, drove them back, loosed the prisoner, and renewed the rough scenes of the day before. At Yim-poo, in 1865, I saw about seven hundred men, whose ages varied from eighteen to forty, engaged in a contest of this sort. The high ground overlooking the plain where they fought was crowded with spectators. Apparently thinking that I was a medical missionary, some of the combatants brought their wounded comrades and laid them down before me. In the intervals of their foolish sport, the men refreshed themselves at the soup and fruit stalls on the ground. Like most Chinese customs, these conflicts have their origin in a superstitious belief. They are occasionally attended with loss of life, and the elders of villages frequently do their best to prevent them.

The second day of the second month is the festival of Too-Tee, the god of wealth. Many of the tradespeople do not re-open their places of business, which closed at the beginning of the year, till after this gala day, for the god of wealth is a very important personage in the empire. All classes, rich and poor, learned and unlearned, religious and irreligious, seem to regard wealth as the chief of blessings, and the homage paid to Too-Tee is very sincere and earnest. His shrines are to be seen at the entrance of almost all the principal streets of Southern Chinese cities. He is represented sitting in state with an ingot of gold in his hand, and on his anniversary his shrines are decorated with lanterns painted in gay colours with various devices. Sweet-smelling flowers are also profusely scattered over them, and the votaries present offerings of pork, and boiled fowls, and pour libations. In all the cities and large towns, a curious custom is observed in front of the principal shrines. It consists in firing from a dais erected in the square which forms the shrine, and which is crowded with men of all ages, a wooded cannon loaded with a small charge of gunpowder, and a ball made of rattan. The ball rises some forty or fifty feet into the air, and innumerable hands are stretched out to receive it, for the lucky man who catches it when it falls is specially favoured by the god of wealth for the rest of the year. He is presented in the name of Too-Tee with an ornament for his ancestral altar. The decorations, consisting of artificial flowers, among which are set representations of the gods of wealth, rank, and longevity, is placed under a gilded canopy, and borne on the shoulders of men wearing red tunics to the house of the fortunate votary. Two or three minstrels head the procession, playing upon shrill musical instruments.

Upwards of thirty balls are sometimes fired from the cannon, but the luckiest man is he who secures the first ball. A large city like Canton presents a very brilliant appearance at this festival, and processions, headed by minstrels, traverse the streets in all directions. All classes are anxious to secure these tokens of Too-Tee's favour. I remember the principal mandarin of the large silk town of Kow-kong pointing out to me with pride an ornament of this kind which his son had won.

On the third day of the third month the *literati* and schoolboys observe the Chaong-tsze, an ancient festival which is alluded to in the writings of Confucius. Those who keep the Chaong-tsze, seek rivers, streams, and fountains, in which to bathe. This is looked upon as a rite of purification, and is supposed to render the votary proof against all evil influences. The festival is more particularly observed in Shantung, the native province of Confucius.

On the fifth day of the fifth month—that is, on or about the 18th of June—the Dragon Boat Festival is observed throughout the length and breadth of the land. This popular holiday is held in memory of Wat-Yuen, a minister of state who flourished about 500 B.C. A man of great honesty and virtue, he served a profligate prince of Cho—a kingdom which included the region now divided into the provinces of Hoopeh and Hoonam, which until recently formed the single province of Hoo-kwang. Obnoxious to the prince for unremitting endeavours to secure his attention to affairs of state, Wat-Yuen was degraded and eventually dismissed. Unable to endure the disgrace, he committed suicide, but before doing so he composed an ode, in which he depicted his sorrows with much pathos. He then flung himself into the river Mek-lo. Some fishermen who witnessed the act hastily rowed towards the spot where he disappeared, but they were unable to recover the body. With the view of appeasing the manes of the departed, they cast into the river offerings of boiled rice. On the corresponding day of the following year—the fifth day of the fifth month—the ceremony of searching for the body of Wat-Yuen,[1] and

---

[1] Near the spot where he is said to have perished, a large temple has been erected in honour of Wat-Yuen.

presenting offerings to his manes, was repeated; and from that
time to the present it has been continued, and is observed
besides on nearly all the rivers and creeks of the empire.   The
offerings of rice were formerly inclosed in small pieces of silk,
which were then tightly bound together by five threads or cords,
each of which was of a different colour.   This custom is said to
have owed its origin to the following myth:—On one occasion
whilst a number of votaries were engaged on the banks of the
Mek-lo river in worshipping and presenting the customary
offerings to the spirit of Wat-Yuen, he suddenly appeared and
addressed them in the following words :—

"I have hitherto been unable to avail myself of the offerings
which you and others have so graciously presented to me, in
consequence of a huge reptile which immediately seizes and
devours all things that are cast into the waters.   I request you
therefore to inclose all offerings intended for me in small
pieces of silk, and to carefully bind the same by means of five
threads, each being of a different colour.   Offerings which are
in this manner inclosed the reptile will not dare to touch."

Leaves of the bamboo tree, or those which by the Chinese are
termed Tuung-ip, are now substituted for the pieces of silk.
The boats which are used at this great annual festival, resemble
in form, as their name implies, large dragons.   Boats so constructed are supposed to have the power of intimidating the
huge reptile of which Wat-Yuen complained.   They are from
fifty to one hundred feet in length, and are decorated with flags
bearing various devices.   In the centre of each boat is placed a
drum, to the sound of which the rowers, who are sometimes as
many as ninety, keep accurate time with their paddles.   Gongs
are also placed in each boat, and the noise is supposed to dispel
the hungry ghosts who may be disposed to prey upon the spirit
of the departed.   In the bow, which is ornamented with a green
sprig called Low-yow-yeep, a man stands as if on the outlook
for the body of Wat-Yuen, throwing his arms about as if
casting rice upon the waters.   A leading feature of the festival
is the races which take place between the different crews.
Sometimes, especially when the contest is between two crews
of different clans, the race ends in a fight, the immediate

cause of which is probably the boats fouling. They often provide beforehand for such an occurrence, many of them being followed at a short distance by boats carrying stones and other weapons. At Canton, where the festival is very popular, the river is crowded with boats of almost all kinds of naval architecture; and the din arising from drums, gongs, fire-crackers, and the shouts of contending crews, is incessant and deafening from ten o'clock in the morning until four in the afternoon. Fatal accidents are not uncommon, as, owing to their shallowness and their peculiar construction, the dragon boats are easily swamped or capsized. For some weeks before the festival, great preparations are made for it by the various clans, and the launching of a new boat is a most exciting event to the clan to which it belongs. The Dragon Boat Festival is celebrated by dinners at all the guilds, and the soldiers and police show their appreciation of the national holiday by "squeezing" gambling houses. At Pekin where there is no river, the people have recourse on this day to horse and cart, and camel races. Even members of the blood-royal resort to the city of Tang-Chow, which stands on the banks of the Peiho river, in order to witness the processions of dragon boats. . In Mongolia, the people generally celebrate this great national festival by theatrical representations.

The Tien-Chung-Ching-Sit, or Feast of the Middle Heaven, falls on the same day as the Dragon Boat Festival, and in observance of it cakes possessing medicinal properties are baked by the Chinese at noon, and sent to friends as presents. Chemists make such cakes in large numbers, and export them to Australia and California, where they meet with a ready sale among the Chinese population. This festival, which is of great antiquity, is also marked by suspending leaves of the sago palm, a branch of the cactus tree, and a bulb of garlic above the outer doors of dwelling-houses, as a preventive against evil influences. Children of tender years have their foreheads and navels marked with vermilion for the same reason; and as a check to insects and vermin, small strips of yellow-paper, with characters written on them with a vermilion pencil, are posted on the doorposts and bedsteads. The inmates of prisons are apparently very careful

A DRAGON BOAT.

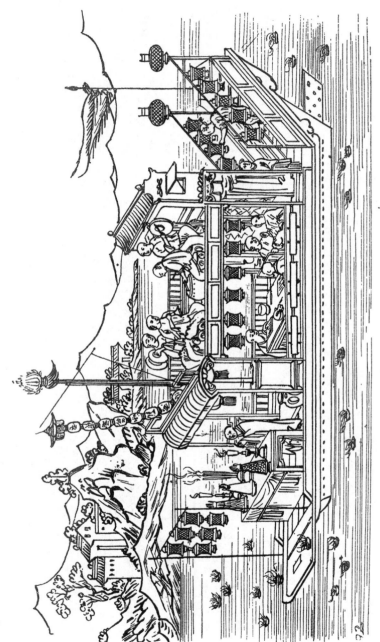

A FLOWER-BOAT—FESTIVAL OF SHU-YEE.

to observe this custom. On a visit which I paid to the Namhoi prison at Canton, on the day of the festival, I found them posting such strips above the doors of the cells, as the clock struck twelve.

From the first to the fifteenth day of the seventh month the Chinese burn vestments made of paper, and gold and silver paper representing money, as offerings to the souls of paupers and beggars who have died unbefriended during the past twelve months. At first sight this would seem to be a great proof of benevolence. Those who have carefully studied their character, however, incline to regard it as a prudent observance of the first law of nature—self-preservation; for, if not appeased in this way, the spirits to whom the offerings are made are supposed to go to and fro disseminating every kind of evil through the land. From eight to ten o'clock during the festival, lanterns are suspended either above the doors of houses, or from the boughs of adjoining trees, and tapers are placed by hundreds along the streets and highways. The towns and villages are lighted up by large quantities of burning paper clothes, paper money, and paper representations of sedan chairs and attendants. A river in the neighbourhood of a large city presents the most animated appearance. Large flower boats, brilliant with rows of lanterns, glide along the stream, which reflects their numerous lights. They carry Taouist priests chanting a requiem for the souls of those who have perished by drowning, supposed to be flitting disconsolately over the surface of the waters. Men stationed in the bow, burn paper clothes and paper money, others throw rice and vegetables into the stream for the spirits. At intervals floating lights are borne quickly past by the rapid current. These are lamps placed in earthenware vessels, and launched on the river or creek to light up the darkness for the wandering souls of the drowned.

This festival, which is called Shu-Yee in the Cantonese dialect, and which we might not inappropriately call the Chinese Festival of All Souls, is also observed in the principal temples, monasteries, and nunneries. Masses are said there continuously for several days by Taouist and Buddhist priests for the spirits of those who had nobody to care for them when they died.

Buddhist priests do not confine their intercessions at this time
to their own gods. They pray for the departed also to the Taouist
deiites, and their liberality is reciprocated. When I visited the
temple of Tsing-poo near Canton, in 1861, at the celebration of
this festival, I found the priests of Taou invoking Buddhistical
deities as well as the gods of their own sect to bless the souls of
the departed poor.

At Canton this festival was observed in 1856 on a grand
scale. The vicinity of the execution ground was appropriately
chosen as the special scene of its rites; for here Yeh, the then
governor-general, had during the past two years slain his
hecatombs, and the headless spirits of his victims were reported
to be seen at night in thousands threatening the citizens. The
father of Yeh, who was a very superstitious man, was amongst
the foremost contributors to the fund provided for the celebration of the festival.

In the course of the fifteen days devoted to the observance of
the Shu-Yee, a festival called T'shat-T'sic takes place. This is
held on the seventh day of the seventh month, and is in honour
of the Seven Stars, which are regarded by the Chinese as
goddesses. They are the patronesses of embroidered work,
and are worshipped chiefly by women—especially unmarried
women—who embroider silk garments and shoes for offerings
on this anniversary. These gifts are tastefully laid out on tables
in the halls of houses, which, as the festival is celebrated by
night, are brilliantly illuminated. Other tables are spread with
flowers, sweatmeats, and preserved fruits, and amongst these are
placed basins containing tender shoots of the rice plant. They
are so arranged as to appear as if they were growing, and in the
centre of each cluster a minute lamp is placed, whose spark of
light reminds one of a glow-worm or a fire-fly. Miniature bridges
formed of garlands and flowers, and also of grains of boiled rice
and almonds cemented by gum, connect these tables. While the
ladies in their holiday dresses wander uncertainly from table to
table—for their feet are very small—to admire the curious art
of delicate fingers, the gentlemen are listening in another apartment to singing men and women; elsewhere Taouist priests are
chanting pæans in honour of the seven goddesses. At midnight

the young ladies with their female attendants go out to draw water, every Chinese house being provided with one or more wells.   The water is poured into large earthenware vases, arranged in order round the mouth of the well.   After the seven goddesses have been invoked to give the water medicinal properties, the jars are hermetically sealed and put in a place of safety, to be opened only when a member of the family requires a draught of the disease-dispelling beverage.   The outer door of the dwelling house is kept open during the night, and the streets in which the gentry reside are crowded with people anxious to witness the display.   The festival is brought to a close at twelve o'clock on the following night, the richly-embroidered garments being burned, in order that they may be conveyed to the goddesses.   The Chinese tell the following legend of the origin of the festival.   The youngest of the seven sisters was sent by the gods to this world as a special messenger.   While here she became enamoured of a cowherd, to whom she was eventually married.   In course of time she was summoned to return to her home in the firmament.   In obedience to the gods she hastened back, and had no sooner joined her fair sisters than a shower of rain fell.   It was the tears of the disconsolate goddess. Before long the cowherd died of a broken heart.   And as his life had been one deserving the approbation of the gods, he was admitted as a reward into the constellation situated on the side of the milky way opposite to that on which the seven stars shine.   Once every year, that is, on the seventh day of the seventh month, the cowherd is supposed to bridge the milky way and pass over on a visit to his fair spouse.   This is the origin of the mimic bridges which span the tables on which the offerings for the seven goddesses are arranged.

The fifteenth day of the eighth month is specially set apart for the worship of the moon.[1]   This festival is known by foreigners

[1] On the first and fifteenth day of each month the Chinese also observe festivals bearing some resemblance to the Mominia, or feasts observed in honour of the new moon by the Hebrews, Egyptians, Persians, Greeks, and Romans.   Courts of justice and yamuns are closed.   The moon is not, however, the object of the worship on these days so much as various other deities, especially the gods of wealth.   At one time it was customary to sacrifice a bullock to the moon on the first and fifteenth days of each month.   Afterwards a goat was substituted.   On

as the Feast of Lanterns, and takes place at night, when families
worship the moon on the roofs of their houses and in their
ancestral halls.   On the altars erected there are arranged offerings of fowls, pork, and cakes.   While these are being offered
the worshippers perform the kow-tow, and gongs, tom-toms, and
drums are beaten.   On the tops of the houses, long poles bearing
lanterns and banners of various devices and mottoes are erected.
The lanterns are sometimes kept burning during the greater
part of the night.   The ships and boats riding at anchor in the
rivers are gaily decorated and illuminated, the festival being
very popular with the nautical population.   Canton, seen from
an eminence during the Feast of Lanterns, presents a very
striking appearance, the illumination extending over the whole
city and neighbourhood.   As at all festivals in China, there is
much eating and drinking.   For several days before, the con-
fectioners' shops are stocked with moon-cakes,[1] for which there
is a great demand.   They are circular in form, so as to represent
the orb of night, and are ornamented with all sorts of devices.
Another custom is the erection in the squares in front of the
large temples and guilds of pagodas from seven to ten feet high,
and filled with firewood.   When the hour of worship has come,
the fuel is set on fire and the blaze is kept up by fresh supplies
for upwards of three hours.   The flames burst forth through
small apertures on each side, and at the top, which is not
covered in.   From a small platform near it seven or eight men
by turns throw saltpetre into the flames.   Gold and silver papers,
representing ingots, are also thrown in as offerings to the goddess
of the moon.   As fresh fuel is added, the men in charge run
round the burning pagoda fanning the flames through the

the day before the festival the bullock or goat was conducted in procession
through the principal streets of the city to inform the people of the near approach
of the new or full moon.

[1] Among the poorer classes, especially in villages, what are called moon-cake
societies are formed.   The head or treasurer of the society is either a baker or a
confectioner, and each member contributes a monthly sum of one hundred cash
or ten cents.   When the festival comes round, the treasurer, who has had full
liberty to employ the subscriptions in trade, provides each subscriber with a full
supply of moon-cakes.   In the cities cakes are given at this season by the con-
fectioners as presents to the abject poor.

apertures, shouting loudly, and, in the lurid glare, presenting a sufficiently wild and barbarous appearance.

Electro-biology is practised to a great extent at this festival. A person willing to be operated upon is placed in the rays of the moon. He has to stand leaning his forehead on the top of a pole which he grasps with his hands, and which is placed slantwise, the other hand resting on the ground. Burning incense sticks are then waved over his head and about his body, the operators—there are generally two or three of them—repeating prayers in a low tone to the goddess of the moon. In the course of half an hour the mesmerized person falls down. He is then raised, and placed upon his feet, and made to go through a variety of movements at the will of the operator. In 1862, I saw a youth at Canton perform the sword and lance exercises under this mesmeric influence. He went through the evolutions, which, it was stated, he had never been taught, with a grace and dexterity that would have done credit to a well-trained lancer. He was kept in a state of great bodily exertion for upwards of three hours. In the Toong-koon district of Kwang-tung mesmerism is much practised at this festival.

What the goddess of the moon is to the Chinese, Ashtoreth seems to have been, in ancient times, to the Sidonians. As the moon is regarded by the former as the correlative female divinity to the sun, Ashtoreth was looked upon by the latter as the correlative female divinity to Baal, the Sun god. It is not unreasonable to suppose that a reference is made to Ashtoreth under the title of "queen of heaven," in the prophecy of Jeremiah (vii. 18, xliv. 17); and from these passages we learn that to the "queen of heaven" incense was burned, cakes were offered, and libations were poured out—rites which are at the present day observed by the Chinese in their worship of the moon. The Chinese have, however, a legend of their own to account for their worship of the moon. On the fifteenth day of the eighth month of the first year of his reign, the emperor Ming Wong was walking in the grounds of his palace attended by one of his priests. The emperor, who was much given to astrological studies, asked his companion if he could inform him of what material the moon was made. The priest, by way of reply, asked his royal master if he would like to visit the moon. The emperor said he would, and thereupon the priest threw his staff into the air. The staff became a bridge, and Ming Wong and his companion passed over it. They found the moon to be a region of vast palaces, beautiful flowers, and fair women. On their way back the priest requested his majesty, who had his lute with him— an instrument which he was noted for playing with remarkable skill—to enliven their way with its melodious strains. The music filled the air, and the inhabitants of Nankin and the surrounding territory, believing that rejoicing angels were traversing the realms of space, ran to the tops of their houses to do them homage.] At the request of the priest, his majesty showered down cash upon the votaries. When Ming Wong was once more in his palace, his adventure seemed so strange that he concluded it was a dream; but whilst he was persuading himself that it was so an official communication was laid before him. It came from the governor-general of the province, describing certain marvels which had taken place on the 15th day of the month—celestial music had been heard in the air, and cash had fallen from heaven. So the emperor was convinced that he had visited the moon, and the people have since continued to worship her on the night on which Ming Wong accomplished his marvellous journey.

On the twenty-fifth day of the eighth month the sun is worshipped. When the great male star, Tai-Yaong, as he is often called by the Chinese, has reached his meridian splendour, the members of each family arrange themselves for worship before a temporary altar in the courtyard of their dwelling-house, or in an apartment whence the sun can be seen. Tapers and incense are kept burning on the altar, and thankofferings are presented. Frequently, especially in the houses of the wealthy, Taouist priests assist at the ceremony. Copies of an address from the sun to the people are gratuitously circulated at this festival, at the expense of persons who have made a vow to do so on recovering from sickness. The address is as follows:—

"I, the great male luminary, when I come forth, the whole canopy of heaven is tinged with my brightness. Morning and night I weary not, but at all hours steadily pursue my course.

My speed is according to my own pleasure. No one can urge
me forward, no one can stay my progress. The dwellings of all
men I visit with my light. You, however, the people, do not
address me with reverence and respect. Were I, in displeasure,
to cease my shining, you would all die of starvation, inasmuch
as the earth would no longer bring forth fruits. The salutary
vicissitudes of day and night would cease.

"To the gods in general all men pay great devotion, but to
me, the great male star, homage is seldom or never rendered.
The twenty-fifth day of the eighth month is my natal anniversary, and on this occasion it is your duty to read this address
and to burn tapers and incense to my glory. Families by which
these, my commands, are obeyed will be kept free from evil.
Hell and destruction, however, are before all those who neglect
them. My title is the great light which rules the world. To
all good and virtuous men and women I now speak. Read
seven times daily this my address : you will not descend
to hell, and all the members of your families will at all times
rejoice and be happy. Your posterity also for seven generations
will ascend to heaven. Address me by the name of the Great
Light which rules the world, and I will stretch forth my golden
hands to give you light, and to guide you to the Paradise of the
Western Heaven."

On the occasion of an eclipse of the sun his worship is also
celebrated. Five months prior to the eclipse the head of the
Li-poo board at Pekin, in obedience to the commands of the
emperor, forwards a despatch to the chief rulers of each province, and through him to the chief magistrate of each prefecture and each county, requesting them at the approaching
eclipse to save the sun. At the time all the mandarins, attired
in black robes, assemble at the official residence of the chief
magistrate. When they have arranged themselves before an
altar erected in the courtyard of the yamun, the chief magistrate
burns incense on the altar and beats a drum three times. At
this stage all the officials present fall down before the altar and
perform the kow-tow. The ceremony on the part of the officials
having been brought to a close, a number of underlings continue,
until the eclipse is over, to beat drums and tom-toms with the

view of frightening and thereby preventing the Tien-Kow or heavenly dogs from devouring the sun. During this din, priests of the respective sects of Buddha and Taou stand before the altar and chant appropriate prayers. Upon the tops of all the dwelling-houses and shops of a Chinese city, men are also stationed who, by means of drums, tom-toms, and horns, add to the general din. The same ceremonies take place during an eclipse of the moon. Formerly in other lands, as in China to-day, an eclipse of the sun or moon was beheld with terror. To rescue the moon from the spell of the enchanter, other nations, like the Chinese of the present day, had recourse to the blowing of horns and the beating of drums and brazen pots and pans. This ridiculous custom was evidently in full force in the days of Juvenal, who alludes to it in a description of a brawling woman—

> " Forbear your drums and trumpets if you please,
> Her voice alone, the labouring moon can ease."

To relieve nature in the full light of either the sun or moon is by the Chinese regarded as an act of great impiety. In both Taouistical and Buddhistical classics such an act of profanity is regarded as more than enough in itself to bring calamities upon the nation. Placards are occasionally by billstickers posted at the corners of the streets, warning the people against such an unseemly and irreligious practice. Throughout the empire of China there is, I believe, only one temple in honour of the sun. It stands within the walls of the city of Pekin, and is of a circular shape, and domed. At the festival of the Sun the emperor worships here.

Besides these festivals of the sun and moon religious cere- monies and rejoicings take place throughout the whole month in honor of Wa-Kwong, the god of fire. In the south of China at all events, the principal streets of the cities are illuminated not by lanterns, but by crystal chandeliers suspended at frequent intervals from beams extended across the streets. The lights are protected from rain by sheets of canvas stretched across the streets, which are very narrow in southern cities. During this month groups of figures in wax-work, attired in silk dresses, are carried in procession. They represent certain episodes in the ancient history of the empire. The figures are very well executed, and would do no discredit to Madame Tussaud's well-known exhibition. In the principal streets are erected temporary altars in honour of Wa-Kwong, and Taouist priests are engaged all night long in chanting prayers. The idols of this deity are occasionally borne in procession through the streets. In 1861, I witnessed a large procession at the prefectoral city of Tak-hing on the banks of the western branch of the Canton river. Numbers of boys riding on horseback, and ladies borne in triumphal chairs, attended the idol, attired in the costumes of the period in which Wa-Kwong flourished. As no foreigners had previously visited the city, the presence of my friends and myself was a source of much curiosity to the vast crowd assembled on the occasion. The young ladies regarded us with surprise and alarm as they were borne past the corner of the street near which we were standing; and, much to our annoyance, the majority of the spectators deserted the procession to follow us in our explorations of their ancient, but uninteresting city.

On the ninth day of the ninth month, the festival termed Ching-Yaong or Tan-Koon is celebrated. The people resort to the hills of their neighbourhood to commemorate the intervention of angels to save a pious scholar and successful teacher who lived about nine hundred years ago in the time of the T'sun dynasty. This personage, called Too Wong-hing, was instructed to go with his wife and family to the top of a mountain in order to escape an impending calamity. The Ching-Yaong is held in honour of his miraculous deliverance. The people picnic on the hills, and fly kites, which they set adrift, cutting the cords when the kites are high in the air. A kite thus set adrift is supposed to carry with it in its downward course all the evils impending at the time on the family of the person to whom it belongs. This superstitious observance brings to a close what the Chinese regard as the season for kite-flying. This pastime, it may be remarked, is much indulged in by men and boys. I remember being considerably surprised when, calling upon a Chinese gentleman, shortly after my arrival in China, I was informed

by the servant that he was on the top of the house flying his
kite. Chinese kites, which are without tails, are of all shapes,
and resemble birds, insects, baskets of flowers, serpents, centipedes, ships, and even men. Those resembling serpents or
centipedes are sometimes of enormous length. The most beautiful kite I ever saw was at Tam-sui, in Formosa, and was in
the form of a Catherine wheel. The largest kites are made at
Tientsin, and some of them require four or five men to hold
them. In the centre of Chinese kites, four or five metallic
strings are fixed on the principle of the Æolian harp. When
they are flying, " slow-lisping notes as of the Æolian lyre " are distinctly heard. The legend which describes how these strings
came to be used in this way is very characteristic of the people.
During the reign of the emperor Low-pong, the founder of
the Hon dynasty, a general who was much attached to the
dynasty which had been obliged to give way before the more
powerful house of Hon, resolved to make a last vigorous effort
to drive Low-pong from the throne he had recently usurped.
A battle, however, resulted in the army of the general being
hemmed in and threatened with annihilation. At his wits' end
to devise a method of escape, he at last conceived the ingenious
idea of frightening the enemy by flying kites, fitted with Æolian
strings, over their camp in the dead of night. The wind was
favourable, and when all was wrapt in darkness and silence, the
forces of Low-pong heard sounds in the air resembling *Foo-Hon !*
Foo-Hon !—Beware of Hon! Beware of Hon! It was their
guardian angels, they declared, who were warning them of
impending danger, and they precipitately fled, hotly pursued by
the general and his army.

Besides the public festivals observed by the Chinese, the
chief of which I have described, there are what may be termed
family festivals. The most important is the celebration of a
birthday, which is invariably attended with much rejoicing.
Sons and daughters usually mark the birthday of a parent by a
great entertainment. Before the banquet is served, the parents,
seated on a dais under a crimson canopy of embroidered work,
receive their children's homage and congratulations amid the
blowing of pipes and trumpets, and the clanging of cymbals.

FLYING KITES.

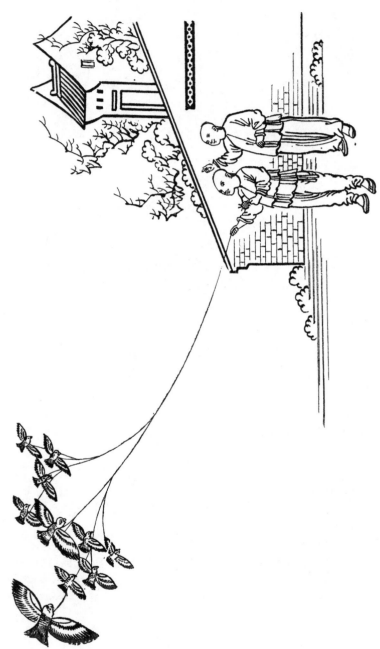

FLYING KITES.

The kow-tow is performed first by the sons in the order of seniority, and afterwards by the daughters in the same order. Relatives and friends are often present in large numbers—sometimes coming from a great distance. In Kwang-tung, the name of one Shou Sing-koon, who in the last century attained a patriarchal age, is used as a term of congratulation at such a time. When travelling in this province in 1862, I saw near the city of Loong-moon, on the banks of the river of that name, a long procession of ladies going to the birthday celebration of the head of their clan. They were preceded by a number of attendants bearing the gifts usually presented on such occasions. When a father completes his fifty-first year, he usually receives from his children, besides other gifts, a large screen of several leaves richly carved in wood and inlaid, in wealthy families, with ivory, silver, and mother-of-pearl. On the panels are various devices, some emblematical of longevity, others of virtue. The screen is placed behind the chairs of the parents when they sit in state to receive their birthday congratulations. Gifts of this kinds are, of course, very costly. I remember seeing one which was valued at the sum of £400. Large pieces of tapestry are frequently presented to parents on the completion of their fifty-first year. When they reach the age of sixty-one they sometimes, incredible as it may seem, receive coffins as gifts from their children. The coffins are either deposited in temples or kept in the house, and are much valued. At the banquet which follows the offering of congratulations and gifts, the person whose birthday it is, is careful not to partake of the flesh of the animal which represents the division of the twenty-four hours in which he was born. These divisions are two hours each. Thus from midnight until 2 A.M. is represented by a n'gow, or cow ; from 2 to 4 A.M. by a loo-foo, or tiger ; from 4 to 6 A.M. by a rabbit ; from 6 to 8 A.M. by a loong, or dragon ; from 8 to 10 A.M. by a shay ; from 10 to 12 noon, by a ma, or horse ; from 12 to 2 P.M. by a yaong, or sheep; from 2 to 4 P.M. by a matou, or monkey ; from 4 to 6 P.M. by a ki, or fowl ; from 6 to 8 P.M. by a kow, or dog ; from 8 to 10 P.M. by a chu, or pig; from 10 until midnight, by a lo-shu, or rat. To eat at his birthday banquet the flesh of the animal which the hour of his

birth proscribes, entails bad dreams upon a Chinese. It is his
duty to purchase such an animal and let it go free. When he
cannot do this, he burns a paper figure of it. Wealthy families
also hold theatrical performances in honour of a birthday. The
houses of the wealthy are generally provided with theatres, and
on the anniversary of a decade of years, performances are sometimes given for a fortnight. The completion of the fifty-first
year, and of every following decade, is celebrated with great
magnificence.[1] I was present at a celebration of this kind held
on the fifty-first birthday of the wife of Howqua, one of the
wealthiest citizens of Canton. In addition to the theatrical
entertainments, which lasted for a fortnight, and the garden
fêtes, there were religious ceremonies at the temple of Longevity,
which was tastefully decorated. For three whole days no fewer
than thirty Buddhist priests were engaged in returning thanks to
God for His preserving care over the lady who had completed
her fifty-first year. When a person completes his eighty-first
year the elders of his village or district usually inform the
local government, which communicates it through the proper
channels to the emperor, who orders a sum of money from the
Imperial treasury for the erection of a monumental arch in his
honour. The arch is erected either in front of the house of the
patriarch or in the country. These arches are very numerous
throughout the empire. They are made of granite, or, in some
districts, of marble. They consist of a triple gateway, like
the triumphal arches of ancient Rome. The slab immediately
above the central gateway is usually elaborately carved, and
inscribed with four Chinese characters selected by the emperor,
and expressive of the virtues of the patriarch. Above the centre
slab, and at right angles to it, is a small one inscribed with the
two characters Sing and Chee, implying that the monument[2]
was erected by imperial order. The most beautiful arches of the

[1] So great is the reverence paid to old men in China that all above seventy
are permitted to wear an official dress, and to affix a copper button to the apex
of their caps; and district magistrates usually send their visiting cards, four
times in the year to all those in their districts who are upwards of ninety years
of age.

[2] There are several such arches in front of dwelling-houses in Canton. They
are kept in a good state of preservation. Several of them are made of brick.

FIREWORKS.

kind which I have seen, are on the banks of the western branch of the Canton river. Two are particularly imposing, one which was erected by Hien-fung in honour of a centenarian, and another erected near Tak-hing, by Ying-chung in honour of his secretary. I may mention a third, recently built at Yim-poo in honour of a woman who lived to be a hundred years old.

The natal anniversary of the emperor is celebrated with much rejoicing by the civil and military officers in all the provinces. At a very early hour they repair to an imperial temple—with one of which every city is provided—to perform the kow-tow before the emperor's tablet. The three days immediately preceding, and the three following his majesty's birthday are devoted to holiday-making. It is usual for the emperor to mark the day by a proclamation of clemency to criminals, addressed to the chief rulers of provinces. Those condemned to death sometimes have their sentences commuted to transportation for life. Others have their term of imprisonment limited; and some are released from captivity. Prisoners also get extra rations on the birthday of the emperor. I remember seeing the walls of all the government offices in Canton posted with copies of a proclamation of this kind, issued when the late emperor Hien-fung completed his thirty-sixth year.

The birthdays of the Chinese are also celebrated after their death. Offerings of fruits and viands are placed on a table in front of the ancestral altar, on which is the tablet of the deceased. His portrait also hangs in the ancestral hall to receive the homage of his children and grandchildren. I was once present at the natal anniversary of a lady who had been dead for several years. It took place in a large ancestral hall attached to the family residence. In an ante-chamber I found no fewer than forty ladies, in their best robes, waiting to pay their homage to the spirit of the deceased lady, who, had she lived, would have then completed her ninety-first year. A master of ceremonies was present, and the ladies performed the kow-tow in the order of seniority. The religious ceremony was followed by a banquet, and all the servants and slaves of the family received small presents of money, inclosed in little envelopes of red paper.

The making of a will is another occasion of feasting and rejoicing in families. In China, as elsewhere in Asia, it is customary for parents, when they are advanced in years, to divide their property amongst their children. On a lucky day, selected by a geomancer, the parents meet their children in the principal hall of the house, or in the ancestral hall. All are attired for the occasion in their richest robes. The parents occupy the chief seats, and the sons stand, arranged according to seniority, on the side of the father, while the daughters are ranged on the side of the mother. Having informed his children of the amount of his property, the father proceeds to divide it equally amongst his sons, so that each may at once have his portion. The daughters although present, are not, as a general rule, allowed to inherit any of their father's property. In many instances, the elder son receives a larger portion than the younger. The father reserves a sum of money, the interest of which he considers will be sufficient to defray the future household expenses of himself and wife. At the death of the parents, the sum thus reserved does not revert to the children, but is set apart for the endowment of the ancestral hall. Such endowments serve to defray the cost of the offerings presented on the ancestral altars, and at the family tombs. They are occasionally used in the event of a son proving a spendthrift, the brothers sometimes saving the prodigal from starvation by an allowance out of these funds.

When a father does not divide his property among his sons during his life-time, it is usual for him to assemble his children, nephews, nieces, and other relatives in the ancestral hall, and to inform his sons of the amount he intends to bequeath to each. He then proceeds to draw up a will, which is given to the firstborn, copies being given to each of the other sons. If nephews be included, they also receive copies. Obeisance is then made to the father by all present, in the order of seniority. Where the testator has houses or landed property, he sometimes divides it into as many equal portions as he has sons, and then calls upon them to cast lots for the portions, according to seniority. Those present at such ceremonies are invited to a banquet in honour of the occasion. Except in cases of dangerous illness, a Chinese father does not make his will until his wife has ceased to bear children.

As a Chinese will may prove interesting to my readers, I venture to give a translation of one taken from the columns of the *Friend of China*, under date June 22nd, 1861. The editor introduces it with some prefatory remarks :—

" Three respectable Chinese," he writes, " came to us the other day, to ask whether it would be possible to induce the allied commissioners of England and France (for the city of Canton was at that time under foreign rule) to adjudicate in a dispute between them and their elder brother, relative to the division of certain lands and houses devised by their father, one of the Hong merchants of Taou-Kwang's palmy days ; and they appeared greatly disappointed when we told them that, being a purely Chinese matter, it was not in the power of the foreign officers to take up the case. According to their account, the doors of the native courts of justice were closed against them, the usurper of their rights being able to fee the understrappers, to keep their petition from reaching the higher officers to whom it is addressed. The will which they brought us to exhibit their rights is an interesting document, and as but little is known regarding the tenure of property in China, we will briefly notice the heads of it. It begins thus :—

" These are the dying behests of Cha-Kar-Ng to his seven sons, the first called Yow-Mun (deceased) ; the second, Yow-Shing, the third, Yow-Yan ; the fourth, Yow-Sün ; the fifth, Yow-Tak ; the sixth, Yow-Him ; the seventh, Yow-Yeung ; and his two brothers named Kar-Ting and Chee-On. The 16th day of 12th month of the 5th year of the reign of the emperor Taou-Kwang.

" I, Cha-Kar-Ng, your father, give you these following departing instructions, which must constantly be observed as rules or guides.

" In my youth I forsook the study of the classics, and for sixteen years have addicted myself to traffic. But though attending to trade with all my heart, I have still cultivated the virtues, and have not been inattentive to the performance of social duties. Suddenly I find myself troubled with dysentery, and as this is a dangerous disease, I apprehend that I shall soon die. The estate which I have founded has been created through many difficulties, and the current business of the firm is weighty and serious, while you, my sons, are still young and unmarried. In managing the business you cannot be too circumspect, and should you be able to resign it and do some other thing (obtain government employment), it will be well; otherwise you must carry on the business as I did, and to aid you I have spoken to several merchants to be your securities when necessary. Also I have consulted with several elders as to the greater fitness for managing tradal concerns, and have found that my fourth son, Yow-Sün, whose trading name is Tai-Wa, is able to be successor and master of the hong called Tung-yü. As there will be trouble in regulating foreign affairs, his salary will be 400 taels of silver per annum, and the rest of you shall be his assistants in the establishment, at salaries of 200 taels each. My younger brother, Chee-On, will still attend to the tea-weighing and delivery, and on account of his old age it is my wish that his stipend be 1,000 taels per annum. With regard to the value of the hong and other property—say, for instance, that it is worth 200,000 taels, the same must be divided into ten parts, one of which must be given to my younger brother in order to comfort the spirits of my parents, as well as to show brotherly love; two of the remaining nine parts must be preserved as hereditary property, the proceeds of which shall be applied to ancestral sacrifices. The other seven must be given to you my sons—one to each. Now my first son died in the middle age (*i.e.* forty) and left but one daughter, so the second son must give up one of his sons to be my first (deceased) son's adopted heir, and all of you must encourage the affairs with union and concord. You must not quarrel nor dispute with each other; you must be harmonious and upright in all respects, careful and sincere, relieving one another with willing hearts, and this by reason of brotherly connection; participating in both prosperity and adversity, and using your exertions to enlarge or increase the possessions. You must not violate or break this on any account; and I write this that it may be law among you.

> " *Witnesses :—*
> " LAM-MUN, *Cashier of the Hong.*
> " SOO-TSOY, *Overseer of Goods.*
> " CHA-PAK, *Book-keeper.*

and sundry relatives."

It appears that, besides the sons named, there were three daughters, but for them no provision was made.

There are other occasions for what may be termed family festivals : such are the putting off of mourning, and the entering upon a new house. I may add that the Chinese are accustomed to observe fasts as well as feasts. Two of their principal fasts are held on the 16th day of the 5th month, and the 16th day of the 8th month, and are called Tien-Tee-How-Tai, or heaven and earth meeting together.   Some days beforehand, each of these fasts is announced by red placards posted in the principal streets, and married people are exhorted to live apart for a time that they may give themselves to fasting and prayer.   The first nine days of the 9th month are also observed as fast days, in honour of the gods who inhabit the nine stars, or " Cerberus."   Altars are erected in houses, and fruits and flowers are offered.   On the altars are placed nine candles, nine incense sticks, nine plates of flowers and fruits respectively, and a tub containing rice, in which a rod or yard measure is placed in an upright position. Taouist priests are engaged to offer up prayers, in which pardon is sought for past sins, and petitions are offered for long life. On the ninth day especially, sparrows are bought from the poulterers by the devout, and allowed to escape, an act well pleasing to the gods.   Gentlemen sometimes go into the country, accompanied by a Buddhist priest, to give the birds their liberty. Sometimes the sacrifice is a fish bought from the fishmonger, and set free in its native element.

CHAPTER XII.

FUNERALS.

THE mourning ceremonies of the Chinese are very numerous, and vary of course according to the rank and condition of the deceased. When the time of dissolution evidently draws near, it is usual, in the case of a male member of the family, to remove him to the *atrium* of the house to die. Here, placed upon a bed of boards supported on tressels, and with his feet towards the door, he remains to take his last departure. It is also usual for the nearest relative to arrange the best robes of the dying man on the couch beside him, in order that just before he dies his body may be arrayed in them. The cap or hat is placed on the pillow, the tunic or coat by the side of the body, the trousers by the side of the legs, and a boot by the side of each foot. The sufferer will regard a proceeding of this nature with the utmost composure, and may sometimes be heard to express gratitude for having such apparel to appear in before the spirits of his departed ancestors. As soon as the last struggle is anticipated, he is washed with warm water in which fragrant leaves, generally those of the pomeloe tree, have been boiled. The clothes are then put on him. Death, it need scarcely be said, is often hastened by this singular practice. The eyes of the deceased are closed by his nearest relative, in order, I suppose, that the corpse may assume a less ghastly appearance. According to Virgil (*Æneid*, ix. 487) and Ovid (*Her.* i. 102, 111; ii. 102 ; x. 120), a custom very similar to this was observed by people of other lands. When closing the eyes of the deceased, the relative calls upon him by name, and addresses him very much to the following effect:—"Be not thou sorry on leaving us; thou hast gone to bliss, and we thy relatives hope to confer upon thee posthumous honours, by being ourselves through thy good influences prosperous upon earth." Shortly after death, a functionary called the Nam-mo-loo, generally a priest of the sect of Taou is called in. The Nam-mo-loo, calls upon one of the spirits—for each Chinese is supposed to be animated by three spirits—to quit the corpse and hasten to Elysium. The prayer which he chants, is termed Hoi-Loo, or open the way. He next casts the horoscope of the deceased, and informs the relatives how far the spirit has ascended towards Elysium, when it will return on a visit to them, and what form it will assume in another state of existence. If they are assured that it will animate the form of a man, they greatly rejoice; if that of a beast or reptile, they grieve and offer up intercessory prayers to the gods, celebrate masses, and present offerings of gold and silver paper, folded up so as to resemble ingots of silver and gold. If the deceased has been a person of consequence, a porch consisting of a framework of bamboo poles covered with matting is erected above the entrance door of the house. From the centre of the porch is suspended a large bunch of strips of blue and white paper. This is to prevent casual visitors from entering the house of mourning, and becoming in consequence unclean. It would appear from Horace (Od. ii. 14, 23), and other ancient writers, that a custom not very unlike this was observed by the ancient Romans. A cypress branch was placed above the door of the house of mourning to prevent the high priest from entering and incurring ceremonial pollution. Should a person die unexpectedly, or before his relatives have had time to dress him in his best robes, the next-of-kin attires himself in sackcloth, and hastens to the nearest river or well to buy from the Hoi-Loong Wong or River Dragon King water wherewith to wash the face and body of the deceased. Four cash, and in some instances a live fish as well, are cast into the stream by way of payment. The fish is supposed to inform the river god that the water has been bought and paid for. The nearest of kin is accompanied to the well or river by several friends, two of whom support him, one on each side, for he is supposed to be bowed down with grief. The procession is headed by two or more minstrels, the discordant sounds of whose musical instruments cannot easily be forgotten by one who has once heard them. The face and body of the deceased are sprinkled rather than washed with the water, the rite implying not so much the cleansing of the body, as the washing away of sin. A few hired attendants belonging to a pariah class called Ng' Tsock,[1] next proceed to undress the corpse with the view of bathing it with warm water (cf. Virg. Æn., vi. 219; Plin. Epist. v. 16) and dressing it in robes becoming the rank of the deceased. Whilst the Ng' Tsock are attiring the corpse, all the members of the family either stand or kneel around the couch upon which the dead body is placed. Women enceinte are not permitted to be present.

Upon the corpse of a person, who was of the first, second, or third rank, three silk dresses are placed. A rank lower than the fifth entitles the deceased to only two silk dresses. Whilst each dress is being placed upon the body, two men stationed near it beat gongs. The cakes of rice flour which had previously been placed on the ground, at the foot of the couch as offerings, are thrown aside during the dressing of the corpse as of no further service. They are afterwards eaten by the persons who dress the corpse, or are picked up by beggars, who on such occasions station themselves in eager expectation at the door. On one occasion I saw a poor half-starved wretch rush into the outer hall of a house where a corpse was being attired. He was anxious to get the cakes, but one of the Ng' Tsock who had all along been keeping his eye upon them, sprang forward, and, to the great consternation of the mourners, knocked the beggar down.

When the corpse has been placed in the coffin, one of the pariah class proceeds to each corner of the chamber, and beats the floor with a large hammer, to terrify evil spirits. If the

[1] So degraded is the position of the Ng' Tsock as to deprive them of the rights of worshipping in the public temples ; and their sons are not allowed to become candidates for literary degrees. They resemble in many respects the *pollinctores* of the ancient Romans.

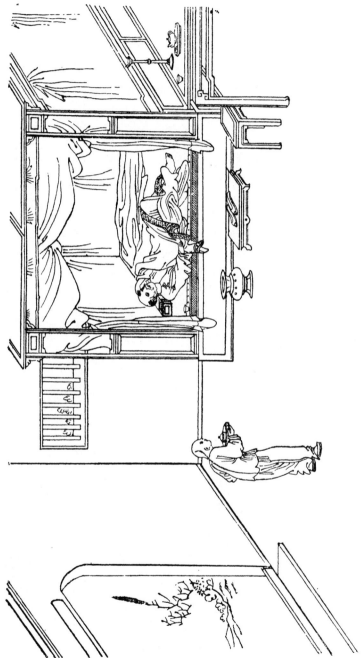

REMOVED TO THE HALL TO DIE.

deceased belonged to one of the first five ranks, a crown [1] of
gold is placed upon his head. The crowns vary in costliness.
The wife of such an official is also entitled to a crown. I
once saw the corpse of a wife of an official of the fifth rank
lying in state. The coronet was made of silver washed with
gold, and her clothing consisted of silk vestments upon which
flowers and butterflies were embroidered in gold. I have also
seen the remains of Tartar ladies lying in state. Their bodies
were attired in robes more costly, if possible, than those just
described. It is also usual for wealthy Chinese to deck corpses
with diamonds, gold earrings, bracelets either of gold, silver, or
jade, hair-pins,[2] &c. These ornaments are sometimes presented
by the friends of the deceased that he may remember them in
the world of spirits. If the deceased was of the first, second,
or third rank, a pearl, a piece of gold, a piece of silver, a piece
of jade stone and of another precious stone—in all five articles—
are placed in the mouth. To have been of the fourth, fifth,
sixth, or seventh rank entitles the deceased to a piece of gold
and very small jade stone ornaments of five different forms. The
eighth or ninth rank entitles the deceased to a small piece of gold
and a small piece of silver. In many instances, however, three
pieces of silver are used; in others, one piece of silver only, and
amongst the poorer classes three copper cash. It would appear
from Juvenal (iii. 267) that the ancient Romans used to place
a small coin in the mouth of the dead, to pay Charon for ferry-
ing him across the rivers of Hades. Grains of paddy or seeds
of three different kinds are in some cases placed by the Chinese
in the mouth of the dead. Whilst the corpse is being thus prepared by the Ng' Tsock, the sorrowing relatives who surround
it, turn away their faces. Faithful servants, however, see that
the Ng' Tsock do not despoil the corpse of any of its ornaments. It is also usual to place in the coffin any small article
which the deceased was accustomed to prize. I was present
when the corpse of a great friend of mine named Lo Poon-qua

---

[1] This reminds one of a custom of the ancient Romans. Cicero (*De Leg.* ii.
24) and Pliny (xxi. 3) state that if a Roman had received a crown for his
bravery it was always placed upon his head when he died.

[2] Cf. Propertius, iv. 7, 9.

was put into the coffin, and his sons placed beside it a copy of an
English and Chinese vocabulary by Dr. Wells Williams. In
this volume, they informed me, their father took great delight,
and he had for several years past spent a portion of each day in
studying it. The hair which has come out in the process of
combing, and the parings of the nails are, in some instances,
inclosed in a bag and placed in the coffin at the feet of the
corpse. The practice of putting valuable articles upon a corpse
offers a strong temptation to thieves to break open the tombs
of the wealthy, and some families are so much alive to this risk,
that they content themselves with using ornaments made of
sandal-wood and gilt. It was also customary at one time to
deposit large sums of copper cash with a dead body. So great
a sum was deposited in the tomb of the Emperor Hwan-tai of
the Han dynasty, who ascended the throne of China A.D. 147
that it was plundered by a band of robbers. During the Tsin
dynasty, therefore, which commenced A.D. 265, the practice was
adopted of burning paper representing ingots of gold and silver
—a custom to which I have elsewhere referred.

When the corpse has been placed in the coffin by the Ng'
Tsock, they ascertain whether or not it is placed in a straight
position, by means of a line which they stretch from the head to
the feet. This proceeding is closely watched by the relatives.
The face of the deceased is now covered with a white silk shroud,
and two or more coverlets are placed over the body. These are
presented by relatives and friends. In some instances twenty
or thirty coverlets are presented, and those which are not used
are committed to the flames of a sacred fire, that they may be
conveyed to the world of spirits for the service of the deceased.
It is possible, however, that in some instances they are not
burned, but made use of by the family. These articles, which
are lined with white silk, vary in texture and colour according to
the rank of the deceased. Thus, if the deceased was of the first,
second, or third rank, his coverlet is of a bright red colour; if he
was of the third or fourth rank, it is dark red; if he was of
the fifth rank it is green; if he was of the sixth rank, it is
purple; if he was of the seventh rank, it is of an ash colour; and
if he was of the eighth or ninth rank, it is white. At the bottom

of the coffin a loose board is placed, upon which the corpse rests. It contain seven holes, which are regarded as representing the seven stars, and is therefore called the "seven stars board." It is fluted as well as perforated, and a quantity of lime and oil is deposited between it and the bottom of the coffin. The duty of placing the lid on the coffin and nailing it down devolves in some instances upon the nearest of kin. Frequently, however, he only presents the nails which are used to the undertaker. He does so, kneeling by the side of the coffin, and holding up with both hands, until the undertaker has finished, a plate containing the nails. At the close of this ceremony, he is presented with an ornament of copper made to resemble a lotus flower, with a long stem and several small pieces of silk of various colours attached. This he places in an upright position on the centre of the lid of the coffin, where it remains until the day of the funeral, when it is laid on the ancestral altar. This ornament, which by the Chinese is termed Tsze-Shun-Tay, is, so I have been given to understand by well-informed Chinese, emblematical of the never-ending posterity of the family of the departed one. The coffin, having been closed, is now hermetically sealed by means of chunam.

The Chinese consider coffins indispensable for the repose of the dead; and in almost all their towns and villages there are what are termed coffin societies, or, as they are sometimes called, Long-life Loan Companies. In the prefecture of Kwang-chow, in the province of Kwang-tung, there are several such companies. Every member is entitled to a coffin and grave clothes. Persons who wish to become members must have attained sixteen years of age. In the third month of each year, a general meeting is held when each member pays his annual subscription of three hundred and sixty cash. The names of those who do not pay their yearly subscriptions are removed from the list of members. The period during which each person is called upon to subscribe to the general fund is sixteen years, and at the close of this period he is regarded as an honorary member. Should any member die from home, the sum due for his funeral expenses is paid to his heirs.

A Chinese coffin is very substantially made, and in shape

resembles the trunk of a tree. Three kinds of wood are especially used. The first, called Chum-Sha, is very heavy and sinks in water. The second is termed Ting-Chow, and the third Lou-Chow. The wood of a coffin is from four to five inches thick, and the cost varies from four to three or four thousand dollars. As a rule the coffin receives two or three coatings of lacquer. That of a duke is covered with red lacquer, and further decorated with representations of flowers in gold. That of a marquis, or an earl, or a baron, is covered with red lacquer, but has no gold flowers. That of a gentleman of any of the first five ranks may be covered with a coating of red lacquer. In the case of the remaining four ranks the coffin is covered with a coating of black lacquer; in the case of the poorer classes it is plain and unvarnished.

All men upwards of sixty years of age are supposed to have their coffins ready, and it is not unusual, when fathers or mothers have completed their sixty-first year, for sons to present them with one as a suitable birthday gift. These presents are sometimes deposited in monasteries and temples, where they remain until they are required. At Shanghai I visited a monastery which contained several coffins deposited for safe keeping. And in a temple in honour of the Sleeping Buddha at Nankin, I saw a coffin brought in by an old man of the age of seventy-five, to whom it had that very day been presented by his sons. At Canton and other cities of the south of China, people sometimes keep their coffins in their houses. This is also the case in the midland provinces; I observed coffins in several houses in Kiukiang and Hankow. During my stay at Woo-see Hien, on the banks of the Grand Canal, I saw a family in the act of moving to a neighbouring town, and the father, a very aged man, carried his coffin with him, regarding it, I was told, as of far more value than all his furniture. The Chinese do not now inclose their dead in two coffins, but in one only. During the Chow dynasty two coffins were invariably used, but this custom was, it is said, set aside during the dynasty of Tong.

But to return to the rites which are observed in a house of mourning. The coffin having received the corpse, is placed upon trestles near the ancestral altar; and upon the ground immediately underneath it a lamp is made to stand upon three bricks. In order that it may be kept burning day and night, it is assiduously replenished with oil by the chief mourner, or his substitute. It is supposed to give light to the spirit which remains with the corpse. On the east side of the coffin is a clothes stand, on which are placed the robes, hat, and shoes of the deceased. So soon as the coffin and lamp have been placed, the relatives arrange themselves on each side, and do obeisance to the spirit. This continues during the first seven weeks of mourning, and is accompanied, especially before the morning and evening meal, with loud lamentations. A portion of food is on these occasions presented to the deceased, whose merits the conductor of ceremonies bids those assembled keep fresh in their memories. In the length and loudness of their lamentations for the dead the Chinese rival the ancient Egyptians. It is indeed well known that all orientals give forcible expression to their grief on such occasions. St. Mark in his Gospel (v. 38) speaks of "them that wept and wailed greatly;" and again, in the Acts of the Apostles (viii. 2) we read of "devout men" who "made great lamentation over Stephen." On the 7th, 14th, 21st, 28th, 35th, 42nd, and 49th days of the period of mourning, the lamentations are louder and more frequent. At early dawn on each of these days, the relatives go into the street, and, kneeling down in front of the door of the house, lament bitterly. Their lamentations at such times are, I believe, more particularly for the soul of the deceased which is supposed to be on its way to Elysium; and food and offerings are therefore placed on the door-steps for the wandering spirit. Offerings on a very extensive scale are also presented to the soul, which is supposed to remain with the body. For example, a wealthy family offers on the 7th day the carcase of a sheep and nine dishes of as many different viands, together with wine. A feast is also made ready for the friends of the family. The offerings are regulated by sumptuary laws. Seven sheep are sacrificed to the manes of a duke, 40,000 paper ingots of gold are burned in a sacred fire, and no less than fifteen tables are spread with viands of various kinds. In honour of a marquis six sheep are sacrificed, 36,000 paper ingots of gold are burned, and thirteen tables are spread with viands. For an earl there are six sheep, 32,000 paper ingots of gold, and twelve tables; for a person of the first rank, civil or military, five sheep, 28,000 paper ingots of gold, and ten tables. In this way the value and number of the sacrifices diminish with each descent in rank. For a gentleman of the ninth rank, or of no rank, one sheep is sacrificed, 5,000 paper ingots of gold are burned, and two tables are spread. The banquet which is served up on the 21st day is especially in honour of the spirit which is destined to find its way to Elysium, and which on the day in question is supposed to return on a visit to the house. On this day all the members of the family carefully refrain from entering the hall in which the repast is spread, generally remaining in their private rooms. The entrance doors of the house are closed, and the neighbours also shut their doors. These arrangements are owing to a dread lest the visiting spirit should be disturbed and provoked to anger. This superstition originated in the Tong dynasty, A.D. 620, its most powerful advocate at the time in question being a literary character named Lee Tsay-pak.

The family of the deceased, as a rule, do not put on their mourning robes until the third day after death, on the ground that it is a duty to entertain, for a few days at least, a hope of the probability of resuscitation. The dresses worn are of coarse sackcloth. The sons or nearest of kin to the deceased wear, in addition, caps of the same material. From the top of each cap small balls, made of cotton, hang by threads. That sackcloth dresses were in ancient times worn by Asiatic mourners is evident from various passages of Scripture.[1] Chinese mourners allow their finger-nails, and the hair of the head as well as the beard, to grow during the first seven weeks of their bereavement. According to Herodotus, these observances were practised by the common people of Egypt, and there is a reference to them in the second book of Samuel (xix. 24). Chinese mourners, it need hardly be said, are very dirty in appearance. Occasionally all the members of the bereaved family fast, and for some time a strict separation is maintained between husbands and wives. They are, moreover, prohibited from giving their sons and daughters in marriage; and must close their ears against

---

[1] Cf. Job xvi. 15, 16; 1 Kings xxi. 27; and Jonah iii. 8.

good tidings of any kind. To frequent theatres, or to listen to music, during such seasons of sorrow is regarded as highly indecorous. The ordinary red covers are removed from the chairs and other articles of furniture in the house, and replaced by others of a blue or mourning colour. The pictures on the walls of the various rooms are either taken down, or turned towards the wall, and frescoes, or ornaments which cannot be removed, are covered with sheets of white paper. All members of the family who were absent at the time of the death are immediately called home. If sons of the deceased, they are made, upon entering the house for the first time after their parent's death, to creep upon all-fours as a mark of their deep humiliation and grief. The married daughter of the deceased, also, leaves her husband for seven days, in order that she too may attire herself in sackcloth and join in the lamentations of the family. On the seventh day, however, she throws aside her robes of sackcloth, and entering a sedan-chair is borne by four bearers to the house of her husband. In front of her sedan-chair, even though it be broad daylight, lighted lanterns of a gay colour are suspended. This is to imply that, though sorrow prevails at the house of her parents, joy and gladness are, or ought to be, found in the dwelling of her husband. On her arrival at the door of her husband's house, she is made to step over a fire of straw with the view of being purified. In passing through the Lin-fa-cheng street of the city of Canton, I once saw an old woman with small feet passing through a fire of this kind. Her dress was partially set on fire, and had not aid been promptly rendered she would have fallen a victim to her observance of the custom. In their *feriæ denicales* the ancient Romans observed a somewhat similar practice. On the tenth day after the death of a person, the house was swept with a broom of a particular kind, and the inmates also purified themselves by stepping over a fire.

For seven days after a man's death his widow and children show the intensity of their grief by sitting not upon chairs, but upon the ground. At night also they sleep, not in their beds, but upon mats spread on the ground near the coffin. During this period no food is cooked in the house, and friends and neighbours are trusted to supply the common necessaries of life. A similar custom was observed in Palestine in very early times.[1] Moreover, in eating the food thus supplied the family are not allowed to use chop-sticks, but their hands only. Nor are they permitted to use needles or knives during this period of grief. On the seventh day, however, it is customary for the sons or nearest of kin to the deceased, that is, if he has died at a very advanced age, to kindle a fire in the court-yard of the house and boil thereon a quantity of rice, they themselves sitting round the fire to superintend the operation. The women sit round the fire, giving vent to their grief. The rice, in the pan in which it has been boiled, is placed before the tablet of the deceased; and the Nam-Mo-loo rings a small hand-bell and utters a few prayers. The pan is then opened, and a bowl of the rice is taken to be presented in due form to the tablets of the family ancestors. Another bowl of it is presented to the tablet of the departed, and the remainder is distributed in small quantities amongst the family and the neighbours and friends. This rice is regarded as lucky, and, in many instances, the neighbours hasten to the house of the deceased lest their share of it should be forgotten. This ceremony is called by the Chinese, Chu-shou-fan, or "the boiling of longevity rice."

Letters are now written to all the relatives and friends of the deceased, informing them of the death. They are written upon paper of a light brown colour, and inclosed in envelopes of the same material. The paper is so folded that the first character that meets the eye is that of sorrow. The letters are stereotyped, and the following is a translation of one which fell into my hands :—

"My sins are many and heinous, and for them I ought to die. My life, however, is spared. The gods, nevertheless, have punished me by causing the death of my father. He died on the 5th day of the 10th month in the large hall of his dwelling-house. Now with reverence, and bowed down with grief, I hereby inform my friends of the sad calamity. My mother is now alone. (The names of the son and grandson of the deceased follow.)

[1] Cf. 2 Sam. iii. 35; Jer. xvi. 7 ; and Ezekiel xxiv. 17.

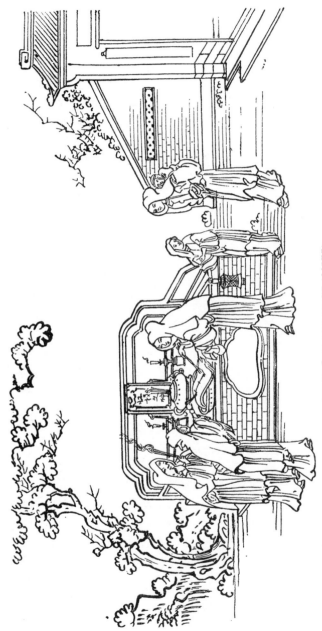

DEDICATING THE GRAVE-CLOTHES.

" Kwock A-tam,   } who shed tears of blood, and who bow
" Kwock A-cheong, } their hearts to the earth with grief."

The names of the nephews are also recorded, and opposite to
their names are placed characters which respectively signify
" Our tears flow, and our heads are bowed down with grief."
These letters are in some instances delivered by the grandsons
or nephews of the deceased, in others by servants attired in
mourning.   This singular custom of a son attributing to his sins
the death of his father, or *vice versâ*, was evidently observed by
the inhabitants of the land of Canaan.   Thus in the First Book
of Kings (xvii. 18) the widow of Zarephath is represented as
saying to Elijah the prophet upon the death of her son, " Art
thou come unto me to call my sin to remembrance and to slay
my son ? "   The period of the day selected for the delivery of
such letters is the evening.   The bearers do not in all cases
deliver them to the servants of the persons to whom they are
addressed, but throw them over the hall doors ; for the Chinese
regard it as unlucky to see at their doors one who is attired in
mourning apparel.   Presents of money are immediately forwarded
to the house of mourning by all persons receiving such letters.
The money, which is termed Fo-yee, " helping money," is spent
upon incense, candles, and offerings for the soul of the dead.
The members of the family in due course present their sympathizing friends with small porcelain bowls, or tea or wine
cups of the same material.   On the steps of the entrance door of
the house a white board is placed, on which are recorded in black
letters the hour, day, and year in which the deceased was born ;
the hour, day, and year in which he died ; his names and titles ;
the names and titles of his sons, and the names of his grandsons
and nephews.   On the 21st day of the period of mourning,
three large paper birds resembling storks are placed on high poles
in front of the house.   The birds are supposed to carry the soul
to Elysium ; and during the next three days, Buddhist priests
address prayers to the ten kings of the Buddhist hades, calling
on them to hasten the flight of the departed soul to the Western
Paradise.

As the coffin is kept in the house of mourning for a period of seven weeks, or forty-nine days, an altar is erected near it in the *atrium*. The altar is placed immediately in front of a chair which stands upon a temporary dais, and upon which a portrait of the deceased and a tablet bearing his name are placed. For this purpose every Chinese gentleman has his portrait taken. Sometimes, although rarely, they have small wooden effigies made instead. Thus, on one occasion I saw an idol of a general named Mūh, who was at the time in command of the Tartar troops at Canton. The idol had been presented to him by the troops, and was kept in the temple of the Five Genii. Mūh afterwards took the idol—a faithful representation of himself—to Tartary. Again, a gentleman named Cham Kom-tsune, who resided in the old city of Canton, had a wooden image of himself in his ancestral hall. In Buddhist temples I have also occasionally seen very small clay or wooden images of priests, made against the day of their death. Offerings consisting of various kinds of fruits are neatly arranged on the altar; and immediately in front of the tablet, a cup of tea, a plate of food, and a pair of chop-sticks are placed. If the deceased has been addicted to the vice of opium-smoking, an opium pipe is placed on the altar, which is also covered with such flowers as are in season. Near the chair on which the tablet is placed stands a long bamboo pole with a streamer made of dark red satin, and bearing in letters of gold the names and titles of the deceased. The streamer, like the other appointments, varies according to the rank of the deceased. In the case of gentlemen of the first three ranks, it is ninety Chinese inches long; streamers of less length being used for those of inferior rank. In the case of each person who dies at a tolerably advanced period of life, two long strings of copper cash are attached to this pole. In the case, however, of a person of middle age, only one string of copper cash is affixed to the pole. Upon the seventh day of mourning, presents of various kinds are sent by sympathizing friends. These are intended for the soul of the dead man, and consist of candles, or cakes, or banners, and a small sum of money. Upon the banners, which are either of a blue or white colour, are letters of gold, which set forth the merits of the deceased; and, as they are thereby supposed to convey sympathy to the mourners, the banners are regarded in the light of letters of condolence. A letter is sent also with the present; and the tenor of this document may be gathered from the following translation of one which fell into my hands :—

" Awong, who is your stupid and young brother, presents to you herewith two banners on which are written words of comfort. He also sends one roast pig, two baskets of cakes of flour, a variety of fruits, a bottle of wine, and a small sum of money, $10. I lament with many and bitter tears your death, but most of all do I sorrow that your stay in this world was so short. The 3rd day of the 10th month of the 3rd year of the reign of Tung-chee."

The letter is cast into a sacred fire, in order that it may be conveyed to the departed spirit. Within the door of the house of mourning a person sits at a table registering the presents, so that when the days of mourning are ended a gift of equal value may be presented in the name of the departed one to each donor. The banners to which I have referred, are, so soon as they are received, placed upon the inner walls of the house of mourning, and impart to the dwelling-house, especially by night when the halls are lighted up, a most imposing appearance. In the case of wealthy persons, the banners are very large and costly, and so numerous as to cover the spacious walls. The other gifts, such as fruits, flowers, cakes, and tapers, are placed upon the altar as eucharistical offerings to the spirit of the deceased. On this same day, each donor calls at the house of mourning for the purpose of worshipping the spirit of the deceased, and presenting a burning incense stick, which is placed on the altar. The friends who come for this purpose do not appear in a court dress, but in a raiment of dark cloth. Those on whom the badge of the peacock's feather has been conferred do not wear it on this occasion. Within the porch of the house of mourning on this day, three or four musicians are seated, who play doleful tunes upon their shrill and discordant pipes when visitors arrive. This practice has many times reminded me of the passage in which St. Matthew (ix. 23) tells how " Jesus came into the ruler's house, and saw the minstrels and people making a noise." Again, on this same day, that is the seventh day of mourning, priests of the sect of Buddha, or of that of Taou, are called in to assist, by their prayers, the flight of the departed spirit towards Elysium. They erect, in a room which immediately adjoins the hall in which the coffin is placed, seven altars. Above these they suspend pictures, which represent respectively the past, present, and future Buddha, and ten other pictures, each of which represents one of the ten kingdoms of the Buddhist hades. At stated intervals, masses are said for the repose of the soul of the deceased. The poorer classes, unable to retain the services of Buddhist priests, seek on such occasions the services of the Nam-mo-loo, a functionary to whom I have already referred. These ceremonies are again repeated on the 14th, 21st, 28th, 35th, 44th, and 49th days of mourning, the 21st being by far the most important of these days. The expenses which are incurred on the 35th day are defrayed by the female members of the family. When the spirit of a deceased person who held high rank is the object of worship, the rites and ceremonies are upon a very grand and expensive scale, and make a deep impression upon the minds of the Chinese.

Thus, on the death of H. E. Phih Wei, the governor-general of the two Kwangs, all the officers, whether civil or military, who were serving at the time in Canton and its environs, repaired on the 21st and 35th days of mourning to the palace where the body was lying in state; and the homage rendered to the deceased was apparently not a mere form. On this, as on many other occasions, I observed that while each votary worshipped the tablet, the sons, who were dressed in sackcloth, prostrated themselves upon the ground in deep humiliation and sorrow. The youths, still in a recumbent position, were then saluted by each votary, and politely acknowledged the compliments which had been paid to the shade of their father. If the house in which a deceased person is lying in state is too small to receive many worshippers, it is not unusual to remove the portrait and tablet of the deceased, with the red satin streamer which bears his names and titles, to the public hall of a neighbouring temple. This, however, is probably seldom done, except at the funeral ceremonies of officials. Thus the remains

of Loi Tsung-neen, a famous general who was killed at the
siege of Soo-chow, were brought back to Canton, which was his
native place, and placed in one of the temples, to receive the
homage of the grandees of the city. I also witnessed a similar
ceremony in honour of a distinguished soldier named Cheong
Kwok-laong, who fell fighting bravely in a battle with the
insurgents in Kong-nam. In the month of August, 1861, I
saw in one of the state temples in Canton the funeral of the
Emperor Hien-fung. The despatch containing the melancholy
intelligence of the Emperor's death was received at Ma-tow—an
official landing place in the vicinity of the city—by the officials
attired in robes of sackcloth. It was then entrusted to a herald,
who, with his hands raised above his head, carried it, in the midst
of loud lamentations, to the Tsip-Koon-Teng, or hall of audience,
where he read it aloud in the hearing of all the officials. The
officials then proceeded to the temple of Kwan-te, where, upon
a dais, stood a throne covered with yellow silk, and screened
from view by curtains of the same material. The officials, *i.e.*,
the civil officers with the governor-general, and the military
officers with the Tartar general, at their head, having arranged
themselves, the former on the left, and the latter on the right
side of the throne, prostrated themselves on the ground at a
command given by the conductor of ceremonies. Each officer,
at the same time, either cried, or attempted to cry. Indeed,
several of them succeeded in working themselves into such fits
of frenzy that saliva was actually oozing from their nostrils and
mouths. This highly ridiculous ceremony was repeated on
several days in succession; and for many weeks the citizens
were not allowed to shave their heads, or to frequent places of
public resort and entertainment.

Let us now proceed to consider the manner in which the
Chinese dispose of their dead. In the very earliest times it was
customary for almost all nations to bury the dead out of their
sight. Thus in the Bible, which is the oldest book we can read
there are only two instances recorded of the practice of getting
rid of the dead by cremation. The one instance, which is contained in the First Book of Samuel (xxxi. 12), refers to the burning of the bodies of Saul and his sons : and the other, in the

Book of the prophet Amos (vi. 10), refers to the burning of the bodies of certain persons who had died during a time of pestilence. The Chinese are no exception to this apparently general rule. Cremation is only resorted to by the majority of the priests of the sect of Buddha. It ought also to be stated that in the province of Kiang-nan it was customary during the Sing dynasty, A.D. 960, to burn the dead. In each village throughout the province in question there was a place for the purpose, called Fa-Yan-Ting, or receptacle for men's ashes. The ashes when removed from the funeral pyre were not unfrequently cast into the neighbouring rivers or creeks. There was also at a later period, in the same province, a Buddhist temple called Toong-Tsze, to which the priest urged the people to bring their dead for cremation, declaring that the souls of the departed would in consequence become Buddhas. The funeral pyre in the monastery having been struck by lightning, many persons who saw in this a mark of Divine displeasure, memorialized the governor of the province not to allow the pyre to be re-erected. With these few exceptions, it would appear that, throughout the whole of their nationa history, the Chinese have observed the practice of burying the dead. The Mongolians, on the other hand, have recourse to cremation, but as the ceremony is a very expensive one among them, it is in a great measure confined to the wealthy classes. The poor of Mongolia expose their dead in remote parts of the plains over which they wander, and leave them to be devoured by wild beasts, wolves and foxes in particular. The summit of a hillock is generally selected for a funeral pyre, and it is customary for the relatives to mark the spot where the body has been burned, by erecting a pile of stones. I passed several such cairns on the plains of Inner Mongolia.

Chinese families who are unable to find or to purchase a lucky place for interment, not unfrequently deposit coffins containing the dead on the sides of hills, which are used as cemeteries, until such time as they shall be able to afford the due rites of burial. In some instances the coffins are allowed to remain exposed for several years, during which, however, the customary acts of homage are paid to the remains of the deceased. In other instances poverty, change of residence, or death, prevents the relatives from removing the coffins, which, neglected for a long time, are at last buried at the public expense. In a temple called Tsze-Tchu-Miu, in the western suburb of Canton, a fund was established in 1870 to purchase a plot of ground for the interment of several coffins which had been left exposed for many years on the hill-sides of Pechung, a village about seven miles distant from the city. Contributors to this fund were of course moved by pity for the unhappy souls of the unburied dead. Shortly after the neglected bodies had been interred I visited the place, and found three or four men who had come, so they informed me, from the distant village of Tai-shek, to exhume the body of one of their ancestors. As the name had been painted on each coffin, and as there was a small head-stone to each grave, they had no difficulty in finding the remains. The bones were put into a cinerary urn for removal to the village, in which generations of the family had probably lived and died.

Like other nations of antiquity, the Chinese regard the rites of sepulture as of the utmost importance. The loss of such rites, which death by drowning or in battle often involves, is regarded as nothing short of a calamity. That the ancient Jews held similar views as to the importance of the rites of sepulture is evident from several passages in the Old Testament,[1] and the ancient Romans believed that the spirits of those whose corpses had not been buried were not allowed, for a hundred years at least, to cross the river Styx. So much, indeed, were the latter impressed with the importance of sepulture, that for friends who had perished, and whose bodies could not be found, they performed the rites at empty tombs. This custom has its parallel amongst the Chinese, who, in their devout respect for the dead, are in no way behind the classical nations of antiquity During the reign of the emperor Chan-tuk, in the first century of the Christian era, it was enacted that if the bodies of soldiers who fall in battle, or those of sailors who fall in naval engagements, cannot be recovered, the spirits of such men shall be called back by prayers and incantations, and that figures shall be made either of paper or of wood for their reception, and be

[1] I refer to 2 Sam. xxi. 9-14 ; 2 Kings ix. 28-34 ; Ps. lxxix. 2 ; Ec. vi. 3.

buried with all the ordinary rites. It is recorded in the annals of China, that the first persons who conformed to this singular enactment were the sons of an officer named Lee Hoo, who fell in battle, and whose body could not be recovered. The custom is now universally observed. On the occasion of a visit which I paid to Tai-laak, the capital of the ninety-six villages, I had an opportunity of seeing so singular a ceremony. An effigy of the missing man, clad in robes of the most costly kind, was placed on the ground, and a number of men and women, dressed in deep mourning, knelt round it. In the centre of the circle a Taouist priest invoked the spirit to come to the body prepared for it, and accompany it to the tomb. Lest the soul of the deceased should be imprisoned in one of the ten kingdoms of the Buddhist hades, miniature representations of the infernal prisons were made by means of small clay flags or tiles. They reminded one of dolls' houses. Prayers in which the kings of the infernal regions were in turn invoked, were then offered, and at the conclusion of each invocation the priest with a short magic wand dashed to the ground one of the miniature prisons. The effigy was eventually, with the usual observances, put into a coffin and conveyed to the grave by the sorrowing relatives. I was told before leaving the spot, that the man who was supposed to be dead had several years before gone as a travelling merchant to the neighbouring province of Kwang-si, but that since then his relatives had not heard of him. They concluded that he had been lost at sea, or killed by pirates. Sometimes persons whose obsequies have been celebrated in consequence of their supposed death, return to their family hearths and altars. I was acquainted with a native of Tsze-kai, a village near Si-nam, in the county of Nam-hoi, who, when a youth, was kidnapped and sold as a slave in Havanna, where he remained for a period of twenty years. His friends naturally concluded that he was dead. The ceremonies necessary in such a case were observed, and his younger brothers, nephews, and cousins performed the customary acts of worship at a tablet bearing his name, and placed on the ancestral altar of the family. The absentee returned to the home of his fathers in 1870, and is now a fruiterer in the Loo-pai-hong street of the western suburb of

Canton. There is a law in China, that the sons of missing
parents shall wear slight mourning, and on no account frequent
places of public entertainment. This law, however, is, I apprehend, more honoured in the breach than in the observance.
The sites which the Chinese—who are great believers in geomancy
—consider most propitious for tombs, are the sides of hills,
whence a view of rivers, creeks, lakes or ponds, can be obtained.
The hills near cities and towns are often literally covered
with tombs—melancholy memorials of the antiquity and popu-
lousness of the habitable places of the empire. The hills by
which the White Cloud mountains are approached from Canton
may be termed vast mounds of human dust. They are literally
bestudded with graves from base to summit. Seen on a summer's
evening, by the light of the setting sun, they present a very
striking appearance, and I shall never forget my feelings, as I
gazed one evening from the monastery of Pak-wan-um[1] upon
the melancholy spectacle of this vast pagan grave-yard.

For a lucky spot for a tomb wealthy families pay large sums
of money. Not content with a space similar in area to that
which is ordinarily allotted in Europe to each mortal, they in
some instances purchase for one tomb an area sufficiently large
for the erection of a spacious mansion. The selection of a site
for a tomb is entrusted to a geomancer. This functionary in the
discharge of such a duty not unfrequently spends several days
on the sides of the mountains. He is provided with a compass,
wherewith to ascertain the exact position of the spot he may
select; and in some instances he is accompanied not only by two
or three of the nearest relatives of the deceased, but by two or
three men with pickaxes and spades, who dig up here and there
portions of the soil for his inspection. The Chinese call the
men of the pariah class who accompany the geomancer, Shan-
Kow, or mountain-dogs. So soon as a site has been obtained,
a fortune-teller is called upon to name a propitious day
for digging the grave. The grave-diggers must not begin
their work before the members of the family of the
deceased have worshipped the genii of the mountain; and a
letter addressed to these gods is read aloud by the nearest of

---

[1] This monastery is situate beyond the north-east gate of Canton.

kin, who on the occasion in question wears not mourning, but court costume. All such letters are written in precisely the same words, and the following is a translation of one which I had an opportunity of seeing:—"We, the sons and relatives of ——, who died on the ——, intend to bury his remains here, and, as it is now our desire to make ready the tomb, we pray you not only to grant your sanction to such a proceeding on our part, but at all times to care for and prosper us. Moreover, we most respectfully beg to offer unto you offerings of fruits and wines, which be graciously pleased to accept." The kow-tow having been performed by each person present, the letter is despatched to the gods by being committed to the flames. When the grave is being prepared, a member of the family is present in order to superintend the operations of the workmen, and a temporary mat hut is erected. The bottom of the grave is lined with a layer, three inches thick, of lime mixed with powdered charcoal. Over this is placed a board, covered with a layer of charcoal dust, which is made very hard by being tramped down. The grave having been prepared, it is necessary that a lucky day and hour should be selected for the burial. This sometimes occasions a delay of several days, or weeks as the case may be. So anxious were the relatives of a person with whom I was acquainted to select a really lucky day for his interment, that they actually delayed it for several months, placing in the prepared grave, as is customary on such occasions, a slab on which the name of the deceased was painted. In some districts it is customary to delay the burial, should one or more of the ladies of the bereaved family be *enceinte*. In such a case the funeral does not take place until the expected birth has taken place. The grandmother of a gentleman with whom I was on very intimate terms, remained unburied for several years, because one or other of the ladies of the family were *enceinte*.

On the day before the burial, the relatives, in mourning garments, repair to the house of the deceased to weep and lament by the coffin. A long white streamer, which is termed the soul-cloth, is borne by the relatives to the ancestral hall, in order that the soul may take leave of the spirits of the ancestors of the family. It was, I believe, customary in former times to take the coffin into the ancestral hall for the purpose. At this leave-taking, the relatives, who place themselves in front of the ancestral tablets, give vent to loud lamentations. In some provinces the mourners, on the day preceding the funeral, purify the streets and houses along the route which the procession is to take. This ceremony, termed Khan-loo-Shuee, is observed as follows : Taouist or Buddhist priests, whichever may be summoned, offer up prayers at the house of mourning for the repose of the soul, and, informing it of the intention of the friends to bury the body on the morning, entreat it to accompany the body to its last resting-place. A procession is then formed, which marches through the streets of the city or village along which the body is to pass. Each priest is provided with a rude musical instrument, upon which he plays, in order to charm the evil spirits in the neighbourhood, and prevail upon them not to appear as the funeral cavalcade passes, lest they should affright the departed soul and cause it to return to the dwelling-house. The procession is headed by a youth carrying in his left hand a small tub of holy water, and in his right a bunch of hyssop. He sprinkles the streets and shops with the water, in order to preclude the possibility of evil spirits lurking in them. On the only occasion on which I witnessed a procession of this kind, it consisted of Taouist priests, attired in costly robes of blue satin, and provided with musical instruments, on which they discoursed what appeared to me a solemn dirge. The youth who, attired for the occasion, carried the holy water, entered each shop and sprinkled the floor. Evidently the occupants, who all seemed to welcome him, entertained no doubt of the efficacy of the rite.

On the night preceding the day of the burial of a person who has died at a very advanced age, it is usual in some villages for the neighbours to assemble at the house of mourning and beat gongs, tom-toms, and drums at frequent intervals, or sing songs. At three or four o'clock on the morning of the funeral all the decorations erected in front of the door are taken down and set on fire, amidst the howlings and lamentations of the bereaved relatives. At a later hour, tables covered with

viands are placed before the tablet of the deceased, and the
spirit is addressed as follows by the Nam-mo-loo : " We are now
about to remove your remains to the tomb ; and as you must
of necessity accompany them to the tomb, and there remain
with them in perpetuity,[1] we have prepared for you a parting
feast. Partake of it, we pray you." The conclusion of this
address is followed by a sudden outburst of lamentation from
the assembled family.

When the deceased had reached the age of sixty years, or
upwards, a man stations himself at the door and beats a gong to
summon the friends and neighbours. The distant relatives and
friends await the arrival of the corpse in the street, the immediate relatives remaining within. Previous to the lifting of
the body, the Nam-mo-loo sets a quantity of paper on fire, and
waves it along and round the coffin, which it is supposed to purify
and light up. The Nam-mo-loo then calls upon the departed
spirit to accompany the coffin to the tomb, while the sorrowing
relatives stand around weeping and lamenting. This ceremony
ended, the eldest son removes the tablet of the deceased, and
places it in a sedan-chair. He places the portrait in another chair,
over the top of which he arranges a streamer of red satin on
which the name and titles of the deceased are recorded in letters
of gold. The various offerings carried in a Chinese funeral
procession having also been placed under gilded canopies, the
coffin-bearers enter the house. As they are in the act of
lifting the coffin, all the relatives rush, in a state of great
alarm, into the adjoining apartments. They are afraid lest
the day selected for the burial by the geomancer should be unpropitious, and the soul of the deceased should in wrath afflict
those present with sickness or other calamities. The first time
I witnessed this superstition was at the funeral of an old Hong
merchant named Lo Poon-qua. Ignorant of the custom, I was
somewhat startled at the stampede of mourners which took
place as soon as the bearers began to lift the coffin. When the

---

[1] The idea that the soul is buried with the body was entertained by the
Romans. Virgil describes Æneas as having entombed the soul of Polydorus in
a sepulchre :—

"Animamque sepulchro
Condimus."

moment of danger was supposed to have passed, the mourners returned from their places of concealment. No warning had been given to me, and I naturally felt that the Chinese were only acting, as usual, on the principle that self-preservation is the first law of nature. As the body is carried across the threshold, offerings are presented to the soul of the departed. The coffin is placed upon a bier in the street, where it remains during other funeral ceremonies. The males and females of the family, for instance, march round it in solemn procession.

The funeral *cortége*, which is now formed, includes, among others, the following functionaries:—two men bearing large lanterns, recording the family name, age, and titles of the deceased; two men, each bearing a gong which he beats loudly at intervals, to give warning of the approach of the cavalcade; and sixteen musicians, immediately followed by men with flags, and by others carrying red boards with the titles of the deceased and of his ancestors inscribed on them in letters of gold. The boards are replaced, after the funeral, in the hall of the house. A similar ceremony was practised in the funeral processions of the ancient Romans—images of the ancestors being carried before the corpse. These ancestral busts were kept in the *atrium* of the house, and bore the titles and honours and a summary of the exploits of the deceased. The ancestral tablets are followed by four richly carved and gilded canopies—carried sometimes by horses, sometimes by men—under each of which are arranged offerings for the dead. The portrait of the deceased comes next, carried in a sedan-chair, and followed by a band of musicians. Next comes a sedan-chair, with a wooden tablet inscribed with the name of the deceased. Then follows a man called Fong-Loo-Tchun-Yan, who scatters at intervals pieces of paper, supposed to represent ingots of gold or silver. The mock money is intended for hungry ghosts, *i.e.*, for the souls of men who have died at the corners of the streets. These restless spirits, if not appeased, will greatly trouble the departed soul. Next come the sons of the deceased, each attired in deep mourning. The eldest son carries a wooden staff in one hand at his father's funeral, and a bamboo staff at his mother's funeral. Strips of white paper are twined round the staff. In the other hand, at the end of a bamboo pole, he carries a white streamer, called the soul-cloth, and supposed to summon the soul to accompany the body. A cock is carried in the funeral procession for the same purpose. On either side of the eldest son, who is supposed to be bowed down by grief, a person walks to support him. Behind him follows the bier, sometimes drawn by horses. When they are not used, sixty-four men are appointed to draw the bier of a person of the first or second rank; forty-eight, that of a person of the third, fourth, or fifth ranks; and thirty-two, that of a person of the sixth or seventh rank. The corpse is followed by the relatives and friends. The relatives wear half-mourning, and the friends wear bands of white cloth round their head. In the procession a man called Pi-Li-Sze-Yan gives each person at the grave a piece of betel nut wrapped in a leaf, and a piece of silver or a copper cash wrapped in cream-coloured paper. The sons of the deceased walked immediately in front of the coffin: but I have seen sons walking on either side of the sedan-chair containing the tablet of their father. At the funeral of Lo Poon-qua, one son was at the time residing in Batavia, and mourning robes, intended for him, were bound to the shafts of the sedan-chair, which was accompanied by the other sons. This singular custom, which is adopted universally, is intended not only to imply that the son though absent in body is present in spirit, but to inform people in the streets through which the procession passes that the deceased left other sons than those present. All who were bound to the deceased by the ties of consanguinity, are expected to walk in the procession. Female relatives, however, unable to do so owing to contracted feet, often content themselves with accompanying it for a short distance. This is the case, for example, in Canton and its immediate environs; but in the district of Sai-chu, which is thirty English miles distant from that city, the women as well as the men must walk to the grave. I once witnessed a funeral procession from the slopes of the Sai-chu mountains. Before me stretched a vast plain, extending from the base of the mountains to the western branch of the Canton river, and literally studded with towns and villages nestling amid umbrageous trees. The long funeral train took a quarter of an hour to pass a given point. All who were present, of both sexes, wore long white dresses, and the effect in the distance was very impressive. Where the women take part in these processions, the sexes are sometimes separated by a cordon of white cloth, which is borne by two men. Women with small feet are permitted to ride, not in sedan-chairs, but on the backs of female servants or slaves. In Sinam, a large and populous town in the district of Sam-shuee, I saw a procession in which numerous ladies, attired in deep mourning, were riding on the backs of female servants or slaves. The bearers of the coffin went through the streets of the town at a smart pace, and one of the slaves, with a very stout old lady on her back, had great difficulty in keeping up with it. At Pekin, Tien-tsin, and other northern cities, especially in Tartary, I observed that at funerals both males and females nearly all rode in covered carts or on horseback. The longest train of wheeled carriages I have ever seen in China or elsewhere, was at a funeral procession in Pekin. The catafalque was very large, and the bearers were dressed in green, and had red plumes in their hats. Each person present carried a small banner in his hand, and the state umbrellas were also very numerous. The procession was headed by trumpeters, who produced very grave and dismal sounds from trumpets larger and longer than those used in the south of China. The sons of the deceased walked on either side of the sedan-chair, which contained the tablet; the widow and daughters rode in carts, immediately behind the coffin. In other parts of the empire those only are allowed to ride who are of greater age or higher rank than the deceased. In all cases those who ride alight when they come in sight of the tomb, and walk the remaining distance.

I have mentioned the Fong-Loo-Tchun-Yan, or scatterer of paper money. To appease or dispel evil spirits, it is customary in some parts to carry in the procession an idol of Hoi-Loo-Shan. This personage was a distinguished minister of state in the reign of Hin-yun, an Emperor who flourished towards the close of the Chow dynasty. The latter was in the habit, with his Empress, of making tours of inspection throughout his northern provinces, and on one of these tours the Empress died. Upon an attempt being made to remove the coffin containing her remains, it was found to be so heavy as to be quite immovable. Hoi-Loo-Shan was, therefore, requested by the Emperor to take charge of the coffin. On a second attempt to remove it, the task was readily accomplished. This was attributed to the good influences of Hoi-Loo-Shan, whose shining virtues the evil spirits were supposed to be unable to resist. In certain parts of the Empire, the dispersion of evil spirits is supposed to be accomplished by carrying at the head of the funeral procession a man dressed as an avenger. His face is covered with a fierce-looking mask, which in a funeral of either the first, second, or third rank, is provided with three eyes, one of which is placed in the centre of the forehead; and in that of a person of lower rank, with two eyes. On the arrival of the procession, this dispeller of evil spirits strikes each corner of the grave with a spear. Wealthy families erect a mat tent over the grave, and the coffin is placed by the side of it on two tressels. The female mourners, if any are present, kneel and perform the kow-tow on the right side of the grave, and the male mourners on the left. The coffin is then lowered by ropes amidst their loud lamentations. These ropes are not removed until the geomancer has assured himself, by means of a compass, that the coffin lies in a straight position, and the utmost care is taken to adjust it exactly to the bed prepared for it under his directions. This functionary, or the priest, as the case may be, then addresses a few words to the soul of the deceased, calling upon it to remain with the corpse. The mourners kneel during this address; and at the close of it, the priest or geomancer offers as an eucharistical sacrifice to the soul a quantity of paper or mock money, paper carriages, and paper images of men-servants and maid-servants, which are burned in order that they may be conveyed to the world of spirits for its use. A hermetically-sealed pot containing rice boiled on the day when the corpse was placed in the coffin, is lowered into the grave as food for the soul. Grains of unboiled rice are also scattered over the coffin, and libations of tea poured upon the ground. Sometimes five effigies of cows, made of the roots of trees, are put into the grave to avert evil influence from the north, south, east,

and west, and from the centre of the earth. When the grave-
diggers begin to cast the earth into the grave, the priest or
geomancer lifts the cock which was carried in the procession,
and, standing at the foot of the grave, bends his body forward
three times. Each mourner, receiving the bird in turn, repeats
the ceremony. The soul cloth is then committed to the flames
of a sacred fire. The tablet bearing the name of the deceased is
next removed from its sedan-chair by the chief mourner, in
order that the dearest friend of the family may make a mark
on it with a vermilion pencil. After this he addresses a few
words of exhortation to the sons of the deceased, calling upon
them to live at all times as their father would have them live
were he present with them. They receive the exhortation
kneeling. Sometimes this ceremony is observed on the return
of the funeral party to the house of mourning, when the
sons put off their sackcloth robes and appear in tunics of
black broadcloth. The red mark on the tablet is made, I suppose, in order that good fortune may attend the sons, and has
a particular reference to the blessings of wealth and posterity.
After the tablet has been marked, every one present does homage
to it, the sons knocking their heads on the ground thrice, and
the more distant relatives twice. Poor families give a small fee
to a schoolmaster or graduate to mark the tablet and deliver
the exhortation.

The funeral procession returns to the house of mourning in
nearly the same order in which it set out. On arriving at the
door of the house, the mourners sometimes purify themselves by
stepping over a fire of straw. On entering they frequently wash
their eyes and sprinkle their faces three times with water in
which the leaves of the pomeloe tree have been boiled. In this
water of purification have been mingled the ashes of a piece of
paper on which a Taouist priest has written a mystic scroll.
The tablet of the deceased is then placed in a private chamber,
where it remains for one hundred days. The funeral party
then proceed to celebrate the feast of the dead. In the hall
in which this banquet is held, a portrait of the deceased is
placed on the wall, and various kinds of food are arranged
before it. This custom is not unlike the *toscar* or feast of

the dead which is celebrated on the death of an Abyssinian. On the third day after the interment, it is customary in some parts of the Empire for the sons or near relatives to revisit the grave, worshipping and marching in procession three times round it. I have seen this ceremony, which is termed Yune-Sha, or seeing that the grave is in order, in the graveyards of the district or county of Heong-shan.

On the hundredth day of mourning, the services of the Nam-mo-loo are again called into requisition, and the tablet of the deceased is taken from the private chamber and placed upon the ancestral altar where it remains. On this occasion the Nam mo-loo addresses the soul of the deceased in the following terms :—" The body which you once inhabited having been dead one hundred days, it is now high time for you, together with the tablet, to take your place on the ancestral altar." Homage is paid to the tablet by all the relatives, and at the close the distant relatives take off their mourning robes and cast them into a fire kindled to consume them. On this day also the sons shave their heads, bind up their queues with blue instead of with white thread, and replace their white shoes by blue ones. At a banquet prepared for the occasion, and at which dishes of ducks' eggs, hard boiled, are noticeable among the many viands, not only the relatives, but the immediate friends of the family sit down. Offerings of food are of course presented to the tablet of the deceased. On the first anniversary of the death, offerings are again presented to the tablet, and all the bereaved relatives perform the kow-tow before it. These ceremonies are termed Tsaong. On the second anniversary, the tablet of the deceased is again worshipped, together with those of the other ancestors of the family. Numerous offerings of paper clothes, paper money, paper trunks, paper sedan-chairs, and paper man-servants and maid-servants are cast into a sacred fire in order to be conveyed to the ancestors. Buddhist or Taouist priests are present to offer up masses for the repose of the departed soul. The ceremonies of the second anniversary are termed Tai-Tsaong.

At the end of the first month of the third year, the members of the family substitute red visiting cards for the white mourning cards they have hitherto used. They write on them the character Tam, which signifies "grief not so bitter as before." At the close of the seventh month of the third year, the days of mourning are considered at an end. To mark this event, a large banquet is prepared to which all the relatives and friends of the family are invited. This ceremony is called Tut-Fuk, or putting off mourning. I was present at a banquet of this nature in 1871. It took place at the residence of a mandarin named Woang Sing-keet, in the Kee-hā Street of the old city of Canton. The feast was upon a most extensive scale, and was attended by all the members and friends of the family. Amongst the ancient Persians it was customary to mourn for a father or mother during a period of three years, and on the completion of the days of mourning a large banquet was given by the members of the family. In all probability the banquet which was given by Ahasuerus, King of Persia, to the great men of his empire at the close of the third year of his reign (Esther i. 3), marked the completion of the period during which he had been mourning for his father. Although children in China mourn for a deceased parent for two years and seven months, or three years as they call it, they and their wives and children observe each recurring anniversary of the death, repairing to the nearest Buddhist monastery, and erecting an altar with a temporary tablet bearing the name of the departed; and engaging priests to offer up prayers for the repose of his soul. At these celebrations the members of the family are not in mourning, but generally in robes of the most costly description. I have often witnessed such ceremonies in the large monasteries of Canton, but more frequently in that which is termed the Flowery Forest monastery. Each officer, civil or military, is at liberty to close his office on the anniversary of a parent's death, and on that of the death of an emperor there is an entire suspension of business by all officers of state. Such anniversaries, which are termed Choy-Shon, or prolonging old age, are regarded by those immediately concerned as days of fasting.

I have already pointed out that the tomb of a Chinese gentleman is remarkable for the extent of ground assigned to it. The size of the plot varies from ninety English yards on each

side of a given centre to nine yards. The former gives the
area of the ground belonging to a personage of the first rank;
and the latter that of the grave of one below the seventh rank.
All tombs of these classes may be inclosed by walls, and the
rank of duke, or marquis, or earl, entitles the deceased to have
two watch-towers built in corners of the square. For a person
of any of the first five ranks only one watch-tower may be built.
Persons of the four remaining ranks may have two watchmen to
guard the tomb by night, but no watch-tower. Burial-places of
the classes I have described are endowed with lands or houses,
the rents from which go to keeping the tomb in repair and
paying the watchmen. The tombs of nobles, and of officers who
were of the first or second rank, may have an approach constructed, consisting of a stone pathway winding through an
avenue of stone figures,[1] in many instances much larger than
life. Two of these represent ministers of state; two, warriors
clad in armour; the others, horses, camels, sheep, and tigers, a
pair of each kind. There is a lofty stone pillar on each side of
the entrance to the avenue. For the third rank the representations are of horses, tigers, and rams, a pair of each kind; for the
fourth they are of horses and tigers; for the fifth, of horses and
rams. The statuary is wrought in granite, and two pillars mark
the entrance. The stone tigers are supposed to prevent the
approach of a wild animal, which the Chinese call Mong-
Tsaong, and believe to feed upon the brains of corpses. The
rams, camels, and horses, may have a reference to the pastoral
pursuits of the Mongolians. In the northern and midland
provinces fir and cypress trees are commonly planted round
graves, to prevent the Mong-Tsaong from approaching. The
epitaph on the tombstone consists of the names of the deceased;
the generation to which he belonged; the date of his birth, and
of his death; his titles; the names of his sons and grandsons;
the name of the village in which he resided, and, in some
instances, a summary of his virtues. The slab, which is placed
in front of the tomb of a duke, marquis, or earl, is ninety
Chinese inches high and thirty-six Chinese inches wide. Im-

---

[1] The custom of erecting stone figures of men and animals in front of the tombs
of men of rank, was, it is said, first practised in the Tsin dynasty about 249 B.C.

mediately above the inscription there is engraved a representation of the head of a reptile, thirty-two inches broad, called by the Chinese, Lee. The stone, which is placed in a perpendicular position, rests upon a figure of a tortoise thirty-eight inches thick. The tombstone of a person of the first rank is five inches lower than that of a nobleman, and two inches narrower, the representation of the head of the Lee being also two inches narrower. The tombstone of each descending class, is marked by a like diminution of size. The carving on the tomb of a gentleman of the second class is that of a Kee-lun—a fabulous animal which is said to appear when a sage is born. An animal called Pek-tsay is engraven upon the tombstone of a gentleman of the third class, and an ancient Chinese character of a circular form upon those of inferior officials. In the rear of the tomb-stone is erected another stone with the titles and names of the deceased, and those of his forefathers. It states which of his father's sons he was, and whether he survived him. At some of the villages at the base of the White Cloud mountains near Canton, and at Nam-tiang, a village in the neighbourhood of Whampoa, there are tombs such as I have described. When I visited the latter place, my servants were warned against touching any of the stone figures forming the avenue. I was told that instances had occurred of persons having become seriously ill in consequence of having done so. One of the most interesting tombs of this description is near the east gate of Canton. It contains the remains of a distinguished Tartar minister of state, who died at Canton ; and was erected at the command of the Emperor Shun-Chi, A.D. 1644. A translation of the inscription upon the tomb appeared in the *Friend of China* (August 24, 1861), and I give the following extracts :—

" The Emperor Shun-Chi receiving the behest of heaven says, The glory of a kingdom is to increase in wealth and to reward the meritorious. Of all the meritorious, those who aid in building up a kingdom should be cherished and exalted, for with prospect of reward others are induced to act nobly in behalf of government. This has been the practice both in ancient and modern times, and it is just."

* * * * * *

[After alluding to the services of the deceased, the Emperor proceeds to say :—]

" You, Pan-Chee-Foo, have been the emperor's arms and legs— exceedingly useful— day and night have you been faithful. And you, Pan-Chee-Foo's wife, ruling well your family, have, also, been of great aid to your husband ; the Emperor manifests his will regarding you also. When Pan-Chee-Foo was major-general, you assisted him to an extent which raised you in excellence far above all other women, and, therefore, shall you be rewarded according to your merits. I, therefore, confer on you a title of the first degree in commemoration of the labour you bestowed and the aid you gave your husband. I confer this unparalleled reward as well also, for your chastity and obedience ; and, although you are dead, yet your spirit is cognizant of the honour bestowed, and you will continue to remember these great rewards."

[The inscription concludes with the following apostrophe :—]

" You truly were of a noble nature and true heart. While an officer you were reverential and diligent. Suddenly you died. Alas, it grieved me sore, and I grant an additional worship. Your soul is not without understanding, may it fully enjoy this. Beyond the door, only your name is great. You have fought bravely. For many years you protected the boundary. But suddenly your body rests in the water and mud. I give you these offerings to show I lament your death. May you live in a city (be prosperous). May your sons return to us."

Of tombs of this class, the most interesting, in point of historical associations, which I visited, is near Hangchow. It contains the remains of one N'gock Pang-koee, a general who flourished during the reign of Fy-chung, a sovereign of the Tai-Soong dynasty. It appears that Fy-chung in fighting the invading army of a neighbouring sovereign was taken prisoner, and that his queen then offered great rewards to any of the officers of his army who should accomplish the overthrow of the enemy, and the restoration of her husband to his throne. The task was undertaken by N'gock Pang-koee, a soldier of distinction. The success of the expedition, however, was not what the prime minister of the captive sovereign desired. He was anxious to bring about the death of the latter, in the hope of occupying the throne. His wife, like another Jezebel, stimulated her husband's ambition, and plotted to procure the execution of N'gock Pang-koee by a false accusation. The prime minister, who was called Chun Poee, accordingly represented to the queen that the general was not only indifferent to the restoration of his sovereign, but was oppressing the soldiers under his command in a variety of ways—that he gave them little or no food, kept back their pay, and took care not to lead them against the enemy, who were daily laughing at his apparent imbecility. On these representations the queen determined on the execution of N'gock Pang-kooee. The general was accordingly recalled, and Chun Poee, fearing lest he should obtain an interview with the queen, secretly issued an order for his decapitation. This was done without her majesty's authority, but in her name, and the order was at once carried out when the general reached Hangchow. The elders of the city, who suspected underhand dealing, memorialized the queen. The case was investigated, and, the guilt of the prime minister and his wife and two others having been established, they were thrown into prison, where, two months later, Chun Poee sickened and died. Two sons of N'gock Pang-koee who had proved themselves as brave as their unfortunate father, were then appointed to the command, and succeeded before long in defeating the enemy, and restoring Fy-chung to his throne. On his restoration, the wife of Chun Poee was strangled, and the two male prisoners were executed by a process of slow torture. The wives and children and other near relatives of the male prisoners were also put to death, as well as the children and nearest relatives of the wife of Chun Poee. Posthumous honours were conferred on N'gock Pang-koee, and the tomb which now stands in his memory was erected It is in the form of a large circular mound, and is built of brick. In front of it, beside a stone altar and a large tombstone bearing an inscription, is a monumental gateway of three arches. The statues forming the approach represent two ministers of state, four warriors, two horses, two rams, and two *kee-luns*. Besides these there are four figures in a kneeling posture, as if in the act of asking forgiveness. These represent the four

murderers of N'gock Pang-koee, with their hands bound with
cords behind their backs, and on each figure the name of the
criminal is inscribed. The area in which the tomb stands is
inclosed by a wall. The upper part of the entrance door of the
area is very graceful, and before it is a small pond of water
encircled by a wall, on the top of which is a stone balustrade.
A neat monumental bridge of one arch spans the pond. Near
this bridge stands a wall in which are inserted four slabs, each
engraven with a Chinese character. The characters, which are
Ching, Chung, Pow, and Kwok, signify allegiance and attachment to the throne. These characters are said to have been
tattooed upon the back of N'gock Pang-koee by his mother,
when he was a child. The tomb remained intact until the close
of the eighteenth century, when a descendant of the wicked
prime minister, having taken high literary honours at Pekin,
memorialized the Emperor Kien-lung Wong to grant him, as an
especial favour, the removal of the figures which commemorated
the infamy of his ancestors. The Emperor acceded, but the
step gave great offence to the people, and he ordered the figures
to be replaced. They continued uninjured until the capture of
Hangchow by the insurgents, when they were more or less
mutilated by these iconoclasts. They were, however, restored by
the provincial judge as a monument which, he declared, ought
to stand for ever. It is usual for visitors, in some instances to
stone,[1] and in others to flog with sticks the iron figures which
represent the vile persons by whose false accusations the hero
was put to death. This, however, is a minor offence against
taste compared with another practice by which the Chinese
are accustomed to express their hatred of the crime thus commemorated. Near the tomb stands a temple in honour of the
unfortunate soldier, whom the Chinese of course deified. It was

[1] The observance of this singular custom recalls to my mind a parallel custom
mentioned by Robinson in his *Travels in Palestine and Syria*. That interesting
writer, in speaking of the sepulchre, or rather mausoleum, of Absolom in the valley
of Jehoshaphat, says that, to the tomb in question, there is no "perceptible
entrance, but the upper story has been opened by violence. Into this aperture
Mahommedans, Jews, and Christians, men and women, old and young, are in the
habit of throwing stones as they pass, meaning to testify their abhorrence of the
rebellion of a son against his father."

destroyed by the rebels, but was restored by Imperial grants of money.

In the prefecture of Hangchow I saw several graves, above each of which was placed a stone pillar resembling a pagoda in form; and on the banks of a small lake near the city I saw a domed sepulchre, which was open at the sides. It contained the remains of a member of the Soo family. On the granite pillars which supported a richly ornamented roof were inscribed prayers for the hastening of the wandering soul of the departed one to Elysium. In many of the central provinces, but especially in the low districts of these provinces, the dead are deposited in mausoleums. The coffins are not placed below the earth, but are made to rest on trestles, or, in some instances, upon the ground. Buildings of this kind differ much in shape. In some instances, they resemble the ordinary brick huts which in English meadows are erected for the service of cattle. One mausoleum which I visited, in the province of Kiang-soo, was erected in the centre of a courtyard of seventy feet by thirty. It was built of bricks, and consisted of three large chambers, each of which was above ground and approached by an arched door. As the bricks by which the entrance had at one time been blocked up had been thrown down, I was able to inspect these chambers, and in each of them I found coffins resting upon trestles. It was evident that either thieves or rebels had broken open the coffins in the hope of finding valuable ornaments and dresses. In the silk districts of the prefecture I observed several garden tombs. They were, as a rule, in sequestered spots, under wide spreading trees or in mulberry plantations. Each tomb was a vast mound of earth in the form of a half-circle. In the southern provinces of the Empire the tombs are not inclosed by boundary walls, nor are they surrounded by trees. They consist of a pyramidal mound of stone, or asphalte, or earth inclosed by a wall which resembles in form the Greek letter Ω. In front of a tomb of a man of rank two granite pillars, surmounted by figures of *kee-luns*, are erected. There are also the customary slabs for inscriptions. Long red flag-poles are in some instances erected in front of the tomb, and on extraordinary occasions, banners bearing the names and titles of the deceased are hoisted. The poles differ somewhat in form according to the rank of the deceased.

In 1865, I had an opportunity of visiting the imperial tombs near Chan-ping Chow, the city in the prisons of which certain English officers and Mr. Bowlby, the correspondent of the *Times*, were confined during the last war, after their capture under a flag of truce; and where they died of the cruel treatment to which they were subjected. The extensive valley in which these imperial tombs are contained, is approached by a large monumental arch of three gateways, and by an avenue of stone figures of colossal size. The figures, which are placed at a distance from each other of several yards, are four lions, four elephants, four camels, four horses, four warriors, and eight ministers of state. They are distributed so that where there are four of a kind, there are two on each side. Each tomb consists of a vast pyramidal mound of earth seventy English feet high, inclosed at the base by a wall which resembles in form the Greek letter Omega. The mound is thickly planted with cypress-trees. In front there is a large temple, whose lofty and vaulted roof is covered with yellow tiles, and supported by tall red pillars. In a niche, there is a tablet bearing the name of the deceased Emperor, and before it an altar on which at stated periods the customary offerings are placed. The tomb at Nankin which contains the remains of an emperor of the Ming dynasty is precisely similar to these. The interior of these vaults is very tastefully decorated. It was usual in former times for the imperial family to place figures of male and female servants in them. This custom is alluded to by Confucius in his writings as absurd. The remark of the sage, however, was misinterpreted, and from about 500 B.C. until the reign of the emperor Kien-lung, who abdicated the throne in 1795, it was customary to place not the effigies, but the servants themselves—a man and his wife—in an emperor's tomb. Two poor people were easily prevailed upon to become the attendants on departed royalty, in consideration of a sum of money settled on their families. Their chief duties were to burn incense, and to light tapers morning and evening at the head—or foot—of the coffin.

At Cheefoo, in the province of Shantung, I visited the cemetery of a prince who was a member either of the former or of the present dynasty. The cemetery was inclosed by four walls, and the tomb was approached by an avenue of cedar-trees and stone figures. On each side of the avenue were several smaller tombs, containing the remains of descendants of the prince, and surrounded by clumps of trees.

Among what are known as the ancient royal tombs, there are some which are said to be of extraordinary antiquity. The most ancient of these is that of the Fok-hi, who reigned B.C. 2852. The tomb is in the district of Wy-ning, in the province of Honam. The second is that of Mi-too, a sovereign upon whom, so say the Chinese, devolved the duty of repairing the vault of heaven. It is in the district of Chu-ching in the province of Shansi. Ten of these tombs belong to the third millennial period before Christ, and seven belong to the second. There are thirty-seven of these ancient royal tombs, the thirty-seventh being that of Hien-tsung, who reigned A.D. 1488. They are to be found chiefly in the provinces of Shansi and Honam, and worship is rendered at them by the officials of the districts in which they are respectively situated, at the equinoxes, on the accession of an heir apparent to the throne of China, on his marriage, on the celebration of each of his natal anniversaries which marks the completion of a decade of years. At such periods, a sheep and a pig are sacrificed before each of the tombs, except those of two emperors of the Kum dynasty, at which the sacrifice is a cow.

In the course of this chapter I have observed that geomancers are employed to choose lucky sites for tombs. Should the geomancer fail to find a site before the time appointed for the burial, it is usual for the mourners to convey their dead with funeral pomp and parade to a public building called " Koong-Tsoi-Chong." Such an edifice consists of several apartments, houses, or cottages, in each of which one or more coffins are placed, waiting for the indispensable geomancer. In each apartment there is an altar, with a tablet bearing the name of the deceased, before which are placed incense burners, candlesticks, and cups containing tea. In Canton the remains of

officials, merchants, or travellers who have come from other
parts of the empire, and died during their residence in the city,
are frequently deposited in this building. To bury them at
once at Canton would be to deprive them of that worship from
the family which is considered essential to the happiness of a
departed soul.[1] Formerly it was, I believe, customary for the
Chinese, when the geomancers failed in finding a lucky site, to
burn the coffin containing the body. Now, however, coffins are
sometimes allowed to remain thirty, forty, or even fifty years
in the Koong-Tsoi-Chong, either because a lucky site has not
been found, or because funds are wanting to celebrate the
obsequies. In the latter case, houses and lands are sometimes
mortgaged or sold ; and there are not a few instances on record
of men selling themselves as slaves to obtain the means of duly
celebrating the obsequies of a father or mother. An entrance fee
and a monthly rent are paid by those who place their dead in the
Koong-Tsoi-Chong, the sums paid varying according to the wealth
or rank of the family.   Should no member of the family leaving
the body visit it for three years, or should no rent be paid during
that period, the body is buried under the sanction and, I believe,
at the expense of the local government.   At Canton, near
the north gate, there is a Koong-Tsoi-Chong for the natives of
the province of Chit-Kong who have died in the city ; and near
the north-east gate there is one inclosed by a high circular wall,
and approached by folding doors, for the natives of the province
of Kiangsi. In addition to rows or streets of private cells for
the dead, it has three large public apartments which, when I
last visited it, were filled with coffins awaiting removal. To
foreigners, the most interesting institution, however, of this
nature is the Wing-Shing-Tsze, which is situated at a distance

[1] When travelling in Mongolia I met several Chinese officials returning to
their respective homes in China Proper, from stations at which they had been
serving for several years. In each case the official was attended not only by
secretaries, clerks, servants, and slaves, but by all the members of his family.
Sometimes the mules and asses, used as beasts of burden, were yoked to biers,
on which lay the remains of a deceased relative. These trains reminded me of
that portion of Joseph's history, when he went up from Egypt to Canaan to bury
his father, and when there went with him " all the house of Joseph, and his
brethren, and his father's house."

of one English mile beyond the east gate of Canton. It is laid
out, like those which I have been describing, in the form of a
small city, and is not inaptly termed "the city of the dead."
Two of its sides are flanked by a lofty wall, loopholed for
musketry. This precaution is taken against robbers, who are
said sometimes to bind themselves by an oath to remove the
body of a person who has bequeathed wealth to his relatives,
and to hold it until a ransom has been paid. When a suspicion
of this is entertained by the relatives of the deceased, a few
armed men are hired to keep watch by night. In this place
it was, and may still be, customary to keep a white cock, in
order that the spirits of the dead when disposed to wander
abroad might be recalled by its crowing. In the courtyard
there is a pond, the east bank of which, lined with trees and
shrubs, affords shelter, it is said, to no fewer than one thousand
"pagoda birds" or herons, which are held sacred to Buddha.
Attached to this same city of the dead there is a garden with a
large garden house. To this bower, persons, when visiting their
dead, resort to dine, and I have been present at many pic-nic
parties in it. In each city of the dead two or three priests of
the sect of Buddha reside, whose duty it is to offer occasional
masses for the repose of their souls. When on a visit to the
city of Chinkiang, I observed that in the absence of a Koong-
Tsoi-Chong, the corridors of the temple in honour of Shing
Wong were occupied by coffins containing dead bodies, which,
I was told, were those of men who had come to Chinkiang from
other parts of the Empire for the purpose of trade.

Where such institutions are not provided, the Chinese deposit
their dead on or near the sides of hills, which are used as cemeteries, or on the open plains, and, in some instances, by the
wayside. Walking once along a road in the immediate vicinity of
Eching, I observed several coffins by the wayside. Behind one of
these, which from its size evidently contained the remains of one
who in his lifetime had been accustomed to receive the good things
of this world, three poor women were sheltering themselves from
the cold north wind. Coffins are also deposited on the banks of
rivers, creeks, and canals. On one occasion I saw a very large
one on the banks of the Poyang lake. The coffins are in most

instances uncovered ; sometimes they are covered with matting, tin, or straw, sometimes with stones. At Kilung in Formosa I saw some which were covered with chunam or asphalte. At Nankin I observed coffins exposed in great numbers, and two or three of them were lying near the west gate of the city, where there is a large market for the sale of reeds. At Woo-see Hien I found one exposed in the middle of a market which is held daily for the sale of timber at the west gate. At Woo-chang, on the banks of the Grand Canal, I found more coffins exposed in proportion to the size of the city than in any other in the Empire. The unburied coffins were so numerous not only in the city itself, but throughout the district of which it is the capital, that I naturally inferred that few or no interments take place in that portion of China. It is not too much to say that from the city of Woo-chang to the market town of Ping-wong-chun, and for miles beyond, the banks of the Grand Canal were more or less covered with coffins. This reluctance to bury their dead is, I believe, to be attributed to the fact that the surrounding country is very flat, and that flat lands are by the geomancers deemed unlucky for tombs. When the coffins decay and fall to pieces, the bones of the dead are gathered together, put into bags, and cast into the water. At Koon-yam-moon, a market town near Nankin, I saw a coffin at the door of the house in which the family of the deceased person were residing. At the cities of Kiu-kiang, Chin-kiang, and at the town of Hankow I also saw coffins at the doors of houses in the less frequented streets. This singular custom, I was informed, arises not so much from a difficulty in finding lucky sites of interment, or funds for the funeral expenses, as from a reluctance to remove their dead out of their sight. This sentiment prevails to a still greater extent at Yang-chow Foo, where it is not unusual for tradespeople and others to keep their dead *within* their dwellings. Such persons often place near the coffin, on each occasion of their sitting down to table, a portion of their own meal. At Canton, I know only of two or three instances of this nature occurring. An old silk merchant, with whom I was very well acquainted, kept the remains of a wife whom he had dearly loved in his house for several years ; and a gentleman named Chay Yow-yan, who was also a personal friend of mine, and who resided in Tai-shap-poo, kept the remains of his father in his house for some time. A family named Ho, whom I knew, kept for many years the remains of their father in their house. In this case the step proved to their advantage, as the landlord of the house, although desirous of ejecting the inmates in consequence of their inability to pay him any rent, was unable to do this, so long as the corpse remained in the house.

In many of the cemeteries of the northern and midland counties, receptacles for human bones are erected. I saw them at Shanghai, Ningpo, Nan-kang Foo, Ta-koo-tang, and Tan-yang. As the bodies of infants are not unfrequently deposited there, they are sometimes called baby towers. They are built of bricks and mortar, and vary in shape : some are in the form of towers ; others are like pagodas. The buildings at Ta-koo-tang, Kam-poo-sheng, and Tan-yang reminded me of Sandys' description of the Aceldama, or field of blood, in the vicinity of Jerusalem.

" On the south side of this valley, near where it meeteth with the valley of Jehoshaphat, mounted a good height on the side of the mountain, is Aceldama, or Field of Blood, purchased with the restored reward of treason for a burial place for strangers. In the midst whereof a large square room was made by the mother of Constantine ; the south side walled with the natural rock, flat at the top, and equal with the upper level, out of which ariseth certain little cupolas open in the midst to let down the dead bodies. Through them we might see the bottom all covered with bones, and certain corpses but newly let down."

At Kilung, Tam-sin, and other ports on the coast of Formosa, each ossuary is in the form of a square hut or shed one side of which is unenclosed. In an ossuary at Kilung I saw not less than one hundred human skulls. At Canton the corpses of infants are generally wrapped in matting or cloth and cast upon the sides of the hills, especially upon the hill near the East gate of the city, which, being the cemetery for malefactors and others, is called the hill for 10,000 men's bones. Here they are devoured by dogs. In some instances they are cast into the water. In a large cemetery, however, at Pechung, near Canton, I observed a plot of ground which had been purchased by a wealthy family named Yeh, and set apart for the interment of infants. In cemeteries at Canton, it is customary for the gentry to employ men to gather human bones together for interment. Over each plot of ground in which the bones are buried, it is usual to erect a low conical mound of asphalte or chunam, in front of which is a small slab recording the number of bones which lie buried beneath.

In the spring time, particularly in the third month of each year, it is customary for the male members of Chinese families to visit the family tombs to pay homage to their ancestors. They present offerings of boiled pork, fowls, ducks, geese, and tea; suits of paper clothes, paper money, paper men servants and maid servants are also burned. All such sacrifices and offerings are, I believe, regulated by a law established in the first year—A.D. 1723—of the Emperor Yung-ching. The singular custom of presenting offerings of food to the dead appears to have been observed from the earliest times by all heathen nations; and we read of the children of Israel that, led away by their example, " They joined themselves unto Baal-peor, and ate the sacrifices of the dead " (Ps. cvi. 28). In the " Holy State " of Thomas Fuller, which was published in 1663, it is stated that " There was a custom in Africa to bring pulse, bread, and wines to the monuments of dead saints, wherein Monica (the mother of St. Augustine) was as forward as any. But being better instructed that this custom was of heathenish parentage, and that religion was not so poor as to borrow rites from paganism, she instantly left off that ceremony, and as for piety's sake she had done it thus long, so for piety's sake she would do so no longer." Fuller goes on to observe, " How many folks nowadays, whose best argument is use, would have flown in their faces who should stop them in the full career of an ancient custom."

The Chinese also pour libations of wine in honour of the departed dead ; and the whole ceremony is brought to a close by a salvo of fire-crackers. Worship is not confined to private family tombs, but whole clans resort to the tombs of their

WORSHIPPING AT THE TOMBS OF ANCESTORS.

founders. On reaching the tomb of their great forefather, they place immediately in front of it the insignia of the rank which he held; and, having first worshipped the genii of the mountain, they worship the souls of their forefathers. While they are thus engaged, musicians enliven the proceedings by playing various Chinese airs upon shrill pipes. After worship, they sometimes dine on the ground by tens *al fresco*. Sometimes the votaries return for dinner to the ancestral hall of the clan. At this banquet, which is called Pi-moo, or finishing the worship, three dishes are served up: the first consists of pork patties, cabbages, and crabs; the second of roast geese, stuffed with cocoa, and the third of baked rice. Similar dishes are presented to the souls of their ancestors. Large quantities of paper money are also burned before the ancestral tablets. The expenses are defrayed by funds arising from the lands by which ancestral halls are endowed.

To repair and ornament the tombs of their ancestors is considered by the Chinese an act of great piety. Devices made of white and red paper are used by them in decorating their tombs, for Chinese families are not permitted to scatter flowers over the graves of their dead. This is a privilege confined to members of the royal family, who, as a rule, use artificial flowers. These are manufactured in China, especially by the inhabitants of Amoy, with much neatness and skill. The Jews, as we learn from certain passages in the twenty-third chapter of St. Matthew's gospel, were in the habit of embellishing the tombs in the neighbourhood of Jerusalem, and it is singular that the season selected by them for this purpose was the return of spring, a little before the celebration of the Passover.

On the ninth day of the ninth month, the Chinese again repair to the hills for the purpose of worshipping at their family tombs. This duty, however, is not so strictly observed as it is during the third month of the year. To worship at the tombs at the appointed seasons is apparently imperative upon men of all classes of society; and in order that families unable through poverty to erect tombstones for their dead, and perhaps ignorant of the precise spot where they have laid their remains, may have no excuse to neglect so important a duty, there stands within the precincts of each cemetery a large stone tablet, with the inscription Koo-Mow-Tsing-Tsi, directing all who cannot find the tombs of their fathers to worship before this stone.[1] The prayers to their ancestors are such as those which Christian men present to the God of all good, when they ask that they may receive grace to preserve them safe in the midst of life's temptations, and to prepare them for eternal glory. It is sad to think that the Chinese should be so blinded by the god of this world as to suppose they can obtain from the creature what emanates from the Creator alone. It is usual for them, at any time of perplexity and trouble, to repair to the tombs and consult the spirits of their ancestors.

Only the males of Chinese families worship the tombs throughout the third month, and again on the 9th day of the 9th month of each year; but during the first few weeks after a burial, female relatives visit the tomb, worshipping and bewailing the departed dead.[2] I have several times seen widows weeping by the graves of their husbands; often relating their troubles to the dead, and seeking consolation from them. The affecting custom of women weeping by the graves of their deceased relatives is, as might be expected, not confined to China. In Palestine groups of women may be seen daily at the tombs, scattering flowers over them, and shedding the unaffected tears of heartfelt sorrow. When Mary rose quickly to meet the Redeemer, of whose coming she had been privately informed, it was natural for the friends, who were gathered together, to conclude that she was going "unto the grave to weep there."

All Chinese sepulchres are extra-mural, and interments are not permitted within the walls of a Chinese city or town. To this rule, however, there are evidently exceptions, as I saw graves within the walls of Ningpo and Nankin. The practice of burying the dead beyond the precincts of cities and towns,—which

[1] Such worship is regarded as equivalent to that paid to the souls of the departed at their tombs. At the base of the slab there is a small stone altar at which to present the customary offerings.

[2] On the two great annual occasions of ancestral worship it is not customary to weep and lament. The inhabitants of the province of Honam, however, are an exception.

has only during the past few years been partially put in force in
Great Britain—has apparently been always observed by the
inhabitants of all ancient countries. The Athenians buried in
the Ceramicus;' the Romans in the fields and gardens near
the Via Appia,' 'Flaminia,' 'Latina,' and other highways, and
in places set apart without the gate.

"Quorum Flaminia tegitur cinis atque Latina."

The Chinese are not allowed to carry a corpse within the
gates of their walled cities.   Should a person who resides
within the walls, die from home, his relatives are not permitted
to take the corpse, even though it is inclosed in a coffin, within
the walls.   In the case of a very distinguished civil or military
officer dying at his post of duty, the Emperor sometimes, as a
mark of very great honour, issues a decree that the body of the
departed shall be carried in mournful procession through the
principal streets of the capital city of the district, prefecture, or
province of which he was a native. The mournful cavalcade
enters the city by the east gate, and leaves it by the west.   In
1859, I saw the remains of a distinguished civil officer, named
Laong Tong-san, who was a native of the western suburb of
Canton, and who had died while in the discharge of his duties,
borne thus through the city.   On its arrival at the east gate, the
procession was joined by all the officers of the city, civil and
military, who accompanied it until it had passed into the western
suburb.   In 1868, I witnessed a similar ceremony.   The funeral
was that of a high mandarin named Lok Pang-chaong, a native
of Fat-Shan in the province of Kwang-tung.   For many years
governor general of the large and wealthy province of Sze-chuen,
he had given many decided proofs of his private virtues and of
abilities as a statesman.   Dying at his seat of government, his
remains were carried in mournful triumph through the city of
Canton, the capital of the province of which he was a native.
To judge from the solemnity which pervaded the crowds of
witnesses, it would appear that in their estimation no greater
honour could be paid to the dead.   A similar honour is paid to
all officials who die in active service at Pekin, the corpse being

removed to its native place at the expense of the Imperial government. A similar mark of reverence is paid to the wife of an official should she have accompanied her husband to Pekin and died there.

The Chinese are not allowed to receive a corpse into their houses. When a man dies from home his remains are placed in a coffin, and borne at once to the grave, or to a Koong-Tsoi-Chong. Many instances of the operation of this rule came under my notice. The most melancholy occurred at Canton in 1870. A fire having taken place in the rear of the foreign settlement, several native fire brigades were speedily on the spot. One of them took up a position on a bridge spanning a creek which flowed round the block of buildings which the fire had attacked. The wooden beams of the bridge, which was an old one, suddenly gave way, and not less than one hundred persons fell into the water. Seventeen were drowned. As each body was recovered from the water on the following morning it was immediately dressed in grave clothes, inclosed in a coffin, and conveyed at once by sorrowing relatives to its last resting-place.

In the common cemeteries, which in China are very large, each family has often its own piece of ground, within which the bones of its ancestors remain undisturbed. In other instances, however, a Chinese family buries its dead in different cemeteries. This custom has prevailed more or less in some parts of the Empire since the Tsin dynasty, B.C. 249, and owes its origin in a great measure to the fact that the geomancers not unfrequently recommend new ground for a new interment, alleging that the spot they have discovered is even luckier than the family grave. In the south of China the remains of husband and wife are buried in the same tomb, if the husband is the first to die. Should the wife die first, the remains of the husband are not deposited by her side, as this would be regarded as most unlucky. Most Chinese cemeteries have a very neglected appearance, more especially in the south of China. Many of the tombs are in a most dilapidated state, though the law makes it obligatory on the Chinese to keep the tombs of their ancestors in excellent order. So sacred are tombs held by Chinese

law, that a desecration of them is regarded as a most heinous
offence. A person caught reopening a grave would, if he had uncovered the coffin, incur the punishment of one hundred blows,
and transportation for three years to a place distant three thousand
li from his home. Should he have removed the corpse, nothing
would await him but death by strangulation. One who opens
a tomb, which in consequence of storms or the lapse of time
has become very dilapidated, is punished with ninety blows
and exiled for two years and a half; and if he has removed the
bones death by strangulation is the sentence. People who steal
the bricks or stones of a tomb are punished in proportion to the
value of the bricks or stones. That Chinese grave-diggers are
occasionally guilty of disturbing the dead is clear from an
edict which the Chief Justice or Provincial Judge of Kwang-
tung issued in the month of June, 1871. He had received information to the effect that the grave-diggers, vulgarly known
as hill dogs, had of late exhumed several corpses, and re-
sold the graves from which they were taken, and he offered to
reward liberally any person or persons who would bring grave-
diggers guilty of such sacrilegious acts to justice. He warned
the grave-diggers that any one of them taken in the act of
removing a corpse, or of opening a grave for this purpose, would
suffer death either by decapitation or strangulation; and that
selling the head-stones of graves which have long since been
neglected and forgotten, would be visited with the very worst
form of imprisonment. Any one who injures a coffin in the
pursuit of rats, foxes, or wild cats which have burrowed into
graves—a circumstance by no means uncommon in the north of
China—is punished with eighty blows and sent into exile for two
years. Should he use fire for the purpose of smoking the foxes
or wild cats out of their holes, and destroy the corpse, he is
liable to one hundred blows and to be sent into exile for three
years. Should a farmer level a tomb on the estate which he
farms, he would be punished with one hundred blows and have
to rebuild the tomb or tombs at his own expense. Should any one
covet the graves of another family as being in a propitious situation,
and prevail upon the grave-digger to remove the remains already
there, he and the grave-digger would be put to death by

strangulation. A man who, regarding a tomb as lucky, secretly buries the dead body of his father in it, is liable to be punished with one hundred blows and exiled for life to a place distant three thousand li from his native place. A man secretly burying a member of his family in a plot of ground set apart as the private cemetery of another family, but in which no body has yet been laid, is punished with ninety blows and transported for two and a half years. People who, in consequence of poverty, are unable to purchase ground for their dead, and who bury them in the private cemeteries of others, incur a punishment of eighty blows, and are to remove their dead. If a purchaser of a plot of ground for a burial-place discovers that corpses have already been interred there, he is required to report the circumstance at once to the district ruler, who examines into the matter, and gives the necessary orders for the removal of the dead. Should he remove the dead on his own responsibility, he would be punished with eighty blows and sent into exile for one year. When the Chinese suffer from drought or any other epidemic, they often attribute the visitation to devils or evil spirits coming from a certain tomb or tombs. Persons, therefore, occasionally conspire to destroy a tomb. Such an offence is dealt with very severely. The law directs that the leader of the gang shall be strangled, that the second and third of his accomplices shall be transported for life, and that each of the other offenders shall receive one hundred blows and be transported for three years. A son or grandson, nephew or grandnephew, who is caught in the act of opening the graves of his ancestors for the purpose of despoiling the corpses of valuable ornaments, is punished with one hundred blows and banished for life three thousand li from his native place. Should he have succeeded in opening the coffin, the sentence is decapitation. To conclude, should a son or grandson, a nephew or grandnephew, exhume the remains of his ancestors for the purpose of selling the ground in which they have been interred, he would be decapitated, and the purchaser of the ground would be punished with eighty blows and mulcted in a sum of money equal to that which he had given for the ground.

It is customary for descendants to exhume the bodies of their ancestors, if they have reason to think that they are resting in unlucky tombs. Should the good fortune or the good health of a family suddenly change, it is not unusual for them to apply to a geomancer with the view of ascertaining the cause. That worthy sometimes discovers that the ancestors are resting in unlucky tombs, and their remains are at once exhumed for re-interment in more propitious spots Should the grave-diggers succeed in finding all the bones of the skeleton, they are rewarded with a liberal fee. The bones are arranged in order on a board, and washed with warm water, in which, to render it aromatic, the leaves of a cypress, cedar, or pomeloe tree have been boiled. They are then marked with a vermilion pencil, and placed in a cinerary urn, which is deposited in the tomb selected as lucky. Sometimes the urn is taken home by the relatives, and either placed in a private chamber, or lodged in the grounds round the dwelling-house. Sometimes it is left for a time in the cemetery. Passing once through a large cemetery beyond the north gate of Canton, I saw several persons standing by the side of a grave. They were descendants of one Laong Chun-ping, who had died many years ago, and were removing the remains of their ancestor, it being supposed that the tomb which contained them was unlucky. A short distance from the grave, a fire was burning in a portable grate, on which was a pan containing water in which leaves of the cypress-tree were being boiled. Anxious to witness the usual ceremonies upon the exhumation of a body, I remained by the side of the grave, and was not a little surprised at the accuracy with which the grave-diggers arranged the bones belonging to the skeleton. These men acquire in this way a most perfect knowledge of the anatomy of the human frame. After each of the descendants of Laong Chun-ping had done obeisance to them, the bones were carefully washed by the grave-digger, separately marked with a vermilion pencil, placed in a cinerary urn, and conveyed away for interment. The descendants of the deceased were in dark dresses, and, as they moved with the ashes of the dead towards the new tomb which had been prepared for them, the nearest of kin carried in his hand a streamer—the call cloth—to induce the spirit which had remained with the corpse to accompany the exhumed bones to their new resting-place. During the three months after the exhumation of the body, it is customary for the family to wear mourning. Exhumation generally takes place in the third month of the year, and it is not necessary to obtain the permission either of the central or local government. During the Ming dynasty, however, it was imperatively necessary to obtain the sanction of the ruler of their county. Although the exhumation of human remains, supposed to be resting in an unlucky grave, is universally practiced throughout China at the present day, I have reason to believe that the act is unlawful. If I mistake not there is a law that any geomancer who persuades people to exhume their dead upon the ground that they are resting in unlucky tombs, shall be severely punished, as well as all who assist him. This law was, I believe, framed in the twelfth year of the Emperor Yung-ching, in the year of our Lord 1735.

CHAPTER XIII.

SUICIDES.

THE Chinese are perhaps more prone to commit suicide than the people of any other country in the world. This cannot be said to be the result of a deliberate opinion that man is at liberty to end his mortal existence when he pleases, for the cases in which suicide is considered praiseworthy are exceptional, and it is generally condemned in their literature. Dire miseries also await the self-murderer in the Hades of the Buddhist, and the people look upon him as one who must have sinned deeply in a former state of existence. A Chinese would find nothing repugnant to his notions in Virgil's lines :—

> " Proxima deinde tenent mœsti loca, qui sibi letum
> Insontes peperere manu, lucemque perosi
> Projicere animas. Quam vellent æthere in alto
> Nunc et pauperiem et duros perferre labores !
> Fas obstat, tristique Palus inamabilis unda
> Alligat, et novies Styx interfusa coërcet."

Notwithstanding this, suicides are, as I have stated, a more numerous class amongst the Chinese than amongst any other race; and this opinion is confirmed in the account given by Captain Bedford Pim in his *Gate of the Pacific* of the suicidal mania displayed by the Chinese coolies engaged in the construction of the Panama railway. Tempted by the very high rate of wages, " men were brought," he writes, " to the locality in great numbers from China, India, Africa, and almost every nation in Europe." "There is no question," he continues, "of the unhealthiness of that portion of the Isthmus over which the railway runs, but of the labourers the Chinese lost the greatest number; for besides those carried off by disease, a strong suicidal tendency developed amongst this singular people, and it was not uncommon in the morning to find half-a-dozen bodies suspended from the trees in close proximity to the road."

The Chinese commit suicide chiefly by taking opium,[1] hanging, or drowning; and the wretched creatures who are guilty of this act are generally, as amongst ourselves, driven to it by immorality or destitution; or overmastered by jealousy, anger, or disappointment. Suicide by cutting the throat is seldom or never resorted to, as the Chinese believe that to destroy the integrity of the body is to add to the misery, or detract from the happiness, of the soul. As they also believe that in the world beyond the grave the shades are clad in garments similar to those which the deceased wore at his death, it is usual for those who have resolved upon self-destruction to put on their best clothes. Thus attired they frequently resort to the summits of hills, or other retired spots; and on several occasions I have found the bodies of men who had taken poison lying on the White Cloud mountains. Very often the deed is committed in some well-frequented thoroughfare when night has made it a solitude. On one occasion I saw the body of a suicide hanging from the balustrade of a bridge in the western suburb of Canton. At Macao I found a body suspended from the bough of a tree which stretched across the street. Several persons were passing at the same time, but the melancholy spectacle seemed to excite no emotion, scarcely to attract attention. No one seemed to consider it a matter of consequence whether the body was to remain hanging or to be taken down.

Females generally commit suicide in their homes. This, however, is not always the case, and I remember an instance

[1] According to Dr. Henderson of Shanghai, in his pamphlet on *The Medicine and Medical Practice of the Chinese*, native orpiment or yellow sulphuret of arsenic is occasionally taken; but he adds that opium is in much greater favour amongst the Chinese as "the irritating poison produces too much suffering and trouble."

—which occurred February 8th, 1871—in which two married ladies of the clan or family Tong became passengers in a steamer in order that they might jump overboard. These ladies, who resided in the Koong-a-lan street of the Western suburb of Canton, were sisters-in-law, and, during the absence of their husbands, had gambled away their money and jewellery. Accompanied by their maids, they came on the deck of the S.S. *Kin-Shan*, and, so soon as the vessel had reached the mouth of Canton river, they jumped overboard, locked in each other's arms. Fortunately, however, Captain Carey, who was in command, promptly lowered a boat and succeeded in rescuing them.

Gambling is, either directly or indirectly, a frequent cause of wives having recourse to suicide; and in 1861 a very sad example of this occurred in a large mansion adjoining the house which I was then occupying. My neighbour's fifth wife had incurred the displeasure of her husband—a member of the Ng family—by losing her jewels at play, and, finding the harsh treatment to which in consequence he daily subjected her unendurable, she took a large dose of opium. When, shortly afterwards, the discovery was made of what she had done, the aid of Dr. Dods, a medical practitioner at Honam, was immediately sought. I was present on the occasion, and I shall not readily forget the indignation with which I saw her carried to an outhouse, in order that she might die there. The removal was effected at Ng's orders, in accordance with an inhuman custom which dictates that an inferior wife or concubine shall not be permitted to die in the house of her husband. The wretched woman recovered, however, under the careful and kind treatment of Dr. Dods—but only, in consequence of the renewed cruelty of her husband, to repeat the attempt, and succeed in ending a life the misery of which she had not strength of mind to endure.

Canton could tell many a sad tale of the miseries which gambling has entailed upon the innocent as well as the guilty, and I cannot forbear recording a singularly melancholy case which occurred in the Cheung-hong Street. Two women were one day discovered lying together *in articulo mortis* by the neighbours. Reduced to destitution by their husbands' losses at play, they had attired themselves in their best robes, and decked their hair with flowers, and then sat down to drink a fatal draught which they had prepared of sugar-water mixed with opium. Before doing so, it would seem these poor women had engaged for the last time in the rites of ancestral worship; for upon the altar of the house where they lived and died together, the customary sacrifices were set out, and the tapers were still burning, when they were discovered by the neighbours.

Of suicide by men who have ruined themselves at play, the following case is perhaps a typical one; and the gambling centres of Europe could tell many a similar tale. A young gentleman, exceedingly well-dressed, entered the Tak-Hing hotel, dined, retired to rest, having given orders that he should be called early, and was found dead in the morning. The proprietor of the hotel immediately laid the matter before the Nam-hoi magistrate, the result of whose inquiry was a verdict to the effect that the deceased had committed suicide by taking opium. In the pocket of the unfortunate youth several pawn-tickets were found, and it was ascertained from them that he belonged to the Chan family. But no other particulars respecting him could be obtained. It was supposed by some that he had come to Canton to attend the literary examinations which were then being held; others conjectured that he was a collector of rents. All agreed that he was a confirmed gambler, and that the loss of his money at play and the fear and shame of meeting his friends had driven him to the fatal act. The inquest was delayed, owing to the non-attendance of the magistrate, until the body had become offensive; and the landlord, compelled to remove it from his hotel, hired a small boat for its reception. After lying in this for three days, the body was removed to the wharf of the Custom-house, where the mandarin, sur-rounded by numerous attendants, held his inquiry over a mass of corruption.

In all probability more cases of suicide arise from quarrels than from any other cause. In 1862 I was walking with some friends in the Western suburb of Canton, when my attention was arrested by a scene of excitement which was being enacted between the elders of the street and some women, whom the former were threatening to take before the magistrate. Upon making inquiries I learned that a poor woman—a neighbour of the viragos who were being threatened—had hanged herself in consequence of the shameful way in which the latter had treated her. They had not only refused to pay her a sum of money which they owed her, but had maltreated her ; and in the excitement of the quarrel the victim of their cruelty formed, and immediately carried into execution, the resolution of hanging herself. The elders contented themselves with saying to the offenders that if they did not defray all the expenses of the funeral of the deceased, they would be taken before the magistrate—a decision to which these worthies had evidently come after carefully considering how they might save themselves all trouble in the matter. As another illustration of suicide arising out of a quarrel, I may mention a case which occurred at Canton in 1853. The quarrel was certainly not one on account of which an Englishman would have dreamed of making away with himself. Ho Akow, who was door-keeper of the Consular church at Canton, was accused by the gardener employed in the old factory garden of having killed his canary. Ho Akow denied the charge, and declared that the bird had been destroyed by a rat. The gardener who in his grief would hear of no such explanation, repeated his accusation, whereupon Ho Akow, deeply resenting the charge, went into the church tower, of which he had the keys, and poisoned himself by taking opium.

The passionate sense of injury which led to suicide in the cases we have just described cannot be said to exclude revengeful feelings, but it is also not uncommon for persons to make away with themselves with the express intention of being revenged on those who have injured them. To quote one example only, I find in the *Pekin Gazette* of June 19th, 1872, that " a family of four persons, having first drawn up a statement of their grievances, threw themselves into a well, in order that they might be revenged on a relation who had cheated them out of a part of their patrimony, and otherwise ill-treated them. Now that the case has been brought prominently forward," the writer adds, "it will go hard with the persecuting relative, but the tragedy is a fearful illustration of how wretchedly justice must be administered, and how difficult it is for the feeble to invoke its protection against the strong and unscrupulous."

Jealousy is, as may be supposed, a fruitful source of suicide in a land where polygamy is extensively practised. In 1863, my attention was directed to a case which occurred in the family of a gentleman named Ho. It seems that the first wife of this gentleman was jealous of the second, who had usurped her place in the husband's affections. It happened, however, that on account of illness the latter was removed to a medical missionary hospital at Canton, which was then, and is now, I believe, presided over by a good and excellent physician named Dr. Kerr. Ho now regularly visited the hospital to the vexation of his first wife, who repeatedly expostulated with him, and used various expedients to prevent his visits. At last one morning he received a communication to the effect that his second wife was dying. He hastened to her death-bed, and was only in time to take a last farewell of her. Meanwhile his absence was observed by his first wife, who, learning its cause from the servants, shut herself up in her room, and, overmastered by jealousy, poisoned herself with opium.

Frequently suicides are the result of immorality, and a melancholy case of this kind came under my notice at Canton. Observing on one occasion a crowd endeavouring to break into a house, and learning that it was suspected to contain the bodies of two suicides, I waited until the door had been forced and then entered. Passing through a kitchen, I came to an inner chamber, where two bodies lay stiff in death. They were those of a man and woman who had bound themselves to each other by their queues. Near them were two small earthenware vessels which had contained opium. The story was a very simple one. The young woman, who was unmarried, had been discovered by the elders of the village to be *enceinte ;* and, as is customary in such circumstances, had been ordered to quit the home and village of her fathers for ever. Provided with a small sum of money which the elders had given her, she had reached Canton, where, of course, nothing but a life of prostitution awaited her.

The partner of her guilt had followed her, and urged, it was supposed, that they should commit suicide together. They then hired the house in which they were found, and poisoned themselves. The harshness which drives such women from their homes is much to be regretted, as, in nearly every case, they are compelled to adopt a life of prostitution. In some instances, however, they are bought as second or third wives by men who are childless. In a case in which the rash act of the suicide followed the discovery of a theft which he had perpetrated, the wretched man, who was one Lee Heong-peng, a native of Sam-woee, left behind him the following letter:—

"Having no occupation, and finding my home uncomfortable in consequence of the irritable temper of my father, I resolved to leave it. My grandmother having provided me with a letter of introduction to one named Cheng Chung-chein, with the hope that he would obtain for me a situation in the family of a foreign merchant or gentleman, and my grandmother having promised him for any good services which he might render me the sum of twenty-three dollars, Cheng Chung-chein obtained a situation for me in the family of a foreign gentleman. Having, however, after a servitude of twenty days been very rude, I was dismissed, and became a vagrant, being in truth without friends in the world. A few days, however, after my dismissal from service, I called at the residence of my former master, who was absent from home, and I was invited by his domestics, my former fellow-servants, to stay and dine. This invitation I accepted. Upon leaving the house in question at the close of the evening it was discovered that certain articles had been stolen, and suspicion resting upon me, I was at once accused of theft. Of this theft I was in truth guilty ; and having greatly disgraced myself, and being in consequence utterly devoid of friends and acquaintances, I have resolved to pawn all my superfluous clothes, &c., and to expend the proceeds in dining sumptuously at an hotel in the city of Canton, and at the close of the banquet, and in the hotel, to commit suicide. When I am dead, let no one accuse the landlord or servants of the hotel in which my dead body may be found of having murdered me. Further, inform my parents of my death, and beg of them to give interment to my remains.—TUNG-CHEE, 10th year, 11th month."

Before passing from this painful list of examples of suicide amongst the Chinese, I may mention that for a period of four years, during which he was most faithful and obedient, I had as a servant a man named Lou-N'g-Fok, whom I rescued from the Canton river into which he had thrown himself. When taken from the water he seemed in a dying state, but with care and attention he soon recovered. Friendless and destitute he had had no desire to live, he told me. He remained under my roof several days; and, observing that he was one in whom confidence might be reposed, I kept him with me as a domestic servant—a step which I never had any cause to regret.

Many Chinese believe that suicides are tempted to their fate by a spirit who presents them with a golden necklace; and when the deed has been perpetrated in the house, a religious ceremony is performed in it by a Taouist priest for the expulsion of this or other seducing spirits. After the priest has made a great many signs, and performed the kow-tow, he receives from the inmates a small black dog, together with a chopper and a block; and when he has severed its tail from its body with a sharp blow, the wretched animal, with a cord round its neck, is led or rather dragged, piteously howling, by the head of the family into every nook and corner of the house. It is then taken to the front door and kicked into the open street. The bleeding and yelping cur is supposed to frighten away the evil spirits, and to pursue them in their flight through the streets. By way of purifying the house, the priest then walks through it with a brass pan containing a burning mixture made of sulphur, saltpetre, and other inflammable ingredients. He is preceded by one bearing a lighted torch, and at intervals he flings portions of the burning mixture into the air. The ceremonies of exorcism and purification are now complete, but lest the spirits should return, the priest before his departure leaves several mystic scrolls written on sheets of red paper, to be posted above the doors of the apartments. Should the deceased have committed suicide by hanging, the beam from which he suspended himself is removed, lest his spirit should return to rest upon it.

The Chinese have also another curious superstition to the effect that the Pak, or power by which a man is able to walk, goes into the floor of the house when he commits suicide, and assumes there, if allowed to remain, the form of a piece of charcoal. They further believe that if the Pak be not removed, other members of the family, or future tenants will be tempted to commit suicide in the same room. It is therefore usual to dig to a depth of two or three feet in order to remove the Pak.

But if the wretched being whom the Nemesis of evil deeds or the overmastering fury of passion has driven to self-destruction incurs the reprobation or contempt of the Chinese, they hold in very different estimation those who have been impelled to this course by a sense of honour. Theirs is the death of the virtuous and the brave, and for them the gates of Elysium open wide. The first class of suicides of this description is called Chung-shan, and comprises all servants or officers of state who choose not to survive a defeat in battle, or an insult offered to the sovereign of their country. Thus, while, on the capture of the Bogue Forts by the British in the first war which Great Britain waged with China, Kwan Tai-poee rendered his name and family illustrious by committing suicide, the famous Yeh, on the other hand, incurred the hatred of his countrymen by not following so noble an example when Canton fell in 1857. When the Takoo Forts were captured in 1860, many of the mandarins committed suicide. We also read in the account given of the Conference held at Pekin in 1861—at which Sir Henry Parkes was present—that when it was shown that the only course open to the Chinese was submission to the foreign force without, one of the mandarins suddenly brought the proceedings to a standstill by deliberately leaving the meeting in order to commit suicide. In some instances the wives of officials also commit suicide. This was done by the wife of the Pun-yu magistrate rather than submit to the insult offered to the august Emperor of China by the attack of British troops upon Canton. While her husband was leading his troops against the enemy—for in times of extremity a civil magistrate is called upon to take military duties—this lady arrayed herself in her most costly dress, presented each of her attendants with a gift of money, and, withdrawing to a private chamber, ended her life by strangulation. A temple was erected to her on the Koon-Yam hill by the Cantonese, and its name, Tchu-Chang-tsze, was bestowed on it by H.I.M. Tung-chee.

Another class of honourable suicides comprises young men who, when an insult has been offered to their parents which they are unable to avenge, prefer not to survive it. A third class, called Tsze-Foo, consists of affectionate wives who refuse to survive their husbands. This custom, which at once reminds one of the sutteeism which used to be practised in India, prevails, I believe, throughout China, but is apparently more generally practised in the eastern province of Fokien. Widows on such occasions are dressed in robes of red, and commit suicide by hanging, either in their own houses in the presence of their relatives, or in the streets or open plains, surrounded by a vast concourse of people. When they ascend the dais on which they are about to immolate themselves, they are worshipped by the people; and after their death, tablets bearing their names are placed in the temples which are erected in honour of virtuous women in every city of the empire. Such a scene of voluntary death is thus described in the *Hong-Kong Daily Press* of January 20th, 1861 :—

" A few days since," says the writer, " I met a Chinese procession passing through the foreign settlement, escorting a young person in scarlet and gold in a richly decorated chair—the object of which I found was to invite the public to come and see her hang herself, a step she had resolved to take in consequence of the death of her husband, by which she had been left a childless widow. Both being orphans this event had severed her dearest earthly ties, and she hoped by the sacrifice to secure herself eternal happiness, and a meeting with her husband in the next world. Availing myself of the general invitation, I repaired on the day appointed to the indicated spot. We had scarcely arrived, when the same procession was seen advancing from the joss-house of the widow's native village towards a scaffold or gallows erected in an adjacent field, and surrounded by hundreds of natives of both sexes; the female portion, attired in gayest holiday costume, was very numerous. I and a friend obtained a bench for a consideration, which being placed within a few yards of the scaffold gave us a good view of the performance. The procession having reached the foot of the scaffold, the lady was assisted to ascend by her male attendant, and, after having welcomed the crowd, partook with some female relatives of a repast prepared for her at a table on the scaffold, which she appeared to appreciate extremely. A child in arms was then placed upon the table, whom she caressed and adorned with a necklace which she had worn herself. She then took an ornamented basket containing rice, herbs, and flowers, and whilst scattering them amongst the crowd, delivered a short address thanking them for their attendance, and upholding the motives which urged her to the step she was about to take. This done, a salute of bombards announced the arrival of the time for the performance of the last act of her existence, when a delay was occasioned by the discovery of the absence of a reluctant brother, pending whose arrival let me describe the means of extermination. The gallows was formed by an upright timber on each side of the scaffold, supporting a stout bamboo from the centre of which was suspended a loop of cord with a small wooden ring embracing both parts of it, which was covered by a red silk handkerchief, the whole being surrounded by an awning.

" The missing brother having been induced to appear, the widow now proceeded to mount on a chair placed under the noose, and, to ascertain its fitness for her reception, deliberately placed her head in it; then withdrawing her head, she waved a final adieu to the admiring spectators and committed herself to its embraces for the last time, throwing the red handkerchief over her head. Her supports were now about to be withdrawn, when she was reminded by several voices from the crowd that she had omitted to draw down the ring which should tighten the cord round her neck; smiling an acknowledgment of the reminder, she adjusted the ring, and motioning away her supports was left hanging in mid air—a suicide. With extraordinay self-possession she now placed her hands before her, and continued to perform the manual chin-chins, until the convulsions of strangulation separated them, and she was dead. The body was left hanging about half an hour, and then taken down by her male attendants, one of whom immediately took possession of the halter, and was about to sever it for the purpose of appropriating a portion, when a struggle ensued, of which I took advantage to attach myself to the chair in which the body was now being removed to the joss-house, in order to obtain ocular proof of her demise. Arrived in the joss-house, the body was placed on a couch, and the handkerchief withdrawn from the face disclosed unmistakable proofs of death. This is the third instance of suicide of this sort within as many weeks. The authorities are quite unable to prevent it, and a monument is invariably erected to the memory of the devoted widow."

With this class of suicides may be ranked young women whose affianced husbands have died before the day appointed for the marriage, and who elect not to survive them. Such instances of devotion are generally set forth by the governor of the province in which they occur, in a memorial to the throne; and posthumous honours are usually decreed. Thus, in 1872, the governor of the province of N'gan-huy brought before the Emperor the signal virtue of a girl of seventeen, who had committed suicide on the death of her betrothed; and we find the editor of the *Shanghai Daily News* remarking in his comments on the case, that "several similar memorials have appeared in the (*Pekin*) *Gazette* during the last twelve months, and they exhibit a curious phase in the native character—that of putting a premium on suicide." Women who have been ravished, and who prefer to die rather than survive the disgrace, are also included in this class.

A corresponding class among men are the Yee Foo, or Faithful Husbands, who in times of war and rebellion follow the example of their wives in committing suicide. Fathers also on such occasions sometimes destroy themselves with their daughters. When our forces captured Amoy, Ningpo, and Chin-kiang, many ladies, evidently thinking that our soldiers were like the brutal soldiery of their own country, committed suicide in the presence of their husbands, who followed their example. Their bodies were found in the wells and ponds with which Chinese houses are invariably provided.

To honourable suicides, tablets bearing their names are erected either in the temples in honour of virtuous men, or in those in honour of virtuous women. Monumental arches of granite or brick, which are in many cases richly carved, are also built in their honour in cities or their neighbouroood, or in open plains. Several of the arches in honour of virtuous women are very imposing—those, for instance, which I saw at Chin-kiang on the Yang-tsze; at Choo-loong-shan near Woo-see Hien on the banks of the Grand Canal; and at Soo-chow.

Before concluding this chapter, I may observe, as a singular fact, that in the early Christian Church suicide under certain circumstances was also deemed honourable; and in Mr. Lecky's

"European Morals from Augustus to Charlemagne" we have the following interesting remarks on the subject:—

"There were," he writes, "two forms of suicide which were regarded in the early Church with some tolerance or hesitation. During the frenzy excited by persecution, and under the influence of the belief that martyrdom effaced in a moment the sins of a life, and introduced the sufferer at once into celestial joys, it was not uncommon for men, in a transport of enthusiasm, to rush before the Pagan judges, imploring or provoking martyrdom, and some of the ecclesiastical writers have spoken of them with considerable admiration, though the general tone of the patristic writings and the councils of the Church condemned them. A more serious difficulty arose about Christian women who committed suicide to guard their chastity when menaced by the infamous sentences of their persecutors, or more frequently by the lust of emperors, or by barbarian invaders. St. Pelagia, a girl of only fifteen, who has been canonized by the Church, and who was warmly eulogized by St. Ambrose and St. Chrysostom, having been captured by the soldiery, obtained permission to retire to her room for the purpose of robing herself, mounted to the top of the house, and flinging herself down, perished by the fall. A Christian lady of Antioch, named Domnina, had two daughters renowned alike for their beauty and piety. Being captured during the Diocletian persecution, and fearing the loss of their chastity, they agreed by one bold act to free themselves from the danger, and, casting themselves into a river by the way, mother and daughters sank unsullied in the wave. The tyrant Marcentius was fascinated by the beauty of a Christian lady, the wife of the Prefect of Rome. Having sought in vain to elude his addresses, having been dragged from her house by the minions of the tyrant, the faithful wife obtained permission, before yielding to her master's embraces, to retire for a moment to her chamber, and she there, with true Roman courage, stabbed herself to the heart. Some Protestant controversialists have been scandalized, and some Catholic controversialists perplexed, by the undisguised admiration with which the early ecclesiastical writers narrate these histories. To those who have not suffered theological opinions to destroy all their natural sense of nobility, it will need no defence."

CHAPTER XIV.

IN China there are orders of nobility which differ in a few minor respects from our own ; and although it is impossible for me to enter into nice distinctions regarding the dignities of the " Middle Kingdom," I may be able to furnish a succinct account of the titles of honour which correspond with those of Great Britain. The Chinese have what may be termed dukes, marquises, earls, barons, and baronets. These ranks are respectively named :—Koong (duke), How (marquis), Paak (earl), Tze (baron), and Nan (baronet). Five in number, they represent, according to Morrison's *Dictionary*, the five elements in nature, namely, water, fire, wood, metal, and earth. Nobles of these various grades rank, I apprehend, above all other subjects of His Imperial Majesty.

Each of these orders of nobility is divided into classes according to the number of generations for which the title is allowed to be inherited. Dukes are divided into three classes, the titles of the first class not descending beyond the heirs male of the twenty-sixth generation. The titles of the second class cannot descend beyond the heirs male of the twenty-fifth generation ; nor those of the third class beyond the heirs male of the twenty-fourth generation. Certain dukedoms, however, continue so long as there are heirs male to inherit them. Marquises are also, like dukes, divided into classes according to the number of generations. These classes, four in number, hold their marquisates for twenty-three, twenty-two, twenty-one, and twenty generations respectively. Some marquisates also, continue to exist so long as there are male heirs to inherit them. According to the same principle, earls are divided into four classes, the number of generations during which the several classes are permitted to retain this rank being respectively nineteen, eighteen, seventeen, and sixteen. The first class of barons only hold them for fifteen generations, the other three classes for fourteen, thirteen, and twelve generations respectively. The title of baronets is only held in the first class for eleven generations, the three remaining classes holding their titles, for ten, nine, and eight generations. Precedence among the members of each order is, of course, determined by the class to which they belong.

Besides these five orders of nobility there is a further degree of rank which is termed Kee-Too-Wye; and a still lower grade termed Wan-Kee-Wye. The former rank descends in families belonging to its first class, no further than the heirs male of the third generation; and in its second class to the heirs male of the second generation. The latter rank, Wan-Kee-Wye, descends only to the immediate male heir. It is apparently not dissimilar to knighthood in Great Britain, and carries with it a right to a title of honour. There is a degree of rank which is termed Yan-Kee-Wye, and which is inherited by the descendants of dukes, marquises, earls, barons, and baronets, when these titles by effluxion of tenure have become extinct. In China as in Great Britain, earls are, in some instances, raised to the dignity of marquises, and marquises to the dignity of dukes. It is customary for an earl, created a marquis, to transfer his dignity of earl, by royal permission, to his younger brother. These various dignities are of very ancient origin and, in the form in which we now find them, may be traced back to the darkest periods of Chinese history. The power and authority which once attached to them, however, have greatly diminished. At one time their possessors were princes, or powerful feudal chieftains, each wielding a sceptre over his own territory. The dukes had almost absolute power over a dominion or principality which was one hundred li, or thirty miles English in extent. The principality of a marquis was nearly equal in area, while earls and barons were allowed to possess estates which did not exceed seventy li, or twenty-three English miles in area; and baronets, estates which did not exceed a limit of fifty li, or sixteen English miles.

In addition to these honours there are other degrees of rank which bring with them the right to certain titles. These degrees are nine in number, and each degree is divided into the classes: Ching, correct; and Tsung, deputy.

Among those who belong to the civil state—using the phrase loosely as opposed only to the military—the four cabinet ministers and members of the great council of the nation, are of the first degree and of the class Ching; and the heads of the six boards are of the class Tsung in the same degree. Governors-General of provinces are of the second degree and of the class Ching; and provincial governors and treasurers are of the class Tsung in the same degree. Of the third degree, criminal judges are of the class Ching, and salt commissioners of the class Tsung. Of the fourth degree, toutais are of the class Ching, and prefects of the class Tsung. Of the fifth degree, sub-prefects are of the class Ching; and the president of the astronomical board, physicians to His Imperial Majesty, and deputy salt commissioners of the class Tsung. Of the sixth degree, the vice-president of the astronomical board, district rulers whose offices are at Pekin, and the superintendents of ecclesiastical affairs—four in number—are of the class Ching, and the chief of the *literati*, deputy treasurers and deputy judges of the class Tsung. Of the seventh degree, doctors of law, district rulers, masters of ceremonies, and *literati* in charge of bachelors of arts, are of the class Ching; and clerks of the palace, and clerks of sub-prefects, of the class Tsung. Of the eighth degree, officials who have charge of temples in honour of Confucius at the place where the sage was born, physicians of the royal household, chiefs or rulers of salt markets, and officials in charge of all provincial, prefectoral, and district Confucian temples, and priests whose especial duty it is to chant prayers not only in honour of Heaven but in that of the Sun and Moon, are of the class Ching; and officials whose duty it is to reside in the offices of provincial treasurers for the purpose

of comparing the impression of seals, are of the class Tsung.
Of the ninth degree of civil rank, interpreters of the Siamese,
Japanese, and Corean languages are of the class Ching; and
superintendents of police, and the heads of various classes of
artificers employed in the palace are of the class Tsung. There
is also another class which is termed Mee-Yap-Lou or "not yet
of rank." Men of this class are either keepers of the doors of
provincial treasuries, or of the gates of the metropolis, Pekin,
or heads of branch custom-houses, or chiefs of the postmen or
couriers. Among those who hold military rank, there are also
nine degrees each of which, as in the former cases, is divided
into the classes of Ching and Tsung. Of the first degree of
military rank, generals of the household troops are of the class
Ching, and generals of Tartar or Chinese troops, and admirals
are of the class Tsung. Of the second degree, the director of
the imperial procession which accompanies the Emperor when
he goes from the palace, generals, and vice-admirals are of the
class Ching, and colonels of the class Tsung. Of the third
degree, members of the body-guard (all of whom are men of
birth and fortune), the general of the royal brigade of match-
lock men, and the keepers (all of whom are military men) of
the imperial tombs, are of the class Ching; generals and
colonels in command of body-guards, who are always in attendance upon the uncle and brothers of the Emperor, are of the
class Tsung. Of the fourth degree, the members of the second
regiment of body-guards are of the class Ching; and the officers
in command of the troops by which the gates of the City
of Pekin are garrisoned, of the class Tsung. Of the fifth
degree, the captains of the third regiment of body-guards are of
the class Ching; and the captains of the troops who have charge
of the canals, of the class Tsung. Of the sixth degree, officers
in charge of three hundred soldiers are of the class Ching; and
officers of three hundred policemen, whose duty it is to superintend the canals, are of the class Tsung. Of the seventh
degree, soldiers who guard the gates of Pekin, the head grooms
of the royal stables, and centurions are of class Ching; and the
head of the herdsmen [1] who have charge of all animals intended

---

[1] This official resides in Tartary.

for sacrificial purposes, is of the class Tsung. Of the eighth degree, officers in charge of twenty or thirty soldiers are of the class Ching; and bearers of the Imperial sedan-chairs are of the class Tsung. And lastly, of the ninth degree of military rank, officers in charge of small military stations are of the class Ching, whilst officers of less note are of the class Tsung.

Officers of the second degree of rank, whether civil or military, can purchase the title of a first degree of rank. The power, however, which as officers they are called upon to exercise, is that only of the second rank. The various degrees confer titles upon those who hold them; and as the title borne by those in the first class of a degree is different from that borne by those in the second class, there are in all thirty-six titles, eighteen for civilians, and eighteen for those whose appointments rank as military. I refrain, however, from inflicting the thirty-six titles upon the reader. If the bearer of a title has received the honour in question from the hands of the Emperor direct, he places the term Shou before his title. The father of a son who receives a title, is, also, allowed to assume a title precisely similar in point of importance to that which has been conferred upon his son. He, however, places before his title the term Foong, which implies that he has received his title in consequence of the renown of his son. If a father die before his son be ennobled, he, though dead, is nevertheless ennobled. It is necessary, however, for the son in speaking or writing of his father, or in erecting a tombstone to perpetuate his memory, to place the term Tsang before the title—a term which implies that the honour is a posthumous one. Great-grandfathers and grandfathers are also, whether they be dead, or alive, ennobled by imperial decree, if their great-grandsons and grandsons be so fortunate as to attain to any of the titles and distinctions of the Chinese empire.

Should a man of title marry, his wife is allowed to bear a title precisely similar in point of rank. Should, however, this lady die, a second wife would bear no title, unless he were to be raised still higher in the scale of nobility during her wifehood. A third wife is not allowed to assume a title even though her husband has one. Should her sons, however, become

nobles, she is, as a matter of course, allowed to bear a title.
Widows of title are on no account allowed to contract a second
marriage ; and widows who marry clandestinely are never permitted to bear titles. The fathers of mandarins who attain to
the eighth or ninth rank, do not, I apprehend, receive any titles
in consequence of the promotion of their sons. Should the
Emperor, however, at the time of his accesssion, or on the
occasion of his marriage, or the celebration of his sixty-first
natal anniversary, confer rank on all the officials, it is regarded
as the duty of mandarins of the eighth and ninth ranks to give
these honours to their parents. If a governor-general have a
father who is a prefect, it is customary for him to confer the
honour which he receives on such occasions upon his father.
The father, however, must then retire from office.

All military officers in China who fall in battle, and all
civil officers who come to an untimely end in the discharge of
their duties, have posthumous honours conferred upon them.
The eldest sons of such officers also receive titles at the hands
of the Emperor. The importance of such titles depends, in each
case, in a great measure upon the rank which the father held at
the time of his death. The distinction which attaches to the
possession of rank in Chinese society, never fails as a stimulus
to exertion, which if it is not disinterested is indefatigable.

The transition from titles of honour to visits of ceremony is
an easy one. The nation which has laid down with such
minuteness the distinctions of rank, has elaborated, with an
exactness peculiar to itself, a system of etiquette which prescribes the forms to be observed in official and social intercourse.
A Chinese is seldom at a loss to know what polite observances
must regulate his behaviour. Etiquette is an essential part of
his education. That a man should have a knowledge of science
would perhaps not seem in the eyes of many a philosopher of
China so important as that he should know how to comport
himself with perfect propriety in his intercourse with others.
He would argue that it is more essential to learn reverence,
respect, and courtesy, than to acquire any knowledge which *per
se* has no moral bearing—a convincing argument, if he could
prove that it were perfectly applicable. These remarks, however,

are suggested by a consideration of the case generally, rather than by the mere details and punctilios of ceremony which follow; and which, although it is consistent with the plan of this work to give an account of them here, may perhaps induce my readers to imagine that they are deep in the contents of a book of etiquette.

The classes from whom etiquette exacts most are naturally the official classes, and the manner in which Chinese officials must deport themselves towards each other, in what are termed visits of ceremony, is regulated, according to rank, with the utmost nicety.

Among those who are of equal rank, and who reside in the imperial capital, a visit of ceremony is conducted as follows. On arriving at the door of his friend's house, the visitor, whether he ride on horseback, or in a carriage, or sedan-chair, presents through his servant, who on such an occasion never fails to accompany him, a visiting card, which the door-keeper delivers to his master. His master inquires how the visitor is dressed, and if the visitor is in full costume, he at once puts on robes of a corresponding description. That done, he goes to the entrance, and invites the visitor to alight and enter. As they are about to pass through the centre door of the inner gate, the visitor is requested to take precedence—a request which, in the first instance, he most politely declines. On his host repeating it a third time, however, the visitor yields, and advances towards the reception hall, at the door of which the same punctilious interchange of ceremonious civility is repeated. Upon entering the hall, the host and his visitor kneel, and knock their heads six times upon the ground. On rising, the former arranges or affects to arrange, the cushion of the chair on which it is intended the latter shall sit, and then, bowing, requests him to be seated. The visitor, who graciously bows in acknowledgment of his host's politeness, seats himself in the chair, which is placed on the east side of the hall; that which the host occupies being on the west side. Conversation ensues, and, after a reasonable time, a servant is ordered to make tea. Two cups are quickly brought, for the visitor and his host. Before drinking it, and as they raise the cups towards their lips, they

bow to each other. The visitor now rises from his chair, and
addressing the host, says, " I wish to take leave; " upon which
the host bows assent, and follows him as he goes towards the
grand entrance of the house. At each doorway through which
they pass, the visitor bows to the host, and requests him not to
advance with him any further. The latter, however, is not
expected to comply with these polite entreaties; and on reaching
the entrance door, he remains standing until the visitor has
entered his carriage, or mounted his horse, and proceeded on
his way.

  If the host be of the first and the visitor of the second rank,
the ceremonies observed differ little from those which I have
described. But, when the visitor, about to seat himself, protests
to the former, who affects to arrange the cushion of his chair
for him, that he is altogether unworthy of such attentions, the
host at once desists. Moreover, the visitor proceeds to arrange
the cushion of the chair which it is proper for the host to occupy,
but is frustrated in his polite endeavour by similar protestations
of unworthiness from the host. The other ceremonies are the
same as I have already described.

  An official or gentleman of the third or fourth rank when
visiting one who belongs to the first rank, is received by the
latter, not at the grand entrance, but at the inner door of the
house, which by the Chinese is termed Yee-Moon, or second
entrance. The ceremonies which are observed in the visitors'
hall are precisely the same as in the former instances; and when
the visitor takes his leave, the host, who only received him at
the inner door, now escorts him to the grand entrance. He does
not, however, wait there until the visitor has entered his chair
or mounted his horse, but at once withdraws to his own
apartment.

  A person of the fifth, or sixth, or seventh rank, when calling
upon a person of the first rank, is received in the large hall
and, as they together enter the visitors' hall, the host takes
precedence. Upon entering this hall, the visitor looks to the
north, kneels at the feet of the host, and is told there is no need
for such ceremonies. He then expresses his respect by three
profound bows towards the north, which the host acknowledges

by similar inclinations towards the east. When the visitor has arranged, as he is allowed to do, the cushion of the chair which the host is to occupy, he requests the latter to sit down, and grant him an interview of a few minutes. The latter readily assents, and proceeds to his seat on the south-west side of the hall, while the visitor places himself in a chair on the east. Conversation at once takes place. No invitation to take tea is given by the host, nor does he accompany him on leaving beyond the second or inner door.

The ceremonies observed in provincial cities and towns are slightly different. A provincial treasurer, a literary chancellor, a provincial judge, a salt commissioner, or any other high provincial official of state does not when calling upon a governor-general, or a provincial governor, present a card. After passing through the great gate of the palace of the governor-general, or provincial governor, he alights from his horse or carriage, and walks to the second or inner gate, where he is received by the high official himself. Should the visitor be either the literary chancellor, or the Tartar general, or the commissioner of revenue, the centre door of the gate (each gate consists of three doors) is thrown open to allow him to pass. A provincial treasurer or provincial judge enters by the east door of the gate. The governor-general or governor immediately conducts him to a reception hall, generally the east hall, which is also called Fà-Teang or Flowery Hall. On entering, the visitor looks towards the north, and says " Pan-sam," or, I respectfully beg to be allowed to kneel and knock the head. On the governor-general or governor replying " Tsze," or I am not worthy to receive such honour, the visitor, instead of performing the kow-tow, bows three times, each obeisance being graciously acknowledged by the host who bows in return. The latter now seats himself on a chair facing the south, and invites his visitor, who bows in acknowledgment of the courtesy, also to be seated. A chair placed on the east side of the hall is then occupied by the visitor, who rises from his seat, and, making a profound bow, respectfully calls upon the host to hear what he has to say. The host assents by a low bow. Both resume their seats, and after conversation the visitor begs to be allowed to take leave.

He is invited to take a cup of tea. On rising to leave, he looks owards the north, and makes three profound bows, each of which is acknowledged by a similar inclination by the host, He then leaves the hall, taking precedence, and walking quickly, being careful not to turn his back upon the host, by whom he is being escorted. At the second or inner gate, they take formal leave by bowing to each other three times. The visitor, however, does not yet cross the threshold of the inner gate, but remains standing there until the host, having retraced his steps to the door of the eastern hall or reception room, looks back towards him, when he makes three parting bows, which the host returns. Passing the inner door, the visitor then enters his carriage, or sedan-chair, and departs. A person of the first rank when calling upon a governor-general or a provincial governor, does not present a card. A document, however, which the Chinese call Lee-lik, is placed by the visitor in the hands of an officer styled the Hoo-Fong. The Lee-lik contains not merely the names and titles of the visitor, but also a brief account of the services which he has rendered to the state. According to the rules of ceremony, this document ought to be read aloud in the hearing of the host by the visitor himself, whilst in a kneeling posture. This ceremony, however, is some-times omitted. On the visitor's departure, the Lee-lik is returned to his servant by the Hoo-Fong. On any subse-quent visit to the same high official, the T'sune-kan is substi-tuted for it, a document with the visitor's names and titles, but with no reference to his services to the state, or to the offices he may have filled. A governor-general or a pro-vincial governor returns the call of an official of the first rank on the following day. The visiting card of an official occupying so distinguished a position bears his name only.

A prefect of the fourth rank, when visiting a governor-general or a provincial governor, is received in the same way as a provincial treasurer or a literary chancellor. The bows, how-ever, which he makes are not acknowledged by the host. An official of the fifth, or sixth, or seventh rank is not allowed to pass through the Yune-Moon or carriage gate of a governor's residence in his sedan-chair, or on horseback. Alighting at this gate and walking towards the palace, he is received at the inner gate, and by servants only. On reaching the visitor's hall, where he finds the host already seated, he kneels, looking towards the north, and knocks his head six times upon the ground, after which, rising to his feet, he makes three profound bows. Meanwhile the host rises from his chair; but he does not bow in return, nor invite his visitor to sit down, nor subsequently to take tea. When the visit is finished the visitor makes three bows and withdraws. If of either of the ranks or classes above mentioned, he presents his Lee-lik on his first visit, but on all subsequent occasions substitutes the T'sune-kan, or card bearing his names or titles. The visits of such officials are not returned by governors-general or governors.

When a governor-general is on his way from the imperial capital to his seat of government, it is customary for each prefect and each county ruler through whose prefecture or county His Excellency may have to pass to meet him, the one at a distance of three miles from the walls of the prefectoral, and the other at a distance of three miles from the county city. On the arrival of His Excellency at a point which is three miles distant from the provincial capital which is the seat of government, the provincial treasurer, the provincial judge, the literary chancellor, and the commissioner of salt send their cards. On his arrival, however, at the provincial capital, he is received outside the gates of the city, by all the officials whether of civil or military rank, and invited to a reception hall outside the walls, where they are expected to make most anxious inquiries respecting the health and happiness of H.I.M. the Emperor. When His Excellency has answered them and has taken tea, he is escorted to his Yamun, or Palace, within the city. When the cavalcade passes the south gate, which is used, not only by the Viceroy, but by all officials, on making their entrance into the city within whose walls they have been appointed to exercise jurisdiction, the guard turns out to receive him, as it does also at each guardhouse or station *en route*.

The etiquette for the officers of the Chinese army does not differ much from that which regulates the intercourse between civil officials. When a military mandarin of the second rank

A VISIT OF CEREMONY.

proposes to visit an officer of the first rank whom he has not visited before, he dons his armour and buckles to his side a sword, and a bow, and a quiver in which are six arrows. On arriving at the Yune-moon, or carriage entrance of the official residence of the officer to whom he is desirous of paying his respects, he alights from his state sedan-chair, or horse. Should the host, to whom the gatekeeper has forwarded the mandarin's Lee-lik, send word that it is unnecessary to wear armour, the visitor retires to an adjoining chamber and puts on a court dress, retaining, however, his sword, which he is obliged to wear on such occasions. The military mandarin, who must enter by the east door of each gate through which he has to pass, now proceeds to the reception hall, where he finds his host standing to receive him. He says " Pan-sam," or I respectfully beg to be permitted to kneel and knock the head ; to which the host replies, " Pay-me," or I pray you no such attentions. Look-ing towards the north, the visitor now makes three profound bows, each of which the host, who stands on the east, returns. They then seat themselves, the host in a chair on the north, and the visitor in a chair on the east side. At the close of conversa-tion tea is served, and the visitor rises to take leave. After three low bows, returned by the host as before, he leaves the reception room, followed by the host. A few yards from the door of the reception hall they halt, and again take leave by bowing to each other three times.

A military mandarin of the third rank when visiting a military mandarin of the first rank wears armour, and, on entering the visitors' hall, kneels and knocks his head upon the ground three times. He then rises, and makes three profound bows, which his superior officer acknowledges by three half bows. After conversation tea is served, and on taking leave he again makes three profound bows, which receive the same acknowledgment. The host does not leave the reception hall, but commits his visitor to the care of servants, by whom he is escorted to his sedan-chair.

Officers of the fourth, fifth and sixth ranks, calling upon an officer of the first rank, also wear armour. The visitor finds the host seated, in the visitors' hall, kneels at his feet and performs the kow-tow, knocking his head three times upon the ground. Still kneeling and looking toward the north, he reads aloud to his host, who remains seated, a document with his names and titles and the name of his superior officer, together with that of the station where he has been appointed to serve. On the host inviting him to rise from his knees and be seated, it is his duty not to take a chair, but to sit or squat on the east side of the hall with his face towards the west. At the close of the conversation he again kneels and performs the kow-tow, before leaving. Tea is not served to a visitor of this rank, and he retraces his steps from the visitors' hall without an escort. The same ceremonies are observed when an officer of the seventh rank visits an officer of the first rank, except that he is not invited to sit down.

It remains for me to describe the etiquette of visits between military officers and officials of civil rank. A military officer of the first rank on visiting a governor-general, receives on his arrival at the Yamun or palace of the latter a salute of three guns, and is borne in his state sedan-chair, not only through the middle door of the street gate, or principal entrance, but also through the middle door of the inner gate. Here the governor-general is waiting to receive him, and bows are interchanged between them. They then walk in company towards the third gate, through which, on the threshold of its centre door, they hesitate to pass, the host urging the visitor to take precedence, and the visitor respectfully assuring his host that he will do no such thing. At last, the visitor ceases to be inexorable. Each, upon entering the visitors' hall, makes three profound bows to the other. The host then seats himself on a couch, arranged on the north side of the hall so as to face the south, making his guest occupy a seat on the same couch, on his left hand. If the latter is noble, the host sits on the east, and the visitor on the west side of the reception hall. After conversation and tea, the visitor on taking leave is accompanied to the second or inner gate, by the host, who remains there until his visitor re-enters his state sedan-chair, or mounts his horse and proceeds on his way. A military officer of the second rank visiting a civil officer of the first rank, alights from his chair or horse at the outside of the

second or inner door of the Yamun or palace. He is received
by his host at the head of the stone steps by which the gate is
approached. The ceremonies are very similar to those I have
just described. On the following day the visit is returned, and
it is an essential point of etiquette that the military officer of
the second rank should receive his visitor at the outside of the
second or inner gate. The visitor does not alight here, but,
attended by his host, is borne to the very door of the reception
hall. The host seats himself facing the south in a chair placed
on the north side of the hall, while his visitor sits facing the
west in a chair on the east side of the hall. Tea is, of course,
presented, and on rising to take leave, the visitor makes a low
bow to the host, which the latter returns. On re-entering his
sedan-chair at the door of the reception hall, he is escorted by
the host to the outside or inner gate. Here the chair-bearers
halt until the host has made three bows, when the bearers
resume their progress. A military officer of the second rank,
and of the class Tsung, calling upon a civil officer of the first
rank, such as a governor-general, must wear armour. He is
also required to alight from his chair or horse at the first or
street gate of the Yamun, and to walk to the second or inner
gate, the east door of which is thrown open for him. Upon
entering the visitors' hall he kneels, looking towards the north,
and performs the kow-tow, knocking his head three times upon
the ground. Upon rising, he takes his station on the east side
of the hall, where he stands whilst engaged in conversation with
the host, and he receives no invitation to seat himself. In due
course he is presented with a cup of tea, but he does not presume
to drink it until he has made a profound bow to the host. Before
leaving the visitors' hall, a master of ceremonies calls upon him
again to perform the kow-tow. A military officer of this
rank calling upon a civil mandarin of the first rank, such as a
provincial governor, is expected to wear armour. On entering
the visitors' hall he also says, " I respectfully beg to be permitted
to kneel and perform the kow-tow." The host however declines
to receive this mark of deference, and the visitor substitutes three
profound bows. The host sits facing the south in a chair on the
north side of the hall, and the visitor in a chair on the east side,

facing the west. After tea, he is accompanied by the host to the door of the reception hall.

A military officer of the second rank calling upon a literary chancellor, or a governor of canals, or a commissioner of revenue, presents a visiting card, with his name and titles. At the street gate of the Yamun, the officer alights from his horse or sedan-chair and walks towards the inner gate, the centre door of which is open to admit him. At the door of the visitors' hall he is received by the host, and makes three profound bows, after which, with another bow, he presents his Lee-lik. The host and his visitor occupy chairs facing each other on the east and west sides of the hall respectively. After they have conversed for some time, tea is served. Upon withdrawing the visitor is escorted by the host, who leads the way, to the outside of the second or inner gate. Almost at each step, he begs the host to advance no further. On reaching the inner gate, they again bow to each other. The visitor, however, does not pass through this gate until the host has retraced his steps to the door of the reception hall, and looked back, to receive and acknowledge the three profound bows which the visitor makes before he re-enters his sedan-chair.

A military officer of the third rank visiting a civil officer of the first rank, such as a governor-general, must appear in armour. He alights from his horse or sedan-chair at the street gate of the Yamun, by the east door of which he is allowed to enter. Here servants appointed to receive him conduct him through the east door of the inner gate to the reception hall, where the host awaits him. After kneeling and performing the kow-tow, he presents his Lee-lik. To a visitor of this rank tea is not served, nor is he invited to sit down. He stands during the interview on the east side of the reception room, with his face towards the west. On leaving the visitors' hall, he makes three profound bows, which are acknowledged by the host with a bow.

A military mandarin of the third rank, when visiting a provincial governor, alights from his chair or horse, at the great gate of the governor's Yamun or palace. He enters through the east door of this gate, and through the corresponding door of the inner gate. At the door of the visitors' hall he finds the governor, to whom he makes three profound bows, each of which is returned. The host then occupies a chair on the north side of the hall, facing the south, while the visitor seats himself on a chair on the east side, facing the west. On taking leave, the visitor bows three times to the governor, who thereupon escorts him as far as the door of the hall. A military officer of the fourth, fifth, sixth, seventh, eighth or ninth rank, when calling upon a governor-general, alights from his chair or horse at the street gate of his excellency's palace ; and, as in the previous instance, walks to the visitor's hall through the east doors of the gates. On entering the hall, he kneels at the feet of the host, and knocks his head upon the ground three times, after which he reads his Lee-lik to the host, in a kneeling posture. A visitor of this rank wears armour on the occasion of such a visit ; and it is not his privilege to be invited to sit down, or to take tea. When visiting a provincial governor, a military officer of the fourth rank wears armour. When, however, he has been admitted into the presence of the latter, and has performed the kow-tow, he withdraws, at the request of the host, to divest himself of his armour, and re-enters, in court costume, making a profound bow. Although he is not invited to be seated, he is served with tea, after which he takes his leave, making three profound bows, which the provincial governor, who rises from his chair, politely acknowledges.

A governor-general of a province or provinces is supposed to go on a tour of inspection through the vast territorial district over which he rules as viceroy, three times in each year. The inspection of troops is the principal object of the tour, and only garrison cities are visited. On his arrival his excellency is received by the Chan-Toi, or commandant of the garrison, who, standing on the right side of the road, makes three profound bows to him. When the Viceroy has acknowledged these salutes, he continues his progress in his sedan-chair, and the cavalcade, which is joined by the commandant, at once proceeds to the parade ground, where the troops are assembled. When the Viceroy has taken his seat under a special marquee, the commandant approaches, and begs to be allowed to perform the ceremony of the kow-tow. This honour, His Excellency declines

to receive, and requests the commandant to occupy a chair on
his left hand.   Before taking the seat the latter makes three profound bows, which the Viceroy rising from his chair acknowledges.   The review of troops now takes place, and, at its conclusion, His Excellency, to whom the commandant again makes
three profound bows, re-enters his sedan-chair, and is escorted
back to his state barge.

Tartar generals and Tartar brigadier-generals visit governors-
general and provincial governors, and all military officers of the
first rank on terms of perfect equality.   Provincial treasurers,
provincial judges, commissioners of salt, and Toutais when
visiting a Tartar general observe ceremonies similar to those
which require their attention when calling on a governor-general.
A prefect, or a county or district ruler of the fourth, fifth, sixth,
or seventh rank, visiting an earl, observes the same ceremonies
as those which are imposed on a military officer of the second
rank, and of the class Ching, when the latter visits a governor-
general ; and when visiting a duke or marquis, they observe
ceremonies similar to those due by military officers of the
second rank, and of the class Tsung, when they visit a governor-
general.   All Tartar military officers visit Chinese officials of
corresponding rank, civil or military, on terms of perfect equality.
Officials serving at Pekin, who are either of the first, second, or
third rank, also the Hanlin of the seventh rank who have duties
to discharge in the imperial palace, and the Hee-Kŭ-Chŭ, or
officials who note the actions or movements of the Emperor, and
military officers of the first, second, or third rank who are also
serving at Pekin, are, on making a visit to any of the provinces,
received at the gates of all the cities through which they pass,
by the chief rulers of the cities, whether the latter be governors-
general, or governors, or Tartar generals, or prefects, or county
rulers.   On receiving any of these officials from Pekin, the first
duty of the host is to make inquiries respecting the health and
happiness of His Imperial Majesty.   A strip of yellow satin on
which expressions of the loyalty of the officials are recorded, is
also given to the visitor on his departure, in order that he may
present it to the emperor on his return.

But let me now record the ceremonies observed by literary

graduates in connection with their degree. Every successful bachelor of arts repairs, within a few days after his degree has been conferred upon him, to a Confucian temple, to pay his respects to the Kow-Koon or government professors, or lecturers, two of whom are in charge of each temple dedicated to the great Chinese sage. The graduate presents his visiting card, and is escorted to the visitors' hall, where the government teachers await him. Approaching this hall by the eastern steps, he looks towards the north on entering, and makes three profound bows, each of which the Kow-Koon or lecturers acknowledge. The graduate then stations himself on the east side of the hall, and looking towards the west, listens attentively to a short address from one of the lecturers, after which he makes three profound bows, and withdraws. This first visit is especially regarded as of a ceremonial character. On an ordinary visit, the lecturers, when a visiting card has been presented, order their servant to invite the graduate to enter, and receive him at the door of the visitors' hall. In the centre of the hall he kneels and performs the kow-tow, knocking his head twice upon the ground. The lecturers, who stand on the east side of the hall, bow. Rising from his knees, the visitor arranges the cushions of their chairs, and is invited to seat himself. Before he presumes to do so, he makes a low bow to the lecturers. The chairs of the latter are in the south-west corner of the hall, facing the north-east, whilst that of the visitor is on the east side, facing the west. Should the visitor have occasion to ask a question in the ensuing conversation, he rises from his seat and bows before doing so. Before leaving he is presented with a cup of tea. On leaving he makes three profound bows towards the north, which are duly returned by his hosts, who then lead the way to the second or inner gate. Here the lecturers and the graduate bow to each other, and part, the former not waiting until their visitor has re-entered his sedan-chair, but at once withdrawing to their apartments.

All schoolboys, great and small, when visiting their schoolmasters have to observe the following ceremonies: — On entering the visitors' hall, the pupil carefully arranges the cushions of the chairs for his host and himself. He then

stations himself outside the door of the hall, where he awaits
the coming of his teacher. When the teacher has arrived, and
invited him to enter, the pupil presents him with a small
packet, which he holds with both hands in an uplifted position.
The packet in question contains a tael of silver. Looking
towards the north, he then kneels and knocks his head twice
upon the ground. The teacher responds by bowing. On rising,
the youth makes inquiries about his tutor and his tutor's parents
—inquiries which, when answered, are followed by similar
questions from the tutor about the youth and his parents.
The teacher then invites his pupil to sit down. In the
course of the conversation, should any question be put
by the tutor, the youth rises from his chair in order to
give the necessary answer. On taking leave, he is not accompanied to the entrance door of the house. Whenever a pupil
enter or leaves the schoolroom, he must make a bow to his
teacher.

A few lines will suffice to describe the ceremonies generally
observed by people outside official or professional circles, on
paying and receiving visits. A visitor is received at the entrance
door of the house by the host, and escorted to the visitors' hall.
On the way to the hall much politeness is exchanged, the host
bowing at almost every step, and requesting his visitor to take
precedence. Upon entering the visitors' hall, each kneels down,
and knocks his head twice upon the ground. On rising, the
host hastens to arrange the cushions of the chair on which the
visitor is to sit, whilst the latter shows equal courtesy. The
chairs of the host and his visitor are respectively on the east
and west sides of the hall, facing each other. After conversation
and tea, the visitor is accompanied to the entrance door of the
house by his host, whom, at almost every step, he requests to
proceed no further. Where the visitor is a youth, or young
man, and his host his senior, the order of procedure is naturally somewhat changed. A young man, when visiting an old
man, is received by the latter, not at the entrance door, but in
the visitors' hall, upon entering which he looks towards the north,
and, kneeling, knocks his head twice upon the ground. This
mark of deference the host acknowledges by bowing, and invites

his visitor to be seated. When they have conversed together, tea is served; after which the latter takes his leave. The senior does not accompany the young man to the door of the house. Ceremonies precisely similar to these are observed on visits paid by nephews to uncles, and by sons-in-law to fathers-in-law.

CHAPTER XV.

THE sumptuary laws of China are very comprehensive. They restrain the expenditure of citizens in the building of houses, in the luxuries of the table, in clothing, and furniture, and similar matters. In almost all ages and nations there have been such laws. As to their utility, different opinions have been expressed by political economists. I apprehend that, in countries of early marriages where the human race increases rapidly, and the arable lands, though tilled to the utmost, scarcely yield enough bread to satisfy the hungry, a free indulgence in luxuries would be attended with bad results. Such a social condition calls for the utmost industry and economy, and if legislators believe that these virtues can be produced or fostered by laws, it is natural for them to have recourse to law-making. The sumptuary laws of China, however, like its civil and common laws, are very badly executed. This is, doubtless, due not to maladministration only, but in part to the reason which Hallam assigns for the desuetude of sumptuary laws among western nations—that they are attempts to restrain what cannot be restrained.

Perhaps the most important matter with which these laws deal in China is the building of houses. With regard to the residence of an official or gentleman of the first or second rank an astonishing number of details are prescribed. The foundations of the house must be laid at a depth of twenty Chinese inches beneath the surface. The house must consist of nine open halls, on each side of which there are suitable private apartments. The pillars which support the vaulted roofs of these open halls must be of wood, and painted black. The ridge-beam of each vaulted roof must be gilded; or, figures of flying dragons may be painted on it instead. On the ceilings of the various private apartments there must be painted representations of dragons, or phœnixes, or cheluns. On the tops of the vaulted roofs porcelain figures of dragons, or dolphins, or cheluns must be affixed as exterior ornaments or decorations. In front of the residence there must be a large entrance gate with a vaulted roof; and the gate must have three doorways; and on the faces of each of the doors, with the view, I suppose, of giving it the appearance of strength, there must be seven rows of large headed nails, each row consisting of seven nails. The doors must be painted green or black, and have two large copper rings supported by lions heads made of the same material. In a smaller house of this class the seven rows of large headed nails on the doors become six, and each row consists of only six nails. In a still smaller house of this class another row of nails is struck off, and another nail off each of the five remaining rows. Houses of officials or gentlemen of the fourth or fifth rank, must consist of seven open halls, with suitable apartments on each side. The beams supporting the vaulted roofs must be painted green, except the ridge beam, the colour of which must be red. The exterior decorations on the top of the roof are porcelain figures, not of dragons, but of cheluns. Each house of this class must be approached by a gateway covered with a vaulted roof, and consisting of three doors or arches. The doors must be painted black, and rings made of block tin, and supported by the heads of animals made of the same material, must be affixed to them. Houses of officials or gentlemen of the sixth, seven, eighth, or ninth rank must consist of five open halls, with suitable private apartments. Each house of this class is to be approached by a folding door, each division of which must have a plain iron ring, supported by iron lions' heads. Though without rank themselves, the immediate or more remote descendants of an official or gentleman of any of these classes, may reside in the house of their forefathers, and there is no law to compel them to alter the form of the houses.

The house of a private gentleman or citizen without rank must consist of five open halls. The beams, excepting of course the ridge beam, must be painted black. The house must be approached by a folding door, with no rings or ornaments. On the ceilings of the private apartments no figures of dragons, or phœnixes, or cheluns are to be painted.

The sumptuary laws are not less specific with regard to dress. What the Chinese shall wear in winter and summer is minutely prescribed from the hat downwards. The law distinctly states with regard to the winter costume, that the hat to be worn shall be covered with dark satin, and the inside lined with black cloth. The brim is to be turned up—which gives it the appearance of what used to be known as the "pork-pie" hat. The apex must be adorned with a tassel of red silk so long and so thick as to cover the entire top. The top of a court hat for the winter season must be covered with red floss silk, so long as to extend slightly over the brim. The summer hat is to be made either of fine straw, or of very thin strips of bamboo, or rattan; the outside covered with very fine silk, with a tassel of red silk cords on the top. The border must not turn up. The court hat for summer is to resemble the ordinary summer hat in all particulars except the following:—The rim must be covered with gold lace, and the inside lined with red gauze. On the apex the tassel must be of floss silk. The travelling hat for summer is to resemble the ordinary summer hat in form. The red tassel, however, must be of cow's hair. In addition to the tassel, a button, indicating by its colour the rank of the wearer, must be attached to the apex of each hat. For example, the hat worn by an officer or gentleman of the first rank is distinguished by a button of a bright red colour on its apex. A dark red button distinguishes the second rank; a dark blue button, the third rank; a light blue button, the fourth rank; a crystal button, the fifth rank; a white button, the sixth rank; a gold button, the seventh or eighth rank, and a silver button, the ninth rank. To the back of each hat is also attached a peacock's feather, which in the case of a person of high rank has two eyes, while persons of inferior rank are restricted to a feather which has only one eye. The peacock's feather is regarded as the gift of the Emperor, and is never worn by its fortunate possessor when engaged in celebrating funeral obsequies, or when worshipping the tablet of a deceased relative or friend. Each of the hats I have described must have a band, which, whenever the hat is worn, is to pass behind the ears and under the chin.

With regard to the form and texture of tunics the specifications are equally minute. The outer tunic is to be made of satin of a dark-purple colour, and its sleeves are to be wide and flowing, but shorter than those of the inner tunic. The body of this tunic is also to be shorter than that of the inner tunic. It is to be made to button in front. It must have on the front and back a piece of embroidered work. The sleeves of the tunic which is worn in spring must be lined with satin; those of the autumn tunic, fringed with fur; those of the winter tunic lined with fur. When travelling, a short outer tunic, made to reach below the hips of the wearer, must be used. Each outer tunic which I have described must have in front a row of five buttons only.

Let me now describe briefly the devices, or decorations, worn on the outer tunics. On that of an official or gentleman of the first rank must be embroidered in dark gold thread a back and breast-plate, and upon each of these a Tien Hok or angelic stork must be wrought in light gold or silver thread. On the outer tunic of a gentleman of the second rank, and upon a similar back and breast-plate, the figure of the Kam-Ki or beautiful bird, a species of pheasant, must be wrought. Similar back and breast-plates are worn by civilians of all the nine ranks; the particular rank being in each case indicated by the device. Among civilians this is invariably a bird—each rank being denoted by a different kind of bird—which is represented as standing on a rock in the midst of a tempestous ocean, with wings outstretched, and gaze directed towards the sun. The devices for the remaining ranks are as follow:—For the third rank, a Hong-Tseock, or peacock; for the fourth rank, a Wan-N'gan, or wild goose; for the fifth rank, a Pak-Ham, or silver pheasant; for the sixth rank, a Loo-Tsze, or cormorant; for the seventh rank, a Ki-Chik; for the eighth rank, a quail; and for the ninth rank, a Leen Chok, or white bird.

On the outer tunic of a person of the class Mee-yap-lou, that is, gentlemen who are expecting positions, the device is the figure of a Wong-Lee, or *yellow bird.*

Military officers must wear similar back and breast plates containing a device in light gold thread to indicate the rank of the officer. The devices are animals represented as standing on a rock in the midst of a tempestuous ocean, looking towards the sun. The devices for the various ranks of military officers are as follow:—For the first rank, the figure of a kee-lun, or chelun, a fabulous animal which is said to have the legs and hoofs of a cow, the head of a dragon, and the body of a sheep covered with scales; for the second rank, a Sze-Tsze or lion; for the third rank, a leopard; for the fourth rank, a tiger; for the fifth rank, a bear: for the sixth or seventh rank, a chetah; for the eighth rank, a sea-horse.

The criminal judge of each province occasionally wears on the back and breast plate of his outer tunic, a figure of an animal called by the Chinese Hi-Chi. This fabulous animal is supposed to have the power of distinguishing good from bad men, and it is said that it butts all bad people with its horns.

On the outer tunic of a nobleman there is embroidered in dark gold thread a back and breast plate with the device, in light gold thread, of a dragon with four claws at the extremity of each leg. In some instances, however, that is where the Imperial sanction has been obtained, the dragon is represented as having five claws on its legs. The device of a dragon is worn by dukes marquises, and earls; barons and baronets wear the device of a lion. Tippets or jackets, having deep gold borders, and embroidered with figures of dragons, are also worn by noblemen. Jackets of yellow satin are also bestowed by the Emperor as marks of distinctions upon officers both civil and military, who have rendered especial services to the state. The inner tunic is made of blue silk. It reaches from the neck to the ankles, and is confined to the waist by a sash or belt. The sleeves are to fit close to the arms, and the cuffs must resemble the hoofs of a horse in form. The inner tunic must have in front a row of five buttons only.　On these tunics the rank of the wearer is indicated by the number of dragons embroidered on them in gold thread.　On the inner tunic of an officer of the first rank, nine dragons are embroidered.　An officer of the second rank, has eight dragons on his tunic; an officer of the third rank, seven dragons; an officer of the fourth, fifth, or sixth rank, six dragons; and an officer of the seventh, or eighth rank, five dragons.　The dragons have at the extremity of each leg four claws only.

The Shee-Wye, a class of officials always in attendance upon His Imperial Majesty, also wear tunics embroidered with figures of dragons.　These officials are divided into four ranks or classes, and the dresses worn by the members of each class are similar to those worn by civil and military officers of corresponding rank.　Officers or gentlemen of rank are not allowed to wear robes of a light or dark yellow colour without Imperial permission; nor are they allowed to wear the fur of an animal called Yune-Woo, which is, I believe, a dark-coloured fox. Court dresses can only be worn on occasions of state worship, or banquets; or on the celebration of the birth or natal anniversary of any member of the Imperial family; or on the first, fifth, tenth, fifteenth, twentieth, or twenty-fifth day of each month. The outer tunic of the court may also be worn by an official or gentleman of rank, when paying or receiving visits from officers of high rank.　Besides the dresses I have described, there are what are termed rain-clothes.　These must be of a bright red colour, for officials of the first rank.　Gentlemen of the second or third rank must have a red hat and purple robes.　Those of the fourth, fifth, or sixth rank must wear a hat with a purple border, and a red dress.　For the seventh rank, the hat and cloak must be purple, and for the eighth or ninth rank, the hat must be purple with a red border.　Rain clothes worn by military officers of various ranks are the same in every respect as those which are worn by civil officers of corresponding rank.　With equal minuteness the laws prescribe the style of dress which graduates must adopt.　The dress of a bachelor of arts is a long, light blue silk tunic with a purple border.　It is girt about the waist of the wearer by a sash or belt.　His boots are of satin.

The hat is similar in shape to that worn by officials and gentle-men. The dress of a master of arts consists of a long, dark blue silk tunic with a light blue border. It is bound to the waist by a sash or girdle. The hat and boots of a master are the same as those of a bachelor. The priests of the sect of Buddha are on no account allowed to wear silk dresses, except when per-forming certain sacred rites. Nor are they permitted to spread silk coverlets on their beds, or to have silk curtains round them. They must not use vessels made of silver or gold, or inlaid with mother of pearl. Their dress is very plain, and consists of a long grey cowl with loose flowing sleeves. In short, it appears to resemble in shape, the cowl of a Christian monk. The materials of which it is made are coarse fabrics. These remarks also apply to the priests of the sect of Taou.

The dress worn by the οἱ πολλοί consists of a jacket reaching to the hips, and a pair of wide trousers. These garments are made of cotton fabrics. In the winter season, a pair of cloth shoes, a pair of stockings, and a skull cap are added. Shopkeepers and respect-able artificers wear cloth shoes, stockings, caps, trousers, and long blue cotton tunics, and, in some instances, a tippet or cape of black, or blue broad cloth. In summer, however, the cap is dispensed with, and a tunic of white calico, or grass cloth is substituted for the long blue cotton tunic. The gentry, in ad-dition to their under garments, wear long plain or flowered tunics of silk. The colour is either blue, purple, claret, or buff. Tippets or capes of fur are also worn by them when the weather is at all cold. To the apex of the cap, which is also made of silk, a button of red silk cord is attached, and to the front bor-der of it a false, or true pearl, or a precious stone is affixed. A person who has attained the age of seventy years, is allowed, if he be of good report, to wear a dress similar to that of an official of the ninth rank ; and one who has reached the ripe age of ninety, and who is of good report, is permitted to wear a dress similar to that worn by an official of the seventh rank. Play actors, slaves, and bastards are denied this privilege, and they are also forbidden to wear silk dresses. They may, how-ever, wear dresses made of what the Chinese call Kan-Chow. This fabric is woven of silk threads obtained from large silkworms which are not reared in houses, but feed, in their natural state, upon the leaves of oak trees. The skins of sheep and goats are the only furs which the sumptuary laws permit such persons to line their dresses with in winter. No ordinary citizen is allowed to wear a dress on which are embroidered in gold or silk thread, figures of dragons with five claws attached to the extremity of each leg. An offender would have to bear the cangue or wooden collar for a month, after which he would receive a flogging of one hundred blows. The people must not wear dresses embroidered with gold thread. They are permitted, however, to embroider their dresses with silk thread.

A lady when attending court, wears a hat precisely similar in shape and texture to that worn by her husband on such occasions. To the back of the hat, however, are attached two long silk ribbons, which hang down over her shoulders. A simpler hat is occasionally worn. The outer and inner tunics are of the same length. From the back of the neck-band of the outer tunic, two ribbons hang gracefully down. In front of her hat, a duchess wears three gold ornaments. Around her neck is a purple satin scarf which hangs down in front. The front portion of the scarf has, in the centre of it, a fringe of gold thread. Above this is the figure of a phœnix, and below it that of a dragon, embroidered in gold thread. Immediately above the fringe is fixed a large pearl. Three ear-rings are placed in the lobe of each ear, and from each ring hangs a valuable pearl. The outer tunic worn by a duchess, is of purple satin, and has a deep border of gold. On the front of the tunic, figures of two dragons are embroidered in gold thread, and on the back a figure of one dragon only. From the back of the neck-band are suspended two long silk ribbons, on each of which are sewn several precious stones or pearls. The inner tunic is of blue silk, and has a deep border of gold adorned with precious stones. On the front of the inner tunic a figure of a dragon is embroidered in gold thread. On each side of the tunic figures of four, on each cuff a figure of one, and on each sleeve figures of two dragons are embroidered. From the back of the neck-band of the inner tunic, two long ribbons are suspended, each of which is covered with pearls. The skirt worn by a duchess is of red satin. Upon it are embroidered in gold thread several figures of walking dragons. The ordinary dress of a duchess consists of an inner tunic of blue silk, on which are embroidered in gold, figures of nine dragons; and an outer tunic, with figures of eight dragons. These representations are in the form of circles. The dress of a marchioness is very similar to that of a duchess, but is not so resplendent with bullion and pearls. The wife of a civil officer of the first rank wears a hat like that worn by noblewomen. Her outer and inner tunics are in form, texture, and colour, the same as those worn by a duchess. The device, however, which is embroidered in gold on her dress, is that of a red-headed egret. Like all other ladies of rank, she wears the device of the class to which her husband belongs. Wives of military officers, however, wear figures of birds, not of beasts, on their outer tunics. Their inner tunics are embroidered with dragons, the number of which is determined by the husband's rank. Thus the wife of a military officer of the first rank has eight or nine dragons embroidered on her inner tunic, and the wife of an officer of the seventh, eighth, or ninth rank has only five. Wives of gentlemen who are without rank, may wear vestments of silk, but they are not allowed to wear tunics, or head-dresses, or pearls like those of the wives of men of rank. Each lady is limited to one gold hair-pin, and to one pair of gold ear-rings. If they feel disposed they may wear silver hair-pins, and earrings, and rings of the same material in great profusion.[1]

We turn to the various emblems or insignia which officials and gentlemen of rank are allowed to use when passing in procession through the streets of a city. In the procession which accompanies an officer of the first rank residing at Pekin, the insignia are as follows :—one large red umbrella; two large

[1] Hair-pins were used at a very early period in China. The date given is B.C. 1122, when the Chow dynasty was reigning. In the first instance they were made of bamboo. In the reign of Siang-Wang, however, the eighteenth emperor of the Chan dynasty, in the year B.C. 651, hair-pins made of ivory were introduced to the notice of ladies of fashion; and in the reign of King-Wang, the twenty-fifth emperor of the same dynasty, hair-pins made of tortoiseshell were regarded as the most becoming of all. In the reign of Chi Hwangte, that is, about the middle of the third century B.C., hair-pins, made either of silver or gold, were held in great requisition. As the head of each gold or silver hair-pin was wrought so as to resemble a phœnix, these were called phœnix pins.

fans, in the centre of which are recorded in letters of gold the name and titles of the officer, and on each of which are painted four representations of the sun; four banners; four spears, and two yellow rods of office. In the procession of an officer of the second rank there are only three representations of the sun on each of the fans, and two spears are carried instead of four. Two of the banners which are carried have the figure of a dragon on the one side, and that of a tiger on the other; and the other two banners have the characters Tsing and Poo, which mean "clear the way," inscribed on each of their sides. An officer of the third rank has only two representations of the sun painted on the fans of his procession; and for the fourth rank, the fans are merely bespangled with gold. One fan only is allowed to officers of any of the remaining ranks. The processions are also regulated according to rank in some other respects. These processions only take place in Pekin, when an officer is leaving the imperial capital *en route* to a station which has been assigned him in one of the provinces. Officers of the various ranks, who reside at Pekin, are usually accompanied when riding through the streets by a certain number of equerries. An officer of the first rank is accompanied by ten equerries, two of whom precede him, while eight follow. An officer of the second rank is preceded by two, and followed by six equerries; an officer of the third rank is preceded by two and followed by four equerries; while an officer of the fourth rank is simply preceded by one. An officer of the fifth, sixth, or seventh rank is followed by one. A red tassel attached to the martingale of a horse indicates that its rider is an officer of one of the first four ranks.. Tartar officers who are of the blood royal, the four high ministers of state who constitute the cabinet council, the presidents of each of the six boards, and officers also of the second rank, if aged and infirm, may when passing through the streets of Pekin, ride in state sedan-chairs. With these exceptions all other officers, and their immediate, retainers, ride on horseback, except when leaving Pekin, *en route* to a provincial station. An officer of the first, second, or third rank then rides in a sedan chair borne by four bearers. So soon, however, as the chair has passed beyond the gates of the city, eight bearers are appointed. To the sedan chair of an officer of an inferior rank, two sedan-chair bearers are appointed on such occasions, and outside the gates of the city the number is increased to four. The sedan chair of the higher official is furnished with dark-coloured curtains, and the top of it is surmounted by a silver globe or ball. That in which an officer of lower rank rides is surmounted by a globe or ball of block tin.

Passing from the imperial capital to the provinces, let me note the nature and style of the insignia of office. To begin with the procession which accompanies a governor-general of a province, or provinces. When passing in his state sedan-chair through the streets of a city, there are borne in his train two large silk umbrellas ; two banners, on each of which are representations of winged tigers ; two rods of office, on the top of each of which, as an emblem of authority over the troops, is the figure of a clenched fist; two swords, each of which is supposed to resemble in shape the feather of a wild goose ; two swords, the hilt of each of which is adorned with the head of an animal in brass ; two yellow rods of office ; two white rods of office, each of which is made of the branch of a tree called by the Chinese, Toong ; two wooden boards painted red, on which are written in gold the characters Wooee and Pee, which are intended to warn persons who are riding in sedan-chairs, or who are bearing heavy burdens through the narrow streets, to turn aside and avoid meeting his excellency's cavalcade ; two wooden boards painted red, on which in gold are the characters Shuk and Tsing, or Be respectful and silent ; four spears, in addition to the two banners, and eight other banners on which are painted figures of dragons. The procession of a provincial governor is distinguished from that of a governor-general by the absence of the rods indicating military authority, by fans substituted for the banners with winged tigers, and by only two swords and two spears being carried. Similar points of difference indicate the lower rank of treasurers and judges of provinces, and of toutais and prefects. The sedan-chair of a governor-general or a provincial governor, or a Tartar general, or a commissioner of revenue, is borne by eight men. Provincial treasurers, provincial judges, literary chancellors, salt commissioners, toutais, and

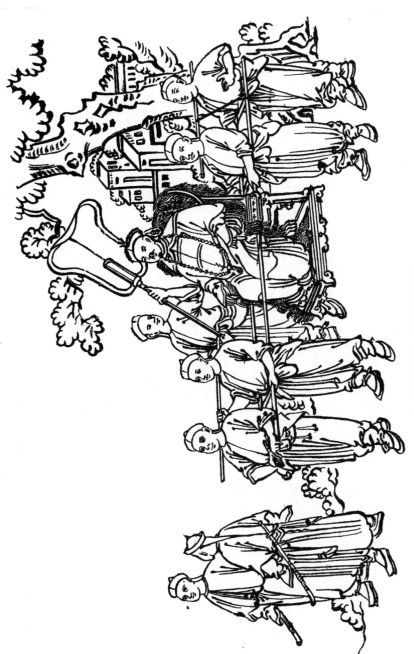

A MANDARIN IN AN OPEN CHAIR.

prefects are limited to four bearers. The number of equerries is in each case, of course, regulated by rank. The procession is headed by lictors, who carry, some whips, and others chains, in their hands, and by men provided with gongs. At intervals the latter beat their gongs loudly, to announce the near approach of the great man who is passing through the city. The lictors also, at frequent intervals, and especially when passing through the gates of a city, call out, " Let all men keep silence." The busy hum which arises from the crowded mart is accordingly succeeded, for the time being, by a deathlike stillness. The custom reminds one of a similar practice in ancient Egypt. In the history of Joseph we read (Gen. xli. 43) that when Pharaoh had exalted that remarkable man to rule as a viceroy over the people of Egypt, a herald went before him as he passed along the crowded streets, and cried aloud, " Bow the knee." In the procession which accompanies an officer of the fifth, sixth, or seventh rank, when he passes in his sedan-chair through the streets of a city, there are borne one blue silk umbrella, one fan, two white rods of office, two wooden boards on which in gold are the characters Shuk and Tsing, and four banners. The procession is headed by two lictors. Officers of the eighth and ninth ranks are entitled to one umbrella, and two rods of office. The procession is headed by two lictors, each of whom carries in his hand a bamboo rod.

A military officer of the first rank has for his insignia, two umbrellas ; two fans ; two banners on each of which are figures of tigers with wings ; two staves each of which is surmounted with a clenched fist ; two swords, the hilt of each of which is ornamented with the head of an animal in brass ; two swords, each of which resembles in form the feather of a wild goose ; two red boards on which in gold are the characters Shuk and Tsing ; four spears, and eight green banners, to the top of each of which a streamer is attached. The procession is headed by two lictors, each of whom carries in his hand a bamboo, and by two gongmen. A military officer of the second rank and of the class Ching, has two battle-axes instead of the staves with the clenched fist ; and he is not entitled to display the two swords which are shaped like the feather of a wild goose. The number of spears is also reduced to two in this procession. Similar points of difference mark other gradations of military rank. The state sedan-chair of each military officer is preceded and followed by equerries and pedestrians, varying in number.

It is worthy of remark that the practice of carrying fans in official processions, as insignia of honour and power, is of great antiquity, and in early ages the custom was not confined to China alone. On the monuments of ancient Egypt are to be found representations of fans carried on the tops of long poles, just as to-day in China, before the mighty of the land.

There is little to be said about the retinue which accompanies the sedan-chairs of private individuals. A private gentleman or wealthy citizen is borne in his chair by four or two men, and is followed by four or two livery servants on foot; and his wife is borne in a chair by four or two men, and is followed by two or one female servant on foot.

The style and furnishing of sedan-chairs is also regulated by the sumptuary laws of China. The state sedan-chair of an official, whether civil or military, of all ranks, must be covered with green cloth. The fringe which is made to skirt the outside of the roof of the chair, and the curtains for the windows, must also be green. For the first three ranks, the ends of the poles or shafts may be tipped with brass moulded in the form of dragons' heads. For the fourth and fifth ranks, the ends of the poles may be tipped with brass moulded in the form of lions' heads. The ends of the poles of the sedan-chair of an official of any of the four remaining ranks, may be tipped with brass on which is engraven in relief representations of the clouds. On the top of each of the chairs in question is to be fixed a globe or ball of block tin. Blue cloth is to be used for the chair of a private gentleman, and the ends of the poles must be tipped with plain ferules of brass. Sedan-chairs, used by persons in the humbler walks of life, must be covered with cloth of a dark colour, and the ends of the poles or shafts perfectly plain.

In all Chinese cities there are public sedan-chair stands, at which chairs are let out on hire by the hour or day. In some parts of the empire, the proprietors have to pay a tax. I found this to be the case in Nankin and Hang-chow, but it is certainly not so in the southern cities of China with which I am acquainted. Upon each taxed sedan-chair the name of the proprietor, and of the street in which he resides is painted in large Chinese characters. At Nankin, aged and infirm persons in the lower walks of life are borne from place to place in baskets, and at Eching I saw a respectable youth of twelve years of age being conveyed in this manner. Of the style and form of carts or carriages, a description will be found in another chapter. I may say here that the wheels of a cart or carriage of a man of rank, are placed not under the centre of, but at the extreme end of the cart. On the sedan-chairs and carts used by officials and people, there may not be painted or embroidered figures of dragons, or phœnixes, or indeed, representations of any imperial emblems.

This chapter would be incomplete without some special notice of state umbrellas. These are a conspicuous feature of Chinese processions. On the top of a state umbrella of a gentleman of the first or second rank must be the figure of a gourd, made of block tin. For the third and fourth ranks, the gourd must be made of wood and painted red. An official or gentleman of the fifth rank, displays a blue cloth umbrella with a gourd made of wood and painted red. In the case of the first four ranks, the umbrella must have three flounces; those who are of lower rank being only entitled to two flounces. It is interesting to observe that in other Eastern countries the umbrella has also its place among the insignia of high rank. It was, and is still, if I mistake not, one of the emblems of royalty and power throughout India, Persia, Arabia and other Asiatic countries, and in that portion of the great continent of Africa which is inhabited by the followers of the false prophet of Mecca. At the time Rome was giving laws to the world, it was used by the sovereigns of Egypt, since Mark Antony is censured for having united the eagles of Rome with the state umbrellas of the unfortunate Cleopatra.

> " Interque signa (turpe !) militiaria
> Sol aspicit cornopeum."

The masses are not allowed to use silk or cloth umbrellas only those made of oil paper. In this, as well as in other respects the sumptuary laws are disregarded, for it is not at all unusual to meet people in the streets of a Chinese city carrying either silk or cloth umbrellas. Red silk umbrellas are occasionally presented by the people to distinguished officials.

From umbrellas to walking-sticks is a much greater transition in China than in our own country; but this has not prevented sumptuary legislators dealing with them. According to some Chinese authors, they were first used as far back as 2357 B.C., and, according to others, were introduced during the reign of Woo-wing of the Chow dynasty, who flourished 1122 B.C. That walking-sticks were used during the reign of Woo-wing, appears from a reference made to a prince named Chow-Koong, who used one in punishing an act of rudeness on the part of his son. During that period the use of walking-sticks was common to all classes of society. For some reason, however, their use was eventually restricted to men who were fifty years of age and upwards. The law, however, was very arbitrary, and prohibited men who were between fifty and sixty years of age from using their walking-sticks except when walking on their own premises! Those who were between sixty and seventy years of age were allowed to use them when walking through the towns and villages in which they resided, and only those upwards of eighty were at liberty to use them wherever they went. During the after-Liang dynasty, A.D. 903, a law which allowed all aged and infirm persons to use walking-sticks was established. I may remark, in conclusion, that precepts not dissimilar to some contained in the code of sumptuary laws framed by Zaleucus, the famous legislator of Locris, are at this very time observed in China. For example, it is enacted that no respectable spinster of the lower orders of society shall wear apparel similar to that which is worn by ladies of rank and fashion. Those, however, who are not respectable may do so, as in Locris a ruffian might wear the gold ring which was denied to the honest man; and in China all prostitutes who reside in cities and towns, wear gold bracelets and embroidered dresses, and paint their faces, like virtuous women of the upper classes.

CHAPTER XVI.

AMUSEMENTS AND SPORTS.

THE Chinese appear to appreciate the drama quite as much as the more civilized nations of Europe. Their dramatic entertainments appear to be connected in many instances with their idolatrous worship, and in front of the principal temples there are permanent stages upon which the plays are performed at festivals. It is not unusual for sick persons to vow in the presence of certain idols that, should their lives be spared, they will give dramatic entertainments in honour of these deities. To such entertainments the people are of course admitted gratuitously; but no seats are provided for them. There are societies or companies, however, who hire actors and give theatrical representations both to amuse the masses and to make money. Each society must include one or two persons who have taken literary degrees, and each is held responsible for the peace and good order of the spectators. Stage plays are generally acted in large tents, as among the ancient Romans. These tents, made of large bamboo frames covered with matting, are in the form of squares. Three sides of the square are occupied by rows of benches for the spectators. Behind these, immediately in front of the stage, there is a gallery for ladies. There are different classes of seats, and the prices of admission vary accordingly, some of the benches having a rest for the back, and others having none. As theatres are made of bamboo or matting, there is great danger from the displays of fire-crackers, which sometimes take place during a performance,

as representations of thunder and lightning. In 1844, a
large theatre in the vicinity of the literary chancellor's yamun
at Canton, caught fire, and, as it was densely crowded with
spectators, upwards of two thousand persons perished. Their
charred bones were afterwards gathered together and buried
in a common grave beyond the north-east gate of the city. A
similar accident occurred in a small theatre at Whampoa, in
1853, when thirty persons, chiefly women with small feet,
perished.

In every large town there are several companies of actors,
each consisting of ten, twenty, or a hundred persons. Though
they afford much gratification to the people, actors are ranked
so low in the social scale, that their children are not allowed to
present themselves for literary distinctions, which, of course,
prevents them ever attaining to any high position in the state.
When boys, they are bought by the conductors of companies
and sent to dramatic schools, where they are carefully instructed
in all the mysteries of their art. They are very harshly treated
at these seminaries, and disobedience is visited with very severe
punishment. Should a refractory youth die under the hands of
a master, no notice whatever is taken by those whose duty it is
to administer justice. A Chinese parent named Lee once called
upon me, to ask me to give advice to his son, who, much against
his father's wish, was bent on selling himself to the manager of
a company. The youth, with whom I had two or three inter-
views, was deaf to all entreaties, and eventually entered a
dramatic school, where I afterwards learned he was very cruelly
treated by the man to whom he had deliberately sold himself
for a small sum. On visiting the school, I found him engaged
in learning the use of the sword and spear, his instructor having
settled that the *rôle* of a soldier suited him best. The usual
period of instruction is one year, at the close of which the
youths are expected to take part in any plays which may
be performed. They are regarded by their purchasers as little
better than beasts of burden, and receive for their services
only food and clothing. Their period of servitude, however,
lasts only for six years, after which they may claim their discharge. If sufficiently influential, they form companies of their

own ; otherwise, they engage themselves to managers at a tolerably remunerative salary. As a rule, women are not allowed to appear on the stage. Female parts are well sustained by men, and their presence does not seem required. There are, however, schools in which females, generally of dissolute habits, are instructed for the stage.

The usual hire for a company of players is from twenty to one hundred dollars a-day. They are frequently rewarded during the performance of a play by presents of food, such as roast pigs, or offerings of money. I have seen a present of roast pigs carried across the stage by the servants of the donor at the very time the most pathetic part of a play was being performed. The gifts are no sooner received than one of the performers not engaged in the play attires himself as a deity, and, coming before the audience with a graceful salutation, unfolds a scroll with an inscription in large characters expressive of the thanks of the company for the presents received. These substantial expressions of approbation may remind the reader of the *corollarium*, or reward given to actors amongst the ancient Romans.

The plays which appear to be the most popular, are those which relate to the history of ancient times, for, like most of the plays of the immortal Shakespere, the productions of the dramatic writers of China are in a great measure historical. The leading principles inculcated are those of loyalty to the throne, filial piety, and entire devotion to the gods of the land. Generally they exalt virtue and condemn vice. What refers to the vices of the age is clothed in very unchaste language, and the acting is attended with coarse and sometimes indecent gesticulation. Performances are accompanied by vocal and instrumental music, the musicians being arranged on the background of the stage. There is no curtain, and the movements of the scene-shifters are witnessed by the spectators. The dresses of the actors are generally of the most elegant and costly description, especially in the theatrical companies of the southern provinces.

In 1861, at Whampoa I witnessed a play the plot of which was laid in the Sung dynasty, that is, about five hundred years ago. Its purport was to set before the minds of the people the great advantages and blessings which attend the exercise of filial piety, an addiction to literary pursuits, and entire devotion to the gods.   Let me give the following *résumé* of the play:—A youth, named Laee Mung-ching, though born in a humble station in life, was conspicuous alike for his filial piety and studious habits.   When his parents were old and no longer able to labour for the common necessaries of life, he resorted daily to a Buddhist monastery, to beg the crumbs which fell from the table of the monks.   The monks, at last growing weary of his repeated importunities, told him to discontinue his visits, and presented him with a small sum of money as a parting gift.   With this he purchased a small quantity of rice and a bundle of firewood.   On his way home he was attacked by a large dog, and in his terror dropped the rice, which was quickly devoured by some fowls.   Upon his return home, he related his disaster to his parents, who at the time were perishing with hunger.   Eventually they died of starvation, and, in order to obtain funds for the decent interment of their remains, the son was constrained to sell his wife.   As he sallied forth with her having this object in view, an aged man chanced to pass that way, whom he accosted.   The old man entered into conversation with him, and, hearing his tale, agreed to become the purchaser of his wife.   Returning home with her newly-acquired husband, the bride did not dream of the good fortune which was about to befall her former lord.   But his filial piety, and the numerous though very small pecuniary offerings which his parents had made in their lifetime to funds established for the repair and erection of temples, were not forgotten by the gods.   In the course of a conversation the aged man informed her that he was formerly the head of the Buddhist priesthood, and that he resided in that capacity, for many years, in a temple which had been erected and endowed by the ancestors of the very man whose wife she had recently been.   These words were no sooner uttered, than he ascended towards the heavens, passing out of sight.   The poor woman was greatly alarmed, and concluded that the person with whom she had been conversing was an angel.   She retraced her steps, and had not gone far, before she met her sorrowing husband.   He was surprised at her unexpected return, and still more so when she related what she had just witnessed. They resolved, however, to hasten home, to expend the money they had acquired, in the due celebration of the obsequies of their parents. When they had reached the threshold of their cottage, they found their parents restored to life, and surrounded by every comfort. Their good fortune did not stop here. Possessing great abilities, the young man soon made himself master of the classics, and eventually succeeded in attaining the highest literary distinctions, and the most important political positions of the empire.

Chinese plays are of great length, and not unfrequently take up three days and nights in acting. Besides theatrical representations on the part of professional performers, families of respectability frequently amuse themselves by private theatricals. Amateur companies are formed by young gentlemen, many of whom display great dramatic power. These entertainments take place in the large family residences, and are seldom witnessed by Europeans, excepting, of course, by those who have succeeded in becoming well acquainted with native families of wealth and respectability.

With the view of preventing actors from performing obscene plays in Canton, the following edict was issued by Wong, the Provincial Treasurer :—

"I, Wong, Provincial Treasurer, hear that the people of Canton are exceedingly fond of dramatic representations. Why ? Because they deem it necessary when worshipping the gods to render them all honour by having dramatic representations. Theatres are, therefore, a source of much rejoicing to the people, and to prevent such things there are of course no laws. It is, however, very necessary that plays should be performed which have a tendency to cause men to worship the gods, to make them true and faithful to the throne, and dutiful to their parents. To represent on the stage lewd plays, is the surest way to destroy morality. Many of the gentry are greatly shocked to find that such plays are not unfrequently performed, and they at the same time state, that in the performance of such plays, actresses usually take parts. They have, therefore, called upon me to put a stop to such obscenities. I therefore command all managers of theatres to take care that, in future, such abominations be not tolerated. I inform them further that should they neglect to carry out my views I shall not only apprehend but severely punish them. Tung-chee, 8th year, 7th day, 10th month."

Another kind of amusement known to the Chinese, which may be mentioned in this connection, is marionettes. Puppet-shows are generally held in front of temples in honour of goddesses, and are attended, as a rule, by females only. Sometimes they take place in the houses of the gentry, for the especial gratification of the female members of the household. I have seen an historical play well sustained by the expert employ-ment of such images, the men behind the scenes giving the dialogue.

I have observed that such shows are generally attended by females only. I may mention an exception to this rule. At Yong-mak in the district of Heong-shan, I attended a represen-tation of this kind at which the spectators were all men. It was given in honour of the god of the markets. A friend accompanied me, and we took up our position at the end of the theatre, immediately opposite the stage. No sooner had the news of our presence spread, than all the spectators turned their backs upon the performance, and gazed with wonder on the two barbarians who had joined them. A somewhat similar scene occurred when, in 1862, I visited the town of Loong-keng, a small country town at the extreme point of the long and mountainous district of Tsung-fa. Two travelling companions and myself entered the town together. We were much sur-prised at the emptiness of the streets, and found on inquiry that all the inhabitants were at the play. We had not ridden far through the streets, when we found ourselves in sight of the theatre. The news of our arrival spread, and the spectators at once left the delights of dramatic fiction to gaze upon a startling novelty in real life. We were the first Europeans the inhabit-ants had ever seen, and literally we proved as "good as a show."

At Soo-Chow, I saw a puppet-show, the marionettes in which were exceedingly small. The figures were set in motion by strings from above the stage, the others I have described being worked from behind the scenes. Whilst the show was going on,

A PEEP-SHOW.

an incessant clamour was kept up by beating gongs. A puppet representing a Chinese soldier armed with a shield and sword, was made to go through the sword exercise with admirable precision, and a spearman was made to perform his evolutions with equal success. A contest eventually took place between these warriors, and it was so well sustained that the spectators became quite excited. Victory after a severe tussle, fell to the spearman. Another puppet was made to represent an old fisherman walking along the sea-beach in pursuit of a stranded fish. The fisherman, who was provided with a basket, made frequent ineffectual endeavours to place it over the sprawling fish. The fish at last escaped into the water, and the fisherman, ignorant of the fact, put his hand into the basket, and groped for his missing prey. The cleverness with which the movements of the fisherman were executed excited great applause.

The musical attainments of the people are at such a low ebb that I had almost written there are no concerts in China. Vocal and instrumental entertainments, however, are given at the celebration of the natal anniversaries of several of the minor deities. These entertainments, which are held in mat houses erected in front of the temples, succeed each other during three consecutive days and nights, and appear to afford great delight to large audiences. The Chinese enliven their summer and winter evenings by song. Towards the close of the day, numbers of blind women, neatly dressed, and guided by aged women, may be seen traversing the streets. They are professional singers, and are invited into the houses and shops of the citizens, where, for small sums, they will sing nearly the whole night long. As artificers of all kinds are very industrious, and often work up to a late hour, their employers sometimes call these women into their shops to amuse them. I have seen a number of cobblers diligently plying their task, with a singing woman seated in the corner of the shop lightening their labour by her songs.

Pyrotechnic displays are very popular. The fireworks consist of catherine wheels, burning moons, fiery flowers, and bright stars. Graceful pagodas are also outlined, and, by means of puppets, scenes are represented in which emperors hold *levées*, officials preside over courts of justice, generals review troops, and ladies lounge in garden bowers.

Conjurors are a tolerably numerous class, and they perform many of the tricks with which the fraternity in Europe seek to amuse their audiences. In my travels I met occasionally with strolling gymnasts, whose performances equalled those of the kind which are common in our own country. One of the most remarkable of these performers threw a bamboo pole thirty feet long and decorated with small banners, into the air, caught it upon his head, chest, shoulders, or hands, and balanced it for a considerable time with the greatest ease. Before receiving it on his head he put on a thickly padded cap. At Pekin, I saw young men, evidently of great strength, amusing themselves by throwing a large stone into the air, and catching it as it fell by a ring which was attached to it. The feat was performed with much ease and grace. Others, also for their own amusement, threw an earthenware vase at each other, the person at whom it was thrown catching it on his elbow, or shoulder, or head. At Hankow, I saw a female with remarkably small feet, going through a tight-rope performance. With a balancing pole in her hands, she executed a graceful dance on the rope, amid the clanging of cymbals and beating of gongs. At Tien-tsin I was amused by a singular procession of children on stilts. The children were beating tom-toms, and showed great ease and grace in their movements. Two men who headed the procession beating tom-toms solicited alms from the passers-by. At Pekin, I engaged the services of a ventriloquist, who, with great skill, represented a conversation between a farmer and his wife on the one hand, and their cow-herd, swine-herd, and dairy-maid on the other. The lowing of the oxen and the grunting of the swine were also admirably rendered. Peep-shows are to be met with in almost every town. In Canton and other southern cities, they are very small ; in the central provinces they are very large, such shows being provided with ten or fifteen large circular peep-holes. Those which I saw at Hankow and Soo-Chow

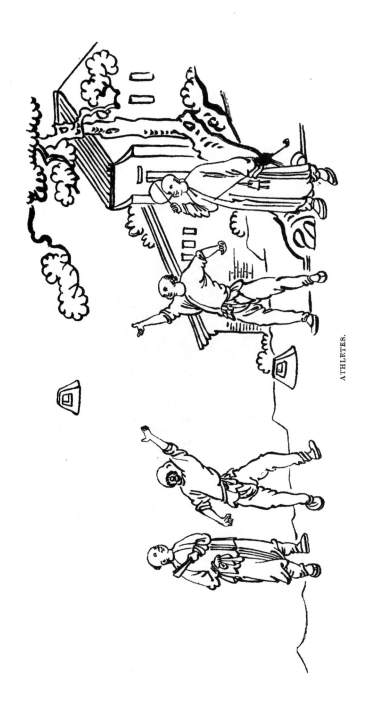

ATHLETES.

GAMBLERS.

were so large as to resemble tents of drill. Obscene pictures
are, it is said, exhibited in these shows.

No amusement is more popular among the Chinese than
gambling. The inordinate love of play is so deeply rooted in
the breasts of the people that men and women of all classes
of society, and of almost all ages, are gamblers. The gaming-
houses are numerous everywhere, and are thronged with players
from an early hour in the morning until a late hour in the
evening. Even fruit-stalls are turned into gaming tables, and
it is scarcely possible to pass one of them without finding it
surrounded by boys of tender age, gambling for its tempting
stores. The boys cannot resist a throw of the dice, although
they know that the chances are greatly in favour of the
fruiterer.

Gambling is, of course, forbidden by law. It is tolerated,
however, by the depraved rulers of the people, who derive,
monthly, considerable sums of money from this source. Indeed
the Namhoi and Pun-Yu magistrates at Canton have actually
converted some spare rooms near the outer gates of their
respective yamuns into gaming-houses. When on a visit to the
district cities of Loong-moon and Tsung-Sheng, I observed that
the rulers of these cities had resorted to a similar device. In
general, however, gaming-houses are in back or side streets, as
the more respectable and wealthy tradespeople object to such
establishments in their neighbourhood. In 1861, all the shopkeepers living in the street called Su-shee-Kai, at Canton, closed
their shops, and refused to open them until the governor-general
of the province, whom they had memorialized on the subject,
promised to issue an order directing the district ruler to close a
gaming-house which he had permitted to be opened in the street.
I remember a similar circumstance in a street at Honam, named
N'goo-chow-Kai. When on a visit to the prefectoral city of
Eng-chow-Foo, or Woo-chow-Foo, in the province of Kwang-si,
I found that the objection of the citizens to gaming-houses
was so strong that they had succeeded in prevailing upon the
prefect to insist on all such establishments being upon the
water. Several large chops, resembling floating houses, were at
anchor in the river for the purpose. The objection to gaming-

houses on the part of wealthy tradesmen, does not arise from the fact that they do not gamble themselves, but from a fear lest a number of needy and abandoned persons should assemble in such establishments, and plunder the neighbouring shops.

Gaming-houses are of various kinds. Those which are called Tan-Koon are conducted by a joint-stock company, consisting either of ten or twenty partners. Such houses consist of two apartments. In the first of these is a high table, on the centre of which is placed a small square board. The four sides of the board are marked respectively one, two, three, and four. For the game played in this apartment the presence of three of the partners is necessary. The first is called the Tan-Koon or the croupier; the second the Tai-N'gan, or shroff, who sits by the side of the former, with his tables, scales, and money drawers, to examine and weigh the money which may be staked; and the third, the Ho-Koon, who stands by the table, keeps account of the game, and pays over the stakes to the rightful winners. The gamblers stand round the high table, and the Tan-Koon, or croupier, places a handful of cash on it before him. Over the heap he immediately places a tin cover, so that the gamblers cannot calculate the exact number of the cash. They are now called upon to place their stakes at any of the sides of the square board in the centre. When this has been done, the Tan-Koon removes the cover, and, using a thin ivory rod a foot long, proceeds to lessen his heap by drawing away four cash at a time. Should one cash remain, the gambler who placed his stake on the side of the small square board which is marked one is declared the winner. If two cash remain, he saves his stake; and in the case of three remaining he is allowed the same privilege. If, however, four cash remain, he loses his stake. This game is called Ching-tow, and the gambler, as the reader will perceive, has one chance of winning, two of retaining his stake, and one of losing it.

A second game played at the same table is called Nim. At this game the gambler has one chance of winning double the amount of his stake; two chances of losing it, and one of retaining it. Should he place his stake on the side of the board marked two, and two cash remains upon the Tan-Koon removing his heap by four at a time, his winnings are double the amount of his stake. If three cash remain of the Tan-Koon's heap, the gambler retains his stake ; if either one or four remain, he loses. A third game played at this table is called Fan. In it the gambler has one chance of winning three times the amount of his stake, and three chances of losing it. A fourth game at this table is called Kok. The rule observed in it, is to place the stake at one of the corners of the board, that is, between any two of the numbers. Should the croupier's remainder correspond to either of the numbers between which the stake is placed, the gambler wins a sum equal to his stake. Should the remainder correspond to one of the other two numbers, he loses.

In the inner apartment of these establishments the stakes are all in silver coin, whereas in the ante-chamber cash only—from fifty up to several hundreds—are played for. Three partners are also required to conduct the games in the inner room. As the stakes are very heavy, they are not placed on the table, lest the vagabonds who are in the habit of resorting to the first apartment in large numbers should rush in and sweep them away. It is customary, therefore, to use Chinese playing cards to distinguish the gamblers; also, corresponding cards from another pack to represent their stakes. The stakes are carefully noted down by the Ho-Koon, to avoid disputes. In spite of this, disputes are not uncommon, and I may add that the only stand-up fight which I ever witnessed during my long residence in China, occurred at the door of a gaming-house at Pit-kong, between the keeper of it and a disappointed speculator.

The proprietors of these gaming-houses realize large sums of money, and the gamblers are frequently ruined, and, driven into desperate courses, often end their days in prison. Sometimes they lose not only all their money, but the clothes they are wearing. On one occasion, passing the door of a gambling-house near the temple of the Five Genii, at Canton, I heard a great noise. Entering the establishment to ascertain the cause I found the conductors of the games actually engaged in stripping the clothes off a man who had staked and lost them. The unfortunate man was then dressed in gunny-bags[1] and turned into the street.

Seven per cent. of the gamblers' winnings go to the proprietors to defray the expenses, which are very great in consequence of the large monthly sums paid to the mandarins.

Sometimes females of bad character conduct gaming establishments. When detected they are put down by the strong arm of the law.

Another mode of gambling is that called Koo-yan or "the Ancients." It is also known under the name of "Flowery Characters." This game is said to have originated in the department of Chun-chow, and was introduced into Canton in the twenty-eighth year of the reign of Taou-kwang. By the "ancients" is meant a number of names and surnames by which thirty-six personages of former times were known and recognized. These names are divided into nine different classes, as follows:—

I. The names of four men who attained the highest literary distinctions.

> In a former state of existence, these men were respectively, a fish, a white goose, a white snail, and a peacock.

II. The names of five distinguished military officers.

> These men were once, respectively, a worm, a rabbit, a pig, a tiger, and a cow.

III. The names of seven successful merchants.

> These men were once, respectively, a flying dragon, a white dog, a white horse, an elephant, a wild cat, and a wasp.

IV. The names of four persons who were conspicuous for their uninterrupted happiness on earth.

> These were once, respectively, a frog, an eagle, a monkey, and a dragon.

V. The names of four females.

> These were once, respectively, a butterfly, a precious stone, a white swallow, and a pigeon.

[1] Gunny is a strong coarse kind of sacking.—[ED.]

VI. The names of five beggars.

These were once, respectively, a prawn, a snake, a fish, a deer, and a sheep.

VII. The names of four Buddhist priests.

These were once, respectively, a tortoise, a hen, an elk, and a calf.

VIII. The names of two Taouist priests.

These were once, respectively, a white egret and a yellow streaked cat.

IX. The name of a Buddhist nun who was once a fox.

The game is played as follows. The gambling company select a person who has an aptitude for composing enigmas, to whom they pay a very large salary. New enigmas are constantly wanted, as the houses where this game is played are open twice daily, namely, at 7 A.M., and again at 8 P.M. Each enigma is supposed to have a reference to one of the creatures enumerated, whether beast, bird, fish, reptile, or insect. So soon as an enigma is composed, it is printed, and several thousand copies are sold to the people. The sale of these enigmas must prove in itself a considerable source of revenue. When a purchaser of one of them thinks he has found out the creature to which it refers, he writes his answer on a sheet of paper. At the hour appointed he hastens to the gaming-house, generally a large hall, where he presents his answer, and the sum of money which he is prepared to stake, to a secretary. When all the answers and stakes have been received, the managers of the establishment retire to an inner chamber, where they examine the answers and count the stakes. The secretary records the names of those who have answered correctly, while his partners wrap up the various sums of money which the successful conjecturers have won. All this time there is suspended from the roof of the chamber where the speculators are assembled, a scroll folded up, and containing a picture of the creature to which the enigma alludes. When the winners' stakes have been prepared for them, the secretary enters the hall and unfolds this scroll. So soon as the picture is seen, it is greeted with a loud shout of exultation from the successful few, and with murmurs of discontent from the many who have guessed wrong. It is hardly necessary to add that the managers take care to provide riddles of such an ambiguous character, that the majority are always wrong in their conjectures. The amount staked in these places is limited.

Ladies lose large sums of money at such establishments. As they are not allowed to appear in public, they are generally represented at them by their female slaves or servants.

Large sums are daily lost by men, women, and children of all classes, in a game called Ta-pak-up-pu, or "strike the white dove." A company is formed, consisting of fifty partners having equal shares. One is selected to act as an overseer, and, for reasons which will presently appear, he is made to live in strict retirement. A sheet of paper on which eighty Chinese characters, respectively signifying heaven, earth, sun, moon, stars, &c., is given to him. With this sheet he enters a private apartment, and remains there without communicating with any one for several hours, during which he marks twenty of the characters with a vermilion pencil. The sheet is then deposited in a box, which is at once carefully locked. Thousands of sheets of paper containing eighty similar characters, are then sold to the public. The purchasers mark ten of the eighty, and take their papers next morning to the gaming establishment to have them compared with that marked by the overseer. Before they give them up, they make copies of them, which they retain. When all the papers have been received, the box which contains the overseer's paper, and which stands conspicuous on a table, is unlocked. The gambler's papers are then compared with the overseer's paper. If a gambler has marked only four of the characters selected by the overseer, he receives nothing. If he has marked five of them, he receives seven cash; if six, seventy cash; if eight, seven dollars; and if ten, fifteen dollars. A person wishing to gamble can buy as many as three hundred copies of the gambling sheet, but he must mark them all alike. There are never more than two such establishments in large cities such as Canton, and the winnings of the firms conducting them must be very great, to judge from the number of sheets sold daily.

In cities, there are also houses in which card-playing for very high stakes takes place both by day and night. Many persons are there brought to ruin. To elude the vigilance of the authorities these establishments are more or less private ; but card-players experience little or no difficulty in finding out such haunts of vice. A private residence was used for the purpose in the neighbourhood of a Chinese house in which I resided for six years. I was induced to visit it on one occasion, and found in it gentlemen card-players with several female companions. The latter were not engaged in the game, as it is altogether contrary to Cantonese notions of propriety that women should play cards with men. In the cities of Nankin and Kam-poo-sheng, I saw to my astonishment men and women playing together, and on making inquiries I found that a similar custom prevails at Shanghai. Cards are a very popular amusement with all classes.

A mode of gambling by means of three thin short rods, like ordinary chop-sticks, is sometimes practised. The gambler holds the three rods in his right hand, taking care to conceal them at one end by the compression of his palm. He has previously attached a sum of money to one of the sticks. His antagonist places an equal sum of money on the opposite end of one of the rods ; and, should he place it on the rod to which the person holding the sticks has attached his stake, he wins it.

Gambling by means of oranges is also greatly practised by the Cantonese. This takes place, as a rule, at fruit-stalls, but it is practised in private houses. A man bets that an orange contains a definite number of pips. The orange is then cut into pieces and the pips are counted. At a fruit-stall the fruiterer pays five cash to a lucky guesser for each cash he may have staked. An unfortunate speculator pays the value of the orange, and in addition, five cash for each cash he may have staked. At fruit-stalls it is also usual to gamble for sticks of sugar-cane. The cane is placed in a perpendicular position, and he who succeeds in cutting it asunder from the top to the bottom with a sharp-edged knife, wins the cane from the fruiterer. Should he fail, the fruiterer retains his sugar-cane, and wins more than its value in money.

Gambling by means of a joint of meat, or pork, or a fish, is a very common pastime in the winter season. The joint or fish is suspended from the top of a long pole, and bets are made as to its weight. At Tien-tsin it is very common to gamble for viands and fruits. The butcher, or poulterer, or fruiterer, provides himself with a long bamboo tube, into which he places several small wooden rods, some with a number or mark on them. Should the speculator draw a rod on which there is no number he loses his stake. Should he draw a rod on which a number is marked he receives a corresponding prize.

In the summer months, cricket-fighting is a very popular sport in the southern provinces. These insects are found in large numbers on the hills there, and men capture them by night. For this purpose they take with them Fo-lam or fire-baskets. These are made of iron rods, and during the time they are being used, a fire of fir or cedar wood is kept burning in them. Sometimes the cricket-hunters drive the insects out of their holes by pouring in water on them. Sometimes they endeavour to entice them from the nest by placing a fruit called "dragon's eyes" at its entrance. Crickets which chirp loudly are regarded as the best fighters. The crickets when captured are kept singly in earthenware pots, at the bottom of which is a small quantity of fine mould, and a very small cup containing a few drops of water for the insects to drink out of and bathe in. Their food consists of two kinds of fish, called Man-yu and Kut-yu. Insects called Loo-kum-chung, Tun-tsit-chung and Pin-tam-chung are occasionally given to them. They get honey to strengthen them, and other items of their diet are boiled chestnuts and boiled rice. For two hours every night a female cricket is placed in the pot with the male. Smoke is supposed to be injurious to their health, and the rooms in which they are kept must be perfectly free from it. A charm or mystic scroll to avert evil influences, is sometimes placed on the crickets' pot. If they are sick from overeating, red insects called Hun-chung are given them. If the sickness arises from cold, they get mosquitoes ; if from heat, shoots of the green pea plant. Chuk-tip or bamboo butterflies are given for difficulty in breathing.

At the cricket-pit, which the Chinese call Lip, the insects are matched according to size, weight, and colour. The stakes are

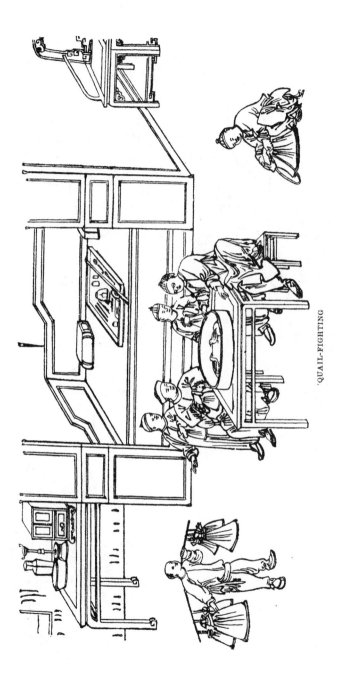

'QUAIL-FIGHTING.'

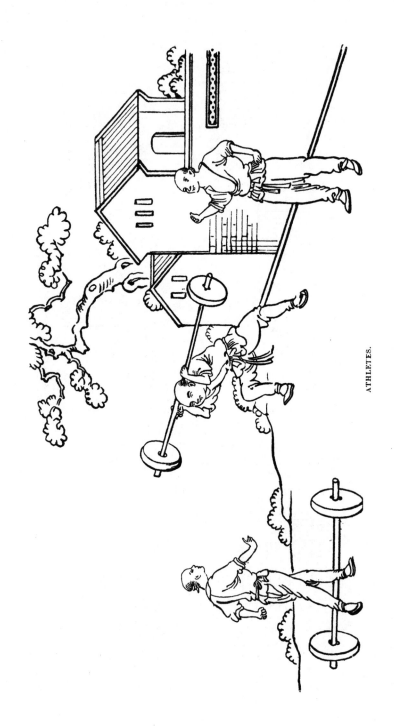

ATHLETES.

in some cases very large. It is, however, generally supposed by
the government that they consist of presents of sweet cakes.
A cricket which wins many victories is called Shou-lip or
conquering cricket, and when it dies it is placed in a small
silver coffin and buried. The owner believes that the honourable
interment brings him good luck, and that good fighting crickets
will be found next year in the neighbourhood where the cricket
lies buried.

The places most notorious for cricket-fighting are Fa-tee, in
the immediate vicinity of Canton, and Cha-pee, near Whampoa.
At these places there are extensive mat sheds divided into
several compartments. In each compartment there is a table
with a small tub on it in which the crickets fight. The sum of
money staked on the contest is lodged with a committee, who
deduct ten per cent. and hand over the balance to the person
whose cricket has won. He is also presented with a roast pig,
a piece of silk, and a gilded ornament resembling a bouquet of
flowers. This decoration is placed by the winner, either on the
ancestral altar of his house or on a shrine in honour of Kwan-te.
In order that betting men may be made acquainted with the
merits of the crickets matched against each other, a placard is
posted on the sides of the building setting forth the various
stakes won by each cricket. The excitement manifested at these
matches is very great, and considerable sums of money change
hands. Crickets which display great fighting powers are not
unfrequently sold for large sums.

During the winter months quail-fighting is a favourite sport.
The pits in which these birds fight are like the cock-pits once
only too popular in England. Great pains are bestowed upon
the quails by those who train them. The trainer first destroys
the tympanum of the bird's ear by blowing upon it through a
small tube. This is to make it deaf and insensible to the
noise caused by the spectators when witnessing a well-contested
struggle. The bird is washed daily in warm water to make it
lean and active. The quail pits are generally very small. They
are provided with two or three tiers of galleries, in which the
spectators have to stand in a stooping posture. In the centre of
the pit, on a table, is a tub with low sides, into which the quails

are put. Before the struggle begins, the birds, one after another
are placed on the table, to give the spectators an opportunity of
judging of their respective merits. Two birds are placed, one in
a blue and the other in a yellow bag. The spectators are
then called upon to make their bets, which are carefully registered by a secretary. The stakes are placed in the hands of an
umpire, who hands them over to the winner when victory has
been declared. Whenever the birds find themselves facing each
other in the tub, a fierce encounter ensues. The fight, however,
does not last many minutes, the vanquished invariably seeking
safety in flight.

The Pan-Kow, or wild pigeon, the Chu-Shee-Cha, and the
Wā-mee are also kept for fighting. Contests between these
birds take place not so much in public pits, as in the dwelling-
houses of the more respectable citizens, and large sums of money
often change hands over them.

The Chu-Shee-Cha is so-called in consequence of its natural
propensity to feed upon the dung of pigs. Great pains are
bestowed upon fighting birds by their owners to prepare them for
the fighting season. They are fed at one time with rice mixed
with the yolks of eggs. At another season—midsummer—
white insects taken from boiled rice which has been exposed to
the sun, are their food. Maggots from dogs' flesh which has been
cut into very small pieces and dried in the sun and pounded, are
given to them at other times. Immediately before the fighting
season, which is in spring, *gensing* is given. Annually at Loong-
kong a large mat-shed is erected in which the birds are made
to fight mains. Round it are hung cages containing the birds,
which fill the air with their warbling.

The fighting birds called Wā-mee also receive much attention.
Each bird of this description is kept in a high cage in which a
small bridge or table is placed as a perch. They are fed with
rice and the yolks of eggs and a small quantity of sand well
mixed together. Each day during the summer, their cages are
placed in tubs of water so that they may wash themselves,
which they do apparently with much delight. To induce the
cock birds to fight it is necessary to place a hen-bird in close
proximity. These birds are remarkably good songsters.

In some parts of the empire cock-fighting is also practised, though to no great extent. The best game cocks are said to be those which have thick combs and sharp spurs. Sometimes a root called Tsoo-Woo-Tow is secretly rubbed on the comb previous to a main. The smell of this root is so distasteful to fighting cocks, that they turn away from a bird whose comb has been so treated. At the close of a contest the greatest care is bestowed upon the birds, and to make them eject any blood or mucus, their throats are probed with a quill. This cruel sport is now seldom or never practised in Canton.

No interest is taken in field sports, such as fox-hunting, shooting, and angling, by gentlemen in the southern provinces. In the northern provinces and in Mongolia, there are apparently a few persons who find pleasure in them. The emperor has hunting-grounds at Je-hole and in Mongolia, and in the immediate vicinity of Pekin. The hunting-forest in Mongolia is, I believe, 400 Chinese li, or 133 English miles in breadth, and 800 Chinese li, or 266 English miles in length. That at Je-hole is inclosed by a wall which is twenty-one Chinese li, or seven English miles in circumference. Of the extent of the hunting-grounds in the immediate vicinity of Pekin, I am ignorant. To judge, however, from the vast extent of the walls by which it is inclosed, it must consist of several miles of land. To one or other of these hunting-grounds the emperor is supposed to repair once annually, to enjoy the pleasures of the chase.

Fox-hunting is not uncommon among the Chinese in the northern provinces. They use two or three dogs only, which are not unlike the English lurcher. Hares are also hunted in the northern provinces. The same dogs are used as in fox-hunting, and no more than two or three of them are allowed to take part in the chase. A hare hunt, therefore, in the north of China, bears some resemblance to coursing in England. In the province of Chili, and also in Mongolia, a falcon is used, in addition to the two or three hounds. The hare when pursued appears to have a greater dread of the bird than of the dogs. When the falcon hovers over it, it at once cowers in the grass, and falls an easy prey to its winged enemy. In the north the falcon is also not unfrequently employed in hawking. Great pains are bestowed upon the training of these birds. When a young falcon has been taken from the nest, it is kept without food for two days. The trainer then allows it to perch upon his arm, which is protected by a leather sleeve. Some ten feet off stands another man who allures the bird to him, by holding out a piece of raw meat. The meat is sometimes attached to a white feather fan. In order to tame old falcons, which are generally captured by nets, they cover the head of the bird with cloth and then bind it to the arm of a figure resembling a man. It is fed very sparingly during the process of training, which extends over a month. At the end of this period the cloth or bandage is removed from its head. Its wings, however, are now bound by a cord. It is again made to perch during a period of seven weeks on the arm of the wooden figure. It is then for the first time allowed to fly in the open air. To prevent its escape a long string is, of course, bound to its leg. Wooden figures of pheasants or other birds to which morsels of flesh are attached, are, with the view of attracting the falcon when soaring in the air, pulled through the long coarse grass by which the hills and plains are covered. The bird darts upon these figures and finds its reward in the tempting bait. At Mow-yow, a city of the district of Yoong-kong, falcons for the chase are sold in large numbers. The market for these birds is, I believe, generally held at night.

In the midland and northern provinces shooting is a favourite sport with some gentlemen. In the south a sportsman is a *rara avis*. This I attribute, in a great measure, to the influence of the Buddhist religion, and to the idea which prevails that birds exercise good geomantic influences over the surrounding country. In every village there is generally a notice to the effect that persons passing that way are not to destroy the birds, or injure the trees upon which they are accustomed to roost. Many men, however, of the poorer classes shoot birds for sale. The birds, I believe, are mostly purchased by foreigners.

The Chinese are not much given to athletic exercises. Of such manly games as wrestling, boxing, cricket, rackets, and football they are apparently ignorant. They are very expert, however, at their own game of shuttlecock, which they play using their feet instead of battledores.   The shuttlecock is sometimes kept up in this way for several minutes.   Athletics are mostly confined to candidates for military degrees, who by constant practice acquire great strength of body.   This is especially true of the Mongolians, who are naturally very strong.   I remember being much astonished at Je-hole on seeing the ease with which a cavalry officer upwards of seventy years of age, pulled the strongest bows, and, armed with a sword.and lance, went through parts of the cavalry exercise.

Regattas are not unknown to the Chinese.   I was present at one which took place in 1866, at the town of Too-kow, and on the first day found no less than forty-two boats contesting in heats for the prizes.   The first prize was a roast pig, a red tablet with a highly eulogistic inscription, a small marble screen on which good moral sentences were recorded, two silver wine-cups of antique shape, and a silk banner.   There were seven prizes, and the distance rowed over was three English miles.   The oarsmen, as a rule, were fine muscular men, and the winners of the first prize seemed to be capable of contending, in their way, with the best-manned four-oar on any English river.   The crews of the winning boats were presented with bouquets of flowers by their friends.   A regatta takes place in the Namhoi district of Kwang-tung every year.   It is advertised by placards, the advertisements being usually of a humorous character.

END OF VOLUME I.

CHINA

A History of the Laws, Manners
and Customs of the People

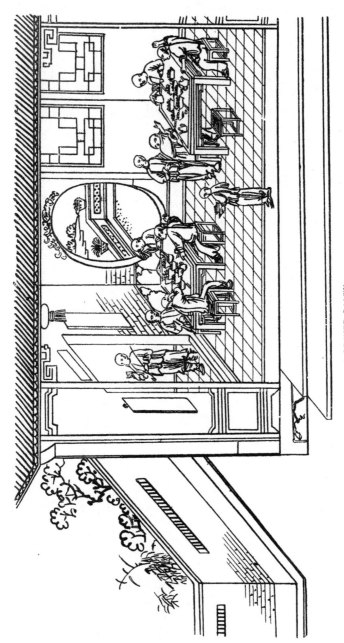

A DINNER PARTY.

CHINA

A History of the Laws, Manners and Customs of the People

JOHN HENRY GRAY

Volume II

DOVER PUBLICATIONS, INC.
Mineola, New York

CONTENTS.

CONTENTS.

CHAPTER XXX.

CHAPTER XXXI.

CHAPTER XXXII.

LIST OF ILLUSTRATIONS.

LIST OF ILLUSTRATIONS. xi

LIST OF ILLUSTRATIONS.

CHINA.

CHAPTER XVII

ASTROLOGERS AND FORTUNE-TELLERS.

IN their knowledge and practice of the various illusory arts for the discovery of things hidden or future, the Chinese are not behind the most superstitious of Asiatic or African races. They have always manifested great anxiety to find out the course of fortune, and to forecast the issue of their plans. There is scarcely a department of nature not occasionally appealed to as capable of affording good or bad omens. Their daily conduct is shaped by superstitious notions in the most momentous as well as in the most ordinary occurrences; and physiognomists, diviners, or soothsayers, fortune-tellers, interpreters of dreams, astrologers enchanters, exorcists, spirit-rappers, witches, or consulters with familiar spirits, necromancers, rhabdomancers, or diviners by rods, belomancers, or diviners by arrows, serpent charmers, are daily,— one might say hourly—called upon to exercise their delusive arts. These impostors either station themselves at the gates of the most frequented temples, or occupy houses or stalls, in streets or very crowded thoroughfares. At Tan-yang Hien, on the banks of the Grand Canal, I saw a fortune-teller plying his trade in a tea saloon, in one corner of which he had his table. He was regarded by the people throughout the neighbourhood as pre-eminently learned in his profession, the proprietor of the tea saloon being equally famous for the excellence of his tea and cakes. Each brought grist to the other's mill; for those who came to have their fortunes told remained to drink tea, and those who came to drink tea remained to have their fortunes told.

The physiognomist, who is always surrounded by numbers anxious to ascertain their destiny, suspends a large white cloth or sheet with painted representations of the human countenance, in front of the entrance of his house, or from a wall near which he has placed his table and chair. Some of these likenesses are supposed to be expressive of rank and station, others of contentment and quiet, of affluence and power, of poverty and shame, or of crime and disgrace. Chinese physiognomists, however, do not confine themselves to a study and knowledge of the human countenance only. They profess to be also able to predict the future welfare or misery of persons of all conditions, and of both sexes, from the formation and appearance of each member of the body. The following particulars, gleaned from the elaborate treatises written by the professors of the art, will give the reader some idea of Chinese physiognomy.

A round head, with hair growing well from a high forehead, eyebrows thin and of equal length, large and thick ears, the upper parts of which extend above the eyebrows, a large mouth in the male and a small one in the female, a large chin, a high and firm nose, high cheek bones, a silky beard, a dark moustache with a tendency to curl upwards, a large neck, a powerful voice, and eyes long and angular, and with much expression, are regarded as most favourable indications. Where such features are wanting, various degrees of trouble and misery are predicted. Thus, a person whose head is not round, or whose eyebrows are thick, is told that he can never attain to celebrity, but must remain in a subordinate position all the days of his life. One whose forehead is singularly low is likely to suffer punishment from the magistrate, and is invariably advised to turn monk and seek the retirement of a cloister. A man whose ears are neither large nor thick is told that he will die at an age varying from fifty to sixty years, and that, should he continue to attain a good old age, he will die in a state of destitution. One with a small chin will be overtaken by dire misfortunes should he reach old age; and a woman with a large mouth has a life of shame

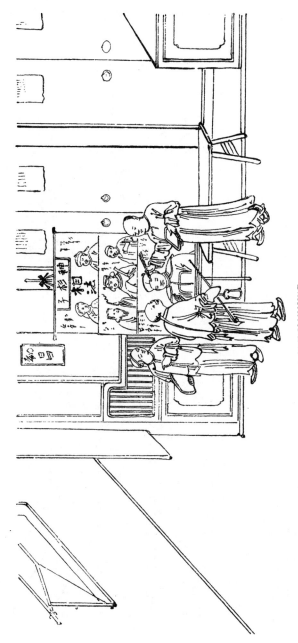

A PHYSIOGNOMIST.

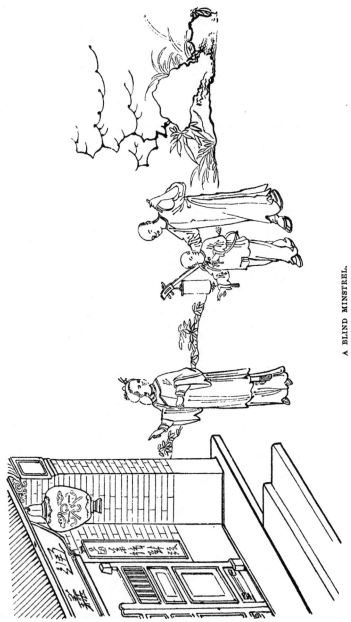

A BLIND MINSTREL.

predicted for her. A man with a small nose and distended nostrils is born to beggary ; and to be without high cheek bones is to be weak in character, and to be shut out from the hope of attaining any post of trust or honour. The wife of a thin-necked man will die shortly after marriage ; and an effeminate voice indicates the slave of vicious practices, who cannot attain to a good old age. Eyes long and angular with large round pupils full of expression foreshadow much good fortune ; while eyes lacking these characteristics indicate a strong propensity to steal.

An examination of the hand generally follows that of the face. A thick hand with a soft red palm without wrinkles is a sign of much good fortune, and the opposite qualities bring corresponding trouble. When the fingers fit closely together, it is regarded as an indication of a happy and prosperous life. Such are some of the physiognomical notions of the Chinese, and it is surprising to find what a number of respectable and influential men throughout the empire resort to the professors of the art. Their belief is so fixed that they are convinced that nothing, save a decree of the gods, can avert the fortune to which they are destined, according to the formation and appearance of their bodies.

Blind soothsayers are to be met with in all parts of the empire. These men, who are generally well dressed, carry over their shoulders a Chinese harp or guitar upon which they have learned to play skilfully. They sometimes wander immense distances from their homes. In a remote valley of Inner Mongolia I met with an aged blind minstrel, who informed me that he had come all the way from the province of Shen-si, and that he was on a journey to the city of Lama-miou, where, by his music and his fortune-telling, he hoped to prosper. At Koo-pee-kow, I saw two blind minstrels resting themselves on a green sward at the base of the Great Wall. They had travelled all the way from the central province of Sze-chuen. These minstrels are generally led by young attendants, though they sometimes grope their own way with long sticks or rods of bamboo. As they traverse the streets of towns, they call aloud the nature of their profession. Though not taught to read, as the blind are in European countries, they are, in some respects, amongst the best informed of their countrymen. When young they are placed under the care of others of the calling, and commit to memory from their lips several volumes regarding the mysteries of their trade. They are well versed in the ancient history of China, and can give the exact date of the accession of all the emperors, and tell with great exactness the principal historical events of each reign. They are chiefly called into dwelling-houses where the inmates are in perplexity through domestic affliction. The soothsayer having tuned his instrument, and learned the cause of their anxiety, breaks forth into singing, accompanying himself upon his harp. Throughout his song he throws light upon the originating cause of the trouble which has befallen the family, and thus, by his prophetic aid, raises their hopes, or increases their sorrows and fears. Such soothsayers have had a place in the empire from its earliest commencement. All blind Chinese musicians, however, are not soothsayers. Many pretend to no prophetic power, and traverse the streets, like men of a similar class in England, to obtain a living by playing on the violin, the lute, or the harp. One of the most remarkable of these strolling musicians with whom I came in contact, was a native of the city of Tien-tsin. Passing along one of the principal streets of this city in 1865, I was surprised to hear some one playing "God save the Queen" upon a violin, and on turning aside I found that a blind Chinese fiddler was the performer. As I was walking away from him, he commenced to play the "British Grenadiers," and subsequently I heard him playing the "Dead March in Saul." On inquiring, I was told that he had picked up these airs listening to the bands of the English regiments which during the late war with China garrisoned the city of Tien-tsin.

The fortune-tellers who draw oracles from words form another important class of those who obtain a living by the practice of superstitious arts. Their method of proceeding has been described as follows, by Archdeacon Cobbold in his graphic " Pictures of Chinese " :—

" A number of important and significant words are first selected ; each of these is then written upon a separate slip of thin cardboard which is made up into a roll like those very tiny scrolls of parchment, inscribed with a verse of Scripture, which are used in the present day by the Jews in their

A ROPE-DANCER.

FORTUNE-TELLING BY MEANS OF WORDS.

phylacteries. These slips of cardboard, amounting altogether to several hundreds, are shaken together in a box, and the consulting party—moved perhaps with solicitude to know the result of an intended expedition or coming engagement in business— repairing to the fortune-teller who is always to be found at some convenient corner of the street, puts in his hand and draws from the box one of these scrolls of paper. The mysteries of the art are now displayed; the fortune-teller, writing the significant word on a white board which he keeps at his side, begins to discover its root and derivation, shows its component parts, explains where its emphasis lies, what its particular force is in composition, and then deduces from its meaning and structure some particulars which he applies to the especial case of the consulter. No language perhaps possesses such facilities for diviners and their art, as the Chinese, and the words selected are easily made to evolve under the manipulation of a skilful artist, some mystical meaning of oracular indefiniteness. Some faint notion of this method of divination may be gathered from remarking the changes of meaning which in our own and other languages arise from the transposition of letters forming a name or sentence. For instance, the name Horatio Nelson becomes by a happy alliteration, Honor est a Nilo. Again Vernon becomes Renown, and Waller, Laurel. Or in the remarkable instance of Pilate's question 'Quid est Veritas,' which by transposition gives 'Est vis qui adest.' . . . . The diviner and his stall," adds the Venerable Archdeacon, " are also sure to be seen at any great fair or religious festival, wherever experience has taught men that the trade might be profitably plied. It is astonishing what a number of persons gain a livelihood by an occupation of which we should think every day's events would prove the fallacy. No one lifts up his voice against it. The Confucianist thinks it may be necessary for the rude uneducated mind. Both the Buddhist and the Taouist encourage all feelings of dependence on the unseen world, as it is sure to bring a reverence to their monasteries. The state religion does indeed ridicule all such superstitions, but it is powerless to keep the people from practising them, nor do any of the influential men of the country see any sufficient reason to interfere. It is not (say they) a question of good government, or good morals, it concerns a man's own mental convictions, and we may safely leave these to take their own course. A very favourite expression of theirs is, if you believe, these things have reality; if you believe not, they have none. By which is meant that every person must be guided by his own convictions; the great matter is sincerity and earnestness,

and a false creed heartily embraced, when it does not oppose
morality, will be of more use to restrain and govern than
a barren orthodoxy."

Another class of fortune-tellers use birds in their divining
operations. Seated in front of a table, with a cage on it containing a bird not unlike an English bullfinch, the fortune-
teller presents a pack of cards to his client, who selects
one. Upon some of these cards sentences are written indicative of very good, or good, or indifferent, or bad, or very
bad fortune. Having selected a card, and noted the sentence
on it, the client replaces it in the pack, which generally consists
of a hundred cards. When the fortune-teller has shuffled them
with an appearance of great thoroughness, and placed them
upon the table, the bird hops out of its cage, and is told to select
one, in order to see whether the client has chosen the very card
which it was decreed he should select by the gods, or fates,
or stars. If the bird pick out the card he drew, the client is
assured that the prediction especially refers to him. The bird,
of course, never fails to select the card. I have occasionally
seen hens, generally white ones, made use of in this way.

There are, also, female fortune-tellers who predict the future
of females only, making use of tortoises instead of birds. The
method these impostors adopt is as follows:—Around the
sides of a large bamboo tray are neatly arranged, a number of
envelopes, probably a hundred, each containing a card upon
which words of good or bad import are written. The client,
having selected and noted one of the cards, replaces it on the
tray. A tortoise is then placed on the tray, and selects the client's
card, as in the former instance. Fortune-tellers of this class
are generally the wives of itinerant tinkers, and are mostly
found in villages and hamlets. Houses called Poo-Shek-Men,
are also kept by women for the superstitious of their own sex.
In each house of the kind there is a shrine in honour of an idol,
before which the female wishing to learn the issue either of a
present or contemplated scheme, kneels and performs certain
devotional exercises. She then makes known her desire to the
idol, kneeling and gazing intently upon a stone placed on a tripod.
After a little she is supposed to see on its surface a figurative or

pictorial representation of the event which awaits her. I visited a house of this description in the Kwong-how-kin street of the old city of Canton, and found an old lady in a state of great distress, in consequence, she informed me, of having seen a green field in the centre of which was a coffin.

Geomancers constitute, as my readers may suppose, a very large class. Diviners of this kind visit the hills and mountains almost daily in search of lucky places for tombs, and they are always ready, on receipt of the customary fees, to direct the attention of clients to suitable burying-grounds. Should the inquirer on examining the spot be dissatisfied, he usually fees the geomancer handsomely to take some pains to find a more auspicious site. Geomancers are sometimes received into the houses of wealthy and influential citizens, and treated with the greatest kindness. Of course, they are expected to be very careful in selecting for their patrons the best places possible for family tombs. The great anxiety of the Chinese gentry on this score arises from their genuine belief that should members of their families be interred in places the geomantic influences of which are bad, direful effects would ensue. The word geomancy is a compound from two Greek words, namely, γη, the earth, and μαντις, a diviner. It probably owes its origin to the fact that in ancient times it was customary to scatter stones or marbles upon the ground, and to form opinions of the issue of certain events according to the arrangement which they presented. In course of time, instead of this plan, dots were made at haphazard, or, it may be, according to astrological considerations, on a sheet of white paper, and good or bad omens drawn from the various shapes or figures which they presented. Polydore Virgil says that geomancy is a species of divination effected through the medium of fissures made in the earth. He considers that the Magi of Persia were its first professors. To the geomancers of China these two methods are altogether unknown. Each Chinese geomancer is provided with a compass to ascertain the position of the neighbouring and distant hills in relation to any plot of ground which he may think of selecting for a tomb. He is very particular in his examination of the soil. Should it be dry, and of an auburn colour, it is pronounced good. Should it be damp and stony, it is at once condemned. Ground towards which a stream of water flows, or which is encircled by a stream, or which commands an extensive view of hill, dale, and water, is supposed to possess very great advantages.

It would be an endless task to attempt to dwell on all the particulars which a geomancer must think of in selecting propitious sites for tombs. The introduction of geomancy in China is attributed to a person named Kwok Pok, who flourished during the Tsun dynasty, and wrote a work named "Tsong-King"; or, the Burial Classic. The Emperor Wu-tai, who was the sixth sovereign of the Hon dynasty, and who flourished B.C. 140, was a great upholder of these principles as well as of the superstition which taught that certain plants and stones had the power of imparting immortality to man. In the Tang dynasty, however, Tai-tsung, who ascended the thrown of China A.D. 627, was very much opposed to them, and employed a *literate* named Lu Tzo to write a treatise setting forth their absurdity. It failed to check the growing superstition. In the Sung dynasty, A.D. 960, a memorial was presented to the throne for the suppression of geomancy. The two ministers of state to whom the Emperor referred the matter advised his Majesty against the memorial, observing that, if the soil is soft and of a good colour, and the grass and trees growing on it are bright and green, all plots of ground ought to be regarded as suitable for tombs, provided that they are never likely to become either sites for cities, towns, or villages.

We now come to interpreters of dreams—a class of men who have from the very earliest times held a place in almost all Asiatic countries. The Chinese have always been very earnest believers in dreams, and in the pages of their ancient books certain dreams are recorded which are said to have been fulfilled, a fact which has no doubt greatly helped to strengthen the national faith. When Moo-ting, the twentieth sovereign of the Shang dynasty, who lived B.C. 1324, was mourning for his deceased father upon whose wisdom he had greatly relied, he dreamed that he saw the gods of heaven presenting to him a faithful minister of state. On awakening he found that the

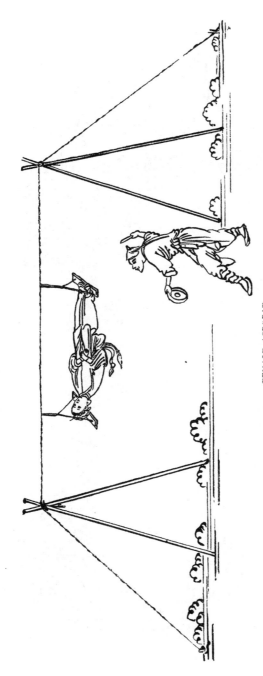

FEMALE ACROBAT.

A MESMERIST AT WORK.

features of the minister revealed in his dream, were indelibly fixed upon his mind. Calling into his presence the most distinguished artists of the day, he described the face which haunted him, and requested each to retire to his studio and try to reproduce it in a sketch from the description. From the portraits which they produced Moo-ting selected one, of which he caused copies to be taken, and forwarded to various parts of the empire, with instructions that the man whom the portrait was found to resemble should be brought to him. In the course of a few months an officer of state, while passing along a high road, observed a man engaged in building a house, whose features bore a striking resemblance to those of the person represented by the portrait. In the course of a conversation the officer learned that the builder was named Foo Yut, and that, though an ordinary bricklayer's labourer, he was a man of great learning. Foo Yut was eventually taken to court and presented to Moo-ting, who was much struck with his resemblance to the figure of his dream, and with his general ability. Foo Yut was immediately raised to the position of chief minister of state, and is said by the historian to have governed the empire well.

Another of these dreams is as follows:—Previous to becoming emperor of China Chow-man Wong, the founder of the Chow dynasty, was the viceroy of one of those petty states which now form portions of China proper. One night, before retiring to rest, he ordered his retainers to be prepared to accompany him on a hunting expedition on the following morning. During the night he dreamed that he saw a winged bear flying from a window of the palace. On the morrow, at an early hour, he summoned the magicians of the court into his presence to interpret his dream. When they had consulted with each other for some time, one of them observed that the projected hunting expedition would not be attended with the capture of any wild animals. The viceroy was about to give it up, when he was advised by the magicians that he would, that day, meet with a very good and excellent man. He proceeded therefore to the hunting forests where, as was predicted, he met with no success in sport. When fording a river on his return, however, he met

with an old fisherman, whom he discovered to be a man of
profound learning. Keong Tai-koong was invited by the viceroy to his palace, and was of great service to him. In a revolution, soon afterwards, Chow-man Wong was enabled through the
wisdom of Keong Tai-koong to ascend the throne of China—
the first emperor of the royal house of Chow.

Another well-known dream is that in which Confucius is said
to have received an intimation of his coming death. In his
sleep he saw the summit of a high mountain in the province
of Shang-tung falling to the earth. On awakening, he interpreted his own dream by observing that his death was at hand.
He died during the course of the same year.

Being earnest believers in dreams, the Chinese pay great
attention to their interpretation; and that the reader may be
able to judge of their ingenuity, I venture to place some of its
results before him in a tabular form. The interpretations of
dreams here given are those of Chow Koong, a very distinguished interpreter in his day, and who is now regarded as the
greatest authority upon such matters.

HE WHO DREAMS	MAY EXPECT
that heaven's gates open to receive him,	good fortune, and is blessed;
of good weather,	immunity for a season from all sorrows;
in sickness of a bright light from heaven shining on him,	to recover;
that the heavens are bright red,	war to break out;
that he looks towards the sky,	wealth and distinction;
of riding heavenwards on a dragon,	official rank;
of flying heavenwards,	good luck in his labours;
that he is commissioned by the gods to undertake important duties on earth,	great happiness here and hereafter;
of the heavens parting asunder,	the empire to be divided;
of the sun or moon setting,	his father or mother to die shortly;
that the sun or moon is obscured,	a son distinguished for his abilities;
that he sees the sun and moon coming together,	his wife to conceive and bring forth a son;
that he sees the sun falling,	a son;
that he sees the moon falling,	a daughter;
that he sees the stars falling,	sickness and judicial punishment;
of the sun or moon setting behind a mountain,	his servants and slaves to revolt;

HE WHO DREAMS	MAY EXPECT
that he hears loud peals of thunder,	misfortunes unless he vacate his house ;
of death by lightning,	rank and wealth ;
of bright clouds,	good fortune ;
of dark clouds,	sickness ;
of much rain and wind,	a member of his family to die ;
of a fall of snow,	to wear mourning soon ;
of an earthquake (if a mandarin),	promotion ;
of an earthquake (if non-official),	great happiness ;
of the earth opening,	great evils ;
of carrying pebbles in his hands,	much happiness ;
of a mountain falling,	calamities ;
of carrying a large package to the top of a mountain,	that his wife will conceive and bear a son ;
of being in a large and beautiful garden,	to be unsuccessful in life ;
of a large, spreading tree,	more of sweetness than bitterness in life's cup ;
that he is planting a tree,	great riches ;
that he is climbing a tree,	much honour and renown ;
that he sees a tree falling,	death, or sickness, or serious accidents ;
of a dead tree bringing forth leaves,	members of his family to be successful ;
of a tree heavily laden with ripe fruit,	his descendants to become rich ;
of the Lan-Fa flower,	a long and illustrious line of posterity ;
that he is sweeping the ground,	his family to be unfortunate ;
of excrement,	to become wealthy ;
that he wears white clothes,	to be injured by bad men ;
that he is shaving or washing,	sorrow to depart from his family ;
that he is in a profuse perspiration,	bad fortune ;
that his body is covered with insects,	freedom from sickness ;
that he is bound by cords,	to attain to a good old age ;
that he has been condemned to wear the cangue or be put in irons,	severe sickness ;
that he is fat,	to be unsuccessful ;
that either his teeth, or hair, or eyes are falling out,	that one of his family is near death ;
that he has wounded himself with a sword or knife,	to be fortunate ;
that he has wounded a fellow-man with a sword or knife,	to be unlucky ;
of sweet music,	friends from a distance to visit him ;
of seeing the empress,	to be unsuccessful ;
of visiting the palace,	to be very fortunate through life ;
of visiting a temple,	to be fortunate through life ;
of being in a wine house,	to be successful ;
of gold, silver, or precious stones,	to be prosperous ;
that he is in the act of going to bed,	to be unsuccessful ;
that he is crossing a high bridge, or walking along a good road, or at a well attended market,	to accumulate a fortune ;

HE WHO DREAMS	MAY EXPECT
that his clothes are on fire (if a mandarin),	misfortune unless he is removed to another sphere of duty (a merchant or shopkeeper having such a dream must change his house or shop ; and a farmer his farm) ;
of losing his clothes (if a mandarin),	to lose his rank (of a non-official who has such a dream, it is predicted that he will lose money) ;
of being well-dressed,	to be fortunate ;
of being badly dressed,	to be unlucky ;
of wearing a rain-coat,	to receive great favours at the hands of his superiors ;
of wearing broken shoes,	to fall sick ;
of wearing another man's shoes,	his wife to prove unfaithful ;
that he sees a man holding an umbrella over him,	to be forsaken by his relatives and friends ;
of corpses, tombs, or funeral processions,	to be prosperous ;
of idols, or priests,	to be fortunate ;
of nuns,	to lose all the goods that he is possessed of.

This list might be extended if we were to give, for example, those dreams which relate to articles of dress. Of this kind is a mandarin dreaming that his clothes are on fire, which betokens that he ought to seek removal to another sphere of duty ; or a man dreaming that he wears broken shoes, which is a sign of coming sickness. Probably, however, my reader has had enough of these—

> " Children of an idle brain,
> Begot of nothing but vain fantasy."

Fortunately, when a man has dreamed a bad dream in China, he need not despair ; for an interpreter of dreams is ready to supply him, should he desire it, with a mystic scroll, which will avert the impending calamity. It is written on red or yellow paper, and the interpreter rolls it up in the form of a triangle and attaches it to the dress of his client. The dreamer is then made to look towards the east, with a sword in his right hand and his mouth full of spring water. In this position he ejects the water from his mouth, and beats the air with the sword, repeating in an imperative tone certain words of which the following is a translation:—" As quickly, and with as

much strength as rises the sun in the East, do thou, charm or
mystic scroll, avert all the evil influences which are likely to
result from my bad dream.   As quickly as lightning passes
through the air, O charm, cause impending evils to disappear."

The charms which are given vary according to the days of the
month on which the dreams are dreamed. One charm is given
for a bad dream dreamed on a day of the month called Tsze, or
snake ; another for one dreamed on a day of the month called
Mow, or rabbit, and so on.   The science of astrology, which was
received and cultivated by almost all the nations of antiquity,
has been perhaps more universally studied in China than in any
other country.   The Chinese apparently do not believe that the
planets are the instruments by which the deities, forming their
pantheon, direct and control the course of events in this sublunary
world, but that the heavenly bodies themselves are the only
agents by which the course of man through life is shaped.
Herodotus (2 c. 82) states that the Egyptians regarded each day
as being under the influence of some star, and that the fortunes,
character, and hour of death, of each man would be according
to the day on which he first saw the light.

The system of astrology taught by the astrologers of China
seems, therefore, to bear on the face of it its own refutation.
If the position of the heavens at his birth establishes the
character and fortune of a man, all persons born on the same day
must have before them a similar career.   Yet all those who are
born in the large city of London on a certain a day in a certain
year do not attain the same eminence or have the same career.

Despite, however, the manifest absurdity of this pretended
science, the Chinese invariably seek to ascertain their future
by a reference to astrological predictions.   Astrology in China,
as in ancient Egypt and Chaldæa, concerns itself with the
determination of lucky and unlucky days, and great attention
is paid to this branch of the so-called science (cf. Job iii. 3,
and Gal. iv. 10).   Astrologers in cities and towns form a
very large class, who are never without occupation.   No marriages are celebrated, nor voyages commenced, no journeys
entered upon, nor works of any kind undertaken, until the
astrologer has decided by a reference to the aspect of certain

stars and planets, what month or what day of the month in the year is most propitious. The horoscopes of parties wishing to contract a marriage are carefully examined. The hour, and the day, and the month, and the year, in which each of them was born, are noted and, by two signs apportioned to each of the periods in question, the desirability of the intended union is determined.

Each day of the lunar month has its appropriate name, and in the official almanac, published annually at Pekin, the days which are deemed propitious or unpropitious for the observance of certain rites and for the performance of certain duties, are recorded by the astrologers. Take as an example, the day which is ruled by the constellation Kok-Sing, which consists of seven stars arranged to resemble a dragon. To enter upon any important commercial transactions, to lay the foundation stones of new houses, to give daughters in marriage, to purchase lands, or to attend literary examinations on this day is to be very fortunate. But children who bury their parents, and all who repair tombs on this day, must expect evil to befall them in some shape or another before the expiration of three years.

The day of the month which is ruled by the constellation Kong-Sing is said to be unlucky. This constellation consists of seven stars placed so as to mark the outline of a long-tailed dragon with a general named N'ghon on his back. To purchase lands or rank, or give daughters in marriage, or celebrate the funeral obsequies of parents on this day, will certainly entail evil consequences.

The day of the month which is ruled by Tai-Sing is very unlucky. This constellation consists of six stars, which mark the outline of a camel, near which stands a general named Kā-Fuh. To enter upon commercial transactions, or to commence to plough fields, or to begin to delve gardens on this day, is to be unlucky in business, or to reap bad crops. If children bury their parents on this day, a member of the family will, ere long, commit suicide; if shipbuilders lay the keels of ships, or merchants permit their ships to go to sea, shipwreck will follow; and the brides of men who marry on this day, will, before many months have elapsed, prove unfaithful. Similarly,

each of the other days of the lunar month is ruled by a constellation, and each constellation has its own special influences.
Nothing under the stars is beyond the reach of their hyper-
physical control. Events in social and official life, commerce,
shipbuilding, silk-culture, cattle-rearing, fuel-gathering, digging,
draining, building, laying foundation stones, literary competition, ploughing, travelling—all are within the scope of their
action.

The appearance of comets, eclipses of the sun or moon, earthquakes, and all other unfrequent and extraordinary occurrences,
exercises, in the estimation of the Chinese, a good or bad influence on empires and kingdoms, on emperors and kings, and
even on ordinary individuals. During an eclipse of the sun or
moon, the people, as I have stated in a previous chapter, go to
the tops of their houses, and beat gongs and tom-toms to frighten
away the heavenly dogs by which they think the sun is about to
be devoured. Comets in particular are regarded as harbingers
of woe. In 1858, when Chinese and foreigners alike had every
reason to conclude that a treaty of lasting amity and peace had
been agreed upon between Great Britain and France on the one
hand, and China on the other, the appearance of a most brilliant
comet at once dispelled from the minds of the Chinese all
expectation of the blessing so long wished for. So well persuaded were they that hostility would be renewed, that at
Canton they began, once more, to remove their families, chattels,
and household goods to a place of security. The board of
astrologers at Pekin is regarded as a very important department
of the central government of the empire. The duties which
devolve upon its members are, I apprehend, very similar to
those which occupied the attention of the monthly prognostica-
tors of the new moon amongst the Chaldeans, to whom reference
is made in the prophecy of Isaiah (xlvii. 13). The board are
the almanac-makers of the country, and, like the monthly prog-
nosticators of Chaldæa, publish statements of the important
events which may be expected to occur in each succeeding
month. The result of their labours is embodied in an almanac
published annually at Pekin. For its republication in each provincial capital of the empire, a certain sum is advanced by the

treasurer of each province. The copies so provided, however,
are intended more particularly for the service of the officials.
The republication of the almanac for the ensuing year takes
place towards the close of the ninth month, and on the first
day of the tenth month the copies intended for the officials of
the city are placed, at the government printing office, under a rich,
carved pavilion of wood, and a procession, headed by banners
and bands of music, conveys them to the residence of the
viceroy, or, in his absence, to that of the next highest official.
All the civil and military officers of the city assemble to receive
the procession on its arrival, and range themselves, the civil
mandarins on the east side of the grand entrance of the Yamun,
and the military officers on the west side. The pavilion with
its contents is carried with much solemnity through the avenue
of human beings, and placed in the centre of a large hall. All
the mandarins then front towards the north and perform the
kow-tow, after which the distribution of almanacs takes
place. A great many copies of the almanac are published for
the service of the people. Each copy has to bear the stamp of
the astronomical board at Pekin. Although each chief official
and the people in general have almanacs, the members of the
astronomical board at Pekin usually call the attention of the
chief rulers of the provinces, prefectures, and counties, to an
approaching eclipse of the sun or moon. These officials sometimes warn the people by means of proclamations. In May,
1872, the chief ruler of the county or district of Shanghai
issued a proclamation, informing his people that on the sixth
day of the following month there would be an eclipse of the
sun. He further informed them that, at Soo-chow, the sun
would be eclipsed seven digits and thirty-two minutes, and that
the eclipse would commence at 9.29 A.M., reach its height at
11.37, and terminate at 12.56. He concluded his proclamation
by earnestly calling upon his people to beat their gongs and tom-
toms loudly during the time of the eclipse, with the view of
preventing the Tien-How, or heavenly dogs, from devouring
the sun. It seemed absurd enough that he should do so, knowing
as he did that all would end well.

At the time when the Jesuits had acquired great power over

A TAOUIST PRIEST EXORCISING.

the members of the royal family of China, the court devoted much attention to the study of astronomy. The Jesuits, who were their teachers, were very assiduous, and succeeded in establishing an observatory, the remains of which, in the form of several magnificent astronomical instruments, are still to be seen. This observatory was erected during the reign of Kam-hi, who ascended the throne of China A.D. 1662. The Jesuit fathers were commended to Kam-hi, in 1688, by Louis XIV. of France, in a communication which runs as follows:—" Most high, most excellent, most puissant, most magnanimous prince. Our dearly beloved good friend, may God increase your grandeur with a happy end. Being informed that your majesty was desirous to have near your person and in your dominions a considerable number of learned men, very much versed in European sciences, we resolved some years ago to send you six learned mathematicians, our subjects, to show your majesty whatever is most curious in sciences, especially the astronomical observations of the famous academy we have established in our good city of Paris."

Besides physiognomists, fortune-tellers, geomancers, and astrologers, there is a numerous class who attribute sickness to the action of spirits, and profess to control these by charms and incantations. Let us suppose that a person is sick, and has recourse to an enchanter. Should the illness have seized him on the first day of the month, it is declared to have come from a south-easterly direction. The enchanter adds that the malady has been caused by the genii of trees, who, on the first day of each month of the year, often send emissaries to and fro to afflict all those with whom they may come in contact in their wanderings. The emissaries are said to be souls of men who have died from home, and who, in consequence, have not received from their friends or posterity that meed of homage which they are supposed to regard as their due. Should the sufferer complain of either fever or ague, or headache, or bodily weakness, the enchanter seeks to restore him to health by inscribing a mystic scroll with a new vermilion pencil upon two pieces of yellow paper, cut in the form of cash. One of the charms is burned, and the ashes having been placed in a cup of cold water, are given to the sufferer to swallow. The other is eventually placed above the door of the patient's dwelling-house. The enchanter then takes in his hand five yellow cash, and, having walked forty paces in a south-easterly direction, commits them, as an offering to the imps, to the flames of a sacred fire, saying in imperative tones: Begone! Begone! Begone!

Should a person complain on the second day of the month of headache, or fever, or weakness of limbs, or vomiting, his sickness is declared by the exorcist to have come from the south-east, and to have been caused by the angry spirit of one of his ancestors. The *modus operandi* is the same as before. A different mystic character however, is, of course, inscribed on the pieces of yellow paper.

The ailments which these enchanters especially pretend to remove, are nearly all of that vague description to which quacks especially devote themselves. Such are listlessness, feverish restlessness, weakness, a wandering mind, loss of appetite, and pains in the limbs, or in the region of the heart. Rheumatism, ague, and bilious attacks are also included in their list. These afflictions come from all quarters of the compass, but noticeably less from the west than from the east. Generally the patient has to swallow the ashes of a mystic scroll in a draught of water, and he always receive a similar charm which is fastened to his dress, or to the head of his bed, or to a door or wall of his house. Like the quarter from which the illness comes, the spirits who cause it are determined by the day of the month. Restless or angry ancestral spirits, the spirits of aged females, of women who have committed suicide, of children who have died in infancy, of old women, whose bodies it may be have not yet been interred, of ancestors who have been Buddhist priests, of beggars who have died uncared for at the corners of streets, and of old men, are amongst the tormenting agents; and among the genii who instigate them to their task are those of pomegranate trees, of the earth, of the western mountains, of gold, of wells, and of fire and water.

When evil spirits haunt a dwelling-house, the proprietor of it loses no time in procuring the services of an exorcist, generally a Taouist priest. Attired in a red robe, blue stockings and a black cap, the exorcist stands, with a sword made of the wood of the peach or date tree in his hand, before a temporary altar on which are burning tapers and incense sticks. Should the tree from which the sword is made, have been struck by lightning, the sword is supposed to be very efficacious. Round the hilt and guard of the sword is carefully twined a strap of red cloth, equalling in length the blade of the weapon. Upon the blade a mystic scroll is written in ink. Placing the sword upon the altar, he then prepares a mystic scroll. This is burned, and the ashes are placed in a cup containing spring water. The exorcist then takes the sword in his right hand, and, still stand- ing before the altar, raises the cup in his left. Next he takes seven paces to the left, eight paces to the right, uttering the following prayer:—" Gods of heaven and earth, invest me with the heaving seal, in order that I may eject from this dwelling- house all kinds of evil spirits. Should any disobey me, give me power to deliver them for safe custody to the rulers of such demons." Having received the authority for which he prayed, he calls to the evil spirit—" As quick as lightning, depart from this dwelling." He then takes a bunch of willow, which he dips into the cup, and with which he besprinkles the east, west, north, and south corners of the house. Laying it down and taking up the sword again, and still carrying the cup in his left hand, he now goes to the east corner of the house and ex- claims, " I have the authority,"—" Tai-Shaong-Loo-Kwan." When he has said this, he fills his mouth with the water of exorcism, which he immediately ejects upon the eastern wall. He then calls aloud, " Kill the green evil spirits which come from unlucky stars, or let them be driven far away." At each corner of the house, and in the centre, he repeats the ceremony, saying at the south corner, " Kill the red-fire spirits which come from unlucky stars, or let them be driven far away ; " at the west corner, " Kill the white evil spirits, or let them be driven far away ; " and at the north, " Kill the dark evil spirits, or let them be driven far away ; " and in the centre, " Kill the yellow devils, or let them be driven far away." The attendants of the exorcist are now ordered to beat very loudly gongs, drums, and tom-toms.

In the midst of the appalling din the exorcist cries aloud, " Evil spirits from the east, I send back to the east; evil spirits from the south, I send back to the south; evil spirits from the west, I send back to the west; evil spirits from the north, I send back to the north; and those from the centre of the world, I send back thither. Let all evil spirits return to the points of the compass to which they belong. Let them all immediately vanish!" Finally, he goes to the door of the dwelling-house, making some mystical manœuvres with his sword in the air, for the purpose of preventing the return of the evil spirits. He then congratulates the inmates on the expulsion of their ghostly visitors, and receives his fee.

The labours of exorcists are not confined to the ejection of evil spirits from dwelling-houses. They have not unfrequently to eject or exorcise evil spirits or devils supposed to have entered the bodies of men, and to have made them sick by preying upon their vitals. The following method is very often adopted. The exorcist places in the invalid's chamber a paper image representing a human figure, to which the name of Tai-Sun is given. Before this figure a small temporary altar is erected, upon which are laid offerings of eggs, pork, fruit, cakes, and paper money. Candles and incense-sticks are also lighted. The exorcist now calls the evil spirit to leave the body of the invalid and enter that of the paper figure. The Tai-Sun having, it is supposed, been taken possession of, is removed to the street and set on fire. Sometimes the figure is placed in a large paper junk, or ship, and conveyed to a tidal stream to be carried seaward.

It is also usual for people who have experienced reverses of fortune, been afflicted with sickness, or lost near relations, to engage the services of an exorcist or Taouist priest. He and his client, the latter accompanied usually by two or three of his nearest relatives, resort to a temple to pray. Here the votary places on the altar as offerings three measures of rice, a boiled fowl, a piece of boiled pork, a small portion of mutton, three hundred cash, and in some instances forty-nine lamps, or candles. He then kneels before it, holding in his hand a tray on which are placed a full suit of clothing and two pounds of rice, whilst the exorcist, also kneeling, calls upon the idol to grant him a long series of prosperous years. After the prayer, the votary, still bearing the tray and its contents, and followed by his relatives, one of whom bears in his hand a bamboo rod to the top of which are attached strings of paper money, marches in procession three times round the altar. The procession is headed by the exorcist, who, at each step, calls upon the idol to grant the blessing sought. At this stage he gives to the votary, to be kept as a sort of talisman, a paper with an address or prayer to the god or gods inhabiting the north star. The Chun-Wan, or changing or turning from bad to good fortune, as the rite is termed, is of great antiquity. It was instituted during the Hon dynasty by Chu N'gam, who was told by a famous astrologer named Koon Loo, that his only son would die at the age of nineteen, and sought to avert the calamity by this singular observance. I have frequently seen this ceremony at Canton in a temple in honour of the idol Pak-Tai. In a monastery on the slopes at the White-Cloud mountains, where, in August, 1869, I saw the same service gone through by Buddhist priests, the votaries were eight or ten well-dressed Chinese ladies.

Spirit-writing is another variety of superstition with which the Chinese are familiar, and it is popular with the *literati* and gentry as well as the uneducated masses. It is frequently practised in private dwelling-houses. There are, however, regular professors of the system, and from morning until night they are visited by persons in every rank and condition seeking to ascertain what the future has in store. In the room of the professor stands a small altar, with offerings of fruits, cakes, and wine; above it is an idol of an angel or spirit named Sow-Yoong-Tai-Sien. The votary kneels before the altar, and, having prayed and presented the offerings, calls upon the medium to inform him what the spirit has to reply. The professor proceeds with his client to a small table which stands in the corner of the room, and the surface of which is covered with sand. Here he writes mystic characters with a pencil of peach-wood. The pencil is shaped somewhat like a " **T**," the horizontal piece being the handle of it. The end of the upright, however, is hooked. The professor rests the right end of the handle of the pencil carefully upon the tip of the forefinger of his right hand, and the left end upon the tip of the forefinger of his left hand. The point of the curve of the pencil is made to rest upon the sanded table. Thus supported it moves —apparently of its own accord—rapidly over the surface of the table, writing mystic characters understood only by the professor and his assistant. These are translated into Chinese by the assistant who is always present, so that the votary may have a perfect knowledge of what the spirit has stated in reply to his questions and prayers. The system is also practised in temples in honour of angels or spirits; one of the most famous of these is in honour of a spirit or angel called Loee-Shun-Yaong-Koon. It is situate in the street of the Honam suburb of the city of Canton, called Wan-chu-kew-keock.

Of the professors of spirit-rapping, the most distinguished in our time was one named Yām Mā-āsow. His establishment at Canton was visited, not only by persons curious to consult the spirits, but by men wishing, if possible, to free themselves from the vice of opium-smoking. Yām Mā-āsow undertook to effect this upon receiving from each opium-smoker a sum of money varying from two to ten taels of silver. Men enfeebled through excess used to resort to him, hoping to regain their strength. I observed that to such patients he gave a liquid which, like the potion prepared by the exorcists, consisted of water in which the ashes of a mystic scroll had been mixed. I was often astonished beyond measure at the degree of confidence which Chinese, apparently in very respectable positions, appeared to place in this practitioner of the deceptive arts.

In China, as in other lands, there are persons—always old women—who profess to have familiar spirits, and who pretend that they can call up the spirits of the dead to converse with the living. It may be said that the familiar narrative of the Witch of Endor has led to women being credited especially with this power. Amongst nations, however, who have no knowledge of the Scriptures, women have always been notorious for the exercise of such arts; and of the witches of a large Chinese city like Canton it may be safely said that their name is

"Legion." Let me describe what occurred on one of the many occasions on which I witnessed the practice of witchcraft during my residence in Canton. One day, in the month of January, 1867, I was the guest of an old lady, a widow, who resided in the western suburb of the city. She desired to confer with her departed husband, who had been dead for several years. The witch who was called in, was of prepossessing appearance and well-dressed; and she commenced immediately to discharge the duties of her vocation. Her first act was to erect a temporary altar at the head of the hall in which we were assembled. Upon this she placed two burning tapers, and offerings of fruits and cakes. She then sat on the right side of the altar, and, burying her face in her hands, remained silent for several minutes. Having awakened from her supposed trance or dream, she began to utter in a singing tone some words of incantation, at the same time sprinkling handfuls of rice at intervals upon the floor. She then said that the spirit of the departed was once more in the midst of his family. They were greatly moved, and some of them burst into a flood of tears. Through the witch as a medium, the spirit of the old man then informed the family where he was, and of the state of happiness he was permitted to enjoy in the land of shades. He spoke on several family topics, and dwelt upon the condition of one of his sons who, since his death, had gone to the northern provinces of China—references which evidently astonished the members of the family who were present, and confirmed their belief in the supernatural powers of the female impostor before them. There can be no doubt that she had made suitable inquiries beforehand. After exhorting his widow to dry her tears, and on no account to summon him again from the world of shades, in which he was tolerably happy, the spirit of the old man retired.

A witch is occasionally called in to ascertain the cause of sickness in a family. Should she declare it to be due to an ancestral spirit from a tomb long neglected by the descendants, they seek to appease the spirit by offering it paper money and paper clothes. Should these fail to cure the sickness, it is customary for the witch to lop a branch from the east side of a peach tree, cut it in the form of a wedge, and drive it into the tomb. This ceremony is supposed to confine the angry ancestral spirit to the tomb for ever. Like the Africans whom Speke describes, the Chinese very often fancy that both men and things are bewitched. A person who suspects that his bed-curtains, or bed-pillows, or counterpanes are bewitched, pins a mystic character to his night-dress. When a kitchen range or any cooking vessels become bewitched, a mystic character is placed on the walls of the kitchen to rectify the evil.

In the district of Shun-tuk, and at Si-chu-shan, a portion of the district of Nam-hoi in Kwang-tung, there are women called Mi-Foo-Kow, who profess by incantations and other mysterious means to be able to effect the death of their fellow-creatures. They are consulted by married women who, being cruelly treated, or for other reasons, are anxious secretly to kill their husbands. The witches gather the bones of infants from the public ceme-teries, and invoke the evil genii of the infants to accompany them to their dwelling-houses. The bones are reduced to a fine powder, and sold in this form. Mixed in tea, wine, or any other beverage, the powder is daily given to her husband by the murderous wife. At the same time the witch daily calls upon the evil genius of the infant whose bones have been used to assist in effecting the death of the object of the woman's hate. Sometimes, in addition to this horrible daily draught, a portion of the bone of an infant is carefully secreted under his bed. Attempts have been made, I believe, not without success, to destroy these witches. In the Toong-Yan-Shan-Hok, or public hall at Kang-hee, near to Si-chu-shan, some of these women were summoned into the presence of the gentry, and made to answer certain grave charges of this nature which had been preferred against them by their neighbours. Upon being con-victed, they were put to death by poison. Not later than the year 1865, several women of this class were put to death in this manner. I believe that a similar wicked custom prevails, or did prevail, in the Sandwich Islands.

In the south of China, it is commonly supposed that a poor man desirous of avenging himself upon a person in the upper walks of life by whom he has been oppressed, may effect his purpose either by bewitching the family or the dwelling-house of his oppressor. This is said to be accomplished in the following manner. He repairs each night for seven weeks to a cemetery to sleep under a coffin in which a corpse is contained. There is little or no difficulty in this part of the programme, as it is usual in almost all Chinese cemeteries to find coffins above ground, generally resting upon pillars. During this period he must lead a most abstemious life, drinking water and eating rice cakes only. At the end of the seven weeks he is supposed either to have received power from, or to have prevailed upon, the spirit of the departed one whose corpse is contained in the coffin, to bewitch the family or the dwelling-house, or both, of his rich oppressor. I called, on one occasion, upon a wealthy Chinese coal-merchant, whose place of business was at Fa-tee. This gentleman, I learned, had gone to his country-house, summoned in all haste because an enemy had bewitched it. On the 14th of July, 1872, my attention was called to a house in the Yan-wo-lee street of the Wong-sha district of the western suburb of Canton. The doors were literally crowded with persons of both sexes, and of all ages, attracted by the report that the house was bewitched. On entering I found the inmates in a state of terror. On the floor of the first hall were scattered broken vases and pots, which but a short time before had been cast from their places by an invisible agency.

Another of the superstitious arts is that by which a class of men predict the fortunes of the living from the appearance of the corpses of their ancestors. If a corpse, for example, be found, when exhumed, in a high state of preservation, great evils are said to be in store for the descendants of the deceased. If the skeleton only be found, the necromancer, if I may use the term in this sense, proceeds to form an opinion as to the good or bad fortune of the descendants of the departed one by observing the appearance which the bones present. Thus, for example, if the bones of the skeleton look yellow, very good fortune is predicted ; if they are reddish, good fortune is foretold ; if they are black, or white, great evils are presaged. Several other systems of telling fortunes are in vogue, as for instance, hydromancy, by water ; pyromancy, by fire ; arithmancy, by numbers.

There is also a mode of divination, rhabdomancy, by the staff. This mode, however, is, if I mistake not, confined in a great measure to gamblers, who before leaving their homes to pursue their vicious courses are anxious to know what road will bring them luck. Placing a staff in an upright position, they allow it to fall to the ground. To a method of divination similar to this, a reference appears to be made in the prophecy of Hosea (iv. 12)—"My people ask counsel at their stocks, and their staff declareth unto them," &c. This method of divination, Jerome states, was much observed by the Assyrians and Babylonians. Herodotus also, in his sixth book, mentions the Alani women as diligently searching for smooth and straight rods or sticks, to be used in this manner. There are, however, fortune tellers, who profess to direct men in what direction they ought to go. On the first day, called Kap-Tsze, of the cycle of sixty days, joyous spirits are supposed to be by the fortune-tellers in the north-west. To go in that direction therefore on the day in question, is supposed to be very fortunate. In the south-west, on this day, honourable spirits are supposed to reside. In the south, five evil spirits are said to dwell. To leave a city, therefore, or a dwelling-house on this day by passing through the south gate, or the south door, is what few Chinese would do, as they regard south gates and south doors on such occasions as gates and doors of death. To take another illustration. On the fifth day of the cycle, called Moo-Shan, joyous spirits are supposed to reside in the south-east, honourable spirits in the south, and the five evil spirits also in the south. The gate of death on this occasion is said to be in the south-west.

The same class of fortune-tellers direct men as to certain days on which they ought to avoid the discharge of certain duties. The Chinese never open their granaries on the day called Kap, which is the first of the cycle of sixty days, believing that, were they to do so, the rice in the granaries would either be spoiled by mildew, or destroyed by insects. On the day called Yut, they neither sow nor plant, as bad crops might be the result. They never repair the grates of their kitchens on the day called Peng, which is the third of the cycle lest their houses should be

eventually destroyed by fire. On the day called Teng, few people
shave, as they suppose their heads would, in the course of a few
days, become covered with boils. They never purchase lands
on the day called Moo, or open bills of exchange on the day
called Kee. To do so would be unlucky. On the day called Kang,
weavers never begin a web, as an inferior fabric would be the
result. A sauce would be tasteless if made on the day called Sun ;
to repair the bank of a river on the day called Yam would be labour
thrown away, and legal proceedings instituted on the day called
Lui, money spent in vain. These ten days are called male days.
There are also twelve female days On the day called Tsze, they
never have recourse to fortune-tellers, who would give them unfavourable answers. On the day called Chow, they never put on
new clothes, *i.e.*, for the first time, for this would be to die from
home. On the day called Yan, they never offer sacrifices, for the
gods would not accept them. Wells begun on the day called Mow
yield bitter waters. On the day called Shan, mourners never
weep for the dead, as to do so is to experience sorrow upon
sorrow. People who go far from home on the day called Tsze,
are in danger of being attacked by robbers. A house must not
be roofed on the day called N'g, otherwise the owner of it will
be called upon ere long to sell his property. To take medicine
on the day called Mee, is to take poison. To erect bedsteads on
the day called Shen, is to admit evil spirits into the bedchamber.
To kill a fowl on the day called Yow, is to cause all the other
fowls in the pen to die of sickness. To eat dog's flesh on the
day called Sut, is to be haunted at night by the spirit of the dog.
Lastly on the day called Hoi, a marriage must not be celebrated,
lest it should end in a separation between husband and wife.

Like other orientals, the Chinese practise the art of taming
and charming serpents. They declare that not only snakes of
an innocuous species, may be domesticated and taught to recognise those who feed them, but that it is in their power to tame
even the most venomous reptiles. To effect this, they deprive
the serpents of their fangs. It is not unusual in the streets of
a Chinese city to see snake-charmers, who, merely by the movements of their hands, cause even venomous snakes to raise
themselves up, as if to dance, remaining erect so long as the snake

charmers continue to move their hands to and fro. It is very
common to see snakes wreathing themselves with apparent affection round the arms and limbs of their respective proprietors.
A still more remarkable performance is that of an itinerant of
this class who opens his mouth wide, in order that his pet snake
may hide in his stomach by wriggling down his throat. He is
however, very careful not to let go the tail of the vanishing reptile.
Men of this class undertake for a small sum to banish snakes
from houses which are supposed to be infested by them. There
is also a class of men who sell an ointment, capable of curing
the most ghastly wounds, and the bites also of the most venomous reptiles. By way of testing the truth of his statements,
a man of this class occasionally takes up a serpent, and allows it
to bite his tongue. Showing the bleeding member to the gazing
crowd, who expect him to fall down dead, the itinerant
quack applies a small portion of his wonderful ointment to the
wound. Seeing that no harm has befallen him, the most gullible
members of his audience readily come forward to purchase the
nostrum. In the pursuit of this vocation, they remind one of
the Psylli, a race who inhabited Lybia, and who were celebrated,
as Roman writers tell us, not so much for their power in taming
and charming serpents, as for their expertness in curing their
bites. Men of this class and Chinese druggists sell besides, a
beverage termed snake wine, or tea consisting of water and wine
in which snakes have been boiled to a pulp. The Chinese regard
it with much favour, as a febrifuge. The flesh of the snake is
also eaten by invalids; the head is cut off by the well-
sharpened edge of a piece of porcelain, and the body, skinned by
the same implement, is fried or boiled. The flesh is then cut
into small pieces, which are eaten well mixed with the minced
flesh of a fowl. For the benefit of the illiterate public, many
fortune-tellers combine with their other duties those of public
scribes or letter-writers. Perhaps it would be more correct to
say, that many scribes are also fortune-tellers. These men
station themselves near temples in honour of popular deities, or
in the most crowded streets of a city. Having been informed
of the various matters which his client is anxious to comuni-
cate to his far-off friends, the scribe quickly writes the letter

required.   He is furnished with a writing table, a smooth board painted white, or covered with shining zinc.[1]   He first drafts the composition, and then copies it upon a sheet of Chinese note or letter paper, which, inclosed in an envelope and properly addressed, he presents, on the receipt of a small gratuity, to his illiterate client.   I was one day attracted to a letter-writer's table by hearing loud sobs.   On drawing near, I observed a youth seated at it, weeping bitterly, and, at intervals, dictating to the scribe certain items of information which it was his desire to convey by letter to his uncle.   The burden of his painful story was as follows :—He was suffering from a lame foot which rendered him altogether incapable of working, and unless a cure were immediately effected, nothing apparently awaited him but death by starvation at the corner of one of the streets.   He was applying to his uncle to forward him the funds necessary to enable him to engage the services of a competent physician. The foot was so much swollen as almost to preclude the possibility of his walking.

Before concluding this chapter, I must describe a number of superstitious ways in which the Chinese attempt to remove and ward off various evils.   Sometimes a man whose son or daughter is sick, humbles himself in the sight of the gods by becoming a beggar, asking alms from house to house.   His calls, however, are generally limited to a hundred houses.   At the door of each he begs that a cash only may be given to him.   When he has collected a hundred cash he expends them in the purchase of rice, which is boiled and given to the patient.   It is called

---

[1] The custom of using such a writing table has been in force not only in China, but in almost all Asiatic or eastern countries, for many centuries.   We read in the gospel of St. Luke that when Zacharias, who at the time was speechless, was asked how he would have his son called, "he asked for a writing table and wrote, saying, 'His name is John.'"   The Rev. J. Hartley, in his interesting and instructing work, entitled, *Researches in Greece*, states that "in Greek schools it is still usual to have a small clean board on which the master writes the alphabet, or any other lesson which he intends his scholars to read.   As soon as one lesson is finished, the writing is washed out or scraped out, and the board may thus be continually employed for writing new lessons.   Not only does this instrument harmonise in its use with the writing table mentioned in Luke i. 63, but the Greeks call it by the same name."   Barnes, in his notes on the gospels, distinctly states that "sometimes the writing-table was made entirely of lead."

Pak-Kā-Mi, or the rice of one hundred houses. A custom somewhat similar is observed by a parent who has been informed by
an astrologer that his son is destined to become a beggar. To
avert the calamity, the father, providing himself with a small
earthenware money-box, goes from door to door asking alms.

To restore to health a child suffering from fever and ague, it
is customary for the mother to place three burning incense sticks
in its hand. The child is then quickly carried out of the house by
a servant. The mother follows them with a broom in her hand, pre-
tending to sweep, and crying aloud, Begone! Begone!! Begone !!!
The evil spirit which is regarded as the cause of the child's sickness is supposed to be driven away for ever by this ridiculous
ceremony. It is also usual, when a child is ill, for the mother or
nurse to walk with it in her arms through the street in which she
resides, throwing two copper cash upon the ground at each ten
paces which she takes. This is to tempt the evil spirit to quit
the body of the suffering infant. The " Chu-pin," " to take away
the sickness," is a similar ceremony. When a child is very sick
and slight hopes are entertained of its recovery, its body is
rubbed with copper cash. These are then thrown into the
street, to tempt the evil spirit which is regarded as the cause of
the sickness, to leave the sufferer. This ceremony is also
practised with adults who are supposed to be seriously ill. The
fortune-teller not unfrequently attributes the malady of a child
to the spirit of a white tiger against which it has offended. The
mother, accordingly, often repairs to a shrine in honour of the
white tiger. With the view of appeasing its wrath she worships
the stone figure or idol of the animal, and presents an offering
of fat pork, which she places in its mouth. In the temple of
Pak-tai there is such a shrine, before which, at an early hour of
the morning, mothers with sick children may be seen earnestly
prostrating themselves. In the temple in honour of Yun-tan
there is a similar figure of a tiger in stone.

In the third month of the year, and on the day called Hon-
Shik, it is usual for the Chinese to pluck two willow branches.
The father of a family places one of these branches above the
entrance door of his dwelling-house, and the other above the
ancestral altar. They are supposed to summon the spirits of his

ancestors to return home for a season. When this is believed to
have been effected, the branches are boiled, and the decoction
carefully preserved as a beverage for children when restless by
night. It is a time-honoured custom for a mother to besmear the
forehead of her children with a paste made of the leaves of the
betel-nut tree, to keep away all kinds of evil spirits. She does
the same when her child has seen a pregnant woman. The
charm is supposed to preclude the possibility of the spirit or
soul of her child going into the unborn infant. Every one who
is suffering under any sickness which has the appearance of an
epidemic, is supposed to be under the influence of evil spirits,
and it is customary to suspend a representation of a sword
above his bed. This consists of several hundreds of cash
bound together with cords, and is supposed to scare away the evil
spirits. The practice is not confined to the "profane vulgar,"
it prevails among all classes. On a visit which I paid to a
sick Chinese gentleman named Poon Heng-kee, I found a "cash
sword" suspended from the top of his bed. Another friend of
mine, named Kwok A-ham, even when in health, had a sword of
this kind fastened to his curtains. Sometimes, for a similar
purpose, people hire from executioners the swords with which
they have decapitated malefactors. In my private museum of
Chinese curiosities, arms, &c., there were two or three such
weapons, and occasionally friends of sick Chinese, aware that I
possessed such weapons, made application to me for them, in
order that they might fasten them to the beds of their sick.
Sometimes a horse's tail is placed in the chamber to terrify
spirits. In some parts of the Empire, people who have sick
relations dip rags into the blood which has come from the
bodies of decapitated criminals. Such a rag, tied to the bed of
an invalid, is supposed to be very efficacious. When a person
is very sick, a suit of his clothes is often taken to a temple, and
placed upon the altar. When a priest of the sect of Taou has
invoked the blessing of the idol, the clothes are taken back and
the invalid clothed in them. While the Taouist priest is calling
upon the god to grant the desired blessings, the nearest relative
of the sick man kneels before the altar, holding in his hands
sticks of burning incense. I have frequently seen this ceremony

in a temple in honour of Tai-Wong in the Si-yow-cho-tee street
of the western suburb of Canton. It is customary when a
person is sick, to cast into the street, so that they may be
trodden under the foot of man, the leaves of any medicinal
herbs from which a decoction has been poured off as a beverage
for an invalid.

The citizens of the prefectoral city of Koo-chow, in
Kwang-tung, annually observe a very curious custom, for the
purpose of getting rid of all evil spirits in their neighbourhood. A canonized serpent is said to have had its abode,
centuries ago, in a large cavern near the city, and the object of
the observance is to prevail upon this serpent to expel the
spirits, and thereby secure for the inhabitants of the city
immunity from epidemics during the next twelve months. The
streets are traversed by a long procession of citizens, carrying
pigs, fruits, and flowers, as offerings to the snake. The most
striking figure in the procession, is a youth with an arrow in
his mouth, borne on men's shoulders. This youth, who is the
snake's representative, is said to be selected by the casting of
lots in a temple erected in its honour. As he is carried through
the streets, all evil spirits are supposed to take their flight.
The youth is regarded by his friends and neighbours as a very
fortunate being, and his services are requited by a present of
money taken from the funds of the temple. The arrow belongs
to the temple, and is borrowed in turn by sick persons, and
suspended from their beds to drive away the evil spirits which
afflict them.

To prevent the approach of evil spirits, it is a very common
practice, at all events in the cities of the south of China, to
place above the entrance of each street a strip of yellow or
white cloth with a mystic character. In front of houses and
streets which are suspected not to have been built according
to the principles of geomancy, it is usual to place stone figures
of lions, which are supposed to avert the calamities which
would otherwise visit the people. In front of the Poon-yu
magistrate's official residence in Canton, a large stone lion
stands on a stone pedestal to counteract bad geomantic in-
influences. In 1865, during the bombardment of the city by

the English, a round shot knocked the lion off its pedestal, and
it was allowed for some time to remain where it fell.   There
was in consequence much sickness in all the streets near the
magistrate's residence, and eventually the lion was replaced.
Sometimes one sees rows of stone lions in front of villages.
In front of Wong-king-tong, a pretty little village in a valley
beyond the White Cloud Mountains, I observed a long row of
them, which, the villagers informed me, kept them safe from
robbers and other calamities.   At each of the approaches to
a village on the island of Honam, I observed a stone lion;
and at Loong-gan-toong, a large village about ten miles east of
Canton, I saw a large stone altar with a stone lion standing
on it.   The inhabitants regarded these figures as the faithful
guardians and protectors of their homesteads.   At the end of
streets it is customary to erect, as antidotes against ills of all
kinds, stone slabs or pillars, upon which are inscribed the characters : Tai-Shan-Shek-Kom-Tong, "the great mountain stone
which dares to face evils."   Boards bearing the words, Yat-Seen,
or "one beatitude," are also placed upon the outer walls of
houses.   These words[1] are also used by the superstitious when
they meet funeral processions in the streets.   Boards with the
character "Shou" or "longevity" inscribed on them are also
suspended from the walls of Chinese streets.   A board of this
kind is in the form of an escutcheon or hatchment, and its
influence is said to be very propitious.   The character "Shou"
or "longevity," is also often carved upon the backs of chairs.
Boards with the characters Ying-He, or "collected happiness,"
carved or painted on them, are placed as emblems of good
fortune upon the walls of Chinese streets.   On the outer walls
of dwelling-houses, generally above the doors or windows,
boards with the characters "Keong-Tai-Koong-Tsoy-Tsze" are
often placed.   These words imply that "Keong-Tai-Koong
is here," and are supposed to prevent evil spirits or noxious
influences entering the house.   Keong Tai-koong flourished
during the reign of Wu-wang, the first emperor of the Chow
dynasty, B.C. 1122, and was raised by the latter, for his great

[1] Those also use these words who inadvertently see the nakedness of their
fellow-men, as this is regarded as very unlucky.

talents and administrative abilities, from the condition of a poor fisherman to be a high minister of state. In many villages in Nam-hoi, more particularly in that part of the country which is termed Si-chu-shan, it is customary for the inhabitants to burn a mixture of straw, human hair, and brimstone, at the doors of their dwelling-houses. This is done on the eighth day of the fourth month, and it is supposed that no snakes dare enter these houses. It is usual to see above the doors of dwelling-houses strips of red paper, upon which are written the characters "Eng-Fok-Lam-Moon," or "Five beatitudes enter by this door." The five characters are occasionally represented by five bats, either made of stucco, or drawn on sheets of red paper. In the estimation of the Chinese bats are birds of good omen. Should an epidemic visit a street, despite all the charms which I have described, the inhabitants generally carry idols in procession through it. Another practice is to engage Taouist priests to worship the god whose temple stands in, or near, the pestilential street. Near the gates of the temple a large paper figure of a heathen deity called Tai-tsze is placed, and upon an altar erected in front of the idol, incense pots and offerings are arranged. Tai-tsze is represented as holding in his hand a board with four Chinese characters, namely, Fan-Yee-Shee-Shik, or "the divider of clothes and bestower of food." He is regarded as a king or ruler of evil spirits, and on such occasions the Taouist priests worship him morning, noon, and night, for three or seven days, to prevail upon him to expel the hungry ghosts supposed to be the cause of the epidemic. In order that Tai-tsze may have the means of satisfying the wants of these angry and hungry spirits, large quantities of paper money and paper clothes are presented to him.

The Fat-Pee, or pillars, or slabs, on which the name of the future Buddha, or Pam-Mo-O-Mee-To-Foo, is inscribed, are erected near rivers, creeks, and ponds in which men have been drowned. On the surface of their waters, enraged devils and imps are supposed to float, always on the alert to effect, if possible, the death by drowning of the unwary. A stone of this kind stands on the banks of the creek which bounds the east end of Shameen, the foreign settlement at Canton. Upon asking the Chinese why they had erected such an unmeaning pillar in the vicinity of the foreign settlement, they informed me that several Chinese had, by the malice of evil spirits, been drowned in the adjoining creek. In various parts of the empire the Chinese exorcise water-devils, by sacrificing white horses on the banks of rivers, creeks, canals, or ponds. The horse is first felled, and then decapitated by a person set apart for this very singular duty. The head of the horse, is placed in a large earthenware jar, and buried either on the banks or in the bed of the rivers at low water mark. Near the place of interment a stone pillar, or slab is erected, with the characters " O-Me-O-To-Fat." Sometimes the figure of a horse's head is substituted for such a pillar. At Tze-tow, a village near Whampoa, I observed such a representation of a horse's head in stone on the banks of a creek which flows past the village. The headless carcass of the horse is not thrown away as offal, but becomes the perquisite of the slaughterer. Cut into pieces to suit purchasers, it is sold by him in the adjacent markets as wholesome food.

In the month of August, 1869, I witnessed the sacrifice of a white horse at Gna-yew, a village ten miles to the west of Canton. During the preceding year, several persons had been drowned at, or near, the village, and the last person who met with a watery grave was one of the *patres conscripti* of the locality. The inhabitants believed that a number of the spirits of men who had died

"Unwept, unhonoured, and unsung,"

were greatly incensed at not having received the usual annual offerings to the departed dead, and that they brought these calamities on the residents. It was considered necessary therefore to appease them with offerings of various kinds. In a pauper cemetery adjoining Gnā-yew, a large mat temple was erected. Numerous altars were raised in it, with tablets bearing the names of the departed poor. In front of each altar stood two or three priests of the sect of Taou, who, from morning until night, chanted appropriate prayers in a dull monotonous tone. Behind the priests, well-dressed ladies with their female attendants knelt, uttering loud

lamentations. In another part of the temporary temple were
arranged more than two hundred ordinary-sized chairs, made
of bamboo frames covered with paper. There were also
numerous figures of the same materials, representing male and
female attendants, and an infinity of gold and silver ingots
made of paper. The religious ceremony, prolonged during three
days and nights, was terminated by a general conflagration of the
chairs, figures, ingots, and other offerings, the priest standing by
the sacred fire and calling upon the hungry ghosts to accept the
sacrifices which a generous public had provided for them, and
to cease from troubling. At this part of the proceedings a
white horse was decapitated with the view of intimidating the
spirits. The stench from the grave-yard in which the ceremony
took place—the bodies, in many instances, having been interred
but a few inches below the surface—was in itself more than
enough to cause a pestilence. Many thousands of persons, say
at the very least 40,000, were present. Large numbers of them
sought amusement in witnessing dramatic representations which
were being performed in a large mat theatre by a company of
first-class actors. Others strolled through the courts of a vast
building in which were exhibited figures representing scenes
taken from the national history; while thousands lined the
banks of the river to witness the processions of dragon boats.
The banners with which these boats were decorated were of
costly silks of the most brilliant colours. Foreigners who were
present on the occasion observed that they had never seen such
a display of dragon boats, even at the great annual boat festival
at Canton. The ridiculous and costly ceremony was not very
successful, for a dragon boat running foul of a Malen-Teng, or
slipper boat, capsized it, and six of the eight women in the boat
were drowned.

On the 6th of August, 1870, I had another opportunity of
witnessing a similar ceremony at Tsing-poo, or as it is sometimes called Leeming-koon, a village not more than five miles
to the west of Canton. The white horse, with its head
crowned with garlands, was led in triumph through the
streets of the village. Over its back was slung a wallet, in
the pockets of which were placed charms bearing the name

and seal of the goddess Chow-Chu-Laong-Laong-Koo. The charms, which were folded in the form of triangles, were bought very readily by the crowd, amounting to several thousands, who had assembled on the occasion. The purchasers placed them on their respective dwelling-houses, with the view of preventing the entrance of evil spirits. At 3 P.M. the horse was brought to the banks of the river to be put to death. Before this was done, however, an exorcist, dressed in robes that gave him a very ferocious appearance, performed a wild dance and uttered all kinds of violent threats against the devils who were supposed to be flitting over the surface of the waters in quest of mischief. This ceremony ended, the legs of the horse were tightly bound with cords. The poor, unoffending animal was then thrown upon the ground and the fatal knife was applied to its throat. The blood was received into a large earthenware jar. A small portion of it was carried into the temple in honour of the idol Chow-Chu-Laong-Laong-Koo, and several hundreds of people madly rushed into the temple, to sprinkle with it the charms they had bought. The head and legs were cut off from the carcase, and placed in the bows of a long open boat, in which was also placed the blood mixed with sand. A young man, whose face, hands, and feet were painted black, supposed to represent the whole family of water devils, was now seized, bound hand and foot, and set near the head and legs of the sacrificial horse. A procession of boats, headed by that containing the representative of water devils, and the mutilated remains of the horse, was now formed, and, as it slowly moved along the waters, handfuls of the sand with which the blood had been mixed were cast into the river to dispel the evil spirits. The second boat was also open, and several village braves in it, at frequent intervals, discharged their matchlocks to increase the terror of the demons. The other boats, which were richly carved and gilded, bore, some of them Taouist, and others Buddhist, priests. When the procession had reached the confines of the district, the young man who represented the devil, having been unbound, jumped into the river, amidst the rattle of musketry, and quickly swam ashore. The head of the horse was eventually placed in an earthenware jar, and, at low water, buried in the bed of the river. This singular ceremony has, I believe, been observed for several centuries by the Chinese. Nor does it appear to have been confined to them for we read in Herodotus (7—114) that when the Persian King, Xerxes, reached the banks of the river Strymon, the magi sacrificed white horses to it.

In connection with these observances I ought to mention that beyond the north gate of each walled city there is a stone altar on which sacrifices termed Li-Tsi are offered twice annually, on the fifteenth day of the seventh month, and again on the first day of the tenth month, for the purpose of appeasing evil spirits. On each of these occasions three sheep, three pigs, three large baskets of rice, and one large jar of wine, are offered. At the time of this celebration there is placed above the altar a tablet on which the name of Shing Wong, the protector of walled cities, is inscribed. When the ceremony is ended the tablet is returned to the temple of the deity, where it remains until it is again required. The ceremony originated during the Chow dynasty (B.C. 1122 to B.C. 255), and has been systematically observed ever since.

Before retiring to rest, *i.e.*, at ten or eleven o'clock, shop-keepers and others perform a superstitious ceremony called Fong-Chow, or letting go the money paper. Two tapers are lighted and placed immediately in front of the door, and three pieces of paper-money are burnt as an offering to poor, hungry ghosts or spirits flitting about in search of food. If not appeased, these hungry ghosts may bring dreadful calamities upon the residents. A similar ceremony is performed nightly by the boat population to appease the water devils.

When the Chinese purchase lands on which to erect houses, they hire Taouist priests to sprinkle the ground with holy water, and so drive away evil spirits. When a house is being built the owner treats the builders with great kindness, in order to induce them to build the house carefully according to the principles of geomancy. Great pains are taken in the selection of a ridge beam which has neither knots nor cracks. It is painted red, and several yards of red cloth are suspended from it previous to its being placed in position. A long strip

of red paper is sometimes substituted for the cloth.   This cloth
or paper is first blessed by a Taouist priest, who slightly besmears it with blood taken from the comb of a young cock.
During the performance of this duty, the priest chants prayers
to Loo-Pan, the god of carpenters and architects, and to other
deities of the sect.   These prayers are continued whilst the
beam is being raised into its position.   During the whole of the
ceremony, candles and incense are burning upon a temporary altar
erected in honour of Chong-Wong-Yae.   In some instances there
is suspended from the ridge beam a sieve or tray containing, as
emblems of good fortune, scissors, knives, a ruler, a rice measure,
red coloured thread, a metallic looking-glass, a few copper cash,
and a small pair of scales.   To bring wealth to the family, a hole
is made in the beam, and a small quantity of gold leaf placed in
it.   The quantity of gold leaf which is deposited varies, I apprehend, according to the rank and wealth of the persons for whom
the house is being erected.   In the ridge beam of a house which
was purchased by a Chinese friend of mine, not less than sixteen
taels of gold leaf were found.   The religious ceremonies which
are observed at such times are prolonged through the night, and,
at their close, ten cakes or dumplings, called Tsin-Toee, or fried
dough, are taken from the temporary altar, and thrown by the
chief officiating priest over the newly-erected ridge beam.   As
he throws each cake, the priest exclaims, " May the sons and
grandsons of the person for whom this house is now being
erected, purchase annually one hundred acres of land."   When
the house is finished, Taouist priests are again called in.   The
ceremony which takes places on this occasion is called Shay-
Too-Gow, or to shoot the earth bow.   The chief priest is provided with a bow and five arrows, and having placed a charm,
and the picture of a soldier riding on horseback, on each of the
four walls of the principal hall of the house, and in the centre
of the floor, he repeats certain incantations, and discharges an
arrow, to the barbed point of which a burning cord is attached,
at each charm and at each picture.   He then casts several live
fish into an adjacent river or pond for good luck, in the presence
of all the members of the family, and with an accompaniment
of gongs and tom-toms.   Should carpenters and bricklayers, in

repairing a house, find occasion to remove any portions of the walls, they suspend a square from the ridge beam of the house, to propitiate evil spirits, which are supposed to be capable of causing the death of the workmen were this observance neglected.

It is usual for workmen to place a portrait of a Chinese deity named Chong-Wong-Yae in a house which they have been called upon to repair. These portraits are bought by them at the temple of this deity; and when the repairs of the house have been effected, they are, as a rule, returned to the person in charge of the temple, to whom a few lucky cash are given. All persons residing in a street in which a house is being repaired, are duly informed by the elders of the day on which the rebuilding or repairing is to commence. This is owing to a notion that, should the day selected by the astrologer for commencing the works prove unlucky, all evil spirits flitting through the air or walking to and fro in the earth, or who have taken up their abode in the house, will visit with sickness, death, or other calamities, all who may be found in the street when the workmen enter on their labours. Sometimes the astrologer discovers that the day for the commencement of the works will be unlucky for all persons of a certain age found in their dwelling-houses, or in the streets in which these stand, when the workmen begin. Such persons, of course, are duly warned of this by the elders. On a day selected for repairing a temple, the people in the street or district in which the temple stands are very apprehensive of calamities overtaking them. They not unfrequently leave their homes for the whole day, sometimes for two or three days. I was walking, on the 7th of July, 1870, through the principal street of Wong-sha, a suburb of Canton, when I noticed that the streets were deserted, and that the doors of the shops and houses were closed. As the circumstance was very extraordinary, I made inquiries as to the cause. I was informed that, as various kinds of workmen had that day commenced to repair a temple in honour of a deity named Chaong-Kwan, the inhabitants of the district, fearing lest the day should prove unlucky despite the well-known wisdom of the astrologer who had chosen it, had placed themselves beyond the reach of danger by leaving their homes on a visit to their respective friends. Many of them, I was informed, had risen from their beds at 3 A.M. for this purpose. I called at an academy which was conducted by a personal friend of mine named Chaong Kai-shek, and found no one within. The " dominie" and his pupils had also sought to place themselves beyond the reach of harm.

It is not unusual for the proprietors to engage the services of Taouist priests, in order that the wells in the streets and houses of a Chinese city may contain pure water. The priests, after saying prayers, write a mystic character upon a piece of yellow paper. The scroll is then burned, and the ashes, with a handful of sugar, and a few leaves from a pomelow tree, are thrown into the well. I have frequently seen this ceremony performed, especially in the month of August, both at Canton and Macao.

Before embarking on a voyage or setting out on a journey, and in the act of leaving his home, an intending traveller often stands with his feet close together on the step of the inner door of his house, gnashes his teeth thirty-six times, and moves his right hand four times in a horizontal and seven times in a perpendicular direction through the air. He then addresses the following prayer to the god Yue Wong :—

"I am now, O Yue-Wong in the act of embarking on a voyage (or setting out on a journey). Do thou, therefore, watch over me whilst I am from home, and turn away from me all evil spirits which may wish to assault and hurt me. From thieves, or pirates, or wild animals, great god protect me, and bring me back in safety to my home. To this my prayer, O god, give ear."

This prayer having been read seven times, the traveller quits the inner doorstep of his dwelling-house, not looking behind him to say farewell.

A person who swears falsely before the gods that he is innocent of charges brought against him consoles himself by means of an observance called Kai-yune. To check all the evil consequences which the gods may permit to overtake him, the perjurer writes on each corner of a clay tile the

four following characters : Peng, Sew, Nga, Kai. He then
places the tile on an altar in honour of the gods of the earth
and rice fields. When several days have elapsed, he returns
to the altar, and breaks the tile with a hammer. By this
simple and ridiculous ceremony, he is supposed to avert all
impending calamities. This custom is also observed by
persons who are sick, and by those who are engaged in
quarrels or disputes. In the former case a Taouist priest
is hired to break the tile. Before doing so he generally
prays.

To protect themselves from all evil influences, the Chinese
are accustomed to place a portrait of Chee-Mee in their houses.
This worthy has at all times been regarded by them as a guardian
angel. He is represented riding upon a lion ; he holds in his
right hand a large seal or stamp, upon which the characters
Chee-Mee-Tsing-Chu are engraven, and in his left a representation
of the Yin and the Yan. It appears from the history of Chee Mee
that at one time a large and fierce lion was accustomed to commit
very serious depredations. To check his inroads Chee Mee
descended from above, and, in an encounter between him and
the lion, succeeded in throwing round his neck a golden
chain, and leading him captive. By a virtue which he possessed, the lion became so tame and docile as to allow his
captor to ride upon his back. In consequence of this extraordinary display of power, and of the singular integrity and
perfection of his character, and his watchful care over men,
wicked spirits are afraid to go into Chee Mee's presence. For
the portrait the name of the deity is sometimes substituted.

It is also usual for the Chinese to place upon the tops of
their houses, either earthenware figures of cocks, or three
earthenware representations of cannons, or tridents made of
iron, to avert calamities and disorders. This singular custom
is due to a person whose history is somewhat remarkable.
During the reign of Man Wong, of the Chow dynasty, B.C. 1122,
a man named Moo Kat, who was daily employed in cutting
grass upon the sides of the hills, was so unfortunate, when
entering the gate of the city in which he dwelt, as to fall
beneath a heavy burden of grass which he was carrying on his

shoulders.   In his fall he inadvertently knocked down a man,
who was so severely bruised that he died almost immediately.
For this Moo Kat was cast into prison.   In consequence, however, of the reverence in which he was held throughout the
district, and of his filial affection, he was permitted by the
emperor to pay his parents periodical visits.   On his way home,
on one of these occasions, Moo Kat met a physiognomist, who,
looking him full in the face, said, " You are a homicide."
Moo Kat at once acknowledged it, and begged the physiognomist to suggest some means by which he could obtain exemption
from further imprisonment.   He was instructed by him to
sleep on the earth, and on the same plot of ground for forty-
nine days, and, during the hours of sleep, to have two lamps
burning, one at his head and the other at his feet.   Moo Kat
carried out these instructions, and the result was as the physiognomist had predicted ; for the emperor being informed of
his non-return to prison, ordered that no officers should be
sent in search of him.   It happened several years afterwards,
the emperor, whilst taking exercise in the vicinity of his palace,
met Moo Kat, and said, " Is that you, Moo Kat ? I thought you
had died long ago."   Moo Kat recounted the interview he
had had with the physiognomist, the instructions which he had
received, and the happy result.   The emperor, anxious to see a
physiognomist of such extraordinary knowledge, commanded
Moo Kat to bring him before him.   In an interview with the
physiognomist, the emperor was so struck with his fund of
information, that he at once resolved to appoint him to a
lucrative and honourable situation in the household.   The
physiognomist never forgot Moo Kat for having been instrumental in introducing him to royalty and affluence, and gave
him as a present certain valuable sybilline works.   Moo Kat
became a diviner, and was resorted to by persons of all classes.
He taught the people that, amongst the most effectual methods
of keeping evil spirits and other obnoxious influences from
houses, was to place on the roof of the house, either an
earthenware cock, or three earthenware guns, or an iron
trident.

Short iron tridents are affixed to the taffrails of junks which navigate the rivers and seas of southern China, to ward off evil. Speaking in his *Juventus Mundi* of the trident of the sea god Poseidon, Mr. Gladstone observes that, " it appears evidently to point to some tradition of a trinity, such as may still be found in various forms of eastern religion other than the Hebrew." I am unable to say whether or not the trident used as a charm by Chinese seamen points to some tradition of a trinity.

Representations of the Yin and Yan, or male and female principle, are placed above the entrance doors of dwelling-houses with the view of averting calamities. Occasionally, however, small circular looking-glasses, around the frame of which are carved mystic emblems of the Pat-kwa, are used instead of them. Charms of this nature are used by the Chinese, especially when they are at all apprehensive that the houses immediately in front of those in which they reside have not been built in strict conformity with the rules of geomancy. Many instances came under my notice. In the Honam suburb of Canton, there is a stately mansion, the owner of which is named Eng. Near it is a lofty pawnshop, or tower, by which the mansion is overlooked. As the pawn-shop had not been built according to the principles of geomancy it was regarded as a never-ending source of sickness to the family of Eng, and the father was most anxious to purchase it, in order to raze it to the ground. The proprietors, however. naturally refused to sell so valuable a property, and Eng was obliged to place before the various doors of his house repre-sentations of the Yin and the Yan.

In the chapter on Festivals, I have described the custom of placing portraits of two Chinese generals upon the outer doors of dwelling-houses. Sometimes portraits of Tung Weng and Chat Chae are substituted for them. Chinese records tell us that Tung Weng was an inhabitant of a planet, and that he was renowned not only for handsome features, but for great virtues. Chat Chae, or the seventh sister, was the inhabitant of the seventh of the seven stars. Their history is, briefly, that of a happy marriage, and for ages past the Chinese have placed portraits of these two fabulous personages over the doors of their houses with the view of being protected from evil, and blessed with male offspring. The practice of placing portraits either of San Too and Wat Looee, or of Tung Weng and Chat Chae on the entrance door of houses, prevails from Canton to Inner Mongolia.

One other custom may be described, although it can hardly be called a superstitious one, which prevails amongst the Chinese. It is that of suspending either from the inner walls of their houses, or from rafters which support the vaulted roofs, boards with good moral words or sentences written on them. In many instances, these are quotations from the writings of Confucius or Mencius, like the following :—" Cleanse your hearts ;" " Turn from impurity ;" " Ensure paths of virtue ;" " Do to others as you would have others do to you." The characters of " Happiness," " Wealth," " Longevity," &c., are frequently so exhibited. In the residence of a Chinese gentleman named Lee, I saw a scroll on the wall with an exhortation to youth. Such sentences remind one very much of the Mezuzoth which the Israelites were accustomed to place not only on the outer doors of the dwelling-houses, but on those of the various apartments.

In concluding this chapter, I may remark that it is very singular that the Chinese, who for ages past have been a most exclusive people, cut off from all intercourse with other nations, not only by their Great Wall and vast deserts, but by their ponderous and difficult language, and jealous laws, should, in the use of charms and spells, present so many points of striking resemblance not only to other Asiatic nations,[1] but to those in the north of Africa, and to the nations in the east of Europe, with whose literature, laws, manners, and customs we have so long been familiar.

---

[1] The observance of such practices by the Jews from the very earliest ages is, I apprehend, clearly implied in the endeavour which Moses made to turn such charms to a becoming purpose by commanding that sentences taken from the law of God should be used instead. See Exodus xiii. 9-16 ; also, Deut. vi. 8 ; and xi. 10.

CHAPTER XVIII.

BENEVOLENT INSTITUTIONS AND BEGGARS.

IN China, as in more civilized lands, there are benevolent institutions. It cannot be said, however, that in China they originate, as in Christian countries, in the pious feeling of willing sacrifice. They are rather works of merit wrought to ensure the favour of the gods than the free-will offerings of grateful hearts. Gentlemen of fortune sometimes spend very large sums in benevolent schemes, in the hope of receiving titles and honours from the Emperor. In 1872, a well-known banker, named Hu Kwang-yung, contributed very large sums in aid of the sufferers from the floods which took place at Tientsin. The Emperor accordingly conferred on him the title and rank of a provincial treasurer, and raised his parents to the first grade. Hu Kwang-yung then gave a further donation of 10,000,000 cash, and it was at once suggested that the rare and signal honour of an imperial tablet or scroll ought to be bestowed upon him. The truth is that, as a rule, the Chinese have little or no sympathy with persons born in or reduced to a state of beggary, or with those afflicted with blindness or any other bodily or mental infirmity. They regard them as suffering for grievous sins committed against the gods, either in their present or in a former state of existence. On a visit to a monastery in the White Cloud Mountains I found a monk who was suffering much from a loathsome disease. He applied to me for medical aid, and his condition excited my warmest sympathy. I urged him to return with me to Canton, so that I might place him under

CHAP. XVIII.]   ANTI-BENEVOLENT PREJUDICES.   47

the care of Dr. Kerr of the Medical Missionary Hospital. On hearing of my intentions, the Abbot took me aside and begged of me not to show any kindness to a man who had doubtless been guilty in a former state of existence of some very heinous sin, for which the gods were then making him pay the well-merited penalty. In the same way death under exceptional and startling circumstances is regarded as a special judgment of the gods. During a storm which swept with great violence over Canton and the surrounding country on the 27th of July, 1862, the house in which an American missionary resided was blown down. This gentleman unfortunately perished in the ruins. His body was eventually extricated from the mass of bricks and beams, and, when it was being conveyed to the cemetery, it was a common remark among the Chinese who stood at the doors of their houses watching the funeral procession, that the violent death of the deceased was due to the disrespectful way in which he had spoken of one of the principal idols of the city in a sermon on the preceding Sabbath. During a thunderstorm which visited Canton on the 27th of May, 1864, a Chinese boatman was killed by lightning, whilst in the act of crossing the river with his wife and children. The boat was damaged and in a sinking condition, and the survivors seeing their danger clung to a large tea-junk. They were at once driven off by the crew, who became much infuriated, positively refusing assistance to a family the head of which they supposed had been so impious as to deserve the condign punishment of the gods. But for timely aid from three American gentlemen who were on the river at the time, the poor woman and her children would have been drowned. Clearly the Chinese do not hold the views of Minutius Felix, who, in his defence of Christianity, observes—"Fulmina passim cadunt; sine delectu tangunt loca sacra et profana; homines noxios feriunt, sæpe et religiosos." [1]

In Canton, as in other cities of importance, there are Asylums for the aged and infirm of both sexes, for the blind, for foundlings, and for lepers. These buildings are all constructed upon the same plan, and consist of large quadrangles with streets or

---

[1] "Thunderbolts fall indifferently; they light upon places profane and sacred without choice; they strike good men and bad alike."

rows of cells for the inmates on each side. The management is in all respects vastly inferior to that of similar institutions in Europe. Indeed, there appears to be no management at all, and the filth and discomfort which everywhere meet the eye lead a foreign visitor to think that the inmates are not much benefited by their admission. These institutions are supported in some instances by a tax imposed upon the salt-merchants, and in others by funds derived from lands and houses. The asylum for aged men at Canton draws its revenues from the former source. The allowance, however, which is set aside for the maintenance of the aged hospitallers, four hundred in number, is so small that occasional appeals have to be made to wealthy residents of the city and neighbourhood. Many of the inmates are very old men, some being upwards of seventy and others upwards of eighty years of age.[1] In the centre of the principal quadrangle is a temple in honour of the god Kwan-te, who is supposed to protect the inmates. In the same quadrangle is the house of the physician whose duty is to prescribe for the sick.

The government of China has another method of prescribing for the wants of aged men. The salt trade being a monopoly, no one is allowed to deal in salt without a licence from the salt commissioner. The government, however, allows a certain number of aged men in each district to do so without a licence— which enables them to undersell the licensed dealers. These poor men traverse the streets crying " Salt for sale! Salt for sale!" and seldom fail to obtain a livelihood for themselves and families. The Asylum for Aged Women is a counterpart of the institution which I have already described. The temple with which it is provided is in honour of Koon-Yam, the goddess of mercy, who exercises a watchful care over women and children.

The inmates of the Blind Asylum at Canton are apparently not

---

[1] Aged men in China not unfrequently carry in each hand a very small piece of wood which they constantly compress against the palm. This is done to promote the circulation. The custom prevails, however, to a much greater extent in the north than in the south, where instead of pieces of wood I have seen walnuts used.

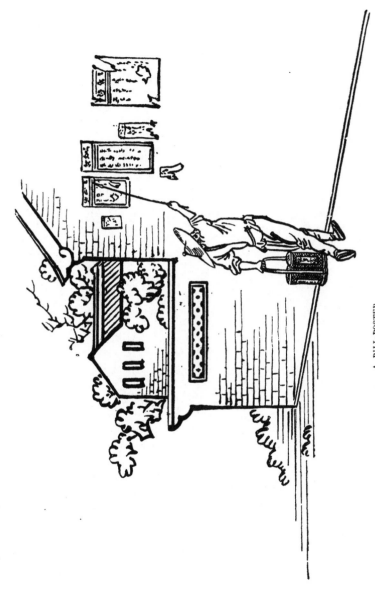

A BILL-POSTER.

so well provided for as the inmates of the two other establishments. Their rooms are in a more dilapidated condition, and the
portion of the tax derived from the salt trade for their maintenance is so small that they are compelled to beg from door to door.
These blind creatures generally sally forth every morning on a
begging expedition in companies of six or seven. They walk in
single file, each resting his right hand on the shoulder of the
person in front of him. The leader of the file gropes his way with
his stick. When they enter a shop they commence beating
the small gongs which they carry, and sing a variety of songs
pitched in a very high key. The din is more than any European
shopkeeper could endure; but noise makes no impression upon
Chinese shopkeepers, who have been born and brought up in
the midst of it. They are obliged to minister to the necessities
of the blind men, and they find it their best policy to allow
them to remain waiting in the shop as long as possible.
Only one company can occupy the shop at a time, and
the longer it stays the less opportunity there is for others
making new demands. If the shopkeeper turns a deaf ear to
the noise of the intruders, they increase their din, and inter-
sperse their songs with remarks not at all complimentary. His
benevolence seldom exceeds a copper cash—the smallest coin of
the realm—or a handful of unboiled rice. At the close of the
day these poor blind men may be seen wending their way back
to the asylum with their wallets over their shoulders, scantily
filled with the proceeds of the day's begging. Despite their
poverty and blindness, beggars of this class contract marriages
amongst themselves. All the husbands and wives whom I saw
in the asylum were blind, and I remember once seeing the
arrival of a blind bride. She was borne to the asylum in a
richly-ornamented bridal-chair, preceded by musicians and men
in red tunics carrying banners and lanterns. When the young
woman alighted she was formally received by the bridegroom.
In the asylum there is a temple in honour of the tutelary deity
of the blind.

The Foundling Hospital at Canton has accommodation for
five hundred foundlings, and, like the other benevolent institutions, is supported out of the salt-tax. In its arrangement

the building is very similar to those already described. The rooms, which are small, are furnished with beds for the nurses, and with cradles made of rattan for the infants. The cradles are suspended from the beams by cords, to protect them from the rats, which are excessively numerous in all Chinese dwellings. One rule of the institution prescribes a wet-nurse for two infants. I have, however, in my numerous visits, not unfrequently seen nurses burdened with three infants each. The cries which always assailed my ears as I entered convinced me that the children received little or no nourishment. The many deaths which take place among them afford the most incontestable proof of the fact. I have more than once seen five or six dead infants huddled together in the corner of a room. On entering the gates at an early hour it is not unusual to see a coolie hastening on his way to the cemeteries in the immediate neighbourhood, with a basket containing dead infants on his shoulder. As a rule the foundlings are female children. When they have reached the age of eight or ten months they are sold. The purchasers are supposed to be childless married people, or to be anxious for female children to bring up as wives for their sons. This plan is not unfrequent among the peasantry of various districts in the southern provinces. Those who come for the ostensible purpose of obtaining by purchase children for adoption, often intend to sell them when they have reached the years of puberty as slaves, or for baser purposes. The hospital is provided with a temple, in which stands an idol of Kum-Fa.

Though they are greatly mismanaged, the foundling hospitals have a tendency to check the crime of infanticide. In parts of the empire where there are none, and even in those where they do exist, this crime prevails, I fear, to a large extent. In the mountainous districts of Loong-moon, Kah-hing Chow, and Chan-ning, in the province of Kwang-tung, it is usual for women in the humble ranks of life who give birth to female children to sell them to their neighbours, to be brought up as future wives for their sons. When, however, female infants are not in demand for such purposes, they are wilfully put to death, if not by their unnatural mothers, yet at their instigation. Nor is this diabolical practice altogether confined to the lower classes. It is sometimes resorted to in the homes of the opulent. When travelling in December, 1864, in the district of Loong-moon, a young gentleman, the son of one of the principal landed proprietors of the district with whom I had been staying, accompanied me at his father's request—for the natives were very ready to insult Europeans—and entered freely into conversation with me respecting his relatives and friends. He told me that three sons and four daughters had been born to his brother, but that of the daughters only one was living, three having been wilfully put to death at their birth. I pointed out to him the dreadful crime which his brother and sister-in-law had committed; but he replied, with much apparent indifference, that what was regarded as a crime in western countries was not considered as such in China. In the autumn of 1863 there was, I believe, a great scarcity of females in this district, in consequence of the prevalence of infanticide. I met three persons at Canton who had come from there for the sole purpose of buying women to re-sell on their return to people in want of wives.

In the southern provinces, more especially in Kwang-tung, lepers are very numerous. There is an asylum for them at Canton, two miles from the gate of the city. It is embosomed in a grove of banyan-trees, and contains accommodation for 400 or 500 inmates. The cause of the disease appears to be unknown. The Chinese think that it is due in some instances to people having sheltered themselves during showers of rain under trees called by them Chee-king-fa. They allege that the rain-water dropping from the leaves of this tree upon the exposed parts of the body causes leprous eruptions. The face and ears, as well as the hands and feet of a sufferer, become enlarged, smooth and glossy. Running sores afterwards make their appearance, and often increase to such a degree as to cause the afflicted parts to drop off by sloughing. Lepers contract marriages amongst themselves, and families are the result of such unions. There is no known cure for this disease; but though Chinese physicians fail to cure, all outward symptoms of it sometimes disappear, and it does not seem to shorten life. The inmates of the asylum at Canton occupy their time in making rope of cocoa-nut fibre. Female

patients from whose bodies all outward symptoms have disappeared are allowed to retail their wares at the famous rope-
market held daily in the Cham-mook-lan street. Lepers of
hideous aspect, from the same asylum, repair every morning to
the adjacent cemeteries, awaiting the arrivals of funerals to exact
money from the mourners. Their demands are invariably complied with, as the mourners believe that the souls of their
departed relatives would be persecuted by spirits of departed
lepers were alms refused. Fees for lepers are always included
in the calculation of funeral expenses at Canton. The demands
made are sometimes so exorbitant that the mourners refuse to
yield to them; and to extort them, the lepers not unfrequently
leap into the grave, and resist all the attempts of the under-
takers to lower the coffin. Should the mourners not have the
sum required at hand, promises of payment are made and accepted.
When they are not redeemed, the lepers exhume the bodies, and
hold them until ransomed. The sum of money demanded is
in proportion to the rank and dignity of the deceased, the lepers
estimating it by the display on the occasion. They are, however,
sometimes deceived in this respect, as the following anecdote
will show: In the spring of 1862, I was present at the funeral
of a Chinese merchant called Lo Poon-qua. The procession
consisted of several gilded pavilions, under which various offerings
were arranged. As is usual at the funeral of a Chinese gentleman, there were also in attendance two or three bands of
mus cians. So soon, however, as the cavalcade reached the open
country near the cemetery, it was halted, and the coffin was
denuded of a richly embroidered pall. It was then borne to the
grave accompanied only by the mourners. Seeing the funeral
procession without the usual accompaniments, the lepers were
reasonable in their demands, and for once, at all events, were
hoodwinked.

As the asylum at Canton is not large enough for the numerous
lepers who seek admission, several anchorages are set apart on
the river for boats in which they are accommodated. The
support of these sufferers depends in a great measure upon their
relatives and friends; but the help they receive is so inadequate
that they are under the necessity of paddling about the river,

asking alms from the crews of the junks and boats with which
the river is crowded. The leper-boats generally go in fleets of
ten or twenty each, and money is almost forced from the sailors.
Not unfrequently the lepers eke out their scanty subsistence by
stripping the dead bodies which are too often found floating on
the river. Should the corpse be that of a person in respectable
circumstances, they often advertise it, in the hope of obtaining
a reward. In September, 1869, I saw a corpse floating past my
residence on the banks of the river. Seeing that it was that of
a person who had been in comfortable circumstances, several
lepers started in eager pursuit. The body was advertised, and
it was found to be that of a young man named Lum A-chung,
the son of a well-to-do butcher. The youth had lost a large
sum of money in a gambling-house, and, being afraid to confront
his father, he had flung himself in a moment of rashness into
the river.

Near Fat-shan, a town fifteen miles from Canton, I entered an
old fort which had been converted some years before into a refuge
for lepers. At the time of my visit it afforded shelter to seventy
of them. At Wing-shing-sha, a portion of the town of Fat-shan,
I found an asylum for lepers which contained no fewer than two
hundred males. It had been founded by a benevolent man of the
clan Yhu, who more than two centuries before had lived and died
in a neighbouring village named Lu-kong. The right of patronage
to this asylum was invested in the elders of this village. The
inmates were engaged in making ropes of cocoa-nut fibre.
Observing how anxious I was to gather information as to the
nature of the disease, and the provisions made for those who
suffer from its effects, they told me of another asylum at a
village named Chong-poo-hom, some five miles distant. I visited
this, and found its inmates living in comparative comfort. They
did not appear to be suffering so much from the disease as the
lepers I had already seen. One woman, however, presented a
very ghastly spectacle, the disease having spread over her whole
body. In the silk districts of Kwang-tung lepers are very
numerous. At almost every town, and on almost every creek
and river, I found anchorages for leper-boats. So far as I could
ascertain there were no asylums in the towns themselves. The

disease in this district was apparently of a virulent character, and the sufferers presented a very painful appearance. Each leper, for it appeared there was but one in each boat, was provided with a long bamboo rod, at the end of which was a bag, which was duly presented for alms as ships passed and re-passed. The sums given were very small, but the bags were never presented in vain. On a voyage which I subsequently made along the western bank of the Canton River to the province of Kwang-si, I found a leper residing in almost every one of the small shrines erected at intervals on the banks, in honour of the Dragon's Mother. Each leper, as on the creeks and rivers of the silk districts, was provided with a rod and alms-bag. They reminded me very much of hermits, and appeared to hold no intercourse with their fellow-men, or with each other. The law forbids lepers to associate with those who are free from the disease, and enjoins them to seek a refuge in the asylums provided for their reception. When there are no asylums in the neighbourhood, or if the asylums are over-crowded, they are sent on board boats, or made to reside in mat sheds or huts erected for them in lonely parts of the country. In the autumn of 1865, I saw two lepers living in such sheds beyond the walls of Nan-kan Foo. There are lepers also living in mat sheds near the eastern gate of Canton, and in various parts of the province. In 1864, I was told of a youth of respectable parentage who on becoming leprous was taken by his father to the banks of the Canton River, and put into a covered sampan or boat, which he was told to regard as his future home. Men of wealth, however, when afflicted with this disease, not unfrequently try to evade the law by shutting themselves up in the most secluded chamber of their large mansions. This evasion of the law is not countenanced by the neighbours, who entertain a great dread of the disease, and consider it to be a mark of the disfavour of the gods. They never hesitate to report the case to the authorities; and there is, I believe, a statute in the penal code, that if a leprous person of rank is killed when his neighbours attempt to remove him to an asylum by force, the person who kills him is exempt not only from punishment, but from censure. In the northern provinces, there were no cases of leprosy, so far as I could ascertain; and, in the central provinces, although the disease is by no means unknown, the cases do not seem to be numerous.

In China there are no lunatic asylums. Violent lunatics are kept manacled in dark, inner rooms in their own houses. Where the family is poor, the want of asylums entails great hardship. I have seen a lunatic lying by the side of the highway bound hand and foot, without a creature near him to render him the slightest assistance. When at large he had manifested violence, and his unfeeling countrymen, instead of conveying him where he might be securely kept, bound him hand and foot, and left him lying by the wayside. On another occasion, I saw a female lunatic traversing the streets of Canton in a state of nudity. The poor woman was being pursued by a number of lads, who were beating her unmercifully with rods. On being expostulated with by some Europeans, they coolly replied that she was possessed of a devil, and well deserved her treatment. The unfortunate creature took shelter in the ruins of a Danish factory, which had been destroyed at the commencement of the war in 1856. After remaining there for some days she was removed, at the expense of three or four European merchants, to a place of comfort and security. Lunatics who are not violent, are allowed to go at large. There appear, however, to be very few of these; and idiocy is very rare in China. I have only seen four harmless lunatics—all women.

There are no workhouses in the empire. There are institutions, however, in which, during the winter season at all events, beggars can obtain food and lodging. At Pekin there is a large refuge of this sort, capable of receiving a thousand mendicants. It is supported by the Emperor, but, like all such institutions in China, it affords unmistakable signs of general mismanagement and decay. When at Shanghai, in the winter of 1875, I observed a notification issued by Yeng, the *toutai*, setting forth that certain houses had been set apart for the reception of homeless wanderers. The vagrants frequenting these houses were, I found, provided with bundles of rice straw, on which they slept, and, twice daily, small quantities of boiled rice were doled out to each inmate. This refuge, I believe, owed

its origin, not to any feelings of benevolence of the *toutai,* or of
the government which he represented, but to a well-grounded
fear that burglaries and other serious offences might become
rife, unless the numerous wanderers traversing the streets of
Shanghai were provided with a home. The notification stated
that those who did not avail themselves of the refuge would be
regarded as bad characters, apprehended, and punished severely.
At Nanking and Eching, cities on the banks of the Yang-tsze, I
saw, during a severe winter, from five to six hundred people, on
one occasion, having boiled rice doled out to them by the government officials. At the latter city a large shed had been erected,
but it was a wretched hovel. At Yang-chow, also on the banks
of the Yang-tsze, I witnessed a distribution of wearing apparel.
The recipients belonged to poor families, and the clothing
was the gift of wealthy residents. The distribution took
place in the courtyard of a large Buddhist temple, and was of
course regarded as a work of merit. It is usual in some parts
of the empire for the members of wealthy clans or families to
administer to the wants of poor members, by allowing them to
receive small sums of money out of the rents accruing from the
tenements or lands by which the ancestral altars are endowed.
This plan undoubtedly helps to keep down the number of
beggars. These sums are doled out twice annually, in spring
and autumn, the seasons in which the Chinese worship at the
tombs of their ancestors. It is the duty of mandarins to provide
accommodation and food at the expense of the imperial treasury,
for persons who have been driven from their homes by bands of
rebels or of robbers. This duty, however, is not, as a rule, faithfully discharged by the officials. Where relief is granted, these
men make the people contribute for the purpose, either because
the imperial coffers do not contain sufficient supplies, or because
they are afraid to let the government at Pekin know that their
districts or provinces are in such anarchy and confusion. In
1860, no fewer than 2,000 persons came to Canton in a state
of perfect destitution. They had been driven from their homes
by the red-headed robbers, so called from the red turbans which
they were accustomed to wear. The mandarins ordered a large
mat shed to be erected on the island of Honam for the accom-

modation of the sufferers. The expense of building this and of supplying them with food, fell upon the Howqua and other wealthy families of the city and the neighbourhood. The contributions of these rich families were so scanty, that the fund would have been speedily exhausted, but for the timely assistance rendered by the resident European merchants, and by those of the adjacent port of Hong-kong.

Sometimes wealthy Chinese contribute largely to these funds, not out of real sympathy with the sufferers, but in the expectation of receiving honours from government. Men who have obtained the first degree at the literary examinations, and who find they cannot by their own abilities take a higher degree, usually seek it in this way from government. Government officials have the management of these eleemosynary funds, and their rapacity not unfrequently tempts them to appropriate portions of them. I am disposed to believe that this was the case with the funds contributed for the support of the poor sufferers whom the attacks of the rebels had driven to take refuge in Canton; and the streets were crowded with these poor creatures, begging from door to door. Many became seriously ill from extreme destitution. An additional mat shed was erected for them, and on being removed to it they were apparently left to die. I shall never forget my feelings on visiting this hospital, if I may so term it. Four women lay stretched on the floor evidently in a dying condition, and without an attendant to render them the slightest service. Two were in a state of nudity, having been robbed, I suppose, in their weakness.

In all walled cities, as well as in many towns and villages, there are imperial granaries, in which rice is supposed to be stored by the government, so that it may be retailed at a reduced price in time of war or famine to the soldiers of the garrison and the poor. These institutions owe their origin, not so much to benevolent feelings as to those of self-preservation. Mandarins are well aware that few things are more dangerous to the peace of the state than a half-starved population. In the towns also there are similar institutions, supported by the wealthy. Although the mandarins are aware of the importance of being able to administer cheap food to the people in seasons of war

or famine, they are very apathetic, and allow their granaries to
remain empty. I have visited very many public granaries, and
have seldom, if ever, found one containing more than a measure
of rice. I found many in a ruinous condition. This was particularly the case with the government granaries of Tai-wan
Foo, in Formosa, not more than two or three chambers of which
were left standing, and these were gradually falling into decay.
On the walls of one of them, I observed some English characters
written with a lead pencil in a very legible hand. It was the
record which the shipwrecked crew of an English brig—the
Ann—had left of their imprisonment here in 1842, when
England was at war with China. They had been heavily
ironed; and had been confined in the granary, because the
prefectoral prison was crowded by the shipwrecked crew, 120
in all, of H.M.'s transport *Nerebuddha*.

In small towns and villages, the granaries are generally
erected by the elders or gentry. As a rule, the rice is not
sold in seasons of famine, but doled out gratuitously. Like
the others, these granaries are erected to prevent uprisings
from a starving population. Villagers, oppressed either by the
gods or men, are very ready to band themselves together as
pirates or highwaymen to obtain the common necessaries of life.
In cities, a few of the wealthy residents sometimes place vases
filled with cold tea at their doors during the summer months,
for the refreshment of wayfarers, and in winter they provide
ginger soup, with the same benevolent intention. During the
hot months of summer, other gentlemen distribute fans to the
poor. These are bought in large numbers for this purpose,
some gentlemen buying three hundred and others as many as
one thousand. Not a few purchase medicine for gratuitous
distribution. Soup-kitchens and clothing-clubs also exist, but
on a very limited scale. Another form which benevolence takes
is the purchase of coffins for paupers. A person is held in high
esteem who makes a gift of coffins, or of money to purchase them,
at a temple where he has been worshipping. Judging from the
number of coffins which I saw, in 1865, in a Buddhist temple at
Shanghai, this form of benevolence must be very popular with
the native gentry. These charitable acts are considered highly

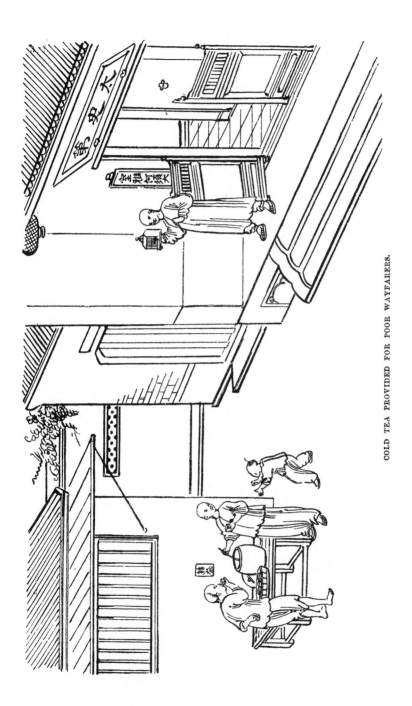

COLD TEA PROVIDED FOR POOR WAYFARERS.

meritorious, and are supposed to commend those who perform them to the favour of the gods, and especially to the providential care of Buddha.

In the absence of workhouses, the beggars form themselves into societies or guilds, which are presided over by presidents called by the community generally, Ti-Quat, a term of reproach for which the beggars themselves substitute a title of honour. The guilds are under the superintendence of a magistrate named Poo-Teng, by whom the presidents are protected. The beggars are sworn to pay due respect to the rules of their societies, and the entrance fee for each member is upwards of four dollars. On the demise of a member, a coffin valued at two dollars is given for his decent interment, and it is the duty of the other members to accompany his remains from the house of mourning to the grave. In the third month of the year, all beggars worship at the tombs of their brotherhood, and afterwards dine together. They dine together also on the 25th day of the 9th month in a tavern. They have a house in which members are permitted to sleep on payment of one cash per night. At the celebration of the New Year, and other principal festivals, and on the occasions of marriages, natal anniversaries, and funeral rites, it is usual for the chiefs of these fraternities to demand alms. Should the family be a leading one, eight beggars are admitted into the porch to dine. A family of secondary rank dines six beggars. Third-rate families give food to four. Sometimes money is given instead of food, in which cases the amount is limited to four dollars. These donations are deposited in a common purse and eventually divided, each mendicant receiving a sum in accordance with his standing in the guild. In acknowledgment of the alms, the chiefs of the fraternities give householders a red card bearing the stamp of their respective guilds. A householder receiving it places such a document above the entrance door of his house as a protection against the importunity of the chiefs of other guilds; and it is a rule strictly observed by the mendicants, that householders who have already given alms shall be exempt from further intrusion during the remaining days of the festival on which the demands were made. As festivals are very numerous, and extend over several days, the begging communities do not fare amiss. The proprietors of establishments where marriage chairs or funeral biers are kept for hire are not unfrequently the heads of these communities. They are thus able to hire the able-bodied members of their guilds at a reduced rate, to carry the chairs, pavilions, banners, and other insignia of processions. Watchmen in charge of the streets of cities are also usually the heads of guilds. This circumstance is owing to the fact that tradesmen consider such persons to be in a position to quell the disturbances which mendicants are sometimes disposed to create. The power of the head of a guild is very great, and never seems to be questioned by his ragged subordinates. In 1853, a friend and myself were accosted by three or four beggars whilst we were walking round the walls of Canton. So determined were they not to be baulked, that they attempted to put their hands into our pockets in search of money. Seeing a watchman at hand we begged of him to protect us from annoyance. He seized the foremost offender, stretched him on the ground, and flogged him severely with a bamboo. The beggar received his punishment without a murmur, his castigator being, as I afterwards learned, the head of his clan.

Twice annually, in spring and autumn, the beggars of Canton are entertained at dinner in one of the public halls of the city by the wealthy shopkeepers. These entertainments are given by the tradesmen on condition that the beggars of the guilds will come to them for alms not daily, but on certain specified occasions. At the hour appointed for the banquet the aged, the blind, the withered, and the maimed wend their way towards the hostelry. Charity of this sort is of very great antiquity. In the gospel of St. Luke we find that our Lord called upon persons of rank and opulence to observe it : " When thou makest a dinner or a supper, call not thy friends, nor thy brethren, neither thy kinsmen, nor thy rich neighbours ; lest they also bid thee again, and a recompence be made thee. But when thou makest a feast, call the poor, the maimed, the lame, the blind : and thou shalt be blessed ; for they cannot recompense thee : for thou shalt be recompensed at the resurrection of the just." On the 3rd November, 1866, I had an opportunity afforded me of being present at a banquet of this nature. It took place at the Tchaong-Heng tavern in the Tsing-tsze-fong street of the western suburb. When I entered the first dining-hall the beggars were called upon by one of their leaders to rise as a mark of respect. They continued standing until they were told to resume their seats. I was then escorted to an upper room in which were a few tables only. My companions at table were the elders of the guild or society of beggars, theirs being the privilege of "sitting in the uppermost rooms at feasts."

These guilds exist in almost every province. In the city of Foo-chow in the province of Fo-kien, there are several very large societies of this nature; and, at a temple embosomed amidst trees of thick and beautiful foliage, the vagrants may be seen each day devouring the broken meats or rice which have been given to them. One peculiar occupation of the beggars at Foo-chow is the rearing of snakes. These are sold, I believe, to the doctors, by whom they are boiled down and used for medicinal purposes.

Besides those who belong to guilds, hordes of beggars of both sexes infest the streets of Chinese towns. These unfortunate creatures are of all ages, and as they are houseless, they are generally allowed to occupy the squares in front of temples. At Canton many of them resort by night to a square in the western suburb, immediately in front of the temple called Mee-Chow-Miu. It is called The Beggars' Square, and by night it is crowded with poor wretches who have spent the day in traversing the streets in search of alms. I once passed through it at midnight, and I shall never forget the number of ghastly countenances which I saw by the light of the moon, which shone with a brightness seldom or never paralleled in western climes. Beggars, and indeed other persons in indigent circumstances, are brought to this square to die. I have frequently seen the sick and dying stretched upon its hard granite blocks apparently without a friend to administer to their necessities, exposed at one hour to a tropical sun, and at another to heavy rain. Upon inquiring why they were brought here to die, I was informed that for several years past, at the guild of the Fo-kien

merchants, which forms one side of the square, there has been a
fund to provide coffins for all who die there in a destitute and
forlorn condition. It is not by any means unusual to see poor
persons dying at the corners of streets. At Macao, in the summer
of 1857, I saw on my way to church, in the course of a walk of a
quarter of a mile, no fewer than three persons dying at the corners
of streets. The bodies are generally interred at the expense of
wealthy citizens, or of those near whose houses they have died.
The rich, however, do not usually come forward of their own
accord, but are called upon to do so by the *tepos* or constables of
their respective neighbourhoods. There are, I believe, plots of
ground set apart by the government for the interment of such
bodies. The graves are distinct from other Chinese graves,
resembling in form the graves which are to be seen in English
cemeteries. At the head of each the *tepo* places a small board,
upon which is written, not the name of the deceased, but that of
the gentleman at whose expense his body was interred.

The beggars,[1] some of whom are very deformed, resort to
various expedients to induce people to give them alms. I have
seen one bearing on his back a leper so much affected by
the disease that his ears and hands and feet were apparently
sloughing off. With this loathsome burden the beggar threatened
to enter each shop he passed, unless the shopkeeper at once
administered to his wants. Alms were promptly thrown into
the street, and quickly picked up. Others go about carrying
sharp Chinese razors, with which they cut themselves to show
their misery, and to extort alms. I have seen mendicants with
the upper part of their bodies covered with blood. At the
town of Pit-kong in the province of Canton, I saw a beggar
literally bathed in his own blood, which also sprinkled over the
floor of the shop in which he was trying to melt the apparently
obdurate heart of the shopkeeper. I have also seen beggars
knocking their heads against the walls of shops, and others
beating their bodies with large stones. At Han-kow, in

---

[1] The beggars of Pekin, Nankin, and Chinkiang are remarkable for their
servility, and kneel, not only before their own countrymen, but before foreigners,
in order to obtain alms. This is a step to which the meanest beggar in Canton
would not resort.

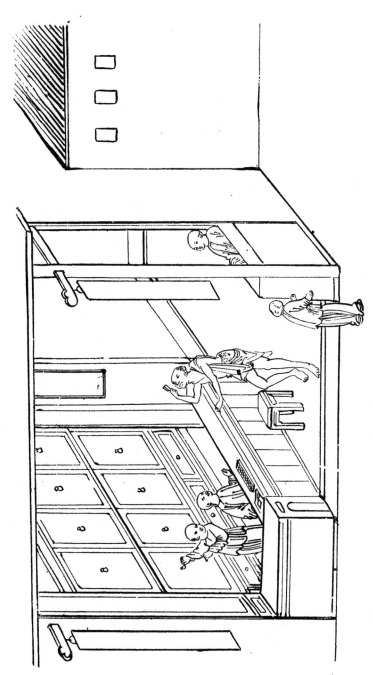

A CHINESE BEGGAR CUTTING HIMSELF TO EXCITE COMPASSION.

the province of Hoopeh, some of them were provided with
two sticks, with which they belaboured themselves about the
head in the most unsparing manner. Others were provided
with long tobacco-pipes made of copper, which they offered to
each passer-by, in order that he might take a whiff or two if he
chose. They received three cash from the smoker. Occasionally a beggar, apparently so emaciated as to be in a dying
state, may be seen to throw himself down on the threshold of
a shop or dwelling-house, declaring that he purposes to remain
there and die. In May, 1864, I saw one apparently perishing
from hunger throw himself down at the doorway of a dwelling-
house, saying that he would die of starvation if he were not
immediately relieved. The householder, who was in a state
of great trepidation, at once offered the starving man a small
sum of money, which was indignantly refused. A friend who
was with me expressed his readiness to relieve the wants of
the sufferer. He held out a half-dollar, and the penurious
householder at once rushed towards him, and eagerly grasped
the coin, which he at once gave to the sufferer. One sometimes
finds beggars on the banks of the various rivers, canals, and
creeks; and I saw several on my voyage along the Grand
Canal. Nieuhoff, in his celebrated work on China, describes a
class of beggars who " knock their heads together like distracted
persons, so that spectators would believe that their brains were
ready to fly out, or themselves to fall down dead on the ground;
for such is their customary manner that they will never cease
beating till they have prevailed with you to bestow something
on them. There is another sort who, instead of knocking their
heads together as aforesaid, strike their foreheads so hard upon
a round stone, four fingers thick, which lies upon the ground,
that it makes the earth seem to redound with the blows; by
means whereof many have contracted such swellings upon their
foreheads that they can never be cured of them. . . . . There
is also another sort of beggars here who set fire to a combustible
kind of stuff upon their heads, which they suffer to burn there
with such excessive pain and torment till they have extorted
some charity from the transient company, howling and enduring
very great misery all the while."

CHAPTER XIX.

HOTELS, INNS, AND RESTAURANTS.

RESTAURANTS, hotels, tea-saloons, and soup-stalls are everywhere numerous throughout the empire. The restaurants are generally very large establishments, consisting of a public dining-room and several private rooms. Unlike most other buildings, they consist of two or three stories. The kitchen alone occupies the ground floor; the public hall, which is the resort of persons in the humbler walks of life, is on the first floor, and the more select apartments are on the second and third floors. These are, of course, resorted to by the wealthier citizens, but they are open to persons in all classes of society, and it is not unusual to see in them persons of limited means. At the entrance-door there is a table or counter at which the proprietor sits, and where each customer on leaving pays for his repast. The public room is immediately at the head of the first staircase, and is resorted to by all who require a cheap meal. It is furnished, like a *café*, with tables and chairs, a private room having only one table and a few chairs in it. On the wells of all the apartments are placards, by which the guests are admonished not to lose sight of their umbrellas, fans, articles of wearing apparel, &c.; and assured that the proprietor does not hold himself responsible in case of loss. A bill of fare is also placed in each room. It probably includes, among other dishes, bird's-nest soup, sharks' fins, and *bêche de mer*. A waiter places it in the hands of the visitor on his entering the establishment, and when he has made his selection the dishes are promptly served. The dinner may consist of ten or twenty small dishes. At a large dinner-party more than a hundred dishes are sometimes placed on the table. The feast is begun by the host or principal person of the party pouring out a libation—a ceremony which is in truth a form of grace before meals. The wine-cups are then filled and the guests, bowing politely to one another, proceed to drink The custom of beginning a feast with wine was practised by the ancient Persians, so that the term " a banquet of wine " was applied by them to such entertainments. The first course consists of fruit, such as oranges, nuts, and almonds. This is followed by various kinds of soups and stews, which with their inseparable concomitants are savoury to a degree. Between each course the waiters, who in the heat of summer divest themselves of the greater portion of their clothing, supply the guests with pipes of tobacco. When the guests have taken a few whiffs, they find the next course awaiting their attention. There are various wines : in this country they would be called spirituous liquors. The strongest, which is a decoction of rice, is called suee-chow. Others are made from plums, apples, pears, litchis, and roses. The custom of taking wine with each other is strictly observed by the guests; and it is not unusual for a gentleman to show politeness by using his chopsticks to place a portion of food from his own plate into the mouth of his neighbour. The table is without a cloth, and by the side of each guest there is placed a piece of coarse brown paper, which he uses between the courses to wipe his chopsticks and his lips. As oil is lavishly used in Chinese cookery, the process is by no means merely formal. The fowls, ducks, joints, &c., are all carved and cut into small pieces down stairs, and served stewed, an arrangement rendered necessary by the all-prevailing use of spoons and chopsticks. This mode of cooking is regarded with favour by the inhabitants of almost all Eastern nations.

During the last course it is not unusual for guests to indulge in a bacchanalian game of chance called Chi-Moee. The game, which is accompanied by much boisterous mirth, is played between two. A guest holding up his hand suddenly shows so many fingers extended, and his antagonist must simultaneously guess their number. Should the latter guess wrong, he must drink a cup of wine. This game is as old as the Pyramids, and travellers state that in the paintings at Thebes, and in the temples of Beni Hassan, seated figures are represented in the act of playing it. From Egypt it was introduced into Greece. The Romans brought it from Greece at an early period, and it has existed among them ever since, apparently without alteration.

When dinner is ended the waiters again appear, bearing towels, which I purposely refrain from calling clean, and copper or brazen basins filled to the brim with hot water, so that the guests may wash their hands and faces. Dipping it into the hot water and then wringing it, the waiter presents a napkin to one of the guests. When it has been used by him, it is again dipped into the basin and presented to the next. The custom of servants going at the close of a banquet from guest to guest with water for this purpose, is very old in the East; and we read in the second book of Kings (iii. 11) that Elisha the son of Shaphat rendered such a service to his master Elijah.

Besides the restaurants there are numerous soup-stalls in the principal streets and squares of Chinese cities. At these stalls soups and patties of various kinds are to be had for a small sum of money, and on the benches round them men may be seen enjoying a good and cheap meal. There are also other restaurants which may be termed pork eating-houses, and which are resorted to by gentlemen. The arrangements in them are the same as those I have already described.

The hotels in China are distinguished, as in Europe, by names or signs. Thus, in Canton, there are such names as the Cum-Lee, or Golden Profits; the Cut-Shing, or Rank-conferring Hotel; the Fuk-On, or Happiness and Peace Hotel; and the Cut-Sing, or Fortunate Star. The hotels in this city are generally very lofty buildings; and as usual with shops of a trade, they are to be found in groups. Thus the Lune-heng Kai at Canton is formed by two rows of hotels. On the ground-floor of an hotel there is an apartment for the proprietor, and a large kitchen where three or four cooks and as many scullions are busily employed in preparing meats and washing dishes. The first floor contains one public and several private dining-rooms, and the second floor is occupied by bedrooms. The bedrooms are divided from one another by thin wooden partitions, and a conversation conducted even in a subdued tone can be heard by the occupants of the adjoining chamber. Should your neighbour be loquacious, you need not think of sleeping. Should he be an opium-smoker, as is not unfrequently the case, you are almost stupefied by the spreading fumes of the drug. In travelling in the less civilized portions of the empire, the differences between Chinese and English hotels become amusingly prominent. When passing from Tam-sui to Kilung—both towns in Formosa —I was obliged to sleep at Skek-kow. On arriving at night, I found the principal hotel full. The landlord, however, who had an impression that Englishmen as a rule paid liberally for their entertainment, resolved that I should not pass his door. He entered an apartment which contained three beds, and awoke the sleepers—a task of some difficulty. They were naturally astonished at being roused, and still more at finding two English-men standing in their apartment. What did it mean? Boniface politely explained that he should like them to give up their beds to the two "foreign devils," who had come from a distance and were very tired. Two of the men at once agreed to do so. The third, however, who was an old pedlar, strongly protested against the intrusion. He had for years patronized the hotel; he had never failed to pay his reckoning; and he considered such conduct highly disgraceful. At the rebuke, which was very effectively administered, the landlord at once became his ob-sequious servant. He appeased him by gentle persuasion, he assisted him to put on his clothes, and, *mirabile dictu !*—for it is a service which the arrogant Chinese are seldom disposed to render to one another—he knelt down and helped the old man to put on his shoes. We retired to rest, but not, as it turned out, to sleep. Three or four men in an adjoining chamber began in loud tones to discuss the merits of a street-fight which had taken place that day between some colliers. Loud at first, the discussion soon became warm, and the vehemence of Chinese in an angry discussion is very startling. The noise aroused others, and at last we came to the conclusion that about thirty people must have joined in the dispute. We begged them to be silent ; but our remonstrances were unheeded. At length, about three o'clock in the morning, my friend got up to call the landlord, and, opening the door, stumbled over the body of the prostrate pedlar, who had stretched himself on a shake-down. The landlord was fortunately again able to adjust conflicting interests.

The dinners served up in these hotels are usually different from those one gets at restaurants, and consist of roast pork, roast duck, boiled fowl and rice, or fish and rice. Besides the large hotels, there are in cities and towns smaller hotels called Yin-fong, and in the country wayside inns. The country inns are very humble, and do not afford much comfort. In the northern provinces and Mongolia, the hotels or caravanseras are in all respects more comfortable than those in the southern and central provinces. Each caravansera is erected in the form of a quadrangle, and, as is necessary in the northern latitudes, the walls are built of clay or mud. It consists of one public room, in which the traveller will meet with carriers, drovers, and muleteers ; several private apartments [1]—some of which are very comfortable—for the gentry ; stables for the beasts of burden so much used in northern provinces—mules, donkeys, and horses ; and, attached to the building, a large compound for the flocks of sheep, and herds of cattle and swine, which are driven in large numbers from Mongolia to China. Occasionally the large hotels have a second quadrangle, consisting of stables only. Some of the smaller caravanseras, on the other hand, have no proper stables at all, only a long trough or rack placed in the centre of the quadrangle, to which the beasts of burden are fastened. As these sometimes fight with one another, one never can be sure at such inns of an undisturbed night. The beds in these caravanseras are called cangues, and resemble furnaces in form. The traveller, protected by a thick coverlet, reclines on the top of a stratum of

[1] There is an entire absence of certain conveniences in Mongolian hotels. Expostulating on one occasion with a landlord, I was told that they were not required, as night-soil was not valued in Mongolia to the same extent as in China proper.

chunam or asphalte, below which is an aperture like the door of a furnace. By means of this, fuel is laid below the asphalte, and a fire kindled to warm the sleeper. The hall for the reception of muleteers, waggoners, and poor travellers is a very broad cangue, and it is their common sleeping apartment.[1] The largest hotel which I visited in the course of my travels in the north of China and Mongolia was at Woo-shee-woo, a town or village midway between Tientsin and Pekin. I found it crowded with visitors, most of whom were returning from a pilgrimage to the temple in honour of three goddesses who preside over parturition, blindness, and deafness. The extensive stables were filled almost to suffocation with horses and mules. These hotels are the resort of all classes of travellers.

At the caravansera at which I stayed at Je-hole or Yit-Hoi, I observed on the walls of the rooms which I occupied a placard setting forth that a prince of the blood royal had occupied the same apartments a few weeks previous. When the bill was being settled, the landlord had the audacity to ask for an extra sum, on the ground that he had lodged me in apartments which a short time before had been honoured by the presence of a prince of the blood royal.

In some Mongolian and Chinese cities there are khans which are depots or godowns for the goods of travelling merchants. The merchants lodge and board comfortably at the expense of the proprietor until the goods are sold, when they give him a fair percentage upon their sales. There are several houses of this description in the southern suburbs of Canton.

It is the duty of the proprietors of a hotel to record in a book kept for the purpose the names and addresses of all visitors. These books are submitted monthly to the magistrates of the district. This practice doubtless proves of some service when the peace of the state is disturbed by great political movements. In 1865, one of the principal hotels in the street at Canton, called Lune-heng Kai, was closed by the mandarins because a notorious rebel, for whose apprehension a large reward had been offered, was found to have lodged in it. When travel-

[1] On the walls of every public room of this sort I observed very obscene pictures.

ling in Mongolia in the same year, I was refused admission to one of the principal hotels at Lama-miou until the proprietor had obtained permission from the authorities to receive me; and at Foong-ling-sheang, also in Mongolia, I met with the same cautious treatment. Women are not received in the hotels in the southern cities; but in the northern provinces and in Mongolia, it is usual to meet with Chinese and Mongolian women of all ranks. When a traveller arrives at a hotel he is invited to choose his bedroom; having done so, he receives the key from the proprietor. Should he leave the hotel even for a few minutes, he must lock his door and place the key in the hands of the landlord, who under such circumstances is legally responsible for the property of his guest. The landlord is informed of the nature of the property by the visitor on his arrival. Placards are often posted on the walls of bedrooms, setting forth all such rules and regulations for the information of visitors. Should a traveller die in a hotel, the proprietor must inform the district magistrate, who at once proceeds to the hotel and takes an inventory of the effects of the deceased. The intelligence of the death is then communicated to his relatives, and his effects handed over to them. Should they reside at a considerable distance, twelve months are allowed for a reply. After this period the effects become confiscate to the crown.

In the large cities and towns there are public buildings which are much resorted to by wealthy travellers, and by students in particular who have come to attend literary examinations. Above the entrance-doors of these establishments are signboards with Hak-yu (Traveller's Rest), or Hit-yim (Lodging-house), inscribed on them. These buildings are very much larger than hotels, and differ from them in this respect, that the lodger is obliged to provide himself with a cook and a body-servant, whose duty it is to furnish him with everything he may require without any reference whatever to the proprietor. Such a house consists of so many bed-rooms, and attached to it is a large kitchen furnished with several grates, at which the cooks may be seen preparing meals for their respective masters. Gentlemen often bring their wives and children to such establishments, as they would never do to hotels. The Koong-Koon are establishments of the same kind resorted to by civil and military officers only. In all large cities such as Canton there are many mandarins waiting for office, and it is in such houses that they take up their abode until the time for their assumption of power. The officials whose term of office has expired also take up their quarters at the Koong-Koon, where they generally remain for some time either in anticipation of the arrival of a lucky day for their departure to their homes, or to arrange matters connected with their giving up office.

The guilds, of which each trade in every city has one, may also be regarded as clubs or hotels. Tradesmen or dealers who come to the various marts from a distance, resort to their respective guilds for board and lodging, and at such places it is usual to meet with persons from various parts of the empire. It is astonishing what an amount of information about the Chinese a foreigner may acquire by visiting these institutions, and entering into conversation—by means of an interpreter, if necessary—with the many respectable and intelligent persons who board and lodge at them. The dinners and breakfasts are furnished by shops called Chow-Koon. These are very numerous and easily recognized by the dinner-services and earthenware pots with which the shelves are crowded. Dinners are cooked and sent out from such establishments to the guilds, and occasionally to private houses, on the shortest notice.

Nine times annually, the trades meet at their respective guilds for festive purposes. These days of recreation are generally the second and fifteenth days of the first month; the fifth day of the fifth month, or Dragon Festival, and the thirteenth day of the fifth month, or God of War's natal anniversary; the fourteenth day of the seventh month, or All Souls' Festival; the fifteenth day of the eighth month, or Feast in honour of the moon; the twenty-first day of the eleventh month, or winter solstice; and at the festival of Wan-shan, which is celebrated on a lucky day towards the close of the twelfth month, and which is observed as a day of general thanksgiving to all the gods for the mercies which they have bestowed throughout the year. Each guild has its patron-saint, and his natal anniversary is celebrated by the members, who hold a banquet in honour of the occasion, and spend the day in mirth and jollity.

In the spring of 1864 I had the pleasure of receiving an invitation to dine at the Lacquer-ware Merchants' Guild. I readily accepted, and a very pleasant evening indeed was the result. In many of the guilds, funds are established by the members for the decent interment of their brothers in trade. These burial societies have existed for centuries, and have not, so far as I have been able to learn, proved such enormities of evil as similar societies in England not many years ago.

The guild-halls are amongst the most beautiful of Chinese buildings. The green-tea merchants' guild-hall at Canton is remarkable for its many singularly formed doorways and windows, some of which resemble fruits, leaves, flowers, fans, scrolls, and vases. In the northern and central provinces I found the guild-halls, though not so large as those of Canton, much superior to them in other respects. At Tientsin I visited a magnificent guild-hall, and at Ningpo I saw one still grander. The pillars supporting the roof of the latter are of granite and wood elaborately carved. Dragons of great thickness are represented by the chisel of the sculptor, twined round the granite pillars. Figures of men and temples also stand out in bold relief. The city of Soo-chow, in the province of Chit-kong, was famous amongst other things for its magnificent guild-halls. Many of these, however, were destroyed when it was captured by the rebels in 1860. I visited the ruins of two guild-halls there which belonged to the Shen-si and Shang-tung merchants respectively, and to judge from the gateways which still remained, the buildings must have been handsome.

Tea-saloons are also very numerous in cities and towns. Many are large and neatly fitted up. Each consists of two large saloons furnished with several small tables and stools. Upon each table is placed a tray, containing a large assortment of cakes, preserved fruits, and cups of tea. A cashier seated behind a counter at the door of the saloon, receives the money from the guests as they are leaving the establishment. There is a large kitchen attached to all of them, where cooks remarkable for their cleanliness are daily engaged in making all kinds of pastry.

These tea-saloons are much visited by men of all ranks. Females, however, are not allowed to resort to such places in the southern provinces. At Nankin, Hankow, Woo-chang, and other cities on the banks of the Yang-tsze, and at Hang-chow and Soo-chow, and other cities on the banks of the Grand Canal, I observed elderly females, evidently of the lower orders, in tea-saloons. In the northern provinces, if we are to judge from a proclamation issued on the subject by the *toutai* of Shanghai, it is not regarded as decorous for females to go there. Visitors to such establishments in the southern cities are expected to leave and make room for others as soon as they have finished their repast. In the tea-saloons, however, of the cities of the central provinces it is not unusual for men with no particular duties to spend the whole of the day in gossiping with the various people whom they meet there. To increase their attractions, it is not unusual for the proprietors of tea-saloons to hire vocalists, who keep the company in a state of hilarity during the whole day, either by singing songs or reciting poems. At Nankin on two or three occasions I visited a saloon which was crowded to suffocation by visitors, in consequence of a vocalist who was hired by the proprietor to sing or recite the whole day long. At Hang-chow and other cities on the Grand Canal I observed that the saloons were kept open until ten or eleven o'clock at night, whereas at Canton they are invariably closed at five or six o'clock in the evening. On visiting a tea-saloon at Hang-chow at nine o'clock at night, I found it crowded by respectable citizens, engaged, many of them, in discussing the events of the day. There were several men verging upon seventy years of age, and they appeared to find great pleasure in one another's society. Each had a cup of tea by his side and in his hand a pipe of tobacco. The scene was one which made me feel how very desirable it was to have such institutions open by night. In the cities on the banks of the Yang-tsze and on the Grand Canal it is customary for poor people to buy boiling-water at the tea-saloons for domestic purposes. They can obtain a large kettleful for two cash, and they find it cheaper to buy boiling-water than firewood. The boilers are placed near the doors of the saloons, so that there is no need for the purchasers to enter.

Tea-saloons are generally erected in the most crowded streets
of cities. In the province of Kiangsoo, however, it is apparently
customary to have them in the public temples. At Tan-yang
Hien I found the large porch of the principal Buddhist temple
in that city used as a tea-saloon. At the Choo-loong-shan monastery, near Woo-see Hien, I found one of the most spacious
apartments set apart for a similar purpose. The apartment was
in the centre of the courtyard, which was ornamented by a
rockery, the stones of which were put together in a most grotesque and fanciful manner. Near the door of the saloon there
was a spring well, a large slab of marble near which bore a
sentence, said to have been composed by Kien-lung Wong,
expressive of the excellence of the waters. At Soo-chow I found
two very large tea-saloons in the great courtyard of the Shuen-
Miou-Tuan temple; and at the city of Kha-hing I was not a
little surprised to find the entrance-porch of the prefect's yamun
or palace used as a similar institution. As temples and yamuns
are places of public resort, the expedient of setting apart rooms
or halls for this purpose is well worthy of adoption by the inhabitants of the southern provinces. It is impossible for a
foreigner who is a lover of order, to visit these institutions without
feeling that they are indeed superior, in every sense of the term,
to the ale-houses or gin-palaces which disgrace the cities of more
civilized lands. On country roads, what may be termed tea-sheds
take the place of tea-saloons. These erections generally consist
of a tile roof supported by pillars of brick, and as a rule the
highways pass underneath them. Large and airy, they are a
grateful shelter from the burning heat of a tropical sun, to the
many wayfarers whose business calls them from home. The tea
which is set before the thirsty travellers is very palatable, and,
judging from the manner in which they drink cup after cup, it
is very much appreciated. Sometimes such tea-sheds are to be
found by the side of comparatively deserted roads. In 1853 I
was travelling with two friends in the district of Heong-shan,
and to reach our destination we had to pass through a wild tract
of country. For several miles it appeared as if the district we
were traversing was without an inhabitant. On arriving at
a mountain-pass, we found it in some parts so rugged and

A RESTAURANT.

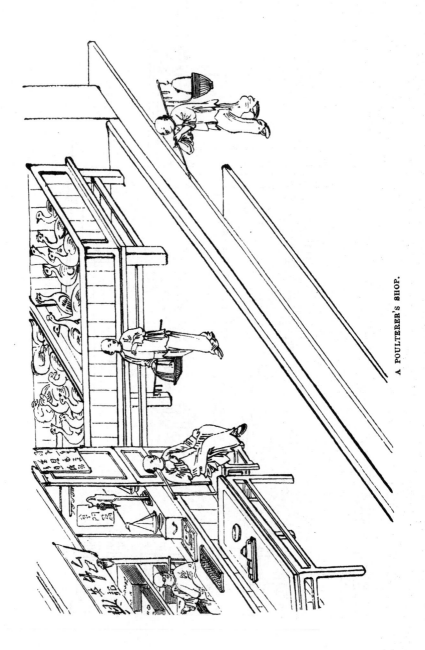

A POULTERER'S SHOP.

precipitous as to render it necessary for us to dismount from our ponies and walk. The fatigue was much increased by the extreme heat of the summer sun. Feeling sure that we should have no opportunity of refreshing ourselves until the end of our journey, we were in a very despairing mood, when fortunately our spirits were revived by the sight of a mat-shed, beneath which, at a table with cakes and cups of tea arranged on it, sat an aged man with a long white beard. We were only too glad to avail ourselves of our unexpected good fortune. Our host and his fare reminded us of the lines—

> "No flocks that range the valley free
> To slaughter I condemn ;
> Taught by that Power that pities me,
> I learn to pity them.
>
> "But from the mountain's grassy side
> A guiltless feast I bring—
> A scrip with herbs and fruits supplied,
> And water from the spring."

Noticeable among the restaurants to be found in cities are the Kow-Yuk-Poo, in which visitors are served with dog's and cat's flesh. Such restaurants, in Canton, are not so well fitted up, nor nearly so numerous as the others already enumerated. I do not think, however, that I exaggerate in saying that there are no fewer than twenty such places in Canton. Each restaurant contains only one public apartment. The approach to this dining-room is generally through the kitchen, where cooks may be seen standing in front of slow fires over which the flesh of cats and dogs is being cooked. The flesh is cut into small pieces, and fried with water-chestnuts and garlic in oil. In the windows of the restaurant dogs' carcases are suspended, for the purpose, I suppose, of attracting the attention of passengers. Placards are sometimes placed above the door, setting forth that the flesh of black dogs and cats can be served up at a moment's notice. On the walls of the dining-rooms there are bills of fare. The following is a translation of one :—

"Cat's flesh, one basin	10 cents.
Black cat's flesh, one small basin	5 ,,
Wine, one bottle	3 ,,
Wine, one small bottle	1½ ,,

Congee, one basin . . . .   2 cash.
Ketchup, one basin   3   „
Black dog's grease . . . . 1 tael 4 cents.
Black cat's eyes, one pair   4   „

All guests dining at this restaurant are requested to be punctual in their
payments."

The flesh of black dogs and cats is generally preferred, because
it is supposed to possess more nutriment than that of cats and
dogs of any other colour. At Ying-tong, a suburban district of
Canton, a fair is held at which dogs are sold for food; and in
one of the streets dogs and cats are daily exposed for sale. The
dogs are put to death by strangling, stabbing, or felling with
clubs. The carcases are usually put into tubs of boiling-water
to remove the hair. They are then disembowelled, and afterwards suspended in front of the windows of the restaurants.
The persons who frequent such eating-houses are respectable
shopkeepers and artisans, and the sum which they pay for a
good dinner is on an average 15 cents, or 7½d. I have occasionally seen poor men dining at these restaurants, but they form
a very small proportion of the visitors. Throughout the vast
province of Kwangtung and other southern provinces, it is more
or less usual for the people, and especially for the Hakkas,
who inhabit Loong-moon, Toong-koong, T'seng-shing, and
other districts, to partake of such food. At Pekin I found
two or three shops in which dog's flesh was exposed for sale as
food; and Dr. Williams has stated that dog hams are exported
from the northern province of Shang-tung. At the commencement of summer a ceremony called A-chee, which consists in
eating dog's flesh, is observed throughout the empire by persons
of all ranks. Dog's flesh is supposed on this occasion to impart
strength to the body, and also to serve as an antidote against summer sicknesses or epidemics. The eating-houses where the flesh
of cats and dogs is usually served up are at this time crowded
with visitors, and many of the street stalls usually spread with
other viands are covered with what are doubtless regarded as
tempting morsels of dog's flesh. The Cantonese think that to
eat the flesh of dogs is to act in opposition to the will of the
gods, and on many Buddhist temples, I have seen placards calling

upon the people not only to abstain from the flesh of bulls, goats, and swine, but from that also of dogs, as these are the faithful guardians of their masters' homes. It is generally understood by the Cantonese that no man who is accustomed to eat dog's flesh can enter a temple for the purpose of worshipping the gods until he has abstained from such food for a period of three days at least. This remark, however, applies to votaries who are accustomed to partake of the flesh of any other animals.

The flesh of rats is also an article of food. In a street at Canton, named Hing-loong Kai, where there are many poulterers' shops, rats are exposed for sale with ducks, geese, and fowls. They are salted and dried, and eaten both by men and women. The women, however, who eat the flesh of these animals are generally those who are becoming bald, it being considered by the Chinese as a hair restorative. In the winter, when rats are in season, the windows of the poulterers' shops in the street which I have named are often crowded with dried rats. The consumption of such food is by no means universal, but the practice of eating rats prevails to some extent in different parts of the empire.

I shall bring this chapter to a close by a brief notice of what may be called floating-hotels. These are to be found at all cities and towns on the banks of rivers and creeks. They are large boats of special construction, and are called Chee-Tung-Teng. As the rivers and creeks may be said to be the highways of the country, these boats are of great service to travellers. The gates of cities and towns are invariably closed at an early hour of the evening, and should a passenger-boat arrive at a city by night, the passengers would be unable to disembark until the next morning were it not for the convenience of these floating-hotels. They are also a great convenience to passengers who on arriving at a city or town find no business to detain them, and wish to continue their journey by other passenger-boats. There are also large boats on the Canton river called by the Chinese Wang Lau, and by the foreigners flower-boats. These boats are neither more nor less than floating-houses; they are often richly carved and gilded. They are illuminated by chandeliers of crystal and lamps, and by night present a gay and animated appearance. In the evening these boats are the resort of citizens who are disposed to make merry. It is not considered decorous for a Chinese gentleman to invite friends to dinner at his family residence, excepting on the marriage of a son or daughter, or when honouring the natal anniversary of a member of his family. He therefore issues cards of invitation to his friends to meet him at dinner on board a certain flower-boat. The dinner is cooked in a large floating-kitchen anchored near. At such banquets there are invariably a number of public singing-women attired in beautiful garments and highly rouged. These women are much more modest than those of their class in the streets of English cities. Whilst some of them are employed in filling the cups of the guests with wine, others sing and play upon various musical instruments. Sir John Barrow in his Autobiography informs his readers that when at Canton with Lord Amherst, he was invited to an entertainment on board one of these flower-boats by the Commissioner who had escorted Lord Amherst, himself, and others from Pekin to Canton. On his arrival Sir John was formally presented by the Commissioner to the ladies who had come to the flower-boat to give their services for the evening. Sir John was struck with their musical powers, and thinking doubtless that they were in all other respects highly accomplished, inquired more particularly about them. He was assured by his host that they were the wives of the Governor-General, the Governor, and the Treasurer of the province of Kwangtung. He did not suspect the deceit, for he records it in his Autobiography in language of perfect simplicity. I remember mentioning this circumstance to some Chinese gentlemen at Canton, and their amusement was great at the cruel hoax practised on the Englishman by their humorous fellow-countryman.

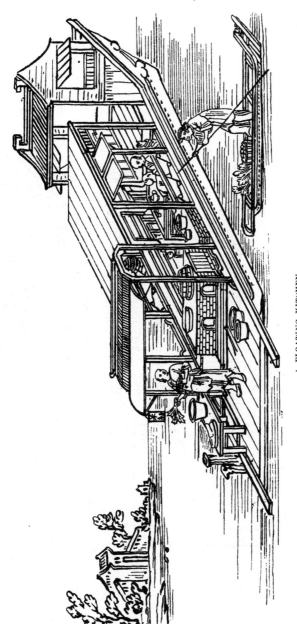

A FLOATING KITCHEN.

A PAWN-SHOP.

CHAPTER XX.

PAWNSHOPS.

PAWNBROKERS form a numerous class, and there are a great many pawnshops. Probably in no country in the world is the trade of lending money on pledge more universally practised than in China. The people who embark in this business are divided into three classes, separate and clearly distinguished. Those of the first class are generally regarded as amongst the most wealthy of the tradesmen. They form companies, and their establishments are known by the name of Tai-Tong. Such a company must hold a licence, for which it pays $100 to the treasurer of the province. A tax of $12 of silver is also paid annually by the firm to the imperial treasury. All kinds of merchandize, wearing apparel, old silver, ornaments, and precious stones may be received on pledge. Arms and soldiers' clothing, and other articles, the property of the imperial government, cannot be pledged. The rule is, that on all sums of money advanced by the proprietors of the Tai-Tong establishments, interest shall be paid at the rate of three per cent. per mensem, or thirty-six per cent. per annum. It is customary during the three winter months to reduce the rate of monthly interest to two per cent. This custom was introduced, I believe, by the Emperor Cha-hing, at the suggestion of a governor of the province of Kwang-tung, named Tsung Yuk, so that the poor might be able to redeem their clothes during the inclemency of winter. Besides, all Chinese are anxious to appear in their best attire at the celebration of the New Year.

One of the most exciting scenes which I ever witnessed was in a pawnshop at the district city of Chun-tso-sheng, on the banks of the Grand Canal. There were more than a hundred persons in the shop, all anxious to redeem their best clothes as the year was just coming to a close, and they had no time to lose in making their preparations for the approaching festival.

No goods can be received on pledge after sunset. This regulation is to prevent fraud, the dim light from the oil-lamps which the Chinese place in their shops and stores in the evening, not admitting of a proper inspection of the articles. It is also a precaution against fires, as, were goods received on pledge during the evening, it would be necessary to use lights in the storehouse of the establishment. After three years, unredeemed pledges are exposed for sale. Under certain circumstances, however, goods left on pledge at pawnshops of the first class are sold before the expiration of this period. Should the district be disturbed by rebels, and the proprietors of the pawnshops apprehend that they are in danger of being plundered, they are at liberty to dispose of all articles which have been deposited on pledge for upwards of twelve months by public auction. As pawnshops of the first class are considered to be very much under the protecting care of government, it is the duty of their proprietors to receive on interest at the rate of twelve per cent. government funds to the amount of 3,000 taels. The interest is paid quarterly, and, in Canton and other cities, is expended by the officials in the support of the benevolent institutions of the city and in providing fodder for the horses of the Tartar garrison. About two per cent. per annum on the imperial loan is divided by the pawnbrokers among the underlings of the treasurer's yamun. Were the pawnbrokers to refuse this gratuity, these harpies would refuse to receive the interest due on the loan, and thus damage their credit with the treasurer. In order to provide against loss, the proprietors of all first class pawnshops are obliged to sign a bond for the payment in full of the sum lent, together with interest at the rate of sixteen per cent. per annum, should the establishment in which it has been deposited be obliged to suspend payment.

Persons of all ranks and conditions resort to these establishments when they are in want of money; and although there are banks properly so-called, the latter are scarcely so much resorted to for borrowing money except by persons in trade. It is by no means unusual for persons of respectability to deposit their winter apparel in such establishments at the commencement of summer, not because they are in want of funds, but to secure its safe keeping. The climate is very damp at this season, and insects of all kinds swarm and devour all wearing apparel, books, and similar articles, unless great care is taken. No pawnshops of this class can be closed, nor a dissolution of partnership take place, without the sanction of the treasurer; and a fee of $100 must be paid to have the name of the firm erased from the tax list.

Pawnshops of the first class are built of brick and faced with granite. With the exception of pagodas, they are the loftiest buildings to be seen in China. They are conspicuous above all the surrounding edifices of a town, and remind one of the keeps which are so numerous on the borders of England and Scotland. In the absence of windows, they are provided with iron shutters or blinds. The entrance-doors are very strong, being made of solid iron. The basement is devoted to offices in which the business is transacted, and where men and women and boys and girls may be heard wrangling and quarrelling with the clerks respecting the amounts offered on the goods. In the various chambers there are several long rows of shelves. None of these are placed on the walls, there being always a broad passage between them and the latter. Arranged on these shelves with great regularity are innumerable parcels of all sizes, neatly packed. Attached to each parcel is a wooden label with the contents written on it in very legible characters, the name of its owner, and the date upon which it was pledged. In the centre of each chamber is a wooden safe in which valuables, such as gold and silver ornaments and precious stones, are carefully deposited. The pawnshops of the second class resemble those of the first, but are considerably smaller.

The style of architecture observed in the construction of the Tai-Tong and Haong-Āt is rendered necessary by the numbers of lawless characters who are ever ready, despite the severity of the laws, to form themselves into bands for the purpose of pillaging their well-to-do fellow-countrymen. The buildings of this description which I visited in the central and northern provinces, and in Mongolia, were not so lofty as those in the south. They were, however, very strong.

The great strength of pawnshops does not exempt them from attacks from robbers. In 1860 several such establishments were attacked in Canton and its neighbourhood, and robbed of their most valuable contents. With the view of rendering their shops more secure in future the proprietors hit upon the expedient of placing large stones on the roofs to throw upon the the heads of future assailants, and vitriol in large earthenware vases to squirt with large syringes into their faces. Several of the robbers who attacked and plundered the pawnshops of Canton in 1860 were eventually captured and decapitated on the public execution ground. The construction of these pawnshops protects them against fire. In 1861 a large fire took place at Canton by night, and on visiting the scene next morning I found that a whole street had been burnt down, with the exception of a large pawnshop.

Pawnshops of the second class are also conducted by joint-stock companies. They are called Kwan-Shuee or Haong-Āt, and are licensed by the Shun-Kum or gentry. The large sum of 200 taels of money is paid for a licence, and the money raised in this way is expended by the gentry in paying the braves and militiamen whom they employ to preserve the peace of the province. As such licences are renewed every two years at the same rate, large sums fall into the hands of the gentry for these purposes. The money advanced on articles pledged in pawnshops of this class bears interest at the rate of 30 per cent. per annum on all articles valued at $14 and upwards; and at the rate of 20 per cent. on all articles valued at from $10 to $13. The pawnbrokers, however, on agreeing to advance $14 or any other given sum on goods, pay the money less one dollar, a custom very much to their advantage. The goods received are similar to those received at the Tai-Tong, or pawnshops of the first-class. The proprietors have the privilege of receiving on pledge wearing-apparel belonging to soldiers, the coat or cape

A MONEY CHANGER.

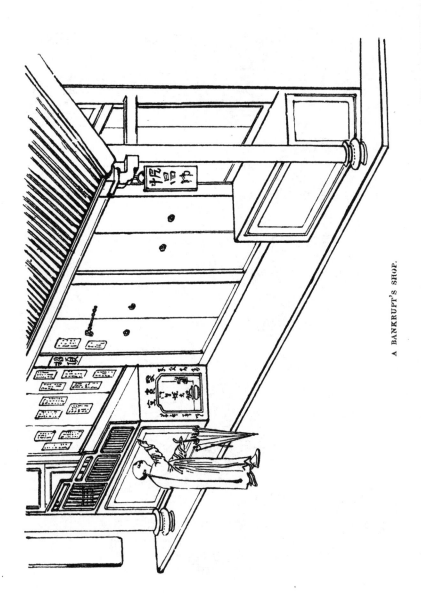

A BANKRUPT'S SHOP.

which is provided by Government excepted. Arms of all kinds, not the property of the Government, may also be received by pawnshops of the second class. One year must elapse before the goods left can be exposed for sale.

Pawnshops of the third class are named Seu-Āt, and are conducted in some instances by wealthy convicts. They are of course under the strict surveillance of the officials, and a great part of the proceeds is appropriated to these harpies, who are so notorious throughout the empire for their grasping proclivities. The goods pawned remain six months at a very high rate of interest before they can be brought to the hammer. Pawnshops, the proprietors of which are convicts, are not now numerous in Canton. There are pawnshops also of the third class called Loi-Koong-Kwang, conducted, as a rule, by joint-stock companies consisting almost entirely of policemen and runners in attendance on the officers occupying the various yanums or official residences. The goods must remain three months, if unredeemed, in the hands of the pawnbroker before they can be disposed of by public auction. The rate of interest on the sum of money advanced is very high, and must be paid, if I mistake not, by the persons pawning the goods at the end of every ten days, or three times a month. Should the owner be unable to meet these requirements, the goods are not held for the three months by the pawnbrokers, but are sold by auction without further delay. There are establishments also of this class called Loi-Peck-Poo. These are more of the nature of benevolent institutions. They are kept under the sanction of the Government by the blind, the halt, the withered, and the maimed. The rules observed at the Loi-Peck-Poo are similar to those at the other pawnshops of the third class. Pawnshops of this class are not built on the same principles as those of the first and second, but resemble ordinary retail shops, the goods deposited in them not being so valuable.

Many persons find themselves unable to redeem their goods after.paying interest on the amounts which they have received, and the pawnbrokers, especially those of the first and second classes realize considerable profits. The pawners carefully preserve their pawn-tickets. Should they lose or mutilate them in any way,

the pledges cannot be recovered. Persons who have pledged
articles and who find that they cannot redeem them, often sell
their tickets ; sometimes to friends, sometimes to men who gain a
livelihood by buying and reselling them. These men are called
Shou-Mi-Tong-Pew-Yan, or buyers and sellers of pawn-tickets.
In the stalls which they occupy at the sides of streets they exhibit,
arranged in order, the tickets which they have bought at a considerably reduced cost, and are prepared to resell at a profit.

Pawnshops of the first and second class dispose of their unredeemed pledges during the 2nd, 5th, 8th, 9th, and 11th months
of each year. The sales take place in the pawnshops, and cash
is paid by buyers in taels of silver before delivery. The articles
of wearing apparel sold on such occasions are generally bought
by dealers in secondhand clothes, and resold in their retail
shops. In all cities and towns there are generally two or three
streets of shops of this kind, the walls of which are covered
with wearing apparel for both sexes. In the cities of the north,
dealers in second-hand clothes are employed from morning till
night disposing of their wares after the manner of a "Dutch
auction." They place a number of garments of all kinds in the
doorways of their shops, and proceed very rapidly to hold up
one garment after another for the inspection of those who have
gathered round them, setting forth volubly the price of the
article. Should any one in the crowd consider the price reasonable, he at once closes with the offer, as the article is immediately
withdrawn. The clothes-dealers invariably ask the highest prices,
and the bidders offer prices much lower, which are often accepted.
The goods which are left unredeemed at pawnshops of the
third class are sold as a rule in the public markets. Thus, at
Canton, there is a market in the western suburb where such
articles are daily exposed for sale from five o'clock A.M. until
nine o'clock A.M. Pawnshops are not only resorted to by persons
anxious to obtain money for the common necessaries of life, but
by those who are in want of funds to celebrate marriages or
funerals, or to meet bills nearly due. Sometimes persons in need
of money resort to money-lending companies. These are of two
kinds, named Lee-woee, or interest-receiving societies, and Yee-
woee or non-interest-receiving companies. The societies called

Lee-woee were instituted by a person named Pong Koong, an official of great wealth, who flourished during the Hon dynasty. Some say that Pong Koong was a benevolent man who acted upon the principle that it is a duty incumbent upon the rich to assist the poor. Others maintain that he instituted them to provide a convenient investment for his money at a fair rate of interest. The way in which such societies are formed is as follows. A person who is anxious to obtain a loan, either to satisfy the demands of his creditors, or to celebrate the nuptials of his son, or to do honour to the funeral obsequies of his father, calls upon his relatives and friends to form such a society. The first rule is, that the company shall consist of a definite number of members; that each member shall contribute an equal sum to the fund; that a meeting shall be held at the end of each quarter; that at such meetings all members must attend, not regarding heavy rains, nor tempestuous winds, nor extreme heat, nor extreme cold as a just excuse; that due notice of the meetings shall be given; that each meeting shall be held at the house of the president of the club; that the various sums contributed to the fund shall be carefully weighed and examined by him; and, lastly, that should important business or severe sickness preclude the possibility of any member attending, the member shall appoint a suitable representative. The second rule is to the effect that at each properly notified meeting the borrower shall pay back an instalment of the loan, with interest at a rate *per mensem* previously agreed upon. The instalment shall be equal to the amount contributed by each individual to the fund in the first instance, the interest to be divided equally amongst the members of the club. The third rule is that each member shall, at each of the meetings duly and properly notified, contribute to the fund a sum equal to that which he contributed at the first meeting; that in order to give each an opportunity of borrowing the collective amount thus formed, each shall deposit in a lottery-box placed on the table for that purpose a tender, written in a legible hand, setting forth the rate of interest which he is disposed to pay on the amount in question; that the tenders shall then be taken out of the lottery-box by the president of the club, and that he who is found to have made the highest offer shall be declared the receiver of the loan; and that should two or more persons make an equal offer, he whose tender was first offered shall be regarded as the person appointed to receive the loan. The fourth rule is that at the close of each meeting there shall be provided a luncheon or repast of some kind for the benefit of the members; and that the meal shall be served up either at the residence of the president of the club, or at a neighbouring tavern; and that every absent member shall be called upon to contribute his quota towards defraying the expenses. The fifth rule is that each member shall be provided with a book in which the minutes of each meeting may be duly recorded, and that, should any member be unable to contribute to the general fund at any one of the meetings the amount required from him, three days grace shall be allowed him. At the expiration of that time should he continue a defaulter, he shall be mulcted in the sum of two mace *per diem* until the sum due be paid up. To illustrate further the working of such societies, I may add that should one consist of thirteen members, and should the loan required by the thirteenth person, or the man for whose benefit the club was established, be $36, each of the twelve remaining members is required to contribute $3 to the general fund. As the person receiving the loan is called upon by the rules of the society to pay back at each subsequent meeting an instalment of $3, together with the interest, and as the meetings take place but once a quarter, three years must elapse before he can refund the amount due. These remarks apply also to the other members of the club, each of whom becomes in turn, according to the rules, the receiver of a loan.

Money-lending clubs of this kind are occasionally formed by women. In 1866 I was present at a quarterly meeting of such a society, and the members were all respectable-looking females of mature age. Judging from the high rate of interest which each of them tendered for the loan, they were all, I am afraid, greatly in need of money. The highest tender was at the rate of 25 per cent., and the woman by whom it was presented rather appeared to rue her bargain. I knew the old lady at whose house the meeting was held, and received a pressing invitation to be present at the repast which was served up on the occasion.

CHAPTER XXI.

PAGODAS.

No one can visit China without admiring its numerous pagodas.[1] These are erected in or near cities, often on the banks of rivers and streams. They are of various kinds. Those of the first class are lofty and graceful towers, consisting of seven, or nine stories; in some instances, of thirteen. The towers, which are generally octagonal, diminish in height and width as they ascend, and above each story there is a projecting roof of tiles. These are generally glazed and of a green colour; and each corner of the roof is ornamented with a bell. As a rule, pagodas are built of bricks, the facing being often of stone. In some parts of the empire they are made of iron. Thus, for example, in the neighbourhood of the city of Chin-kiang I saw one of iron consisting of nine stories. This structure, which is not more than sixty or seventy feet in height, stands within the grounds of the Kham-Loo Sze, or Sweet Dew Monastery. It is of great antiquity, having been erected during the Tong dynasty, and on each of its sides are numerous representations of Buddha. The monastery, which is famous in Chinese annals, stands on a hill and commands a very extensive and charming view of the surrounding country. At Nan-kang Foo, on the banks of the Poyang Lake, I saw, five miles from the gates of the city, a graceful pagoda standing on the

---

[1] In Formosa, which constitutes a portion of the province of Fokien, there are no pagodas, and in Mongolia I saw only two, one of which was in the Imperial ground at Yit-hoi, and the other within the precincts of a Lama temple in the immediate vicinity of the same city.

top of a peak which rises two thousand feet above the level of the sea, in the form of a sugar-loaf from the rocky sides of the Loo Shan range. This pagoda, I afterwards learned, is made of iron, and upon each of its sides, as on the iron pagoda at Chin-kiang, are representations of Buddha in relief.

The ascent from story to story is effected by a spiral staircase consisting of stone steps, and constructed within the outer and inner walls, of which almost all pagodas consist. The most beautiful pagoda which I visited was that at Woo-see, a city on the banks of the Grand Canal. The largest which I saw was that at Soo-chow, also on the banks of the Grand Canal. The circumference of the base of this tower is about 200 feet. It consists of two walls, an outer and an inner, between which the staircase winds to the summit. There are nine stories, each containing within the inner wall a spacious chamber paved with limestone flags, and entered at each of its eight sides by an arch. These chambers reminded me of so many churches of the Holy Sepulchre. In the walls there were niches, which were probably at one time occupied by idols of Buddha. The pagodas do not appear to be plumb in every case, and two or three of those I visited were certainly leaning towers. For example, the pagoda on the summit of the Hoo-choo Shan, near Soo-chow, reminded me greatly of views which I have seen of the leaning tower of Pisa. This structure, which, like the Soo-chow pagoda, consists of two walls, each six or seven feet in thickness, was erected during the Hon dynasty, and bears every mark of great antiquity. I was unable, to ascend it, as the staircase had been destroyed by the rebels. A grand Buddhist monastery which formerly stood near the pagoda shared the same fate. Twelve Buddhist friars who lived for many years in this monastery had taken up their abode in the lower story, which, with its walls of vast thickness and its ornamented roof, reminded me of the crypt of a Christian church. It is so spacious that the priests found it large enough for their shrines, refectories, and dormitories. Some pagodas are without staircases, and consist of solid masonry. At a small village not far from Hang-chow I visited a structure of this kind. In the stone facings of this tower I observed representations in *basso relievo* of Poon Koo forming the world out of chaos. In some of the provinces there are square pagodas. Amongst the most beautiful square pagodas which I have seen, I may mention one at Woo-chang, a city on the banks of the Tai-Hoi or Great Lake, and another at Song-Kong, a city not far distant from Shanghai. These pagodas are from 120 feet to 130 feet in height.

The origin of pagodas is still involved in more or less of obscurity, although much has been said and written upon the subject. From their being built so frequently on the banks of rivers or creeks, it has been supposed that they were designed to serve in the first instance as beacons to announce the approach of invading fleets or armies.[1] This is a supposition, however, which need not be discussed. The importance of building pagodas as towers sacred to Buddha was probably in the first instance impressed upon the minds of the Chinese by the Indian bonzes who came as Buddhist missionaries to China in the early part of the Christian era ; and it appears that these structures were unknown in the empire until the introduction of Buddhism. The pagodas of China, though they differ in point of architecture from the Gopuras or tower temples of the Hindoos, are analogous structures ; and it is customary to find in many of the most ancient of them representations of Buddhistical deities. I have already alluded to pagodas containing such representations ; but as a further example, I may cite the pagoda at the prefectoral city of How-chow. In outward appearance it is very similar to that at Soo-chow. It differs, however, in its internal arrangements, being without floors or lofts, with which such buildings are generally provided. Thus on entering the basement the visitor sees at one view the whole of the interior. In the centre stands a graceful marble column of a pagoda shape, which reaches from the ground-floor to a height of fifty feet. Upon the sides of this are 10,000 small idols of Buddha. Around the inner wall, at intervals from the basement to the summit, are over-

---

[1] Instances have come under my notice of the Chinese on the approach of danger having discharged fire-crackers from the summits of such towers for the purpose of calling the peasants in the adjacent villages to arms.

hanging verandas approached by a spiral staircase constructed between the outer and inner walls.

In not a few instances pagodas are erected within the precincts of Buddhist temples, the court by which they are inclosed being often of considerable extent. For example, in the first court of a large Buddhist temple in the city of Shee-moon, on the banks of the Grand Canal, there are two pagodas which from their appearance I was disposed to conclude were structures of a very early date. In the vicinity of the city of Soong-kong, also on the banks of the Grand Canal, I visited a Buddhist temple, in the courtyard of which there was a very lofty and graceful pagoda. In the southern provinces, also, we often find pagodas erected in the courtyards of Buddhist temples. Thus, the walls of the Luk-yoong Sze monastery, situate in the Tchu-tin Kai street of the city of Canton, contain the famous Flowery Pagoda, erected during the Liang dynasty, in the sixth century of the Christian era. It was erected by one Sù Yu, a governor of Canton, at the suggestion of a Buddhist abbot, named Tam Yu, as a necessary appendage to the monastery over which the abbot presided. It has an extremely weather-beaten appearance. At one time an overhanging veranda incircled each story, and some of the decayed beams by which these verandas were supported may still be seen projecting from the walls. To this pagoda, the Chinese have for centuries been accustomed to attach much importance. It is said that when the work of building it was brought to a close, the builder, who was named Laong Tai-toong, predicted that if ever the vane, which consisted of nine iron balls placed on a perpendicular rod, fell down, evil would befall the city. To prevent the fulfilment of this prediction the authorities at Canton and the people have at various times throughout the course of centuries expended their funds in keeping the structure in good repair. About five or six hundred years ago it was thoroughly repaired by a famous Chinese architect of that period named Loo-Pan, a worthy who was canonized at his death, and whose idol is now worshipped in many temples, by carpenters and joiners, as the tutelary deity of their craft. In the vicinity of the pagoda there is a small shrine in honour of Loo-Pan, which is resorted to on

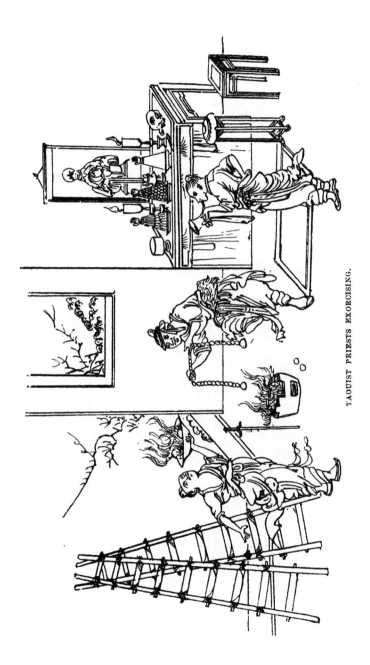

TAOUIST PRIESTS EXORCISING.

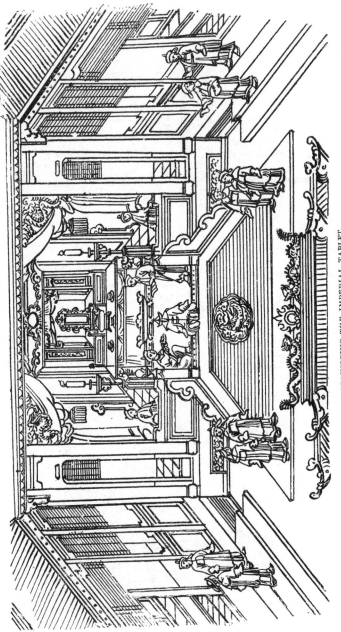

WORSHIPPING THE IMPERIAL TABLET.

the anniversary of his canonization. Those of the craft who are suffering from ulcers seldom retire from the shrine on such occasions without having helped themselves to some of the lime by which the bricks forming the pagoda have for so many centuries been held together. The mortar is reduced to a powder, and taken mixed with water. After the repairs which the pagoda underwent at the hands of Loo-Pan it was neglected for several years, and 220 years ago the vane fell. Within a few months after it had fallen, the city was invaded by the Tartars. The invasion was crowned with success, and the Tartar dynasty Tai-Tsing, which superseded that of Ming, rules to this day over the fair provinces of the Celestial land. During the invasion the citizens of Canton suffered very severely, several thousands having been butchered in cold blood. Their remains were gathered together and entombed in a compound in the rear of the Tsoi-Shan temple, which stands in the Chu-nā-kong street of the western suburb of the city. A large mound which was raised to mark the spot still remains. It is occasionally visited by foreign travellers as an object of interest, and frequently by the Chinese, who go there to worship, with the view, it is supposed, of propitiating the troubled spirits of the slain.

The Cantonese of that period felt deeply this fulfilment of a prophecy made so many centuries before, and at once resolved to re-erect the vane. The resolution was speedily carried into effect; and the dread of troubles again befalling the city should the vane once more fall to the ground, caused them to pay careful attention to the pagoda for several years. Like all Chinese institutions, however, it came to be neglected; and in the month of August, 1856, the vane again fell with a heavy crash, breaking the roof of an adjoining temple, and striking a priest who was in the act of saying matins to Buddha. When the Cantonese discovered that the vane of the pagoda had again fallen, they inquired eagerly of the soothsayers what calamities were likely to befall the city. The mystery was soon disclosed, for in the following month, September, the affair of the lorcha *Arrow* took place, which led to an angry and unsatisfactory correspondence between the English and Chinese officials. In the following month of October, Sir Michael Seymour declared war against the Viceroy Yeh, and proceeded to bombard the city—a measure which eventually led to a general war with China. At the close of the war a fund was again established for the rebuilding of the pagoda, with the view of averting further catastrophes. The work of rebuilding, however, has not yet been commenced, and it is likely to be still further delayed, not because the superstitious feelings of the Chinese are on the wane, but from the growing inactivity of the people.

Many pagodas have been erected by private individuals, as evidences of the pious feeling of willing sacrifice, or the generous wish to do something for the glory of Buddha. At Tung-chow, there is one of thirteen stories, which was erected out of funds contributed by pious Chinese ladies residing in the cities of Tung-chow and Pekin, which are within a distance of ten miles from each other.

It would appear that after a time the Chinese began to erect such structures over tombs containing the remains of Buddhist priests. In my travels through the central and northern pro-vinces, I found that amongst the most ancient pagodas of the country were those erected over the tombs of Buddhist priests distinguished for their zeal and earnestness in the discharge of their sacred duties. The pagodas, however, are now no longer erected for this purpose. In the fifteenth century they were sometimes built to perpetuate the memories of distinguished men and women. Native writers inform us that the once famous porcelain pagoda at Nankin was erected in the year of our Lord 1413, by the third sovereign of the royal house of Ming, in sign of his gratitude towards his mother. It is also stated by native writers that in order to exercise a good influence over the city of Nankin and its environs, no fewer than five pearls of great price were placed on the roof of the pagoda. One was to prevent the overflowing of the adjacent river Yang-tsze; a second to ward off conflagrations; a third to avert tempestuous winds; a fourth to check the prevalence of dust-storms; and a fifth, called a night-shining pearl, to render futile all attempts made to disturb the peace during the hours of darkness. The outer walls of this once graceful tower were built of bricks of the finest white porcelain. The Chinese say, however, that the

XXI.]   PORCELAIN PAGODA AT NANKIN.   93

predominating colour of the pagoda was green, owing in a great measure to the fact that the eaves by which each story was defined were of that colour. The inner walls, it appears were built of ordinary bricks of clay, and not of porcelain, as the Western world had been led to suppose. They were, however, encased by fine porcelain bricks, yellow and red, and, like the porcelain bricks forming the outer walls, so richly enamelled as to impart a very imposing appearance to the structure. This pagoda was an octagon, and nine stories high, each story being nearly thirty English feet in height. As with Chinese pagodas in general, the summit was crowned with a large gilded ball, fixed to the top of a strong iron rod or bar, which was incircled by nine iron rings, each of considerable circumference. The time occupied in building the pagoda is said to have been nineteen years, and the sum of money expended not less than 200,000l. sterling. The city of Nankin was captured by the rebels in the year 1853, and in 1856 these Vandals razed to the ground the porcelain tower which for upwards of four centuries had been regarded as one of the wonders of the world. The citizens of Nankin say that this act was the result of a speech made by one of the rebel kings, of whom there were several, during the course of an angry conversation with his colleagues. He said that from the pagoda in question he would bombard and witness the downfall of Nankin, and with the downfall of the city the defeat and disgrace of his coadjutors. These immediately issued an order for the destruction of the pagoda, and, unfortunately for antiquities and fine arts, the order was promptly obeyed. I visited Nankin in the month of January, 1866, and on arriving at the place where the pagoda stood, I did not find one stone left upon another. I observed a few white porcelain bricks, which, I was told, were the only vestiges left of this once graceful column.

> "We build with what we call eternal rock:
> A distant age asks where the fabric stood;
> And in the dust, sifted and searched in vain,
> The undiscoverable secret sleeps."

Pagodas also seem to have been erected on the ground that

they exercise a good geomantic influence over the fields, hills, rivers, and groves, as well as towns and villages in their vicinity.

In a work entitled, *A History of the Province of Canton*, we read that a nine-storied pagoda, which stands near a village called Check-kong, on the banks of the Canton river, midway between the provincial capital and the port of Whampoa, was erected A.D. 1573, at the command of Man-lick, an emperor of the Ming dynasty. This sovereign, also known as Shin-tsung, ordered its erection because two high officers had represented to him that the country surrounding Canton could not possibly be productive, nor the provincial capital itself enjoy peace, unless a pagoda were erected to exercise a good geomantic influence over the adjacent lands. The Pā-chow pagoda, which is near the port of Whampoa, was erected by him at the same time, in order to bring peace, wealth, and learning to the neighbourhood. Indeed, Man-lick regarded the building of these structures as a work of such importance that he despatched three envoys extraordinary to Canton for the proper superintendence of it. The Check-kong and Pa-chow are nine-storied, octagonal pagodas, each 120 feet high. Other pagodas of this class might be mentioned, which were erected by Man-lick and subsequent emperors for their evil-dispelling properties; but *ex uno disce omnes*. In Mongolia I saw only one pagoda. It is situated in the imperial hunting-grounds of the city of Jehole, and is by far the most beautiful of all the pagodas I have seen. It is nine stories high, and is surmounted by a gilded dome.

Besides pagodas of the first class, consisting of seven, nine, or thirteen stories, there are others which consist of three or five stories.[1] Those constituting the second class are very numerous in the south, and are, as a rule, called literary pagodas, and occasionally pencil pagodas, from their supposed resemblance to a Chinese pen or pencil. They are found not so generally in the vicinity of cities and towns as in the neigh-

---

[1] The only pagoda which I have seen of one story in height is a tower of a pagoda shape erected near a portion of the western suburb of the city of Canton, known to the Chinese by the name of Poon-Tong.

bourhood of villages, and on the banks of rivers, streams, and creeks. Like those of the first class, they are considered to exercise a good geomantic influence over the adjacent country, causing peace, wealth, and literature to flourish and abound. The most beautiful pagodas of this class which I visited were one situate at Shek-moon, a village about eight miles to the west of Canton, another near Kow-pew, a village in the immediate vicinity of Fa-tee, Canton, and a third at Teng-yune, a district city in the province of Kwang-si.

Many persons think that pagodas are not now erected by the Chinese. This, however, is a mistake. At the district city of Sam-shuee in the province of Kwang-tung, one of nine stories was erected in 1827; and at a large market town named Cum-lee-hoi, in the district of Sam-shuee, I visited, in 1861, a pagoda which had been erected during the preceding year. A military mandarin, whose station was not far distant from it received me most courteously, and in the course of conversation informed me that it had recently been erected by the towns-people to secure for them wealth, peace, and learning. In times past the district had been renowned for the wealth and learning of its inhabitants, and for the tranquillity it enjoyed; but during the last few years, the wealth of the people had been much dissipated, the youths of the district had been unsuccess-ful as candidates for literary honours, and the inhabitants had experienced nothing but anarchy and confusion, in consequence of the many inroads made upon them by the red-headed rebels.[1] At his invitation I ascended the pagoda. It consisted of three stories only, and contained idols of three heathen deities, namely, in the lower or first story an idol of the god of wealth; in the second story an idol of the god of peace; and in the third and highest story an idol of Fooee-sing, one of the gods of learning. Pagodas are occasionally resorted to by beggars who have no homes. Persons also seek retirement in them from worldly cares by taking up their abode in such of them as are erected on remote hills. In one near Yung-hu, in the province of Kwangsi, I found the skeleton of a man in the lower story,

[1] So called, as I have elsewhere observed, in consequence of the red turbans which they are accustomed to wear.

which was furnished with chairs, tables, a bed, a Chinese oven, and three or four culinary utensils. The general appearance of the apartments led me to the conclusion that the inmate had been in the condition of a peasant or cottager rather than that of a beggar. In a pagoda near Teng-yune, I found the dead bodies of two men who were supposed to have been hiding there from justice.

Besides pagodas, there are temple towers in China called Man-Kok, which are erected for the purpose of exercising a good geomantic influence over the localities adjacent. In the uppermost story of such temples there is generally an idol in honour of Man-Chang, the god of learning, before which the youths of the neighbourhood go through various ceremonies so as to obtain great success at the literary examinations. These temple towers are very numerous in the province of Kwang-tung, and more particularly in the large and thickly populated island of Honam at Canton. The highest structure of this kind which I have seen is at the village of Wang-kong-kew. At the time of my visit (in 1868) it was quite new, having been built in 1866.

There are also in some of the cities of China other structures called pagodas, erected for the sake of the good geomantic influence they are supposed to exercise. On the north wall of the city of Canton there stands an edifice of this kind which was erected in the fourteenth century. This tower was destroyed by fire in the fifteenth century, and was not rebuilt until the reign of Kang-hi, in the latter half of the seventeenth century. This rebuilding took place at the suggestion of a governor-general of Canton who believed that the prosperity of the city had been gradually declining since the destruction of the tower by fire. In the first instance it was named Chan-Hoi-lou or Ocean-ruling Tower. It is now, however, more generally known by the name of Eng-T'sang-lou or the Five-Storied Tower. It commands an extensive view over the vast city of Canton and its environs. In the year 1854, the famous viceroy Yeh was accustomed to witness from the top of this tower the engagements on the neighbouring hills between his troops and the insurgent forces. A smaller

KOONG-YUNE; OR, M.A. EXAMINATION HALL.

tower of the same kind is the Kung-Pak-lou, which stands on
the top of a piece of masonry which at first sight resembles
the gate of a city.   In it is contained the famous water clock [1]
of Canton, which was erected during the Yuen dynasty by
Chan Yoong, who, in the fifth year of the reign of Jin-tsang,
A.D. 1317, was governor-general of the province of Canton.   At
the time of its erection it was called T'sing-Hoi-lou, or Sea-
purifying tower.   A similar tower was erected at Nankin by the
emperor Kam-hi in consequence of the sickly state of the inhabitants, few of whom ever attained to a good old age.   In the
early part of the chapter I observed that pagodas were not
erected by the Chinese as beacons.   If any proof were wanted
for this, it is supplied by the fact that beacons are provided
throughout the empire.   They are supposed to occur at intervals
of not more than three English miles apart.   In the south,
however, they are not so numerous as the law prescribes.
In some instances they are built on the plains, and in others
on the high hills.

In point of situation and height they are erected in strict
conformity with instructions received in the first place from the
geomancers, as they are supposed, like pagodas and other towers,
if built according to the principles of geomancy, to exercise
a good influence over the surrounding country.   In 1859 the
Chinese Government erected four beacons, resembling in form
Chinese pencils, on certain rocks in the Canton River, in the

---

[1] Of the clepsydra, or water-clock, the following account, taken from the *Chinese
Repository* (vol. xx., p. 430), may prove of interest to the reader.—" The clepsydra
is called the Tung-Wu-Ti-low, *i.e.* copper jar water-dropper, and is placed in a
separate room under the supervision of a man who, besides his stipend and
perquisites, obtains a livelihood by selling time sticks.   There are four covered
copper jars standing on a brickwork stairway, the top of each of which is level
with the bottom of the one above it.   The largest measures 23 inches high and
broad, and contains 70 catties or 97½ pints of water ; the second is 22 inches high
and 21 inches broad ; the third is 21 inches high and 20 inches broad ; and the
lowest 23 inches high and 19 inches broad.   Each is connected with the other by
an open trough, along which the water trickles.   The wooden index in the lowest
jar is set every morning and afternoon at five o'clock, by placing the mark on it
for these hours even with the cover, through which it rises and indicates the time.
The water is dipped out and poured back into the top jar when the index shows
the completion of the half-day ; and the water is renewed every quarter.   Two
large drums stand close by, on which the watchmen strike the watches at night."

immediate vicinity of the city. The year following the erection
of these beacons, three or four natives of the city of Canton
succeeded in obtaining high literary honours at the examination
which was held at Pekin. As this had not occurred for years
before, the geomancers and citizens of Canton agreed that the
success was due entirely to the good geomantic influence
exercised over the city by the newly-erected beacons.

佛身恵高五丈但自髪除
至膝坐高四尺三寸。周圍
十七間二合石量高二尺五
寸。面長入入五寸横一丈
尺。字眉間圓一尺五寸。
眼長四尺C看長四尺寸。
耳長六尺六寸。鼻壁三尺
八寸横二尺三寸。口貫三
尺二寸五分。陰螺髮高八
寸徑一尺四寸。螺髮各高八
膝徑六間。佛手大拇屆
三尺餘。

鎌倉大佛

清淨泉寺高德院

SAKYAMUNI.

CHAPTER XXII.

HIGHWAYS AND BRIDGES.

THE Carthaginians, Phœnicians, Israelites, and Romans devoted much of their time and attention to the construction of highways. Probably the reasons which first induced them to do so were of a military nature. Good roads, however, were found to be of vast utility for the purposes of commerce, and at a very early period were regarded as an evidence of the civilization and wealth to which a nation had attained. Thus, Josephus (*Antiq.* 8—7, 4) says, " Solomon did not neglect the care of the ways, but he laid a causeway of black stone (basaltic) along the roads that led to Jerusalem, both to render them easy for the traveller, and to manifest the grandeur of his riches." Milestones were placed regularly on these ancient ways. The Chinese, however, although clearly entitled to rank amongst the earliest civilized nations, have never been distinguished either for the vast extent or solid construction of their highways. The reason why they are unlike other ancient Asiatic races in this respect, is that their vast and fertile country is everywhere intersected by noble rivers with numerous tributaries, which not only themselves afford great facilities for inter-communication between the most distant parts of the empire, but render possible that great system of canals which existed when a navigable canal was hardly known in Europe. The canals of the Chinese must be taken as a better index than their highways of the degree of civilization to which this wonderful people have attained. Their rivers, indeed, are the highways, built for them in their

vast empire by the hand of a beneficent Providence. Had our
own civilization two centuries ago been tested by the state of
our highways, it would have been thought deplorably deficient.
" On the best lines of communication," says Macaulay, writing
of the state of England in 1685, "the ruts were deep, the descents
precipitous, and the way often such as it was hardly possible to
distinguish, in the dusk, from the uninclosed heath and fen which
lay on both sides." We read in the pages of the same historian,
of journeys in which travellers of exalted station were five
hours in going fourteen miles, and six hours in going nine
miles ; while that from Leeds to London is described as involv-
ing " such a series of perils and disasters as might suffice for a
journey to the Frozen Ocean or to the desert of Sahara."

Notwithstanding the little importance which seems to have
been attached to the construction of roads in China, there are,
of course, many highways running in all directions through the
vast empire. Those, however, by which the southern and
central provinces are traversed are no better than ordinary pathways. In the great majority of instances, these roads are so
narrow as to render it impossible for travellers either to ride or
walk two abreast. The roads which lead to the more secluded
villages are of course much inferior. In the northern provinces,
however, where water communication is not so great, and
where travelling in carts, or wagons, or on horses or mules, is
almost universally practised, the roads are wide ; but they are
much neglected, and the ruts in them are so deep as to render
travelling—more especially in Chinese carts or wagons, which
are invariably without springs—a thing to be avoided by delicate
persons. In the wet seasons they are neither more nor less than
mud pools, as no metal, so ar as I could ascertain, is ever
placed upon them. From Pekin to the Yuen-ming-yuen, or
summer palace of the emperor, a distance of eight or nine
English miles, there is a broad road called the Imperial Highway. It is paved throughout with flag-stones, and is broad
enough to admit of two large family carriages travelling abreast.
The flag-stones, however, are so much worn as to render travelling upon them a most uncomfortable and disagreeable duty.
From Pekin to the city of Tung-chow there is also an imperial

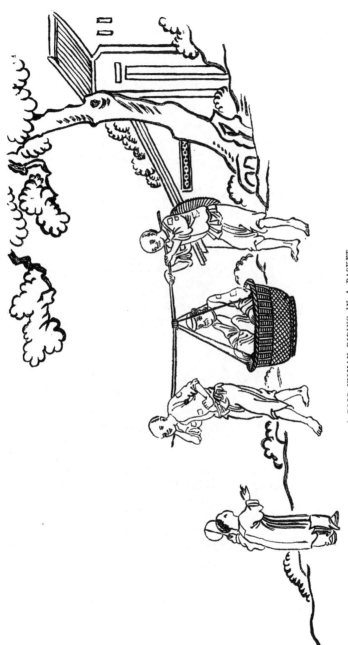

A POOR WOMAN RIDING IN A BASKET.

CHINESE CONVICTS.

highway, which is similar in every respect to the one which I have just described. A third imperial highway on which I travelled is the one which extends from Pekin to Siling, the latter city being distant from the former eighty English miles. Of this road, six miles only are paved with flag-stones. From Soo-chow, in the province of Kiang-soo, to Hang-chow in the neighbouring province of Chit-kong there is a high road which when built was doubtless regarded as a work of great magnitude. It does not seem, however, to have been solidly constructed, for although of comparatively recent date, it sustained material injury. At intervals between the cities in question portions of this road remain to testify to the neatness, if not to the solidity, of this once great undertaking. From the city of Woo-chang to the market town of Ping-wang-chun, and thence to a distance of three English miles, this road is supported as it runs along the margin of the grand canal by a stone wall, and the various creeks, minor canals, and natural obstacles, are traversed by well-built bridges of the same material.

Along all the highways and byeways of China, mile-stones and guide-posts of granite are erected at intervals. It is provided by law that at the end of each distance of ten li, or $3\frac{1}{3}$ English miles, there shall be along every highway, a beacon, on which, if need be, a fire may be lit to announce the approach of an invading army. This law, however, is not universally obeyed, and the beacons along the highways of the southern and midland provinces of the empire are few and far between. At intervals, also, along the roads which traverse the northern provinces, there are wells from which water is drawn for the service of passing beasts of burden and cattle. The water is poured for them into an adjoining trough, and is paid for at the rate of one cash per head. At one of these wells before which I halted when travelling in the province of Chi-li, a priest of the sect of Buddha, who was in charge of it, came forward, when he had supplied the horses and mules with water, and with much politeness presented our party with cups of tea ; for which he refused to receive any recompense. With the view of keeping the highways of China clear of robbers, there are occasionally, by the sides of the roads, small shrines in which are placed idols, into whose sacred presence, it is supposed, highwaymen are afraid to come. All imperial roads are constructed and kept in repair by the central government. Ordinary highways are formed and kept in repair by the people, and in some instances, as works of merit, by private individuals. By the side of a road which has been constructed or repaired at the expense of a private citizen, there is erected a slab either of black marble, or granite, on which an account of the deed of merit is faithfully recorded.

Let me say a few words about Chinese bridges. In the northern provinces of the empire I saw several beautiful structures of this kind. On my way to the valley in which are the tombs of many of the emperors of the Ming dynasty, I passed over, near the city of Chan-ping Chow, a very fine stone bridge of three or four arches. The balustrades of this bridge were more or less ornamented. The frontier town of Chun-chee-kow is also approached from the south by a road which leads over a fine stone bridge. The handsomest structure of the kind, however, in the northern province of Chi-li, is the marble bridge in the city of Pekin. It consists of three large arches, and is so broad as to admit of three large family carriages passing over it abreast. The balustrades are richly sculptured. It commands a fine view of the surrounding country, and though it is in close proximity to the imperial palace and grounds, it is always opened to the general public, except on two days in the year. The reasons assigned for this apparently arbitrary restriction are that on the fifth day of the sixth month, the emperor passes over the bridge to inspect his flowers, which grow in rich profusion in an imperial garden not far distant. On the eighth day of the twelfth month, His Majesty passes over it on his way to the same gardens, but for what purpose I was unable to ascertain. In the city of Nankin, also, and in the country by which it is surrounded, I saw the remains of many fine stone bridges of three, five, or seven arches. One, which conducts to the ruined palace of the Ming sovereigns, had evidently at one time been a noble structure. Little of its former magnificence however was then remaining. The bridges in the city of Chinkiang, though not large, are exceedingly well-built. Had they been the work of a European architect, they would have brought him considerable reputation. The most

CARRIERS.

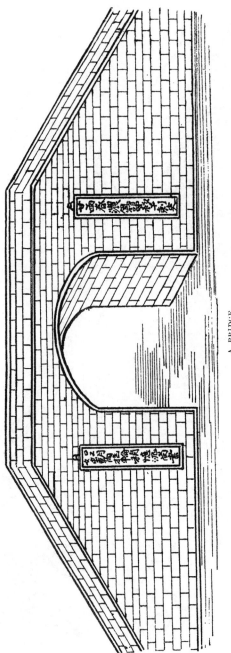

A BRIDGE.

graceful is a one-arched bridge not far from the temple in honour of the heathen deity Shing Wong.

The Chinese town which appears pre-eminently rich in bridges, is that of Tang-yang Hien, on the banks of the Grand Canal. It was once a rich and flourishing place, and within its walls, it is literally intersected at almost every angle by canals or creeks. When in a more perfect state than at present, its bridges must have been highly ornamental. Tang-yang, when I visited it, was more or less in ruins, having been captured, and in a great measure destroyed, by the rebels—a barbarous horde, who seem generally to have made defenced cities ruinous heaps. Over the Grand Canal also, there are thrown, at not unfrequent intervals, very graceful one-arched bridges. The arches are generally of great span. At Tang-shek, on the banks of the Canal, in the prefecture of Hang-chow, there is a very graceful bridge of seven arches. At Chang-chow I saw one, equally well constructed, of three arches.

Nor ought I fail to mention a beautiful one-arched bridge in the city of Yang-chow, on the top of which there is a graceful pagoda, through the lower story of which persons crossing the bridge are obliged to pass.

Besides these there are in some of the northern and midland provinces several very extensive bridges. In the province of Shan-tung there is one of seventy-two or seventy-three arches. In the city of Woo-chang, on the banks of the Grand Canal, I passed over a bridge—leading towards the east gate—which had fifty-three arches; and on my way from this city to that of Soo-chow, I observed near the ingress of the Tai-hoi lake, one of twenty-six arches. The latter bridge, previous to its partial destruction during the rebellion, consisted of fifty-three arches. At Foo-chow, also, the river Min is spanned by a bridge of very considerable length.

Bridges in the southern provinces of the empire are, I think, very inferior to those which I have described. Had I not visited the north of China, I should certainly have returned to England under the impression that the art of bridge-building was all but unknown to the inhabitants of the Celestial Empire. Thus the bridges in the south of China consist as a rule of two or three long slabs of granite, resting on buttresses of the same material. In not a few cases they are, like the bridges in Syria and Asia Minor, unfenced. This is seldom attended with any fatal results, as the inhabitants are not only a sober race, but are fond of returning home at an early hour. Some of these flat-arched bridges are built of granite and are very imposing, like the bridges at Shek-ching and at Lee-shuee, both in the vicinity of Canton. The latter is supported by lofty granite pillars, each of which is a monolith. The only bridges which I have seen in the province of Kwangtung, having highly carved arches, are the five-arched bridge at Fatee and the new bridge at Nam-tai-chung in the district of Heong-shan. On many of the bridges which span the Grand Canal there are characters carved in *basso-relievo*. On some of them are good moral sentences; others indicate the distance of one place from another; others give the names of the members of the family at whose expense the bridge was built as a work of religious merit.

Bridges are sometimes built by the government, sometimes by the people. The bridge at Shek-ching was built at the expense of the inhabitants of thirteen villages in the centre of which it stands. The building of a bridge by a private individual, is a beneficent enterprise most highly commended by the Buddhist religion. When a new bridge has been completed, a lucky day is especially selected for its inauguration. Taouist priests are called upon to bless the undertaking by prayer, and an aged man, the oldest in the district, is the first who is allowed to cross the structure. This patriarch crossing it for the first time, carries an infant in his arms. By this ceremony, it is implied that the bridge will last from generation to generation. There are dramatic representations provided for the gratification of the visitors. The occasion is honoured by more than ordinary salvoes of fire-crackers. At the end of such bridge, a small permanent altar is erected in honour of its genius, and before this burning incense sticks are placed by the devout each morning and evening.

Bridges with houses erected along their sides, are to be found in some parts of the empire. Thus, on one of five arches within the walls of the city of Nankin and near the south gate, and on

A BRIDGE.

BRIDGE WITH PAGODA.

one beyond the walls of the same city, I saw rows of houses—
much as in engravings which I have seen of old London Bridge
—in which each side of the roadway appears occupied from end
to end by rows of shops and dwelling-houses. At Chinkiang I
passed over a bridge with several houses on it; and I found
dwelling houses on both sides of a wooden bridge spanning a
mountain river which empties itself into the Fung-hwa branch
of the Ning-po river.

It has been maintained by some writers that the Chinese were
the inventors of chain or suspension bridges. In the *Wonders
of the World in Nature, Art, and Mind,* published in New
York by Walker in 1850, we are told that " there is a famous
bridge of this kind on the road to Yun-nan, in the province of
Kwei-chow. It is thrown over a rapid torrent between two
lofty mountains, and was constructed by a Chinese general, in
the year 35 of the Christian era. At each end of the rocky
mountain a gate has been erected between two stone pillars, six
or seven feet high by seventeen or eighteen feet wide. Between
these pillars four chains are suspended by large rings, and united
transversely by smaller chains. Over these chains is a flooring
of planks of timber, which are renewed as often as they become
decayed. Other chain bridges have been constructed in China
in imitation of this, but none of them are either so large or have
been so durable." Nor are the Chinese strangers to pontoons or
bridges of boats. There is a bridge of this kind across the river
at Ning-po, in the province of Chit-kong; and another, on a very
small scale, across the Grand Canal at Tien-tsin. The largest
of the kind, however, with which I am acquainted, is one
thrown across the northern branch of the Canton river. It
almost rivals those which, for military purposes, Darius threw
across the Bosphorus and the Danube; or that famous bridge
which the impulsive Xerxes, on the occasion of his disastrous
expedition into Europe, flung across the Hellespont.

CHAPTER XXIII.

AGRICULTURE.—ARABLE FARMS.

IF we may judge from their historical records the Chinese were, at a very early period after the Deluge, entitled to be ranked amongst the first agriculturists of the world. In recent times the nations of Europe, and notably our own, have by the discoveries of modern science obtained a knowledge of the theory of agriculture which has placed them far in advance of the Chinese. I do not think, however, that any of them is more devoted than this singular people to the cultivation of the soil. Their love of agriculture may be regarded as providential, as the population depending on the fruits of the earth is so enormous. But although the Chinese are, and have always been, devoted to agriculture, vast tracts of fertile land are still uncultivated. This neglect cannot be due to the portion of country already under the plough being enough to supply the wants of the people, as rice in large quantities is imported to China from Siam and other contiguous rice-producing countries. Great inducements are held out by the government to all landed proprietors to reclaim and cultivate waste lands. Such reclaimed lands are exempt from taxes for two or three generations; at all events, until they have become sufficiently fruitful to recompense the investment of labour. In very remote districts it is, I believe, sometimes customary for the government to make all those who reclaim lands the proprietors of them; and the government has sometimes great trouble in getting men to quit lands which they have reclaimed. In copies of the *Peking Gazette* of the 7th and 8th of March, 1872, reports were published, giving an account of the great annoyance which the Chinese government had experienced in ejecting some banner-men, from certain lands lying on the outskirts of the imperial hunting-grounds at Jehol, a city of Inner Mongolia. From these reports it appeared that the lands, when in a waste state, had been given to the banner-men for cultivation, on the express understanding that they should eventually revert to the Crown. When the time for that had arrived, however, the banner-men, who during their term had been allowed to enjoy the full fruits of their labour, having paid neither rent nor taxes, positively refused to quit. *Vi et armis*, however, they were eventually evicted.

As the farmers are very industrious, they become great adepts in reclaiming land; and all along the banks of the rivers the traveller may observe the fruits of their industry. They turn the slopes of the hills to account; and, in the absence of natural levels, form artificial terraces, preventing the earth from being washed away by the former and latter rains. It is intended that by this arrangement a sufficient supply of water should be retained for the irrigation of the crops. Such cultivated terraces are numerous at San-chune, Tai-shek, Sze-tow, Kan-chung, and other villages in the rear of Whampoa, as well as in the neighbourhood of Fow-chow.

With the view of superintending farmers and agricultural labourers in their operations, an agricultural board is established in almost every village throughout the empire. This board is presided over by three or four aged agriculturists, upon each of whom the eighth degree of rank is conferred. This board insists upon each farmer cultivating his lands to the fullest extent, and sowing and reaping in due season. A farmer who is negligent in these respects is taken, at the suggestion of the board, into the presence of the magistrate to receive a flogging. The number of stripes is in proportion to the quantity of land which he has left uncultivated. Nor is the law confined to renters. There is a decree which enjoins all landed proprietors to see that their estates are kept in high cultivation; and the penalty inflicted for a breach of this law is an entire con-

fiscation of the neglected property to the Crown. Farming in
Great Britain and in China involve very different outlays. In
Great Britain it is impossible for a man without capital to
enter upon a farm. In many of the provinces of China, however, the reverse is the case, as a Chinese farm—I speak more
particularly of the south of China—is without stock. The
government authorities frequently receive petitions from poor
farmers asking to be appointed tenants of the public lands, as
the government sometimes appoints men who are acquainted
with husbandry to farm its estates. Like their masters, the
agricultural labourers are very industrious. As in some parts
of England, women are employed as well as men.

The lands in China are all freehold, i.e., held by families
under the sovereign on the payment of a certain annual tax.
The taxes are regularly paid to district rulers, who generally go
on circuit through their respective districts. The landowners
receive receipts, which they carefully preserve, as they have
to produce them when called for the current taxes next year.
Without them, they would most assuredly be called upon to
pay their taxes over again. Should the crops be destroyed
either by inundation or the ravages of insects, the land-tax
is not, according to law, to be exacted. The iniquitous mandarins, however, when in want of money, too often disregard
this law. In the twenty-fifth year of the reign of the Emperor
Taou-kwang, a gentleman named Wong-Kap-Sze-Chung, incensed against the mandarins of Canton for exacting taxes
from farmers whose crops had been destroyed by an inundation, memorialized the emperor, who immediately issued an
imperial decree against the practice. When the farmers have
been deprived of their crops by inundation, the representatives
of all provincial governments are authorized to advance money
to them to enable them to purchase fresh seed. They must
repay the sum advanced, on or before the expiration of a period
of ten years.

The lands and houses in each district are carefully registered
at the office of the district ruler, and no sale can be effected
without his cognizance. The person to whom the property
belongs must make an offer of it to his father, or to the next

of kin, in the event of his father being deceased or declining
to purchase. Should all the members of his family—the list
ending with cousins—be indisposed, or unable to buy the estate,
it is then offered for sale to others. The intended sale is generally announced by advertisements in the form of handbills,
which are given to the middleman or auctioneer, who distri-
butes them to likely purchasers. The reason the Chinese give
for not posting these advertisements on the walls of the public
thoroughfares, is that the public would thereby be made
acquainted with the poverty or reduced circumstances of the
person wishing to sell his estate. The following is a translation
of an advertisement of this nature, which is called Chaong:—

" The family Cheang have an estate, situate at Poon-tong on
the banks of the Canton river, for sale. The estate in question
consists of 224 acres, according to imperial measure of the
present time, and is let to one named Ching Yee-chak, at an
annual rental of 1,400 taels of silver. The price which the
Cheang family require for this estate is 21,500 taels of silver.
The purchaser must also pay the sum of 200 taels, which
includes the necessary fees of transfer and the amount to be
expended on the occasion in wine. Any person wishing to
purchase the estate, let him come to see me, bearing in his hand
a copy of the advertisement which I have issued. The estate
contains nineteen fish and water-lily ponds. Along the banks
of the ponds are growing several hundreds of fruit-trees. The
estate is also intersected by three tidal creeks, and the whole is
inclosed by a stone wall.
" Upon a lucky day of the sixth month of the seventh year of
Tung-chee."

The nature of the placards announcing the sale of houses,
may be readily understood from following translation of one of
them which came into my hands :—

" Tsay Yow-yan has a large family residence for sale. It is
situate in the street called Tai-shap-poo, and looks towards
the north. The frontage of the house is seven halls or rooms in
extent, and the back part of the residence is eleven halls or
chambers in extent. The back door looks upon the Cham-loo
street or lane. In the centre of the house, there is a handsome
altar. There is a hall for the reception of male visitors, and one
for the reception of female visitors. There are also a great

many rooms, sitting and sleeping. The materials of which the
house is built, are of the strongest and most durable nature.
The price required for the property is the ordinary market price.
Any person who may have a desire to purchase the property can,
by bearing a copy of this advertisement in his hand, and being
accompanied by the middleman, inspect the property, and treat
with regard to the price.

" Sixth month of seventh year of Tung-chee."

When the estate is sold, the purchaser repairs to the office of
the district ruler, and informs him of the purchase. The district
ruler then gives the purchaser a document—a sheet of white
paper on which is written an account of the transfer. For this
he receives six per cent. on the purchase-money. It is necessary to report the sale of an estate to the district ruler, at the
earliest convenience of the purchaser. Should the latter not do
so before the expiration of three years, the estate would be confiscated. The deed of transfer which the purchaser receives
from the district ruler, is a very important document, and, in
the event of his wishing to mortgage the estate, he can always
do so by placing this document in the hands of the mortgagee.
When a sale has been effected, a document, written in the
following strain, is presented by the seller to the purchaser.

" I, Wong Ahong, late owner of the estate, or house, known
by the name of Fa-tee, do hereby declare that I give, with no
intention of receiving the same again, this document to Loong
Afoong. In the document in question, I declare that in consequence of my poverty, I have sold to him my estate of Fa-tee,
Loong Afoong and the middleman having agreed to give me for
the same 10,000 taels of silver. I further declare that, should
I ever become wealthy, I will not seek to recover the estate in
question. Further, let it be recorded herein that Loong Afoong
must in future pay the necessary land tax.

" This step on my part is taken with the full consent of all the
members of my family or clan, to each of whom the estate was
in the first instance offered. Thus Loong Afoong need not be
apprehensive of an uprising at any future time, on the part of
my family or clan, to recover by force, the estate which he has
this day legally bought from me. Further, let it herein be
recorded that the estate is not mortgaged, and that it passes
from my hands into those of Loong Afoong, not because I am

indebted to him, such a sale being illegal, but because I am poor and require money, being greatly indebted to others.

" To the truth of these statements, the middleman is a witness.

" To the sale of my estate all parties are fully agreed. I, Wong Ahong, present, therefore, this document to Loong Afoong, as a sufficient guarantee that he is now the rightful owner of the estate Fa-tee.

" Fifth day of seventh month of sixth year of Tung-chee."

For the sale and purchase of lands, a lucky day is, of course, selected. One day is regarded by the Chinese as above all others very unlucky—the fifth day, Moo, of the cycle of sixty days. The farms in the northern and central provinces are, as a rule, divided into small fields of one or two acres, which fields are separated from each other, not by beautiful hedgerows of thorn as in England, but by low, narrow embankments. They frequently present another feature unfamiliar to an English eye. In the centre of many of the rice fields, mounds of earth are allowed to remain. These are supposed to exercise a good geomantic influence on the lands. In the neighbourhood of villages, long rows of cedar-trees may frequently be seen extending across the rice plains. Though they occupy much space, they are allowed to grow on the same geomantic principles.

The walls of farmhouses are generally built of clay. The roofs which, as a rule, consist of tiles, are made to extend considerably over the walls, so that the houses have the look of Swiss cottages. In front of each farmhouse in the southern provinces, there is a compound or fold, the walls of which are also of clay. It is not unusual to see posted upon the walls in remote valleys of the southern provinces a mystic scroll, or character, which is supposed to have the effect of keeping foxes, badgers, and wild cats away from the fold. This foolish notion is not confined to the southern provinces. When travelling in the northern province of Chi-li, and also in Inner Mongolia, I observed a mystic character in the form of a circle painted upon the walls of almost every farmhouse, to preserve the folds from attacks by wolves, panthers, foxes, and other wild animals.

The stock on the great majority of farms in the southern and central provinces of China, is very small, and consists chiefly of

a yoke or two yokes of draught cattle, either buffaloes or bullocks. Milch cows are very few in number, and, as in the southern
and central provinces, there are no grazing farms. The stalls
for the cattle are immediately contiguous to the dwelling-house.
As in Great Britain, many of the farmhouses are in very
lonely and retired positions, others are erected in villages. Some
are so large as to contain accommodation for several families
of people. In the same farmhouse it is not unusual to find
members of three generations, together with their attendants.

The villages generally look well, being surrounded by lofty
trees. Most of those in the south are embosomed in the midst
of trees of the banyan species ; and, as the inhabitants entertain
the notion that trees exercise a good geomantic influence over
the villages they inclose, they at all times regard them with superstitious awe. On the walls of the ancestral hall of the village,
or above the gate by which it is approached, there is generally
posted a notice forbidding all the inhabitants, and all strangers
and visitors within the gates, to injure the trees. On one occasion,
passing with two or three Chinese friends through a village
named Chung-pew, near the market town of Yim-poo, I saw,
above the gate of the village, a board with the following
notification :—

" The elders and gentry of the village of Chung-pew hereby
give notice to the inhabitants of the village, and to all who
may pass this way, that they are on no account to fell or injure
the trees by which the village is surrounded. Nor are they to
shoot the birds which lodge in the branches of these trees.
Let this command receive implicit obedience at the hands of all,
as the trees and birds exercise a good geomantic influence over
the village and adjacent rice plains. Upon all persons who shall
in future offend, a fine will be inflicted.

"Dated this fourth day of the fourth month of the 27th year
of the Emperor Taou-kwang."

In many of the remote and mountainous districts of the
province of Kwang-tung, the farmhouses are constructed very
much in the form of border castles or strongholds—a style of
architecture which is deemed necessary to protect the farmer from
attacks by armed robbers who occupy the mountain passes,

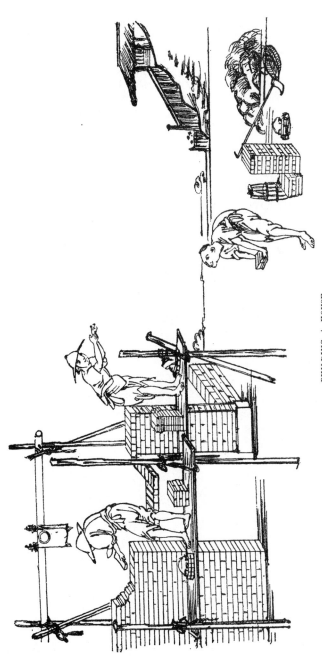

BUILDING A HOUSE.

or by neighbouring families or clans. On my journey in the
month of December, 1862, through the districts of Tsung-fa, Chan-
ning, and Loong-moon, I found nearly all the farm-houses and the
residences of the gentry very strongly fortified. These keeps, as
they would be termed on our own Border, are generally erected
in the form of a large rectangular square. The outer walls of
this square are very thick and strong, and rise generally to a
considerable height. As a rule, they are not made of stones or
bricks, but of a composition consisting of lime, sand, and earth.
Walls built of this are, the Chinese assert, much stronger and
more durable than walls of brick. The walls, which entirely
conceal the interior of the tenement from outward observation,
are pierced with loopholes for musketry, and at each of the four
corners of the rectangle which they inclose, a turret is erected
with similar provisions for defence. Along the sides of the
rectangle run rows of houses, some of which are occupied by
the farmer, others by his servants, and the remainder by cattle.
The largest edifices of this kind are the residences of landed
proprietors, who generally, as in England, farm a portion of
their own estates. On a tour through the district of Tsung-fa,
I was invited, when at the market town of Huet-tee-pai, to
become the guest of a gentleman who lived in one of these
baronial residences. The residence of my host, which was not
more than a quarter of a mile from the market-place, was strong
enough to be quite capable of bidding defiance to a considerable
force of besiegers. The room allotted to me for the night was
in one of the towers of the building. Although in a strange
land, and surrounded by people who were most hostile to
foreigners, I slept in it with a sense of the greatest security.
My host, who was of the clan or family called Lo, was a person
of great wealth, and had evidently gained such influence over
his clan as to hold the position of a feudal chieftain amongst his
neighbours.

In the vicinity of the city of Canton, there are very few
residences similar to those which I have just described. The only
house at all approaching the description I have given is situated
at Cha-shan-heung, a small hamlet in a remote valley beyond the
White Cloud Mountains. Within the walls of this fortified

residence I spent two or three pleasant hours with its proprietor, a gentleman named Shan, on the afternoon of February 5th, 1868. Various parts of the province, however, are provided with fortalices to which it is usual for the farmers to resort, with their wives, little ones, labourers, and cattle, when in danger of being attacked by robbers, or, as in recent years, by rebels. These fortalices are often strongly fortified, and are calculated to resist an opposing force of considerable strength. Such buildings are not confined to the province of Kwang-tung. When travelling through the province of Kiang-soo in the winter of 1865, I visited a large building of this kind, near the market town of Ping-wang-chun, capable of affording accommodation to a large number of persons. In the neighbourhood of the market town of Toong-chee, in the prefecture of Hang-chow, I had an opportunity of inspecting one of the largest of them. Its chambers were all bomb proof, and the accommodation for families and cattle was very extensive. It was provided with wells, from which, I was told, an abundant supply of water could be obtained at all seasons of the year. In the island of Formosa also, I found several similar erections. They were so small as to be unworthy of comparison with those which I visited on the mainland of China.

The agricultural implements which are in use among the Chinese include the ordinary kinds, and are very simple. They consist of the plough, the harrow, the spade, the hoe, the flail, the reaping hook, the winnowing machine, and various appliances in connection with irrigation.

The plough "consists of a beam handle, and a share with a wooden stem, and a rest behind instead of a moulding board.' It is, I apprehend, altogether similar to the plough which is at this day in general use throughout Asia Minor and Palestine. With such an implement it is impossible for the farmers to plough their lands to any great depth ; and, were the Chinese to make use of a subsoil plough, their crops would be much more abundant. A change like this, however, is not the simple matter which it may perhaps seem to the reader, for it would necessarily lead to the use of more beasts of draught. The Chinese plough is so light that the ploughman, on his return from his labours at the

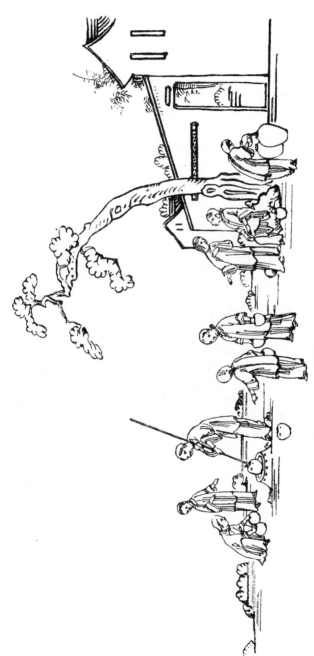

DRAWING WATER.

A CARPENTER.

close of the day, often carries it on his shoulders; and, among the aborigines, a farmer may sometimes be seen guiding the plough to which his wife is yoked. Instead of the plough, a large wooden hoe tipped with iron is not unfrequently used by small farmers for breaking up their fallows, its use doing away with the expense of a yoke of oxen. In the cultivation of the hill lands, which when formed. into terraces yield a considerable return of grain, the hoe is invariably used by all classes of farmers. The harrow used in the cultivation of rice lands is provided with three rows of iron teeth, above which there is a handle by which the labourer holds the implement, and presses it into the earth. That used in the central and northern provinces of China, where wheat, barley, and millet are the principal produce, is very similar to the harrow used in England, although not so large.

The farmer's year is solemnly inaugurated in China, and the season of spring ushered in by a festival. No farmer is supposed to begin to plough his lands until certain state ceremonies have been performed in honour of the respective deities of spring and agriculture. These ceremonies, which indicate the deep veneration for agriculture which is characteristic of the people, and the political importance of the cultivators of the soil in an empire whose cultivated lands are said to be little short of six millions of English acres, are performed at Pekin by the emperor in person; and in all provinces, prefectures, and districts by the respective governors, prefects, and magistrates. On the first day of spring the governor of a province, borne in an open chair over the back of which a tiger's skin is spread, and attended by all the mandarins of the city and neighbourhood, repairs, at an early hour in the morning, to the east gate of the capital of his province, to meet and welcome the season of spring, which begins that day. When the procession, headed by banners and bands of music, arrives at the east gate, the governor and his followers are escorted to a mat shed, in which an idol is placed of the god of spring, with a paper buffalo as large as life. Tsai-Soee, for so the deity is called, is represented as holding a branch in his right hand, his left resting on the horns of the buffalo; thus indicating that the season for husbandmen to plough and sow their lands has arrived.

The governor and his retinue having worshipped and offered sacrifices, the idol, with the paper buffalo, is placed upon a chair of state, and borne in triumph into the city. When the vast cavalcade which attends, has traversed a few of the principal streets, its course is directed to the official residence of the prefect, where the idol and the paper buffalo are placed above a temporary altar erected under the roof of the inner door-way. When the governor and his attendants have again worshipped the idol, they return to their official residences. On the following day, at noon, the prefect, attended by four or five minor mandarins, again repairs to this temporary altar, and, having worshipped, performs one of the most ridiculously childish ceremonies which it has ever been my lot to witness. The paper buffalo is placed in the centre of the court-yard of the prefect's official residence. This functionary and the minor mandarins, having provided themselves with rods, range themselves on each side of the effigy and walk round it at a slow pace, beating it severely at each step. The fragments of the buffalo are now set on fire, and, as many of the Chinese labour under an impression that to become possessed of a portion of the paper of which it is made is to ensure their being fortunate throughout the course of the year, a scramble takes place round the fire.

Another ceremony remains, before farmers and labourers can commence to plough their lands. It is the opening of the ploughing season at Pekin, the capital of the empire, by the emperor in person; and in provincial capitals by governors-general, treasurers, salt-commissioners, commissioners of revenue, literary chancellors, judges, &c. ; in prefectoral cities by prefects ; in district cities by district-rulers. To continue my description of these ceremonies as I have seen them at Canton : the governor-general, the governor, the treasurer, the commissioner of customs, the literary chancellor, and the criminal judge of that city repair, at an early hour, on the fifth day of the ploughing season—that is, in the second month (March) of the year, on a day called Hoi— to the temple in honour of Shin-Nung, the god of agriculture. This temple is situated at an English mile beyond the eastern gates of the city. Its principal shrine is two stories high. In the court-yard, inclosed by walls of brick, there are three cham-

A PAPER BUFFALO BEING CARRIED AT THE SPRING FESTIVAL.

bers, in the first of which certain implements of husbandry are kept; in the second, grain for seed and offerings; in the third, stalled sheep or swine, intended victims in honour of the god. The officials, having arranged themselves before the altar, proceed to perform the kow-tow. The governor-general then offers to the god, as expiatory sacrifices, a sheep and a pig. Nine kinds of grain and vegetables are also presented as thank-offerings. The kow-tow is then performed once more, the officials knocking their heads upon the earth nine times. Upon rising to their feet, a letter addressed by them to the idol of the god of agriculture is read aloud in the hearing of all assembled—the reader looking towards the idol. The letter, which is written according to a form prescribed by the Board of Ceremonies, runs thus :—

" Upon this auspicious day, we, the principal officials of this city and province stand, O god, before thy altar, and render to thee, as is just, heartfelt homage. We depend upon thee, O god, to grant speed to the plough, and to give food sufficient for the wants of the people over whom we rule. As high as the heaven is above the earth, so great are thy virtues. The ploughing season has this day begun, and all agriculturists are now prepared to prosecute their labours with diligence. Nor is His Imperial Majesty, the emperor, though so high in rank, at all behind in his preparations for the discharge of such important duties. We, therefore, the officials of this city pray to thee, as in duty bound, to grant us favourable seasons. Grant us, then, we fervently beseech thee, five days of wind, and afterwards ten days of rain, so that each stem may bear two ears of grain. Accept our offerings, and bless us, we pray thee."

When they have again performed the kow-tow, knocking their heads nine times upon the ground, the officials put off their tunics, and proceed to certain government lands which are adjacent to the temple, for the purpose of ploughing nine furrows each. Here each official, having been presented with a whip, is escorted to a plough to which a buffalo is yoked; and, when the word is given by a conductor of ceremonies, the ploughs are set in motion. At the head of each buffalo, to direct its course, a peasant is stationed, who is permitted on this occasion to wear a yellow jacket. Behind each of the illustrious plough-men walk three or four officers of the civil service, whose duty

it is to sow, at each step, seeds of grain in the newly made
furrows.   While the governor-general and his colleagues are
engaged in ploughing, youths in gay dresses, stationed at each
side of the field, sing, at the very top of their voices, pæans in
praise of the god of agriculture. In a long line at the south end
of the field stand aged husbandmen, wearing gay garments suited
to the occasion, while at the north end are a body of graduates
corresponding to our Bachelors of Arts.   When each high official
has ploughed his nine furrows, the ceremony [1] is brought to a
close.   The duties of the governor-general do not terminate
here, however, for, on his return to his official residence he holds
a *levée*, at which he receives the congratulations of all the
officials, and of many of the landed gentry.

When this great festival has inaugurated the agricultural year,
the first duty of Chinese farmers is to follow the good example
which their rulers have set before them, by putting their own hands
to the plough.   To prepare the fields for rice-crops, they cover
them with lime, which serves to manure the land, and to destroy
noxious insects.   The lime is, as a rule, obtained from oyster or
cockle shells, which are burned in large quantities in the various
lime-kilns throughout the country.   The land is then irrigated,
except when the rain has fallen in frequent and heavy showers.
Several ingenious and useful methods of irrigation are in use
among the Chinese.   One of them is by the water from deep
wells, with one of which, in some districts at least, almost every
field is provided.   A post or pillar of wood about ten feet in
length, is erected near the well.   Upon the top of this a lever is
carefully balanced, with a weight, generally a large stone at
one end ; and at the other a long rope, to the end of which a
bucket is attached.   On being raised to the mouth of the well
the water is poured by the labourer into furrows, previously

[1] The ceremony is, of course, observed on a much grander scale at Pekin than
in any of the provinces.   The emperor, who in person holds the plough, is
assisted in his duties by all or several of the princes of the blood royal.   The
ploughs which are used by the members of the imperial family are yellow,
whereas those used by the provincial officials are red.   This great agricultural
festival was, it appears, instituted by the Emperor Shun, who, according to
native historians, reigned over China about the year B.C. 2,200.   This emperor
was a great patron of agriculture, and occupied a portion of each day in attending
to the cultivation of the imperial lands.

A WATER-WHEEL.

made for the purpose of conveying it to all parts of the field.
In this way the whole surface of the field is soon covered with
water. With this rude machine the principal labour is not to
raise the bucket when full, but to overcome the resistance of
that end of the lever to which the heavy weight is attached, in
lowering the bucket when empty. In cases where no heavy
weight is attached to the end of the lever, the bucket is simply
drawn up by means of a rope to which the labourer applies the
strength of his arms. In the northern provinces it is much
more usual to have—what is not uncommon in England, in
country districts—a windlass erected over the mouth of the well.
In some parts of China, a bucket is fastened to the end of a
long rope or chain which passes over a pulley, and is attached
to the neck or collar of a bullock. In all rural districts where
the fields are not provided with wells, there are ponds, from
which the water is drawn in two or three ways. The first is
very simple. Two men hold a bucket suspended between them,
by means of ropes attached to each of its sides. This vessel
they keep in a swinging motion, dipping it with great rapidity
into the pond, and, as quickly, pouring its contents over the
field which they wish to irrigate. Another appliance is the
chain-pump, which is thus described by a writer on China :—

"This pump consists, in the first place, of a hollow trough
of a square make. Flat square pieces of wood corresponding to
the dimensions of the trough, are fixed to the chain which turns
over a roller or small wheel, placed at each extremity of the
trough. The square pieces of wood fixed to the chain move
with it round the rollers, and lift up a volume of water equal to
the dimensions of the trough, and are, therefore, called the lifters.
The power used in working the machine is applicable in three
different ways. If the machine be intended to lift a great
quantity of water, several sets of wooden arms are made to
project from various parts of the lengthened axis of the rollers
over which the chain and lifters turn. These arms are shaped
like the letter T, and made round and smooth for the foot to rest
upon. The axis turns upon two upright pieces of wood, kept
steady by a pole stretched across them. The machine being
fixed, men treading upon the projecting arms of the axis, and
supporting themselves upon the beam across the uprights, communicate a rotatory motion to the chain, the lifters attached to

which draw up a constant and copious stream of water. The chain pump is applied to the purpose of draining grounds, transferring water from one cistern to another, or raising it to small heights out of rivers or canals. Another method of working this machine is by yoking a buffalo to a large horizontal wheel connected by cogs with the axis of the rollers over which the lifters turn."

In those provinces where buffaloes are scarce, asses, mules, or ponies work the chain pump. I noticed this at Tien-tsin, and at the cities of Chin-kiang and Nankin. To protect the animals engaged from the inclemency of the seasons, a mat shed is erected near the machinery. In the district of Heong-shan in Kwangtung, and at Nankin in Kiang-soo, I have seen chain pumps worked by the hand. This method of keeping the chain-pump in motion was apparently unattended by any great exertion. It was effected by means of a small horizontal wheel, united by cogs with the axis of the rollers.

In districts where the land is high above the channel of the river the farmers are obliged to have recourse to the water-wheel. In the districts of Tsung-fā and Loong-moon, I have seen many of these water-wheels in motion. They are described as follows, in one of the many works on China:—

" The wheel, which is turned by the stream, varies from twenty to thirty feet or more in height, according to the elevation of the bank; and, when once erected, a constant supply of water is poured by it into a trough on the summit of the river's side, and conducted in channels to the field. The props of the wheel are of timber, and the axis is a cylinder of the same material; but every portion of the machine exhibits some modification or other of the bamboo, even to the fastenings and bindings, for not a single nail or piece of metal enters into its composition. The wheel consists of two rims of unequal diameter, of which the one next to the bank is rather the least. This double wheel is connected with the axis by sixteen or eighteen spokes of bamboo, obliquely inserted near each extremity of the axis, reaching the outer rim; and those proceeding from the exterior extremity of the same axis, reaching the inner and smaller rim. Between the rims and the crossings of the spokes is woven a kind of close basket-work, serving as ladle boards which are acted upon by the current of the stream, and turn the wheel round. The whole diameter of the wheel being something greater than the height of the bank, about sixteen or eighteen hollow bamboos, closed at one end, are fastened to the circumference to act as buckets. These, however, are not loosely suspended, but firmly attached with their open mouths towards the inner or smaller rim of the wheel, at such an inclination that, when dipping below the water, their mouths are slightly raised from the horizontal position. As they rise through the air their position approaches the upright sufficiently near to keep a considerable portion of their contents within them; but when they have reached the summit of the revolution their mouths become enough depressed to pour the water in a large trough, placed on a level with the bank to receive it. The impulse of the stream on the ladle-boards at the circumference of the wheel, with the radius of about fifteen feet, is sufficient to overcome the resistance arising from the difference of weight between the ascending and descending, or loaded and unloaded sides of the wheel. This impulse is increased, if necessary, at the particular spot where each wheel is erected, by draining the stream, and even raising the level of the water, where it turns the wheel. When the supply of water is not required over the adjoining fields, the trough is merely turned aside or removed, and the wheel continues its stately motion, the water from the tubes pouring back again down its sides."

In the Island of Formosa the fields are supplied with water from the slopes of the lofty mountains, so that the chain-pump and water-wheel are seldom needed there. When I was at Kilung, the northern port of the island, in the summer of 1864, the vast rice plains, under this process of irrigation, presented the appearance of a large lake.

When the land has been irrigated it is covered with manure. This consists of various kinds of excrement, feathers of birds— those of geese, ducks, and fowls in particular—human hair, which is preserved by the barbers, and sold to the farmers for this purpose, Peruvian guano, bone dust, bean cake, and a composition consisting of the dung of horses, cows, and pigs, and fine mould. A compost of this nature is made in large quantities by the inhabitants of several villages in the vicinity of Canton. One of these villages, called Chu-shee, about two English miles beyond the eastern gates of Canton, is specially noted for the manufacture of this preparation. In the northern provinces of

Chi-li, also, and in the valleys of Inner Mongolia, I found a similar compost much valued. The graziers, however, of Inner Mongolia, who dwell in tents on the vast rolling plains of that country, appear to use the dung of their horses or cows rather as fuel for their fires during the winter than as manure. Thus in the vicinity of every tent in Inner Mongolia, the traveller may see large stacks or mounds of dung, intended for winter fuel. The Chinese as well as the Mongolians employ the dung of animals for this purpose, preference being given to the dung of cows. This is gathered and formed into small cakes, each equal in circumference to an ordinary dinner-plate. These are exposed to dry on the sunny sides of the houses or cottages, whose appearance, it may be easily imagined, they are far from improving. When dry the cakes are deposited in an outhouse. Cowdung is used as fuel both by the Mongolians and the Chinese, in baking food. They either use it for heating their portable ovens, or, more simply, lay their cakes, yams, cocoas, potatoes, or turnips, as the case may be, on the fire itself. Occasionally the food is placed *in* a fire of this description, and covered over till penetrated by the heat. The ashes are then removed, and the food served. At a cottage in which I rested on an excursion from Canton to Fat-shan, I found cowdung asserting its existence in a very unmistakable manner. Indoors, my kindly and matronly hostess was deftly illustrating the process of cooking food *in* it; while, outdoors, the sun was drying with his rays, for the use of the inmates, the cakes with which one side of the cottage was covered. This plan is adopted in many other Asiatic countries, more particularly in Media and Armenia. In the book of the prophet Ezekiel (iv. 15) there is evidence that the Hebrews used the dung of animals for fuel. The passage indicates at all events that the prophet was accustomed to bake bread over a fire of cow's dung. This substance is also regarded by the Chinese—and the opinion is shared in by some of the peasantry in our own country—as an excellent salve for boils, inflammation, abscesses, &c. It is used by basketmakers in China for the purpose of making a paste with which to smear the outside of baskets made of rattan canes or bamboo, so as to render them waterproof. In this case it is freely mixed with the

gum or resin which exudes from a certain tree.   These baskets
are in great request among farmers.   The urine of cows and of
horses is appreciated not only as a good liquid manure, but as
an excellent lotion for cutaneous diseases.   In some instances it
is used for the destruction of white ants.

The manure, however, which is regarded as most valuable by
Chinese farmers is night-soil.   A tolerably high price is given
for it; and the people, always desirous of making money, are
very careful to collect any manure of this description, both solid
and liquid, for the agriculturist.   It is usual to see rows of
large earthenware jars as receptacles for it at the entrance of
every village.   In a village near Pekin, through which it was
customary for many travellers to pass, I observed in front of
nearly all the cottages a public privy; and, when passing through
the province of Kiang-si, I found them at the fords of many of
the rivers.   These had been erected by the farmers and cottagers
of the neighbourhood.   In Canton, and all the other large cities,
there are markets at which night-soil is daily sold in large
quantities.   They are held in squares on the banks of the creeks
by which so many of the cities and towns in China are intersected.   The squares consist of several vats or pits in which the
night soil, which men bring in pails on their shoulders, is deposited.   When at Foo-chow in the autumn of 1864, I was
much surprised to see females engaged in this filthy occupation.
They were by far the prettiest women I have seen in China;
their dresses also were remarkable for neatness and cleanliness;
and each woman had her headdress ornamented by a small
bouquet of beautiful flowers.[1]   When sold, the night-soil is conveyed in large flat-bottomed boats to the agricultural districts,
where the farmers deposit it in cisterns, rendered water-tight by
thick coatings of chunam.   In these cisterns, which are usually
in the corners of fields, it remains until the arrival of the proper
season for manuring the land.   Of the advantages of urine as
a liquid manure the Chinese are, and have been, for centuries
fully aware; and cisterns, inclosed by walls and roofs, are

---

[1] The suggestion is ascribed to Fourier that scavengers, chimney-sweepers, and
other workers in disgusting employments should be rewarded for their self-sacrifice
in behalf of the public weal by a laurel crown, or other badge of honour.—ED.

attached to nearly all the farm-houses, with the view of preserving it.

Excrement is regarded by the Chinese not merely as a valuable manure for land, but as a useful medicine for the sick. Before, however, it is used as a medicine, it undergoes a lengthy preparatory process. Seven years elapse before the medicine is ready for use. If I mistake not, it is given by physicians to persons suffering either from fever or small-pox. The Buddhist monks who reside in a monastery, called Hoi-fok Sze, or Ocean Happiness Monastery, at Honam, are famous for their preparation and sale of this singular medicine. A Chinese acquaintance of mine, named Eng-a-Kit, was also renowned as a preparer and vendor of this strange mixture, which he regarded as an elixir of life.

When the fields have been covered with manure, the plough is put in operation. The object of a Chinese ploughman is not so much to make straight furrows, as to mix the earth thoroughly with the manure and water by which it has been previously overspread. In the southern provinces, and in the island of Formosa, buffaloes draw the plough through the soil set apart for the rice crops, and, the fields being literally saturated with water and manure, it is usual to see the ploughman and his buffaloes above their knees in slush. In ploughing lands for wheat, barley, or millet, the difficulty of drawing the plough is considerably lessened, as the fields are not irrigated for these crops. For what by the Chinese is termed " wet ploughing," the buffalo is not, as some writers on China suppose, reserved. I laboured under this impression until on a visit to the central provinces of Hoonam and Hoopeh, in 1865. I observed that buffaloes were frequently employed in dragging the plough through lands which were being prepared for crops of wheat, barley, or millet. Among the Miau-Tsze, or wild tribes, it is not unusual to see the plough kept in motion by a yoke of asses or mules, or, as I have already stated, by men and women.

When the plough has done its work, the fields are harrowed. The fortune-tellers are now called upon to select a lucky day or days on which to sow the seed. One day which amongst many others is invariably avoided as unlucky, is the second day of the cycle of sixty days. Upon that day, which is designated Yut, the farmers neither sow nor plant, as they are assured by the soothsayers that to do so is to have very indifferent crops. The seed of the rice plant, which has been well soaked in water, is not thrown broadcast, like wheat, barley, or millet, over the field. It is sown very thick in a corner of the field which has been previously banked up for that purpose ; and, when the shoots have grown a few inches, they are taken up and transplanted over the surface of the field. If there are more shoots than can be used in this way, they are taken to the market, where they are bought by farmers and cottagers. On visiting a market near Sai-chu-shan, I found large quantities of these shoots being sold. The labourers, who are very expert in the work of transplanting them, are able to prick out upwards of twenty in a minute. Whilst engaged in this work, they have their backs protected from the rays of the sun by mat coverings, which resemble in form the shell of a turtle. The holes dibbled for the plants run in straight lines, and are close to each other. So quickly does the rice plant grow, that in the course of a few days the whole country presents a rich, green appearance. Perhaps one of the most charming scenes on which I ever gazed was the vale of Manka, in the Island of Formosa, seen from the slopes of one of the neighbouring mountains, when the rice plants were putting on the fresh green of their early growth. The vale, through which the Tamuri river was directing its slow, steady, meandering course, resembled a vast park of soft verdure, and its beauty was enhanced by clusters, here and there, of the ever-green and ever-graceful bamboo. The extensive plain on which the ninety-six villages stand at Canton, has also a very pleasant aspect at such seasons ; and the clumps of tall wide-spreading trees amid its green expanse, stir up in the heart of an Englishman pleasant memories of the scenes of his native land. A walk over a portion of this plain on a still, quiet evening in spring or autumn, cannot fail to gratify any who loves the picturesque.

After the rice has been planted, the farmer must see that his lands are well supplied with water, for a scarcity of that element would prove fatal. In general the rains, which fall at

such seasons in heavy showers, are enough for this purpose.
In 1864, however, so great was the drought in Kwang-tung,
that the farmers were obliged to have recourse to the chain-
pump and other methods of irrigation, which are only resorted
to, as a rule, when the fields are being made ready for the
seed. The labourer must watch the plants carefully, lest they
should be destroyed by noxious weeds. A labourer who observes
a weed growing in close proximity to a plant immediately removes the latter, so as to destroy the weed, after which he
replaces the plant. It is the duty of other labourers to gather
a kind of worm, like our common earthworm in form and
size, and said to be very destructive to the rice plant. As
the Chinese are utterly unembarrassed by prejudices in the
matter of food, and consider nothing common or unclean which
is at all edible, these worms are not thrown way, but conveyed
to the various markets, and sold to ready purchasers as a delicate
article of diet. There is also an insect resembling a grasshopper
by which the rice crops in China are often in danger of being
blighted or destroyed, and which flies about in large numbers.

When the rice is ripe unto harvest—generally in the month
of June, _i.e._, one hundred days after it was first sown—the
reapers come upon the field. Each reaper is provided with a
sickle, which bears a strong resemblance to the reaping hooks
in use in Great Britain. In some of the agricultural districts
reapers gather only the tops of the ears of rice. To this
mode of reaping grain a reference is made in the Book of Job
(xxiv. 24), where it is written, " They are taken out of the way
as all other, and cut off as the tops of the ears of corn ;" and
again in Isaiah (xvii. 5), " And it shall be as when the harvest-
man gathereth the corn, and reapeth the ears with his arm; and
it shall be as he that gathereth ears in the valley of Rephaim."
According to this mode the ears are cut off near the top, the
straw being left standing. This is the earliest method of reaping
grain of which we have any mention in the Scriptures, but it
was not that adopted by the Hebrews in later times. To some
extent, indeed, it may have been practised; but the Jews appear
to have reaped their grain as it was reaped in England before
the very recent introduction of the reaping machine. As it is

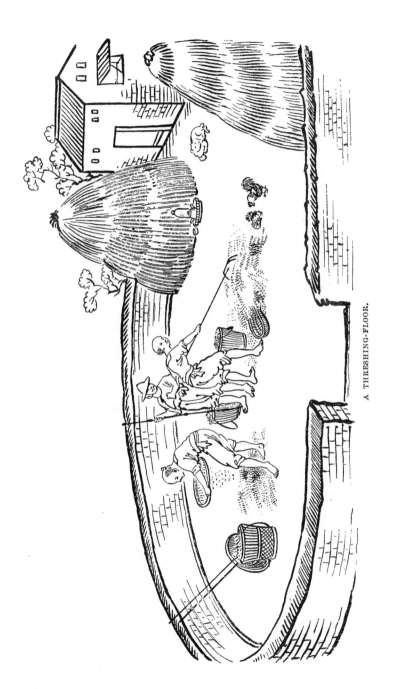

A THRESHING-FLOOR.

cut, the grain is bound into small sheaves, each of which is placed on the ground in an upright position. In this position, however, the sheaves are not allowed to remain for any length of time; they are threshed, then and there, by labourers, who take them in their hands and strike them with force against the inner sides of tubs, into which, of course, the grain falls. Certain kinds of rice, however, cannot be threshed in this way; and it is customary for the labourer to carry the sheaves of this rice to the homestead on bamboo rods, so that they may be threshed there by flails. The threshing does not take place in a barn, but on a threshing-floor, with one of which every farm is provided. Before the sheaves are laid on this floor, it is very carefully swept. The Chinese farmers consider this of the greatest importance. The farmers of ancient Egypt were also very particular in this respect, if we may judge from the works of Egyptian artists lately brought to light, in which this practice is clearly indicated. To this careful cleansing of the threshing-floor an allusion is surely made in the gospel of St. Matthew (iii. 2), where St. John the Baptist describes our Lord as one " whose fan is in his hand, and he will thoroughly purge his floor, and gather his wheat into the garner."

Each village as well as each farm is provided with a threshing-floor which is for the public good, and is used by the peasants to whose cottages small portions of arable land are attached. In some villages several of these threshing-floors, which are made of chunam or asphalte, and are open to the heavens, are contiguous to one another; and, at the time of harvest, it is a sight to see men and women vigorously plying their flails. According to the book of the prophet Isaiah (xxviii. 27), and the book of Ruth (ii. 17) this mode of threshing grain is very ancient. It would appear, however, that the Hebrews principally used the flail in threshing small quantities of grain, or for lighter kinds, such as vetches, dill, or cummin.

I have not yet enumerated all the modes of threshing grain made use of by the Chinese. When travelling on one occasion in Heong-shan, a district of Kwang-tung, I saw buffaloes engaged in treading out the corn. The farmers in this district were certainly obedient to the injunction, " Thou shalt not muzzle the

ox, when it treadeth out the corn." The buffaloes, however, did
not enjoy any advantage from this, as the young peasants who
led them to and fro on the threshing-floor were evidently careful to give them no opportunity of snatching a mouthful of the
grain which their ponderous feet were pressing from the sheaves
of rice. The treading-out or threshing of sheaves of grain
by oxen is the only process to which any allusion is made
in the writings of Moses; and it is clear from the evidence of
ancient writers, that this method was almost universally practised by the farmers of ancient Egypt. In a description of a
subterranean apartment, discovered at Eilethyas, and belonging to the reign of Rameses Meiamun, Champollion writes:—
" Among other things, I myself have seen there the treading-out
or the threshing of the sheaves of grain by oxen." Homer, also,
who flourished, it may be assumed, about the ninth century
before the Christian era, alludes to no other plan of threshing
grain but driving cattle over the sheaves. Chinese farmers do
not restrict themselves to the employment of oxen for the
treading-out of grain. In some parts of the empire, I have
seen mules, asses, and ponies engaged in this work. The
Romans, by whom this mode of threshing by oxen was practised, preferred, if we are to believe Virgil, horses to oxen:—

> " Sæpe etiam cursu quatiunt, et sole fatigant,
> Quum graviter tunsis gemit area frugibus, et quum
> Surgentem ad Zephyrum paleæ jactantur inanes."
> GEORG. iii. 132.

The Chinese also thresh their grain by means of rollers—
a method which I have seen in operation in the provinces of
Hoo-peh, Kiang-si, and Kiang-soo, and which, according to
various writers, is still employed in Egypt, and in some of the
contiguous countries. The rollers are drawn by oxen, mules,
asses, or ponies.

For winnowing the grain, the Chinese use a machine similar
in all respects to that which was, and is still, used by many of
our English farmers. In some instances, however, they adopt a
much more primitive method of winnowing. Having selected
a day when a fresh breeze is blowing, labourers stand with

TREADING OUT THE CORN.

WINNOWING.

their backs towards the wind, and let the grain fall gently
from a tray. I have often seen gleaners in Leicestershire, winnowing the grain gleaned from the harvest-field in a manner
precisely similar. Another mode resorted to by the Chinese, is
tossing up the grain with a fork against the wind. The grain
undergoes a further sifting or cleansing by being tossed up on
bamboo or rattan trays, and occasionally on wooden shovels.
To these processes of winnowing an allusion is evidently made
in the first Psalm, where we read that the ungodly "are like
the chaff which the wind driveth away;" and in the book of
Isaiah (xxx. 24), where it is predicted, as a feature of the prosperity which is promised, that "the oxen likewise, and the
young asses that ear the ground, shall eat clean provender,
which hath been winnowed with the shovel and with the fan."
Again, in the book of Jeremiah (iv. 11, 12), we find the
following allusion to the same process—"At that time shall
it be said to this people and to Jerusalem. A dry wind of
the high places in the wilderness toward the daughter of my
people, not to fan, nor to cleanse, even a full wind from those
places shall come unto me."

When the crop planted in February has been harvested in
June, the ground is again made ready, by a similar process, to
receive seed a second time towards the end of July; and in the
early part of the following November, the whole country is
again adorned with fields of golden beauty. I have stated that
the farmers usually thresh their rice crops almost as soon as
they have been reaped. This, I think, is especially the case
with the first crop of rice. When the second crop has been
reaped, the farmers frequently remove the sheaves to the homestead, in order that they may be formed into stacks. In the
autumn it is not unusual to see nearly all the farm tenements
surrounded with stacks of grain—and the sight never fails to
remind an Englishman of home. These stacks are generally
placed on high granite pillars, to protect them, I suppose,
from rats and other vermin, with which all dwellings appear to
abound.

Like those of other countries, the farmers of China are sometimes disposed to hold back their grain, until they are in a

position to command high prices. The law enjoins that, in times of scarcity, the farmer shall, on no account, withhold his grain—a provision which reminds one of the inspired saying, " He that withholdeth corn, the people shall curse him; but blessing shall be upon the head of him that selleth it." Unfortunately, the law is frequently evaded; for the mandarins are too apt to be turned away from the path of duty by the bribes which the grain dealers, or corn merchants, are able and ready to offer. The principal grain dealers of Canton reside at Tchun-tchun, and at Fa-tee, in both of which places there are extensive granaries. In the Si-woo-Kai street of the old city, there are two such buildings under the immediate supervision of the gentry. As these are large, they belong to the class which are called Ye-T'song, or justice granaries. In the Sze-how-Kai street of the old city there is another granary, also under the supervision of the gentry. It belongs to the class called Shay-T'song, or small granaries. This provincial capital also contains other large government granaries, one of which contains rice for the Tartar troops who garrison the city. These granaries are annually replenished, I believe, by the expenditure of a tax levied on salt merchants. The provinces which contain the greatest number of the government granaries, are those of Kong-nam, Hoo-peh, Chit-kong, Shen-si, and Kwang-si. In Kwei-lum, the provincial capital of the last-named province, there is one of great size in which grain is stored, for sale according to demand in the rice markets of Canton. The farmers in the province of Kwang-tung, are on no account allowed to send rice as an article of merchandise to any of the provinces. Canton merchants are greatly encouraged, however, to import it from other countries, and more especially from the neighbouring kingdom of Cochin China. In times of scarcity, rice merchants who import rice from Saigon to such an extent as to reduce its price at Canton, sometimes receive, as a reward for their meritorious enterprise, degrees of rank at the hand of the Emperor.

Besides the larger granaries there is a Shay-T'song or small granary in nearly every village, for the benefit of the people during seasons of famine, or in times of war. The rice on such occasions is sold at a mace per picul cheaper than the ruling market prices. In the spring of the year indigent farmers and cottagers to whose cottages arable land is attached, often receive rice seed to sow their lands with, on loan from these granaries. In the autumn, when it is the duty of the gentry to see that the granaries are replenished, indigent farmers and poor cottagers have to repay with interest the seed which had been advanced to them in the preceding spring. The granaries attached to the wheat, barley, and millet-producing farms of the northern provinces are very small, and consist of a wooden structure shaped like an English wheat stack. Several of the large landed proprietors have, also, private granaries. One of the largest I saw of this kind, was situate on the Bay of Macao, near a large village named Choy-mee. It was the property of a wealthy gentleman, named Eng Kun-chong, who was not only proprietor of the large village in which he lived, but of all the adjacent lands. Grain in the husk is stored in all granaries in large quantities, as in this state it does not require so much vigilance from those in charge of it as grain from which the husk has been taken. The latter, which is separated from the husk by a process which I shall presently describe, requires great care and attention. To preserve it from the ravages of weevils and other insects, to which it is much exposed, Chinese farmers adopt the following singular expedient. As every one knows carbon is destructive to animal life, and, as the husks of rice when reduced to ashes yield white carbon, the farmers mix this freely with the rice, and by this simple process place it beyond the reach of destructive insects of all kinds. But, despite the well-known properties of carbon, many Chinese corn merchants and farmers, quite as superstitious as the masses, will not open their granaries on the first day of the cycle of sixty days. They believe that were they to do so, all the rice stored in them would be immediately affected by insects, or mildew, or some other of the many plagues to which it is liable.

The Chinese, who are a great rice-consuming people, seldom grind or pound their grain into flour, except for the occasional purpose of making rice-cakes. They use the ordinary eastern handmill for grinding it. It consists of two flat circular stones, which they rub one on the other, turning the upper one by means

of a wooden pin, which is fixed on it as a handle near the rim.
The grain passes through a small aperture in the centre of the
upper stone, whose circular motion spreads it over the lower
stone, and reduces it to powder. The flour is expelled at the
edges of the stones, and it falls into a stone receiver.

In some parts of the empire, it is usual for the farmers, when
they have reaped their rice crops, to plant their fields with
esculents, of which they have a very great variety, such as
potatoes, cocoas, cabbages, turnips, onions, &c. For crops of this
sort, liquid manure is held in great estimation ; and, long before
the sun has risen, and again when it has set, labourers may be
seen running along the sides of the beds which contain plants
of this description, for the purpose of pouring the liquid manure
upon them from tubs provided with long spouts. The smell
which arises from the fields thus treated, is most offensive to
Europeans ; but the natives do not seem to be much disturbed
by it, being probably consoled by reflecting that the nastier the
smell the better the crop. I have been informed that the smell
arising in this way can hardly be much worse than that which
is sometimes to be experienced in some of the hop gardens of
Kent. I can scarcely, however, credit an Englishman who has
not been in China, with being equal to the task of forming an
adequate conception of the intolerable stench which sometimes
arises from Chinese fields.

In the autumn, when the fields which have already produced
two rice crops have become perfectly dry, many of the farmers
of Kwang-tung prepare portions of their lands for crops of
Chā-Yow, or tea-oil. A crop is reaped in the early part of the
following spring. I have several times ridden through the
agricultural districts of Fa-yune and Tsung-fa, and have always
seen great portions of the arable lands of these districts covered
with luxuriant crops of this plant. Its flower is of a pale
orange, and impregnates with its fragrance all the surrounding
atmosphere. The Chinese ladies anoint their heads with tea-
oil, and the demand for it is of course very great. The oil is
extracted from the seed of the plant, which, for this purpose, is
placed, after being well pounded, over pots of boiling water to
be steamed and made soft. When in this state, the seed is

POUNDING RICE.

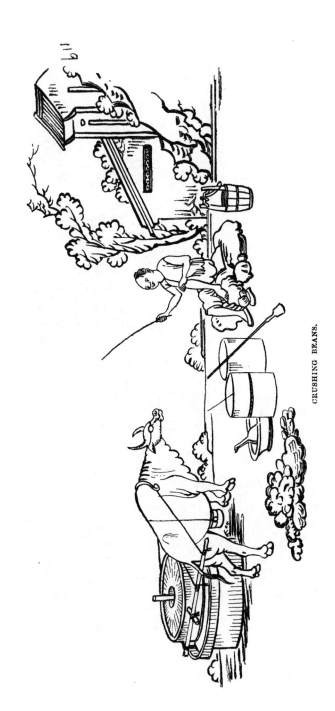

CRUSHING BEANS.

pressed, and the oil flows out.   The cakes of pressed seed are cut into small pieces and then reduced to a powder, resembling sand.   This powder is used as soap by the Chinese in washing their bodies.

Many of the farmers in the southern provinces of Kwang-tung and Kwang-si prepare their lands so soon as they have reaped their second crop of rice, for crops of wheat and barley.   As in England, wheat and barley are sown broadcast over the fields. The seed sown in the autumn yields its harvest in the early part of the following spring, i.e., immediately before the approach of the season in which it is necessary to prepare the fields for the first crop of rice.   In the north, however, as the seasons are almost as well defined as in England, and as, excepting the great heat of summer, the climate there is not very dissimilar to our own, the wheat, barley, and corn crops are sown and reaped at and about the same times as in England.   These remarks apply also to Inner Mongolia, the valleys of which I found, when travelling there in June, 1865, had been brought to a high state of cultivation by Chinese farmers who had migrated thither from the northern provinces—chiefly Shansi and Shensi.   So thick did these valleys—and I may include at the same time all the lands between Pekin and the Great Wall of China—stand with corn, that I was frequently reminded of the striking language of the Psalmist (Ps. lxv. 13), "The valleys also are covered over with corn ; they shout for joy, they also sing."

All the arable lands of Inner Mongolia are occupied by Chinese farmers—a circumstance due, I suppose, to the fact that the Mongolians are essentially a pastoral people.   When the farmers were reaping their corn crops, I observed that the sickle or reaping-hook was not the only implement in use.   In some cases each reaper had a species of scythe very similar to our own, and a few men very quickly cut down large fields of grain.   To the back of each scythe a basket was attached, into which the stems and ears of corn fell at every stroke.   When the basket was filled, its contents were immediately emptied into a cart, drawn by a horse or bullock, which followed the reaper, and conveyed the grain to the homestead.   I was astonished to see reapers, in some instances, plucking the corn up by the roots.   Wheat, barley, or oats, if reaped by the sickle or plucked up by the roots, is bound into sheaves and allowed to stand in the fields in the form of shocks or "stooks" until it is sufficiently dry, when it is conveyed in carts to the homestead.

The mill common amongst the Chinese for grinding wheat and barley, is very similar to that in daily use throughout India, Egypt, and all the countries of Northern Africa. It consists of two circular stones three or four feet in diameter. The lower or nether millstone is fixed to the floor, and has a slight elevation in the centre. The upper stone, or rider as it is called, has a concavity in its under surface, into which the convexity of the former fits. In the centre of the upper stone is a hole into which a large funnel of basket-work is fixed, and through this the grain passes down to be ground between the stones, and to fall over the edge of the lower stone as flour. The rider is rotated upon the lower stone by means of a bar three or four feet in length, projecting from it at right-angles, to which a bullock is yoked. In all the large towns and villages there are mills of this kind. In the mills of Canton, many of which are in the street of the western suburb called Cham-muk-lan, it is not unusual to see fifty head of draught cattle working by relays. To prevent them becoming giddy by the constant rotatory motion, the bullocks are blind-folded. In the northern and central provinces of China I have seen ponies, asses, and mules engaged in this labour. Water-mills are also known to the Chinese. In the province of Che-kiang I observed many such; in Kwang-tung, I saw only two or three, and these were in the vicinity of Macao. Each mill contains an altar in honour of the inventor of mills. After his death he was canonized, and is now by all millers honoured as a god.

On many of the farms in the central and northern provinces, I observed most luxuriant crops of millet. In those fields the soil of which was sandy, the crops were particularly heavy. Between each plant a certain space was allowed, so as to admit of the labourers weeding and hoeing between with facility. Of this grain, which grows to a height of eight or ten feet, there are, it appears, two kinds cultivated. The first or finer kind is used for food by the people, and the second or coarser kind is used for feeding fowls and cattle. From the latter the Chinese also decoct a wine. When travelling in the province of Kiangsi, I had an opportunity of visiting an establishment in which wine was made from this plant; and the process seemed altogether similar to that carried out in the brewing of malt liquor in England. The stalks of millet, which have the appearance of tall, jointed reeds, are used for making fences; while the broad leaves, which spring from each joint, are, together with the panicles, made use of by the practical Chinese as fodder for cattle. The way in which they grind their millet may be described as follows :—A large circular daïs of stonework, about three English feet in height, is erected on the homestead of the farm; or, if for the service of a village, in one of the most convenient places that can be selected. In the centre of the daïs is erected a wooden post. Round this, drawn by an ass, moves a framework, also of wood, in which a large stone roller revolves, like that which is used in gardens in England. Mills of this kind, I observed, were invariably superintended by women. In all probability they were used by the ancient Hebrews, as in the Talmud we are informed that the Jews had mills larger than the ordinary hand-mill, turned by asses. The millstone which is alluded to in the Gospel of St. Matthew, is in the original called an ass-millstone.

Besides the cereals whose cultivation I have described, a formidable list of crops, including beans, peas, the sugar-cane, indigo, cotton, cassia, and tobacco, remains to be noticed.

The bean farms in the northern provinces are very extensive; and, as the soil as a rule is a rich strong loam, the crops are very luxuriant. The varieties of this plant which the Chinese cultivate, are the tick and horse beans; and they prefer to sow them in February and March. After the fields have been well ploughed and harrowed, and manured with a compost consisting of rich mould and the dung of horses and cattle, or with gypsum, which appears to possess the property of forcing the growth of all leguminous plants, the beans are drilled or set in rows, either by an instrument or by hand, with spaces of about two English feet between. These spaces are regularly hoed, and weeds in the rows are carefully removed by hand. Hoeing is so essential

a part of the cultivation of beans that the success of the crop
depends in a great measure upon the manner in which it is performed. So soon as the leaves begin to wither, and the pods to
assume a dull dark appearance, the bean harvest begins, and the
fields become the scene of the greatest activity. From the rising
to the setting of the sun, labourers with sickles may be seen
busy reaping the rows, and gathering them into sheaves. These
remain in the field to dry, after which they are conveyed to the
homestead, and threshed by means of flails. These extensive
crops of beans and peas are grown for the sake of abundant
supplies of oil. For this purpose the beans are placed in a
circular trough, and crushed by a massive stone wheel drawn by
oxen. The fragments are placed in large presses until all the
oil has been expressed into vats. The bean cake from which
the oil has been pressed is given, in part, to cattle, and, in
part, sent to Swatow, Canton, and the ports of Formosa, where
it is regarded as the best possible manure for sugar-producing
lands.

In Kwang-tung there are also extensive bean and pea farms.
The crops, however, which are produced on these farms are not
crushed for oil, but used as food by the people. When threshed,
they are sold in large quantities, and bought extensively by
persons who gain a livelihood by selling bean curds. For this
preparation the beans are reduced to flour by the ordinary
Eastern handmill. The flour is then passed first through a
strainer of coarse calico, and afterwards through one of a finer
quality. It is then boiled for an hour over a slow fire, till it
attains the proper consistency, and can be sold as food. The
Cantonese are very fond of bean curds, which are prepared
during the night to be ready for the morning meal. No sooner
has the sun arisen than men may be seen in almost every street
of the large cities and towns of Kwang-tung, selling the much
relished preparation. It resembles *blanc mange* so much that
for many months after my arrival at Canton, I quite thought
that it was something of that kind. The Chinese also salt beans.
For this purpose they place four catties of beans in a jar,
together with one catty of salt, a half catty of ginger, and a few
taels of almonds and other spices. The jar is then hermetically

CRUSHING BEAN CAKES

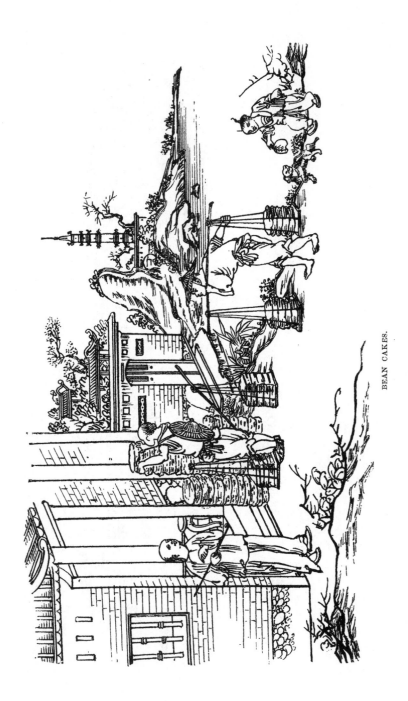

BEAN CAKES.

sealed, and placed in the pantry. At the expiration of a month it is opened, and the contents are always agreeable to the Chinese palate. The most singular use, however, to which beans are put is yet to be recorded. Great quantities of them are purchased by a class called N'ga-Tsoi, who subject them to the following treatment in the large establishments in which they carry on their occupation. The beans are deposited in coarse earthenware jars, which are filled with very clear spring water. In a few hours the water is drawn off by the removal of plugs; and this process is repeated six times in the twenty-four hours. At the end of seven days the beans are inspected, and each is found to have produced a tender shoot. The beans with the shoots are then sold in the vegetable markets as great delicacies. There is an establishment of this kind at the gate of the old Sam-kai Miu, a temple in the western suburb of Canton. There are two wells in this establishment, containing water which in point of purity cannot be surpassed.

Peas are cultivated in much the same way. The soil which the Chinese consider best adapted for them is a light, unctuous earth or marl; and it appeared to me that they thought it could not be too much pulverized by the plough and harrow. Great attention is given to keeping the plants free from weeds; and the traveller passing through the pea districts may often see numbers of labourers engaged in weeding. When the seed on the lower part of the stem is ripe, the harvest begins, as the seed is apt to be lost through the pods bursting if the crops remain longer unreaped. The straw is either pulled from the root, or cut by reaping-hooks. It is then gathered into heaps and left to dry, being frequently turned over by forks in order to facilitate drying. It is next conveyed to the homestead, and made into stacks, which are eventually threshed by flails. The seed is then pressed for oil. The pea-cake which remains after the oil has been expressed, is, like the bean-cake, sold as manure for the sugar plantations of Kwang-tung and Formosa.

Pea-nuts are also produced in very large quantities, especially in Kwang-tung. The harvest of this plant takes place during the months of December, January, and February. The nuts are exposed for sale in all fruit shops, and their consumption by

the people is very great.　Large quantities are grown by farmers
who value them highly for their oil; and it is usual to find a
chamber on the farms, containing all the necessary appliances
for extracting it.　The following is the process :—The pea-nuts
are placed in set pots or coppers, in which they are well
steamed preparatory to being pounded.　The pounding is performed so carefully and gently as to remove the skin or shell of
the nut without breaking in the least degree the kernel, which
is then placed in a press where it remains until every drop of
oil has been expressed into the vat.　The cake formed in the
press is sometimes used as manure for rice lands, sometimes as
food for cattle ; while the shell of the nut, which was in the
first instance removed, is used as fuel.　One of the largest
pea-nut farms which I had an opportunity of visiting was at
Shā-lee-yune, a village situate thirteen English miles to the
north of Canton.

We now pass to the culture of the sugar-cane.　Of this plant,
which in point of importance ranks next to wheat and rice
among the vegetable products of the world, and which has
become the first article of maritime commerce in the western
hemisphere, China is, I believe, the parent country.　It is conjectured that the original word in the Old Testament which has
been rendered sweet cane,[1] has a distinct reference to this plant.
It is certainly clear that the sweet cane or calamus was an
article of merchandise in ancient times, and, as it is spoken of
as coming from a far distant land, it is equally clear that it was
not the production of Palestine, or of any contiguous country.
The conjecture, however, that it is the sugar-cane of commerce,
has, in my opinion, been shown to be highly improbable by Dr.
Moseley in his treatise on sugar.

The cane of the *saccharum officinarum*, as this plant is termed
by botanists, is very like the common reed, and its stem,
which is very knotty, not unfrequently exceeds twenty feet in
height.　From each of its knots or joints, which number from
thirty to forty in each stem, grow long, narrow leaves.　The
land set apart for its cultivation is well manured in the first

---

[1] The passages of Scripture which contain a reference to the sweet cane are
Ex. xxx. 23; Song of Sol. iv. 14 ; Is. xliii. 24 ; Jer. vi. 20 ; Ezek. xxvii. 19.

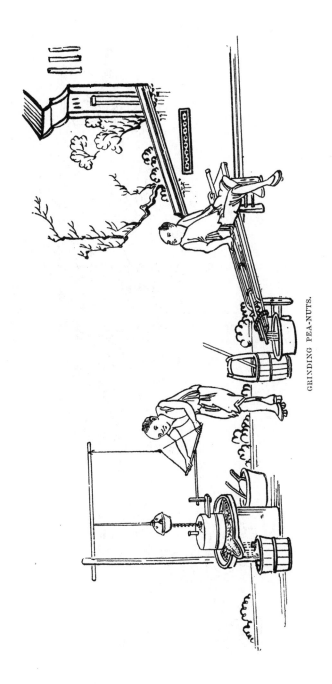

GRINDING PEA-NUTS.

CRUSHING THE SUGAR CANE.

place with bean or pea cake, after which it is formed into long rows or ridges, with four feet between each ridge. Holes two feet apart are then made in the ridges with a hoe, and cuttings or slips of the cane are placed in them, each about a foot and a half long. These slips consist of the tops of the cane with two or three of the upper annular joints, the leaves being snipped off. Between the ridges it is now necessary to pour liberal supplies of water. The canes are preserved upright by means of poles, from the tops of which stretch thick bamboo rods or cords, against which the slips incline. To keep out vermin of various kinds, the brakes are inclosed by fences of matting from two to three feet high. This acts as a strong protection against land crabs, pests which, when once admitted into a sugar plantation, prove very destructive. Like the rice crops, the sugar crops are two annually. When ripe the canes are cut down, great care being taken to cut them as near the ground as possible, as the longer joints contain the richest juice. The canes are then bound together in bundles and carried at once to the mill, which is a very rude and simple contrivance. In the compound of the mill many male and female peasants are busily engaged in cutting away the two or three topmost joints, a preparation thought necessary before they can be placed in the hands of the miller. The tops lopped off are used as fodder for cattle, or as fuel for the fires over which the juice is boiled.

The canes are now ready to be pressed. They are passed between two stone cylinders, which work in an upright position. One of these is set in motion by a yoke of buffaloes, and, by means of cogs, makes the other revolve with it. The juice of the canes crushed between these cylinders, is received in a tub, the contents of which are immediately poured into a large set pot to be boiled. The boiling of the juice immediately on its expression from the cane, is rendered necessary by the fact that it would certainly become acid if it were allowed to remain in the tub from thirty to fifty minutes. Before it is boiled, lime is added to separate the feculent matters which it contains from the juice. The boiling effects the evaporation of the watery particles, and brings the syrup to such a consistency as to crystallize when cool. With the view of draining the molasses from the crystallized sugar, the contents of the pot are poured into small wide-mouthed earthenware jars, each narrowing down to a point where there is a perforation. After a few days the syrup granulates, and, when this stage has been reached, the hole in the lower end, which had been previously closed, is unstopped to allow of the molasses gradually draining off. The sugar is now rendered white and pure by the following simple process. A quantity of it is spread upon the ground, and above it is placed a layer of the cellular portion of the trunk of the banana tree. Upon this layer another layer of sugar is placed, and so on, until a pyramid has been erected. These layers of the trunk of the plantain tree absorb the colouring matter, and render, the sugar pure and white.

All the canes, however, are not used for the manufacture of sugar. Many are sold to fruiterers, by whom they are cut into lengths of from six to ten inches, and exposed in this form for sale in the shops or stalls. For these sticks of sugar-cane, of which the Chinese are very fond, there is a great demand.

The lands best adapted for the sugar-cane are in the district of Shek-loong, in the vicinity of the Low-fow range of mountains, in the province of Kwang-tung. The sugar which is grown in this district sells at the highest price.

Another of the most valuable agricultural products of China is the indigo plant (*indigofera*). It has been supposed that this plant cannot be produced on lands outside of the tropics. This, however, is a mistake. I have seen indigo growing, not only on lands near Canton, which is within the tropics, but on lands in some of the central and northern provinces in Inner Mongolia, and in the Island of Formosa. The seed is sown in long, narrow furrows, about two and a half inches in depth. Between each furrow is a space of ten or twelve inches. The seeds quickly take root, and, in the course of a few days, the plant shows above ground. Great care must be exercised in keeping the ground clear of weeds. After two months from the sowing of the seed the plant, which is of a shrubby nature, is in full flower, and contains its greatest quantity of colouring matter. It is now reaped. The reaper holds the plants in his left

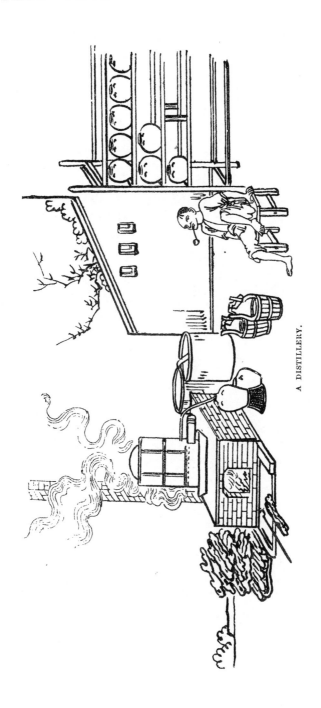

A DISTILLERY.

hand, and with his right hand cuts them with a sickle. He then binds them into sheaves. In six or seven weeks more, a second crop from the same roots is ready for harvest. So prolific is this plant that from the same roots three or four crops are not unfrequently gathered in the year. The roots, however, are considerably weakened after the second harvest, and the yield is much inferior. When the sheaves have been conveyed from the field, they are placed in stone or cemented vats, containing water, with which lime is frequently mixed. After they have remained in these vats for some hours, fermentation takes place. The time, however, which elapses, depends in a great measure on the temperature. At Tai-wan Foo, the metropolis of Formosa, I saw several vats, containing indigo plants, in which, I was informed, fermentation had taken place in ten or eleven hours. This was a remarkably short space of time, as eighteen or twenty hours not unfrequently elapse before the plants ferment. I ought to add that the weather at the time—the summer of 1874—was intensely hot. When fermentation has taken place for a sufficient time—a point of the utmost importance, and requiring skilful judgment—the liquor is drawn off by cocks into other vats, in which it is well beaten with paddles. This makes the colouring matter dark blue, and gives it a tendency to precipitate. After two hours the liquor is drawn off from the precipitate, which is then boiled to the necessary consistence, after which it is transferred to straining cloths or bags, in which it is suspended from beams to drain. After being well drained it is exposed to the burning heat of the sun until its moisture has been perfectly evaporated. The indigo is then ready for use, and is formed into the cakes familiar in commerce. In the East Indies, the processes of gathering the plant and preparing the dye for the market, differ to some extent, I believe, from those which I have described.

The lands most famous for their yield of indigo are those of Pak-loo, in the province of Kwang-tung; and the principal indigo market in Canton is in the street Tai-luk-poo.

Although it was not cultivated by them, cotton, which the Chinese call Min-fa, was known to this people at a very early date; and it is supposed that a reference to it occurs in the

Shoo-king. The Chinese did not cultivate cotton for themselves until during the dynasties of Sung and Yuen, A.D. 1127
to 1333. The provinces in which it was first cultivated were
Kwang-tung and Fo-kien. These, doubtless, owed their priority
to the fact that their ports were the first, and probably for a
considerable time the only, ports at which foreign vessels were
permitted by a jealous government to touch. It appears, however, from a book on the cultivation of cotton, written by a
literate named Lu Kwong-kee, who flourished in the Ming
dynasty, A.D. 1368 to 1628, that the provinces of Shansi and
Shensi were scarcely, if at all, behind those of Kwang-tung and
Fo-kien in this enterprise. This statement may at first sight
seem improbable, as foreign ships are not known to have proceeded further north at that time than the Fo-kien port of
Chin-chew. It is an historical fact, however, that between the
provinces of Shansi and Shensi on the one hand, and India on
the other, there was frequent communication at the earliest
time ; and that, whilst foreign vessels were conveying cotton to
the ports of Kwang-tung and Fo-kien, beasts of burden were
carrying it in equal quantities over the western. provinces of
China to Shansi and Shensi. A knowledge of the cultivation
of the plant is said to have been conveyed to the province of
Kiang-soo by an intelligent and enterprising lady of the Wang
family. This benefactress of a vast portion of the human race
lived in the Yuen dynasty. From the province of Kiang-soo
a knowledge of cotton cultivation spread quickly throughout
Hoonam, Hoo-peh, Honam, Ngan-hwuy, and other provinces.
The lands upon which cotton is grown in these provinces, are
clearly well adapted for this purpose; and, in the summer of
1865, I observed vast plains teeming with the plant. In Kwang-
tung the lands which are said to produce the best cotton are
those of San-tsoo, or San-tchow, in the district of Pun-yu. In
the country surrounding a village named Sheung-king, which
lies in a pretty valley miles beyond the White Cloud mountains,
I observed crops of the plant in 1868.

The cotton plant is grown upon land from which crops of
wheat or barley have been taken. Having been well manured
with bean cake, the soil is carefully ploughed and harrowed.

CARDING COTTON.

The seed is sown in June, either broad-cast, or by depositing it by hand in holes dibbled for its reception. As its growth is very rapid, it soon appears above ground. It seldom, however, reaches a greater height than a foot and a half. The foliage is dark green, and the flower, which comes in the month of August, is yellow. When the plant is in flower, the pods become very much enlarged, and eventually so ripe as to burst, when the cotton is at once reaped, as the heat of the sun at meridian affects its colour. The winds at this season are also a powerful enemy to the cultivator, and carry away the contents of the capsules which have become over-ripe. The harvest is reaped by women and boys, each of whom is provided with a basket, into which the cotton is deposited as it is plucked. On being taken to the homestead, the cotton is passed between two wooden rollers, set in motion by a hand wheel. The seeds, being too large to pass between the rollers, are pressed out of it, and fall into a basket placed to receive them. The seed intended for the next year's crop is exposed to the sun to dry, and preserved in earthenware jars. What is not so required is sold to oil merchants, who press it by heavy weights in order to express the oil. The seeds are regarded by some people as wholesome food, and are sometimes boiled and eaten. They are supposed to impart strength to the 'kidneys. They are also held in great esteem by delicate women, as they are believed to give fresh vigour to the debilitated female system. The stems of the plant are not thrown away, being regarded by this thrifty people as an excellent fuel.

After it is sold, the cotton is sent, before being spun into thread, to establishments where it is placed on the ground, and loosened and cleansed by an instrument called the Tee-kung, or earth-bow. It is then spun into yarn, by an ordinary spinning-wheel, which is to be found in every cottage. The looms which this supply of yarn serves to keep going, are plied by women as well as men; and in all cotton-producing districts weaving is pursued to a very great extent. The cloth called nankin, generally written nankeen, is of the greatest durability. It obtained its name from the fact that it was first manufactured at Nankin. During my stay in this

yellowish city, I was informed that it was woven from a
cotton for the production of which the lands in the vicinity
were very famous.   At the time of my visit these lands had
been lying fallow for several years, in consequence of the
great paucity of labourers, many of whom had been killed
or sold into captivity at the time of the great Taiping
rebellion.   This cloth is also produced in large quantities
in the province of Kiang-soo.   At Han-kow, a large town
in the province of Hoo-peh, I found many cotton-weavers.
In several of the shops which I visited, I found them
busily engaged in the manufacture of material used for
the lining of dresses worn by the Chinese in the winter
season.   In the loom, this fabric resembled a kind of coarse
towelling, but when it was taken out, well brushed, and
vigorously shaken by the weaver, a thick nap appeared on its
surface, giving it the appearance of white fur.   At Han-kow,
and at Nankin, I saw many weavers engaged in making
cotton velvets.   These fabrics were of a dark-blue colour, very
soft and smooth to the touch, and apparently very durable.
What, however, afforded me most amusement in these weaving
shops was a machine for winding silk threads from bobbins.
The threads as they were wound off were made to pass
through water for the purpose of rendering them soft and
flexible.

The dying establishments to which the weaver sends his
cotton fabrics—at least in the localities which I have enumerated—consist of one large room, in which several vats are
arranged.   The dye which is generally used is indigo ; and an
infusion of it is made with water, to which are added wine and
a little lime of the shells of cockles.   The ratio in which
these ingredients are mixed together is as follows :—One picul
of indigo, three catties of wine, and a little lime, to thirteen
piculs of water.   In this infusion the fabric steeps for half an
hour. It is then removed, and, when the water has been squeezed
out, it is dried in the sun.   Each web is subjected to this process
no fewer than eleven times ; after which it passes into the
hands of a workman who spreads it out in the sun, and damps
it by filling his mouth with water, which he ejaculates, to use

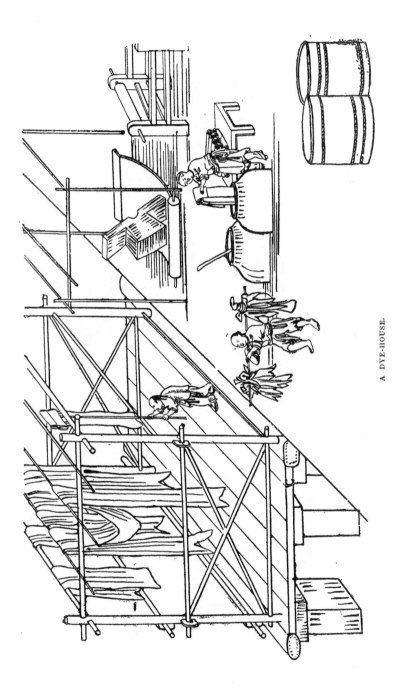

A DYE-HOUSE.

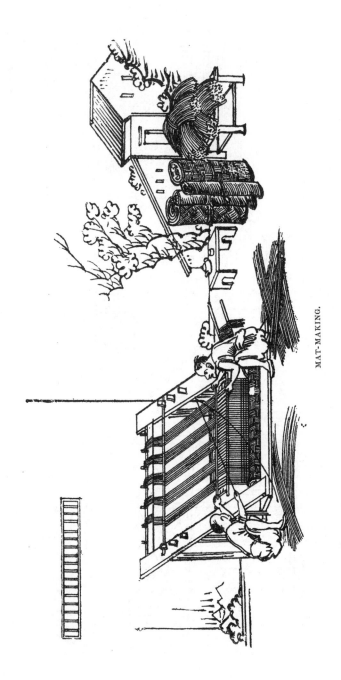

MAT-MAKING.

Lord Jeffrey's expression, over the fabric. When sufficiently exposed to the action of the sun, the cloth is placed in the hands of the calenderer, each dyehouse being provided with two or three of this class of workmen. The Chinese mode of calendering is very rude and simple. A wooden roller, round which the cloth has been wound, is placed on a board about three feet square, which is made fast to the earth. Upon the roller is placed a large stone (see engraving). The workman, standing upon the stone, sets it in motion with his feet, and succeeds in imparting to the cloth a bright glossy appearance. This mode of calendering appears to be universally practised throughout China. At Nankin, Woo-see, and other cities on the banks of the Grand Canal, I observed that the stones used for this purpose were much heavier than those used at Canton. The calenderers, however, in the northern cities are much inferior as workmen to those of Canton.

Prussian blue is also much used for dyeing. At one time it was largely imported by the Chinese. According to McCulloch, however, a Chinese sailor ascertained, when in England, the manner in which it is manufactured, and on his return home gave his country the benefit of the information which he had acquired, so that importation stopped. At Fat-shan, I visited several large establishments where it is manufactured. On the hills near the Shu-hing pass of the western branch of the Canton river there are, I believe, water-wheels by which pestles are kept at work pulverizing the dye.

Another noteworthy plant among the agricultural products of China is cassia, or wild cinnamon, a tree of the bay tribe. The cinnamon gardens are in the provinces of Kwang-si and Yunnan. When found in their natural state, the trees are often upwards of forty feet high, and seldom less than a foot and a half in diameter. It is customary, however, to fell the large stems, as the best cassia is obtained from the tender shoots from the roots, which are not allowed to grow higher than nine or ten feet. The shrubs thus formed generally consist of five or six shoots, and are covered with foliage, which, from reddish yellow in the first instance, eventually become green. They are in full bloom in the month of January, and the flowers, which are in clusters, are white. A supply of plants is maintained in some instances by seed, and in others by transplanting saplings. The latter are planted three or four feet apart, and are pruned at stated intervals, so that they never reach their natural height. In two years they yield bark, after which they are barked twice a year, at the close of the former and of the latter rains. The heavy rains with which tropical lands are visited are said to render this process—in which knives specially made for stripping the bark are used—an easy one. When removed, the bark is exposed to the sun for a couple of days, so that it may in some measure ferment. The epidermis is then stripped off, after which the bark gradually dries and assumes a tubular form. The broken twigs and leaves of the cassia-tree are not wasted, being used for the distillation of an oil to which the Chinese attribute medicinal properties. Large quantities of cassia are sold at Canton to foreign merchants, by whom it is exported chiefly to German ports. It is also used by the Chinese themselves for culinary and other purposes. The largest and most flourishing cassia hong at Canton, is that of Chow-hing.

I observed the cultivation of tobacco in quantity sufficient for an immense consumption, to be carried on in all parts of the empire, and in Inner Mongolia and Formosa. As it requires considerable heat to bring the tobacco plant to perfection, it is of course cultivated with greater success in the provinces nearer to the tropics. Large quantities are produced in Kwang-tung. At Kong-moon, in the district of San-wooee, the tobacco-fields are very extensive. The best Kwang-tung tobacco, however, is produced in the prefecture of Nam-hung. Tobacco requires a very rich mould, and the land on which it is grown must be free from inundations. To hasten its growth as much as possible, the ground should have been deeply trenched, and well manured with bean or pea cake. This manure, which we have seen to be very extensively used by the Chinese, is preferred to the dung of horses and cattle, as the latter has a tendency to impart a disagreeable flavour to the leaves. The seed is sown in spring in a well-cultivated seed-bed. In provinces where the nights are at all cold at this season, the beds are covered with straw or mats. The fields into which the plants are to be transplanted,

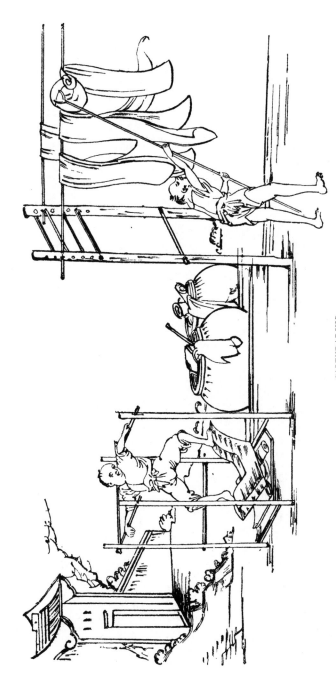

CALENDARING.

are formed into ridges about two feet in width on the surface, with a space of not more than a few inches between each ridge. The plants are carefully removed from the seed-bed by small, spades, great pains being taken not to shake the earth from the roots. They are then placed in the holes sixteen inches apart, which have been prepared for them in the ridges. While the plants are growing, much pains is taken to keep the rows free from weeds, the growth of which would greatly interfere with the luxuriance of the crop. At frequent intervals, the earth is loosened between the plants. The observance of this duty greatly accelerates their growth. When the leaves have attained a certain size, it is necessary to pluck the lower, with the view of increasing the size of the upper leaves. The stem grows to a height of from four to six feet, and is laden with ten or twelve large juicy leaves. In the autumn these assume a pale green colour with a slight tinge of yellow. This is a sure indication that the plants are ripe. They are, therefore, immediately reaped, the plants being cut very close to the ground, where they are left lying for a few hours to dry, great care being observed to hasten the process by turning them over very frequently. Exposure to the dews of night would prove very injurious to the crop, and it is gathered into the garner before the close of day. Here the cut stems with the leaves, are arranged in heaps, so that they may sweat. At the end of four days, the sweating process at this stage is regarded as having come to an end. The stems with the leaves still on them are then hung up in light, airy rooms to dry. When quite dry, they are laid in heaps upon trays of trellis-work, and covered over with mats to sweat again. At frequent intervals the heaps are carefully examined, lest the heat should become too great. When the fermentation is complete, the leaves are stripped from the stems, bound together in bundles, and conveyed to the market for sale.

When a tobacconist has purchased several of these bundles, they are conveyed to his manufactory. Here, the first process to which they are subjected, is the removal of the leaf from the stalk. This is performed by women, girls, and boys, who hold the leaves in the left hand, and remove the stalks by a sudden pull with the right. The leaves are now conveyed to another chamber, where they are broken into shreds, and scattered upon a wooden daïs, which may suitably be compared to an English threshing-floor. The shreds are trodden under foot by men, and, at frequent intervals, sprinkled with oil. Should the manufacturer desire to give a reddish colour, he sprinkles the leaves with a powder called Hung-tan, or Chu-sheak, *i.e.*, red stone. The fragments, having been well trodden and well sprinkled with oil, are gathered together, and packed in certain quantities between boards. These boards with their contents are then removed to a large press, where the tobacco is squeezed into, at most, one-third of its former bulk. Near this press there is a tub to receive the oil, which under the great pressure exudes freely. To destroy their elasticity, the leaves remain for several hours in the press, and are taken out in large hard cakes. These are forwarded to the cutting chamber, where they are distributed to workmen, each of whom is provided with a plane, like that which a carpenter uses for the surface of boards. The cutter works in a slanting position, and, placing his cake of tobacco between his knees, planes it into small heaps. Other workmen place these heaps upon tables, and, wrapping them in paper, make them up into packages of various weights, as is done with shag in England. To each manufactory is attached a shop, where much of the tobacco planed in the manner I have described is sold by retail. In the provinces of Shang-tung and Kan-su the tobacco is not cut, but prepared in the form of cakes. In this form it is brought to Canton in large quantities, where it finds a ready sale. The Cantonese invariably use the hookah when smoking this tobacco, as it is necessary to purify its smoke by passing through water.

One other kind of tobacco requires notice. It is that known as " pigtail," and consists of a rope as long and as thick as the queue of a Chinaman. The process of making it, which is done by a single workman, is similar to that of plaiting the hair. It appears to me, however, that " pigtail " tobacco is prepared not by the Chinese, but by the aborigines who inhabit the mountain fastnesses of Formosa. The Chinese also prepare tobacco for sale in the shape of cigarettes, which are to be bought at the

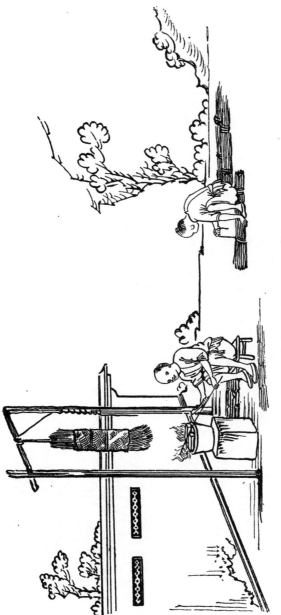

PREPARING REEDS FOR PIPE STEMS.

CHINESE PIPES.

cheap rate of three for one cash. These are manufactured by hand, and consist of a small quantity of broken tobacco rolled in a narrow strip of white paper, which they call Soon-tsoo-chee.

In all probability, the seeds of the tobacco plant were brought to China by the Portuguese, or the Spaniards, during the sixteenth century, after which the cultivation of the plant soon became general. In 1641, Tsung-ching, who was at that time Emperor, issued an edict to his Manchu subjects, in which he strictly commanded them to abstain from its use. Seeing that the great majority of Chinese men and women in all ranks and conditions of life are smokers, and that it is the fashion for girls of even eight or nine years of age to have as an appendage to their dress a silken purse or pocket to hold the pipe and tobacco to which they aspire, even if they do not already use them, it will be acknowledged that the invectives of this sovereign, and of some of his successors, have not been very effectual. Curiously enough, a few years prior to that in which Tsung-ching's edict was issued, we find James I. of England also engaged in endeavouring to suppress the habit of tobacco-smoking in our own country by his famous *Counter-blast*. To show the rapid spread of the practice at that time, I may quote a sentence from the Commission which was then addressed to the Lord Treasurer. His Majesty observes :—" Tobacco, being a drug of late years found out and brought from foreign parts in small quantities, was taken and used by the better sorts, both then and now, only as physic to preserve health; but that persons of mean condition now consumed their wages and time in smoking tobacco, to their great injury and to the general corruption."

As materials for making pipes, the Chinese use metal, cane, bone, and different kinds of wood. The forms in which their pipes are made are very various. The most singular is the hookah, to which allusion has already been made. Aged and infirm men have pipes the stems of which are long, so as to admti of their using them as staves.

In this account of the tobacco plant in China, from its first appearance as a seedling to its consumption as a narcotic in the bowl of the smoker, we have wandered from the fresh fields where we found it growing; and we must wander once more afield before concluding this division of the subject. The very extensive reed-fields to be found along the banks of the Yang-tsze, deserve to be noticed. In passing through the prefecture of Cha-yu, or Kia-yu, in the province of Hoo-peh, I found reeds being conveyed to the homesteads in bullock waggons of two and four wheels; and it appeared to me that the wealth of this prefecture was derived in a great measure from this source. On a visit to Kam-poo-sheng, a walled city not far distant from Nankin, I walked over several acres of reed lands, and found that they formed an excellent cover for hog-deer. At frequent intervals I disturbed pelicans, wild geese, and ducks. The reeds are cut down by farmers in autumn, and conveyed to the nearest markets and sold for a great variety of purposes. They form an excellent material for boat-covers, and are purchased in large quantities by boat and ship builders. They are also very extensively used in the construction of cottages and huts, both the outer and inner walls of which are made of them, and rendered impervious to wind and rain by thick coatings of mud. Of the feathery tops of the reeds the Chinese make shoes which, in cold weather, are very comfortable. In some districts they are used extensively as fuel. One of the most prosperous reed-markets I visited was held at the West Gate of the city of Nankin.

CHAPTER XXIV.

AGRICULTURE.—STOCK FARMING.

I HAVE confined my observations on agriculture, so far, mainly to the cultivation of the soil, and to the various crops raised by the Chinese farmer. In the present chapter I shall notice in detail, with occasional digressions, which I trust the reader may find not without interest, the various kinds of live stock to be found on Chinese farms, and the principal features of the treatment of these animals in health and in disease.

Upon the open plains of the southern and central provinces it is customary to see herds of buffaloes graze. This animal—the *Bos bubalus* of naturalists—is of immense service to farmers by its capacity for great and long-continued exertion in the yoke. Its colour is dark, its hair is thin and coarse, and its long horns lie back, nearly level with the neck, and curving upwards as they taper to a point. Its proportions indicate very great strength, and its spirit and courage are very high. Indeed, in India one of the pastimes in which native princes sometimes indulge, is a contest between a trained buffalo and a tiger, and it is stated that in these combats, the former is generally victorious. The wild buffalo of India, the *arnee*, is a much larger animal, however, than the domesticated buffalo of the Chinese farmer. Indeed, there are so many points of difference in the varieties to be found in different parts of Asia, that naturalists have been led to affirm the existence of separate species· In the breed which the Chinese rear, I found the specimens vary considerably, and the measure of strength and size to which they attain depends largely upon the way in which they are reared. With liberal feeding, the buffalo is capable of becoming a very fine animal, standing about six feet high at the shoulders, and measuring about ten feet from the tip of the nose to the root of the tail. The largest specimen which I saw during my long residence in China was on the occasion of a visit which I made to the Golden Island, in the Toon-ting lake, in the province of Hoonan. In the look of the animal there is something very treacherous; and it appears to be suspiciously watchful of Europeans in particular, regarding them with quick, furtive glances, and often attacking them without the slightest warning. From its great fondness for bathing, the Chinese give it the name of the Sui-Ngow, or Water Cow. Its greatest happiness is in a deep pond, shaded by wide-spreading branches of the banyan-tree. Immersed in such a pond, its reclining horns beneath the surface of the water, and with no portion of the powerful frame visible but its eyes—sometimes drowsily closed—and its nostrils, its enjoyment seems to be intense. The flesh of this animal is very coarse, and it is generally bought for food by the lower orders.

The yak, or grunting ox, although it is not a portion of the stock of a Chinese farm, deserves notice as a beast of burden. It is a native of the range of mountains which divide the exclusive country of Thibet from Bhootan, and derives its name from its peculiar voice, with which it is wont, especially when overloaded, to express its feelings in a loud, melancholy, monotonous, and persistent grunting. Its colour is generally black, but the hair, which—especially in the finer varieties—grows in rich profusion on the forehead, neck, chest, hump, and tail, is quite white and of great length. The hair of the tail in particular, is so long that the French give this animal the name of *Bœuf à queue de cheval*. The tail reaches to the ground, and becomes quite clotted with mud when the roads are wet and dirty. Consisting of an abundance of fine silky hair, it is much prized by the Tartars and Chinese. When it has been dyed red, they use it for the tufts with which they decorate their summer caps or bonnets, and adorn their standards and bucklers. When mounted on a handle, it serves as a *chasse-mouches*, or chowrie, to whisk off mosquitoes and other insect pests with which eastern countries are infested. Among the Turks, mounted on the point of a spear it is one of the ensigns of a pacha's dignity. The yak is domesticated by the Tartars, and its milk, of which it yields an abundant supply, is a useful and nourishing article of diet. For the purposes of a team, the animal does not appear to be well adapted, and consequently it is not used, in China at least, as a beast of draught. It is much employed, however, as a beast of burden, and as the roads are steep and rugged, it is fortunate that it is very sure-footed.

Although herds of buffaloes may be seen grazing upon the plains of the southern provinces, the sight of rich pastures well-stocked with milch cows, so common and delightful in England, is rare in these regions. There are scarcely any grazing farms in the south of China. What may be termed the milch cow of the southern farmer, although he uses it for the purposes of the team, belongs to the humped or zebra kind, and is similar in point of size to the smallest breeds which are reared in the north of Scotland, and in the Isle of Skye. The hunch or fatty excrescence on its shoulders is not large, although it sometimes reaches a weight of ten catties. It might be supposed that this hunch, with the loose, deep dewlap, which is also characteristic of the animal, would give it a clumsy and heavy look. But the compactness of its body, especially from the shoulders backwards, the clean-cut shapeliness of its limbs, and the elegant proportions of its head, combine to distinguish it as an animal possessing great symmetry of form. The general colour of the breed is yellow, although a large number of them are black. Their horns, which are bent backwards, are short and round; yellow at the base, and white at the tip. These cattle are easily fed and afford very good beef. It is, however, to supply the tables of foreign residents in China that they are killed, a Chinese, by the laws of his country, being strictly prohibited from slaughtering an animal of such essential service to the farmer in the cultivation of his land. A man who slaughters a draught cow, or ox, exposes himself by the first offence to receive a flogging of one hundred blows, and to be imprisoned in the cangue for a period of two months. For a second, he is sentenced to a flogging of one hundred blows, and extra-provincial exile for the period of his natural life.

A short digression may be permitted here on the use of milk in the southern provinces. I refer especially to Kwang-tung. Fresh milk is not used by the Cantonese. It is a great mistake, however, to suppose that milk has no place in their dietary. On the contrary, the curdled milk of these cows, as well as that of buffaloes, which is very rich, is highly esteemed. In the evening and at night, more especially in the heat of summer, they partake of curdled milk which is prepared with sugar and vinegar, at their homes, or at restaurants call N'gow Ni-poo, or Cow Milk Saloons. It is supposed by many that the milk which Abraham set before the angels in the plains of Mamre, and which Jael gave to Sisera, was a preparation of this nature.

Although the Cantonese do not use fresh cow's milk, many of them do not hesitate to partake of milk from the breasts of women. These persons are aged men and women, whose infirmities have made an ordinary diet insufficient for their support. In a very popular Chinese work, which gives an account of twenty-four remarkable instances of filial piety, we read that a lady of the family, or clan, Tong, was so much devoted to her mother-in-law, who was a very aged woman and without teeth, as to deprive her child of his necessary supplies, in order that she might have some left in her breasts for the old age of the former. The work to which I refer is illustrated, and there is a representation of the old woman being suckled by her daughter-in-law. I have occasionally seen similar representations painted on porcelain cups. Dr. Hobson, a learned physician, and one of the greatest philanthropists that ever resided in the city of Canton, writes in one of his medical missionary reports :—

"An infant a few months old, in consequence of the mother being unable to continue nursing, was committed to a Chinese wet nurse, and, as money was no object, the woman that had the best supply of milk was chosen for this purpose. For a few days, the child seemed to go on tolerably well; but it soon became affected with head symptoms; and, as one child had died a year before from symptoms somewhat similar, the parents became alarmed, and begged that I would come in consultation to see the child. I found the child lying listless, and almost insensible, on a friend's lap, labouring under the symptoms so graphically described by Dr. Marshall Hall and Dr. Watson, of spurious hydrocephalus. I examined the nurse, who was a young, healthy-looking woman, with breasts full of milk to overflowing. I had some put in a cup for inspection; it threw up no cream, and looked pale and watery. On further investigation, I discovered that the woman had been in the habit of selling her milk in small cupfuls to old persons, under the idea of its highly nutritive properties; and thus her milk, though abundant in quantity, soon became quite degenerate in quality, and instead of being nutritious, was actually poisoning the child dependent on it, and now fast sinking from inanition. I recommended the nurse to be changed immediately. Happily, a suitable one was found in a few hours, and in two or three days afterwards I saw the child laughing and playing on the sofa by the side of its new nurse."

In the northern parts of China, and especially in Mongolia, where the grazing lands are very extensive, milch cows are kept in large numbers. When traversing the vast rolling plains of Inner Mongolia in 1865, I saw several very large droves of cattle; and at all the Mongolian encampments at which I stopped I obtained copious supplies of fresh milk. Essentially pastoral in their mode of life, these people, like the patriarchal fathers of Israel, dwell in tents ; and, in all probability, the tents to which we have frequent allusions in the writings of Moses, were very similar to those beneath which the Mongolians live at the present day. The first mention of the former takes us back to antediluvian times, and in Genesis (iv. 20) we are told that Jabal " was the father of such as dwell in tents, and of such as have cattle." From the minute account given in Exodus (xxvi. 14) of the tent made for the tabernacle, we may conclude that, in early times, it was usual to cover tents with the skins of beasts; and at this day they may be seen on the plains of Mongolia covered with skins. The material generally used for tents, however, is drill. In construction, they are very similar to those which I saw in Arabia when at Aden, *i.e.* of an oblong shape, and twelve or fifteen feet high in the centre. They require more or fewer poles to support them, according to their size. Like the patriarchs who pitched their tents near wells of water, the Mongolians encamp by pools and rippling streams. Each encampment is arranged in the form of a circle, the whole being enclosed by a wall, within which the cattle are driven at the close of the day. When resting, the Mongolians squat on the ground; and, if the weather is cold, they arrange themselves round the fire, which is usually kindled in the centre of the tent, at the top of which is a wide aperture to admit of the smoke escaping. Round each encampment numerous small white banners are displayed, on each of which are written prayers in the Thibetan character. These are supposed to avert all impending calamities. I observed white silk handkerchiefs sometimes suspended before the household gods. These are termed " hadacks," and, having been previously blessed by the living Buddha, or by distinguished Lamas, are supposed to possess great virtue. They are said to impart earnestness and sincerity to the prayers of the members of the family, and to earn for them a ready hearing from the idol. These handkerchiefs are also given as presents to very dear friends.

The cattle in the northern provinces of China and Mongolia are very similar to the middle-horned which are reared in Devonshire and in Yorkshire. They are red, and are well adapted for the yoke, the shoulder-points being formed as if for the collar. As dairy cattle the cows are much appreciated; and milk is used in its fresh state, as is common among people who have much cattle. It is also prepared as butter and cheese. Their bulls, or bullocks, are of inestimable value for the purposes of the team, being not only quiet and active, but capable, in harness, of enduring great fatigue. Between Pekin and Llama-miou, I met at the lowest computation between three and four thousand bullock carts. These were laden with soda, and other articles of merchandise, which it was the intention of the travelling merchants to offer for sale in the markets of North China. On my way from Llama-miou, to Koo-pee-kow, I observed that the bullock carts were not less numerous.

Before passing on, let me briefly notice the mode in which the Chinese farmer feeds his cattle, and look at one or two of the prescriptions which the Chinese cow-doctor makes up for them in sickness. The aim of the cowherd is not only to give the cattle good grass, but clear water at regular intervals during the day. During the winter months, when grass is scarce, straw chopped into small pieces and mixed with beans or peas, the husks of rice, and a little water, forms their staple food. Care is also taken that they are well housed. Their bedding consists of the straw of rice, wheat, or barley. It is the duty of the cowherd to shake this up daily, and to renew it every ten days. Chinese farmers and stock breeders are not unskilled in the diseases of cattle. If a cow is supposed to be sick, it is customary in many parts of the empire to attach a bell to her horns, especially at night, so that it may be readily ascertained whether she is able to chew the cud. If the cattle suffer from any of their ordinary sicknesses, a draught is administered, consisting of five mace of rhubarb and five mace of salts, mixed together in a bowl of water. This is poured down the throat of the animal, without any apparent difficulty, by means of a bamboo tube. When the cattle suffer from murrain, the owner burns incense sticks, the smoke and odour of which are very powerful, at the head of each stall, to dispel the epidemic. When the animals refuse to graze, draughts are administered, consisting of Tsing-muk-haong (four taels), and Koon-n'gan (one catty), well mixed together in pure water, and then boiled. If cattle suffer from lice, the cowherd besmears their bodies with an ointment, the principal ingredients of which are oil and hog's lard. In the case of scab, he rubs them with a paste made of black peas. If they pass blood, draughts of salt water are given; and should this remedy prove ineffectual, a preparation of Tong-qui and Hung-fa is administered. These medicines are boiled over a slow fire, after having been well mixed with two catties of Chinese wine. For ophthalmia, the farmers regularly and copiously bathe the eyes of their cattle with salt water. When a cow has a propensity to butt, they account for the circumstance by the supposition that she has a large gall-bladder; and accordingly the cowherd is called upon to give her a draught consisting of rhubarb (five mace), wine (one catty), and a hen's egg, mixed together. It is very necessary for a Chinese owner of stock to check this propensity, for were one of them to butt or gore any one to death, the law would deal with him severely. When a cow dies, it is customary to send for three or four Taouist priests to drive away the spirit of the dead beast. It is gravely supposed that, should a farmer neglect this ceremony, the spirit would infect and cause the death of the whole herd. After the various incantations, the priests march round the premises, as if in the act of driving away the spirit of the dead beast.

I must not quit this subject without mentioning a very curious custom which prevails in many parts of the empire. Many farmers and breeders of stock keep a monkey in their folds, believing that his presence is a safeguard to the cattle against all the ailments to which they are subject.[1]

The Chinese convert the hides of cattle into leather. They are placed to steep in vats containing water, saltpetre, and lime. At the end of thirty days they are taken out, the hair is scraped from them, and they are well washed in spring water. Each hide is then divided into three sheets or pieces, and pared, after which it is well smoked by being drawn several times over a smoking furnace. It is then stretched upon a flat board, and secured by nails, until it has been thoroughly dried by the heat of the sun. When it is desirable to give a yellow colour to the leather which the smoking furnace has rendered black, it is besmeared with a dye, which consists of water in which the fruit of a tree called Wong-chee is soaked. Of the parings of the hides, glue is made by boiling them for twelve hours in pans placed over slow fires. The glue is then poured into coarse earthenware pots, in which it remains to congeal for three days. It is then cut into sticks with sharp knives, and carefully arranged on trays of lattice work, which are deposited to dry on shelves in an open shed, or Dutch barn. The time required for drying these sticks varies according to the season of the year.

---

[1] The goat seems to hold an analogous position on English farms. It is a common custom in many parts of England for farmers to have a goat or goats along with the cattle in the fold, and also in the field. The reason given for this —I speak from information obtained from a Hertfordshire man—is that the smell from the goat is regarded as healthy for the cattle. In Kent, where the custom also obtains, the reason given is that the goat is a lucky animal. Perhaps in the latter case we have an example of a custom appearing to be merely a superstition, because the original reason for it has been lost sight of.—ED.

Should the north-west monsoon prevail, five days only are required. During the south-west monsoon, forty or fifty days are found to be necessary. The sediment in the pans in which the glue has been boiled, as well as the hair which has been scraped from the hides, is sold to agriculturists for manure. At Pak-sha, a village near Canton, there is a large establishment for the manufacture of leather which is worthy of a visit.

What I have written about the infrequency of herds of cattle in the southern provinces is also true respecting flocks of sheep, which are very rarely indeed to be met with in these regions. In the north of China, however, and in Mongolia, flocks of sheep are very numerous. The breed is that known as the broad-tailed sheep. Their colour is generally white ; in some instances it is a pleasing mixture of black and white. The wool of the lambs has a great tendency to curl, and it is so much prized on this account that the owner of a flock some-times slaughters the ewes which are great with young for the skin of the unborn lamb, in which the tendency to curl is more marked, and which is highly valued as an article of commerce.

In the eighth month of the year—which corresponds with our October—the rutting season commences. At this time, ten ewes are allotted to each ram. Rams without horns are pre-ferred. In the second month of the year—which corresponds with our March—the lambing season is at hand, and the watchfulness of the shepherd is greatly increased. Mongolian sheep-breeders not unfrequently confine the ewes during the lambing season within ring fences. They also often give hay to their flocks, as well as pasture. Though the lambing season usually commences in March, many lambs are dropped at the end of the twelfth month, which corresponds with our January. The lambs dropped in the first month—which corresponds with our February—are regarded as likely to become the largest and finest sheep in the flock. The first reason which the breeders give for this opinion, is that during this month the udders of the ewes contain an abundant supply of milk ; and the second, that on the arrival of the time for weaning, or speaning, there will be an abundant supply of grass.

Sheep-shearing takes place in the month of June. The custom

which obtains at home of washing the sheep in a running stream before shearing them, so far as I could observe, is not practised in China. The wool, however, is well washed as soon as it has been removed from the back of the sheep. For this purpose it is put into large wicker-baskets, which are placed along the bed of a shallow creek or running stream, and the wool is washed by men who stand in them, performing this operation with their feet. The wool is greatly used by the Chinese, who value it much more than the flesh.

For sheep-shearing as performed in the south of China, where the method adopted is very similar to that practised in England, the Mongolians substitute a process which inflicts great pain on the animal. The legs of the sheep are bound together, and the wool is plucked from the body with an iron instrument in the form of a human hand.[1] At a sheep-shearing, if it may be so called, at which I was present, I ventured to point out to the Mongolian shepherds the cruelty of the method which they adopted for removing the fleece. They endeavoured to justify themselves by saying that their method was more practical than shearing, as it removed only such portions of the fleece as were ripe. The sheep evidently suffered very great pain, and so incessant and piteous were their bleatings that it was impossible for me long to remain a spectator of the scene. In withdrawing, I could not help thinking how little it accorded with the descriptive language of the prophet Isaiah, in the memorable passage—" As a sheep before her shearers is dumb."

In countries like the north of China and Mongolia, it is necessary on account of the wild beasts to have large and well-protected sheepfolds. During the winter months—so great is the inclemency of the weather—it is absolutely essential that the flocks be taken under cover by night. Sheepfolds are therefore generally attached to the farmer's house; and, in order to facilitate the superintendence of the flock by night, it is customary to have a small doorway or window in the wall which divides the dwelling-house from the fold. The floors of

---

[1] Within a comparatively recent period it was the custom in England to deprive the sheep of its wool by "rowing," or tearing it from the back with the hand.—ED.

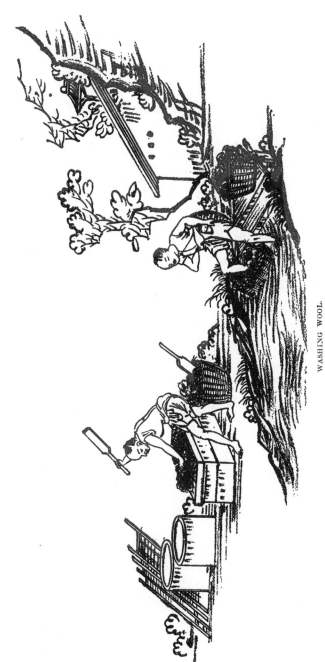

WASHING WOOL.

the folds are usually covered with perforated boards, so as to keep the sheep dry and the fold clean. Twice a-day they are carefully swept. In spring and summer the shepherds lead their flocks to the pastures at an early hour; but in autumn and winter the same regularity is not considered necessary. I say "lead," for in China, as was the case in Judæa, the sheep are wont to follow their shepherds, who walk before them. To an Englishman who has never seen such a sight in his own country, but to whom the idea of it is familiar from his youth, connected, perhaps, with many a tender memory of his mother's early religious training, the spectacle of sheep being gently led by their shepherd is singularly interesting. This practice does not seem to have been observed by the shepherds of ancient Greece or Rome; for neither in prose nor verse do we find anything from which we may infer that sheep were taught to follow instead of being driven by their shepherds. The custom would seem to be a characteristic distinction between the shepherds of European and of Asiatic countries, in ancient as well as in modern times. No doubt it is one of very great antiquity. In Exodus (iii. 1) we read that Moses " led the flock to the backside of the desert ; " and in the book of Psalms (lxxvii. 20), we read, " Thou leddest thy people like a flock by the hand of Moses and Aaron." As the sheep is of all animals the most gentle, the Chinese contend that those make the best shepherds who are tender-hearted and have passed the middle age of life. To overlead the sheep is very injurious, and the Chinese say that this is a fault which the young and inexperienced shepherd is disposed to commit.

The wild beasts from whose attack the flocks require to be protected, include the wolf, the panther, the fox, and the badger. The first is especially dangerous, prowling about the Mongolian plains in a very deliberate manner. While I was travelling across these plains a large specimen crossed our path, with an air of *nonchalance* which led me to suppose that it was a dog belonging to a neighbouring encampment. When it neared the encampment, however, a number of Mongolian women rushed from one of the tents and raised a shout of alarm. Two or three men whom the outcry summoned from a neighbouring tent

were quickly in the saddle, and, with their dogs, gave hot chase
to the prowler.   One of my companions followed their example,
on one of the riding horses which we had always in attendance.
The wolf was now in what Touchstone declared the shepherd to
be—" a parlous state."   If numbers were to win the day, he
was clearly in a painful minority.   If strategy were to succeed,
the men, horses, and dogs, following in his wake, were evidently
of opinion that, overcome by his desire for creature comforts like
a stray lamb or two, he had committed a serious strategical
blunder.   The wily old bandit, however, the deliberate character
of whose movements at the outset probably resulted from a
well-tested knowledge of his own powers, had his retrograde
movements carefully planned, and succeeded in safely reaching
the slopes of a neighbouring mountain, where further pursuit
was useless.   On the following morning I observed another
wolf sporting in the sun, with such lively indications of perfect
satisfaction with himself, as to show that he must have partaken of a substantial meal.   When passing a night, in the June
of 1865, at an inn a few miles to the north of the Koo-pee-kow
Pass of the Great Wall of China, a wolf, at the dead of night,
entered a pigstye adjoining the room in which I was sleeping,
and bore off in triumph two out of a litter of nine pigs.   The
occupants of the inn were roused by the almost unearthly sounds
of terror which ensued; and the sow, bursting open the door
of her stye, rushed wildly across the yard of the inn, followed
by the rest of her bewildered progeny.   To guard their sheepfolds from such attacks, it is customary for the inhabitants of
these regions to place a " scare wolf" in each fold, and to paint
a large circle of white round the outer walls.   It is supposed—
not without reason—that the wolves regard these circles of white
paint with suspicion, and withdraw under the impression that a
trap has been set for them.   The effect which any unfamiliar
object has in deterring wolves from making an attack is well
known, and travellers have often owed their escape to it.

One of the most troublesome diseases of sheep in Asia, as
well as in Europe, is the scab.   It is more prevalent during the
summer.   Sheep suffering from scab show evident symptoms
of distress, and may be seen scratching themselves with their

feet, or rubbing their bodies against the walls and gates of the sheepfold. The cause of this disease is a small insect, and the Chinese endeavour to extirpate it, by washing the sheep daily with rice-water in which the roots of a long grass that grows by the banks of rivers and creeks have been soaked for several days. This grass makes the water very sour. For ophthalmia, which is also common enough among sheep in China, the same remedy—bathing the eyes with salt water—is used as in the case of cattle. For murrain, or a discharge of rheum from the nostrils and eyes, the shepherd washes the parts with pure water, and then applies rags which have been well soaked in salt water. To protect sheep from foot disease, owners are careful not to allow them to graze on lands which are at all of a marshy nature. They refrain from giving boiled food to their flocks, believing that "hoove"—a diseased distention of the belly—would be the consequence of their doing so. To remove this disease the shepherd rubs the tongue of the sheep with salt. As Chinese sheepowners are well aware that "one sickly sheep infects the flock, and sickens and poisons all the rest," they carefully isolate the infected animal until a complete cure has been effected. To prevent apoplexy—which usually results from pressure on the brain, and is of frequent occurrence among sheep—a most absurd antidote is employed. From the roof of the fold is suspended a porous vessel containing salt water and poisonous snakes. The vessel, from which the liquid exudes, hangs only a few feet above the ground, and the sheep licking its sides imbibe what is regarded as a preventive of apoplexy. When an epidemic prevails, it is usual, in some parts of the empire at all events, for the farmer to call in the services of a monkey, to whose presence among cattle, as I have already stated, the Chinese attach a superstitious value. In order that he may be in a proper position to exercise the remarkable influence he is supposed to possess over the flock, the monkey is bound to the top of a high pole, which is erected in the centre of the fold.

At all the hotels in the north of China and Mongolia, the *table-d'hôte* is never without the very best of mutton; which is not surprising, as the price of a sheep in these regions

averages from one to two dollars. In the south of China, however, sheep are very dear, owing to their scarcity. The flesh of
the sheep is sometimes salted in the same way as bacon. I have
often seen it in this preserved state on board the large junks
trading between Tien-tsin and Canton. The mutton hams are
apparently as good and savoury as those which I have tasted in
the southern counties of Scotland. Of the broad tails of their
sheep the Mongolians make what may be termed "mutton
wine." The tails are skinned, cut into several small pieces, and
boiled for some time in ordinary wine. So strongly does the
wine smell of mutton fat, that it requires no ordinary degree
of courage to raise a glass to one's lips. A jar or bottle of this
wine was given me once by a Tartar family. It was, however, so offensive both in smell and taste, that neither I nor my
Chinese servants could drink it.[1]

Although sheep are not reared to any great extent in the
southern provinces, goats are bred in great numbers. I have
often seen vast herds grazing on the hills which bound the north
wall of Canton, and in the valley which leads from that city to
the White Cloud mountains. It seemed to me, however, that
the herds in the southern provinces were not as a rule so large
as those in the north. The goats are almost invariably black,
which renders them of greater value in the estimation of the
Chinese. This remark applies, indeed, to animals and birds of
all kinds, those of a black colour being greatly preferred as
articles of food. At the north gate of Canton there are establishments in which goats are reared for the market, as there is a
greater demand for the flesh of this animal than for that of any
other, except the pig. Many goats are slaughtered for funeral
purposes, as their carcases are used as offerings to the spirits of

---

[1] It appears from a report by Dr. Dudgeon of Pekin, that mutton wine is also
distilled by the Mongolians from cow's milk wine. The latter wine is flavoured
with the bones of a two-year-old sheep, and with white and black sugar, raisins,
honey, and various vegetable drugs well known to Chinese apothecaries. The
prescription is as follows:—"Cow's milk wine, 40 catties; honey, 4 oz.; white
sugar, 1 oz.; black sugar, 8 oz.; raisins, 1 catty; dragon's eyes (fruit of the
Nephelium Longan) 4 oz.; cloves, 5 candareens; nutmeg, 5 candareens; rad.
caraganæ flav., 3 candareens; sien-fen-chang, 1 candareen; pai-chi, 3 candareens; shan-nai, 1 candareen. The last six are various aromatics."

the dead. At the celebration of the obsequies of a wealthy person several carcases are borne by men, on their backs, in the funeral procession. Curdled goat's milk is used by the Cantonese as an article of diet. So far as I am aware, they never drink it fresh.

The skins of goats are essential articles of dress in the wild regions of Mongolia, and there are few better and more durable defences against cold and rain. When the hair is removed from the skin, small carpets and mats are manufactured from it. In the south of China the skin is eaten; and the hair is sold sometimes to farmers, who consider it a useful manure, or to tradesmen, who employ it in the manufacture of Chinese pens. The blood is supposed by the Cantonese to possess medicinal properties, and is taken internally. It is regarded as a powerful emetic, and is not unfrequently given to persons labouring under the effects of opium and other poisons. The Cantonese often smear with it the foreheads of persons supposed to have been made sick by evil spirits. At Pekin in the north, and at Nankin and Chin-kiang, cities upon the banks of the Yan-tsze, and at Yang-yang-chang-chow, and other cities on the Grand Canal, I observed goats employed to drag the small carriages of children of the wealthier classes.

I saw several herds of wild goats grazing on the plains of Mongolia. These were called "yellow sheep" or "yellow goats;" and from the observations which I was able to make, I gathered that they were the species spoken of in the Naturalist's Library edited by Sir William Jardine, (Vol. IV.) as the "Jewtah goat." The Mongolians and Chinese stalk these animals with matchlocks of a very rude description. Near the muzzles of the guns are two wooden prongs attached to the forepart of the stock, upon which the sportsman rests his gun as he lies on the ground taking aim. The flesh of the wild goat is said to be little inferior to that of deer.

As might be expected from the fact of their flesh being the principal animal food consumed by the crowded population of so vast an empire, swine occupy an important place in the Chinese farmyard. The pigs are not quite so large as those of our own country. They are very well formed, and except for a slight, hollow in the back, they bear a striking resemblance to the prick-eared pig of England. They are mostly white, or white and black. This remark, however, applies only to the pigs of the south of China. In the northern provinces and in Mongolia they are all black. Were it not for the fact that the black pigs of the north are covered with hair, I should be disposed to conclude that there was consanguinity between them and the smooth black pig of the Neapolitan breed. In Mongolia, I saw several very large herds of black swine; and as they were being driven across the plains they seemed to live on grass, like the vast droves of cattle around them.

For breeding purposes, sows which have short snouts and bristly hair are considered the best; and those boars are preferred which, from the time of their weaning, have been kept apart from sows. As a rule, the boars are kept by aged and indigent cottagers, who suspend sign-boards from the doors of their cottages, indicating in large letters that a boar is kept upon the premises. The owner takes the animal to the various farmyards, and the fee does not exceed two hundred cash. While the boar remains at the farmyard, the owner is boarded and lodged by the farmer or pig-dealer. Such an occupation is regarded by the Chinese as one of the most degrading which a man can pursue. The sows are of a very prolific nature. They bear two litters in the year, and have from ten to fifteen, and sometimes from eighteen to twenty, young at a time. I remember one instance of a sow—the property of a Chinese friend of the name of Yik Afi—which had a litter of twenty-three. I never heard, however, of any Chinese rival to the famous sow of which Gilbert White recorded that, when she died, she was the mother of three hundred pigs. The Chinese seldom or never allow a sow to suckle more than twelve pigs at a time; and all above that number are sold. A market for sucking pigs which opens at 7 A.M., and closes at 9 A.M., is held daily at Canton, in the street called Chaong-lok-ki. The young pigs are bought, as a rule, by pig-breeders whose sows have given birth to fewer pigs than they are considered capable of suckling. Lest the sow should regard the new comers as intruders, and gore them to death, her own

FEEDING PIGS.

litter are taken from her, and sprinkled like the others with
wine. When driven into the stye, all of them have the same
smell of wine, and it is supposed that the sow regards them all
as pigs of the same litter.

When a sow is near the time of farrowing, she is put into a
stye by herself. On the floor a small quantity of chopped straw
or of the husks of paddy is strewed as bedding. The straw is
cut into short pieces, to prevent the young pigs becoming
entangled in it. The sow is apt to overlay her young when
they bury themselves in long loose straw. In some parts of
China, the pigs get a vapour bath when they are a few hours
old. They are confined in a cage above a large pot of boiling
water. The steam, it is said, gives strength to the bones of the
cranium. In some districts, pig-breeders cut off the tails of
their pigs when they are three days old. They are foolish
enough to imagine that this prevents those sicknesses which
arise from cold, and causes the pig when sixty days old to fatten
rapidly. When a sow gives birth to a litter, a meal of fried
rice, with which a little Chinese vinegar and a small quantity
of charcoal soot are mingled, is given her. When weaned, the
young pigs are fed upon well-boiled rice and water. Should
rice be very dear, sweet potatoes, well boiled, are given as a
desirable substitute. The female pigs are spayed when two
months old. During the spring and summer months it is
usual to let pigs out to graze on the sides of the hills, and on
waste lands. When they have reached the age of twelve
months, the non-breeders are confined to pens in order to be
fattened for the market. At first, beans and the husks of rice
are given to them : afterwards, pease-meal or bean-meal and
water. The food given to fatten pigs varies in different parts
of the country. Some farmers fatten their hogs upon yellow
peas and wheat-shoots, mixed with roots called Kun-chung and
Ho-show-wo. A little salt is added to this mixture, and four
taels (weight) of it are supplied to each pig daily. For the
twelve hours before he is killed, a hog is deprived of food.
His feet are then bound, and he receives his death-blow by a
resolute stab in the neck. When all the blood has flowed out
of it, the body is scalded and well scraped with knives to take

off the hair with the cuticle. Of the hairs, the Chinese make brushes; and they use the bristles for sewing the soles of shoes. The cuticle is sold to farmers as manure for rice-fields, or to florists, who use it in making a rich mould for their flower-pots. The hog is then hung up, and the entrails taken out. After the inside has been washed clean with a cloth, the body is cut into many portions, and exposed for sale in the butcher's shop. Portions of the carcase are sometimes bought by hawkers, who go from door to door crying fresh pork for sale. Bacon is seldom, if at all, cured in the south of China. The province of Fo-kien, however, which lies immediately to the north of Kwang-tung, is very famous for its excellent bacon. In the summer season the entrails of the pig are fried and eaten; in winter they are made into sausages. Nor is the skin wasted. It is either made into glue by being boiled in vinegar and water, or prepared for human consumption by being baked in an oven and boiled in water. The fresh blood is also sold as food. It is generally bought by poor persons, who regard it, when it has been well boiled with water, as an excellent soup. When old, it is bought by painters, who mix it with lime and use it for smearing the doors and walls of dwelling-houses before painting them. The bones of the pig are burned; and reduced by means of a pestle and mortar to a fine powder, which is bought by farmers as an excellent manure.

Chinese pig-breeders profess to have a great knowledge of the maladies to which these animals are liable, and of the modes of treating them. When they are afflicted with the scab, the diseased parts are washed with tobacco water. During an epidemic, five mace of rhubarb and a small quantity of salt are given to each pig. When bleeding is deemed necessary, they puncture a vein in the tail of the animal. Loss of appetite is often treated by puffing musk into their nostrils. During the great heat of summer, a cooling medicine is given, which consists of a mixture of what are called Wong-sham and Tam-tuk. Two taels of the former and forty taels of the latter are well mixed together and boiled.

Chinese pig-breeders are careful to act upon the principle, that much of the profit to be derived from rearing and fattening

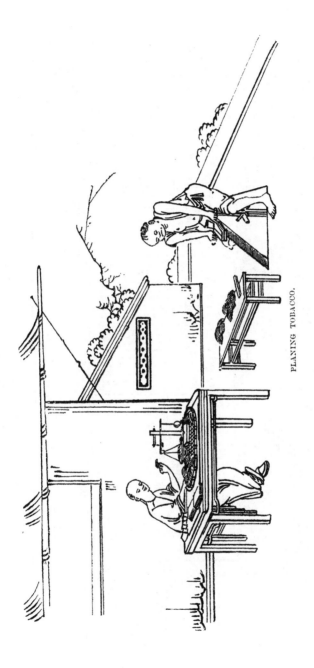

PLANING TOBACCO.

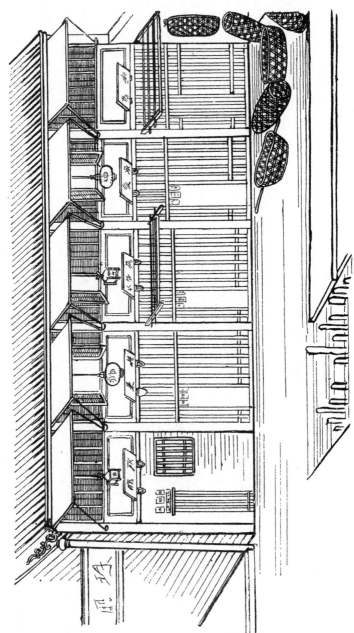

THE PIG-MARKET AT CANTON.

these animals depends upon the manner in which the food is prepared, and the construction of the styes and pens in which they are kept. Each stye consists of a long and lofty chamber, paved with red flag-stones, and divided into several compartments or pens. Each pen is large enough to contain a litter of pigs; and great pains are taken to keep breeding sows, porkers, and hogs in separate pens. The animals are allowed no straw to lie upon, and the flagged floors are, by constant washing, kept as clean as the floor of an English kitchen. Swineherds are always in attendance to remove without delay every particle of excrement. It is possible to visit a stye containing two hundred pigs, without the most sensitive olfactory nerves being offended. It ought, however, to be mentioned as an exception, that in Mongolia, and, again, at Chin-kiang, I saw styes which were neither more nor less than pools of mud. Taouist priests are engaged to drive away all evil influences from the styes. The ceremony in which they profess to do so, is, of course, performed before the pigs are allowed to enter their new domicile. In each stye an altar is erected in honour of the Chu-Lan-Too-Tee, or Genii of pigstyes; and upon the walls of each compartment into which the stye is divided, a strip of red paper is posted, with four Chinese characters, signifying " Let the enemies of horses, cows, sheep, fowls, dogs, and pigs be appeased."

The markets where the animals are exposed for sale are worthy of a visit. Those situated at Cum-lee-fow, Canton, consist of very large buildings, which include both the homes and markets of the pig-dealers. These markets are covered with high roofs, and are divided into pens, each of which contains pigs of the same litter. The pens are boarded with deal planks, and are equal in point of cleanliness to the breeding establishments which I have already described. At the end of the block of buildings is a counting-house, in which the pig-broker attends to his ledger and daybook. Above this office stands an altar, in honour of the tutelary deity of the house, formed of elaborately-carved wood, and gilded or painted. On the walls of the markets are strips of red paper, enclosed in black frames, on which are emblazoned in large characters, written by a calligraphist, sentences having reference to the great advantages of peace, prosperity, and happiness. The buildings are erected on the banks of the river, for the convenience of receiving the pigs which are daily brought by the boats from the surrounding agricultural districts. The number of pigs slaughtered every day in a large Chinese city is, I am assured, very great.

In the southern provinces, herds of swine are not driven through the streets of cities, as is customary in the north. The pigs are carried through the streets in baskets by labourers. Those which have been bought at the market are removed in a similar manner at the expense of the buyer. To the baskets in which, as sold, they are removed from the market, sprigs of the banyan-tree are affixed, as emblems of good fortune. At the house of the purchaser these are removed from the baskets, and placed on the altars of the styes. Worship is also paid to the genii of pigs, and much paper-money offered in sacrifice. The practice in the southern cities of carrying pigs through the streets, instead of driving them, is doubtless owing to the fact that the streets are so narrow. When a pig rushes into a house or shop, it is considered by the southern Chinese that bad fortune will soon overtake the inmates. To avert the impending evil, they will not allow the pig to leave the premises till he has parted with his tail. Where we would ring our pigs, a muzzle is sometimes used; and the use of the ring is not known in China.

The Chinese—I include the Tartars and Mongolians—are not famous for any remarkable breed of horses. In this respect they are unlike most of the nations of Europe, and many of Asia. There is a great scarcity of horses in the southern provinces. In many parts of Kwang-tung and Kiang-si there may be said to be none. This scarcity of horses in the south, and in other parts of China Proper, explains some features in their political economy. To substitute men and draught cattle for horses, and to use as few quadrupeds as possible, so as to have at command a greater quantity of farinaceous and esculent food for human beings, is an idea no way strange to political economists in our own country. In China there are palpable reasons why such a policy should prevail. There are comparatively few cities, towns, or hamlets in this vast empire which do not possess

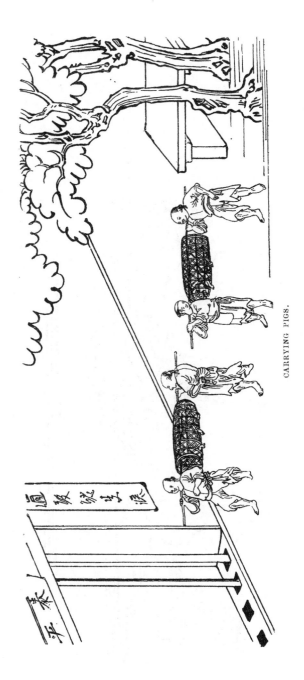

CARRYING PIGS.

A FARMER'S WIFE RIDING TO MARKET ON A WHEEL-BARROW.

their near river, canal, or creek, to render navigation easy, and land transit for travellers, or the bulky commodities of commerce, unnecessary.   To the Chinese the question of an adequate supply of food is a pressing one, which has to be solved by the immediate production of what will support so vast a population. The enormous consumption of grain by horses in England would fill the mind of an honest Chinese with horror.   Were the Celestial Empire suddenly overspread with the powerful breed of quadrupeds which cover the face of our own country, he would read in their sleek and well-fed forms the starvation of many a family.   It is not surprising, therefore, that he is un-willing to encourage the breeding of an animal which in our own and other European countries is considered of such importance.

A word upon one or two of the modes in which the land transit of goods and passengers is accomplished, will show to how large an extent the Chinese make themselves independent of horses.   So powerfully has the food question impressed itself on the Chinese mind that, even in parts of the empire where water communication is not easily accessible, the Chinese refuse to make broad roads, for fear of encroaching on the sur-face of the bread-producing earth.   It is customary on many of the narrow main roads which intersect the provinces—more particularly those of Hoonam, Hoo-peh, Honam, Shan-tung, Chili, and certain districts of Kwang-tung—to see men con-tinually passing and repassing laden with heavy burdens which would elsewhere be borne by animals.   The toil which some of them undergo is of the most painful nature.   I allude to those labourers or carriers who convey passengers and their baggage, and occasionally cumbrous loads of merchandise, in large wheel-barrows both to near and distant parts of the empire.   It is necessary sometimes to yoke several stalwart labourers to these vehicles.   When the wind is fair, they avail themselves of its assistance by means of small sails, which are fastened to slender masts which they erect near the wheels.   In the province of Chili, and in Inner Mongolia, where the roads are very rough, I observed that when their barrows were heavily laden with oil, the labourers occasionally used mules or asses to help them. Sedan-chairs take the place of carriages in China; and persons of all classes are carried in them on men's shoulders both to near and to distant parts of the country. In some parts of the empire—at Nankin, in particular—I observed that many persons, generally women, rode not in sedan-chairs, but in baskets. At Eching, a city on the banks of the Yang-tsze, I noticed a lady, apparently going on a visit to a neighbouring town or village, walking in front of a man-servant who was carrying two baskets, in one of which was a child, and in the other the lady's luggage. The streets of all cities south of the Yang-tsze are so narrow, indeed, as to render traffic by horses quite impracticable. In consequence packages of every kind are borne by porters on their backs.

What I have said about the limited use of the horse in China will find confirmation if we look at the breed which the Chinese rear, and the occasions on which the animal is employed. In the south of China the ponies—for they do not deserve the name of horses—are used principally by government servants. The saddle is very large and clumsy. Round the pony's neck is a band of leather, to which are attached several small bells to warn the people who crowd the narrow streets of southern cities of the animal's approach. These ponies are bred, as a rule, in the province of Kiang-si. In the north, however, where the population is not so dense, and where there are vast plains, more attention is paid to the breeding and rearing of horses by the Chinese, and by the Mongolians, Tartars, and Mantchurians in particular. Even their horses, however, although as a rule handsome, docile, and intelligent, do not generally exceed ten hands in height. In Mongolia I saw horses, about twelve hands high, which appeared to be very strong. For want of a better name, I may term them galloways. The usual colours were chestnut, gray, and bay. They are generally bred in an almost wild state, the stallions and mares being allowed to form herds on the plains at their will. There are also throughout the empire various specimens of what is termed in natural history the tangum, or pie-bald, or skew-bald horse. They are marked with large patches of white and bay; sometimes as to resemble the spotted horses which are found wild in portions of Eastern Tartary.

Respecting the general management and treatment of the

horse, the Chinese, despite their indifference to the animal, are not without some general knowledge. They set forth in their treatises that he is of a fiery nature, and greatly dislikes low or damp ground ; that in the third month of the year (April) he ought to be well fed; that in summer he should be permitted occasionally to graze by the banks of rivers or streams ; that in winter he ought to be kept in a stable having a southern aspect, and be well clothed, as a protection against the cold north wind ; that he ought to be regularly exercised, since confinement to his stall may subject him to swelling of the legs and inflammation of the joints ; that he ought not to be over-ridden or over-driven, as very violent exercise has a tendency to affect his circulatory system ; that after a journey he ought to be carefully rubbed by the groom until perfectly dry ; that neither water nor food should be given to him when in a state of perspiration, lest his wind should be injured ; that he should be watered and fed three times a day ; that the water should be drawn from a well ; and, lastly—not to multiply instances—that his food should consist of wet grass and well-washed beans and peas, or paddy. As a rule, their stables are very rude, resembling cart-sheds. Each possesses an altar in honour of Ma Wong, or the Ruler of Horses ; and in cities and towns there are temples in honour of this god. The largest temple of this description is in Canton, in the street named Chong-yune-tong. One of the attendants of the deity is represented bearing a horse in his hand.

The knowledge which the Chinese possess of the veterinary art is very limited, and some of the prescriptions to be found in their pharmacopœia are ridiculous. If a horse suffer from what they term the " black sweat," some horse-dung which has been dried in the sun is mixed with a quantity of hair, heated over a slow fire, and applied by means of a nose-bag to the nostrils of the afflicted animal. If he suffer from boils, which by the Chinese veterinary surgeon are termed " wart-boils," he is bled by puncturing a vein near the anus, or the lips. At the same time caustic is applied to the roots of the boils, while over them is spread an ointment of which musk is the chief ingredient. The Chinese and Mongolians often bleed their horses by puncturing a vein either in the breast or neck. In the northern provinces it is usual to slit the ears and nostrils of horses. The reasons which were given to me, in justification of this extraordinary practice, were as follows :—It appears that the Emperor Kang-he, after spending a considerable portion of his time in deep study, discovered, amongst other things, that by slitting the ears and nostrils, horses, mules, and asses would be rendered secure against the power of lightning. So soon as he had made this remarkable discovery, the Emperor issued an edict in which he communicated it to his subjects. A general slitting of the ears and nostrils of all the horses, mules, and asses in the empire was instituted at once, and as the Chinese have at all times been earnest believers in the wisdom of their forefathers, the people of to-day continue, more or less, to observe this very singular practice.

Many of the horses in the north are shod with iron shoes as in England. The mode, however, in which the blacksmith accomplishes this, would be laughed at here. The horse is placed under a framework of wood, resembling a gallows ; and raised from the ground by pulleys, and ropes which pass under the belly, and shod while suspended. In the south of China horses are not shod. Their fore-feet, however, are enclosed in shoes of leather which fit the hoof.

The flesh of the horse is eaten both by the Chinese and the Mongolians. On one occasion, while resting near a Mongolian tent, I observed a housewife frying for dinner steaks which I had seen her cut from a haunch of horse. She invited my friends and myself to partake of the hospitality of her tent. We were very reluctant to refuse : but the idea of eating horse-flesh was so repugnant to us that there remained no other alternative. A young woman, apparently a maid-servant, then presented each of our party with a cup of milk. All but one politely declined, as it was the general impression that it was not cow's but mare's milk. The Mongolians not unfrequently preserve the milk of their mares to extract from it a spirituous liquor, which they call koumiss. To this they are very partial, particularly during the summer months.[1] I have read some-

---

[1] A curious reference to this spirit occurs in one of Goldsmith's charming essays, entitled, *On the Advantages which might arise from sending a Philosophic*

where—how much truth there is in the assertion I do not know —that mare's milk, when freely partaken of, gives pain to the eyes.

The Chinese possess a handsome and docile race of mules. Many of those which I saw reminded me of the common grey mules of Egypt. Not a few bore a striking resemblance to the dun-coloured breed of Volterra. Asses—which in every country are essentially the poor man's horses—are very numerous in the northern and central provinces. Slow, patient, laborious, obstinate, as in other countries, the ass of China is remarkable for its strength. In proportion to its size, it can carry heavier weights, and continue to toil longer without sustenance, than any other beast of burden. The flesh of both mules and asses is eaten in many parts of the empire. At Chin-kiang, large quantities were exposed for sale in a butcher's shop which I visited ; and a French priest who lived in this city, informed me that the citizens of Nankin consumed it in considerable quantities.

This account of Chinese *equidæ* would be incomplete without some account of the various kinds of work in which they are employed. Horses and mules are much used in the saddle for travelling, where the distances are very long. For a journey of five hundred miles they have to travel at the rate of from twenty to twenty-five English miles *per diem ;* and so admirable is their training and management, that they perform this work, in the saddle, or as beasts of burden, with apparent ease. Horses and asses are also sometimes used in this way by ladies in travelling, and women in going to market. The women ride them in the same fashion as men. Indeed, the dress of a Chinese lady is not altogether unsuitable for an *equestrienne ;* and among Tartar ladies it is the custom to wear riding-habits of a very modest description. I was much struck with the ease and skill which

Traveller to Asia. He writes :—" There is scarce any country, how rude or un-cultivated soever, where the inhabitants are not possessed of some peculiar secrets, either in nature or art, which might be transplanted with success. Thus, for instance, in Siberian Tartary, the natives extract a strong spirit from milk, which is a secret unknown to the chymists of Europe." One cannot help thinking that Goldsmith must have been somewhat at a loss for examples when he put koumiss first in his list of Asiatic secrets whose discovery would confer a boon upon European nations.—ED.

the latter, accustomed to ride from their infancy, display in the saddle ; and the judgment and dexterity which, near one of the northern towns, I saw a lady display in the management of a restive chestnut, in difficult circumstances, could not have been surpassed by the best English horsewoman. In harness, or, more characteristically, in the yoke, for which they are well prepared by good feeding, horses and mules accomplish, without difficulty, from thirty to forty miles a day. The pace, however, cannot be calculated at more than four or five miles an hour. This is owing, in a great measure, to the heavy tilted carts, or wagons, which are employed by the Chinese. Two mules or horses, and, in some instances, a horse and a mule, are yoked to each cart, and invariably driven tandem. Very great distances are traversed in this way. On one occasion I travelled over eight hundred miles in one of these tilted carts ; and while performing this journey I met with a Chinese merchant from Pekin, whose intention it was to proceed considerably beyond the frontiers of the Russian possessions to purchase a supply of broad cloth, in a cart precisely similar to that in which I was travelling. His cart was followed by two similar vehicles, containing the treasure he was going to invest. By the side of these carts rode three or four men dressed as soldiers, and armed *cap-a-pié*. The merchant himself wore the garb of an official. This disguise of himself and his retinue was, he said, very necessary, as highway robbers, who might not scruple to deprive a travelling merchant of all he possessed, would hesitate to attack an official.

Cart horses and mules are generally in the yoke from eight to ten hours daily. Their pace varies from two to three miles per hour, and the weight which they draw generally exceeds a ton. Horses and mules in the plough work from six to seven hours a day. The severity of their labour depends, of course, upon the nature of the soil and the breadth of the furrow. While the ploughing season continues, the animals engaged in it receive an extra allowance of food. The carts to which I have alluded, are covered vehicles made entirely of wood. The body rests on a strong axle-tree supported by two wheels with six or eight spokes in each. As it is without springs, this is the most unsuitable of all carriages for travelling. The carts

A LADY ON HORSEBACK.

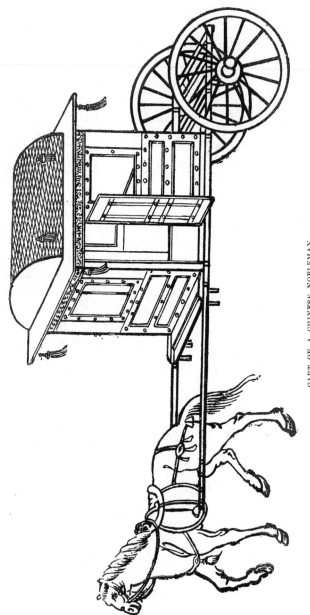

CART OF A CHINESE NOBLEMAN.

used by the nobility differ very slightly from those of the
people. The only difference which I observed, was this—that
the after end of the cart, and not the centre, was made to rest on
the axle-tree. From illustrations which I have seen, it appears
that this was also characteristic of the chariots of ancient Persia.
The wagons are not unlike those which are used in our own
country. In the north of China, more particularly in the
provinces of Shansi or Shensi, wagons appear to have been
used long ago by a nomadic people in their migrations. Wheel-
carriages were first introduced by the Emperor Tay-yu, who was
the founder of the Hia dynasty, B.C. 2205. At this early period,
however, they were not, it appears, drawn by horses, but by men.
Their use was in a great measure restricted to royal and noble
families. The cars in which the Emperor of this dynasty rode
were invariably drawn by twenty men. During the Shang
dynasty, which was founded by Chin-tang, B.C. 1766, the Imperial
car was drawn by eighteen men. Later on, throughout the
Chow dynasty, which was established by Wu-wang, B.C. 1122,
fifteen men seem to have been considered sufficient: and in the
Han-tsin dynasty, which was founded B.C. 246, the Emperor
Che Hwangte, being annoyed by the noise caused by the wheels
of his chariot, ordered them to be taken off; and directed that
in future his car should be borne on the shoulders of men.
During the Shang dynasty, in the seventeenth century before
the present era, it was usual to yoke horses to the cars.
This custom was very generally observed during the succeeding dynasty of Chow. In B.C. 1705, wagons very similar
to those which were then, and still are, used in China, were
employed in Egypt. From a passage contained in Genesis
(xlv. 19, 27) we learn, that the King of Egypt sent wagons to
assist in transporting the family of Jacob from Canaan. These
conveyances were, of course, not war chariots, nor the vehicles
in use among the gentry, but wagons, which must have been
in many respects similar to those of China. When travelling in
Mongolia, I was reminded of this patriarchal journey by the
many tilted wagons which I met, containing Chinese families
migrating from the provinces of Shansi or Shensi to the
extensive plains and rich valleys of Mongolia. In the city of

Chan-chu-kow, which is near the Great Wall of China, I observed vehicles of this description employed as omnibuses. There is, also, a very rude cart, or wagon, drawn usually by oxen or by horses and oxen, and employed by farmers for the carriage of their agricultural produce. In the north, the Chinese use a horse litter, consisting of a light frame, resembling a sedan chair, and fixed upon two strong poles. The framework is covered with cloth, and has a door on each side. The litter is borne by two mules, one between the poles in front, and the other behind. These conveyances are used by the gentry during a journey, when disposed for retirement or comfort, or when sick, or feeble from age. They are also frequently used by ladies of position, in their travels. They are let out on hire, at many of the stations in the north, and I proceeded in one of them from the town of Nan-kow to the walled city of Cha-tow, and found it a most comfortable conveyance. The road between these two towns extends over fifteen miles, and leads the traveller through one of the most rugged mountain-passes, which I apprehend, this world can boast.

The harness of draught horses is very similar to that which is used in Great Britain. The curb-chain, however, which consists of cord, is placed, not under the chin, but between the upper lip and the nose. The harness of the horses or mules employed to draw the carts of members of the Imperial Family is covered with yellow cloth; and that of the gentry is sometimes mounted with silver rings and buckles. When wealthy families are in mourning, the harness of the horses and mules is invariably covered with white cloth.

Besides horses and mules, asses and oxen, the camel is much employed in carrying agricultural and other produce. The species used by the Chinese is that which is supposed by naturalists to have been originally discovered in Bactria. It is large and robust, and capable of enduring a great variety of climates. It is distinguished from the camel of Arabia by the presence of two humps on the back. The height of a full-grown camel of this species is upwards of seven feet. The hair, which is long and shaggy on some parts of the body, is of a dark brown colour, though light varieties frequently occur. By the Mongolians, as by the Arabs, its milk is regarded as a very nutritive beverage ; and in regions where firewood is scarce, its dung, like that of the cow, is used for fuel. Its flesh—more particularly the fatty substance of · the hunches—is also in great request among this singular and interesting people. The burdens which the Chinese place upon the backs of their camels are not nearly so ponderous as those under which the camels of Arabia groan. For the saddle, camels of a lighter build are bred, and carry their riders with great swiftness, accomplishing from sixty to nearly a hundred miles a day. One of the pictures which my memory frequently reproduces as characteristic of the scenes through which I travelled in the northern regions of the empire, is that of a Mongolian who passed me on camel-back. A noble patriarch of a man, with bronzed face and flowing beard of white, resting high in saddle and on stirrup on the mountainous back of this singularly-fashioned steed, he was borne with ungainly motion and astonishing rapidity across the plains. Occasionally, especially when intent upon long journeys, ladies mount these uncouth steeds. On one occasion, leaving the city of Wi-li-sheang, I witnessed the migration of a nomadic family. They were Mongolians, two ladies—who, by the dresses they wore, were evidently of rank—three or four gentlemen, and several attendants, all mounted on camels ; and I could not help thinking of the days when " Jacob rose up, and set his sons and his wives upon camels."

As in Arabia and Egypt, these animals, when used as beasts of burden, follow each other in single file, the halter of the second camel being bound to the trappings of the first, that of the third to those of the second, and so on. From the neck of the last animal a bell is suspended, the tinkling of which makes known to the camel-driver, more especially at night, that the line continues unbroken. This is very essential where, as in many parts, the roads are scarcely distinguishable even by daylight.

Bells are also attached to pack-horses, pack-mules, and asses. In explanation of the almost universal prevalence of this custom, two or three arguments were mentioned to me. Its many-sided advantages had not occurred to me until I discussed

the subject. Thus I learned that the bells by their cheerful
tinkle encourage, on long journeys, the toiling beasts of burden;
that, in the streets and marts of cities, they warn busy crowds
of bipeds that beings with four legs and heavy bodies are
approaching; that " far from the gadding crowd" on lonely
plains and in gloomy mountain-passes, they cast a spell over
wondering wild beasts; and that, above all, by night, in regions
where the roads are ill-defined, their constant music is a guide
to lead those who have strayed or loitered behind to their companions whom the darkness has swallowed up. The custom of
suspending bells from the trappings of horses and beasts of
burden must have been observed by Oriental peoples from the
earliest times. Thus the prophet Zechariah introduces it as a
feature of the glory of the kingdom of the Messiah, that " In
that day shall there be upon the bells of the horses, HOLINESS
UNTO THE LORD."

Chinese farms, like English, have their ducks, geese, and
fowls. Pigeons are also reared by farmers in considerable
numbers. The subject of Chinese poultry might be dismissed
more summarily, if they only occupied the place of delicacies as in England. In China, however, they constitute,
together with rice, fish, and pork, the food of the masses as well
as of the upper ten thousand.

There is one curious exception to this statement. A numerous,
class, who are followers of a god named Hong-Yuen-Shuee,
refuse to eat ducks. It is said that the mother of this
deity when pregnant was cured of a severe distemper, by eating
herbs which were daily brought to her, during her illness, by a
duck. She bore a son, whom she named Yan Shing, who was
brought up under strict injunctions never to eat duck. He was
careful to mind her commands, and his filial obedience was
rewarded in a very striking way. On one occasion, when
seeking safety by flight from a band of desperadoes who
were pursuing him, he was suddenly concealed from their view
by a large flock of ducks, which in their flight darkened the
very heavens. In due course Yan Shing died. He had lain
but a few hours in his grave when it was resolved, on
account of the holiness of his life, to canonize him. After this

solemnity he was regarded as a god under the name of Hong-Yuen-Shuee, or Hong-Kung-Tchu-Shuee. In the presence o the altar in his honour it is usual for his votaries to vow that they will abstain from the flesh of his favourite bird. Parents sometimes dedicate their infants, when a month old, to the service of this deity; vowing in the name of the infant, that, in return for his protecting care, they will ever hold ducks in sacred regard. The inhabitants of Sa-tow, a village on the island of Honam, are his most devoted followers. There is not a duck to be found in their village. The inhabitants are content to be neither buyers, nor sellers, nor eaters of ducks ; and it does not seem to occur to them that they might keep a few as pets, in honour of their favourite god. Their only, or principal, temple is in honour of Hong-Yuen-Shuee ; and on the seventh day of the seventh month there are great rejoicings to celebrate his natal anniversary. A large mat shed or pavilion is erected on this occasion ; and for three days the whole population—the males seated on the one side, and the females on the other—feast in it to their heart's content. The food which is served up for breakfast and dinner on these anniversaries is of the most substantial description ; and, to judge from the quantities which they cheerfully consume, it must be very wholesome.

Non-consumers of ducks are, however, in a very decided minority; and farmers and cottagers accordingly rear these birds in great numbers throughout the provinces. The breed is very similar to that with which we are familiar in England. In the north, however, and more especially at Tien-tsin, I found a much larger variety. In the island of Hainan, and in other parts of the empire, a very fine strain of Muscovy ducks is to be found.

Great attention is paid to the rearing of this bird. The number of ducks allowed to each drake is ten. The companionship, however, between a drake and his ten ducks does not last longer than twelve months. At the end of that period, the old drakes are sold, and new ones bought to supply their place. To make the ducks lay the herds pluck feathers from their wings and tails, and sometimes withhold food from them for several days, and then feed them lavishly. The number of eggs

upon which a duck is allowed to sit is twelve, and, throughout
the breeding season, food is given them in very moderate quantities. Those which are sitting are very carefully attended
to, and once every five days the person in charge drives them
to an adjacent pond or stream to wash. While they are
sitting, women who are in what is called an interesting condition are not allowed to approach the ducks—a prohibition
which has its origin of course in the superstitions to which the
Chinese mind is prone. During the five days immediately after
their leaving the shell, ducklings are not allowed to hear the
sound of tom-toms, or gongs, or the barking of dogs, or the noise
which arises from machinery in motion. The food which is given
to them on the first day consists of congee, which is the water in
which rice has been boiled. On the following days boiled rice is
substituted. Clean spring water is set before them at such
times, as the duckherds believe that the mud in muddy water is
apt to stop up the nostrils. For the first fortnight of their lives
ducklings are confined to a coop, the bottom of which is covered
with soft grass.

Throughout the empire there are institutions called Poo-ap-
chong, in which ducks' eggs are artificially hatched in large
quantities. The process of incubation as practised in such
establishments is as follows: A large quantity of rice-husks, or
chaff, is placed above grates filled with hot charcoal embers.
When heated, the chaff is placed in baskets, and the eggs are
laid in it. The baskets with their contents are then taken into
a dark room, and placed on shelves of lattice-work which are
arranged in tiers on the walls. Underneath the lowest of these
shelves several portable earthenware grates are placed, containing hot charcoal embers. In this dark and heated chamber the
eggs are kept for a period of twenty-four hours. They are then
removed to an adjoining room, where they are deposited in
rattan baskets, which are three feet high, the sides being two
inches thick, and lined with coarse brown paper. Here they
are allowed to remain for ten days. In order that they
may be equally heated, it is usual to alter their position
once during the day, and once during the night. If the servants
are careful, the eggs which in the day are in the upper part of

the basket will be in the lower part during the night. After fourteen days they are removed and arranged on long and very wide shelves. Here they are covered up, for warmth, with broad sheets of thick paper, made apparently of cotton. After they have occupied these shelves for fourteen days, hundreds of ducks burst into life. The principal establishments of this kind in the vicinity of Canton are at Fa-tee and Poee-tai-shuee. The duck-lings are immediately sold to the duck merchant, by whom they are carefully reared in premises conveniently situated on the banks of creeks or rivers. A very large establishment of this sort is at Nam-tong, a village not far from Canton. Here I have frequently seen many thousand ducks in one compound or enclosure. Similar establishments are to be found in the midland and northern provinces. When sailing on the Grand Canal, I saw several large flocks of these birds.

The food given to the ducklings, during the first twenty-four hours, consists of congee, succeeded by boiled rice. Afterwards they are fed on bran mixed with chaff; and occasionally, that is, during the summer months, on maggots gathered from cisterns, or cesspools containing night-soil. Small land-crabs, which the Chinese capture in large quantities, are also given them; and, judging from the manner in which they devour these, the young birds find them very palatable. When sufficiently large, the birds are sold by the duck merchant to itinerant vendors, who anchor their large boats near the establishments I have described, in order to take in a cargo of several hundreds at a time. The duck boats are well adapted for the purpose, and it is not unusual for one boat to carry a living freight of from fifteen hundred to two thousand of these birds. The boats, however, being very clumsy, are in danger of being capsized when the weather is at all tempestuous. In the ever memorable typhoon which took place on the 27th of July, 1862, several of these boats were capsized in the vicinity of the Bogue forts; and so numerous were the ducks released from captivity, that for upwards of a mile the surface of the Canton river was crowded with them. The expense which the itinerant duck vendor incurs by having so many of these birds to feed, is not great: all that he has to do, is to allow them to spend an hour or two, twice a day, on the muddy banks of the river or creek, which he navigates, or in the adjacent fields. The worms, snails, slugs, and frogs, with which these places abound, afford a delicious and ample repast for his feathered freight. On many occasions, I have seen from fifteen hundred to two thousand ducks busy at these meals at low tide. The birds are so well trained that they return from the river banks or adjoining fields to the boats at the call of the herd. Provision dealers are the duck vendors' best customers, and purchase the birds in great numbers with the view of salting them. The itinerant vendor, however, does not confine himself to the wholesale trade, but sells his freight in the numerous cities, towns, and villages which are to be found on the banks of streams. Establishments in which ducks are salted are both numerous and extensive. This is more especially the case in Lin-chow, a prefecture in the province of Kwang-tung. I had an opportunity of inspecting an establishment of this sort at Pak-ok-tung, near Canton. No part of the bird seemed to be regarded as offal by the various hands engaged in the process of salting. In one portion of the premises, the bodies of the ducks were opened, salted, and exposed in the sun to dry. In another department, men were placing the bills and feet of the birds, with quantities of brine, in earthenware jars; while in the courtyard men and women were occupied in exposing to the sun the hearts, gizzards, necks, and entrails. This process may be seen in operation, during the eleventh and twelfth months of the year, in the Lin-hing Kai street of the western suburb of Canton, where large quantities of ducks are at all times exposed for sale.

Although my residence in China has extended over many years, I never remember to have seen a Chinese eating parboiled eggs. Hard-boiled eggs, however, are occasionally eaten; and at the birth of a child, or the celebration of a natal anniversary, it is their custom, as I have elsewhere stated, to eat dyed eggs. In every city which I visited the on banks of the Grand Canal, I saw these exposed for sale in considerable quantities. Of preserved eggs the Chinese are very fond, and they are prepared in large quantities. An account of the process of preserving eggs may prove interesting to my readers.

Some vegetable is well boiled in a few pints of water, together with the leaves of the bamboo, fir, or cedar tree. This is done to render the water aromatic. In this water, as soon as it is lukewarm, the eggs are first washed, and then steeped for a few hours. Where a hundred eggs are being preserved, ten taels of salt, five taels of the ashes of firewood, and one catty of lime are formed into a kind of paste by being well mixed in the vessel which contains the aromatic water from which the eggs have been removed. This paste is then placed in a tub or coarse earthenware jar, the eggs being carefully embedded in it, and allowed to remain for three days. They are then taken out, so that the mixture may be stirred up, after which they are replaced. After three days more, this process is repeated again; and repeated again after three days more. The jar, or tub, is now hermetically sealed, and allowed to continue so for thirty days, when the eggs are fit for use. Another mode is as follows: Four taels weight of Bohea tea-leaves having been well boiled, the water is drawn off, and poured upon as much lime as will go in three basins of ordinary size, as much ash of firewood as would fill seven of these basins, and salt weighing twelve taels. These ingredients are then well mixed into a paste, and the eggs to be preserved are smeared with it. They are then carefully deposited in tubs or jars which contain wood-ashes, so as to prevent the eggs from adhering to one another. As wood-ashes are in great request for this purpose, they are carefully stored by cooks, who sell them to egg preservers at the rate of eight cash per catty. After forty days the eggs are found to be well preserved. In smearing them both men and women are employed: they wear gloves to protect their hands from the effects of the lime. Occasionally eggs are preserved in tubs or jars containing either a mixture of red clay and salt water, or a mixture of soot and salt water. These are called salted eggs, and are regarded as wholesome food for the sick.

What I have written with regard to the rearing and breeding of ducks, is almost equally applicable to geese. The breeds are apparently of great variety. Those which I have seen in the south of China bear a resemblance to the Egyptian goose. The two sexes are very similar; the goose being rather smaller than the gander, and the colouring of its feathers somewhat lighter. In other portions of the empire, I have seen geese very similar, in size at all events, to those of Great Britain. The eggs are hatched in large numbers; but it does not appear that this is done, as in the case of ducks, by artificial means. The reason is, I was informed, the thickness of the shell. As a rule, geese are reared by farmers and cottagers whose lands are contiguous to rivers and creeks. In the districts of Tsung-fā, Fā-yune, Sam-shuee, and Tai-laong, in the province of Kwang-tung, I have seen several large flocks of geese: but as they are not hatched artificially, they are not to be found in such large numbers as ducks. The largest flock I ever saw was at Wang-kong, a village near Canton. It consisted of nine hundred. While they are sitting, the birds are not unfrequently lodged in the houses or cottages of their owners, who bestow the greatest attention upon them. To a large goose ten, and to a small one seven, eggs are allotted; and they seldom fail to hatch all of them. When a fortnight old, the goslings are conducted by the herd to fields on the banks of creeks, where they find plenty of food, in the shape of tussocks of rushes, herbs, slugs, and worms. At the ploughing seasons, the geese may be seen closely following the plough, devouring the worms which are turned up. It is amusing to observe the method the herd adopts to protect the goslings from the hawks, which are very numerous in China. He is provided with a hollow bamboo tube which he swings with great force round his head by means of a rope. The whizzing of the tube through the air scares the hawks from attacking. The establishments in which geese are kept are provided with long rows of wicker shelves, erected against the wall at a distance of five feet from the ground. The wands of which these shelves are formed cross each other at short distances, so that the droppings may fall to the ground. This arrangement is adopted because the moisture of the earth is thought to be prejudicial to the growth of the birds. The dung realizes tolerably large prices. The goose market which is held daily at Canton, in the street called Luen-hing Kai, is almost as large as the annual goose fair for which

Nottingham is so famous. Flat-bottomed boats discharge large numbers of these birds, at the wharf immediately in front of the market. I have seen no fewer than three hundred geese removed from one boat, several others, each containing an equal number, awaiting their turn alongside the wharf. On being removed from the boat, the geese are thrown into the river to have a swim, not, however, before the boat has been surrounded with a wicker-work fence, as the tide might otherwise soon carry them beyond their owner's reach. The geese are thrown into the river by the person in charge of the boat, who is held responsible for their safe delivery. He throws them in, five at a time; and keeps count of them, calling out the number as he throws. The clerk of the goose merchant is also present to see that his employer is not cheated. When they have had their swim, the birds are driven to the market, where they are exposed for retail sale.

The Chinese are also proficients in breeding and rearing fowls. The hens which they regard as the best breeders, are short, have short plumage, and their cackling is not loud. For twenty days after the hatching of her chickens a hen is confined in a coop, the floor of which is kept perfectly dry. During this period she and her brood are fed upon un-boiled rice, as boiled rice is supposed to cause water to form in the crops of the chickens. At the large establishments in which fowls are reared, it is customary to scatter congee upon the floors of the courtyards. In a few days, the congee becomes infested with insects, and the fowls when they are admitted, make very short work both of insects and congee. On such food, the hens not only become fat, but lay plentifully. To promote their laying, they are occasionally fed with Chee-ma, or linseed mixed with hog's lard. In this preparation, a half catty of linseed goes to three taels' weight of the lard. For the same purpose, rearers of poultry are very careful, when feeding the hens, to administer water in very small quantities. When fattening fowls for the market, they give them flour mingled with oil. This paste is formed into pills, several of which are given daily to each bird. Rice, mixed with flour of sulphur, is not unfrequently given for fattening purposes; and fowls which are of a yellowish colour when boiled, are preferred to those which are white. For capons there is a great demand. In fattening both cocks and capons, the birds are, in many instances, bound to their perches by means of cords, and fed daily upon rice and water. In the course of twelve months, they become very fat, and are prescribed by physicians, as suitable food for patients suffering from consumption ; and for polygamists who have become weak, both in mind and body. A species of fowl, the flesh and bones of which are black, is often prescribed by physicians, as suitable food for sick or feeble women. The flesh is cut into small pieces ; and its bones, reduced to a fine powder, are mixed by the Chinese followers of Æsculapius with medicines of various kinds.

Rearers of poultry profess to have it in their power to impart a beautiful plumage to their birds. This, they say, is easily accomplished by giving them as food, cuttle-fish which have previously been stuffed with sulphur, and dried for four or five days in the sun. They profess also to be able to check the growth of chickens, so as to be able to produce dwarf fowls. To accomplish this, the chickens—generally cocks—are confined to coops, and fed for a considerable time daily upon the seeds of opium, mixed with an ingredient called Hung-wong. For sickness the breeder refers to a book which contains rules for the preparation of suitable medicines. In some instances, lamp oil is administered to the feathered patient. Where fowls are afflicted with an epidemic, the dust which is produced by rubbing iron upon soft stones is given, together with rice water. A paste made of a certain kind of pea, which acts very powerfully, is also given. When fowls suffer from contagious diseases, it is not unusual to bleed them under the left wing, and to give them rice mixed with oil, after the operation. Fowls which gasp and are troubled with shortness of breath, have to swallow salt water; and a lotion of alum water is used in cases of ophthalmia.

Many varieties of pigeons are to be found in China. Tumblers, carriers, fantails, and croppers are reared in large numbers. The carrier is of great service to merchants, by whom it is employed in conveying intelligence to the producing districts, of the arrivals of cargoes, and the ruling prices of the markets. Merchants at Hong-kong use them in conveying news of the arrival of the English, French, or American mails to their partners in trade at Canton. To defend the pigeon during its flight from attacks on the part of falcons or hawks, a whistle is attached to its tail, and the shrill noise of this contrivance, as its bearer flies through the air, terrifies the birds of prey. This mode of conveying letters is not by any means new to the Chinese. To them it was as well known in ancient times, as it was, not only to the inhabitants of other Asiatic countries, but to those of Greece. Anacreon alludes to it in one of his Odes. Ovid sings how Tamosthenes, when he had obtained a victory at the Olympic games, sent swift intelligence of the same to his father, at Ægina, by releasing a carrier pigeon, whose wings, as a token of victory, were stained with purple. During the siege of Modena, a correspondence is said to have been held between Brutus and Hirtius by the same means. That carrier pigeons were used by the Jews in the time of Solomon is, also, I think, very clear from a passage in Ecclesiastes (x. 20) which runs, "Curse not the king, no not in thy thought; and curse not the rich in thy bedchamber: for a bird of the air shall carry the voice, and that which hath wings shall tell the matter." It is, I apprehend, impossible to understand this passage of Holy Writ, unless we regard it as referring to the use of pigeons as a means of communication. The speed with which these birds wing their course through the air is astonishing. A case is on record in which thirty-two pigeons were brought from Antwerp, and liberated in London, on the morning of November 22nd, 1819. Of these one arrived at Antwerp, at noon, on the same day; and a second, fifteen minutes latter. The others reached their destination on the day following.

Pigeons are regarded as a delicacy by the Chinese. They are generally placed upon the table at banquets in honour of marriages, and at private festivals; and they are served daily, as a rule, at restaurants, as an attractive *entremet*.

The dung of pigeons is regarded by the farmer as of great value, being especially serviceable in promoting, as in Persia, the growth of esculent plants. It is also given as a medicine by

Chinese physicians—more particularly to women during and immediately after pregnancy. It appears from the Second Book of Kings (vi. 25) that when, in consequence of a siege, the famine in Samaria was very great, pigeons' dung was actually bought and sold by its distressed inhabitants as an article of food. In an abridged chronicle of the history of England, it is recorded that, during the famine in 1316, which caused such desolation in our land, this substance became more or less the food of the poor. I was unable to ascertain whether, among the Chinese, it is taken for other than medicinal purposes.

During my residence in China, I was present at many of the fairs held at all the large towns and villages of the empire. The largest which I attended in the south, were at Yow-loong, in the district of Fā-yune, and at Tai-laak, the capital of the ninety-six villages near Canton. Here, as in the other gatherings of this sort in the towns and villages of the southern provinces, the live stock which changed owners, consisted of buffaloes, cows, pigs, goats, ducks, geese, fowls, dogs, and cats : in addition to which large quantities of grain, vegetables, and seeds of every description, as well as agricultural implements, were exposed for sale. At Tai-laak I observed large quantities of cotton sold, at apparently very remunerative prices. The town of Tai-laak, deserves to be especially noticed for the excellence of its market accommodation. Its principal streets, dark and dirty though they are, resemble arcades, and conduct to large markets for the sale of cattle, pigs, goats, poultry, grain, vegetables, &c. As a rule, however, all Chinese towns and villages where fairs are held—and especially those of Kwang-tung—are provided with excellent accommodation for dealers in agricultural and other produce, and their markets are almost invariably covered with tiled roofs supported by lofty pillars of brick. In this respect, the towns and villages of China are in advance of the majority of those of Great Britain.

The largest fair in the northern province which I had an opportunity of attending, was at Lama-miou, in Mongolia. It commenced at sunrise, and the sale of live stock was brought to a close at 10 A.M. Great droves of horses, herds of cattle and swine, and flocks of sheep were exposed. I was informed that, at the fairs which are held at this town during the sixth, seventh, and eighth months of the year, horses are exposed in very large numbers indeed. The horse fair at Lama-miou reminded me very much of similar scenes in England. Dirty street boys, who were in great requisition, put horses through their paces, with all the skill and cunning of Yorkshire dealers. They endeavoured to impart as much spirit as possible into their steeds, and the way in which the poor horses carried their tails, disposed one to think that they were under the effects of ginger. While I was closely watching them, especially one, with the view of purchasing it, a man who was passing through the market with a bullock-cart allowed the wheel of his cart to pass over my left foot. Probably I was as much to blame as the carter, but I am not quite sure that this reflection was uppermost in my mind at the moment. The injury, however, did not prevent my bargaining for the horse, and the owner of it, a Mongolian, after some very businesslike and amicable wrangling with me, at last suggested the propriety of our adjourning to some inn where the matter might be discussed with greater deliberation. We repaired to an inn accordingly in the neighbourhood of the market, and across a table on which the innkeeper had placed some wine of the country, we fought our commercial battle fairly and in good faith on both sides. It was finally settled that the animal, which was one of the best horses I met with in China, should change owners on reasonable terms. At Pekin also, I attended a very large horse fair. The stables and courtyards of the inns near the market, were crowded with horses of every description to be found in the empire. The sellers were most obliging, giving persons who were desirous of purchasing steeds every facility for riding them on trial, along the adjacent thoroughfare. At this fair I purchased a horse, which candour compels me to confess was not at all remarkable either for proportions or speed. I also visited the sheep and pig market at Pekin. The sheep were not confined to pens, but were bound together by ropes in lots of five or six, and tethered to posts. Each pig was rendered completely *hors de combat*, by being bound by the legs, and lay upon the ground with a doleful expression of utter helplessness.

The sellers of the stock at this fair were Mongolians; the purchasers, Chinese. The concourse of people at these large fairs was very great; and had I not been surrounded by Chinese farmers, I might have fancied myself at an important gathering of the kind at home. There, as here, were to be found the strolling playactor, the conjuror, the fortune-teller, the acrobat, and the itinerant vendor of fruits and mysterious cakes. The ubiquitous pickpocket was also present; and the skill with which the Chinese members of this miserable fraternity practise their detestable art, cannot fail to secure for them a tolerable harvest.

A WORKER IN METAL.

CHAPTER XXV.

IF prizes for profitable gardening were competed for by nations, the Chinese would have a very fair chance of being successful competitors. A Chinese is born with the two great instincts of a profitable gardener—firstly, not to waste such a valuable thing as land by letting it lie uncultivated; and secondly, not to waste anything, because in ninety-nine cases out of a hundred, anything may be utilized as a manure. We have seen the extraordinary care with which they collect from the butcher, the poulterer, the tanner, the gluemaker, the hairdresser—no matter whom—everything that can possibly contribute to enrich the soil. Add to this, that they are an eminently persevering race, and that they have a climate which smiles benignly, if sometimes too warmly, upon their "patient continuance in well-doing" as tillers of the ground. Esculents of every species and variety, such as sweet potatoes, yams, turnips, carrots, beans, peas, celery, radishes, broccoli, cabbages, lettuces, cucumbers, melons, pumpkins, tomatoes, &c., &c., are produced in large quantities in the market-gardens which are to be found in the neighbourhood of every city, town and village. In consequence of their great abundance, they sell at most reasonable prices; and the high state of cultivation in which the market-gardens are kept, would draw from our English gardeners expressions of admiration and respect.

A great variety of trees, some of which are little known out of China, are to be found in the orchards. In addition to the peach, apricot, custard-apple, rose-apple, pine-apple, pear, plum, walnut, date, cocoa, plantain, banana, persimmon, citron, orange, lemon, quince, guava, olive,[1] pomegranate, and vine—the last mentioned being grown in many varieties— there are the li-chi, the fruit of which is of the size of a strawberry, the stone being inclosed in soft succulent pulp of a very delicious flavour; the lung-ngan, or dragon's eye; the wampee, whose fruit, about the size of a pigeon's egg, is much esteemed, and the carambolo. Of these fruits the carambolo is, perhaps, gathered in greatest abundance. The orchards in which it is produced are very numerous, at all events in the province of Kwang-tung; especially at Leep-tak, and other villages which at intervals stud the banks of the Pearl river between Canton and Whampoa. At Fa-tee, a suburban district of Canton, there are many orchards of the same class. Round the trunks of the carambolo trees in the orchards of Leep-tak, and other large villages, quantities of earth are piled, but for what reason I was never able to learn. In the autumn of the year when the fruit ripens, its orchards are in a state of perpetual clangour from the beating of gongs by boys hired for the purpose, and without whom the birds would consume more than half the fruit. On one occasion I occupied, as a study, a small Chinese cottage in the centre of a carambolo orchard, at Fa-tee. So loud and incessant was the din in autumn as to be almost distracting. The orange orchards or groves are not by any means large. They are, however, very numerous, and supply the natives with an abundance of excellent fruit. The principal fruit-market at Canton is held in the Woee-sin street in the southern suburb, the Covent Garden of Canton.

But the Chinese do not confine themselves to cultivation on dry land only : they also cultivate the bottom of the waters, and in the beds of shallow lakes, ponds, and brooks, produce fruits unknown to Europeans. The water-chestnut, or Mai-tai as they

---

[1] The stones of this fruit are much appreciated by the Chinese. They carve them in an elaborate manner, and convert them, by setting them in gold, into very beautiful brooches or bracelets.

WATER-CHESTNUT GATHERERS.

term it, the fruit of which is inclosed in a case formed by its root, is one of the most noteworthy of these products, and is grown in large quantities. It is very wholesome and of a delicate flavour, and is gathered by women, who tuck up their wide trousers, and wade above their knees into the ponds, where they grope for the chestnuts with their hands. As soon as her basket is full, the gatherer repairs to the nearest town or village, which she perambulates with her trousers still tucked up, crying her water-chestnuts. These esculents are much appreciated, and meet a very ready sale. They are prepared for food by removing the rind and boiling the bulb. Occasionally the bulbs are cut into small pieces, which when boiled are eaten as hominy is in Europe. They are often reduced with a pestle and mortar, to a fine powder, which is sold in packages. I have frequently partaken of this food, and found it quite as agreeable, at all events as either corn-flour or arrowroot. At Poon-fong, a district which borders on the western suburb of Canton, it is prepared in large quantities.

There are very extensive water-lily or lotus ponds in the vicinity of the cities and villages of the southern provinces. In the western district of Canton, such ponds are also very numerous. The water-lily, which is I apprehend the Shushan of the Scriptures, is regarded by the Chinese as a sacred plant. It flourishes during the months of July and August; and when, in consequence of the latter rains and high tides, the Canton river during these months overflows the adjacent lands, its large tulip-like flowers—some of a bright red, others of a milk-white colour, and not a few combining the red and the white—may be seen raised, as if in triumph, above the surface of the swollen waters. With these flowers, the Chinese decorate their houses. The leaves of the plant are also used by shopkeepers—grocers especially—instead of paper to wrap their customers' purchases in. The seeds of the lotus, which are almost as large as filberts, are boiled and eaten. From the beds of the ponds, the Chinese also gather the root of the plant, which is of an elongated form, and in colour like a turnip. When opened, the root, which consists of a variety of cells, has somewhat the appearance of a honey-comb. The lotus of China is, I

apprehend, of the same species as that of Egypt, of which
Herodotus writes (2. 92) :—

"So soon as the waters have reached their culminating
point, there is to be seen above the surface a large quantity
of the lily species, which by the Egyptians are termed the
lotus."

It would appear that the Egyptians were in the habit of
eating the seeds of this plant, which they boiled and made into
a paste, and then baked as bread.

Flowering shrubs, flowers, and herbs are exceedingly numerous,
and flowers, as well as fruits, may be had in abundance at
any season of the year. The Chinese have their gardens, as a
rule, on the banks of rivers, creeks, or canals, so as to have
greater facilities for irrigation. This, I believe, was also the
case with gardens in Palestine (v. Genesis ii. 10, and Isaiah i. 30).
When the gardens in China are not on the banks of rivers or
creeks, water is drawn for irrigation from deep wells or from
ponds. Hollow bamboo tubes are used for distributing the
water, which is drawn by means of a balanced lever. These
rest upon wooden supports, and branch in almost every direction
from the mouth of the well. Where the water is drawn from ponds,
two buckets are used. Each is provided with a spout, and they are
attached to the ends of a bamboo pole, which a labourer bears on
his shoulders. Having filled his buckets with water by dipping
them into the pond, he pours their contents upon the vegetable
or flower-beds, without removing the pole from his shoulders.
Pliny, in his "Natural History," (9, 14), describes methods of
irrigating gardens in his time, not dissimilar to those employed
by the Chinese.

As a rule, gardens in China are not contiguous to, or in way
connected with, the houses of those to whom they belong.
Situated beyond the precincts of the city, they are often a
mile or two distant from the homes of the proprietors.[1] It is
evident also from the allusions that the gardens mentioned in

---

[1] This remark applies only to gardens properly so called ; for trees and flowers
are not unfrequently found in the courtyards of the residences of Chinese gentlemen.

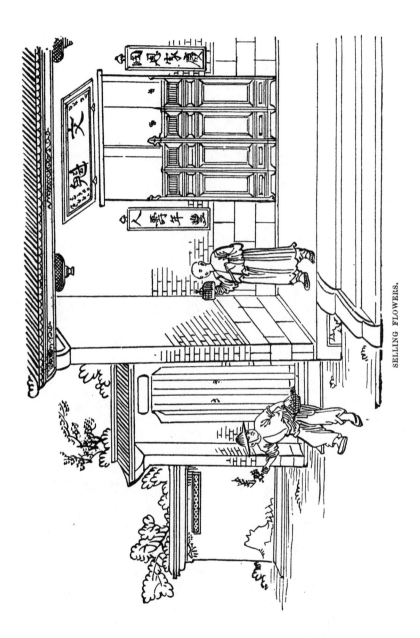

SELLING FLOWERS.

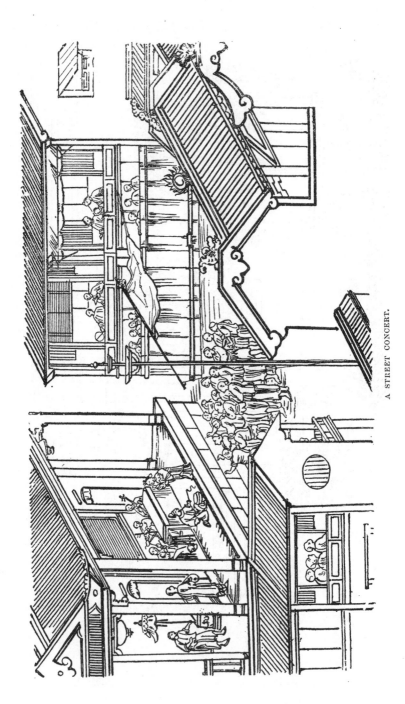

A STREET CONCERT.

Scripture, were generally beyond the walls of the city. Each garden is provided with its complement of garden houses. Some of these bowers are built in the form of pagodas ; others of flower boats, and not a few of domed towers. They are furnished with chairs, couches, and tables, remarkable for their simplicity and neatness. To these pleasant retreats it is customary for families and their friends to betake themselves out of the noise and bustle of the town. Garden dinner parties are frequent, at which singing men and women usually sing and play popular Chinese airs for the entertainment of the guests. Occasionally, these banquets are enlivened by the performance of dramas, by professional actors. Jewish banquets which were given in gardens, were also it may be remarked, accompanied by singing and instrumental music (v. Isaiah lvi. 3, and lxv. 3).

With the general style of gardens in China—both nursery and private gardens—nearly every one may be supposed to be more or less acquainted. The dinner services and rice-paper pictures, which for some years past have been sent in such large quantities to Great Britain, and which have met with purchasers from Land's End to John o' Groat's House, must have made most people familiar with the singular scenery for which these gardens are famous. One or two of the landscape gardens which I have visited, are worthy, however, of particular notice. The largest in the vicinity of Canton is that of a gentleman named Punting-qua. It consists of several acres, and is surrounded by a brick wall fifteen or sixteen feet high. A path, paved with flagstones and covered with a roof of tiles supported with wooden pillars, runs round it, and protects visitors alike from rain, and the glare and heat of the sun, which, during the summer months, is almost unendurable. Each of the paths also by which the garden is intersected is covered in a similar way, so that it is possible to pass with comfort in all weathers from one part of the garden to another. Along these paths, at suitable intervals, there are well-built bowers—some of them two stories in height—which are furnished, according to Chinese taste, with great neatness. Large slabs of granite and huge stones of a yellow colour are placed here and there as seats along the margins of the walks. In the centre of the garden stands a large summer residence to which Pun-ting-qua and the ladies of his family not unfrequently resort. This residence, which is surrounded by water, is approached by a zig-zag bridge. It contains on the ground floor a withdrawing-room and a dining-room; and on the first floor three or four bedrooms and a library. Immediately in front of the dining-room there is a theatre, where plays are performed for the gratification of the guests. At the far end of the garden a white pagoda is erected upon an insulated mound, the summit of which commands a very extensive view of the surrounding country. The mound is covered with a variety of flowers, mosses, and shrubs; and round about it are winding paths, with masses of rockwork here and there breaking the continuity of their lines. On a rocky eminence of this mound stands a small building, which bears a striking resemblance to a miniature temple. The garden is studded with numerous ponds, producing most luxuriant crops of the water-lily, whose bright, gay flowers, conspicuous above the surface of the water, add greatly to the beauty of the scene. Along the banks of the ponds are planted li-chi, lung-ngan, and wampee trees, which yield in season an abundance of fruit; whilst along the sides of the walks which encircle and intersect the garden, are placed pots containing flowers and shrubs of the most beautiful forms and brilliant colours. For the benefit of the citizens of Canton, this garden is open at the celebration of certain festivals to the general public. It is so popular as a place of resort, that, almost weekly, parties of the leading citizens are admitted to dine. The dining-hall, of which pleasure parties are accustomed to avail themselves, is very large and commodious; and as the front and ends of the building consist of glass windows, it is not inaptly termed the crystal chamber. The back wall of the chamber is a panelled wainscot; and on the panels flowers, birds, and insects are portrayed with great accuracy and minuteness.

Such landscape gardens, however, are not in any way peculiar in the south of China; and near Pekin I had an opportunity of exploring the natural and artificial beauties of those which adjoin the Yuen-ming-yuen, or summer palace of the emperor. I also visited what may be termed a very extensive rockery in the grounds of a house situate in the prefectoral city of Yun-chow, on the banks of the Yan-tsze. This garden, which is, or was, the property of a gentleman called Pow Chia, greatly interested me. It was a perfect labyrinth, consisting of intricate paths winding in every direction, with here and there caverns formed by large pieces of rock. At Soo-chow I visited a rockery very similar to this, which stood in the grounds of a small yamun in a street called Pan-loo-cheng. This garden, it is said, was a favourite resort of the Emperor Kien-lung on the occasion of the three imperial visits which he paid to the city of Soo-chow. The attention of visitors is invariably directed by the guide to a tablet suspended from the garden wall, and bearing a sentence consisting of two Chinese characters. It was written by Kien-lung to express his delight in visiting a place so singular and grotesque.

In these parks and gardens it is usual to find one or two deer. This animal is regarded as bringing good fortune to its owner, and the word " deer " is represented in the Chinese language by a character similar to that which implies happiness. Rich families attach so much importance to the possession of a deer that they invariably make a point of keeping one; and the revolutionary forces which disturbed the peace of China for several years during the present century always marched with a deer at their head, in the hope of thereby securing success. With the deer they kept an egret, a bird which is also associated with good fortune in the estimation of the Chinese.

In many of the gardens it is customary to find apiaries ; and it may be observed that in the practical management of bees this people are not one whit behind accomplished disciples of the illustrious Huber. They are aware, as judicious bee-masters, that the principal requisites for an apiary are a sufficient protection from the heat of summer as well as from the cold of winter, and a situation far removed from noise. To screen their hives from the north and north-west winds, and shelter them from the rays of the sun, they place them under covered pathways, or under the broad eaves of their dwelling-houses, or, if these are not convenient, under the eaves of garden walls with a southern aspect. By adopting the plan of placing the bee-hives close to their dwelling-houses, they make their bees so tame that the approach of a person to the hives does not excite their anger as in England. That the bees may not mistake their respective hives, they do not crowd these together, but arrange them at a distance of from twelve to fourteen feet from each other. As water is very necessary to the successful operations of bees in spring and summer, they place their apiaries on the banks of rivulets, or near ponds of water. Rattan canes or bamboo rods are the materials of which the hives are made, the structure being covered sometimes with mud, and sometimes with cow-dung, which has been previously well-mixed with a gum which freely exudes from a tree called Koo-shu. A hive of such materials possesses this advantage over the ordinary straw hives of England, that mice cannot build their nests in it, and eventually penetrate unseen into the interior. To each end of the hive a movable circular door is attached. These doors are perforated, the holes being just large enough to admit the bees. By this arrangement, all large insects which are enemies to bees are, of course, unable to enter. Every morning the walls of the hives are carefully brushed to remove dust and prevent the formation of cobwebs.

In the spring of the year, when quantities of young are reared, should there be a deficiency of food, the bee-masters are very diligent in providing the bees with honey. Nor are less care and skill displayed in their management in the swarming season. Should the bees upon leaving the hive ascend high in the air, and seem disposed to fly far away, the bee-masters endeavour to bring them down by throwing fine mould amongst them. Occasionally I have seen grains of rice thrown with great success among high soaring bees. A swarm which alights upon a low shrub or tree is swept into the hive by a feather-brush, or driven into it by the smoke ascending from a quantity of paper which is set on fire at the foot of the tree. The swarming season terminates in June, and in the eighth month of the year, what the Chinese call the black or "minister bees" die in large numbers. The Chinese think that were they not to die, there would be a great dearth of food for the survivors. It is generally during the night that the hives are deprived of their honey. The bees are driven out by means of smoke. A man

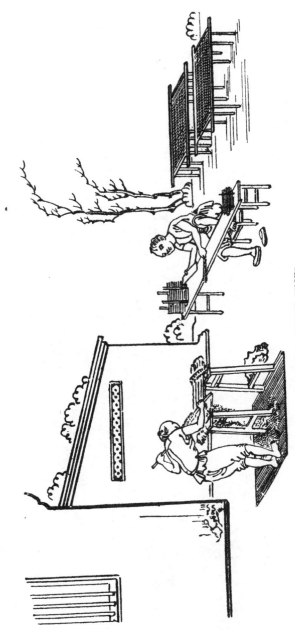

MAKING INCENSE STICKS.

CHINESE PLAYING AT SHUTTLECOCK.

with a thin knife then cuts out the comb; and, when this has
been done, the bees are permitted to return to the hive.
Before cutting the comb the bee-master refers to the calendar to
ascertain whether the day which he has selected for this purpose
be a propitious one.

The comb is put into a muslin bag, through which the pure
honey gradually filters into a vessel for its reception. The wax
is put into a bag made of cotton-cloth, the mouth of which is
closely tied. The bag with its contents is then placed in a
vessel of boiling water, and the pure material oozes through
the bag and floats on the surface. It is then skimmed off and
stored in an earthenware jar. During the winter months, when
there is a scarcity of flowers, the hives are well supplied with
sugar.

An aquarium with gold-fish of various kinds is another very
general and interesting feature of Chinese gardens. For the
aquarium old earthenware jars are preferred. The mouth of the
jar used for this purpose is about fifteen feet in circumference;
the base of the vessel, however, is much contracted. Should it
be necessary to replace an old jar by a new one, the sides of the
latter are in the first place well rubbed with slices of turnip.
It is then filled to the brim with spring-water; and in consequence of this treatment the sides of the vessel are in a few
days covered with moss. Early in spring male shrimps, the
claws of which have been cut off, are, for what purpose I never
could learn, thrown into the jars, which are then immediately
covered with wooden lids. During the great heat of summer,
the water contained in these vessels is changed on alternate
days. The approach of the spawning season is indicated by the
fact that each female fish is accompanied by two males, one on
each side. The jars in which the fish are placed to deposit their
spawn contain very little water, and bunches of weeds or long
grasses are placed in them for the reception of the ova. As the
surface of each egg is of an adhesive nature, it remains attached
to the weed upon which it happens to be deposited. To keep
them from the rays of the sun, the jars are placed under shady
trees. The times which elapses before the appearance of the
young fish is not more than two or three days. When they

are hatched, they are fed during the first ten days of their existence upon the yolk of hard boiled eggs. Afterwards young insects are given to them. These are usually caught upon the surface of stagnant pools, and the fish-breeder washes them carefully in water before giving them to the fish. In winter, when insects are more difficult to be had, the blood of pigs, fowls, or ducks, mixed with rice-flour, and then dried in the sun, and afterwards well pounded in a mortar, is given as food. Small earthworms chopped into pieces are not unfrequently used during this season for the same purpose. During the first four hundred days of their existence, the fish are black. For several days after this period they are marked with gold or silver spots. Eventually this speckled appearance gives place to that bright golden hue, for which the gold-fish of China are so justly celebrated. The time required to effect this change of colour depends upon the constitution of each individual.

The Chinese bestow great pains and attention upon keeping their gold-fish in good health. Where sicknesss occurs they have recourse chiefly to the following remedies :—Should the fish show signs of distress by floating on their sides and gasping, a fresh supply of water is immediately poured into their jar. As an all prevailing remedy, the fish-breeder next proceeds to throw into it a fine powder, made by pounding the root of the plantain-tree in a mortar. When the fish become lean and spotted, he concludes that they are suffering from lice. If not destroyed, these prove fatal to the health of the fish, and to kill them at once he places in the jar strips of the bark of a tree called Foong, together with strips of the white willow. In some instances a newly made brick, which has been well soaked in nightsoil and then dried in the sun, is placed in the jar for this purpose.

The *Cyprinus auratus*, or gold carp, is the most beautiful gold-fish which the Chinese possess. It is indigenous to the country and, according to Pennant, was introduced into England towards the close of the seventeenth century. In China, silver-fish are of greater value than gold-fish, a circumstance which is probably due to their comparative rarity. The Chinese do not value gold-fish which have dorsal fins. When provided with such

an appendage, they are called Tsak-Yu-Chu. Those which are
of greatest value in their estimation are the Chan-Chu-Tun, or
pearly-scaled fish. The males of this variety are distinguished
from the females by certain small white spots, which are
uniformly arranged on the edges of the fins. A fish of this kind
weighs about four taels. In writing upon this subject I have
alluded to the earthenware jars which are used as aquariums.
It ought to be observed, however, that, in some instances, the
fish are kept in troughs and ponds.

CHAPTER XXVI.

TEA.

THE tea-plant is an evergreen, and in appearance not unlike the myrtle. It grows to a height varying between four and eight feet, and is so robust as to flourish in almost every variety of climate. I have seen it cultivated with much success in Hok-shan, Fā-yune, and other districts of the province of Kwang-tung, which are within the tropics; and I have also found it in large quantities not only in the central and northern provinces of China Proper, but in various districts in Inner Mongolia, where the winter season is extremely severe. It, however, flourishes best in the provinces of Fo-kien, Kiang-su, Hoonam, and Hoopeh. An Italian, named Giovanni Botero, who in 1590 wrote a work treating particularly of the causes of the splendour and wealth of cities, is the first European author who alludes to the tea-plant. " The Chinese," he says, " have a herb, out of which they press a delicate juice, which serves them for drink instead of wine: it also preserves their health and frees them from all those evils which the immoderate use of wine produces amongst us."

The culture of this plant, which is propagated from seed, gives employment to large numbers of Chinese labourers. When the seeds are gathered—which takes place about the middle of the ninth month of the Chinese year, that is, in October—they are exposed to the rays of the sun until they are perfectly dry. This is preparatory to their safe preservation during winter. About the middle of the first month of the Chinese year, that is

February, or at the commencement of the second, they are placed in cold water for the space of twenty-four hours. During this time they become perfectly soaked. On their removal, they are deposited in cloth bags, and placed in a moderately warm chamber, so as to admit of their becoming gradually dry. The cook-house is generally chosen for this purpose, the warmth of a fire being preferred at this stage to the heat of the sun. When the seeds are partially dried, they are moistened with water, after which they are again partially dried, and then once more moistened. The process of moistening and drying the seeds, is continued until they begin to sprout, when they are placed half an inch apart, in thin layers of earth, spread over basket-work, or matting. During the first four days great care is taken of the seedlings. Every morning they are well watered and exposed to the sun ; and, at the close of the day, they are placed in a chamber where they remain during the night. On the fifth day, they are strong enough to be exposed to the night air, although the dew is not beneficial to them. Rain, however, must be carefully avoided. When the shoots have grown four inches high, they are planted in the ground at a distance of two feet apart. Hilly ground, as affording good drainage, which is of vast importance, is better adapted for the growth of the plant than flat ground ; and tea plantations, with their rich dark foliage, resembling, as they do, extensive shrubberies of evergreens, present a charming contrast to the wild scenery which surrounds them on all sides.

The tea plant yields its first crop at the end of the third year. If stripped of leaves before it has reached this age, it is apt to be spoiled, or seriously injured. After this age, if the annual stripping which the tree ought now to undergo were omitted, the following year would be marked by a very poor and comparatively useless crop. The first crop of leaves is gathered in the latter part of April, the second towards the end of May, or in the early part of June, and the third about thirty days afterwards. Great pains are taken not to exhaust the plants by plucking them too bare. Despite every care they eventually become unproductive, having, when eight or ten years old, only a few coarse leaves. Hence, it is usual for tea farmers to cut the shrubs down to the stems, so that there may be a plentiful supply of new shoots and leaves in succeeding summers. The leaves are plucked with great nicety, not more than one being plucked from the stalk at a time. Before commencing their labours, the gatherers have to wash their hands, and they deposit the leaves which they pluck in clean wicker-work baskets. An expert labourer can, with comparative ease, gather from ten to thirteen pounds of leaves in a day.

The Chinese teas, which are exported by British and other foreign merchants, to Europe and America, include the following kinds, viz., Congou, Souchong, Flowery Pekoe, Oolong, Scented Orange Pekoe, Scented Capers, and Green Tea.

Congou is made in the following manner. The leaves are spread out in the open air to dry. They are then trodden by labourers, so that any moisture remaining in them after their exposure to the air, or sun, is pressed out. At the close of this process, which not unfrequently lasts two or three hours, the leaves are again heaped together, and covered with cloths. In this state they are allowed to remain all night, when they undergo a great change, spontaneous heating changing their green to black or brown. They are, also, now more fragrant, and have undergone a very decided change in flavour. The labourers now proceed to rub the leaves between the palms, of their hands so as to twist or crumple them. In this crumpled state, they are again exposed to the sun. Should the day be wet, or the sky at all overcast, they are baked over a charcoal fire. The baking is done in the following manner. A basket frame, not dissimilar in form to a corset, i.e., wide at both ends and contracted towards the centre, is placed over the grate containing the hot embers of charcoal. In the contracted part of the basket is placed a sieve, upon which the leaves are arranged, and a person is employed to stir them up at certain intervals so that they may be equally heated. After the processes just described, they are ready to be sold to the proprietors of tea hongs, many of whom reside in the towns in the vicinity of the tea-producing districts. The leaves, although previously fired by the planter, are now—for a space, I believe, of two hours—again subjected to this treatment by the proprietors of tea hongs, after which they are sifted. The use of the sieve, however, although it renders it comparatively easy, does not dispense with the additional labour of separating by hand the bad leaves, and the stems, from the good leaves. This task is allotted to women and girls, who, seating themselves with baskets of the leaves on their laps, dexterously use both hands in picking out all the stems and bad leaves which the sieve has failed to get rid of. A winnowing machine, similar to that used by farmers in England for winnowing grain, is now employed to effect the separation of the light and useless leaves from those which are heavy and good. Teas of first quality are winnowed more frequently than those of inferior descriptions. Having been carefully winnowed, the leaves are put into boxes lined with paper. When sufficient boxes have been filled to constitute one parcel, or chop as it is called by the trade, they are sold to foreign merchants.

Black Leaf Congou, is a term applied to certain descriptions of Congou, and implies that the leaves, so called, are blacker than the teas which are termed respectively Red, or Brown Leaf Congou, Oonan Congou, Uing Chou Congou, and Ho-Chow Congou. Oo-pack Congou is produced in the province of Hoo-peh, and comprises the numerous descriptions which are grown in the various districts of that province. The leaves are bold in form and black in colour, with a grey tinge. In former years Oo-pack Congou was sent to Canton for sale. It is now, how-ever, sold in large quantities at Han-kow—a new port opened to foreign trade, some years ago, in conformity with the Elgin Treaty.

Oonan Congou is produced in the various districts of the province of Hoo-nan. The leaves have a greyish, blackish colour, and, in some instances, a tinge of red. Oonan Congou was also sent to Canton for sale in former years. The prin-cipal market for this tea nowadays is Han-kow. Ning Chow Congou is produced in the north-west of the province of Kiang-si. The finest kinds of this tea, however, are grown at Wuning, a place which is south-west of the city of Kiukiang. The leaves are of a brownish black colour. The chief market for teas of this kind is Kiukiang. In the marts of Hangchow and Canton, however, chops of this tea are occasionally sold. Ho-how Congou is produced in the north-east portions of the province of Kiang-si, and on the north of the Bohea hills. The leaves are very rough and irregular in form, and of a brownish black colour. In the Ho-how district several tea hongs are established, the proprietors of which purchase, in the Oonan and Wing-chow districts, large quantities of partly prepared leaves, which they finish and pack in their own district of Ho-how. The Ho-how teas are almost all sent to Kiukiang for sale. The chops, which are not sent thither, find their way to Canton and Foo-chow respectively. Those, however, which find their way to the latter port are very few in number. Chops of Ho-how Congou are, in some instances, sent direct to Shanghai. The finest chops of Oopack teas consist of the best black leaf teas. Fine Oonan teas are superior to those of Ning Chow, whilst the Ho-how teas rank lowest of all. Black leaf teas are sent to the United Kingdom, with the exception of a few chops, to Australia, and, *viâ* Siberia, to Russia.

Red or Brown Leaf Congou is so called on account of the reddish or brownish colour of the leaves. The Red or Brown Leaf Congou is produced in the province of Fo-kien. The finest teas, however, of this class are produced in a district which is in the vicinity of the city of Shama, and the name of Kai-shan is applied to them. The leaves of the red or brown Congou are small and closely twisted. The principal market for these teas is Foo-chow. Those which are produced in the southern part of the province of Fo-kien are forwarded for sale to the port of Amoy.

In the province of Kwang-tung a large quantity of leaf is grown, which is made into teas resembling those made in the central provinces of the Empire. The principal or best Congou made in Kwang-tung, is called Tay-shan Congou. The leaves of this tea are long and wiry, and of a brownish black hue. Much of the Tay-shan Congou is packed at Macao, and sold there. During the last few years a very good imitation of Red-leaf Congou has been made at Canton. The leaves which are of a reddish colour are small and twisted. Red-leaf and Canton Congous are, as a rule, forwarded for sale to Great Britain, but small quantities are sent for sale to the United States. Black-leaf Congous are generally packed in chests, each of which contains from 85 lbs. to 110 lbs. Red-leaf teas are also usually packed in chests. It is sometimes customary to pack them in half chests, each of which contains from 40 to 50 or 60 lbs. Tay-shan Congous are almost invariably packed in boxes, each of which contains from 20 to 30 lbs.

Souchong is a class of tea very similar to Congou. It has the same brownish or reddish colour as the Red-leaf Congou. The make of its leaf, however, is much bolder and more irregular; and, in flavour, this tea is very different from Congou. Fine Souchong is produced only in one part of China, viz., in the north-east parts of the province of Fo-kien. Its leaf is prepared in the following manner. In the first instance, it is spread out in the open air to dry. It is then trodden by labourers. This process ended, it is piled in large heaps, each of which the labourer is careful to cover with a cloth. In this state the tea remains till the following morning, when every particle of it is well rubbed between the labourer's hands. It is then placed in separate portions, for the space of three hours, over charcoal fires. The method of making Souchong is similar in all respects to that of preparing Congou. The first crop of Souchong, in consequence, I believe, of its superior strength, does not, as a general rule, require to be fired a second time. In most instances, however, it is deemed necessary to expose it to the rays of the sun.

Souchong is packed in chests, or half chests, and the lead with which the inside of each chest is coated is of a very superior quality to that with which the chests are ordinarily lined. It is known by all who are engaged in the tea trade as Souchong lead. The bulk of Souchong tea is sent to the markets of the United Kingdom, and the remainder to those of Australia and the United States.

Flowery Pekoe, which is a fancy tea, is not made to any great extent. It is prepared from leaf buds, which are exposed to the sun to dry as soon as they are gathered, and then sold to the proprietors of tea hongs. By them the leaves are finally fired, over a slow fire, and then packed. The leaves, which have a downy appearance, vary in colour, some being yellow and others

black.   Flowery Pekoe is chiefly exported from Foo-chow.
Small quantities of it are also sent to Canton for exportation.
It is in England that Flowery Pekoe finds consumers.

Oolong, a tea of some importance in the trade, is prepared in
the following manner.   The leaves are first of all spread out to
dry.   They are then sprinkled, or moistened, with water, and
eventually fired in the same manner as Congou.   The planters
then sell the leaves to the proprietors of tea hongs, whose
labourers pick out all the stems and bad leaves.   When this has
been done, the leaves are again moistened with water, and once
more fired.   When leaves have been gathered in quantities
sufficient to constitute a "chop," they are all mixed together
and once more exposed to the action of fire.   In appearance,
they are yellow, with a black or dark green tint; in form, they
are bold, irregular, somewhat wiry, and not closely twisted.
Oolong is produced in the province of Fo-kien, and is, in consequence, exported from the ports of Foo-chow and Amoy.   The
greatest quantity of this tea is sent to the United States, the
remainder being forwarded to England and Australia.

Scented Orange Pekoe is made in the provinces of Kwang-
tung and Fo-kien.   Teas of this description, prepared in the
former province, are called Canton Scented Orange Pekoe, whilst
those made in the province of Fo-kien, are called Foo-chow
Scented Orange Pekoe.   The preparation of these teas takes place
in the following manner.   The leaves are spread out in the open
air to dry.   Labourers then rub them between the palms of
their hands, to impart a twisted, or crumpled, appearance to
them.   At this stage of preparation, they are packed and sent
to the markets of Canton and Foo-chow, where they are immediately unpacked and baked over a slow fire.   Pains are taken
to scent the leaves by mixing them with flowers of the Arabian
jessamine.   When they are supposed to have sufficiently im-
bibed the fragrance, they are separated from the jessamine
flowers by means of sieves.   Fine kinds of Scented Orange
Pekoe are twice scented.   It is unnecessary for them to undergo
a second time the action of fire.   The leaves of Foo-chow
Scented Orange Pekoe are small and closely twisted.   In colour
they are yellow, with a brownish or blackish tinge.   Those

which are called Canton Scented Orange Pekoe, are long, wiry, closely twisted, and black, with, occasionally, a yellowish or greenish tinge. The 'black colour is produced by a mixture of powdered charcoal. Scented Orange Pekoe, which is invariably packed in boxes, is exported for sale to the United Kingdom. A small quantity is also occasionally sent from the port of Foo-chow to Australia.

Scented Caper is made in the same way. It consists, in fact, of leaves separated by a sifting process from the leaves of Scented Orange Pekoe. The leaves thus separated, are in the form of pellets. Those which are prepared at Foo-chow are yellowish and brownish, or blackish, whereas those manufactured at Canton are black or brown, with an occasional tinge of yellow or green. The tea made into Caper at Canton, is grown upon an extensive range of hills in the district of Hok-shan, one of the counties forming the prefecture of Kwang-chow Foo. The tea leaves having been well dried and fired in the first instance, are forwarded, when in sufficient quantity, to the city of Canton, where they are made into Caper according to the following rules. Seventeen or eighteen handfuls of leaves are placed in each of the pans with which the tea hong is furnished. Having been moistened with water, the leaves are now well stirred up by hand. Rendered thus soft and pliable, they are immediately put into small coarse sackcloth bags, each of which, when filled and tightly closed, has the appearance of a foot-ball. These bags are all arranged on the floor of one of the largest chambers of the hong, and are moved to and fro by labourers, who stand upon them, and who, in order to roll them backwards and forwards with their feet without the risk of falling, support themselves by grasping long wooden poles. Under this process, the tea leaves in each bag assume the form of pellets, or capers. The coarse leaves gathered from the finer leaves thus made into Caper, are not thrown aside as useless, but after being well fired, are put into wooden troughs, and cut into several pieces by means of choppers not unlike in shape to large spuds. The pieces of leaves are then made by the process already described, into a tea which is also called Caper. A very inferior kind of Scented Caper, is made by mixing tea dust with Congee water and sifting it, to give it the form of pellets. Scented Caper is exported to the United Kingdom.

Green tea is prepared in the following manner. The leaves of the tea-plant are placed in iron pans as soon as they are plucked, to undergo, for two or three minutes only, the action of heat over a charcoal fire. They are then rubbed together for a short time, after which they are again exposed to the action of fire. The process of firing the leaves a second time, is continued not for two or three minutes only, as in the first instance, but for two or three hours. To the care of each person engaged in the firing department of a green-tea factory, a bundle of leaves, weighing eight or ten catties, is entrusted; and while the leaves are being fired a second time, they are kept constantly stirred by hand. In the case of fine tea, the leaves are constantly fanned during the first hour of the second time of firing, so as to preserve their green colour. When the leaves have undergone this process, they are packed and sold to the proprietors of tea hongs. By them the leaves are again exposed to the action of fire for the space of half-an-hour. They are then cleansed by the usual methods of sieving, picking, and winnowing. In manipulating green teas, much care and attention must be given to the separation of leaves which differ in size and shape. The extent to which this process is carried, varies of course according to the intention of the manufacturer. When separated, the leaves are sold to foreign merchants. Those which are small and resemble pellets in shape, comprise what is termed Gunpowder. Those of a larger size, though similar in form to Gunpowder, are called Imperial. Small sized leaves which are wiry and twisted, are called Young Hyson, whilst those of a larger size are called Hyson. Twankay is a term applied to leaves which are light, large, coarse, and irregular, whilst those which are thin, skinny, and broken are called Skin, or Hyson Skin. To the last-mentioned leaves, the name Hyson-Twankay is also occasionally given. When these leaves have been separated and classed under their respective names, they are again fired, viz., Gunpowder for twelve or fourteen hours, Imperial for eight hours, Young Hyson for ten hours, Hyson for eight hours, and Twan-kay and Skin for three hours. When each of these kinds is half fired, small quantities of powdered gypsum, Prussian blue, and turmeric are mixed with them, the two latter giving them the desired tint. All green teas, whether fine, or common, are mixed with the ingredients I have enumerated. The quantity of colouring matter, however, is optional. Tea-men who wish to make their teas very blue, use, of course, a greater quantity than those who wish their teas to be of a pale colour. When the different kinds of green tea leaves have undergone the action of fire, they are well stirred up, and fired once more for half-an-hour. Green tea is generally packed in half chests. Sometimes, however, it is placed in boxes. The finest description is made in the neighbourhood of Wuyune, and is known by the name of Moyune. All green teas, with the exception of a few chops, which find their way to other ports, are forwarded, for exportation, to Shanghai, Kiukang, and Ningpo.

On a visit to Formosa, I observed tea growing upon the hills of that beautiful island. The tea of Formosa, however, is of very inferior quality. Quantities of it are sent to the province of Fo-kien, of which the island is regarded as a political division. By the inhabitants of Fo-kien this tea is said to be appreciated for certain medicinal properties which it is supposed to possess. Of late years, however, Formosa teas have, in some instances, been forwarded for sale to Macao, where, before exportation, they are freely mixed with Canton teas. Oolong is also produced in Formosa. This tea is bought from the tea growers of the island by European merchants, who, as a rule, forward it for sale to the marts of the United States.

When travelling in Inner Mongolia I also saw the tea-plant growing, though not in large quantities. The leaves of the plant are very large, and are produced, I was told, for the service of the nomadic tribes of Mongolia only. The process which the Mongolians adopt, to prepare the leaves for the palate, is very simple. So soon as the leaves are plucked, they are placed in an iron pan to be well steamed over a slow fire. After this simple process has been repeated seven or eight times, they are regarded as fit for use. What is known as brick tea, is of two kinds, viz., green and black brick tea. Green brick tea is made of leaves which have fallen to the ground either in consequence

of the violence of the winds, or the changes of the seasons. So
soon as these leaves have been gathered, they are mixed with
stalks or stems, which have been separated by the processes of
sieving, picking, and winnowing, from the leaves which have been
carefully gathered by the hand of the labourer. They are then
put into wicker-baskets, each of which is placed on an iron pan
filled to the brim with boiling water. These pans are placed over
slow fires of cow-dung, which keep the water in a boiling state,
and the vapour, as it ascends, permeates the mixture in the baskets.
Having been well steamed, the contents of each basket are
placed in moulds, and eventually pressed with heavy weights.
The time required for these processes in the manufacture of
green brick tea, is one month. Black brick tea, also, consists of
fallen leaves and stems, and is prepared in a precisely similar
manner. Three weeks only, however, are required for its manufacture. Thirty large bricks of green brick tea constitute one
package, while sixty-four are required to form a package of
black brick tea, the bricks of the black tea being much smaller
than those of the green. The bricks of both teas vary much in
point of quality, some being very coarse in appearance, and
others quite smooth. In some instances, the surface is plain;
in others, it is decorated with raised representations of flowers.
Green brick tea is made at Toong-shan, in the province of
Hoonam, and black brick tea at Soong-yang, and at Yang-lou-
toong, in the province of Hoo-peh.

The last-named town recalls to my mind a journey which
would have been one of uninterrupted pleasure, but for an
incident which filled me with horror. It was the capture and
summary punishment of a thief at Tien-hshin, a town at which
I spent a night *en route* from Hankow to Yang-lou-toong. The
unhappy man was taken at midnight in the act of stealing a
package of tea from a junk which was lying alongside the
wharf; he was forcibly dragged on board the junk, and the
crew, having been roused from their slumbers by the policeman,
vented their rage upon him in a most violent manner. For
three hours, at least, the stillness of the night was interrupted,
and the very air, as it were, rent by his painfully agonizing
shrieks. At the end of the third hour they suddenly ceased.

No doubt he died under the torture to which his hard-hearted countrymen had subjected him. Such barbarity towards pilferers of cargo is not confined to the province of Hoo-peh. In 1871, in crossing the Canton River from Shamien to Honam, I found in the bows of a sampan, which was drifting with the tide, the dead body of a man, who, I afterwards learned, had been beaten to death by the crew of a junk for stealing cargo. At Tien-hshin the people were much disposed to maltreat our party; and, passing through the principal streets of the town, in the darkness of the evening, we were assailed by a number of men who pelted us with stones in the most violent manner. As we were traversing a dark alley which leads to the wharf, a man, who was evidently lying in wait for us, threw at my head a stone so large that, had it hit the frail target, the result would probably have been fatal. The formidable missile whizzed past my right ear, and rebounded with great force from the opposite wall of the alley. On arriving at Yang-lou-toong I found many extensive tea hongs, in which black brick tea is made. From the experience which I then acquired, I may venture to affirm that a statement made by Professor Johnson in his work entitled *Chemistry of Common Life*, that the bricks are often made harder by mixing the leaves with the scum of sheep and ox blood, is without foundation. At Yang-lou-toong I bought several bricks of tea. They are still in my possession, and the dimensions of some of them in inches are as follows :—

Length.			Breadth.			Thickness.
13¾	...	...	6	...	...	1
10½	...	...	5	...	...	1
10	...	...	5¼	...	...	¾
8¾	...	...	4¾	...	...	¾
8½	...	...	5½	...	...	¾
8½	...	...	5	...	...	1

The various packages of brick tea are carried from the tea hongs in wheel-barrows to the banks of the nearest navigable creek, or stream, where they are placed on board vessels, and conveyed to Hankow. At this treaty port they are bought by Russian merchants, and forwarded for sale, by retail, to the markets of Mongolia, Mantchuria, Thibet, and Siberia. From fifty to seventy thousand packages of brick tea are forwarded annually to these markets by the Russian merchants. In the well-known work, to which I have already alluded, Professor Johnson states that "the Mongols and other Tartar tribes, in order to use brick tea, rub it to a fine powder, boil it with the alkaline of steppe-water, to which salt and fat have been added, and pour off the decoction from the sediment. They mix this liquid first with milk, butter, and a little roasted meal." Sir Joseph Hooker, in his work entitled *Himalayan Journals*, says that the beverage of the Thibetans is "a sort of soup, made from brick tea, of which a handful of leaves is churned up with salt, butter, and soda, then boiled and transferred to the tea-pot."

In the province of Yun-nan and in the district of Nang-nee-uen, which is a division of the prefecture of Poo-nee Foo, brick or cake tea is also made. The bricks, or cakes, are moulded in the form of circles, each of which is twenty-one inches in circumference. The brick tea of Yun-nan is termed Poo-nee Foo tea, and regarded with much favour by the Chinese, not only as agreeable to the palate, but on account of certain properties which, in addition to their tendency to rid the body of humours and bile, are efficacious in the case of sufferers from bleeding piles. The longer these bricks or cakes of tea are kept, the more powerful is the decoction made from them. Several packages are annually sent to Pekin for the special use of the Emperor and other members of the Imperial family. Brick tea is also made in the province of Fo-kien. The bricks are much smaller than those made in the provinces of Hoonam and Hoo-peh. They consist of coarse tea leaves, which have been gathered and stored upwards of ten years, and which are mixed with other ingredients. This tea is used by the Chinese generally as a febrifuge.

There is, also, a preparation of tea called Cha-peng, or tea cakes. The leaves of which it consists are compressed into the form of thin circular cakes. It is made of coarse tea leaves, which have been first reduced by means of a pestle and mortar to a fine powder. The gum of a tree is added to the powder, so

as to form a paste.   Cake tea is used by the Chinese, and
more particularly by those who inhabit the province of Kwang-
tung, as a febrifuge.   It is made at Loo-loong, in the prefecture of Wei-chow Foo, in the province of Kwang-tung, and
at Su-kwan in the prefecture of Su-chow Foo, also in the same
province.

CHAPTER XXVII.

SILK.

SILK, which is the cloth woven from the fine soft thread produced by the *bombyx mori*, or silkworm of the mulberry tree, was originally exported from China. The silkworm being a native of China, there is the strongest presumptive evidence that its culture and the manufacture of the fabric woven from its cocoons were confined for a very considerable period to that country. In Europe, the manufacture does not appear to have been practised until early in the sixth century of the Christian era. Long before that a large trade in silk was carried on between China and Persia. So soon as the latter had fallen before the Macedonian troops under Alexander the Great, B.C. 325, the silken stuffs of China were exposed for sale in all the marts of Greece. It has been supposed by some that several centuries before this date, the Hebrews of Palestine had a knowledge of silk as a fabric of which dresses were made; and they appeal to the use of the term מֶשִׁי (*meshi*) or silk, by Ezekiel (xvi. 10). Even if it were certain, however, that the prophet alluded to silk, it would not follow that the Jews had intercourse with the Chinese. The allusion might be readily accounted for by the fact that Ezekiel was for several years a captive in the hands of the Babylonians. The whole question, however, is so much a matter of conjecture that it has not yet been decided, whether the Babylonians had any knowledge of silk. At Rome, silken stuffs appear to have been known towards the end of the Republic. Later on, in the reign of Tiberius, a law was enacted by the Roman senate which forbade men to be so effeminate as to wear silk garments, which were regarded as fit only for women. This law, however, was eventually rescinded, for we read that in A.D. 220, the Emperor Heliogabalus appeared clad in robes of silk. At this time the cost of silk fabrics in Greece and Italy placed them beyond the reach of all but kings and millionaires.[1] The extraordinary market value of silk was not owing, however, to its scarcity in China, but to the great difficulty which the merchants of Persia and India experienced in procuring it from there in sufficient quantities. Between the merchants of Persia and India on the one hand and those of China on the other, imperfect and irregular communications were kept up in the face of very formidable obstacles; and if we consider the extreme length of the great caravan route across Asia from Byzantium to Serica—by which there can be little doubt we are to understand China—it is not surprising that silk should have commanded exorbitant prices. A journey of more than two thousand miles lay between Byzantium and the bases of the stupendous Himalayan mountains; and the time occupied by a caravan from this region in reaching its destination in Serica was, according to Ptolemy, not less than seven months.

For several centuries after the introduction of silk as an article of sale into Greece and Italy, it was regarded by some Europeans as a species of down gathered from the leaves of trees, and by others as a very delicate skin of wool or cotton. From the language which he employs in his Georgics (ii. 121), Virgil evidently imagined that the Chinese (Seres) carded the silk from leaves; for he writes—

"Velleraque ut foliis depectant tenuia Seres."

At the commencement of the sixth century, however, all such conjectures were set aside by more correct information from China. Two Nestorian monks, belonging to Persia, having travelled to China, regarded it as a duty to make themselves well acquainted during their stay in that country, with the

---

[1] The Emperor Aurelian refused, because of the cost, to purchase a silk dress for his wife.—ED.

natural history of the silkworm, and to learn how silk was manufactured by the Chinese. When they were in possession of this knowledge, they returned at once to Europe, and, on their arrival at Constantinople, immediately laid the results of their investigations before the Emperor Justinian. Fully alive to the great commercial advantages which would accrue from the manufacture of silk, the emperor persuaded the monks to return to China, to obtain, if possible, a collection of silk-worms' eggs. They had little or no difficulty in collecting them, and they packed them in hollow bamboo tubes, for safe conveyance to Constantinople. The eggs thus introduced to Europe, were, it is said, hatched by the heat of a manure heap. The larvæ were fed upon the leaves of the mulberry tree, and the silkworms multiplied so rapidly in the land of their adoption, that they were to be found, before many years had elapsed, in great numbers throughout the southern countries of Europe.

The first silk culturist of China, and, therefore, of course, of the world, is said to have been Si Ling-chee, the excellent consort of the Emperor Hung-tai, who reigned B.C. 2700. Since the time of this empress it has been customary for all succeed-ing empresses, and for the ladies of the imperial household, to interest themselves in the rearing of silkworms, and to super-intend the weaving and embroidering of webs intended to be used as vestments for the principal idols of the empire. The Chinese annually hold a festival, called the Cocoon Festival, in honour of the illustrious discoverer of the utility of the silk-worm :—" On a fortunate day "—I quote the description given by Mr. Murrow in his *Hongkong Chronicle and Directory* for 1865—" of the ninth month, the empress, either personally or by proxy, accompanied by a train of princesses and honourable ladies, repairs to the altar sacred to the discoverer of silkworms. After sacrificing, the empress with golden and the princesses with silver implements collect the mulberry leaves to feed the imperial silkworms. They, then, wind off some cocoons of silk and so end the ceremony. This very ancient festival is con-sidered as the counterpart of the agricultural one, observed by the emperor in the spring." This, however, is not the only honour which is paid to Si Ling-chee. As the goddess of silk-worms, she has several important temples in the province of Tche-kiang, and, on a fortunate day in the spring of each year, her state worship is duly solemnized by the mandarins. The example set by the empress, the princesses, and ladies of the imperial household naturally finds many followers among the ladies and women of the silk-producing districts.

In endeavouring to give some account of the processes connected with this important branch of Chinese industry, the first point to be noticed is the mode in which the silkworms are reared. Those who are engaged in this work, select a certain number of male and female cocoons. They have no difficulty in distinguishing the sex, as the cocoon which contains the male is strong, very pointed at each end, and smaller than that which contains the female, which is thick, round, and soft. At the end of a period of fifteen or twenty days, the moths come out of the cocoons. They free themselves by first ejecting a fluid which dissolves a portion of the cocoon. All moths the wings of which are expanded at the time of birth, are regarded as useful, whereas those which have crumpled wings, no eyebrows, red bellies, dry tails, and are without down, are considered useless, and at once destroyed. Male moths are permitted to go together only with such female moths as have left their cocoons on the same day as themselves, and any departure from this practice would be most repugnant to the notions of the Chinese breeder and rearer of silkworms. After a day the male moths are removed, and the females, each having been placed on a sheet of coarse paper, begin to lay their eggs. In the silk districts of the north, owing, I suppose, to the severity of the climate, pieces of cloth are used instead of sheets of paper. The number of eggs which one moth lays, is generally five hundred, and the period required for her to perform so great a labour, is, I believe, about seventy-four hours. The females often die almost immediately after they have laid their eggs, and the males do not long survive them. The egg of the silkworm, which is of a whitish or pale ash colour, is not larger than a grain of mustard seed. When eighteen days old the eggs are carefully washed with spring water. The sheet of

coarse paper or piece of cloth on which they were laid, and
to which they adhere, is very gently drawn through spring
water contained in a wooden or earthenware bowl. During the
autumnal months the eggs are carefully kept in a cool chamber,
the sheets of paper or pieces of cloth being suspended back
to back from bamboo rods placed in a horizontal position. In
the tenth month of the Chinese year, which corresponds with
our December, the sheets are rolled up, and then deposited
in a room which is well swept, and free from all noxious
influences. On the third day of the twelfth month the eggs
are again washed, and then exposed to the air to dry. In
the spring of the year, the eggs being now ready to bring
forth, the sheets are placed on mats, and each mat placed on
a bamboo shelf, in a well-swept and well-warmed chamber
containing a series of shelves arranged along the walls. The
shelves are almost invariably made of bamboo, the wood of
which emits no fragrance, aromatic wood being especially avoided
as unsuitable for the purpose.

At the time of their birth the worms are black, and so small
as scarcely to exceed a hair in breadth. Owing to their
diminutive size, those in charge of them cut the leaves of the
mulberry tree into very small pieces. This is done with very
sharp knives, so that the leaves may retain as much sap as
possible. When the worms are quite young they are fed not less
than forty-eight times in twenty-four hours. In course of time
their meals are reduced to thirty in twenty-four hours ; and when
they have attained to their full growth, they get only three or
four in the day. Occasionally, that is once or twice during the
first month, the worms are fed upon mulberry leaves well mixed
with the flour of green peas, that of black beans, and that of
rice. This mixture is supposed to be cooling and cleansing to
the worms, and to tend to the production of strong and glossy
silk. Like all other creatures, these insects have their seasons
of rest, and to these seasons the Chinese give distinguishing
names. The first sleep which takes place on the fourth or fifth
day after birth, is termed the " hair sleep," and lasts but one day.
The second sleep takes place on the eighth or ninth day, and
the third on the fourteenth ; the fourth and last sleep, which

XXVII.]   SILK-WORMS.   223

takes place on or about the twenty-second day, is styled in consequence of its long duration, the great sleep. On the near approach of each period, the worm loses its appetite. It erects the upper part of its body, and sleeps in this position. During each period of sleep, it casts its skin, continuing in a state of repose until the new skin is fully matured. It relieves itself of the old skin by wriggling out of it at that part which covers the head, and which is broken. Sometimes the worm dies in consequence of its inability to free the end of its body from the old skin. The skin being cast, the worm grows very quickly in strength and size. Between the first, second, and third periods of rest, there are, generally, intervals of three or four days, during which these little creatures eat most voraciously. During the four or five days which immediately follow the great sleep, they have a greater appetite for food than they have hitherto manifested. When they have reached the age of thirty-two days they are full grown, each being about two inches in length, and almost as thick as a man's little finger. When the worms are gradually increasing in size they are separated, periodically, into several lots so as to give them more room. Now that it is full grown the worm, which before was of a whitish hue, assumes a tint resembling that of amber. At this period they cease to partake of food, and begin to spin the silk from their mouths on the frames or shelves on which they have been placed. In spinning, they move the head first to one side and then to the other, and continue the operation until the whole body has been enveloped in a cocoon. The time which a worm requires to accomplish this labour, is, I believe, from three to five days ; and so soon as it has inclosed itself in the cocoon, it falls into a state of coma, casts its skin, and eventually becomes a chrysalis. The attendants then place the bamboo shelves on which the cocoons lie, near a slow fire of charcoal or wood, in order that the chrysalids may be destroyed by its heat, otherwise these would in three weeks more break from their prison and appear in the imago form—the last perfected state of insect life.

The chrysalids having been destroyed, the cocoons are removed from the frames and placed in baskets. Women and girls, carefully selected for the task, now unwind the cocoons—a process which they make easy by placing them in boiling water. These workers must be deft of hand, and expert in the business, fully capable of making the threads of equal size, and of producing them bright, clear, and glossy. When the cocoons are put into boiling water, the outer layer, which is called the silk rind or shell, is first unwound. Another set of women and girls who are equally expert, are then engaged to unwind the inner layers of the cocoon, called the silk pulp or flesh. In the course of a day one woman can unwind four taels of silk in weight. The most expert workers cannot, I believe, turn off more than five or six taels weight. Industrious workers who are masters of the business, will finish one season, or silk harvest, in the course of eighteen or nineteen days. Ordinary or second-rate workers will require twenty-four or twenty-five days to get through the same amount of work. From long, white, and shining cocoons a small and good thread of silk is obtained ; from those which are large, dull in colour, and not firm of texture, a coarse thread is produced. This coarse thread is used in making the stuffs with which dresses are lined. The chrysalids are not thrown away as refuse, but are eaten by the workers as food of an excellent kind. On a visit to the large silk town of Kow-hong in the province of Kwang-tung, I was respectfully invited by the proprietress of a silk farm to join her in eating a dish of boiled chrysalids. This invitation, so politely given, I as politely declined.

In the Canton silk districts there are no fewer than seven seasons, or harvests. The first of these commences, as I have already observed, in the month of April. During the first, second, and third seasons, the cocoons are, generally speaking, green. Some few, however, are silvery. In the fourth, fifth, and sixth seasons the silvery, or white cocoons, as they are called, are very numerous. I ought to have observed that, in the first season, the eggs require little or no care, and the hatching takes place without any assistance from those in charge. This is, of course, attributable to the spring season of the year. During the second, third, fourth, fifth, and sixth seasons, the attendants practise the following method, in order that the eggs may be hatched earlier and all at the same time, as great losses would be sustained by the proprietors if the eggs were hatched at intervals. They mix together equal quantities of hot and cold water, and then gently pour the water upon the eggs. The eggs all share in this way one common artificial heat, and the worms come to life at the same time. This practice is one of great antiquity, having been adopted, so I understand, when the culture of silk was first practised. I have hitherto spoken of six seasons or crops only. There is, however, a seventh, which takes place in the month of November, and is not inaptly termed the cool weather, or small season. When it has come to a close, labourers at once cut the mulberry shrubs close to the ground. The cut branches are bound in bundles, and sold as firewood. In cutting down the shrubs, which in the southern silk districts are never allowed to attain a greater height than four or five feet, much care is taken not to injure the roots. In the following spring, if uninjured, they will again produce tender shoots or stems, laden with leaves.

All persons who grow mulberry trees upon their estates are not rearers of silkworms. In many instances, farmers cultivate the tree only to sell the leaves. On the occasion of a visit which I paid in 1868 to the silk town of Wong-ling, a very busy scene presented itself. In the market-place, which was tolerably crowded, as brisk a trade was being carried on as it has ever been my lot to witness. There was but one article of merchandise for sale, namely mulberry leaves. The farmers of mulberry lands were offering these in large quantities to breeders and rearers of silkworms. As I was leaving the market, I observed innumerable boats, heavily laden with cargoes of the leaves, hastening to increase, if possible, the business and excitement of the market. At Luk-low, a town which I subsequently visited, I witnessed a similar scene of excitement in the market-place. In the silk-producing districts of Kwang-tung, the surface of the earth is covered for many miles with mulberry shrubs or trees. The land on which they grow appears to be made ground and is slightly undulating. There are also at frequent intervals throughout these plains, large pits or ponds from which the soil has been thrown out. These pits which are full of water, abound with fish, which are evidently a principal food in the silk-producing districts. In many of these ponds fish are bred to supply the fish markets of the city of Canton.

From this sketch of the processes connected with the breeding and rearing of silkworms, it will be evident that very great care is bestowed upon these delicate creatures. I must further point out some of the conditions under which the Chinese think it desirable to rear them. One of the most important is, of course, the temperature in which the worms are kept. Extremes of heat and cold are not only carefully avoided, but the worms are kept as much as possible in a uniform temperature. The Chinese ascertain the temperature in the chamber in which the worms are placed, not by a thermometer, but by the sensations produced upon the naked body of the person in charge. At intervals, he divests himself of his clothes, enters the chamber, and if he finds the air at all cool or damp, heat is obtained by means of Chinese stoves. Lightning is thought injurious to silkworms, and great pains are taken, when a thunderstorm is apprehended, to cover the shelves on which they are placed with thick brown paper—a precaution which darkens them and intercepts the vivid glare. Thunder is also supposed to be injurious to these little reptiles, as it alarms them. So easily are they frightened and disturbed by noises of all kinds that those in charge of them are required to speak in a subdued tone of voice when administering to their wants. It is very important not to feed them upon mulberry leaves which are at all damp, as they fill them with water instead of silk. The leaves, which are all carefully plucked by hand, are well dried in the wet or rainy seasons, before they are given as food to the worms. They should also be quite fresh, as old and withered leaves fail to nourish the worms, and make them costive. They are supposed to thrive best when the sky is bright and clear, and care is usually taken to place them on the shelves in fine, clear weather. Should this precaution be neglected, the cocoons, the Chinese say, would assuredly prove defective, and yield rough, broken, and dull looking threads. The houses in which the worms are kept should be wide and clean, and free from all

noxious smells.	Punctuality in attending to their wants is also
considered a very important duty.

The two principal diseases which are incidental to silkworms
are called Foong-Tsun, or a sickness arising from flatulence ; and
Tsak-Foong, or thief-wind sickness.	The former is regarded as
very fatal, and should the worms survive, the injury which they
have sustained is so great as to make their silk of a very
inferior quality.	The sickness called Tsak-Foong, or thief-wind
sickness, arises from the wind having been carelessly permitted
to blow into the chamber in which they are kept.	When
suffering from this disease they become in colour very red, and
in their movements so stiff as to be almost unable to crawl.	A
servant neglecting to keep the doors of the chambers closed
would expose himself to the anger of his master.	Great pains
are taken to keep flies from the worms.	Flies not only suck
blood from them, but lay eggs upon their bodies, from which
larvæ, destructive to the worms, are often hatched.	The utility,
however, of some of the precautions taken to defend the little
weavers from harmful influences is far from being apparent,
and some of the notions of the Chinese on the subject seem
equally strange and superstitious.	Thus they will on no account
allow females who are *enceinte* to enter the chambers in
which silk-worms are kept.	Persons in mourning are not
allowed to go near them until seven weeks or forty-nine days
of the period of mourning have elapsed.	Those who attend
upon them must abstain from eating ginger and beans called
Tsam-Tou.	They are also forbidden to fry meats in oil, or to
have about their persons anything which emits an aromatic
smell.	They are careful never to cross the thresholds of the
chambers in which their valuable charges are kept without
having sprinkled themselves with water, which is kept for this
purpose in a basin at the door of each apartment.	When at the
city of Tai-laong, in 1862, I visited an establishment, in the
chambers of which several thousands of silkworms were being
reared.	As I entered each chamber, I was sprinkled with water by
means of a small bunch of mulberry leaves.	This rite of purifica-
tion reminded me of a similar rite observed by the Hebrews,
in which a bunch of hyssop was used.	In the silk districts

of the north, grains of sand are thrown on the heads of persons when they enter and when they leave a chamber in which silkworms are kept.

The silk towns in the province of Kwang-tung are very neat and clean, and, in many respects different from others throughout the empire. Excepting those parts of the silk towns which are especially set apart for marketing, each house is detached and stands in its own mulberry plantation ; partly, I suppose, because they are in consequence removed from noises and bad smells. The houses are generally large, and invariably built of bricks. The pathways which conduct the traveller from one silk town to another are well paved.

In 1862 I made a walking tour through the silk districts of Kwang-tung. Only one disagreeable incident occurred to mar the pleasure of this excursion, which I shall always regard as one of the most agreeable which I ever made. The citizens of Kow-hong had never seen foreigners before the arrival of our party, and unfortunately at the time they had some excuse for regarding us with hostility, as the capital of the province had a short time before been taken by the allied armies of Great Britain and France. They followed us into the yamun of the principal mandarin of the place, and frequently threatened us with instant death. The mandarin appeared to have no power whatever over the people, and was much more alarmed for our safety than we were ourselves. Eventually, thinking that a critical moment was at hand, he called out a number of braves, for the purpose of escorting us to the neighbouring town of Kum-chok. We quitted the town amidst the most unearthly yells from the infuriated populace, and were kindly received by the people of Kum-chok, who proved to be of a much more amiable disposition. I visited several silk towns of equal importance to Kow-hong and Kum-chok on the same occasion, viz. :—Loong-shun, Loong-kong, Sha-tow, Nam-poon, Lak-low, Wong-sui, Yoong-āk, Tai-laong, See-ne-lam, Hung-tan, Shooee-tung, Kat-ngawn-kwei-chow, Yoong-kee, Kòo-loong, Kut-yow, Law-shoo-ee, Loong-tam, Ko-chune, Wong-ngwawn, Foong-kan, Kwang-wa, and Pak-kow. The whole amount of silk produced in the silk-districts of Kwang-tung is estimated at three millions of taels. At each of

WINDING AND WEAVING SILK.

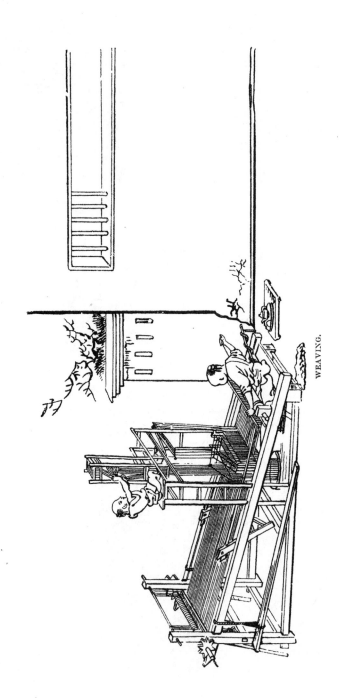

WEAVING.

the principal towns which I have enumerated there is a market at which silk is sold in its raw state. These markets are covered with tile roofs and inclosed with high walls. They are divided into compartments, like the stalls in a stable. On a market day a silk-producer may be found sitting in each compartment, with specimens of the silk which he has for sale arranged on a table before him. The silk is, to a large extent, bought by European merchants, who send it in its raw state to the markets of England. Much of it, however, is wrought into texture by the weavers at Canton, who form no small portion of the residents of that city, and of several of the adjacent villages. The loom for plain weaving is very similar to that in use in England and other European countries. The frames for warping and beaming differ, however, in some respects from those in daily use amongst European weavers. For weaving flowered or figured silks and satins, the draw-loom in its very primitive state is still in use in China. The draw-boy sits above the frame and, with unerring precision and the utmost regularity, pulls the strings or cords by which he can bring down the necessary warp-threads preparatory to the movement of the shuttle. Canton is famous for its gauzes, as well as for its webs of silks and satins. Of the towns of China, however, that which appeared to me to be most deserving of note for the quality of its gauzes was Tang-yang Hien, on the banks of the Grand Canal. This fabric is much required for dresses for the mandarins and gentry during the summer months. On visiting Tang-yang, Hang-chow, Hoo-chow, and Soo-chow, I observed that the looms in which the fabrics were made were arranged on one side of the shop, while on the other stood the counter at which the fabrics were sold. As the Chinese are very much opposed to innovations, many years, I am afraid, must of necessity elapse before the draw-loom and draw-boy give way to the excellent contrivance of M. Jacquard.

There are a large number of weavers in Canton who gain their daily bread by weaving the broad ribbons used by Chinese ladies to cover their small feet. The ribbons, or sashes, to which I refer, are not used, as many foreign residents have supposed, to contract the feet—bandages of a coarse material being employed for this purpose.   They are stockings, that is, they are made as ornamental coverings for contracted feet, and are long enough to admit of their being bound round the leg.

The Chinese are as famous for their skill in embroidery as for their dexterity in weaving.   At Canton, for instance, numbers of men and women—chiefly men—are daily employed in embroidering altar-cloths, banners, and vestments of all kinds.   The principal shops at Canton in which this work—so exquisitely beautiful in design and in the blending of colours—is executed, are situated in Chong-yune-fong street, near the Tai-ping-moon or Great Peace Gate of the city.   The fabric which it is intended to embroider is stretched over a horizontal frame, at the side of which the embroiderer is seated upon a stool.   The crape shawls, for the manufacture of which the Chinese are so justly famous, are embroidered at the town of Pak-kow, in the province of Kwang-tung.   I was much surprised on visiting this town to find work so really beautiful, executed in houses so mean and dirty as are those which form the streets of Pak-kow.

Before concluding this chapter I ought to add that in China Proper, more particularly, I believe, in the neighbourhood of Cheefoo, in the province of Shan-tung, and also in Mongolia, and Mantchuria, there are silkworms which produce what is termed by Chinese silk merchants "mountain silk."   These worms are very large, and are found upon oak trees.   The silken stuffs made of mountain silk are very coarse.

CHAPTER XXVIII.

POTTERIES:

THE art of moulding vessels of clay for domestic and other purposes is in all probability one of the most ancient of industries. It appears to have been práctised in the earliest ages by the most civilized as well as by the most barbarous nations. References are frequently made to the potter in the Bible. The earliest of these references to earthenware vessels is in the book of Judges (vii. 16-19). In Genesis (xxi. 14, 15) allusion is made to a vessel which is rendered in our translation by the word "bottle"; but there can be no doubt, I apprehend, that vessels of this kind were not made of earthenware, but of skins. Some commentators are disposed to think that Rebecca's pitcher, to which reference is made further on in the same book (xxiv. 14, 15), was formed of baked clay. I believe it utterly impossible to arrive at any certainty on the point. Many profane records of great antiquity allude to the potter's wheel, and we have most undoubted evidence that great taste was displayed by the Chinese in the manufacture of porcelain vessels of a superior quality at a very early date. The art of fabricating porcelain, so early practised by the Chinese, extended in time to other parts of Asia, more particularly to the adjacent empire of Japan. A Jesuit missionary named Entreolles, who visited China in the discharge of the duties of his sacred office in the early part of the eighteenth century, states that earthenware or porcelain vessels were then extant which, the Chinese affirm, had been manufactured prior to, or during, the respective reigns of the sovereigns Yaou and Shun. If this statement be correct, the manufacture of porcelain in China is indeed of very great antiquity, as, according to Sacharoff's chronology of the Chinese, the Emperor Yaou flourished B.C. 2357, and his successor Shun B.C. 2355. The literary labours of M. Julian of Paris throw much light upon the antiquity of the potter's art in China. That great sinologue informs us that during the reign of the Emperor Hoang-tai, or Hwang-te, who occupied the throne of China from B.C. 2697 to B.C. 2597, there was always an official called the superintendent of potteries duly appointed by the government. M. Julian says that it was during the reign of Hoang-tai that the art of moulding earthen vessels was invented by an enterprising Chinese named Kouen-Oa. In the early centuries of the Christian era several porcelain vases were discovered buried in the earth. They are reported to have been of a colour resembling the very whiteness of snow. In point of quality and symmetry, however, they were evidently regarded as very defective. According to the statements of Wilkinson, and other modern writers on Egypt, vases evidently of Chinese manufacture were discovered in the ancient sepulchres of the once proud and flourishing city of Thebes. One of the Theban sepulchres from which a Chinese vase was removed was, it is stated, of the age of the Pharaohs. One of these vases is deposited, if I mistake not, in the museum of the Louvre, where it is regarded as an object of extraordinary interest.

Of the eighteen provinces into which China Proper is divided, the one most distinguished for the quality of its plastic clays is Kiang-si; and of the districts of this province, Ping-lee and Kot-how occupy the first position. In the prefecture of Wy-chow in the province of Ngan-huy, very excellent plastic clays are also found. The clays are soft, smooth, and with one exception uniform in point of colour. The exception to which I refer is marked with streaks, or veins, which are like the antlers of deer, and it is greatly preferred by many potters. The town which, from a very early period, has always been pre-eminent for its chinaware factories is Kin-tee-ching. It is situate in the vicinity of Ping-lee and Kot-kow, the two districts I have just mentioned as the best clay-producing districts

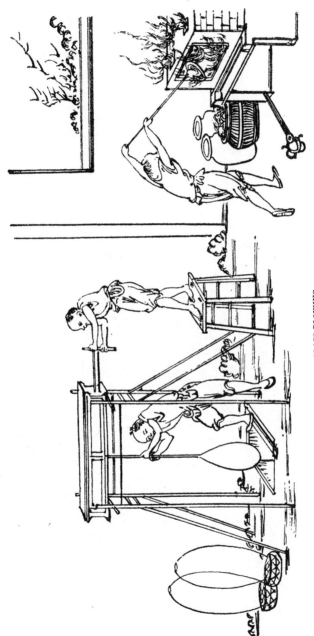

GLASS-BLOWING.

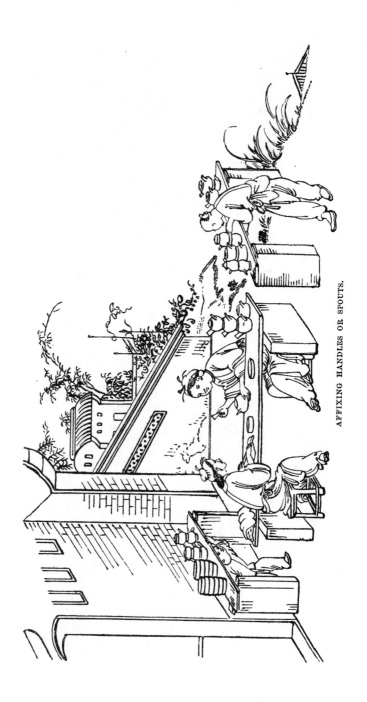

AFFIXING HANDLES OR SPOUTS.

in China. It is approached by the mountain river Chaong-kong, and, in consequence of the position which it occupies on the south bank of this stream, is sometimes called Chaong-nam-chun. The navigation of this river, which is very shallow in many parts, is carried on by flat-bottomed vessels. Where the rapids are very strong these boats are literally dragged up the stream, and they bump on its rocky bed so frequently as to start occasionally one or two of their planks. The boat in which I sailed suffered so much that many times, during the course of the night which I passed on board after arriving at Kin-tee-ching, the crew, which consisted of three or four stalwart men, had to get up to bale the water out. A boat which was riding at anchor alongside of us, laboured under similar difficulties. The water of the Chaong-kong is as clear as crystal, and a most agreeable beverage to the water-drinker. When we were within ten, or twelve, miles of Kin-tee-ching, the dense clouds of smoke which we saw rising from the furnaces, which were just being kindled, assured us that we were approaching a large manufacturing town ; and the broken pieces of earthenware with which the bed of the river was literally strewed at this point would have afforded evidence, had we required it, that we were approaching a city which is still, as it has been for centuries past, famous for its potteries. On our arrival at the town, the full moon had risen ; but, despite its powerful illumination, the midnight heavens were lurid with the glare from the numerous furnaces. On the following morning we made our preparations for inspecting the town and its potteries. They were somewhat elaborate, as owing to the jealousy with which foreigners are regarded by the potters of Kin-tee-ching, who, like workers in clay in every land, are inclined to be rough and lawless, it was deemed expedient that we should visit the potteries in disguise. I afterwards learnt that it was fortunate we did so, as a subsequent party of French *savants*—whom at the time I regretted being unable to wait for and join, as they were furnished with letters from the French ambassador at Pekin, and from high Chinese officials—were not allowed to see anything of the usual processes of manufacture. The men, it was alleged, were released from work for their holidays ! In fact, the Chinese did not relish the idea of agents of the French government closely inspecting their potteries. While showing every politeness, they behaved like the lady who, seeing an unwelcome acquaintance coming to call upon her, instructs her servant to say that she is not at home. My preparations consisted in donning the costume of the country, of which, as the weather was very cold, one of the large hoods worn in winter by the people of the district formed a part. It covers not only the head, but a portion of the face. A very ample pair of spectacles completed, as I thought, my disguise. The captain of the vessel, as he surveyed my tall figure marching along in independent English fashion, was clearly not of this opinion. With anxiety on every feature, he pointed out that it would never do to perambulate the streets in that way. Pacing along the deck, he exactly imitated my gait. He would show me how to walk, and his body collapsing into a somewhat drooping attitude, he returned from the bows in Chinese fashion. Thanks to my monitor, whose cautions throughout the day were vigilantly prompt, I succeeded in traversing Kin-tee-ching in safety. Only once I was an object of suspicion. A sharp Chinese lad, either concluding that my height indicated a being of a barbarous race, or observing some movement which was the reverse of Chinese—for one thing my Chinese stockings troubled me sadly, as they were too short, and I had nothing to strap them up with—walked alongside of me for a short time, scanning me with dubious glances. Eventually, however, he went on his way.

The town of Kin-tee-ching is described by Entreolles as "a league in length, and containing a million of souls." In all probability, when he was residing there in the early part of the eighteenth century, it was as populous as he makes out. I am disposed, however, to conclude that at the present time the population is much smaller. For the great decrease of population which has probably taken place since the days of Entreolles, at least one important cause may be assigned. During the Taiping rebellion, which desolated the fairest portions of China from 1847 to 1854, Kin-tee-ching was captured by the insurgents, who commenced, as was their custom, a massacre of its inhabitants, to which neither the past nor the present century, at all events, can furnish a parallel.[1] Incited by their lust for pillage, the rebels fired promiscuously in the streets and courts of the town upon the people, irrespective of age, sex, or condition, with the same fury as in the day of battle. None of the assailants behaved like men. Not one manifested a sign of compassion. When perfectly masters of the town they disbanded themselves, and commenced to enter the houses for pillage. Murder was perpetrated in the most cold-blooded manner. Neither the aged, nor the sick, nor the young, found any mercy at the hands of the invaders. By this time the greater part of the city was in flames, and, as the fire began in various places at once, it cannot be attributed to accident. The majority of the principal buildings, and a vast number of the tenements of the poor were razed to the ground, so that on the restoration of peace those citizens who had succeeded in escaping from the fury of the insurgents, and who wished to return to the town of their forefathers, found in many instances that they had no longer a dwelling-house in which to find shelter. The town to which Entreolles attributes so large a population in the eighteenth century, and which, notwithstanding the terrible massacre of its people in 1854, probably possesses as many inhabitants at the present day as our own Birmingham, appears to have been devoted to the manufacture of pottery from the commencement of the Chun dynasty in A.D. 557. In A.D. 1280, during the reign of the Yuen dynasty, a high officer was appointed by the Chinese government to superintend the potteries. With a view to the fabrication of vases and other vessels from baked clay for the especial use of the Royal family, an imperial edict was issued in the second year of the reign of the Emperor Hung-wu, A.D. 1366, that a large factory and furnaces should be erected on the Chu-Shan, or Pear Hill; and, in order that the works of this imperial factory might be properly regulated, a very high functionary was appointed with power to exercise a general authority over the

[1] This was written before the present war. The atrocities of which the Turks have been guilty towards the Bulgarians, have caused men everywhere to wonder how such things can be permitted in the nineteenth century, not in regions remote from European influence, but in the presence, it may almost be said, of the leading powers of Christendom.

whole establishment. This edict was obeyed; but the building then erected perished in the conflagration kindled by the rebels in 1854. Chinese annalists inform us that this factory was inclosed by a wall more than a mile in circumference. In the centre of this plot of ground there stood a public hall, in which the superintendent of the establishment was accustomed to consult with the subordinate officials. On the east and south sides of the inclosure were the offices; and on the east and west sides treasuries, in which funds were deposited to defray the current expenses. In the vicinity of the south gate stood a tower with a large drum on it. Not far from the tower was a prison, in which it was customary to incarcerate refractory workmen. A more pleasing feature was found in two large halls, where all the workmen were accustomed to assemble for recreation. There were also three temples, the first of which was in honour of Yow Too-ling, the inventor of the potter's art, the second in honour of Pak-te, the god of the north, and the third in honour of Kwan-te, the god of war. Outside the walls, but in connection with this establishment, there was another temple containing an idol of the tutelary god of the district. Each of the six furnaces was designated by its own peculiar name. The first, being that in which green porcelain vessels were baked, was called the Green Furnace. To the second, owing to its being used for baking vessels bearing representations of dragons, was given the name Kong-Yu. The third was called Fung-Fo-Yu, or the wind and fire furnace; the fourth Shik-Yu, or colour furnace; the fifth Lam-Wong-Yu, or Blue and Yellow Furnace; and the sixth Hap-Yu, or the furnace in which to bake the saggers. In front of the principal gate of the factory there was a screen wall with a large dragon painted on it, as is the case with all government buildings in China.

The workmen employed were chiefly from the two districts of Fow-laong and Pan-tong; and the mandarins at one time had power to compel persons residing in these districts to work in the imperial factory. An official, however, of the name of Chu Tsun, regarding such a measure as one of a most arbitrary nature, suggested that labourers should be invited to come from all the adjacent districts. After some delay, this suggestion was approved and adopted, and it was open to all labourers in the neighbourhood to come forward and engage themselves as workmen in the imperial factory at renumerative wages.   The workmen were divided into five classes, to which the names of " Fire," " Water," " Wood," " Metal," and " Earth," were respectively given.   The duties allotted to these five classes were arranged as follows under no less than twenty-two different heads :—

1. Tai-ee-Tsok, or large ware.

2. Su-ee-Tsok, or small ware.

3. Koo-Tsok, or vessels made after the ancient patterns.

4. Tew-Saong-Tsok, or carved work.

5. Yan-Tsok, or vessels made according to moulds.

6. Wāk-Tsok, or painting porcelain.

7. Chong-San-Tsok, or vessels made after new patterns.

8. Choy-Loong-Tsok, or vessels on which are representations of dragons in *basso-relievo.*

9. Say-Tsze-Tsok, or vases on which are painted Chinese characters.

10. Shik-Tsoy-Tsok, or porcelain of various colours.

11. Tsat-Tsok, or lacquered porcelain.

12. Hap-Tsok, or making boxes and cases for porcelain.

13. Yin-Tsok, or dyeing.

14. Nye-Shuee-Tsok, or bricklayer's work.

15. Tai-Mūk-Tsok, or carpenters engaged in large works.

16. Su-Muk-Tsok, or carpenters engaged in small works.

17. Shun-Tsok, or shipwrights.

18. Tit-Tsok, or iron founders.

19. Chuk-Tsok, or workers with bamboo.

20. Sok-Tsok, or rope makers.

21. Tung-Tsok, or coopers.

22. Tung-Toee, or pounders of clay by means of pestles and mortars.

Besides this imperial factory there were in the same town, Entreolles tells us, no fewer than three thousand ovens, which were the property of enterprising citizens. At the time of my visit, the imperial factory was still in a state of desolation. No doubt it has since risen, like the fabled Phœnix, from its ruins and is once more in full working order.

I have already said that the best plastic clays are found at
Ping-lee and Kot-how, districts in the vicinity. These clays
are of two kinds, the one being denominated Kao-lin, the
other Pe-tun-tse. Let us follow the latter through its various
stages, until it reaches the hands of the potter. The quarry
from which it is taken gives ample evidence, in its numerous
mines or caverns, of the value set upon the grey masses of its
uninviting store. To support the roofs, the quarrymen, as they
have advanced in their excavations, have erected strong wooden
pillars. The clay, where the workmen are busy, is being detached in pieces of various sizes by means of pickaxes. Another
set of labourers place these pieces in baskets, which, when full,
are borne on men's backs to the pounding mills, the large sheds
of which stand at no great distance from the quarries. The
pe-tun-tse is then placed in large mortars, with several of
which each mill is furnished. It is thoroughly crushed by
means of pestles kept in regular motion by water-wheels. The
plastic earth having sufficiently undergone the process of pounding is now carried in baskets to a neighbouring pond, into
which it is thrown, so that it may become well mixed with the
water. The mixture thus formed is permitted to remain undisturbed for some time, and the heavier portions of the pulverized matter sink to the bottom. On the surface of the pond
a liquid of cream-like appearance is eventually found. This is
drawn off and poured into another basin, where it is well stirred
by the feet of labourers, who walk to and fro in the basin. The
heavier particles of the pulverized pe-tun-tse, which sank to
the bottom of the first basin, are conveyed back to the pounding
mill to be reduced to a finer powder. After this they are brought
back to the pond, and the process is repeated. Meanwhile, the
cream-like liquid which was poured into the second basin, is,
after its thorough agitation, allowed to remain undisturbed for
some time. When all the fine matter has sunk to the bottom
the water is drawn off, and the pe-tun-tse is removed, and
formed by means of moulds into bricks. In consequence of
their colour these are called "pak-tan," or white bricks. The
preparation of the kao-lin for the service of the potter is
similar in almost all particulars to that of the pe-tun-tse.

The bricks into which the clays are moulded are afterwards reduced to a powder, and, when this has been carefully washed in spring-water, the two clays are mixed and formed into a paste, which is kneaded sometimes by men, sometimes by buffaloes. When thus employed, the buffaloes are driven to and fro in the large basin in which the paste has been deposited. When ready the paste is placed in the hands of the potter to be formed into vessels. He accomplishes this by means of the " potter's wheel." According to a well-known writer this is " kept in rotation by a man who holds the end of a flat strap, which he presses lightly against the edge of the wheel, when he impels it by drawing one end of the strap, and yielding to its motion at the other; and after each impulse the strap is loosened and restored to its first position on the edge, in order to repeat the impulse. The strap is prevented from slipping over the surface of the edge of the wheel by pins, or points projecting from its surface." Clay prepared to the size required for the vessel to be manufactured is given to the potter by a boy, who is termed in the Worcester-shire potteries the baller. The potter places the portion of clay upon the circular whirling table which is kept in motion by the wheelman, whose eye carefully watches the potter's motion, and adjusts the swiftness of the movement with perfect accuracy. The potter, or thrower, as he is technically called, first forms the clay into a pillar, then presses it into the form of a cake. He next opens the centre of the cake with his thumb, and continues to draw the clay out, or squeeze it inwards until the desired form is given to it. Vessels of square or angular shape are, of course, formed by the use of knives. When formed they are placed in the sun, or, in some instances in a chamber to harden. After hardening, such of them as are intended to have handles or spouts are transferred to workmen whose especial duty is to make and affix these appendages, which are attached by means of liquid clay. When the making and drying of the vessels have been completed, the next process is that of glazing. This is accomplished by dipping them in a mixture of varnish and water. As each vessel is taken from the vat which contains the mixture, it is rotated in the air in a dexterous manner, so as to cause the varnish to settle evenly over every part of its surface.

Only small vessels, however, are treated in this way, as a glaze is applied to large vessels in the following singular fashion. The workman takes a bamboo tube, one end of which is inclosed by a piece of gauze. He fills this with a glazing mixture, which he ejects on the sides of the vessel by blowing through the tube. A pea-green varnish is very much used by the Chinese. One of a light green colour has many admirers. The best varnish or glaze is obtained, so I was informed, in the province of Chit-kong. The provinces of Yun-nan, Kwang-tung, and Kiang-si, also produce a glaze which is in great requisition, and which is not very inferior in quality to that for which Chit-kong is famous. Blocks of this glaze are conveyed in great quantities to the town of Kin-tee-ching, where it is exposed for sale in a large building erected for the purpose. Before the blocks can be used, they are softened by placing them in kilns. The glaze is then reduced to a powder, and mixed with water, when it is ready for use.

Let me now describe the process of baking the vessels. The furnaces are often at a distance from the factories where the vessels are made, and it is not unusual to see workmen passing along the streets of the town, with flat boards on their heads on which several china vases are carefully arranged. These vessels are being conveyed to the furnaces to be baked. They are not made fast to the boards, and it is astonishing to observe the apparent ease with which the bearers thread their way through the narrow and crowded streets. " The ovens in which the vessels are baked "—I quote the description of Du Halde—" are placed in the bottom of a long porch which serves instead of bellows ; it has the same use as the arch in the glass houses. The ovens are, at present, larger than they were formerly, for then, accord-ing to a Chinese author, they were but six feet high and broad, but now they are two fathoms high, and are almost two fathoms deep. The arch, as well as the body of the oven, is sufficiently thick, so one may walk upon it without being incommoded with the fire. This arch or vault is not flat on the inside, nor does it rise in a point, but grows narrower and narrower as it approaches the great vent-hole at the extremity, through which the flame and smoke arise. Besides this mouth the oven has five or six

POTTERIES.

openings above, like so many eyes, which are covered with broken pots, and yet in such a manner that they assist the air and fire of the oven. It is by these eyes that they judge if the china ware is baked; they uncover the eye which is a little before the great vent-hole, and with iron tongs open one of the cases. When the fire is lighted they immediately shut the door, leaving only a necessary opening to throw in thick pieces of wood."

With regard to the nature of the fuel used in heating the furnaces, my experience differs from that of Du Halde. At the time I was visiting one of these establishments, the fuel which was thrown in by the workmen did not consist of thick pieces of wood, but of several large faggots of brushwood and coarse grass or reeds. Moreover, I observed on the adjacent hills several labourers busily engaged in cutting long coarse grass, reeds, and brushwood. They informed me that they obtained their livelihood by supplying the various furnaces of the town with this fuel. On the river I also passed several large flat-bottomed boats, heavily laden with faggots of the same material. These barges, which presented the appearance of so many floating stacks, were directing their course towards the town, where their owners were certain of a ready market for their cargoes.

To resume the description of the process by which the vases and other vessels are baked. Before they are put into the oven they are placed in cases or "saggers," so that they may not break, or become discoloured. The saggers are made of three kinds of crucible clay, which are, respectively, dark-coloured, red, and white. The clays are found in mines—the first, at Ma-an-shun; the second at Su-tsune; and the third at Koon-chong. They are mixed in equal proportions, with a little gum; and the cases or saggers into which they are moulded are very coarse. As the saggers cannot be used more than once or twice, the consumption of them is very great, and forms a large item in the accounts of a Chinese pottery. When the oven is filled the doorway is closed by brickwork, which is sealed up with a compost so as to exclude any current of air. The fire, in the first instance, is kept at a moderate heat, until the vessels are

perfectly dried. It is gradually brought to a white heat, and when
the chinaware has been in the oven for three days, in which time
it is supposed to be sufficiently baked, the fire is allowed to go
out. Twenty-four hours are then permitted to elapse before the
doors of the oven are opened, as, were there a less gradual change
in temperature, the vessels would crack. The saggers, however,
are so hot when taken out that the persons who remove them are
obliged to cover their hands with thick gloves, and their heads
and shoulders with wet blankets. All cracked vessels are rejected, and thrown upon the banks of the river Chaong-kong,
where they lie till the former and latter rains wash them into
the stream. The force of the current at such times is very
great, and carries them a considerable distance beyond the town.
To this circumstance it is to be attributed that the bed of the
river, for several miles down, is literally paved, as I have already
stated, with broken pieces of porcelain. So soon as the baked
vessels have been removed from the oven, the workmen at once
proceed to fill it with others which are requiring to undergo the
same process. This is done without delay, as it is possible in
this way to place in the oven, on the very day on which they
have been shaped, vessels not yet sufficiently dried by the sun,
the warmth remaining in the oven being such as to prepare them
to endure without cracking the greater heat to which they are
about to be subjected.

The baked vessels are now ready for the decorator's art. As
artists, the Chinese do not excel. In the painting of birds and
flowers, however, some degree of credit is due to them, and
their delineations of these objects often show very considerable artistic skill. In the painting of porcelain, as in other
branches of industry, there is a great division of labour. One
artist draws the design ; a second paints landscapes ; a third,
rivers ; a fourth, trees ; a fifth, butterflies ; a sixth, birds ; and
a seventh, human figures and buildings. These artists have a
perfect knowledge of the pigments which are best suited to
undergo the action of fire. An oil which they call Wān-
shaong-yow, is mixed with the pigments for the purpose of imparting smoothness. Gum-water is also occasionally used for
its property of retaining the colours ; and for thick painting, clear

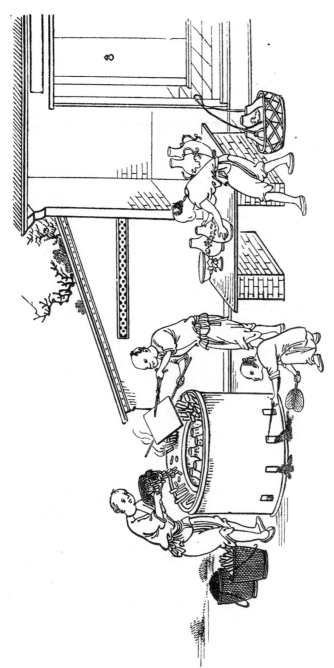

BAKING PORCELAIN.

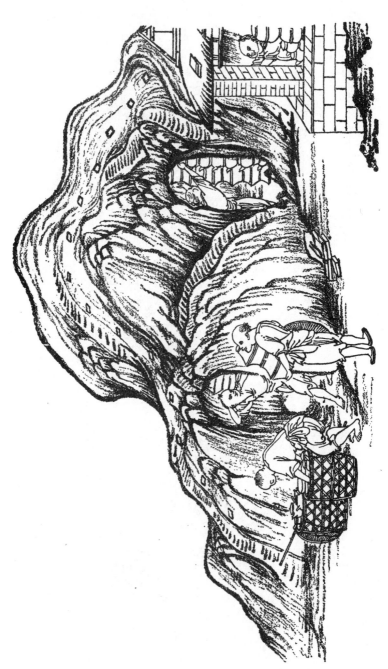

A POTTERY KILN.

water is held in much estimation. The brushes of the artists
are altogether similar to those which are in ordinary use for
painting. The vessels to be decorated are placed upon a table
—if large, upon the floor. When they have received their
decoration, they are again placed in the ovens, that the colours
may be fixed. Of these ovens there are two kinds, the one
termed Ming-fo, or bright fire, and the other Om-fo, or dark fire.
The former is used for small, the latter for large, vessels. They
are of a circular shape and consist of two walls, the inner wall
being formed of flat tiles, the outer of bricks. At the base of
the oven there are several small openings or grates. The fuel,
which consists of charcoal, is placed between the walls, and the
top of the oven is inclosed by broken pieces of tiles which rest
upon the porcelain vessels which are being baked. Hot charcoal embers are placed upon these broken tiles or flags for the
purpose of giving additional heat. This description, however,
applies only to the Ming-fo, which is used for small vessels.
In the Om-fo, and with vessels of a larger size, the fuel is
placed on the top of the oven only. The period during which
these ovens are kept heated is twenty-four hours.

The art of moulding coarse earthenware vessels for domestic
purposes is practised at the town of Shek-wan, in the province
of Kwang-tung. The clay which is used for this purpose is of
a very inferior quality, and the process of manufacture differs
in some respects from that at Kin-tee-ching. The machine
employed by the potter consists of a horizontal wheel which is
attached to the top of a very short perpendicular stake securely
fixed in the ground. A boy who steadies himself in an upright
position by holding fast by his hands to a chain or rope suspended from the roof of the building, gives the necessary motion
to the wheel by means of his feet; whilst the potter, who has
assumed a kneeling or squatting posture by the side of the
wheel, works the clay with his hands. It would appear from a
passage in the book of Ecclesiasticus that, in the ancient days
of Judæa, the potter's wheel was set in motion by means of the
feet,—" So doth the potter sitting at his work, and turning the
wheel about with his feet," &c. The furnaces in which earthenware
vessels are baked at Shek-wan are also very different from those

which I had an opportunity of seeing on the occasion of my
visit to Kin-tee-ching. For example, they are of great length
at the former place, and erected on inclined planes. At intervals along the side of each furnace there are doors through
which the potters enter to fill the furnace with the vessels which
are to be baked. Between the vessels they pile firewood. After
these preliminaries the entrances are blocked up by firebricks.
At the lower end of the inclined plane is a grate, also containing firewood. The workmen now set fire to this, and the flames,
shooting up the inclined plane, ignite the fuel which was
placed between the vessels. On the top of the kiln there are,
at frequent intervals, small apertures, into which broken pieces
of firewood are dropped during the process of the baking. I
may mention that on the occasion of the last visit which I paid
with a friend to the potteries at Shek-wan, we were very nearly
murdered by an infuriated mob. The danger arose from the
following simple circumstance : My friend would go nowhere
without his walking-stick, and upon my telling him that the
Chinese were not accustomed to use such things themselves—
indeed their sumptuary laws prohibit the use of walking-sticks
by any except very old men—he ridiculed the idea that a
walking-stick would be regarded as a proof of a hostile disposition.
On passing through the streets, however, the Chinese began to
make remarks, and to call out one to another, " Beware of
that foreigner, he will club some of you ! " As my friend had
a habit of swinging his stick about when walking, the excitement increased as we progressed. Eventually a large crowd
gathered, and becoming exceedingly angry, attacked us, and
forced us to seek refuge in a pottery, whence we were with
difficulty conveyed through back streets to our boat.

In various parts of China the manufacture of flat clay tiles,
which resemble flags, is carried on. At Pak-hin-hok, near
Canton, and at other places in the vicinity, these tiles are made
in large quantities. The plastic clay of which they are formed
is brought to Canton from the neighbouring counties or districts
of Toong-koon and Pun-yu respectively. As rivers and creeks
are the highways of Kwang-tung, the clay is conveyed to the
tile-yards of Pak-hin-hok in boats. It is piled up in stacks,

THE POTTER'S WHEEL.

from which it is taken as required, and placed on a threshing-floor to be kneaded or tempered by being trodden by the feet. Tiles are made of the clay thus tempered by means of moulds, according to the size and pattern required. The kilns in which the tiles are baked are very large, and the process of baking extends, I believe, over nine or ten days. They are not removed, however, from the kiln until the sixth day after the fire is extinguished.

In many parts of this vast empire bricks are now, and for centuries past have been, made in great numbers. They are made in the following manner: the surface soil, or encallow, as it is termed by brickmakers, is first removed. The clay is then tempered or kneaded by the feet of buffaloes, which for this purpose are led or driven over it by boys, backwards and forwards for several hours. At the town of You-tou, however, which is near Woo-see Hien, the clay is trodden by men. In Persia also, I may observe in passing, a similar plan is practised. When the clay has been rendered soft and pliable, it is at once formed, by means of wooden moulds, into bricks, which are placed on what may be termed tracks, in rows, and at short distances from each other, so as to dry. As a protection from the inclemency of the weather, the tracks, with their contents, are not unfrequently placed under long mats, sometimes under tile sheds. Brickmakers, if poor, often cover them with straw only. When the bricks have been well dried they are conveyed to the kilns, which, like those in which clay tiles are baked, are very large. The largest which I saw—and some are so large as almost to resemble fortifications—are those at You-tou.

CHAPTER XXIX.

SHIPS.

CHINA possesses an extensive sea-board, and there is scarcely a city, or town, or village in it which has not the advantage of an arm of the sea, or a river, or a creek, or a canal. These are to this vast empire, whose length and breadth they intersect in all directions, what railroads and highroads are to more civilized countries; and ships and boats of all kinds are of course very numerous. Some travellers have not hesitated to say that there are more vessels in China than in all the rest of the world put together—an assertion which is not so very extravagant as it seems at the first blush. The trade of shipbuilding is, therefore, one of great extent and importance. The claim of the *Argo*, which carried the famous Argonauts to Colchis in B.C. 1263 in search of the Golden Fleece, to be the first vessel that ever sailed the sea, is, according to Chinese annals, simply preposterous. They assert that Tā Yu, who was the founder of the Hiaki dynasty, and who flourished B.C. 2205, was the first to introduce the art of shipbuilding, and that, long before the close of his reign, vessels of various kinds were navigating the waters of China Proper.

There are numerous dockyards for the building and repairing of vessels at all Chinese coast and river ports; and at each of the principal ports there is one large dockyard specially set apart for government vessels. As a rule, they are not built upon stocks, as in Europe, but in dry docks. The day on which the keel of a ship is laid is regarded by the shipwrights and the owners as one of great rejoicing. It is not devoted to merry·making only, but to the observance of certain religious ceremonies. Taouist priests are engage to chant pæans of praise to the gods, and to call upon them by prayer, to prosper the work. A holiday is observed also on the day when the bow of the vessel is raised. The bow is gaily decorated with streamers of red cloth and strips of red paper, whilst Taouist priests in front of a temporary altar supplicate the gods for the good success of the ship. Ships are never built by Chinese merchants or traders till permission has been granted them by the local authorities. To obtain a license, the merchant must inform the authorities of the class and tonnage of the vessel he wishes to build. The authorities also ascertain what number of seamen she will require for safe navigation. When the vessel is completed, they inspect her, to ascertain whether she has been built in strict accordance with the specifications they have approved.

The vessels navigating the seas, rivers, creeks, canals, and lakes of China, include every variety in naval architecture, from the ocean-going war-junk to the small craft that ply between river ports.

The ocean-going war-junks are sometimes of great size. Captain Basil Hall, who, in 1823, accompanied Lord Amherst, the British ambassador, to China, says that a Chinese war-junk which came alongside the ship of war under his command was so large as to resemble a floating castle. They are divided into several water-tight compartments. The bulwarks are very high, and are pierced for several guns, the port-holes being generally pentagon-shaped and surrounded by a border of red paint. Each vessel has three masts. The mainmast, as in square-rigged ships, is in the centre of the vessel; the foremast is placed well forward in the bows, and the mizenmast is near the taffrail. To the top of the mainmast a vane in the form of a dolphin is attached, and to the tail of the dolphin is bound a streamer, generally red, and of a length almost sufficient to reach the deck of the vessel. Ships in the Imperial navy generally fly at the main a flag on which is a representation of the Yin and the Yang, or in other words the male and female principle. This representation is surrounded by a number of

red lines, some of which have a reference, if I mistake not, to
the Taouist Trinity of persons, and others to good geomantic
influences. A flag bearing a device of the Yin and the Yang
is regarded by the superstitious sailors as a safeguard against
all evils. In the absence of this flag, a tricolour, not unlike
the Dutch flag, is hoisted at the main. At the stern of the
vessel is displayed a triangular flag, with the name of the
official under whose supervision she is, in large red characters.
The sails are made of matting, the mainsail, in particular, being
very large, and shaped like a butterfly's wing. The sails, which
are made fast to the mast by rings, are strengthened at short
intervals by long poles which stretch across the entire sheet.
I have stated that the sails of ocean-going war-junks are
made of matting: this material is very generally used for the
sails of Chinese vessels. Other materials are also used. I
observed, when travelling in Formosa, that many of the vessels
which navigate the rivers of that island and the channel which
separates it from the mainland, were furnished with suits of
sails made of the fibres of the cocoa-nut. On the Shanghai river,
and on the Yang-tsze Kiang, more especially in the neighbourhood of the city of Nankin, and in other cotton-producing
districts through which the Yang-tsze flows, the sails are made
of dyed cotton. Thus at Nankin, and other towns on the
banks of the Yang-tsze river, I noticed several shops filled with
bark for dyeing sails. Being strengthened by long poles at short
intervals, the sails of Chinese vessels do not bend to the wind
like the canvas sails with which all European ships are furnished.
Vessels are generally rigged with ropes made either of rattan, or
bamboo, or hemp, or the fibres of the cocoa-nut. The cables by
which they are moored are of great thickness, and as a rule are
made of rattan. Near the anchorages, at almost all Chinese
ports, there are very extensive rope-walks, where ropes, cables,
and twine are made in the same way as in England.

The guns of these junks are arranged on the upper deck only,
and are placed so near each other that one is at a loss to conceive
how the sailors, who are very numerous, and amongst whom
there is apparently an utter absence of discipline, can work them
all together. They appear to have little or no knowledge of

CANDIDATES FOR MILITARY DEGREES.

training their guns, and the carriages upon which the guns are placed are as inferior as the guns themselves. Very indifferent accommodation is provided for the seamen, and the accumulation of filth in almost every part of the ship is sufficient to engender fevers or epidemics. Standing high out of the water, these vessels form excellent targets for the guns of the enemy. They are strongly built, and present a good front to vessels like themselves. In contests with British ships of war they have invariably been found wanting—a fact of which the Chinese authorities were more or less convinced at the close of what is generally termed the "Opium War." At the commencement of the second war which Great Britain in alliance with France waged with China, a large fleet of these war-junks was destroyed in a creek leading to the important town of Fat-shan, by a boat expedition under the command of Sir Henry Keppel.

The ocean-going war-junks do not form the bulk of the Imperial Navy. This consists of vessels of much smaller dimensions, capable, in consequence of their light draught, of navigating shallow rivers and creeks. Of great length, and broad of beam amidships, they have two masts, and are good sailers. Each vessel of this class carries several guns, some of great calibre. At the main-top there is a basket, filled with a rude species of hand-grenades, called by the Chinese Fo-yok-poo, and by foreigners stink-pots. Another class of war-junks is the Fi-hi, or fast crabs. These vessels, which are also two-masted and of great length, are very narrow in the beam. A certain number of them is apportioned to each of the eighteen provinces of China Proper, the number varying, of course, according to the size and requirements of the province. In the province of Kwang-tung there are—and have been since the last year of the reign of Kien-lung Wong, A.D. 1795, previous to which year there were ninety-three only—no fewer than 161 always in commission. These are classed in three divisions, the first of 10 junks, the second of 115, and the third of 36. Each of the first division costs in building 4,378 taels of silver, or about 1,300*l.*; each of the second division 3,620 taels of silver, or about 1,100*l.*; each of the third division 2,677 taels of silver, or about 800*l.* They are classed for nine years only, and are

not allowed to go into dock for a general overhaul until they
have been three years in commission. At the end of the first
three years, the provincial authorities are empowered by the
board at Pekin to expend in repairs—on each vessel of the
first class, 1,926 taels of silver; of the second class, 1,593 taels of
silver; and of the third class, 1,178 taels of silver. When they
have been in commission six years they are again docked for
general repairs, the amount authorized in the case of vessels of
each class being strictly defined by an unvarying rule. After
nine years, they are regarded as no longer fit for service. Before
a vessel can go into dock, the magistrate under whose supervision she sails forwards a despatch to the governor-general or
governor of the province, certifying that the vessel has been in
service three years, and requires, in consequence, a general over-
hauling. A reply is forwarded empowering the magistrate to
dock the war-junk; the expenses incurred being defrayed, not
by the provincial treasurer, but by the salt commissioner. The
vessels have an annual allowance for suits of sails and ropes.

The crew of a vessel of the first class consists of a commander, a helmsman, and forty-six seamen; of a vessel of the
second class, a commander, a helmsman, and twenty-seven
seamen; of a vessel of the third class, a commander, a helmsman, and eighteen seamen. The allowance for the mess-table, per
diem, to each commander, is eight kandareens; to each helmsman, eight kandareens; and to each seaman five kandareens.

In a calm these vessels are propelled by oars, and move at a
great speed. It is I suppose to this that they owe the name " Fi-
hi," or fast crabs. Under sail their speed is very great. They are
often employed in the Revenue service, and seldom fail to give
a good account of all smugglers. But although they are, as a
rule, employed in suppressing smuggling, I am disposed to think
that the mandarins under whose direction they are placed, not
unfrequently use them to carry on illicit trade. Besides the war-
junks of various kinds which constitute the Imperial navy,
there are others, belonging to the gentry, manned and equipped
without reference to the Imperial government.

A navy composed of vessels such as I have been describing
may, perhaps, excite a mild contempt in the European mind.

The Chinese, however, are now evidently aspiring to a place among the nations as a maritime power, and the importance of square-rigged war-ships and war-vessels like those of European navies has been at length recognised by them. There are now several gun-boats in the service of the Emperor of China, built for His Imperial Majesty in Europe, officered by Europeans, and manned by Chinese sailors. The Chinese have, now arsenals of their own, in which they are constructing vessels for their navy of considerable dimensions, suited to the requirements of modern naval warfare. The first frigate turned out from a Chinese dockyard was launched at Shanghai on the 24th of May, 1872. A description of the Chinese Government's first specimen of a large modern war-ship may prove interesting to my readers, and I quote some particulars regarding the vessel from the *North China Daily News* :—

" Her height," says this report, " from face of sternpost to taffrail is 263 feet 6 inches; extreme breadth of beam, 44 feet 10 inches; depth of hold from kelson to the top of spar-deck, 29 feet 4 inches. There are four decks; on the upper there will be two 90-pounder rifled pivot guns; while the main-deck will be occupied almost along its entire length by a battery of twenty-six 40-pounder rifled broadside guns. She is to be a full-rigged ship, and will have a spread of 22,500 superficial feet of canvas. Her engines are, we learn, designated, in engineering phrase, the horizontal return connecting type; with two cylinders, the diameter of which is 64 inches, while the stroke of piston is 3 feet. The nominal horse-power will be 400, but, as we stated in a former issue, is capable of being worked up to 1,800; the propeller is of Griffiths' lifting, variable pitch description, so that, when at sea, and entire dependence is placed on the wind as the propelling power, the propeller may be raised from the water by the lifting apparatus. . . . . Some of the castings of the engine weigh no less than seven tons; 40 tons of copper (including 3,400 sheets of copper-bottoming) have been used in her construction. Everything, with one exception—viz., the shaft—has been made at the arsenal by Chinese artizans, under the superintendence of only five foreigners."

The sailors and marines who form the crews of these vessels are, as a rule, first-class men. Many have been trained to the arts of war by foreign instructors, and they are armed with

approved modern European weapons. The guns are also constructed and mounted according to the most recent types, and
the drill of the men often equals in severity that which takes
place on the decks of the best regulated of Her Majesty's ships
of war.

These signs of change and progress in the Celestial Empire
are astonishing when we consider the tenacity with which the
Chinese cling to the forms and fashions of the remote past. It
might be supposed that the launch of a modern frigate from a
Chinese arsenal would slightly impair the complacency with
which Chinese officials invariably regard· the products of their
indigenous national civilization. How far it is so the following
extract from an article on the Navy of China, which appeared
in the *North China Daily News*, may perhaps illustrate :—

" At first sight," the writer observes, " one would imagine that
Chinese officials would regard these foreign-built ships with
a certain amount of pride; but it appears that such is not the
case. It is too humiliating altogether to admit for a moment
that a ship built after the barbarian's fashion is fit to be compared with the good old shape which has existed since the days
of Yao and Shun. As an instance of how the Chinese pride
themselves on their ancient notions we may mention, that at
the launch of the frigate at the Kiangnan Arsenal the other day,
a foreign gentleman remarked to one of the officials present that
a larger ship had never been launched in China, or even in the
East. What was his surprise to be told, in the politest manner
possible, that for an intelligent foreigner, he displayed a remarkable ignorance of Chinese history; and that he had better look
up the annals of the Ming dynasty before he ventured to make
such a sweeping remark again, because the Chinese had built
ships almost large enough to carry the frigate as part of their
cargo !

" On reference to the history in question, it will be found that
in the third year of Tung-lo, or A.D. 1406, the Emperor, who
had· usurped the throne, thinking his predecessor had escaped
from the country and was hiding beyond the seas, and wishing
to have him tracked out, and at the same time by a grand
display of troops to manifest to surrounding countries the
wealth and prowess of the Middle Kingdom, commanded the
celebrated warrior Ch'ing-ho, a native of Yunnan, together with
certain of his associates, to go through the Western Ocean.
Whereupon Ch'ing-ho collected officers and troops to the

number of above 28,786 men, and a great quantity of silver and treasure. He then built sixty-two large ships, each 44 chang long and 18 chang wide. Reckoning the chang as no more than ten English feet; the ships were therefore 440 feet in length and 180 feet beam.[1] Starting from the Loo-ka river, near Soo-Chow, they went out to sea and came first to Foo-chow. From Foo-chow they went over all the foreign countries. It would be foreign to our purpose to narrate the wonderful exploits and victories which Ch'ing-ho achieved with these immense tubs at Ceylon, Sumatra, and other places in the Western Ocean, whose names we cannot at the moment identify. Any one who has a great deal more faith in Chinese history than we have, would no doubt be amply repaid by looking up this interesting subject, which forms an important feature in the history of the Chinese navy."

The above incident is quite in harmony with the intensely conservative spirit with which the Chinese, while introducing into their navy the formidable structures of modern science, still cling to their belief in the efficiency of their old modes and appliances of naval warfare. Indeed the former are as yet conspicuous exceptions on a background of effete antiquities. While the Chinese launched their first frigate from their own arsenal in 1872, and arm several of their ships and their crews with approved modern weapons, we find them holding a naval review at Ningpo, in August, 1873, the evolutions in which would be sadly out of place in a conflict with the fleets of the West. I extract the following account from the *China Mail*:—

" On the 14th day of the moon, and for a few days previously, some thirty-five or forty of the men appeared at dead low or the top of high-water—when there was no current—each with a pair of small life-buoys made to fit round the waist, one in front, the other behind, and having sufficient buoyancy to float the men with the lower part of the chest level with the water. Each buoy is made of a light bamboo frame covered with strong oiled paper and a network of twine outside. These marines are armed, some with pitchforks, some with a pair of clubs, others with short sword and shield, and imitated in the water

---

[1] If the above figures are correct, Ch'ing-ho's ships were 92 feet broader than the *Great Eastern*, although the latter exceeded them in length by 252 feet.—Ed.

the evolutions of the junks, sometimes in two lines, sometimes in one, and sometimes as a Saint Andrew cross. There were two leaders, each with a flag fastened to his back, *tout comme au théâtre*, and each armed with a tube filled with sulphur, or something of that kind, which threw out a yellow smoke. The men stand well upright in the water, and seem to propel themselves by taking short steps and moving their shoulders; they usually stayed in the water about half an hour.

"A certain degree of proficiency having been attained, the 15th was named for a grand naval review. A large number of mandarins attended, some on board a large junk, and some—the greater in numbers and rank—in a large pavilion erected on the bank of the river, just beyond the Salt Gate, on a piece of ground that was prepared and often used for this purpose thirty years ago. . . . . Every available standpoint on the banks or the city wall was crowded; there must have been, at a moderate estimate, 8,000 or 10,000 spectators; and all showed an interest in the proceedings worthy of their picturesque importance. The programme I have described from rehearsal, was gone through by the junks and the water heroes with admirable skill and discipline; and then came the grand and final effort, which would in itself suffice to paralyse a foe unaccustomed to Astley's. On the mast of a large junk appeared a structure similar in shape to the cages you see on the poles in front of yamêns and temples. This was covered with flags, and eventually six or eight men went up into it, shinned to the mast-head, swinging their arms, legs, and heads about after the most favourite circus fashion, fired off one bullet from one gingal, shot one arrow from one bow, and tried the two sulphur tubes, which wouldn't go off. They then resumed gymnastics, winding up with a splendid *tableau*, all clinging to the upper part of the mast and sticking out a leg, while the mandarins bow gracefully to each other and the assembled world, back awkwardly into their respective chairs—and are gone.

"From commencement to finish, including stoppages, the affair lasted about one hour and a quarter, and is said to have cost the moderate sum of Tls. 5,000, as the junks are of course never fully manned, and crews had to be specially engaged and taught for the occasion. But the cream of the whole joke is that the mandarin in charge of the display is a lieutenant-general who has travelled over Europe, and was at Paris during the siege. Yet I am credibly informed that he kept his countenance, and that he hopes to succeed in penning a serious despatch to the Emperor, congratulating him on the efficiency of his nautical braves."

It may not be out of place to add a short narrative of a naval engagement which I witnessed in the Canton River during the rebellion of 1854-55. Near an insulated fort, called by the Chinese the Cha-may-pow-toi, or Tee-totum Fort, but by foreigners the Macao Fort, a cordon of imperial war-junks was stretched across the river with the view of commanding all the approaches in that direction to the city of Canton. This precaution was rendered necessary by the presence of a large fleet of rebel junks, which were anchored at a distance of not more than a mile from the position which the imperial junks had taken up. For the purpose of approaching the city, the commander of the rebel fleet proceeded to engage the junks of the Imperialists. During the engagement which ensued, and which lasted the whole afternoon, not one vessel on either side, so far as I could learn, received the slightest injury. It was not at all surprising, as the great majority of the shots fired from the guns of the fleets met half-way. I was on board one of the imperial vessels during the greater part of the engagement, and the only danger to which I felt myself exposed, was, not from the fire of the enemy, but from the chances of an explosion of gunpowder, of which I was in momentary dread. Near each gun, and on the decks of the vessels, lay large quantities of loose gunpowder, near which the gunners stood with burning matches in their hands. In the course of a few days the rebels, who had become more emboldened, brought their vessels along-side the cordon of imperial junks, and succeeded, by means of stink-pots, in setting three or four of them on fire. The rebel fleet, however, though it broke the line, failed to reach Canton, as the Tee-totum or Macao Fort, which was in the rear of the now scattered imperial junks, drove it back by a rolling fire of round shot. I was present at the close of this engagement, and assisted in rescuing several of the imperial seamen from a watery grave. Upon landing these men on the banks of the river, I discovered that many of them were seriously wounded. One man, indeed, owing to the explosion of a stink-pot, was literally raw from the top of his head to the soles of his feet. Another, who had received a very severe gun-shot wound, was determined not to survive the defeat, and madly rushed into the

waters from which he had so recently been rescued, to seek
death by drowning, suicide under such circumstances being regarded by the Chinese as highly honourable. I hastened to
rescue him a second time from the strong current into which he
had plunged. So great, however, was the despair which had
taken possession of him, that he made a third attempt at suicide,
when I was compelled once more to frustrate his rash design.
As the shades of evening were now beginning to fall, I requested
the soldiers who were in garrison at the Macao fort to take
charge of their wounded compatriots, and to convey them with
as little delay as possible to the London Missionary Hospital
at Canton, at that time very ably presided over by Dr. Wilson.
They cheerfully complied, and when I left they were actually
getting their boats ready. Apparently, however, they abandoned it as soon as they were left to themselves, as on the
following day I found the dead bodies of all these men—save
one, who had succeeded in reaching a neighbouring village—
at the very place where I last saw them alive and suffering.
I attributed this melancholy hard-heartedness of the Chinese
soldiers in garrison at the Macao fort, towards wounded countrymen, their own companions in arms, either to the dread which
many of the Chinese entertain of rendering any assistance to
those who are unfortunate, because they regard such persons as
objects of the displeasure either of angry spirits, or of some
avenging deities; or to a fear of leaving their posts at so critical
a juncture, as they might have been punished for such an
act with an ignominious death at the hands of the common
executioner.

As the war junks of China are apparently unable to clear
the seas and rivers of the pirates with which they are infested,
the various classes of trading vessels are licensed by the
government to carry armaments for their own protection.
Licenses for the purpose are granted to vessels navigating the
waters of Canton by the sub-prefect, who is stationed, if I
mistake not, at the Bocca-tigris. The armaments which vessels
are allowed to carry vary of course according to their class and
tonnage. To prevent them becoming dangerous to the peace
and good order of the state, by attacking unfortified towns or

peaceful vessels, with the view of extorting money, it is provided by law that nine other vessels become sureties for each trading vessel. Should a junk for the good conduct of which nine others have become sureties, be guilty of piracy on the high seas, not only are the owners and sailors of the offending vessel arraigned as pirates before the tribunals of their country, but also, the owners and sailors of the vessels which are her securities. In the case of a conviction all the crews are punished, and the ten vessels become confiscate to the imperial crown. There is also a statute that all vessels shall, on arriving at a port, deposit their guns in the warehouses attached to the custom-house, until the vessel is again ready for sea. This law, however, like many others in China, is much more honoured in the breach than in the observance.

Let us now turn our attention to the various kinds of trading junks, passenger-boats, and other craft navigating Chinese seas, rivers, creeks, and canals.

The large ocean-going junks which trade between the northern and southern ports, and those which sail between China and Batavia, Singapore, and Siam, respectively, are very singular in their construction. They have a carrying capacity equal to several thousands of tons, and, like the war junks, they are divided into several water-tight compartments. They have three masts, each consisting of one solid piece of wood. The mainmast is placed amidships; the foremast well forward in the bows; and the mizenmast quite near to the taffrail. Upon the masts, strips of red paper are pasted, with sentences of the following import in large Chinese characters :—" The mast is as a general commanding ten thousand soldiers;" "From every side of the compass may fair winds blow;" "May this mast scorn tempests, from whatever quarter of the heavens they may come." To the top of the mainmast a vane is attached, from the tail of which a long red streamer flutters in the breeze. On the first, and on the fifteenth day of each Chinese month, that is at the new, and again at the full moon, there is on the taffrail an array of small triangular-shaped banners, whilst a large red, or white, or black flag adorns the main-top. The sails are made either of matting, or cotton, or the fibres of the cocoa-nut. They are very large, the mainsail in particular being of great extent, and they are of the same shape, and are straightened in the same manner as are those of the war junks. The hull, which is very heavy and strong, is usually painted white, and the bulwarks, which are very high, are painted according to the custom of the port to which the junk belongs. The bulwarks of junks from the province of Fo-kien are painted black, with a green border; those from the ports of Chit-kong are painted black, with a white border ; and those from the ports of Kwang-tung are painted black, with a red border. These modes of painting vessels are not merely fashions regulated by the customs of the different provinces, but are prescribed by law, as the colours of their bulwarks serve when Chinese ships pass each other on the high seas to indicate the ports to which they belong. For the effectual carrying out of this purpose it is imperatively enjoined upon shipowners to repaint their vessels at the end of each period of two years. The stern-board in vessels of this class is broad and high, and on it is painted, in gaudy colours, a large bird with outstretched wings. This bird resembles the fabled phœnix, and is called by the Chinese " Foong." It is represented as standing on a rock in the midst of a troubled ocean. It is regarded by the mariners as an emblem of speed, and is supposed to assist very materially in urging the vessel onward. Its standing on a rock in the midst of the deep and scorning the tempest, is regarded by the sailors as emblematical of safety. There are also on the stern-board representations of the sun and moon, which, of course, are regarded by the seamen as indicative of light by day and night. Immediately beneath the sternboard is another, but smaller, board, on which are representations of foreigners —Europeans, Burmese, Siamese, Indians—the inhabitants of what the Chinese are pleased to term the tributary nations of the south, bearing tribute to the feet of his imperial majesty. Below these delineations, and standing out in bold relief, are three or four characters, which set forth the name of the ship. The names of Chinese vessels are identical in purport, one being named the " Good Success," another the " Golden Profits," a third the "Never-Ending Gains," &c., &c., &c. The prow of the ocean-going junk, like the stern, is very high and broad, and

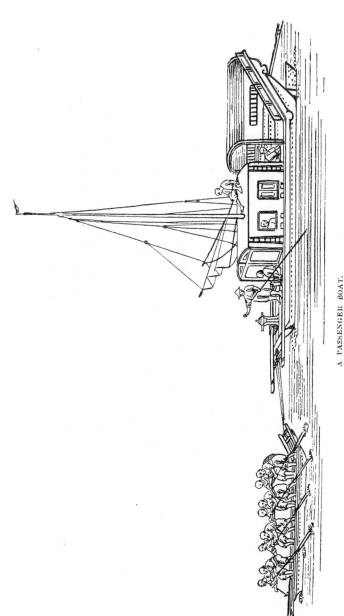

A PASSENGER BOAT.

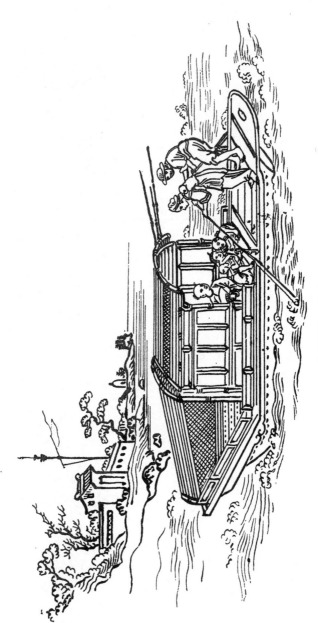

A SLIPPER BOAT.

is supposed to bear a resemblance to the mouth of a dolphin, or other large fish. On each side is the representation of an eye, by which the sailors imagine that the vessel can espy sunken rocks, shoals, and other dangers of the deep. The helm is very large, and extends considerably beyond the stern, in every class of junk. These large rudders are of course of great service to Chinese vessels, which, generally speaking, are provided with very small keels. That they may be moved with ease through the water, they are perforated. On the poop there is a pavilion of wood richly carved and ornamented, above the doorway of which are inscribed three or four sentences, such as: "May the winds not cause angry waters to arise!" or "May this vessel brave the storms of a hundred years."

On the deck of each junk there are three or four wooden cisterns, which are filled before the vessel leaves port, with spring water for culinary purposes. The boards of these water-tanks are joined together by nails, and chunam, of which thick layers are placed in each seam. The quarter-galleries are placed aft, and are resorted to not only by the owners and masters of the vessels, but by the sailors, who are taught to regard the bows as the most sacred part of the ship, and to consider it profanation to let fall filth of any kind over them. In every large junk there is also a neat shrine in honour of the goddess Tien-how, who, as I have elsewhere stated, is the tutelary deity of sailors. The idol of the goddess, which is carefully inclosed in a glass case, is daily worshipped by the crew. Above the altar there is generally inscribed an ejaculatory prayer such as, "Wherever this ship may sail, O goddess, grant her a prosperous voyage." On each side of the altar are inscribed sentences to the following effect:—"Enable us by trading to acquire wealth;" or, "When on the wide waste of waters, fail not, O goddess, to show us thy favour." At the commencement and termination of each voyage, the goddess Tien-how receives a special homage. When a junk is ready for sea, a number of Taouist priests are invited to go on board for the purpose of chanting prayers and offering sacrifices to Tien-how. But should a violent storm arise after all these religious observances and threaten the safety of the vessel, there is an all-prevailing opinion amongst Chinese sailors that it is owing to the anger of the gods against some sinful person, or persons, on board. A similar notion prevailed amongst mariners in ancient times. We read that when a storm overtook the vessel in which the prophet Jonah was seeking to escape to Tarshish, in order that he might evade the Divine command to preach repentance to the inhabitants of Nineveh, the terrified sailors cast lots to know for whose cause the evil was upon them; and when the lot fell upon the disobedient prophet, they reluctantly cast him forth into the sea. Again, the Argonauts of Orpheus were disposed to act in a similar manner towards Medea, when they attributed to her presence the storm by which the "Argo" was overtaken:

> " And much they doubted in their prudent minds
> Whether to kill and cast a prey to fishes
> Wretched Medea, and avert their fate."

We are told that when the vessel which carried Diagoras, surnamed the Atheist—who flourished in the fifth century before the Christian era—was beset by tempests, the sailors at once concluded that it was owing to the atheistical principles which the philosopher professed. Instances are known in which Chinese sailors during very severe storms have cast into the sea persons whose wickedness they have believed to be the cause of the tempests, hoping by the sacrifice to appease the anger of the gods.

The departure of a vessel from port takes place on a lucky day, selected by Taouist priests, or, in their absence, by astrologers. The day generally selected is either the first or fifteenth of each lunar month, at the new or full moon. As a junk is leaving port, other crews which hail from the same port mount the poops of their junks with the view of propitiating the winds and waves in favour of the departing vessel, some of them energetically beating gongs and tomtoms, whilst others, to dispel all evil influences, increase the din by discharging popguns and fire-crackers. When the vessel reaches the port, religious ceremonies are again observed in honour of Tien-how. The services on such occasions are not usually held on board the junk, but in a temple in honour of the goddess. They consist of thanksgiving, prayers, and offerings of boiled fowl and pork, or of small portions of the merchandise which the junk has brought to port. In 1864 I entered a temple dedicated to Tien-how on Fishers' island, one of the Pescadoré group,[1] and observed on the altar a number of small red bags of the size of an ordinary purse. On each bag was written the name of the person by whom, and the purpose for which, it had been placed on the altar. These bags, I was told, contained salt, large quantities of which are brought by junks to the Pescadoré group for preserving fish. In the same temple there was a large model of a Chinese junk, which I was informed it is the custom of the islanders to carry in procession through the streets of their villages when celebrating the natal anniversary of Tien-how. As I was leaving a mandarin entered. He was attired in his robes of state, and wore white buttons on the apex of his hat. This worthy, with whom, through an interpreter, I entered into conversation, was desirous of paying his devotions to the goddess previous to his departure from the island, where he had served for some years as a magistrate. At Chin-chew, Amoy, Foo-chow, and indeed all the ports of Fokien, and at those of Formosa, there are ocean-going junks which in point of naval architecture resemble the large junks which I have already described. They are, however, considerably smaller, and are chiefly employed in a trade which is carried on between the merchants of the province of Fokien and those of Formosa. Their size adapts them for the navigation of the Formosa Channel. Moreover, the harbours on the west coast of Formosa are so few, and surrounded by so many obstacles, as to render navigation dangerous for junks of large tonnage.

At the port of Canton there is a class of still smaller junks which are employed in the salt trade with the provincial city of Canton. They receive their cargoes at See-toong, Tien-pak, and Fan-lo-kong, ports on the coasts of the province of Kwang-tung, and situate east and west respectively of the colony of Hong-kong. These salt vessels are very numerous, and their anchorage, near what are termed the salt flats, has the appearance of a forest of masts. Some years ago, a vast fleet of them, whilst at anchor at the salt flats, was by some unexplained means set on fire, and

---

[1] These islands are regarded as a portion of the province of Fokien.

as the tide was low, and many of the junks were aground, the loss was very great. As the fire, however, which at one time threatened the destruction of the entire fleet was eventually extinguished, and as the result was brought about without any very apparent exertions on the part of the mariners, this was attributed to the merciful interposition of a goddess called Chow-Chu-Laong-Laong-Koo. In honour of this goddess there is a temple at Tsing-poo, a village not more than five miles to the west of Canton. All sailors serving on board salt junks which are in the port of Canton on the twenty-third day of the fifth month of each year, go to worship at this temple. Plays are also performed on the occasion in a temporary theatre. The expense of these performances is defrayed by a fund which was established as a mark of gratitude to the goddess by the owners, masters, and sailors of the vessels which were saved from the conflagration.

The ocean-going junks which trade between Shanghai, Chefoo, and Tien-tsin, have very high sterns and prows, and at midships are very low in proportion. Each vessel has four masts, the foremost being lashed to the side. Occasionally a fifth mast is added. It is placed between the mainmast and aftermast, and is so small as to resemble a boat's mast. On each side of the junk, and not on the stern, as in vessels already described, is painted in large characters the name of the vessel, and that of the person, or trading company, and that of the port, to which she belongs. When at sea these vessels have in place of bulwarks, stanchions through which ropes are made to pass, and light combings are erected over the hatches for the purpose of keeping out the wash amidships. In a gale of wind, such craft are hove to by means of a large basket, which the sailors veer away to windward by a rope which is attached to two other ropes made to cross each other under the basket. This basket forms, as it were, a large parachute, and by holding the water keeps the ship to the wind. When at Tien-tsin, I observed that the decks of the junks became so leaky in consequence of the dryness of the air, that the junkmen had to pour water upon them to render them watertight. At the port of Tien-tsin, there are dry docks in which, on the approach of winter, it is customary for shipowners to place their vessels, with the view of protecting them from the destructive effects of the sea.

The mode in which all the ocean-going junks of China are rigged, precludes the possibility of their working to the windward in the same manner as European or square-rigged vessels. It is well adapted to enable vessels to sail with great speed before the wind. I observed that Chinese sailors, in navigating their vessels, carried the sheet to the windward, and not to the leeward, like European seamen. This circumstance caused me no astonishment, as Chinese modes of action so often differ from our own. The mariners serving on board the coast junks, direct their course by observing the heavenly bodies. The large ocean-going junks, however, use the compass, the directive properties of the magnet having been known to this ancient people several centuries before the Christian era. According to a letter which Klaproth addressed to M. A. Humboldt on the invention of the compass, and of which Mr. Davis has furnished us with a translation in his History of the Mariner's Compass, it appears that it was known to the Chinese 2634 years prior to the birth of Christ.

Large vessels, not dissimilar to those which ply between Shanghai, Chefoo, and Tien-tsin are to be seen on the waters of the Yang-tsze Kiang. I noticed that the boards or planks of which the bows and sterns are constructed, are bound together not by nails but by iron dogs or clasps, which are so small as to seem incapable of giving much strength to the ship. The masts of these vessels consist not of one solid piece of wood, like the masts of ships in many other parts of China, but of two or three pieces carefully bound together by iron bands or hoops. Nearly all the Chinese vessels I saw engaged in navigating the Yang-tsze Kiang were flat-bottomed, and were in consequence provided with the boards which enabled them to pursue their course during strong gales without danger of capsizing. The ocean-going junks are generally owned by joint-stock trading companies, with whose merchandise the vessels are laden. So distrustful are the partners of each other, that it is not unusual for several of them to go to sea in the craft which they own.

Besides those already enumerated, there are the trading

junks of the estuaries, bays, lakes, and rivers. Let us look at those which navigate the estuaries and rivers of the province of Kwang-tung, premising that the river junks of one district differ only slightly from those of another. They are three-masted, two-masted, and one-masted, and pay duty according to their tonnage. Before these river junks, and indeed the ocean-going junks also, may leave the port to which they belong, on trading voyages, the district ruler or magistrate must be informed of the port of destination, the nature and value of the cargo, the number and names of the seamen serving on board, and the time which must of necessity elapse before the vessel can return. Should she be detained beyond the time specified, the owner or master must obtain from the magistrate of the port of destination a note explaining the cause of the ship's detention. This note is handed to the authorities either by the owner or master, on her return to the port from which she hails. Should he neglect to produce it, he is compelled to appear before the tribunal of the place, and then and there receives a flogging of forty blows. A similar punishment is also, if I mistake not, inflicted upon each member of the crew. This strict vigilance is observed by the government to prevent vessels setting out on piratical excursions—a sort of excursion for which Chinese sailors have a great predilection. Trading vessels of the first and second classes, though they are, strictly speaking, river craft, not unfrequently proceed on voyages to Cochin-China, Siam, Singapore, and Malacca.

The Koo-Tay, or fruit boats, are numerous on the Canton river. They ply principally between Canton and Macao, and are supposed to carry fruit only, on which supposition only a small tax is imposed upon them by the government. Merchandise, however, of all sorts is carried in them. They are about ninety feet in length, and from twenty to twenty-five feet in beam. They have two masts, the mainmast being in front of a flat-roofed house, which extends over one half of the deck. The foremast is in the bows. The crew of a vessel of this description consists of twenty men.

Another and a very numerous class of river-boats, is called the "Si-qua," from a real or supposed resemblance which the hulls of these vessels are supposed to bear to a water-melon. The deck of such a vessel is semicircular in shape, and on each side there are three or four large ports through which the cargo is received and discharged. Each vessel has one mast with a large mat sail. In case of calms, it is provided with two large sculls (which are, in short, neither more nor less than twin screws), each so long and so heavy as to require the active exertions of six or seven sailors to keep them in motion. By a diligent use of these sculls the vessel is enabled to make headway even when the winds and currents are most adverse.

The Mā-Yong-Shun are much larger vessels than the Si-Qua-Pin. Each has a mast in the form of shears, which the sailors can raise or lower. A vessel provided with such a mast cannot, of course, tack, and as she is not provided with sculls, the sailors are obliged in case of adverse winds and tides to take to their boats and tow her. These vessels are chiefly employed as lighters. They receive cargoes of salt from the salt junks which arrive at Canton, and convey the salt to the towns and villages on the banks of the many rivers and creeks which intersect the provinces of Kwang-tung and Kwang-si. On a voyage along the western branch of the Canton river in 1861, I observed many of them, heavily laden with salt, directing their course to the province of Kwang-si, whilst many others were returning to Canton with cargoes of sundries, consisting mostly of oil and fire-wood.

On the Canton river, as also on the Yang-tsze, there are cargo boats which are inclosed fore and aft by means of mat covers. These covers, which are impervious to rain, can be removed at pleasure, and are, of course, invariably taken off when the vessel is receiving or discharging cargo. Vessels of this class, some of which are of great length, are each provided with one mast. They bear the name of San-Fo-Teng.

The various cargo vessels and boats which I have described, advertise the cargoes which they have for sale when in port by hoisting a small portion of the cargo to the mast head. A vessel with fire-wood for sale, hoists a bundle of fire-wood; with oil, an oil cask; with rice, a rice measure.

Tea-boats, which navigate the Canton river, are called How-

Tow-Shun. They are about ninety feet in length and fifteen feet in beam. The hold, which is four feet in depth, is divided into several water-tight compartments in which the tea is stored. These vessels are not restricted to the conveyance of tea only, and they not unfrequently arrive at Canton laden with products of various kinds. The roof of the tea-boats is semicircular. In order, however, that the sailors may have the advantage of a level deck, a platform is erected above the semicircular roof. On each side of the vessel there are three doors which also answer the purpose of ports. The mast is in the form of a triangle or shears, and can be raised or lowered at the pleasure of the seamen. The sail, however, which is attached to such a mast, can be of service only when the wind is fair. The sailors have often to take to their boats and tow. These vessels are, like nearly all the river craft, provided on each side with a narrow platform running fore and aft, or from stem to stern. It is customary for the boatmen to stand on this platform and propel their boat with long bamboo poles.

On the Canton river there are also boats to which the name of Chā-Shun, or tea-boats, is more especially applied. Boats of this class are about forty feet long, and about eight feet broad. They are inclosed with a high mat roof of a semicylindrical shape, impervious to rain. Though called Chā-Shun, or tea-boats, they are frequently engaged to carry all kinds of cargo, and are employed as lighters by almost all the trading vessels which arrive at the port of Canton. Those which I saw on the Yang-tsze, and on the Poyang and Toong-ting lakes, were inclosed with mat covers removable at pleasure. These boats, however, are, in point of architecture, very much superior to the great majority of the river craft which I have hitherto described, being built upon very graceful lines. They are of great length and of narrow beam. The stem and prow, which are rather high and pointed, are light and graceful, and the vessel has a neat and finished appearance.

In 1865 I made a voyage in one of these boats from Han-kow, one of the most important ports on the Yang-tsze, to the Toong-ting Lake. It was very convenient and comfortable, and the sailors, who were ten in number, were most obliging, and seemed to have pleasure in doing everything in their power to make the voyage agreeable to my fellow-traveller and myself. We were much struck with their excessive superstition, which surpassed even that of the sailors who are engaged in navigating the rivers of the southern provinces. On one occasion our boat ran aground, and as the waters of the Yang-tsze were rapidly receding, the men became much alarmed, and used their best endeavours to get her off. Whilst the majority were exerting themselves for this purpose, others were busily engaged in propitiating the evil spirits who were supposed to have caused the mishap. After great exertions they got the vessel off, but as it was now dark they let go the anchor, and waited for the following day. We had not been at anchor many minutes, when we observed that the sailors, who crowded around us, were ill at ease. They seemed to anticipate further disasters; and when we were retiring to rest the servant of my companion in travel entered the saloon in a state of great anxiety, informing us that many evil spirits were flitting about, and that the sailors were desirous that we should discharge a revolver or fowling-piece to frighten them away. We refused, however, to connive at what we did not approve. On another occasion they were thrown into a state of profound alarm because, when some ravens hovered over the vessel, my companion wished to shoot one or two of the birds. The ravens were larger and of more beautiful plumage than those of their species in England. The sailors threw pieces of meat to them, which they caught cleverly on the wing. They were evidently accustomed to do so, and not unfrequently alighted upon the mast and rigging. Some of them strutted about the deck. Only the solemn assurance of my companion, that he would not molest the birds, allayed the excitement to which his proposal to shoot them had given rise.

The cassia boats on the Canton river are very similar in construction to the Cha-shun, or tea-boats, which navigate the Yang-tsze. Their bows are made very sharp in order that they may shoot the rapids, which, as in many other Chinese rivers, render navigation perilous. The province of Kwang-si is the cassia-producing district of China; and these vessels have to descend the numerous tributaries which flow from it into the Canton river.

The rivers are also navigated by boats which, in the language of the country, are called Too-Shun, that is, passenger boats. In form they bear little or no resemblance to the vessels which I have been describing. They are divided into five classes. The first class consists of vessels each of which is seventy-two feet in length, and fifteen feet in beam. Each is licensed to carry sixty passengers. The second consists of vessels, each fifty-nine feet in length, and twelve feet in beam, and licensed to carry fifty passengers. Vessels of the third class are forty-three feet in length, and ten feet in beam, and are licensed to carry thirty passengers. Vessels of the fourth class are thirty-eight feet long and five-and-a-half feet in beam, and are licensed for ten passengers. Each passenger boat has a mast and sail in proportion to the length and beam of the vessel ; and two very large sculls, which, in the absence of wind, form a very powerful means of propulsion. Above the hold, running fore and aft, is a saloon for the accommodation of cabin passengers. As there are no bunks, the passengers sleep either upon the floor of the saloon, or upon the narrow benches with which it is furnished. For females there are private apartments, the comforts of which, however, do not exceed those of the public saloon. It is provided by law that the saloon shall have numerous ports, so that the air may have free circulation throughout the ship. It is also enacted that an awning shall be spread for the comfort of the passengers during the summer months, and that it shall be of matting, not of wood. A board must be attached to the lower part of the mast, bearing the name of the captain, the dimensions of the ship, the names of the ports between which she plies, and the anchorages or wharves at which she is accustomed to moor. To prevent quarrels one vessel loads at a time, the vessel which arrives first in port having the precedence. Each of these passenger boats receives a licence from the prefect, which is not granted except on evidence that the master in charge of the boat is of a robust frame, understands the duties of a seaman, and is well acquainted with the dangers of the rivers which the boat is to navigate. Sureties, also, of great respectability, are required by the prefect for his good conduct; and in the licence the name of the captain, his age, his place of birth, that of his residence,

A PASSENGER BOAT.

TOWING A BARGE.

and the names of his sureties, are carefully entered. It is also stated that so soon as the master shall have attained the age of sixty years he shall vacate his office, and that in the event of his having a son or nephew equal to the duties of the situation, the latter shall, with permission of the prefect, be appointed in his stead; otherwise he must sell his boat. No one can own and sail two boats without the permission of the prefect, and boats are not allowed to anchor at other wharves than those named in the licences. A master of a passenger boat upon being proved guilty of a violation of any one of these rules, is immediately deprived of his licence, and made to stand on the wharf daily for the space of one month with a wooden collar, or cangue, round his neck, as a public example. At the end of the period he receives a flogging of thirty blows. The captains and crews of these boats are obliged to exercise every precaution for the safe preservation of the passengers entrusted to their care. Should an accident occur through want of proper management, the captain and crew subject themselves to a severe penalty. In 1861 a passenger ship plying between Canton and Sai-chu-shan was capsized during a sudden and heavy squall, and three of the passengers were drowned. The mandarins at Canton at once gave orders for the immediate arrest of the captain and crew. The prisoners, of whom the mandarins were determined to make a public example, were consigned to the common gaoler, by whom they were detained in prison for three months. Should a boat be capsized in consequence of having a taller mast and larger sails than are prescribed by law, the captain is made to wear a cangue for three months, after which he receives a flogging of forty blows. Should one or two of the passengers be drowned, he has also to pay a fine of two taels of silver to the family of each of the deceased. Should three of the passengers be drowned, the captain and sailors have each to wear a cangue for one month, after which each receives a flogging of forty blows, and the vessel is confiscated. Should a passenger fall overboard and perish, the master of the boat is by law obliged to let go his anchor and to remain at the place of the accident until the corpse of the unfortunate man has been recovered. The passengers, of course, avail themselves of the services of the first boat passing that way, passenger vessels passing and re-passing along the various rivers and creeks of the country at almost all hours of the day. The Hoi-Teng, or marine magistrate, whose duty it is to see that the dimensions of all vessels are such as the law prescribes, is punished where compliance with the provisions of the law has not been enforced. Indeed, should many lives be lost by the capsizing of a passenger boat, the ruler of the district in which the accident occurs may be seriously involved, inasmuch as the principal magistrates of the respective ports have the power to prevent vessels proceeding on their voyages when the general appearance of the heavens indicates an approaching typhoon or very strong winds. Should a very heavy squall be at hand whilst a vessel is on her voyage, the passengers can call upon the master to strike sail and cast anchor until the danger is past. Should the master of the vessel, however, continue the voyage despite these expostulations, he incurs a punishment of forty blows.

These five classes of passenger boats are not the only vessels which are called Too-Shun or passenger boats. The name is also applied to vessels which ply between Canton and Hong-kong, and which are one hundred feet in length and twenty-six feet in beam. The stern of such a vessel is very high, and she has three or sometimes two masts. All these vessels carry large quantities of various kinds of merchandise and cattle between Canton and Hong-kong. The crew consists of a master mariner, eighteen seamen, three or four helmsmen, a purser, and a cook. The fare for a single passenger, including food, is sixty cents; but passengers by these boats are not so numerous as they used to be. Chinese travellers have discovered the advisability of availing themselves of the speed, comfort, and security of the foreign steamboats now plying between these ports.

The Cho-Kā-Shun, or boats in which the mandarins travel, are not unlike large floating caravans. On each side of such a boat there are three doors painted red. The mast is in the form of a pair of shears, and the sail is therefore only of service when the winds are fair. In contrary weather the sailors, who are eighteen or twenty in number, are obliged to take to their boats. In shallow water they shove the vessel forward with long

bamboo poles, calling at the same time in a singing tone to the
spirits of their departed ancestors to grant them favourable winds
and tides.   A narrow platform of wood runs from stem to stern
for the use of the sailors when using their poles.   Most of the
vessels in the coast and river trade are provided with similar
platforms.   Where the torrents are so rapid as to render poling
impracticable, a long rope is made fast to the top of the mast,
and the sailors go ashore and tow.   Nearly all the rivers,
creeks, and canals are provided with towing-paths.   They must
be expert swimmers, as the towing-path is not unfrequently
interrupted by a tributary river.   Cho-Kā-Shun are better
adapted for river travelling than other boats, as their saloons
are spacious and comfortable ; but they are most inefficient in
point of speed.

In the large ocean-going junks the sailors pay their devotions
to the goddess Tien-how.   Those on board ships engaged in the
river traffic are devotees of the deity called Loong-moo, or the
Dragon's Mother.   In honour of this goddess there are small
shrines at frequent intervals on the banks, and a religious ceremony of a very singular nature is usually observed by the
masters of river junks at the beginning of a voyage.   In the
autumn of the year 1861, when setting out in a Cho-Kā-Shun
on a long river voyage, I witnessed a ceremony of this sort.
Previous to weighing anchor the master took his place in the
bows, which the Chinese regard as the most sacred part of the
ship, and proceeded to propitiate the Dragon's Mother.   On a
small temporary altar, which had been erected for the occasion,
stood three cups containing Chinese wine.   Taking in his hands
a live fowl, which he continued to hold until he killed it as a
sacrifice, the master proceeded in the first place to perform the
Kowtow.   He then took the cups from the table, one at a time,
and raising each above his head, poured its contents on the deck
as a libation.   He next cut the throat of the fowl with a sharp
knife, taking care to sprinkle that portion of the deck on which
he was standing with the blood of the sacrifice.   At this stage
of the ceremony several pieces of silver paper were presented to
him by one of the crew. These were sprinkled with the blood, and
then fastened to the door-posts and lintels of the cabin.   This

last ceremony reminded me of a somewhat similar rite which formed an essential part of the observance of the Passover among the Jews. On my arrival at the town of Yuet-shing, which has long been famous in the historical annals of Kwang-tung for a large temple in honour of the Dragon's Mother, the master and his crew went ashore for the purpose of propitiating the deity once more. I accompanied them to the temple and witnessed their religious ceremonies. These were brought to a close by their presenting an offering of two boiled fowls and a piece of fat pork to the goddess; and as they were in the act of leaving there was the usual salvo of fire-crackers for the purpose of dispelling all evil and obnoxious influences.

A well-known class of boats on the Canton river are Wang-lau, or Fā-Shun, *i.e.*, flower-boats. These are to all intents and purposes floating cafés. Each boat consists of a large saloon which extends the whole length of the vessel. They are usually decorated with carvings in wood, and rendered brilliant with gilt and green paint. The windows—which, in many instances, consist of stained glass—are on each side, and extend to the whole length of the vessel. At the close of the day boats of this description are much resorted to for festive purposes by the upper and middle classes, and, the lamps, with which they are profusely furnished, being lighted, they present a very gay and animated appearance. Not very dissimilar to the flower-boats are the boats called Chee-Tung-Teng, which are considerably smaller, and not so gaily decorated. These vessels are used as floating hotels, and are sometimes hired as boats of travel, the sum charged each day varying from two and a half to four dollars.

The boats called Tan-Poo, or bed boats, are of the same class, and are much frequented by Chinese travellers. They are much smaller than the Chee-Tung-Teng, and are somewhat differently constructed. The carved wooden window-shutters or venetians with which they are provided are bright green, and give a gay appearance. The sum for a night's lodging on board a Tan-Poo, varies from fifty cents to a dollar. Travellers are not the only patrons of them, as they are frequently made use of for immoral assignations. Besides these there are the Chu-Teng, or floating

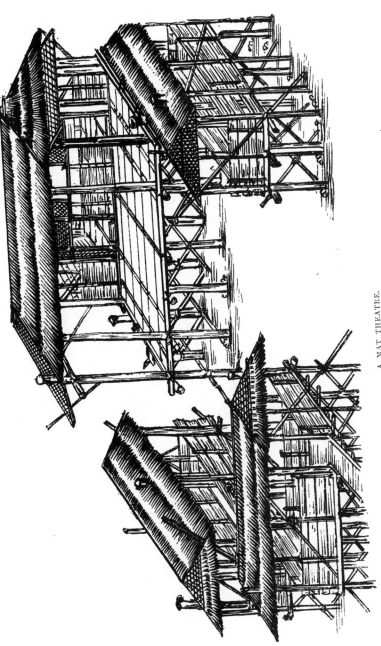

A MAT THEATRE.

kitchens. In size and shape these are very similar to flower-boats, but they are devoid of all decorations, and look neglected. In the front part of each boat is a large kitchen range of brickwork, provided with all necessary culinary utensils. These boats are used for preparing large dinners at the celebration of the marriages of boatmen, and on other festive occasions. The dinners prepared in them are generally served on board other boats. The floating kitchens serve also as floating restaurants for persons in the humbler walks of life, the stern being, in a rude and simple manner, fitted up as a café. At all festivals in towns or villages situate on the banks of rivers, creeks, or canals, these boats are invariably to be found, and are used as cafés by sightseers among the poorer classes.

The Koong-Sze-Teng, or Hong-Mee-Teng, or Hong boats are from thirty to forty feet in length, and are somewhat like the gondolas of Venice. They are in many instances carved and gilded, and the saloon is so spacious as to afford sitting room for eight or ten persons. Abaft the saloon there is a cabin for the boatmen. The boats are propelled by a large scull, which works on a pivot made fast in the stern post. Oars, consisting not of one but of two pieces of wood, are plied by five or six boatmen in the bows. In breezy weather a mast is erected immediately in front of the saloon, and the sail is sufficiently large to give great speed. Hong boats are much used by persons in search of a day's recreation or amusement.

The Lou-Shun or chamber-boats are very numerous on the Canton river. In many respects they resemble "flower-boats." The purposes, however, for which they are used are altogether different. They may be regarded as floating temples or shrines. The marriages of boatmen are solemnized in them by Taouist priests, who also resort to these boats for the purpose of saying masses for the repose of the souls of persons who have either perished by drowning, or who have died at the corners of streets, "unwept, unhonoured, and unsung."

Boats called Nam-Mo-Teng are the residences of Taouist priests, whose services, day and night, are required by the boat population. These boats are similar in construction to the Chee-Tung-Teng. They are not provided, however, with glass windows, and do not possess that air of comfort which characterizes the floating hotels. In the absence of glass windows, they are furnished with sliding-boards. The principal part of the boat forms a saloon, which is furnished with a few chairs and tea-tables. At the end of the saloon there are low narrow shelves, on which are arranged idols of Taouistical deities. In front of the idols there is an altar on which incense sticks are burning at all hours of the day, and upon which offerings of fruits, fowls, and pork are placed when religious rites are being performed for the benefit of devotees. Near this altar there stands a smaller one, on which are placed tablets, bearing the names of the departed members of the priest's family. Behind the saloon, which occupies nearly the whole part of the boat, are two or three cabins in which the priest and his family pass the night. On the door-post of the principal entrance there is a sign-board on which are painted the names of the priest, and the rites which he is prepared to perform. These boats never remove from their anchorages. Should the services of the priest, however, be required on board another boat, to exorcise an evil spirit, or to say prayers in behalf of a sick person, he is ready to go.

The Chu-Kā-Teng are very similar to the Nam-Mo-Teng. As a rule, however, they are much smaller. Men who are employed in a variety of ways on the rivers and creeks of China, make them their homes. Like the class of vessels which I have just been describing, these boats are never removed from their anchorages. They are the floating homes of sailors engaged in navigating ocean-going junks, river-trading junks, lighters, and fishing boats, who, although they may be absent on voyages extended over several months, look on their return to find these vessels, in which, in all probability, they were born and brought up, safely moored at their familiar stations. These floating homes are generally arranged so as to form streets of boats ; but at Canton this arrangement is not so perfect as it was ten or twelve years ago.

The Shā-Teng, or Sampans, as they are called, are very numerous on the Canton waters. They are in great requisition by persons whose business takes them on the river, or who wish to cross it. There are many different kinds. The Shā-Teng

of the first class are about twenty-eight feet in length, and eight
or nine feet in breadth. The centre part of the boat forms a
saloon, which is inclosed on each side by green venetians, and
covered by a circular mat roof. The saloon is entered from the
bows, and has a fixed bench or seat on each side, and one at the
further end. The seats, which are covered with cushions, are
capable of accommodating five persons. On each side of the entrance door is a door-post of carved wood, painted either green
or red. From the arched roof of the saloon a branch of the
sago palm is suspended, to dispel all evil influences; and on the
side of the saloon there is either a picture of the god Yune-Tan
or of Hung-Sing Wong, the god of the Southern Ocean. In the
stern sheets of the boats is a small ancestral altar; also a cup-
board for the crockery, chopsticks, and culinary utensils required
by the boatman and his family. The wife and daughter stand in
the stern to manage the scull, and in the bows the boatman and
other members of his family use oars. On the bow of the boat,
and also on the stern, is pasted a piece of red paper on which
mystic scrolls are written. Such charms are not peculiar to the
Shā-Teng, but are to be seen in almost all river boats. The Shā-
Teng or shallow boats of the second class are about twenty-four
feet in length, and six feet in beam. The saloon, similarly constructed to that of the Shā-Teng of the first class, is much
smaller; and a long narrow board is substituted for venetians.
Owing to the absence of carved wood and bright paint, these
boats present a very plain appearance. The Shā-Teng, or
shallow boats of the third class, are still smaller. Each boat
is tenanted by one man only, who, as a rule, is an old bachelor
or a childless widower. He stands in the stern, and propels
and directs his little craft with a scull. Such boats seldom carry
more than one passenger at a time.

The Shā-Teng at Macao are very similar to the second class of
Shā-Teng or shallow boats at Canton. They are not, however,
provided with fixed benches, but with stools, which are in
danger of tumbling over when the water is at all rough.
These boats are generally navigated by two women, one of
whom is stationed in the stern to scull, and the other in the bows
to row. The Whampoa sampans are sufficiently large to admit

of a mast being erected. It is placed, when required, immediately in front of the saloon or covered part of the boat. These boats are much more comfortable than any others of the class on the Canton river. Another variety of shallow boats consists of those called Ma-Leng-Teng. They resemble a Chinese slipper in form. The covered part, which terminates in a point at the bow, affords a shelter to the owner and his family, and the open part or heel answers the purpose of a deck. The boatman stands looking towards the bows, and by means of oars, the handles of which are made to cross each other in the form of a St. Andrew's cross, propels his craft rapidly. These small boats go occasionally three or four hundred miles along the Canton river. When on a voyage along it, in 1861, to the province of Kwangsi, I overtook, near Tak-heng Foo, two shallow boats which had come from Canton, and which were bound to Woo-chow Foo, on the western frontiers of Kwangsi. Each boat contained a married woman and her children. The women were on their way to join their husbands, who were serving as sailors on board a vessel plying between Woo-chow Foo and Chan-chow. The poor women were much delighted when we overtook them, and earnestly begged that they might be allowed to keep near our boat, as they were afraid of being attacked by pirates.

In the absence of bridges, ferry-boats are very numerous in China. Those which ply for hire on the Canton river, and which are termed Wang-Shuee-Too, are considerably larger than the Shā-Teng or shallow boats. Like all Chinese boats, they are propelled by a scull made to rest on a pivot at the stern. Each of the Canton ferry-boats is licensed to carry six passengers, and the fare for each person is two cash. Passengers carrying luggage are charged one cash for a bundle or basket. The only persons allowed free passages are beggars. The proprietor of each boat, however, is at liberty to take only one beggar at a time, and the ragged fellow, not being allowed to sit beneath the mat cover with which such boats are provided, takes up his position in the bows. The indulgence which proprietors of ferry boats thus show towards beggars is regarded by all Buddhists as highly meritorious. As several thousands of the citizens of Canton cross the river daily, the ferry-boats, there being no bridges, are kept very well employed. The whole of the passage money, however, does not go into the purse of the proprietors. One half is claimed by the householders owning the wharves at which the passengers embark. Clerks are placed on the wharves to record the number of persons landing at them. On many branches of the Canton and other rivers, and more especially in the agricultural districts, the ferry-boats are of great length. . Each is provided with a flush deck, so as to be capable of embarking horses and cattle. The largest ferry-boats which I observed were at Koong-su, a market-town twelve miles distant from Canton. The ferry-boats on the Yang-tsze Kiang, and on the Poyang lake are, in consequence of the great strength of the currents, provided with sails, and are constructed to carry from ten to fourteen passengers each.

Of boats which are propelled by short oars or paddles, the largest are the Loong-shun or Dragon Boats, which I have described in a previous chapter. When the festival for which these boats are required is over, they are buried at low water in the beds of rivers and creeks, to prevent their rapid decay. Other boats of this class are called Chaong-Loong, or long dragon boats. They are much used by pirates, who infest the rivers and creeks, as well as the seas of China. As I was returning with other Englishmen, on one occasion, at the dead hour of the night, from Whampoa to Canton, a boat of this description pursued the gig in which we were seated. As she gained on us, our Chinese boatmen, six in number, became greatly alarmed, and attempted to leap overboard. Prevented by us from doing so, they called to the pirates not to approach, as the English gentlemen seated in the gig were heavily armed and fully prepared to take life. We were without arms, but the statement of the terrified boatmen, was readily credited by the pirates, who probably aware of the danger of attacking foreigners, deemed discretion the better part of valour, and withdrew.

Amongst the most singular boats, however, which I have seen in Chinese waters, are the long, narrow-beamed, snake-like craft which are to be found on the rivers, creeks, and canals of the eastern and midland provinces. These boats are not unfrequently used as post-boats, and as such are obliged to travel night and day. They are very fast, and sometimes traverse a distance of seventy miles between the rising and setting of the sun. The frail craft is propelled by one man, who, when rowing, wears as little clothing as possible in the summer months. He sits in the stern sheets, and with his feet plies a short but broad oar; whilst with another oar, the handle of which he tucks under his arm, he directs his course. In each of these boats there is room for one passenger. The unhappy traveller, however, is obliged, whilst the boat is under way, to place himself in a recumbent position.

Boats not dissimilar to the Chaong-Loong, and called Tcha-Ho-Teng, are also to be seen on the Canton river. These boats are employed by water-policemen, whose duty it is to row guard by night. These night-guardians of the boat population announce their approach by blowing conch shells, the shrill notes of which may be heard at all hours of the night.

The small boats, or punts, which are propelled by short oars or paddles, are a numerous class. They are called by the general name of Sampans, which means, "three boards," such boats being constructed of two or three planks only. They are very narrow, without keels, and draw very little water. From before sunrise until after midnight, boats of this class navigate the waters of the Canton river, each having for sale the common necessaries of life. The Chu-Teng, or hot congee boat has a small galley for the purpose of enabling its proprietor to boil congee. Sitting in the stern he directs her course, by means of paddles or short oars, through the vast fleet of vessels and boats with which the Canton river is crowded, calling aloud Mi-Chuk, or "Congee for sale." Among other boats of this class are the Yu-Teng, or fish boats; the Choy-Teng, or vegetable boats; the Chu-Yuk-Teng, or pork boats; the Ngow-Yuk-Teng, or meat boats; the Tow-Foo-Teng, or bean curd boats; the Kow-Teng, or cake boats; the Hā-Teng, or shrimp boats; the Na-Choy-Teng, or green pea boats; the San-Kwo-Teng, or fruit boats; the Chay-Teng, or sugar-cane boats; the Yow-Teng or oil boats; the Mi-Teng, or rice boats; the Fa-Teng, or flower boats; the Chu-Teng, or fish boats; the Tchi-Teng, or fire-wood boats ; the Kong-Nga-Teng, or chinaware boats ; the Tai-Tow-Teng, or barbers' boats. These boats are too small to be used as floating homes by the hawkers and their families, many of whom reside in the larger vessels which I have described as being used as homes by the boat population. The Tai-Tow-Teng, or barbers' boats, are the smallest of this class. They are small open boats or punts, in the stern of which the barber sits, and paddles among the crowded craft on the river, ringing a small hand-bell. The river barbers of China seldom or never shave the heads of those who reside ashore.

On the Canton river I also observed large floating rice stores or warehouses. At the time to which I allude, a large number of these were moored together near the west end of Shameen, and presented the appearance of a floating town. The stores were built upon huge barges, and had lower and upper stories, which made them look like dwelling-houses. At this semblance of a floating town, a rice market was held daily, at which extensive sales were effected. When the blockade of the Canton river was raised at the close of the late war which England waged with China, I saw these boats returning from the Fa-tee creek, where they had sought refuge, to the anchorage which they had occupied before the commencement of hostilities. As they sailed down the river in company, they presented the extraordinary appearance of a town under way. In 1865 the greater number of these floating warehouses were destroyed by fire. It appears from Nieuhoff's *History of China* that it is not unusual to see floating towns on the large rivers which flow through the country. He describes one of these in the following terms :—

" We saw likewise upon the Yellow river, which is continually ploughed with all manner of great and small vessels, several floating islands, which were so artificially contrived that the best artist in Europe would scarcely be able to make the like of the same stuff, being common reed, which the Portuguese call bamboo, twisted so closely together that no moisture can penetrate. Upon these reeds the Chinese set up huts and little houses of boards and other materials, in which they live with their wives and children as if they had their dwellings on firm land. Some of these floating islands are large enough to

contain at least two hundred families ; and those who live there
subsist for the most part by commerce and traffic in all manner
of commodities, which they carry from place to place upon the
river, being hurried down with the stream, and towed up again
by toilsome bargemen. Whenever they intend to make any
stay they fasten their floating towns with poles fixed in the
ground. They keep and feed aboard the island all manner of
tame cattle, but especially hogs."

I saw nothing in the course of my travels at all answering
to this description. I saw, however, on the Yang-tze Kiang
large timber rafts, to each of which the many well-constructed
huts erected on them gave the appearance of a floating village.
The largest raft which I saw was on the Toong-ting lake. Seen
from the highest lands of the Golden Island, it so much resembled
a large village erected on an island in the centre of the lake, that
I at first thought that it was indeed an island. On the western
branch of the Canton river I have also seen rafts of timber and
others of bamboo, upon each of which a few huts were erected
as dwellings for the raftsmen and their families. Whenever
these rafts entered a port they were made fast, as Nieuhoff states
respecting the floating villages or islands which he saw on the
Yellow river, by means of long bamboo poles fixed in the earth.
It is not unusual to see wooden huts erected on stakes on
Chinese river and creeks. I visited a settlement of this kind
on the Canton river, not far from the island which is called by
foreigners the " Dutch Folly." I found a population of about
one hundred and fifty souls, who gained their livelihood by
selling fire-wood and making coarse matting bags for salt.
The largest floating populations which I saw were at Hankow
on the river Han, at Canton, and at Fat-shan, a large market
town standing on one of the many tributary streams of the
Canton river. The water population on the Canton river has
during the last few years, owing, I suppose, to a variety of causes,
considerably decreased.

The regulations which affect the boat population are enforced
by an official who is called the Hoi-Teng, or river magistrate.
This functionary is assisted in the discharge of his duties by a
river or water constabulary, who row guard during the night

for the purpose of protecting the boat population from the attacks of thieves and pirates, by whom Chinese rivers are much infested. At the approach of the New Year's festivities these lawless characters become very daring, and not unfrequently seize wealthy citizens when crossing the river by night, and hold them as prisoners until a ransom has been paid. In 1861 a native merchant, named Pin King, with whom I was acquainted, was seized when crossing the Canton river by night, and conveyed by his captors to a secluded bay on the banks of the Canton estuary. He was detained until a sum of three thousand dollars had been paid for his ransom. In 1867 another native merchant, named Yow Loong, was carried off in a similar manner, and was detained by his captors until a ransom of six thousand dollars had been paid by his friends. Occasionally the pirates are bold enough to enter flower-boats, and carry off persons of wealth and respectability who may be dining on board. In the month of June, 1867, a wealthy person, named Loong Tai-su, was seized whilst dining on board a flower-boat by an armed party of thirty men, and conveyed to a remote part of the district in which he lived. He was detained as a prisoner until a ransom of three thousand dollars had been paid by his friends. This seizure took place at eight o'clock in the evening, and it was generally supposed by the Chinese that the water police had received a bribe from the pirates to absent themselves from the neighbourhood of the flower-boat in which Loong Tai-su and his friends were dining. These custodians of the public peace have a very bad reputation. A frequent charge brought against them is that of stopping boats by night and exacting black mail from the owners. On one occasion I saw a number of these harpies overhaul a boat which was laden with fire-wood, and deliberately remove several bundles of fuel. The owner of the boat was in such a state of terror lest the rascals should drag him before one of the city tribunals on a false charge, that he allowed the robbery without even uttering a word of protest. Indeed when the water police demand blackmail from the boat population, it is seldom refused. The latter are in terror of being brought before the Hoi-Teng, or river magistrate, on a false or frivolous charge.

Various opinions have been expressed about the origin of the boat population of China. Sometimes they are said to be the descendants of persons who have been convicted of treason, and in consequence deemed unworthy of homes on *terra firma*. The boat people of Canton, at all events, are said by native annalists to be the descendants of a person named Loo Tsun, who during the Tsin dynasty, 200 years before the Christian era, was the head of a large clan or tribe which occupied the village of Namkou on the island of Honam. It is recorded of Loo Tsun that he was at one time a general in the Chinese army. Attaining to great power and influence, he raised the standard of revolt, and, after many successful skirmishes with the imperial troops, he succeeded in making himself master of the city of Canton, where, for thirty years, he continued to rule. After the death of Loo Tsun, his descendants were much persecuted by the imperialists as an accursed race, and were eventually made to take up their quarters in boats, not being considered worthy to reside ashore. During the Tong dynasty they were apparently much persecuted, and made to pay a poll-tax. During the reign of Hoong-moo, the founder of the Ming dynasty, all boatmen between eighteen and forty-five years of age were ruthlessly seized by press-gangs and made to bear arms.

The Emperor Yung-ching appears, however, to have taken a deep interest in their welfare, and in 1730 issued the following proclamation :—[1]

" We hear that in the province of Canton besides the natives of that province there is a class of people called Tan, similar to the Yao and Man tribes, who make boats their houses, and catch fish as a means of gaining a livelihood. The rivers of this province are now full of these people, and they are increasing very rapidly. The Cantonese look upon them as low wanderers, and do not permit them to live on shore ; and as the Tanka people do not dare to put themselves on a level with the other people, they, in fear, submissively remain confined to their boats, passing their whole lives without knowing the security and pleasures of living on land. The Tanka people are naturally well-meaning, and there is nothing (in their character) to be despised, or that they should be rejected by other people.

[1] V. *Notes and Queries*, vol. i. p. 107.

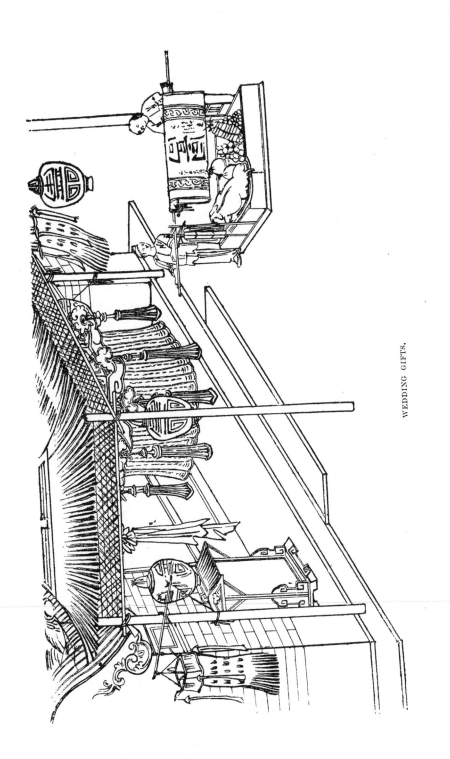

WEDDING GIFTS.

Moreover, they also contribute to Government by paying taxes on fish just as others do.   Why then should they be looked down on, simply because it is customary to do so, and forced to keep separate, passing their days floating about in constant jeopardy of their lives ?   Let the Governor of the province direct the magistracy to promulgate for general information, that if any Tanka people choose to live in their boats they are not to be forced to live on shore ; and if any having means wish to build houses or tents on shore, they are at liberty to do so in villages adjacent to the water ; also to let them be enrolled in the census, and have head men selected in order that an account be kept of them.

" All men in authority, the wealthy or the poor, are in no way to molest or annoy them, or drive them away ; and further- more let the magistrates enjoin them to engage in cultivating the waste land, so that by their own industry they may become men of means ; thereby assisting us in showing that we look on all people with the same benevolent feeling."

Despite, however, this proclamation on the part of Yung- ching, the boat population are all regarded as a pariah class, and their children are not allowed to attend the literary ex- aminations.   Neither are they allowed to intermarry with people who reside ashore.   The term Suee Ki, or water-fowl, is applied to the women by the ordinary Chinese, in sign of their contempt for them.   The *physique* of the boatwomen, however, is vastly superior to that of their countrywomen who live on *terra firma*. The marriages of the boat people appear to be attended with more religious observances than those of the ordinary Chinese, and are solemnized at the dead hour of the night in the floating temples.   Taouist priests are present, who, for three days and nights, chant prayers to the Kow-Wong or Nine Kings, to whom the children of boat people are solemnly dedicated shortly after birth.   A vow at the time of the child's birth is also made by the parents to the Kow-Wong to the effect that if the child be preserved from all evil, masses will be said, and offerings of fruits presented to the deities at the time of the child's marriage. Much feasting takes place on these occasions.   Indeed, one wonders where all the money for the expenses attendant on the due celebration of a Chinese boatman's marriage, comes from. It is, I believe, not unusual for the parents of the bridegroom to spend the greater part of the earnings of several years in celebrating, according to usual customs, the marriage of a son.

It is remarkable how few deaths by drowning occur amongst the large water population on the Canton river. With the view of preventing the children from falling into the river, they are often tied by long ropes, or cords, to the doors of the boats. Children of three or four years of age have floats attached to their backs. When a child falls overboard his parents quickly plunge into the stream after him, knowing that there are few persons in the south of China who would stretch forth a hand to rescue him from drowning. This reluctance of the Cantonese to rescue a person from drowning arises from a superstitious dread. They believe that the spirit of a person who has been drowned, continues to flit along the surface of the water until it has caused, by drowning, the death of a fellow-creature. A person, therefore, who attempts to rescue another from drowning is supposed to incur the hatred of the uneasy spirit which is desirous, even at the expense of a man's life, to escape from its unceasing wanderings.[1] Not a few instances of persons perishing by water who might have been rescued came under my notice. In 1867, a boat-girl named Acheen fell into a creek in the rear of the foreign settlement at Canton. When she was struggling in the water and calling piteously for aid, several boats were passing. Their crews, however, turned a deaf ear to her entreaties, and, as a matter of course, she was drowned. The mother of this unfortunate girl came to me in a state of great distress and complained bitterly of the cruel indifference shown by the people who were passing along the creek at the time her child was struggling in the water. Whilst I sympathised much with this bereaved mother, I could not avoid the thought that though she felt the untimely

---

[1] A superstitious dread of saving a drowning man used also to prevail in Shetland, and other islands in the north-east of Scotland. It was owing to the belief that the person saved would sooner or later do an injury to the man who rescued him. A similar belief existed not very long ago in the south-westernmost part of England. Many readers will remember the scene in Sir Walter Scott's *Pirate*, in which Bryce, the pedlar, warns the hero not to attempt to resuscitate an inanimate form which the waves had washed ashore on the mainland of Shetland. "Are you mad," exclaimed the pedlar—"you that have lived sae lang in Zetland, to risk the saving of a drowning man? Wot ye not, if you bring him to life again, he will do you some capital injury?"—ED.

death of her daughter so much, she would, nevertheless, not have stretched forth a helping hand to save the child of another from drowning. In the same month—July—of the same year, a Chinese with whom I had been acquainted for several years was drowned at Canton, whilst going on board the steamship *Kin-Shun*. At the time this man fell into the water there were many boats close at hand, but not one would render aid. On the corresponding day of the following month, another man was drowned whilst going on board the same steamer. An opinion prevailed amongst all classes of Chinese who were cognizant of these two deaths, that the latter had been dragged beneath the surface of the waters by the spirit of the former. The Hongkong *Daily Press* of July 2nd, 1861, records a noticeable case in point. It describes the *Sir J. Jeejeebhoy* as being delayed on her passage from Macao in taking four Chinese from the wreck of their capsized boat, to which they had been clinging for some time; and adds,

"There were no less than forty-four native boats close by, none of which made any attempt to render assistance, but as soon as the men were in the steamer's boat and on their way on board, the fishing boats launched their sampans and proceeded to the wreck. So much for Chinese humanity."

To show how general is this mischievous superstition, I may mention another scene of which I was a spectator. During a storm which occurred in September, 1864, at Tam-sui, a port on the north-west coast of Formosa, a number of Chinese lightermen were going ashore from a Hamburg ship on board of which they had been engaged discharging ballast. The wind was high, and their boat capsized. Several of the men clung to the keel and called for aid in the most importunate manner. At this moment a Chinese boat passed, but made no attempt whatever to rescue them. All the time, the capsized boat was being driven by a rapid tide towards the mouth of the river. The master of the Hamburg ship, seeing the perilous position of the men, lowered one of his boats and went in pursuit. He was too late. The capsized boat with her crew could no longer be seen, having been carried out to sea, which at the time was running high. I witnessed this heartrending spectacle, and learned on the following day from the mandarin of the place, that the unfortunate lightermen who perished were twenty-five in number.

During squalls the boat populations are much afraid, and with the view of propitiating the evil spirits who are supposed to be the origin of all troubles, they burn paper money in large quantities. In the excitement of the moment others scatter bundles of sacrificial papers to the winds, to appease the spirits that have "put the wild waters in this roar." Such senseless devices are more strictly observed during the summer months, when squalls called Sui-Tow-Foong, or devil's head winds, are of frequent occurrence. It is, however, during a typhoon or cyclone that these poor boat-people sustain their greatest losses, both of life and property. I witnessed a very severe typhoon at Macao in 1857. Hundreds of boatmen perished, and when the storm had subsided the inner harbour of that port presented an almost indescribable scene of devastation. It was a chaos of wrecked boats. So great had been the violence of the wind that some of the boats were actually piled one upon another. The storm, however, which was attended with the greatest loss of life and property, was one which occurred at Canton on the 27th of July, 1862. It is said that throughout the province of Kwang-tung no fewer than forty thousand persons perished on that occasion. Some of these were drowned by the capsizing of boats and vessels, and others were killed by the falling of houses and trees. That portion of the Canton river which flows from Canton to Whampoa, devoured its hecatombs of human beings; and so great was the stench from the dead bodies which for several days after were floating upon its surface, that the governor-general, in the hope of preventing a pestilence, issued a proclamation offering a reward of one dollar for each body recovered from the waters. To lepers and other poor people living in boats this proclamation proved a great boon, and they applied themselves most assiduously to the work. The dead bodies, as they were picked up, were bound together by ropes in lots of four or five each, and towed to certain places on the banks, where mat-sheds had been erected to serve as dead-houses. At each of these temporary dead-houses a mandarin was stationed to superintend the interment of the bodies.

I visited two or three of these morgues with the view of searching for the bodies of three or four Englishmen who had perished
in the typhoon, and I shall not readily forget the sad scenes
which I witnessed.

The fishing vessels of China form another numerous species
of craft which I have yet to describe; but as what falls to be
said under that head will lead me into matters connected with
pisciculture and fishery, I shall treat of them in a separate
chapter.

CHAPTER XXX.

FISHING BOATS AND FISHERY.

As China possesses such an extensive seaboard, its fishing vessels are naturally very numerous. Fishing-boats require a licence from Government—for which they pay—and are divided into three classes. The first class consists of vessels which carry three masts, and are eight cubits in breadth at the bows; the second, of vessels which carry two masts, and are seven cubits in breadth at the bows; and the third, of those which carry one mast, and are six cubits in breadth at the bows. No fisherman, or company of fishermen, can build a vessel for the fish trade until permission to do so has been obtained from the proper authorities, who require specifications. When the vessel is launched, the mandarin of the district is fully informed of the waters over which it is intended she should fish. To prevent piracy, it is enacted that each fishing-boat shall be secured by nine others. Each ten tens of boats, or a hundred boats, form one company, presided over by a chief. The president, who is elected for five years only, is, in general, an old fisherman of independent means and of good reputation. He holds himself responsible for the good conduct of the owners and crews of the hundred vessels forming the company. Should the owner of any vessel wish to dispose of it by public auction, or to convert it into a merchantman, he must inform the president of the division to which the boat belongs. The president submits the application to the proper authorities. All fishing vessels of the first class are allowed to remain at sea for the taking of fish for ten days. Each vessel receives on board at the commencement of each voyage, four hundred piculs of salt to be used in salting the fish. Vessels of the second class are allowed to remain at sea five days, and receive on board three hundred piculs of salt; and vessels of the third class remain three days at sea, receiving on board two hundred piculs of salt. Should vessels at sea discover that they require, in consequence of great draughts of fishes, additional quantities of salt, they are not allowed to enter any of the neighbouring ports for the purpose. To do so is a gross violation of the law, and the penalties incurred are the confiscation of the ship to the crown, the imprisonment of the captain and crew, and the cancelling of the licence of the salt merchant from whom the salt was bought. Vessels employed in the salt-fish trade must not carry stone ballast. This enactment is intended, I apprehend, to prevent the fishermen smuggling granite slabs under the plea that such slabs are required as ballast. In order that all vessels in the salt-fish trade may be recognised when on the high seas, and reported, the names of the vessels, of their owners and commanders, and of the ports to which they belong must be painted on the mainsail in large characters. The proprietors of fishing vessels are required to renew their licences half-yearly. On the coast of the province of Kwang-tung there are many markets at which these vessels meet with a ready demand for their cargoes of salt fish. One of the largest which I visited is that of Tchun-tchun, on the banks of the Canton river. At this market there are very extensive stores—in some cases constructed of wood—in which the fish are exposed for sale.

These vessels not unfrequently sail a considerable distance from the mainland. In 1865 the steamship *Fusi-Yama*, in which I was returning from Japan to China, ran down a fishing smack of the third class near a group of islands called the Saddles. The *Fusi-Yama* was commanded by Captain Dundas a skilful navigator and a most amiable gentleman, who did everything in his power to rescue the unfortunate crew. The shrieks of the men as they were carried past our vessel by a very strong current, were truly heartrending. The *Fusi-Yama* was " put about," and, after a diligent but unsuccessful search

of half an hour, and hearing no cries across the waters, we concluded that the fishermen had perished. Captain Dundas, however, was determined to continue the search, and, in ten minutes,
we again heard shrieks. A boat was immediately lowered, and
eventually four men were found clinging to the wreck. The
fishermen, when received on board the *Fusi-Yama*, informed us
that two of their companions had perished. The missing men
were the father and uncle of a fine young man who was one of
the four we were so fortunate as to save.

The vessels employed in the fresh-fish trade are very
numerous. The principal vessels engaged are not dissimilar in
naval architecture to those which we have just described. All
along the coast of the province of Kwang-tung large numbers
may be descried as far as the eye can reach. They sail two
abreast, and at a distance from each other of three hundred
feet. A net is stretched from ship to ship, and as they proceed,
it seldom fails to inclose large draughts of fishes. On the
western branch of the Canton river there are also large vessels
engaged in this trade. In the bows of each vessel there is
erected a large pair of shears, which can be raised or lowered at
pleasure. To these shears a large dip net is attached. When
the net has been immersed for some time it is drawn out of the
water by raising the shears, and the fish which it contains
are removed from it and cast into the centre compartment of
the hold, which is neither more nor less than a vast cistern.
The sides of this compartment are perforated so as to admit of
the flowing in of an abundant supply of fresh water—a contrivance which enables the fishermen to convey living fish to
the market.

There are also other boats of a medium size, somewhat
sharp in the bows, and of narrow beam, which arrive daily
at Canton with large freights of live fish artificially reared.
Each boat is provided with one mast. The hold from stem
to stern serves as a large cistern, into which the fish are thrown
as they are caught. That they may have an abundant supply of their native element, two or three plugs are removed
from the side of the hold. To prevent the vessel becoming
water-logged, the fishermen work a chain-pump by relays of

two, until the boat reaches the market for which her living
freight is intended.   The chain-pump is worked by means of a
tread-wheel, and the fishermen who keep it in motion seem to
a stranger to be undergoing punishment for mutinous conduct.
The fish which these boats bring in such large quantities to the
market, are not taken from the river, but from artificial ponds
in which they have been most carefully reared.   At Tai-shek,
Lee-chun, Sai-chu-shan, Kow-hong, Kum-chok, &c., &c., there
are several ponds of this description.   In the second and third
months of the Chinese year, that is during the months of March
and April, the spring-tides bring great quantities of fish up the
river.   The spawners deposit their ova amongst the long grasses
or reeds, which grow in large quantities at the banks.   The eggs
adhere to the grasses and in a few days the fish make their
appearance.   At first they are almost as small as the point of
a needle.   The young fish are captured by nets and deposited
in the well-boats.   While they are kept in the boats, the fishermen who live on board are careful not to use oil in cooking
their food, as the smell of any unctuous or greasy matter is considered to disagree with the fish, and sometimes to make them
blind.   They are fed with a paste, made of the flour of wheat
and beans and the yolks of the hard-boiled eggs of hens or ducks.
When the fish become large, they are cast into artificial ponds
which contain no great depth of water, a great depth being
regarded as prejudicial to their growth.   In the centre or at the
sides of many of the fish-ponds it is usual to erect rockeries
beneath which the fish can shelter themselves from the sun.
For similar purposes trellis-work for vines is also occasionally
erected over portions of the ponds.   Along their banks in some
localities it is usual to see rows of plantain, or banana trees
growing in great abundance.   The breeders of fish give a reason
for this custom; they say that the water which, after heavy
showers of rain, falls from the wide leaves of the plantain-tree
promotes the health of the fish.   In other districts, trees called
Foo-lin are also planted by the sides of fish-ponds, the fruit
being regarded as very fattening food.   Along the margin of
many of the fish-ponds I have also observed water-lilies growing in rich profusion.   This beautiful plant is regarded by the

Chinese as sacred, and its presence in a pond is supposed to prevent the intrusion of other aquatic plants. The banks of the ponds are, in some instances, supported by low stone walls. The north bank, however, is invariably left without any such protection. The Chinese prevent anything which they suppose to be hurtful from finding its way into the ponds. They are careful never to wash hemp in them, or any vegetables which may have an injurious effect on the fish. It is also unusual for people in the districts where the rearing of fish is extensively carried on to keep pigeons, as where the ponds are numerous pigeon's dung, which is reckoned very destructive to the fish, would be certain to fall into the water. No willow-trees are allowed to grow in the vicinity of the preserves, as the leaves of the willow are included in the list of hurtful substances. The fishes are fed with grass twice a day, and as the lands are all arable, this is only to be got for them on the banks of rivers. Grass growing at the water's edge is avoided, lest it should have attached to it the ova of fishes of prey. The grass is invariably thrown in the ponds from the north side. The reason for this we were not able to ascertain. It is only during the summer months that the fishes are fed. At all seasons, however, they have an abundant supply of food. The fish-ponds, as I have elsewhere stated, are very numerous at Kow-hong, Kum-chok, and Sai-chu-shan, and also at Tai-shek and Lee-chun. The breeders of fish at Kow-hong farm, for the capture of young fish, that branch of the Canton river which extends from Kow-hong to Tsing-yune and Shu-kwan. For this monopoly they pay an ordinary tax. The breeders who reside at Kow-hong pay frequent visits to the villages adjacent to that town, for the purpose of selling a supply for the village ponds. The Kow-hong men carry the young fish for sale, in some instances in boats, and in others in baskets rendered water-tight by means of gum. Each basket contains five or six hundred fish, and that the fish may have plenty of air, the mouth is inclosed by a piece of network only. In carrying these baskets it is necessary to observe every precaution, as to shake them may kill the fish. The bearers, however, through long practice carry their baskets with the utmost steadiness. When the fish are sold they are

FISHING BY NIGHT.

removed, five at a time, from the baskets by means of small wooden calabashes, and the fishermen are so expert that it is a pleasure and amusement to watch them.

But to return from this digression on pisciculture to the fishing-boats, which we left ready to dispose of their living freights. Almost all fishmongers are provided with large stone or wooden troughs or cisterns, into which fresh water is allowed to flow by day and night; in these the fish are placed upon being removed from the boats. At the Woo-see Hien I visited a large fishmonger's shop, and observed that the proprietor kept his fish alive by depositing them in very large creels or baskets immersed in the Grand Canal, the waters of which flowed immediately in front of his shop. In the streets of most cities and towns on the coast, it is usual to meet with men hawking fish. The fish hawker bears on his shoulders a bamboo rod, which has a tub filled with water and full of live fish at one end, and at the other a block upon which it is his custom to cut his fish, by means of a chopper, into portions of a ¼lb., a ½lb., or a 1lb. weight, to suit purchasers. On the rivers also, it is usual to meet with men or women in small boats, the bows of which are wells filled with live fish, which they hawk amongst the boat population. At Nankin, I observed that all vessels engaged in the trade hoisted a small white flag, by which it was understood that they were duly licensed for fishery.

There are also boats called Pā-pāk-teng, which are not unfrequently employed on the rivers for the purpose of taking fish. These boats, which are used by night only, are long and narrow. On one side running fore and aft, and inclining towards the water, there is placed a long white board, the breadth of which does not exceed twelve inches. Amidships, a stone, which is made fast to the boat by means of a cord, is lowered into the water. In the stern of the boat the fisherman sits, and, by means of a short paddle, makes his boat glide along the waters. The course of the boat causes the stone suspended in the stream to make a rushing noise. Terrified at this, and seeing the reflection of the white board, the fish spring towards the latter, and, nine times out of ten, make such a bound as to overleap it and lodge themselves in the centre of the boat.

In the fish trade there are also other small boats employed. These are quite open, and require the service of two fishermen ; one uses a pair of oars in the hinder part of the boat, whilst the other stands in the bows and throws a large cast-net into the water.   Fishermen of this class appear to be men of great perseverance, for I have seen them casting their nets into the waters without ever taking a single fish.   Judging, too, from their wretched appearance, they are also very poor.   On the streams in the neighbourhood of Macao I saw a very simple and, at the same time, very successful mode of capturing fish.   Having anchored his boat in the middle of the river, and taken up his position in the bows, the fisherman lowered a dip-net into the water by means of shears made of bamboo.   He then threw, in a direct line from the bows, large cork balls, to each of which several baits were attached.   These balls were borne towards the boat by the tide, hotly pursued by a large number of fish, eager to seize the bait : so soon as they floated above the dip-net, it was quickly raised with a take of fish.

At the port of Ki-lung in Formosa, I had an opportunity of witnessing another very simple method of catching fish.   Every night at eight o'clock—an hour at which in China it is quite dark—the fishermen here go to the mouth of the river, or harbour as it may be more properly termed, in small open boats, the sterns of which are in the form of swallow-tails.   From the boats a large circular net is cast into the water.   In the centre of the circle formed on the surface of the water by the corks attached to the net, a boat takes up her position.   She is kept steady by a fisherman plying a pair of oars.   In the bows two men are stationed, whose duty it is to make a large blaze by setting on fire bundles of rattans.   Several other boats, containing two or three men each, are stationed outside the circle formed by the floats, and at a given word they commence to beat the water vigorously with long bamboo poles.   This is done for the purpose of terrifying the fish, which now leap wildly towards the bright fire burning in the bows of the centre boat, and become entangled in the net.   The net is then hoisted up, almost invariably filled with small fishes.   These fishermen are employed by several of the citizens of Ki-lung, who, it appears, have a monopoly of the fish trade in that part of the island of Formosa. The fish caught in this way are salted and sold in large quantities, not only at Formosa, but also in the province of Fo-kien. Large quantities of flying-fish are caught at San-o-bay by the aborigines of the islands in a similar manner. The scene of excitement which is witnessed nightly on the waters of Ki-lung almost beggars description. The night on which I went on the waters to witness it, there were not less than eight boats containing large fires, and surrounded by other boats containing men to beat the waters. It was very dark, and the fires cast a deep lurid glare not only over the surface of the waters, but over the sides of the adjacent hills : in this light the men engaged in beating the waters looked more like infuriated savages than inoffensive fishermen. At Hong-kong, and at Kow-loon, large quantities of fish are caught during the dark by means not very dissimilar to those which are adopted at Ki-lung. The only difference consists in the fact that the fishermen terrify the fish not by beating the surface of the water, but by a loud noise made by striking bamboo rods the one against the other.

In my voyages along the Yang-tsze Kiang I observed that dip-nets quite as large, in some cases much larger, than those which I have already described, were in constant use all along the banks of the river. The shears, however, to which they were attached were not erected in the bows of the vessels, but on the banks of the river, and were, in many instances, lowered and raised at the pleasure of the fishermen by means of windlasses. To many of these dip-nets live fish were bound by cords so as serve as decoys. Many of them, however, were provided with what may be termed wells, into which the decoy fish were thrown, where, unimpeded and uninjured, they were able to exhibit their natural movements.

Near each dip-net was erected a small hut, in which the fisherman sheltered himself from the inclemency of the weather during the time his net was immersed in the waters. In the upper part of the Poyang lake I found the dip-net much used. The shears, however, to which the nets were attached were not erected on the banks of the lake, but on extensive wooden platforms made to rest on thick stakes or posts. In many of the tidal rivers and estuaries stake-nets are used, and by means of them large quantities of fish are caught daily.

In the central provinces, the fishermen dye their nets, with the view of making them more durable. For this purpose a tanning bark is used, and it is not unusual to see numbers of poor fishermen holding on to the rafts of the wood merchant, which the rivers carry slowly onwards with the current, and stripping the timber of its bark. When their nets have ceased to be of use in catching fish they are sometimes suspended from the ceilings of houses for the purpose of warding off evil spirits. Sometimes they are spread over the beds on which sick men are laid, for the same purpose. They are also, in the south of China at all events, bound by means of small twine to the sails of junks, with the view of warding off baleful influences.

On the Poyang lake, and on the Yang-tsze river and its tributaries, and on the Grand Canal, I observed another method of catching fish. A large number of strong hooks were attached to short lines, each line being suspended from a thick cord of great length made fast at the ends to wooden buoys. These hooks were neither baited nor barbed, but were very sharp, and seemed intended to pierce and hold all fishes which might swim against them. On several of the mountain streams which flow towards the Yang-tsze river and the Poyang lake, I saw men spearing fish. They handled long tridents with great dexterity, seldom failing to strike their prey. On the Grand Canal, and near the city of Chun-tso-sheng, I saw men groping for fish with their hands, and was surprised to find how successful their efforts were. The fishermen on the Canton or Pearl river also practise this method in catching eels, and are able to remain under water for an astonishing time. In the southern provinces of China I have very seldom seen the Chinese fishing with the rod. In Formosa, however, where the rivers are in all probability better adapted for angling, I have frequently seen the Chinese throw their lines with a grace and skill worthy of Isaak Walton himself. On the banks of the Min, in the province of Fo-kien, and also on the northern branch of the Canton

DIP-NET.

FISHING WITH CORMORANTS.

river, anglers use a very strong rod, not more than four or five feet long. A large wheel is attached to it, and round this a line of twenty yards long is wound. With this clumsy rod the angler seldom fails to fill his creel. Worms are often used as bait. At Pekin the bluebottle fly is in great request for this purpose.

The most singular method, however, of capturing fish is by employing cormorants. In the river on which stands the city of T'sung-fa, the capital of an extensive district of Kwang-tung I saw fishermen capturing large quantities of fish by means of these birds; and again, in 1862, two years later, in a mountain river in the same district, I had another opportunity of witnessing this singular method. The fisherman, standing on a raft or catamaran, took up his position in the middle of the stream. On the catamaran there were stationed four or five cormorants, which at a signal dived into the waters to search for fish. To prevent the birds swallowing the fish, each had a band, or ring made of bamboo, round its neck. They swam with their prey to the catamaran, and the fisherman at once extracted the fishes from their throats, and deposited them in a creel; when fatigued the cormorants rested for a little on the raft, resuming their task whenever the fisherman gave the signal. In 1865, when on a visit to the Toong-ting and Poyang lakes, I saw large numbers of fish captured by means of cormorants. At the prefectoral city of Yau-chow Foo, in particular, which is on the banks of the Poyang lake, I noticed numbers of these birds fishing for their owners. The boats which the proprietors of the cormorants used there were not dissimilar in size and shape to the ferry boats in daily use on the Canton river. On the sides of each boat, running fore and aft, were roosts on which the cormorants perch when taken from the water. It appeared to me, however, that the birds employed in catching fish in the Poyang lake were not so industrious as were those which I saw on the rivers which flow through the district of T'sung-fa. At the city of Yau-chow Foo, and also on the Poyang lake, the fishermen were obliged, in order to make the cormorants dive, to beat the water with long bamboo poles; and blows were sometimes aimed at the birds themselves. When a fish had been caught, the fisherman received it from the bird in a small hand-net which he held out; and when he observed his birds to be in need of rest, he stretched forth his bamboo pole so that they might perch on it and be lifted into the boat. At Woo-see, Soo-chow, Hoo-chow, and other cities on the banks of the Grand Canal, I observed large numbers of these birds at work.

At Hang-chow, a prefectoral city at the southern extremity of the Grand Canal, I saw not less than five hundred cormorants engaged in fishing at one time, and within a space of one-eighth of a mile. Many of the birds were young and imperfectly trained; and when it happened that one of them caught a fish, he was instantly pursued by a great many other cormorants, each bent upon robbing him of his prize. A scene of great confusion and excitement was the result of this undisciplined behaviour. It was interesting to observe the ease with which, in the midst of disorder, each fisherman recognised his own birds. The boats they used differed from those which I have described as used elsewhere, being very light, and in shape not unlike canoes.

When sailing along the river Yang-tsze, my attention was directed to some men who were fishing for small fresh-water turtles. The rod used for this purpose is very similar to that which I have described as used by anglers on the banks of the river Min, and on those of the northern branch of the Canton river. To the end of the line are attached small hooks and a few leaden pellets. When the fisherman, who is generally seated on a stool with one leg, sees a turtle floating on the surface, he immediately takes aim and casts his line. The hooks penetrate the shell of the turtle in consequence of the impetus acquired by the pellets. The fisherman then hauls his prey out of the water by winding his line round the large wheel attached to his rod. When sailing along the small river or creek which flows under the walls of Nankin, I met with fishermen engaged in spearing fresh-water turtles. They were standing in their boats with a trident in each hand, probing the muddy waters in search of the turtles.

On the same river or creek I saw others similarly engaged; standing not in boats, but on vessels much like ordinary

SPEARING FRESH-WATER TURTLES.

washing tubs. Each fisherman was provided with one trident only, with which he not only speared the tortoises, but propelled and steadied his strange-looking craft.

Shrimp-fishing is also carried on to a great extent in many parts of the empire. In the Canton or Pearl river large draughts of shrimps are almost daily taken. In each boat employed there are two men, one of whom handles the oars, while the other stands in the bow and lowers into the water several small baskets, all attached to the same rope at a distance of two feet from each other. Each basket is baited with the sediment of wine. Attracted by the bait the shrimps enter the baskets, and when these have remained in the water during a reasonable period, they are drawn out and the captured fish emptied into a creel. There is, at all times, a great demand for these fish. Sometimes they are kept alive by the fishermen, as many epicures prefer eating live shrimps. They are served up for the table in a vessel which contains yellow wine, strong vinegar, and sesamum oil. Becoming tipsy, they leap about in an extraordinary manner : while they are in this condition they are eaten by Chinese epicures. The inhabitants of the northern and midland provinces are especially partial to live shrimps.

Oyster-beds are also very numerous, and, in season, yield a plentiful supply of oysters, both large and small. The Chinese never eat oysters in a raw state, thinking them food too cold for the stomach. They fry them, therefore, with flour. They eat small oysters which have been preserved with salt, without any further preparation. The shells are either used in building walls, or converted into lime. For this purpose large quantities of soft coal are procured, and threshed by means of strong flails into small dust. The shells are then mixed with the dust, and the mixture placed upon a fire of coals in the centre of a large kiln. The walls of the kiln, which are about thirty-six feet in circumference, are formed of bricks, strengthened or lined at intervals with strong bamboo poles. Close to the walls of each kiln is a large bellows, which has the appearance of a huge box. The fire is kept burning, and a uniform heat is maintained by the constant use of the bellows. After twelve hours, it is allowed to go out. When the lime to which the oyster-shells have been reduced is sufficiently cool, it is removed from the kiln to a large room and sprinkled with water. Lime is also made in this way of the shells of mussels. These' bivalves are also put to another use. Fishermen sometimes place in freshly-caught mussels six or seven small wooden or leaden representations of the Buddha of Longevity, or some other popular deity. The mussels are then thrown into a pond, where they are allowed to remain for some time. When they are taken out and re-opened the small figures are found to be coated with mother-of-pearl. The shells are then sold as objects of great curiosity ; and ignorant and credulous Chinese are sometimes prevailed upon to believe that the representations of the Buddha of Longevity are natural to the mollusc.

In the Canton river there are many extensive cockle-beds. These are re-stocked twice annually, that is, in the first and again in the twelfth month. At these periods large quantities of young cockles are brought from the district of Toong-koon and other places to Canton. Upon being cast into the beds especially set apart for them, they soon increase in size, and in the seventh month of the year they are removed and sold in large quantities as a great delicacy. The beds are strictly preserved, watchmen being at hand by day and night, not only to drive away poachers, but all kinds of water-fowl. The cockles, however, are often washed away in vast numbers by the strong tides, for which the Canton river is famous ; and many of the boat population may be seen daily dredging for them. While dredging, they keep the bows of their boats towards the rising or ebbing tide, and, in order that they may not be borne along too swiftly by the current, suspend large baskets or pieces of matting in the water, by means of ropes carefully made fast to the bows. Cockles, as well as oysters, are preserved by the Chinese by means of salt. As a rule, however, cockles are boiled and eaten when fresh. As the water in which they are boiled is supposed by the Cantonese to possess certain medicinal properties, it is used as a wash for the body by persons suffering from cutaneous diseases, and by those in particular who are recovering from small-pox. At the celebration of the New Year festivities cockles are in great demand, being regarded as lucky food. This superstition arises, I believe, from the fact that the word which stands for cockle in Chinese is not very dissimilar to that which in the same language signifies brightness, or shining—a property which is associated with happiness and prosperity, just as gloom has come to be a synonym for sadness and adversity. Lime is also made of cockle-shells, and, when mingled with oil, it constitutes a most excellent putty, used for cementing coffins, and in forming a surface for the frescoes with which the gables of temples and private residences are ornamented.

In China, women are engaged as well as men in the business of catching fish. When sailing on the waters of the Mou-hoi-tai lake, a number of large boats the crews of which were capturing fish with nets, were all women. In dredging for oysters, mussels, and cockles, women also are very frequently employed.

CHAPTER XXXI.

ABORIGINAL TRIBES.

In some parts of China, and in the islands of Formosa and Hai-nan, numerous tribes of the aboriginal inhabitants are to be found at the present day. They are distinguished by names which have a reference either to personal appearance, or to manners and customs. When China Proper was overrun and conquered by the reigning Tartar dynasty more than two hundred and forty years ago, the aborigines appear to have maintained their independence, as they do not wear the queue, or tail, which was imposed upon the Chinese as a mark of subjection. The independence of some of these tribes, however, was more or less curtailed in the middle of the eighteenth century by the Emperor Yung-ching, who declared war against them on some frivolous pretext. They now acknowledge the authority of the emperor, and are presided over by mandarins appointed by him. These officials, however, are selected from amongst the most enlightened members of the tribes themselves. Previous to the war which Yung-ching waged against the tribes, they were, it appears, scattered over a vast area. While some of them were occupying territory in the provinces of Kwang-tung and Kwang-si, others were dwelling on the plains, and in the mountain fastnesses of Kwei-chow. At the close of the war, most of the tribes dwelling in Kwang-tung and Kwang-si were compelled by Yung-ching to proceed to the northern frontiers of Kwei-chow, where they were told that lands bordering on those already occupied by similar tribes would afford them homes and occupation. It was, I believe, enacted at the same time that farms or fields belonging to the wild tribes already inhabiting that region, and offered for sale by them, should only be purchased by aborigines. In all probability, Yung-ching resolved to have the tribes located in one neighbourhood, so that he might crush them *en masse* should they become rebellious. The aborigines are, I believe, frequently oppressed by their Chinese neighbours. Not more than forty years ago, an official named Low Tin-chee, having represented to the Emperor Taou-kwang that the aborigines at Kom-suk had become rebellious, was ordered to wage war against them. Low Tin-chee marched into one of their principal settlements, and put to the sword more than forty thousand of the vanquished. This disgraceful war is said to have originated in a dispute between his followers or attendants, and the heads or elders of the tribe against which he marched. The followers of Low Tin-chee desired to appropriate to themselves a piece of ground which the tribe at Kom-suk had from time immemorial occupied as a market-place. This attempt met with a resistance at the hands of this tribe, and of the other tribes who espoused their cause, which eventually led to the loss of several hundred men by the Chinese, and to the slaughter of more than forty thousand of the aborigines.

The aborigines are regarded by the Chinese as a savage and barbarous race, and their manners and customs are very dissimilar. Among nearly all the tribes—one or two being an exception—the "go-between" is an unknown functionary, and each swain, as in more favoured countries, is at liberty to select a bride for himself. At the celebration of the New Year, the season when matrimonial alliances are entered upon by the members of the several tribes, it is customary for young men and maidens to resort to the fairs which are then held in the courtyards of the various temples. As the maidens pass to and fro looking at the various articles exposed for sale, the young men follow them; and when a swain sees a maiden who pleases him, he unhesitatingly enters into conversation with her, and eventually makes his proposal of marriage. The maiden having accepted him, the affianced pair resort to the temple and worship the idol; and, at the close of the religious ceremony, the accepted suitor accompanies his *fiancée* to the home of her parents, where certain necessary documents are prepared and signed. On the celebration of the marriage, no fewer than six days are devoted to convivial purposes. Should the union be blessed with offspring, the first-born is sent as an offering to the parents of the husband, and the second child is presented to the parents of the wife. The husband must reside for a period of seven or ten years with the parents of his wife. At the expiration of this period, he is at liberty to return to the home of his fathers; and, as it is usual for wives amongst the wealthy families of these wild clans to receive dowries—a custom unknown amongst the Chinese in general—and as these are usually bestowed on them during the lifetime of their parents, the portion of goods which falls to a wife is allotted to her on the day that she leaves her father's house to become an inmate of the house of her husband's father.

In the tribe called Luuk-Tuung-Ye-Yau, the bride-elect, attended by her bridesmaids and an umbrella-bearer, goes to the house of the bridegroom's parents, and is married there. After remaining three days as the guest of her father-in-law, she returns with her husband to the house of her parents, where the newly-married couple remain until their first child is born. They then, taking the child with them, return to the home of the husband's parents, where they continue to reside. In one of the tribes—the Long-Tchee-Miau—it is the duty of the father especially to attend to the wants of the children—an arrangement which is recognised in a singular funeral custom. When a father dies, the corpse is buried with the face twisted round—an attitude supposed to imply the father's watchfulness over his children in the world of shades.

On the death of a member of a tribe, it is usual, if the deceased has borne a good character, to carry his corpse, decorated with flowers, through the principal streets of the town or village in which he lived. In the winter months, this singular custom is observed on each of the three days immediately following the death; but during the summer months it is observed for one day only. Should the relatives of the deceased be wealthy his remains are inclosed in a stone coffin, or sarcophagus. The body, however, is not permitted to remain undisturbed in the grave for any length of time, its exhumation being deemed necessary on the ground that the surviving relatives are able by its appearance to predict their future good or bad fortune. If the face of the corpse be but slightly decayed, they conclude that a happy future awaits them. If it is much disfigured, they are forewarned of the approach of dire calamities. To this custom, the tribe called Luh-N'zeh-tsze do not conform. With them, the remains of a member of their tribe are exhumed when they have been in the grave for one year, not that the members of the family to which the deceased belonged may judge of the future that awaits them, but that the bones may be carefully washed. Should any one belonging to the family of the deceased become sick, the bones are at once exhumed and washed, without reference to the period of time which has expired since the interment. This is owing to a curious superstition that their health or sickness depends in a great measure upon the cleanliness or non-cleanliness of the bones of their departed relatives. They are called bone-washers in consequence by the Chinese. The tribe called Lan-Ku-Heh-Miau have also peculiar funeral customs. Among this people interment does not take place until a considerable time after death. In the interval, the bodies of their dead remain inclosed in coffins hermetically sealed; and only on the arrival of certain auspicious days, which, according to their astronomical calculations, do not occur more than four times in the year, do the living commit the bodies of their dead to the dust. A striking exception to the customs is to be found in the practice of the tribes called respectively, Chin-Tau-Hat-Loo, Kwoh-Lo, Paak-Kwoh-Lo, and Chang-chuuk-Luung-Ka, who do not bury their dead, but dispose of them by cremation. Previous to burning a dead body, the members of the tribe Kwoh-Lo cover it with a silk shroud, whereas the people of the tribe Paak-Kwoh-Lo use for similar purposes the hides either of horses, or cows, or sheep, or goats. Sutteeism is also practised, it being a law, as unalterable amongst one or more of the tribes as any of the laws of the ancient Medes and Persians, that all widows shall perish in the fires kindled for the consumption of the bodies of their departed husbands. The people of these tribes observe a fast of three months' duration on the death of a parent or grand-parent, or when the head of the tribe dies.

One of the most wealthy of the aboriginal tribes, called Shurii-Kia-Miau, is remarkable for the practice of a singular and revolting religious ceremony. The people possess a large temple in which is an idol in the form of a dog. They resort to this shrine on a certain day every year to worship. At this annual religious festival, it is, I believe, customary for the wealthy members of the tribe to entertain their poorer brethren at a banquet given in honour of one who has agreed, for a sum of money paid to his family, to allow himself to be offered as a sacrifice on the altar of the dog idol. At the end of the banquet, the victim, having drunk wine freely, is put to death before the idol. This people believe that, were they to neglect this right, they would be visited with pestilence, famine, or the sword. The wealth which it is said they possess, is derived in great measure from traffic in salt, which they place not in barrels or bags, but in large tubes formed of the stems of bamboo-trees. Among some of the other tribes, another practice is resorted to as a protection against pestilence. A man of great muscular strength is selected to act the part of a scape-goat. Having besmeared his face with paint, he performs all sorts of gesticulations and mummeries, with the view of entic-ing all pestilential and obnoxious influences to attach themselves to him only. He is assisted by a priest. At the conclusion of these proceedings the scapegoat, hotly pursued by many persons of both sexes beating gongs and tom-toms, is driven with great haste out of the town or village.

In the third month of every year a great festival takes place, in which many of the tribes take part. It is held by way of a general rejoicing over what these people believe to be a total annihilation of the ills of the past twelve months. This is supposed to be effected by the performance of the following ceremony. A large earthenware jar is filled with gunpowder, stones, and pieces of iron, and then buried in the earth. A train of gunpowder, communicating with the vase, is then laid.

A match being applied, the explosion which ensues scatters the vase with its contents to the four winds. The stones and pieces of iron represent the ills and disasters of the past twelve months, and the dispersion of them by the explosion is supposed to remove the unpleasant realities of which they are symbols. This festival is attended with much conviviality and drunkenness. An ingenious mode of inducing men to drink is resorted to on these occasions. An oil-lamp is duly lighted, and then quickly passed by the revellers round the table. One of them walks round and endeavours to blow it out as it is passed from hand to hand. Should he succeed, the person in whose hands the lamp happens to be when it is extinguished must empty a bumper of wine.

Among many of the tribes a species of bull-fight is indulged in as a pastime. The farmers of one tribe match their bulls against those belonging to their neighbours, and, at a certain season of the year, the poor beasts, infuriated by an intoxicating drink, are brought into the arena to afford amusement to a large concourse of spectators. The tribes bring these games, which extend over several days, to a close by the sacrifice of the conquering bull to one of their principal deities.[1]

It is worthy of remark that one of the aboriginal tribes is presided over by a woman. To this female sovereign or ruler, the title Noi-Tak is applied by her subjects, from whom she receives the most profound respect; and the tribe is known under the name of Nue'-Koon, or the woman-governed people. The right or privilege of ruling over this tribe is confined to the female descendants of one family, so that, in the case of the death of a ruler, there is little probability of a dispute arising as to the descendant to whom the right of succession belongs. The Chinese in general, who think it strange that Great Britain and other European kingdoms in which the Salic law does not prevail, should occasionally be governed by a female sovereign, are somewhat disposed to regard the inhabitants of such

---

[1] The Paak Miau are said to devote special attention to the selection and training of bulls with hard craniums and strong, well-pointed horns for this cruel pastime. This rude people find their chief sport in hunting deer and other wild animals, which they pursue, armed with spears, either on horseback or on foot.

countries as being little, if at all, superior to the wild tribe of Nue'-Koon.

The aboriginal tribes which I have been describing have the reputation of being very good agriculturists, and are further famous for their breed of cattle.[1] The labourers are very industrious, and capable of undergoing great bodily fatigue. The plough, which in the south of China is drawn by buffaloes or bullocks, and in the north by horses or mules or asses, as well as by the animals just mentioned, is, in some of the districts occupied by wild tribes, dragged by male and female peasants. This custom is especially practised by the tribe called Yae-Tau-Miau. The power which the farmer is permitted to exercise over his labourers is very great. When a labourer engages to serve a master, an agreement is drawn up in which the age of the servant, the period of time which he agrees to serve, and the penalty to which he exposes himself should he desert, are carefully noted. The punishment which, as a rule, is undergone by a runaway slave is so severe, as not unfrequently to be fatal. The manufacture and dyeing of linen or cloth also afford employment to many of the tribes. Of the tribes who weave webs of cloth, that which is styled Shui-Ka-Miau is, perhaps, the most famous.

In the province of Kwang-tung various aboriginal tribes are still to be found. The prefecture of Lin-shan, which is one of the political divisions of this province, contains in all probability the greatest number of such uncivilized people. The tribes dwelling in this prefecture are said to occupy not less than eight distinct settlements, five tribes being located in the eastern, and three in the western division of the prefecture. It was formerly customary for these aborigines, also, to rule themselves, and their plan was very simple. One hundred men constituted one *curia*, or company. Each *curia* was presided over by an

---

[1] An exception to this general description of the aborigines is to be found in the condition of the Tching-Miau, who are lamentably ignorant of agriculture, and subsist in a great measure on the wild fruits of the earth. The Ping-Faat-Miau, it may be added, not unfrequently feast on dog's flesh. The Paak-Kwoh-Lo, by whom it would seem creatures of almost every kind are eaten, uniformly cook their food in frying-pans, and eat it, as probably do many of the other tribes, by using their hands instead of chop-sticks or forks.

officer who may be termed a centurion rather than a *curia ;* and
to the head, or heads of the tribe, each centurion was called
upon to pay proper respect, and to manifest at all times due
submission. The affairs of the tribe called Kwoh-Lo are, or
were, directed by nine elders chosen from the people. In the
twelfth year of the reign of the Emperor Taou-kwang, the
various tribes dwelling in the prefecture of Lin-shan rose in
arms against their Chinese neighbours, and by their depredations
made themselves particularly obnoxious to the governor-general
of the province. To suppress what threatened to be a most
serious and perplexing rising, his excellency requested Ha-
Foong-O, the Tartar general at the time, to proceed with a
military force against these savage hordes. After a few engagements, in which he defeated their undisciplined troops, he
succeeded in establishing peace. At the close of this war, an
imperial mandate was issued directing that in the eastern
division of the prefecture each settlement should henceforth
be under the administration of a president, a vice-president,
and eight assistants ; and that, in the western division, each
settlement should henceforth be under the administration
of a president and four assistants. These officers, who are
appointed by the Imperial Government, are, all of them, selected
from amongst the most enlightened and intelligent of the tribes
themselves. At Yang-shang, in the prefecture of Wei-chow,
another political division of Kwang-tung, various aboriginal
settlements are also to be found, each of which, as is the case
with the tribes in the western division of Lin-shan, is under
the administration of a native president who holds his office
under the Imperial Government, and who is assisted by four
subordinate officials.

It is also stated that there are aborigines in the districts
of Luung-Moon, Foong-Chuen, Koo-yu, Yaong-chien, Sze-woee,
Kwong-hing, Yau-ping, Hoi-kin, Hop-poo, Lo-ting, Toong-on,
Si-ning, Pok-lo, Tsang-sheng, Yong-kong, Yoong-yuen, Huk-
kong, and Lok-chaong. In passing through some of these
districts I learned that the aborigines found in them, in the
great majority of cases, form no longer distinct tribes, having
adopted the manners and customs of their Chinese neighbours.

We now come to consider the aborigines who are to be found in Formosa. Among the tribes of this island there is great diversity as to their character and mode of life. While some are kind and gentle, others are singularly savage and inhuman. Some support themselves by agriculture, and the employments of a peaceable community; others, like the Song-Miau, and Hoo-Loo tribes—the most barbarous of these clans—live by the spoils of the chase, and by their lawless and predatory practices on all travellers crossing their path. Among several of the tribes the manufacture and dyeing of cloth is carried on. A specimen of this manufacture which I have in my possession is a fabric of very strong linen. The only part of the body, however, which the male savages in the north of Formosa cover is the loins. The women also cover their breasts. Towards the Chinese, and indeed towards all foreigners, the more savage tribes—among whom the Mow-Tau are conspicuous for their cruelty—entertain a most deadly hatred, which they evince by putting to death all who are so unfortunate as to fall into their hands.

The two tribes which constitute the aboriginal population of the island of Hai-nan are located in the several prefectures of King-chow, G'nai-chow, and Tam-chow. To one of them the name Shang-Lai, or "secluded tribe," is given, and its people are said to be dull, stupid, and barbarous. As agriculturists, however, they are said to be very industrious, but very ignorant. A former governor-general of Canton, who was named Loo Kwan, took great interest in the welfare of this tribe, and appointed persons well acquainted with agricultural pursuits to teach them how to farm their lands to the greatest advantage. At the suggestion of Loo Kwan their attention was much directed to irrigation. The people of this tribe seldom leave their mountain fastnesses, and live for the most part in caves and dens. The other tribe is known by the name of Shuk-Lai, or "bold tribe," and its people are said to be probably the most expert thieves on the face of the earth. Quarrels of a serious nature at one time took place between the aborigines and the Chinese, by the latter of whom the island is now almost entirely overrun; and, in the thirteenth year of the reign of the Emperor

Taou-kwang, the Shuk-Lai tribe waged a fierce war against the Chinese inhabitants of Hai-nan. It was owing, it is said, to the fact that the Chinese would insist upon visiting the mountain fastnesses of the aborigines for the purpose of felling trees, which the latter had always regarded as their own property. When the Chinese had brought this war to a successful termination, the emperor, to prevent, if possible, any future outbreak, placed an important officer, or magistrate, to rule over each tribe.

Many of the best disposed members of the tribes enrolled themselves as soldiers under the imperial standard, and faithfully promised that they would do all in their power to assist the magistrates in maintaining peace and order. At the same time, that the aborigines and the Chinese might come into contact as seldom as possible, a law was enacted that the aborigines should not pass beyond the frontiers of the district, or prefecture, in which their respective tribes were located, and that any transgression should be visited with a severe penalty. That they might be at liberty to visit their markets for purposes of trade, it was ordered that, at least, in the prefecture of Tam-chow, the several markets of San-yaong, Nam-toong, and Tewnam should be open to the Shuk-lai tribe. It was also ordained that these markets should be kept open at one time during the course of five successive days. So strict is the law which was framed at the time I speak of to prevent uprisings of the wild tribes, that each man as he enters the market is obliged to record his name at an office for the purpose. During the time when the markets or fairs are held, soldiers armed with spears are quartered in barracks not far distant, and the market is no sooner brought to a close than all the aborigines are ordered to their respective homes. At the close of each year, when the wild tribes have little or no occupation, great vigilance over them is exercised. For this purpose, five companies of Chinese militiamen, or " braves " are, I believe, placed under arms. For the purpose of defraying the expense which is incurred by keeping this force in arms during the winter months, a sum of $20,000 was, in the fifteenth year of the reign of Taou-kwang, placed at a high rate of interest in the hands of the proprietors of certain pawnshops, which stand in the districts of Pun-yu and Nam-hoi. The daily pay of a militiaman does not exceed forty cash, and the daily pay of each officer does not exceed five hundred cash. As the wild tribes are called upon to pay a land-tax, it might have been expected that the pay of the militiamen and their officers would have far exceeded these respective sums; but the lands which the tribes occupy are as a rule unproductive, and doubtless the people are very often defaulters. It would at all events appear that they are very poor, as there is a law which empowers the Chinese government to advance at each seed time a certain number of *shaaks* of rice for seed. This loan the aborigines repay, if possible, to the government, but without interest.

On the walls of the public hall of each village occupied by the aborigines the following code of laws is supposed by the Chinese government to occupy a prominent place :—

(1.) The elders of each wild tribe, and only such persons, shall receive at the hands of the wild people, and pay to the mandarins, the land-taxes due on the part of such people to the Imperial Government.

(2.) Should any person or persons of the wild tribes violate the law, such person or persons shall be apprehended by the guards or soldiers who are appointed by the government to watch over them.

(3.) A Chinese shall on no account lend money to the aborigines.

(4.) A Chinese shall not, when selling goods to the aborigines, demand for such goods an unreasonable price.

(5.) The aborigines shall not on any account be permitted to have fire-arms in their possession.

(6.) Blacksmiths who are detected making fire-arms for the use and service of the aborigines shall be severely punished.

(7.) Above the door of the dwelling-house of each aboriginal householder a notice shall be posted, stating that *for strangers and visitors* there is no accommodation within.

(8.) All aborigines who form themselves into *banditti* for the purpose of plundering their neighbours shall be severely punished.

(9.) The presidents, or elders, of the aborigines shall make it their duty to see that those who live under their rule are regularly taught to handle the plough, to fell timber, &c.

(10.) All aborigines receiving protection at the hands of the Emperor of China shall throw aside their rude ornaments, and shall shave their heads, and adopt the dress, manners, and customs of the Chinese.

(11.) Any Chinese who kills an aboriginal who does not conform to the preceding law shall receive a free pardon.

(12.) The chief of each tribe of aborigines shall communicate once in every month with the ruler of the district within the frontiers of which the tribe is located.

It was at one time customary, and may be so still, for Chinese who had violated the laws of their country to seek a refuge amongst these tribes; and a further rule was established to the effect, that all aborigines who assist the Emperor in apprehending and bringing to justice criminals of all classes, or who assist His Imperial Majesty in war, shall receive rank not higher than the fourth degree; that this rank shall be hereditary throughout six generations; and that the age at which a son shall be entitled to inherit the rank of his father shall be sixteen years and upwards. The power rests with the provisional treasurer to examine the claims of all who make application for this rank, and to confer it upon them, should he find grounds for doing so.

CHAPTER XXXII.

PHYSICAL FEATURES.

CHINA is a great basin surrounded by lofty mountains on the north-west and south-west, with the sea on the south and south-east. The surface thus inclosed is divided into hilly and champaign country. In the interior there are mountains some of which are of great height. The Loo Shan mountains, for example, five hundred miles from the sea-coast, include five high angular peaks, each of which is not less than five thousand feet above the level of the sea. Seen from Nam-kan Foo on the banks of the Poyang lake, their lofty summits tower grandly into the sky. On the northern frontier of the midland province of Hoonam, there is a range of mountains which appeared to me to be more than six thousand feet high. They were so far off, however, that a journey to them was out of the question. In the northern[1] and midland provinces the mountains are frequently covered with snow in winter. It is seldom very deep, and soon disappears. In the southern provinces a fall of snow is almost unknown.

There are several mountains and hills in China which have, for various reasons, been regarded as sacred from the earliest times. In spring and autumn these are worshipped by the government officials, and sacrifices are offered to them. The

---

[1] In the city of Pekin and its environs it is usual for the people to fill coarse earthenware jars with snow, and hermetically seal them. Snow-water is greatly valued there as a febrifuge, and as a lotion for sore eyes. In the villages at the base of the mountains to the north of Pekin, I observed that the majority of the inhabitants were suffering from *gottre*.

dreadful typhoon, which, on the 27th of July, 1862, visited the city of Canton, was attributed to the angry spirit of Kwei-foong Shan, a sacred mountain in the district of San-woee. New titles of honour have, I believe, been conferred upon some of the sacred mountains by various sovereigns of the reigning dynasty.

In the picturesque ruggedness of its mountain passes China is not probably inferior to any other country. My journey from Pekin to Chan-chee-kow led me through the famous pass of Nan-kow. It is fifteen English miles in length, and is very narrow. The portion which extends from Nan-kow to Cha-tan is, strictly speaking, called the Kwan-kea pass. The first section consists of limestone hills, the latter portion being granitic. In the middle of the pass is a large monumental arch which the Tartars erected some centuries ago to commemorate a decisive victory obtained over the Chinese in the early part of the thirteenth century by the famous Genghis Khan. Various representations are carved on the arch, and inscriptions, in five different languages, give an account of the triumph of the warlike hordes of Tartary over the peace-loving myriads of China. Such arches, I believe, are to be found in many of the cities and towns of Mongolia. On my return from Inner Mongolia to Pekin, the road between the city of Chun-poo and Jehol led me through the short but beautiful mountain pass of Lan-chee-leang-ko.

Of the plains of China, some are of vast extent. The great plain which occupies the north-east part of the empire is six hundred and fifty miles long, and extends from the great wall in the north to the south of the provinces of Ngan-hui and Kiang-soo. The breadth of this plain varies from one hundred and fifty to two hundred miles. Its amazing fertility tempted the Tartar hordes to quit the colder latitudes of their mountain fastnesses, and make predatory incursions into the territories of their Chinese neighbours, and it was from such incursions that the Chinese sought to protect themselves by the erection of a stupendous walled frontier. I passed this vast alluvial plain on the left, on my way from Pekin to Sha-ho, and beyond this city to Nan-kow. On leaving the frontier city of Chan-chee-kow

I crossed the extensive rolling plain of inner Mongolia, as far as
the town of Lama-miou. The monotony of the journey was
broken at intervals by numerous Mongolian encampments, in
the vicinity of which flocks of sheep, herds of cattle, and
droves of horses were quietly grazing. At frequent intervals
I noticed large numbers of prairie squirrels, some of which
were singularly spotted. At brooks or pools of water I occasionally saw large wading birds. Under what name these birds
were recognized in the western world was to me at the time a
matter of some dubiety ; but on since paying a visit to the
attractive gardens of the Zoological Society of London, I at
once recognized in their precincts my magnificent, long-legged,
wading friend of Mongolia. The species in question is known
as the Mantchurian Crane (*Grus montignesia*, Bp.).[1] The journey
was made memorable to me by the spectacle of several striking
mirages. In one of them the optical illusion was so complete
that for a time we all believed that we were approaching a
large sheet of water. As the reflection was vertical, the
objects which we saw reflected were of course reversed, as
they would have been if mirrored in a lake.

There are few countries in the world that are so well watered
as China. Probably the only country which can at all compare
with it in this respect is the United States of America. There
are three principal rivers, the Yang-tsze Kiang, or child of the
ocean; the Hoang Ho or yellow river, and the Chu Kiang or
pearl river. The largest of these is the Yang-tsze Kiang, or
child of the ocean. Its source is in the north west of Great
Thibet, whence it flows in a direct line with the neighbouring
range of mountains, until, by a flexure towards the north, it
enters China proper, through the very centre of which it pursues
its course, skirting extensive and fertile plains, and emptying
itself finally into the Eastern sea. Its length is said to be
nearly two thousand two hundred miles. Its breadth may be
estimated in some parts at a mile and a half. At a distance of one

---

[1] "It is much to be regretted," says the official *Guide to the Gardens*, "that
only one individual of this fine crane is now left in the Society's collection. No
more valuable present could be made by the Society's correspondents in China
than additional specimens of this species."

hundred miles from the sea, it is almost three miles broad.   This noble river is studded with alluvial islands, the largest of which, Tsung-ming, situated at its mouth, ‡s not less than sixty miles in length and eighteen in breadth.   The banks of the Yang-tsze are crowded with towns and villages, the most famous of which are Nankin, and the new treaty port, Hankow.   A large export and import business is now carried on at Hankow between Chinese and European merchants.

The Hoang Ho or Yellow River takes its rise in Chinese Tartary to the north of the mountains of Thibet. Its course is very tortuous.   Making a great bend in a northerly direction, it pursues its way for many miles beyond the Great Wall into Tartary.   It again enters China Proper at Loo-Meoo-Voan, and, flowing nearly four hundred miles in a southerly direction, divides the provinces of Shan-si and Shen-si.   Near latitude 35°, it makes a sharp turn to the eastward and flows through the provinces of Ho-nan and Kiang-soo, until it mingles its waters with those of the Eastern Sea.   The current of the Hoang Ho is very rapid, and it is subject to frequent overflowings.   A short time ago, in the vicinity of Howchiatin, it burst the vast embankments by which it was restrained.   The destruction of life and property was immense.   The officials and inhabitants of Howchiatin were very active in replacing the embankments, and the work must have been speedily effected, for in the *Pekin Gazettes* of the 23rd and 24th of April, 1872, we find memorials to the Throne from the Governor of the province of Shan-tung respecting its completion.   In an edict subsequently issued by the Emperor, the Governor of Shan-tung was highly commended for the zeal and ability he had displayed, and thirty other mandarins were honoured with titles and peacock's feathers.   With the view of appeasing the river-god, the Emperor sent him as an offering, six sticks of incense.   Taking into consideration the sinuosities of the Hoang Ho, it cannot, in point of length, be far inferior to the Yang-tsze Kiang.

The Chu Kiang or Pearl River, or, as it is more frequently called, the Canton river, is not nearly so large as the Yang-tsze Kiang or the Hoang Ho.   It is, however, a river of considerable length, and is of great importance.   Innumerable vessels of all sizes, and of almost every kind of naval architecture, trade on its waters, and carry rich freights of almost every kind of merchandise to different parts of the provinces of Kwang-tung and Kwang-si. There are, strictly speaking, three branches of this river, namely, the great western branch which is called the Kan Kiang; the Pei Kiang or northern branch; and the Tong Kiang or eastern branch. Until 1859, the Kan Kiang or western branch was, except by name, quite unknown to foreign residents in China. In the course of this year, a gunboat expedition organized for the purpose of surveying it, penetrated as far as the prefectoral or frontier town of Woo-chow Foo in the province of Kwang-si. A very correct chart was the result. The Kan Kiang, the course of which I followed to the district city of Teng-yune, which is fifty English miles beyond the prefectoral city of Woo-chow Foo, flows through mountain scenery of great grandeur.

At some points of its course the mountains form narrow gorges. At others they admit of the river spreading into lakes, as large as those which add so much to the beauty of Cumberland and Westmoreland. One of its most magnificent gorges is that which foreigners call the Shu-hing pass in consequence of its close proximity to the prefectoral city of Shu-hing, the ancient capital of the province. The Chinese call it Foo-yung-hap. It is four miles in length, and is formed by mountains eighteen hundred feet high. Between their rugged and almost precipitous sides the waters rush with the impetuosity of a vast mountain torrent. After passing the frontier city of Woo-chow Foo, or Eng-chow Foo, as it is sometimes called, the voyager arrives at the first of the eighteen famous rapids. During the journey to Teng-yune I had to pass over nine of these cataracts. They are formed of extensive ledges of basaltic rocks, by which the river, certainly a mile in breadth, is traversed at intervals. At such points the navigation is attended with considerable risk. The narrow passages by which vessels can pass and repass with comparative safety are indicated by beacons, or cairns, erected on the rocks in the bed of the river. In the rainy seasons the junkmen must find it almost impossible to tow their vessels against its torrent. The well-manned craft in which I sailed, did not, in the dry season, make more than ten English miles per day. According to Chinese accounts, the names which are given to the Canton or Pearl river are "legion," almost every reach having its peculiar name. For example, the portion which extends from Whampoa to Bocca Tigris is called Foo-moon, that which flows from Canton to Whampoa is termed the Pearl river; that which flows from beyond Shek-moon towards the provincial capital, is known as the Covetous river; and the famous branch of the river, known to foreigners as the Macao passage, is called the White Goose river by the Chinese. The singular designation of the Covetous river carries us back many centuries, when it was believed that every one who drank its waters, or used them for culinary purposes, was in danger of becoming possessed by an irresistible desire to appropriate the goods of others. No well-principled person would drink of the Covetous river. In the reign, however, of Kien Wan, of the Tung-Tsin dynasty (A.D. 366), Woo Yan-chee, the Governor of the province of Kwang-tung, resolved to prove to the people the absurdity of such a notion. He proceeded in solemn state to Shek-moon, and publicly drank copious draughts of the dreaded water. By a subsequent faithful discharge of the duties of his responsible office, he succeeded in convincing his superstitious subjects, that, although he had done so, he was still able to respect the distinction between *meum* and *tuum*.

Amongst rivers of less note, perhaps the most important are the Peiho, the Min, and the Shanghai, which are open to foreign ships. Not one of the numerous rivers of China probably flows through scenery more singularly beautiful than that through which the Min directs its course. Of what may be termed mountain rivers, there are vast numbers, most of them more or less navigated by boats or vessels of light draught. One of the most interesting streams of this kind in the South of China is that upon the banks of which stand the district cities of Loong-moon-yune, and Tang-sheng. It empties itself into the Canton river at a point not far from the Polo temple in the vicinity of the port of Whampoa. On one occasion, I spent seven days upon this river. Its rapids are, I think, more formidable than those of the western branch of the Canton river.

They seemed to me to realize the familiar descriptions of the rapids of Canada and America. Another mountain river which I navigated is that on the banks of which stands the town of Kin-tee-ching, so famous for its potteries. This stream empties itself into the Poyang lake. In its course from Kin-tee-ching to Kwan-gan, it is inclosed by mountains, some of which are from eighteen hundred to two thousand feet high. At one part of its course it assumes the appearance of a small lake. When travelling in Inner Mongolia, I forded several shallow mountain-rivers, and was greatly impressed with the grandeur of the scenery through which they flowed. One of these streams, called, I believe, the " Opposing river," is so sinuous in one part of its course where it meanders between high lands at no great distance from each other, that in one day's travel I had to ford it not less than thirty times.

The canals of China are very numerous. The Grand or Imperial Canal, which is by far the most important, was con-structed as early as the seventh century, and in the thirteenth century it was extended. It traverses the great and fertile plain in the north east of the Empire, which I have already described. Commencing at the town of Hang-chow Foo, 30° N. lat., it flows— for in very few places can it be said to be without a perceptible current—over a distance of seven hundred miles to the city of Lin-tchin Chow, where it unites with the river Oo Ho. Its breadth is at some points very considerable, in other parts it is very narrow. So numerous are the drains and creeks which have been made to communicate with it at many points of its course, that it plays a most important part in the drainage and irrigation of the surrounding lands. Like all the rivers of China, its banks are lined with cities, towns, and villages. Owing to the extreme richness of its soil, and the advantages which it derives from internal navigation, the great plain through which it passes, has become one of the most thickly inhabited and flourishing parts of the Chinese empire.

The rivers and canals are guarded, at many points, by high banks, with the view of preventing inundations. These embank-ments—some of which are constructed of earth, others of stone —are standing monuments of the energy and enterprise of the

Chinese of past ages. On various branches of the Canton river I have seen many vast works of this nature. The most important are at Lew-ko-koong, Kok-ki, and Chuk-kee-tow. Near Si-chu-shan there is a large mud embankment. It was for many years kept in repair by the interest arising from the sum of eighty-thousand taels, which was deposited for this purpose by the emperor Ka-hing, at a high rate of interest, in the numerous pawn shops of Canton. Not long afterwards, a rich citizen of Canton, named Eng Yune-lan, expended one hundred thousand taels of silver in strengthening this mud embankment by facing it with stones. The emperor Ka-hing rewarded him with high literary rank. Not far from Canton there is a similar embankment called Sheak-kok-why. Were this to give way, the waters of the Pearl river would—so say the Cantonese—inundate the western districts of their ancient city. I saw other dykes of this kind at Foong-lok-why and Sze-mi-kow in the silk districts of Kwang-tung. To reach the top of these banks from the river, one has in some cases to ascend sixty or seventy granite steps. The vast plains through which the Yang-tsze directs its course are protected at intervals by embankments of a similar nature. A party of travellers who in 1861 endeavoured to go overland from China to India, described themselves, in a letter to the editor of the *North China Herald,* " as reaching the immense plain, which, indeed, may be said to extend the whole distance from Hankow to the north side of the Yang-tsze," and finding it " so low that inundation is only prevented by the existence of embankments (enormous works) of great age." These embankments occasionally give way, and when they do so the results are most calamitous. In the thirteenth year of the reign of the emperor Taou-kwang, an embankment named Sheak-kok-why, which incloses a branch of the Canton river, gave way, and the flood extended as far as the streets of the western suburbs of Canton. In the twenty-third year of the same reign, a bank, named Lew-ko-koong, which confines the river Han to its course through a portion of Kwang-tung, gave way, and the waters of the Han deluged the entire district of Hoi-yong. The emperor is said to have advanced the munificent sum of twenty-four thousand taels for the repair of this embankment. In 1864, this embankment once more gave way, and the waters swept several villages from the face of the earth. A box which was floating on the surface was found to contain a male child of a few months old. By the side of this babe, who was asleep, a Chinese purse containing ten dollars had been placed, doubtless by anxious parents, for the support of the hope of the family. The rivers and creeks often overflow their banks, owing to the periodical heavy rains. In 1871 there was great distress in various parts of the empire from this cause.

In the northern part of the empire there was great distress during the same summer owing to the incessant rains causing rivers to overflow. A "Hongkong tourist," writing to the editor of the *China Mail*, from Tien-tsin on the 25th of August, 1871, says of such an inundation :—

"About twenty-five miles up the river its fearful ravages are seen in fallen houses and flooded fields; but it is only on nearing Tien-tsin that its extent can be appreciated, where beyond the raised bank there is nothing to be seen indicating dry land save a few trees and clay cones indicating the burial-places of the dead, or a small island with the broken mud walls of deserted houses. On our right and left as far as the eye can reach one can see nothing but a vast expanse of water, dotted here and there with the sails of trading junks that have left the tortuous course of the river, and are sailing in a direct course for Tientsin. It requires but one or two incidents to convey an idea of the suffering of the poor villagers. It was raining heavily during the entire day. I noticed at one place a group of houses that had fallen down, and among the damp clay ruins I could see a miserable woman and her children crouched beneath a mat covering, exposed not only to the damp of the cold clay, but to the drenching rain that filtered through the temporary cover. It requires no effort of fancy to picture the sufferings of these poor creatures, deprived of shelter from the rain and the cold night winds, and of the means of sustenance. This is but one instance among thousands, and the result has, in some cases been but too clearly shown in the bodies that have been seen floating down the stream. The richest crop in many places is lost—the crop on which the people depend for food and fuel during the winter. Gardens and orchards are submerged, and their position only indicated by the withered branches of the peach trees that rise above the water. Horses and cattle are seen clustering on small islands, where the last blade of grass has been consumed, or wading in the water seeking in vain for food.

"Thousands of the suffering villagers have flocked to Tien-tsin, and have sought a temporary shelter on the walls, where they are furnished with twenty cash a-day a-piece, and a small supply of food.

"One of the most revolting aspects of the flood is that around Tien-tsin. It literally submerges a *plaine des tombeaux*, where tens of thousands of graves have been disturbed by the watery element. We saw coffins adrift, and coffins fixed down with stakes to the plain and moored to trees; and in some instances, they have been seen burst open and the contents distributed. When one reflects that this is the water used by all, it makes one tremble to think of the probable results of imbibing such impurity.

"I will now conclude my letter by suggesting that the matter should be placed before the wealthy Chinese of Canton and Hongkong, with a view to their contributing something for the relief of their suffering countrymen of the north, and that if an effort is to be made it should be done promptly to prevent the ravages of the flood being followed by famine."—*China Mail, Hongkong*, Sept. 9, 1871.

Meanwhile, his imperial Majesty Tung-chee, alarmed at the incessant rains, issued an imperial edict in which the princes of the blood royal were commanded to offer sacrifices and prayers for fine weather at various temples; and the Emperor arranged to do so himself at the "Temple in honour of the Highest."

Another imperial edict, on the memorial of one Ha Tung-shin, ordered a day of universal prayer to the gods on the 20th day of the eighth month (Sept. 4, 1871), and directed that officials should dole out alms with a liberal hand to the sufferers in their respective districts. Imperial messages were sent to all judges and magistrates requesting them to be merciful in the administration of justice, and to enter upon all cases for trial without any further delay, in order that innocent persons might be set at liberty.

Not a few of the rivers are regarded as sacred, and sacrifices of a sheep and a pig are offered to them, in some instances twice annually. To each of these rivers an imperial communication is at the same time addressed. This is read aloud by a herald in the supposed hearing of the genius or spirit of the river, and is then cast into the flames of a sacred fire, with a view to its being conveyed officially to the spirit.

So far as I know, the only river on which a bore or tidal wave occurs is the Tchen-tang, near the mouth of which stands the important city of Hang-chow. The height of the wave increases by degrees until it reaches the city of Hang-chow, when it subsides. No junks can stem this vast rolling wall of water, which is sometimes ten, sometimes as much as fourteen English feet high. It occurs at spring tides only, and more especially at those which flow during the seventh month of the year, so that the Chinese are, of course, able to calculate on its coming, and to save themselves and their craft from destruction.

Many of the rivers are interrupted in their course by picturesque waterfalls. At a village called Pak-shum-chi, in the Tsung-fa district of Kwang-tung, a stream falls from a height of two hundred English feet. In the dry season of the year its volume is exceedingly small. Water from this stream is conveyed by long lines of bamboo tubes to the doors of the inhabitants of the village. Near the Poyang lake, and about four English miles from Nankan Foo, the capital city of the prefecture of that name, I saw two waterfalls formed by streams rushing over the precipitous sides of the Loo Shan mountains. The water forming what the Chinese call the Greater Fall, sweeps in an unbroken torrent over a rock two hundred feet high. The Lesser Fall is equally high, but it is not so grand. Its waters are interrupted in their descent by a rocky projection. These falls ought to be visited either during the former or the latter rains. In the dry season they are not by any means imposing. The summit of the Greater Waterfall is reached by a climb of one thousand two hundred feet up the almost precipitous side of a spur of the Loo Shan range, and it commands a magnificent view of the Poyang lake, and of the valley by which at this point the Loo Shan mountains are approached. At the foot of the Lesser Fall there is a pool clear as crystal, from which the water gently glides over rocks to the Poyang lake. Near this pool, a Chinese bower affords one a pleasant shelter from the rays of a burning sun. Chinese characters, expressive of the grandeur and sublimity of the surrounding scenery are carved on the rocks. At the foot of the smaller fall, there was once a large Buddhist monastery, the ruins of which still testify to its former extent and beauty. There are ruins of a Buddhist monastery at the top of the Greater Waterfall, and in these we found two or three friars seeking an asylum from the cares of the world. Near Snowy Valley, which is in the Fung-hwha district of Chit-kong, there are three waterfalls. The first, which is immediately below the valley, is two hundred and forty feet high ; while the third, further on, is about four hundred feet high.

Of the lakes of China, which are very numerous, the principal are the Poyang Hoo, the Toon-ting Hoo, and the Tai Hoo. The two former are on the south bank of the river Yang-tsze, the Poyang being in the province of Kiang-si, 116° E. long., and the Toon-ting Hoo, in the province of Hoonam, 113° E. long. As they closely adjoin the river Yang-tsze, they form a receptacle for its superfluous waters, and prevent its inundations being so extensive as those of the Hoang Ho. The Poyang lake is said to be nearly three hundred miles in length during the rainy season, and as it receives the *débris* and superfluous waters not only of the Yang-tsze Kiang, but of other rivers of less magnitude, a great portion of the country by which it is bordered is a perfect morass. This is especially the case on the north-east margin of the lake, and it accounts for the absence of luxuriant vegetation, which the traveller naturally expects to find in a country verging so closely on the tropics. The waters of this lake are sometimes lashed by sudden tempests into a sea of foaming billows. Indeed, so great is the violence with which they roll against the bank on which Nan-kan Foo stands, that a strong stone harbour of refuge for vessels has been provided. In the dry season the waters abate with great rapidity, and the Poyang Hoo resembles not so much a lake as a river winding its course towards the Yang-tsze between low banks of mud. From the summit of the Shang-gang pagoda, in the vicinity of the prefectoral city of Yan-chow, an excellent view is obtained of the vast extent of land in the vicinity which is under water during the wet seasons of the year. In the dry season Chinese peasants—the servants

probably, of the proprietors of the neighbourhood—erect huts
of straw on the land from which the waters have retired, and
set themselves to cut down the coarse grass and reeds which
a rich alluvial deposit yields in very great quantities. These
are piled before the huts in stacks, which are afterwards removed
in boats to the neighbouring towns or villages, and sold as fuel
for the winter months.

On the waters of the Poyang lake are abundance of wild
fowl, chiefly geese, ducks, teal, divers, and pelicans. Great
numbers of these are captured by native fowlers, and exposed
for sale in the markets of the cities which stud the banks of the
Yang-tsze Kiang. For the purpose of capturing these birds
the fowler has recourse to very singular methods. Sometimes
he fixes two gingals in a boat which is constructed to sit low
in the water, and, laying hold of the stern, wades or swims
as the case may be, gently pushing the boat towards the wild
fowl. When he has come within gun-shot, he discharges his
gingals into the midst of the birds by means of a long fuse.
At other times the fowler floats a number of baskets on the
water, and when the wild-fowl have become used to them, and
swim close to them without fear, he covers his head with a
similar basket and wades into the lake. By a gradual approach
he tries to get into the very centre of the flock, and then he
suddenly stretches out both hands, and generally succeeds in
capturing a brace of them, which he at once deposits in a
creel on his back.

The Toon-ting lake is two hundred and fifty miles
beyond the Poyang Hoo, and, therefore, six hundred and fifty
miles from the sea-coast. A great many streams empty themselves into this lake ; but as their waters are not impregnated
with so much sand and clay as those which flow into the
Poyang lake, their banks are not so sterile and unproductive.
The lake is studded with islands, and one of these which I
visited is evidently regarded by the Chinese as a very sacred
spot. It contains many temples in honour of the religion of
Buddha, and numerous priests of the sect live on the island.
Their duties consist in serving the altars not only of
Buddha, but those—and there are several of them—in honour

of the Toon-ting Wong, or king of the lake. From the highest˙ point of the island, which is very undulating and intersected by neat paths, a very fine view of the whole may be obtained. I observed the tea-plant growing in great profusion, and the friars kindly prepared us cups of the refreshing beverage.

There are many Buddhist shrines on what is called the Golden Island. The tea-plant grows here also in large quantities, and as tea grown in this locality is said to promote longevity, a quantity of it is forwarded annually to the palace at Pekin for His Imperial Majesty.

On the occasion of our visit to the Toon-ting lake, my companions and myself were attacked by an infuriated mob, and narrowly escaped being killed. Returning from a sail on the lake, we entered Yo-chow, the prefectoral city, which stands at the head of it. As we walked through the streets we were followed by a vast crowd of young men and boys, who, for no reason that we could conceive, were very angry at our presence. At a certain ward of the city, the houses of which had been destroyed during the rebellion, they called out "Kill the foreign devils," and suiting the action to the word mercilessly pelted us with brickbats. My companion fell to the earth, and how it was that his skull was not fractured by the missiles which were literally showered upon it I am at a loss to say. On his recovering his feet we rushed, hotly pursued by the mob, into the house of a Chinese gentleman, who, for our greater safety, lodged us in the rooms set apart for the female portion of his household. The ladies were not abashed at our unexpected presence, but were full of interest in our safety. The mob continued their violent assault on the house, and we thought it advisable to escape to the Yamun or official residence of the Prefect of the city. We quitted our retreat by the back entrance. Our assailants, however, who were apparently determined to make an end of us, were immediately on our track, and on our way down a slight declivity they favoured us with such a shower of brickbats that on reaching the foot of the hill, we were somewhat surprised to find ourselves in the land of the living. At this crisis, an official who chanced to pass in a sedan chair, alighted and came to our rescue. We were escorted by this officer to the Yamun of the Prefect. That dignitary received us kindly, and lodged us for protection in a room within the porch of his residence. By and by the mob outside the gates, which were closed against them, became more furious, and the Prefect, fearing lest they should force an entrance, ordered us to be removed to a room in the centre of the Yamun. Even here, however, we were not considered safe, and we were eventually lodged in the private apartments of the Prefect himself. At half-past nine o'clock, the night being very dark, we were conveyed—having previously, at the suggestion of the Prefect, put on a few Chinese garments —by a back way which led through some deserted gardens to the Yamun of the military mandarin, or commandant of the city. This officer, who apparently had few soldiers under his command, took us in charge, and a procession having been formed like that by which Chinese officials are escorted to and from a city, we were carried out of Yo-chow in sedan-chairs of state with all the blinds drawn. Beyond the gates a small open boat was waiting to take us to our junk. So soon as we were safely on board she weighed anchor, and carried us in the darkness to a more friendly port. This occurred in November, 1865, and on the twenty-fourth day of the August preceding, a French priest had been deliberately murdered by an infuriate mob in a city not very far distant from Yo-chow. He sought refuge as we did in a native gentleman's house. Feeling, however, that his position was not safe, he left it with the view of going to the Yamun of the Prefect. On his way thither, he was stoned to death.

At the south of the province of Kiang-soo I visited the large oval-shaped lake of Tai Hoo. The circumference is estimated at two hundred and sixty miles. The country by which it is surrounded is most interesting. To the north of the lake is an extensive cotton district, whilst the lands bordering on the south-west are famous as green tea and silk districts. The plastic clays of which the best porcelain is made are found in this vicinity as well as at Kin-tee-ching on the banks of the Poyang lake.

In the course of my travels I visited several lakes besides these three principal ones. Many of them, although comparatively speaking, insignificant sheets of water, are very picturesque. They reminded me of those charming little lakes for which my native county, Cumberland, is so justly famous. None of these smaller lakes, however, gratified me more than one which is near the city of Hang-chow. On three of its sides this lake is inclosed by high lands, and on the remaining side stand the walls of Hang-chow. A singular-looking pagoda overlooks the water from the side of a hill, and on the south-west bank there is another erection of the same kind. The latter is apparently of great antiquity. On the smaller of the two islets in the lake stands a neat China building, in which the Emperor Kien-lung Wong is said to have resided when he visited Hang-chow. In front of this palace, and abutting on the lake, is a stone esplanade which forms an extensive walk. From the mainland to the island in the centre, a good broad pathway leading across, two ornamental stone bridges has been constructed. Whether this road was made in honour of this Emperor's visit I was unable to ascertain.

Three of the lakes of China are, I believe, regarded as sacred. State worship is paid to the spirits who are supposed to preside over them, and a sheep and a pig are sacrificed on such occasions. An imperial communication addressed to the genius of the lake is also read aloud, and afterwards committed to a sacred fire. The three lakes which are thus honoured are the Tçong-ting, in the district of Pa-ling, in the province of Hoonam, the Poyang, in the district of Poyang, in the province of Kiang-soo, and the Hoong-chak, which is in the same province.

The geological formations of this great and interesting country are as yet not generally known. It is a subject, however, upon which a learned German baron is now throwing much light.

Until the last few years, the great jealousy which the Chinese entertain towards foreigners prevented the latter penetrating beyond the ports thrown open by treaty. Since the last war, however, the foreigner lives under a new *régime*, which admits of his travelling, though not without danger, from north to south and from east to west, of the vast empire which for centuries was closed against him.

As an illustration of the dangers to which travellers are exposed from attacks by robbers in many of the wild and mountainous districts of the interior, I venture to introduce here an episode of travel, the incidents of which are not likely ever to be forgotten by those of whom they are related.

In 1862—on the 12th of December—the Rev. John Preston, of the English Wesleyan Society, the late Rev. W. S. Bonney, of the American Presbyterian Board, and myself, set out from Canton, on an excursion into the interior. Our intention was to go through the north-west of the province of Kwang-tung, and to enter the province of Kiang-soo by the wild gorge ravine, called the Dragon's Neck. During the first week, our journey was very successful. On reaching the city of Tsung-fa, we were warned by the chief magistrate of the district on no account to proceed further, as the country beyond was infested with robbers. Thinking, however, that it was the usual cry of " Wolf! Wolf! " when there was no wolf, or that the mandarins wanted to keep us back, we pushed on. On nearing the long gorge or ravine of the Dragon's Neck, which is five English miles in length, we were stopped by the elders of a village, who told us on no account to pass through the Dragon's Neck without an escort, as only three days before two Chinese wayfarers had been robbed and murdered, so that, to prevent the robbers from lurking in the brushwood, they (the elders) had caused portions of it to be set on fire. We replied that we were prepared to place ourselves under their protection. They immediately offered us thirty armed braves to escort us through the gorge to a town called Huet-tee-pie, adding in the same breath that we must requite the services of each brave by a dollar. This demand put a new complexion on the matter, as we intended to go a long distance. Feeling that thirty dollars would be too great a drain upon resources which it was necessary for us to husband, we decided not to avail ourselves of the proffered protection, and went our way. The gorge was safely traversed, and we were congratulating ourselves, and inclined to hope that we had passed the most dangerous part of our journey. On our arrival at Huet-tee-pie, we were not well received by its inhabitants. Many of them—I must explain that this was shortly after the occupation of Canton by our troops had come to an end—were rude to us, and all appeared to refuse us ordinary hospitality Indignant at their conduct we remounted our horses, and our party of five, consisting of Mr. Preston, Mr. Bonney, and myself, and two servants, rode onwards, hoping to reach some hospitable farmhouse, where we might spend the night. We had not ridden more than three or four miles when this hope was realized, and we found excellent accommodation with a benevolent Chinese farmer. Although we had provisions with us (for travellers in China generally find it advisable to carry food), this good man insisted on killing the fatted calf for us, in the shape of fowls, ducks, and one of his pigs, and did everything in his power to make us happy and merry. His children, too, greeted us on our arrival with evident pleasure, and gazed with wonder for the first time on men from the west. During the evening, a report having spread throughout the neighbouring hamlets that foreigners had arrived, many persons assembled at the farmhouse solely to see the barbarians. During the conversation between us and our visitors, we noticed four or five villainous characters in the crowd whose presence augured no good, and who probably wanted to gain information about our movements. The general opinion of the crowd seemed to be that we were travelling merchants, going to distant markets to expend much capital in the purchase of Chinese merchandise. On the following morning at eight o'clock, we remounted and proceeded on our way, accompanied, for better protection, by a brave or militia man. When we had ridden some eight or nine miles, we were travelling in the following order. Preston was riding ahead attended by the servants and the brave ; I followed at some little distance, and Bonney was not far behind me writing up his notes of travel. It was a fine genial day, and on either side of the road rose the sloping sides of hills covered with coarse grass. Presently the sound of angry shouts reached us, and looking ahead we saw that Preston had disappeared round a turning where the straight line of the road was interrupted by a deflection in the shape of the letter V. There could be no mistake, however, as to what had occurred. The shouts were plainly, " Kill him ! kill him ! " and they seemed to come from an appalling number of throats. We afterwards discovered that the robbers were twenty-five in number. I at once rode forward, the brave who had accompanied us deeming it his duty to ride with equal promptitude in the opposite direction. When I reached the scene of disaster, I became the centre of a circle of muskets which were pointed at my head, and when Bonney came up he was immediately subjected to similar treatment. Each captive had now to deal with his own captors, and a man of villainous aspect came up to me and said in truculent tone, "I want your clothes." I replied that if he wanted them he must take them off my back, for I would not give them to him. He at once commenced operations by trying on my hat, but it did not fit him and he flung it on the ground. He proceeded to remove my coat and waistcoat, and after closely inspecting the latter, a clerical vestment in which I had often addressed my people, he evidently came to the conclusion that it was a garment better suited for him than for myself. Putting it on, and buttoning it up to the throat, he resumed his operations on my dress, stating that he must have *Wong-Kum*, *Wong-Kum* (yellow gold). Finally he left me standing in what may be termed the garb of old Gaul; strange to say, behind his back, the captain, who had been watching both victim and robber, indicated by energetic and friendly gesticulations that I should offer no resistance to his subordinate's proceedings. This gave me hope when matters seemed tending towards a fatal issue. Presently, however, a sinister-looking robber, whose cadaverous and lantern-jawed face was made more repulsive by a white bandage which was bound round it, stepped up to me and said with a leer, "He's had your clothes; now I am going to have your life." He raised his gun, and whilst he was on the point of drawing the trigger, a very faithful servant of mine, named Awa, since dead, seized hold of the barrel and pushed its muzzle away from me. Still holding on to the gun, Awa begged and entreated the robber on no account to shoot me. The earnestness and energy with which this faithful man pleaded for the life of his "good master," as out of a full heart he called me, saved my life; and since then the thought has often recurred to me that, if I could preach for Christ with the self-forgetting earnestness with which Awa pleaded for me among the mountain robbers, I would surely turn many sinners from the broad road. The robbers now marched us across a hill, five taking charge of each prisoner. In crossing a brook, Preston had a very severe fall and was much shaken, and he had scarce recovered himself when he fell again. As we proceeded, Bonney's guard began to discuss the expediency of getting rid of their prisoner at once by killing him; and our friend told us that it was evidently time for us to make our peace with God. He requested Preston to offer up a prayer aloud in which we might silently join as we were marching along, but Preston shaken by his fall begged me to undertake the duty. While I was in the act of praying, the robber who had stolen my clothes, and who doubtless thought it likelier that I was imprecating vengeance upon the heads of our captors than lifting up my voice to the God of mercy, dealt me a severe blow on the head with an oaken stick which he had taken from Preston. At this stage another band of robbers appeared in view on the same side of the hill which we were descending. They were beginning to take to flight in the belief that the gang who had captured us were Chinese villagers who had armed themselves and come out against them, when some of our captors called out that we were prisoners, and that there was no occasion for alarm. They proved to be a distinct band. No sooner had we come up to them than the leader asked the captain of our gang why he had not shot his prisoners, and, without waiting for a reply, he covered Preston and myself, who. were standing close together, with his gun. Again, it seemed as if the end was near, and I said to Preston, " You and I have to die together; let us stand true, and fall as we ought to fall." No sooner were the words uttered than the captain of our gang, who from the first had shown a singular interest in my preservation, ordered that we were not to be shot. The bands then separated, and we continued our march into the valley. On our way we passed a cavern which, from the fire outside, where cooking had evidently been going on, seemed to be the haunt of the band. After a little hesitation as to whether they should halt here, the robbers proceeded till they reached the bottom of the valley, where a distribution of our property was commenced. The fellow who had taken nearly all my clothes, and who was now conspicuous in my high-breasted waistcoat, again came up to me. He had found no yellow gold —for we carried that in our portmanteaus—and, if I did not at once give it up to him, he would club my brains out. Suiting the action to the word, he aimed a blow at my head. I put up my right arm to ward it off, when the captain of the gang rushed before me, thrust back the weapon with both hands, and wrested it from my tormentor. At this point a new danger threatened us. The band who were dividing the spoil quarrelled amongst themselves, and high words were quickly followed by threatening gestures. They presented their guns at each other, and a scene of bloodshed seemed imminent, in which it was not likely that we would be spared. Suddenly, like a storm in summer, their anger seemed to cease, and they prepared to resume their march. Without us? It would seem so; yet we could hardly credit the welcome possibility. Making no remark, and with a rough and ready, though not unkindly, action, the captain of the gang flung my coat at me, and we soon saw the lessening forms of the robbers on the opposite hill-side. At last we were alone in the valley.

We now began to retrace our steps. One of the party was so overcome by the fatigue of the ascent and the perils through which we had passed that he begged us to rest a little. But we pointed out the necessity of going on at once, lest the robbers, disappointed with their booty, should return and wreak their vengeance on us, and he nerved himself for the ascent. We moved on, following the direction in which we had come as closely as we could. On reaching the top of the mountain we made a halt; but we had no sooner seated ourselves than we heard a war-whoop, and looking back we saw the other band of robbers in the distance. Clearly, the only course was to move on faster. After some time we came to a point where the long coarse grass on the mountain side was pressed down in two directions, and left us to choose between two tracks. Our Chinese servants were decidedly in favour of one of these paths, and as I was not less decided for the other, a discussion arose. Eventually, although my friends urged that the Chinese servants were likely to know better than myself, they yielded to my representations, and resolved that we should keep together, allowing the servants to go by the other route. The party accordingly divided; but we had not gone more than a hundred yards, when Bonney rushing forward and picking up some sheets of paper which were lying on the ground, exclaimed, " We are on the right path." It appeared that these sheets of paper were copies of the Lord's Prayer in Chinese characters, and that he had given them to his robber guards when they were so earnestly discussing the propriety of killing him, to convince them that they had not captured travelling merchants, but ministers of religion. The robbers had thrown them roughly on the ground, and thereby unwittingly rendered us this great service. It was an almost literal fulfilment of the royal Psalmist's words—" Thy word is a lantern unto my feet; and a light unto my paths."

Presently we reached the place of attack, and on one of our servants kicking over one of the hampers which the robbers had left behind, we found to our surprise a bottle of sherry which had formed part of our *impedimenta*. Never surely was sherry more prized than that which our careless captors had left behind.

But our troubles were by no means over. On the way back we halted at the house of the hospitable farmer with whom we had lodged, and who was truly sorry for us. We soon pushed on to Huet-tee-pie. At this village a rough crowd quickly gathered, and we were taken into an opium shop, which was immediately filled with the natives, rushing into it after us in their eagerness to see the Englishmen with the naked legs. We managed to get off, and when we had got as far as the market-place, after much rudeness from the crowd, it was suggested to us by some of the leading men of the town that we should stand upon a trestle to gratify the people. Whether wisely or not I refused, declaring that I would not be put up like an ox for exhibition. Managing to make our way out of the inhospitable village, we came to a farmhouse, occupied by a major of braves or militia, of the clan or family Ho, and which, like all the farms in this lawless neighbourhood, was constructed as a fortalice. We asked him to let us pass the night under his roof, a request he at once granted, telling

us that he had heard of our misfortunes, and that he would
willingly render us any service which lay in his power.
Meanwhile a crowd of stragglers and inhabitants of Huet-tee-
pie who had followed us, collected round us as we were sitting
in the lower room of the house, and Preston, who said he felt
that his mind was unhinged by the events of the day, was
enabled, by the kindness of the host, to retire to an upper
chamber. In the evening we dined off buffalo flesh, which was
very coarse; but the quality of the meat was amply compen-
sated for by the quantity of excellent vegetables and rice which
were served with it. At night, while I was in bed, the elders
of the village, who had come to consult with the major what
steps were to be taken, entered my room, and carried on their
discussion in low whispers. About one in the morning, before
they left, they informed me that they had agreed to send us
safely out of the district under an escort of thirty braves.
When they had gone, and just as I was beginning to realise how
grateful were the darkness and quiet after so much excitement,
I heard the footsteps of one stealing softly into my room on
tiptoe. On calling out, Who goes there? I at once received
a reassuring reply. "Massa, massa, b'long my (it's me),
Awa, Awa." It was my faithful servant. "You no got
trows," he proceeded to say, somewhat complacently, I thought,
considering the nature of the statement—"You no got trows;
that tief he take all my chow-chow (baggage), but I got one pair
clean trows. I see that bobbery (I foresaw the mess). I chop
chop (quickly) get that clean trows out of my basket, and put
inside my jacket. That tief man no see. You got no trows.
My pay you (I give them to you). Truly this trows number
one clean O! Have wash, have wash. No fear. Number one
clean O!" I got up and, well assured of the truth of his
remarks, put on the Chinese trousers.

At breakfast we reassembled. Bonney had occupied the
same room with Preston, who was now much better, although he
had suffered a great deal. The major reported that the resolution
to which the elders of the villages and himself had come,
viz., that we should be placed under the protection of an escort
of thirty braves, and conducted in safety through the Dragon's

Neck. Strongly impressed with the idea, however, that dangers might await us beyond the gorge, we resolved to go to the nearest district city, and throw ourselves into the hands of the county rulers. Mr. Ho then agreed to escort us to Loong-moon-yune. Passing through a bold and romantic country, not unlike the Highlands of Scotland, we found on reaching the city in question that the district ruler was absent.[1] His deputy, however, received us courteously and entertained us kindly, expressing great sympathy. He also provided us readily with board and lodgings, and procured clothing for us; and before we set out on our way back to Canton, bought for us certain articles of which we stood in need—to wit, haircombs, tooth-brushes, and chopsticks. During the interview in which we gave an account of our misfortunes to this deputy, we spoke in the Kwang-tung dialect, and an interpreter was present to render the narrative to this official in the mandarin or court dialect. We did not of course think this strange, as the two dialects are very dissimilar. We were, however, not a little astonished shortly afterwards, when one of the elders of the city, or at any rate one of the leading men of Loong-moon, who had come in during our audience, began conversing freely with the mandarin in the very dialect for which he had just required an interpreter. In fact, the mandarin was himself a Canton man. The incident was singularly characteristic of Chinese officialism.

The deputy provided two boats for us, one for ourselves and one for our servants; and on the following morning we embarked for Canton, the mandarin himself accompanying us. Our course was down a mountain torrent, and the frequent rapids we had to shoot prevented the journey from being monotonous. But there was little danger of monotony. We were passing through a district the people of which were keenly smarting with resentment at the recent occupation by English troops of Canton, the pride of the southern provinces of China. When boats passed us, their crews execrated us. At one city at which we stopped in order to purchase provisions (the mandarin catering for us

---

[1] The county ruler, Ming-Tai-Loo-Yae, had gone to a town some twenty miles off to hold an inquest on the body of a man who had been killed in a brawl which took place at a theatre.

and defraying all expenses), the people attacked us, and before we could push off into deep water, one of the sailors had his foot injured by a stone. After this the mandarin said that we must not expose ourselves to observation, but so soon as we had taken our morning bath, we must retire and remain under cover.

This official was somewhat of a character. I well remember one of our conversations with him on the social position of women in China. I pointed out to him that Christianity alone gave woman her true place in society, and endeavoured to convince him that China would be much benefited, if her people would consent to emancipate their wives and daughters from the social bondage in which they were held. The mandarin defended the social arrangements of his country, and turning the tables upon me, dwelt upon the dangers and temptations to which the freedom which women enjoyed in England exposed them; and in doing so, he showed himself to be possessed of some knowledge of the present state of society in this country. My two friends then took up the argument, and each in turn addressed him at considerable length. The mandarin heard them patiently, and when they had concluded, he showed the impression which our united efforts had made upon his mind, by drawing himself up to his full length, and exclaiming with an emphasis which can be better imagined than described, " Man is as heaven, woman is as earth!" We parted with him at the capital of the neighbouring county, where we were consigned to the protection of its county ruler, who, like the courteous mandarin, supplied us with whatever was necessary in the shape either of money or provisions, and looked after our safety. This fact deserves to be mentioned, as it shows the good faith in which these various Chinese officials observed the spirit of the treaty which had just been concluded with the British government.

On the sixth night we arrived at a market town, which some of Her Majesty's gunboats had bombarded during the occupation of Canton, and the inhabitants of which were full of hatred towards foreigners. We were unwilling to pass the night here, but it was impossible for us to navigate this part of the river after dark, as it was infested by pirates. From this point, however, we had no difficulty in continuing our journey in the morning; and it was with very lively thankfulness that we found ourselves once more at Canton.

During my long residence in China I had frequent cause to regret that I did not devote my attention to the study of geology when an undergraduate of the University of Cambridge. There, by a regular attendance on Professor Sedgwick's lectures, I should, doubtless, have acquired a pretty fair knowledge of this science, and might have been enabled to lay before my readers some valuable information respecting the geological features of the Celestial Empire. In venturing to say anything upon the geological formations of China, I trust the reader will kindly grant me that indulgence which I feel to be necessary.

In the southern provinces of Kwang-tung and Kwang-si, the plains which form the fertile and thickly-inhabited rice and silk districts are all deposits, many of which are alluvial. In one of these plains in the district of Sam-sui, I found large quantities of shells which would indicate that it must have been formed under the water. The mountains in the provinces of Kwang-tung and Kwang-si, through which the western branch of the Canton river directs its course, are all of granitic and schistose formations, and often rise into bold and angular peaks. The mountains in the north-east of the province of Kwang-tung, that is, in the districts of Loong-moon and Chong-ling, are of a similar formation. In these mountains the granite is, as a general rule, concealed by limestone and sandstone. Some of the hills which abut on the Poyang lake have the appearance of sand-hills, and when the rays of the setting sun rest upon them they look like mounds of gold. These are, I believe, hills of a granitic formation, covered with sand blown over them after the dry season has exposed the bed of the lake. In my voyage along the western branch of the Canton river, I saw in the neighbourhood of the market town of Yuet-ching, a large hill of limestone in strange contrast with the granitic and schistose formations by which it is surrounded. In this hill, which I suppose is upwards of one thousand feet in height, a great number of labourers were working quarries, whilst in the absence of beasts of burden, women were carrying blocks of limestone to the kilns by means of baskets. The kilns are on the banks of the river, and several large barges were anchored near them. The limestone of Yuet-ching is capable of receiving a polish and of being used by the sculptor, and nearly all the temples in this part of the province are furnished with idols and incense burners either of pure white or mottled marble. On a plain near Shu-hing Foo, a city on the banks of the same river I saw seven large rocks of limestone. These rocks, which are about two hundred and fifty feet high, are very singular in their outlines, and are called by the Cantonese Tsat-pak-sing, or the seven stars. They are regarded as one of the seven wonders for which their province is said to be famous. Upon examining them I found that they contained very extensive caverns. One of these, which I explored by torchlight, extends from one side of the rock to the other. The roof of this cavern is adorned by stalactites which hang down in a variety of curious and beautiful shapes. That portion of the cavern which forms the vestibule, is used as a temple, and I observed standing above the altar an idol of the popular goddess Koon-Yam. At one of these limestone hills called the saddle hill, I remember noticing several labourers engaged in making lime for agricultural purposes. Several hills of the same kind in the district of Fa-yune, are of no use to the people, as the mandarins have given strict injunctions that they should not be quarried, lest the good geomantic influence they are supposed to exert over the surrounding country should be destroyed.

Of all the caverns which I had an opportunity of visiting the largest is at Kilung in the island of Formosa. Some years later when I was travelling through the midland and northern provinces my attention was directed to several grottoes at Silver island, which stands in the middle channel of the Yang-tsze not far from the city of Chinkiang. I visited a small grotto in which was an idol in honour of the god Chu-Yan-Chee, who is regarded by the Chinese as one of their minor water deities, and to whom prayers are not unfrequently addressed with the view of prevailing upon him to check inundations on the part of the waters of the mighty Yang-tsze. Near this grotto there stands a large Buddhist monastery which, together with the grotto, was twice visited by the Emperor Kien-lung Wong. In front of this temple are two tablets, on each of which is engraven an inscription said to have been composed by him. Each tablet is placed under a canopy the roof of which is, as a mark of royalty, covered with bright yellow tiles. A number of women were lodged in several of the principal apartments of the monastery. They had been driven to seek an asylum in consequence of their villages being inundated by the waters of the "Ocean Child." Not far from the grotto is a cemetery, and I observed amongst the many graves which it contained, there were three in which British sailors had been interred.

Golden island, which is also in the channel of the Yang-tsze, has two grottoes. This island, it may be observed in passing, has always been held in high estimation by the Chinese, not only for its sanctity and beauty, but for the place it has held in the regard of several of their emperors. In one of the grottoes there was a Buddhist hermit, who, I was informed, had not lain down for a period of twelve months, or held any communication with his fellow-men. In the course of a conversation I had with him, he informed me of his earnest desire to enter Nirvana, the heaven of the Buddhists; and to qualify himself for this he was afflicting both his body and soul. On the door of the grotto, two Chinese characters, viz., Chee and Ching, or Rest and Silence were written in a bold hand. The door was provided with a small port through which the food of the hermit was passed. Upon the inner walls the hermit had written in large letters the sacred vows which he had taken. Near these grottoes were three slabs on each of which were engraven sentences said to have been composed by Kien-lung Wong, who thrice visited this, as well as the sister island of Silver, and on each occasion left behind him a donation for the repair of certain monastic buildings, and of a pagoda in the vicinity of the grottoes. In the crevices and on the ledges of these grottoes, a number of broken reeds had been placed. I found this to be the case also on Silver island. The reeds had been left there by pilgrims and votaries who were either suffering from, or desirous to avert, that terrible malady known as Bright's disease.

In 1865, I visited the grottoes near Nankin in the company of Captain Macleod of the Chinese government transport *Willamette.* These are seven in number, and the first 'is about a mile and a half from the city. The second, which is not far distant from the first, measures thirty-five feet by twenty-one, and is fifteen feet high. This grotto is on the slopes of a limestone hill, and is approached by a steep and rugged ascent of fifty feet from the base of the hill. We found a broken idol of granite in it, standing above a dilapidated brick altar. The rebels, who were vigorous iconoclasts, and who for many years disturbed this portion of the empire, had probably visited this grotto. On its walls I noticed a stanza in Chinese characters, which I learned had been written by a soldier in the imperial army. This soldier poet, having descanted on the beauties of the grotto, proceeded in stirring song to congratulate himself on the recent capture of Nankin from the rebels, not because he was now once more free from the alarms and dangers of war, but because the re-establishment of peace had enabled him to derive so much real pleasure from visiting a place so singular and so interesting as the Eu-Tai-Toong grotto. The third grotto, which is near this, is called the Sam-Tai-Toong, and is by far the most interesting of any which we visited. In the centre of it is a small pool of spring water which is spanned by a stone bridge of one arch. On the top of the bridge stands a stone idol of Buddha. The better days of this idol were probably before the rebellion, for its head, though resting in its proper position, has been broken off from its body. By mounting a flight of very imperfect steps a large natural aperture is reached, through which we were told the spirit of the idol occasionally wings its way to Elysium. The seventh grotto, like the sixth, is nothing more than the rugged and precipitous side of a limestone hill, and is also regarded by the people of the district with superstitious awe. On the side of this hill I observed a marble slab on which was cut a representation of the goddess of Mercy. Above the slab were carved several Chinese sentences. These I was told by a Buddhist priest had been composed by the prime minister of the emperor of the Ming dynasty, whose dilapidated tomb on the south-east side of Nankin is one of the sights of the place. In the crevices of these grottoes we found several pieces of broken reeds left by pilgrims.

A Chinese work which treats on the various places of interest which the province of Kiangsoo can boast, gives an account of a grotto which is at a distance of ten miles from Nan-kan, a prefectoral city on the banks of the Poyang lake. The native annals to which I refer, and which, of course, deal greatly in the marvellous, set forth that in this grotto there are apertures through which the winds, blowing with great violence and causing loud hissing noises, exerted at one period most baneful influences, not only on the various fruits of the earth, but also on the people themselves. The inhabitants, therefore, of the surrounding country placed in this grotto an idol of the goddess of Mercy. A grotto I visited had for several years been the residence of a learned recluse. A rock in the form of a table stood before the entrance, and round it were stone seats. On the surface of the table was carved a representation of a Chinese inkstand; and I was told that the hermit was accustomed to write at this table in the still evenings of summer. The life which he led was so holy, said the friars, that he was translated to Elysium without dying.

In the neighbourhood of Canton, there are several indications of volcanic action; and many of the rocks and hills are of most singular shapes. I may particularize those at the mouth of the Canton river, one of which is said to resemble a tiger in outline and gives, in consequence, the name of Tiger's river to that portion of the river. Near the village of Sooee-foong-chun, which is in the vicinity of the port of Whampoa, I observed a hill greatly resembling in its outline a lion couchant; and in the same neighbourhood my attention was directed to another elevation whose configuration bears a striking resemblance to the head and trunk of an elephant. At the village of Kumchai-laing, which is also at no great distance from Whampoa, I observed a hill which is supposed to bear a striking resemblance to a rat. The inhabitants of this village were at one time very much addicted to thieving, and were a source of much trouble to the magistrates of Canton. The geomancers having eventually decided that this thieving propensity was owing to the bad geomantic influences which the Loo-shune Shan or rat hill exercised over the village, the mandarins, at the suggestion of these fortune-tellers, erected in front of it, with the face towards the "rat hill," a huge iron cat! This tribute to the beneficent influences of the familiar representative of the feline race is supposed effectually to counteract the bad influence of the volcanic rat, to which nature, prompted one would say by the familiar line, "Parturiunt montes, nascetur ridiculus mus," had given birth in one of her sportive moments. The iron cat was placed in its present responsible position in the fourth year of the reign of Ka-hing, A.D. 1800, by the provincial judge or chief justice, and other leading officials of Kwang-tung. It was repaired in the fifteenth year of the reign of Taou-kwang, A.D. 1856, and so great is the importance with which this novel guardian of the interests of justice is invested, that it occasionally receives worship and offerings at the hands of the provincial magistrates. At the opposite approach to the same village there is an iron statue of a Chinese official, which is also supposed to exercise a good geomantic influence over the much-tempted inhabitants of Kum-chai-laing. In the right hand of the iron statue is placed a fan, also of the same material, with which the figure is supposed to waft away all pernicious and soul-contaminating influences which may impend over the neighbourhood. Such striking objects ought surely to remind the inhabitants of Kum-chai-laing of the difference between *meum* and *tuum*.

Near the Lin-Shan pass or water-lily pagoda, which stands on the banks of the Canton river, there is, near the Second Bar, a line of rocks which are clearly indications of volcanic action, and which are termed, I believe, Shek-Sheang or Stone City. At Whampoa there is a rock which from its shape is called the "Stone Fish." Immediately in front of it I noticed one of smaller dimensions and of a spherical shape. This I was informed was the Shek Chu or stone pearl. Respecting these two rocks, the guide proceeded to relate for my edification a legend contained in the annals of the province of Kwang-tung.

It was to the effect that in ages past a large fish was stranded
at this spot, and whilst in the agonies of expiring nature
ejected from its stomach a large pearl.   From the earnest
manner in which he told this story, he evidently believed that
the rocks in question were petrifactions.   Another most curious
formation is that of a large conglomerate rock near to the town
of Teu-chun, which is on the banks of the western branch of
the Canton river.   This rock, which is called the Flowery Table
Monument, is eight hundred feet high, and in outline resembles
a human head.   As it is approached from the east, it seems inaccessible.   Its western side, however, shows a jagged and
almost perpendicular wall by which the ascent may be accomplished, though not without much difficulty.   I made an
attempt to scale it, but so soon as I had reached the high
shoulder of the rock, I became so giddy as to be unable to
advance; my fellow-traveller, however, was more fortunate.
With apparent ease and great dexterity he reached the top, and
thereby performed what the Chinese regard as a very great
feat.   On my way from Foong-ling-shan to Jehol in Inner
Mongolia, I observed some very singular geological formations
in the vicinity of Chan-poo-cur.   At Jehol, my attention was
directed to a rock standing in a perpendicular position, and
reaching to a height of several hundred feet.   But amongst the
most singular geological formations I saw, may be reckoned the
Great and Little Orphan.   In the very centre of the river Yang-
tsze, and at a distance of twenty English miles from the
egress of the Poyang lake, stands a bold limestone rock in the
form of a sugar-loaf, which is termed the Little Orphan.   On
the slopes of this rock, there is a Buddhist monastery in which
reside three or four friars.   In the Poyang lake, and at a distance
of seven English miles from its egress, stands another limestone
rock of considerable altitude.   This is termed the Great Orphan.
As, when seen from a point near the market town of Ma-foo-
shan, its outline resembles that of a Chinese shoe, the additional
name of the "Shoe Rock" is occasionally applied to it.   Upon
its summit there are the ruins of a Buddhist monastery, and near
them stands a pagoda of seven stories high.   It was the dry
season, and I was obliged, in consequence of the waters of the

lake having abated, to wade for a distance of half an English mile through very thick mud. As I was wandering through the ruins of the monastery, a Buddhist monk arrived from the town of Kin-tee-ching to resume possession of the ruins of what, previous to the rebellion, during which it was destroyed, had been an extensive cloister. He, more lucky than myself, sat in a flat-bottomed boat which was shoved over the mud by three or four boatmen. There was only one small chamber in the middle of the ruins for this devout pagan recluse to occupy, and it was so remarkable for its true Spartan simplicity that, had it been in Lacedæmon in the days of Lycurgus, it would have been regarded as a model of perfection. Respecting these three rocks, the Chinese have a singular legend in which many of them most implicitly believe.

The legend, which was narrated to me, is very much as follows:—During a storm of wind, a boat containing a man, his wife, and their two children, was capsized on the Yang-tsze river. The man and his wife perished at once. A large frog, however, upon seeing the lads struggling in the midst of the waves came to their rescue, and having received them upon his back made haste towards their home, which was on the banks of the Poyang lake. But the younger of the orphans, grieving sadly at the untimely death of his parents, threw himself into the river and was drowned. After the lapse of a short time, he appeared in the form of the bold angular peak which is therefore known as the Little Orphan. The humane frog, after vainly endeavouring to save this youth from the watery grave which he sought, pursued his course with the surviving orphan still clinging to his back. When he had entered the Poyang lake, and attained a distance of seven English miles from the mouth of it, the elder orphan, being now broken-hearted, fell in a moment of anguish from the back of the frog into the depths of the lake and was drowned. In due course of time he appeared in the form of the large rock, which is therefore known as the Great Orphan. When the frog had gone a little further from the scene of this last disaster, he began to lament bitterly over his unsuccessful endeavours to save the orphans, and, being filled with intolerable anguish, he yielded up

his life.   In due course of time, he also emerged from the waves
in the petrified form, as the "Frog Rock."

The Chinese state that many aërolites or meteoric stones fall
in China.   In the city of Canton, for example, there are nine
such stones, which they call the "nine star-stones."   The name
may perhaps imply that in the opinion of the Chinese, these
stones fell either from Cerberus or Toucan, or Ara, each of which
constellations consists of nine stars.   They are of various shapes,
and upon one of them there is said to be an impression in large
size of the human hand.   A poem which is said to have been
composed by a person named Mi Yune-chaong, who flourished
sometime during the Tung dynasty, is said to be inscribed on
this stone.   Another is said to have its surface marked in such
a manner as to resemble bubbles of water.   Of these supposed
meteoric stones, six are now in the literary chancellor's
Yamun, two in that of the provincial treasurer, and one
in the Confucian temple of the Kwang-Chow-Foo.   These
aërolites were brought in the first instance, it is said, from
the Tai-Hoi lake.   This was done at the suggestion of a
rebel chieftain named Lou-Chan, who, with his barbarous
hordes, overran the province of Kwang-tung; and the stones
stood for several centuries on the margin of a fish-pond,
which now no longer exists, but which at the time in
question was in the vicinity of the double arch of the city
called Kung-pak-lou.

On the walls of many of their caverns and grottoes, and on
the walls of their rocks and singular geological formations,
the Chinese paint in very large characters, sentences of prose
or stanzas, generally expressive, I suppose, of sublimity and
grandeur.   These writings reminded me of what I had
read of "the written valley,"—Wady Mokattel—which is
in the wilderness of Sinai.   I allude of course to the singular
inscriptions which, it appears, are engraven upon the
rocks in a tongue that is no longer known.   To this
singular custom of writing upon rocks allusion is evidently
made by Job, when he exclaims, "Oh that my words
were now written!   Oh that they were printed in a book!
That they were graven with an iron pen and lead in the rock

for ever!" It would appear from Chinese annals, that one named Soo Toong-po, who flourished towards the end of the seventh century of the Christian era, during the reign of Chung-tsung, the fourth emperor of the Tong dynasty—and his son-in-law, one Chan Sue-yow, were famous for the many beautiful stanzas which they painted upon many of the most singular geological formations in China. The former is also said to have visited the city of Canton, and to have written above the entrance door by which the nine-storeyed pagoda is approached, the characters Luk-Yung-Sze, or Six Banyan Tree Monastery—a name by which the monastery near which the pagoda stands has ever since been known. Of this same Soo Toong-po there is a portrait engraven on the marble slab, which is contained in the Cum-Shan-Sze or Golden Hill Monastery. The monastery is at a distance of fifteen or twenty miles English from Canton.

Besides the indications of volcanic action, to which I have already referred, there are the hot-springs at Yung-mak ; these are at a distance of fifteen English miles from the Portuguese colony of Macao. I boiled eggs in them quite hard, in the short space of two minutes. I filled a bottle with the water for the purpose of having it analysed on my return to Canton. As I was leaving, some of the loafers of the neighbourhood gravely informed me that the water when removed from the springs became cold, and that I should be disappointed if I thought that it would always continue to boil. I also visited some hot springs at a place called Chung-ling-tow, in the district of Tsung-fa. Persons suffering from cutaneous diseases wash their bodies with the water of these springs, and they are highly prized by the people of the neighbourhood. They are also occasionally used for other purposes. Goats and pigs, the carcases of which are sometimes required in large quantities for the proper celebration of marriages, or for funeral obsequies are not unfrequently slaughtered near them, the water being used in scalding the carcases. Hence visitors sometimes find the banks strewed with the hair of these animals. At Foo-chow Foo there are hot-springs which have baths attached to them. These are used by persons suffering from cutaneous diseases.

Besides these sulphurous wells, which are greatly valued by the Chinese, there are wells of spring-water which, superstitious in all things, the people regard as sacred. In Canton alone there are a great many of these wells. One of the most ancient is the "Sun-Well," so called from the supposed fact that it was usual during the night to see on the surface of its waters a reflection resembling the sun. In consequence of this the well came to be regarded as so sacred that people were forbidden to draw water from it. Eventually a temple in honour of the heathen deity, Lung Wong, or the dragon king, was erected upon its site, and the pedestal on which the idol of this god is placed now stands over its mouth. Next in point of importance is the "Moon-Well," on the surface of which the Cantonese declared they saw during the day a reflection of what resembled the orb of night. The people were forbidden to disturb its sacred waters; and eventually a temple in honour of the heathen goddess Kum-fa was erected on the spot, and over the mouth of the spring was placed the pedestal of her idol. Then there is the "Star-well," from which a star-like ball of fire shot up while the well-sinkers were busy sinking the well. The Ki-Pa-Tsiang, so called because it was discovered by the scratching of a fowl, has fortunately not been honoured by having a pedestal placed on the top of it, and is of very great service to the citizens. It is said to have been sunk at the expense of one Ying Tsung, who was not so much a tea-drinker as a water-drinker. The waters of this well, which is in the vicinity of the small north-gate of the city, are greatly used for the purpose of boiling down balls of opium, and it is conveyed for this purpose to villages at a considerable distance from Canton. There is a man in charge of this well, to whom all persons wishing to draw water pay a small sum of money. A former custodian of this neverfailing spring endeavoured on one occasion—it was in the year 1854—to incite a number of idle and evil-disposed persons who were standing by, to kill and rob the ex-bishop of Victoria, Bishop Smith, the late Rev. William Samuel Bonney, and myself, whilst we were passing that way.

Another of these wells, which ranks the most ancient, is the

" Nine-Eyed Well," so called because it has nine mouths. It was sunk, so Chinese annals narrate, by one Chu Tan, who, sometime during the Hon dynasty, was in possession of Canton. He was one of the ministers of the Emperor Chi-Hwangti, by whom the Great Wall of China was built. Chu-Tan attained, so it is reported, the patriarchal age of one hundred and twenty years ; and his longevity was attributed to the copious draughts of this water which it was his custom to take. At one time it was usual for all mandarins who came to Canton to take office to initiate their administration by, among other things, taking a draught of its water. It is of great depth, and is never without a plentiful supply.

These are fair specimens of the stories which one finds connected with Chinese wells. The well, however, with which the most childish superstition is associated is in the quadrangle of the Yamun or official residence of the prefect of Shu-hing Foo. The mouth of it has been covered with large stones for many centuries, and it is supposed to contain an evil dragon, called Kon-Loong. This monster is said to have been the cause of pestilences and earthquakes until, several centuries ago, a prefect named Pow Man-ching, cast him into this well; and, in order that the imprisonment of the wicked dragon may be perpetual, each succeeding prefect, on entering office, affixes his seal to the stones. Nor is the monster alone in his confinement, for many devils and evil spirits have joined themselves to him in this prison, from which, however they may have got in, they are now unable to get out.

I have referred in the course of this chapter to traces of volcanic action; and a proof of the continued existence of this agency is still afforded, although in a very mild form, by the occasional earthquakes which make themselves felt in different parts of the country. These are not at all frequent, and, except in very rare instances, they are not attended with any very serious results. During my residence of twenty years in China, I experienced shocks of earthquakes on two occasions only. The first occurred in 1854. The bed in which I was sleeping shook so much one morning that I concluded a large Newfoundland dog was shaking himself below it. I was so sure of this that I actually looked under the bed to inspect the intruder.

My second earthquake occurred in 1860. At the moment I was sitting at breakfast in a small upper room in a Chinese house which I occupied at that time. The apartment was without a ceiling, and I saw the rafters by which the roof was supported, swaying very slightly from side to side. Two small tea-tables which were in the room, and upon which were standing two porcelain vases which I greatly prized, shook so as to make me fear that the vases would fall to the ground. My Chinese servants, who had become very much alarmed, rushed in hot haste into the adjoining street. I quickly followed them, and found several of my Chinese neighbours, who were evidently much terrified, congregated together. One of them, with terror in his countenance, observed that the great dragon was moving to and fro, and thereby causing the earth to shake. This statement, which it was somewhat difficult for a European to hear gravely propounded without laughing, met, it appeared to me, with a very ready assent from his assembled countrymen.

At Chin-kiang, a port on the banks of the Yang-tsze river, an earthquake took place on the night of the 24th of July, 1872. It was described as follows by the Chin-kiang correspondent of the *North China Daily News* :—

" "We had an earthquake here last night which startled us somewhat. Folks in Manilla or Japan, who are used to these sort of things, would probably consider it nothing, but I can assure you we thought a good deal of it, and are not at all anxious for a repetition. It took place, according to the time of H.M.S. *Leven*, at ten minutes to 8 P.M., and lasted, I should think, fully five seconds. I was lying down at the time, and the first intimation I got of the shock was by my couch being raised as if by a big dog underneath endeavouring to crawl from below, which was followed by an undulatory motion accompanied with a low rumbling noise and the shaking of everything in the room. A friend in the veranda was reclining in a long chair when it occurred, and to him it appeared to shake the house so much, that he jumped up almost expecting from the noise overhead that a portion of the roof had given way. If the noise is any indication of the earthquake's motion, I should judge it was travelling from north to south as the wardrobe was the first thing in my room to become fidgety, and when it had resumed its usual sedate manner the dressing-table seemed to have caught the infection, and began vibrating. There were two other slight shocks preceding the big one, hardly noticeable, however. A fellow resident says he actually saw the pillars in his house shaking. The natives say they have not had such a severe shock for the last eighteen years, when some people walking in the street were thrown on their faces."

In these three instances the action of the earthquakes was not violent. It would seem, however, from an account which Mr. Lowe, the American minister to China, forwarded in May, 1871, to the secretary of state at Washington, U.S.A., that on the 11th day of April of the same year there was a very violent earthquake in the province of Sze-chuen. Mr. Lowe's account of this earthquake, which I quote from *Nature*, June 22, 1871, is as follows :—

"Bathang lies on a very elevated spot beyond the province, about two hundred miles west of Li-Tang, and about thirty post stations from the district town of Ta-Tsien on the high road to Thibet. About eleven o'clock on the morning of the 11th of April, the earth at Bathang trembled so violently that the government offices, temples, granaries, stonehouses, storehouses, and fortifications, with all the common dwellings, and the temple of Ting-lin, were at once overthrown and ruined ; the only exception was the hall in the temple grounds called Ta-Chao, which stood unharmed in its isolation. A few of the troops and people escaped, but most of the inmates were crushed and killed under the falling timber and stone. Flames, also, suddenly burst out in four places, which strong winds drove about until the heavens were darkened with the smoke, and their roaring was mingled with the lamentations of the distressed people. On the 16th the flames were beaten down, but the rumbling noises were still heard under ground like distant thunder, as the earth rocked and rolled like a ship in a storm. The multiplied miseries of the afflicted inhabitants were increased by a thousand fears, but in about ten days matters began to grow quiet, and the motion of the earth to cease. The grain collector at Bathang says that for several days before the earthquake the water had overflowed the dikes, that the earth cracked in many places, and black fetid water spurted out in a furious manner. If one poked the earth, the spurting instantly followed just as is the case with the salt wells and fire wells in the eastern part of the province, and this explains how it happened that fire followed the earthquake in Bathang. As nearly as can be ascertained there were destroyed two large temples, the offices of the collector of grain-tax, the local magistrate's office, the Ting-lin temple, and nearly seven hundred fathoms of wall around it, and three hundred and fifty-one rooms in all inside ; six smaller temples, numbering two hundred and twenty-one rooms, besides one thousand eight hundred and forty-nine rooms and houses of the common people. The number of the people killed by the crash, including the soldiers, was two thousand two hundred and ninety-eight, among whom were the local magistrate and his second in office. The earthquake extended from Bathang, eastward to Pang-Cha-Hemuth, westward to Nan-tun, on the south of Lin-Tsah-Shih, and on the north to the salt wells at Atim-toz, a circuit of over four hundred miles. It occurred simultaneously over the whole of this region. In some places steep hills split and sunk into deep chasms, in others mounds on level plains became precipitous cliffs, and the roads and highways were rendered impassable by obstructions. The people were beggared and scattered like autumn leaves, and this calamity to the people of Bathang and the vicinity was really one of the most distressing and destructive that has ever occurred in China."

China, possessing as it does a great variety of surface, is rich both in minerals and in metals. Of coal there is evidently a very large supply in almost every part of the empire. In the province of Kwang-tung there are several coal districts, the principal and most important of which are in that portion of the province which is termed the Fa-yune district.

This coal is found in a number of low sandstone hills. In the autumn of 1861 I had the gratification of visiting the pits, four of which were close to one another. The shafts of three of them, though not of large circumference, were two hundred feet deep. They were, however, no longer of service, being full of water. At the fourth there were apparently no labourers. Upon expressing a wish to descend the shaft of this pit, I was informed that the ladders had been taken away. The shafts of mines in China are divided into several stories or lofts at intervals of twenty feet, and the pitmen pass and repass by means of ladders. In the same neighbourhood there was, on the side of a hill, another pit, which I found to be in the form of winding galleries of no great extent. The roofs of the galleries were supported by rafters of wood resting on pillars of the same material. Only a small number of hands were employed. The coal of this district appeared to be very inferior, its degree of inflammability being about that of culm or stone coal. Surface coal is also found in the immediate vicinity of Canton. At Fa-tee, a suburban district of the city, there are several large coal depots, which receive abundant supplies of surface coal from Yun-tuk, a city on the banks of the northern branch of the Canton river. The coal is conveyed in bullock carts to the banks of the river, and thence by boats to the depots.

At the town of Ki-lung, and more particularly at the coal harbour of that port in the island of Formosa, I also visited several coal pits. They are constructed in the form of galleries, and contain, apparently, much coal. The roofs of the galleries here are not supported by rafters and pillars of wood, but by pillars of earth or seams of coal, which for that purpose are left standing. While I was at Ki-lung, the pitmen engaged in contiguous pits inadvertently broke down a middle wall of partition, and unexpectedly found themselves face to face in the bowels of the earth. A fine seam of coal being at hand, a quarrel at once took place with regard to it, and many very severe blows were exchanged. Indeed, one of the combatants was so much injured that he died on reaching the pit mouth.

The coal mines in the neighbourhood of Ning-po, according to general account, are much more extensive than those which are in the more southern provinces. Coal is not at all in demand in China. It is used to some extent for smelting iron. At the town of Fat-shan, which is the Birmingham of the province of Kwang-tung, a great quantity of coal from the Fa-yune district is consumed. On my way from the northern province of Chi-li to Lama-Miou in inner Mongolia I passed several strings of camels carrying coals towards Pekin from extensive coal mines in the vicinity of Kiming. In the neighbourhood of this city I also saw strata of coal, sandstone, and shale alternating with seams of anthracite. I saw coal formations near the city of Suien-hwa-fa, formerly the summer residence of the emperors of Mongolia. At this stage of my journey I also saw porphyry in large quantities; and again at Chan-chee-kow.

In the vicinity of Newchang, in Mantchuria, there are also coal mines. The Newchang correspondent of the *Shanghai Courier*, in a letter dated April 3rd, 1872, writes regarding the Newchang coal mines in the following terms:—

"Some time ago I wrote you about coal being produced in this district. Since then I have tried many varieties. There is both bituminous and anthracite to be obtained at mines variously situated from eighty to one hundred and twenty miles from this port. The coal obtained from them supplies the city of Moukden and the surrounding district, besides being extensively used for iron smelting, there being a great number of furnaces in the vicinity of the coal and iron mines. The best coal comes from the district of Pin-Su-Hoo, about one hundred and twenty miles distant. It resembles Welsh coal, burning splendidly and giving great heat and no smoke. In fact, it is just such an article as you in Shanghai would appreciate, not only for steam, but for household purposes.

"The coal is brought all the way to this in carts, each carrying one-and-a-half to two tons, drawn by six ponies and guided by two men. It can be brought only in winter when the roads are hard, as in summer the roads of this plain are mere quagmires, and carts sink in the ruts up to the axles. When you consider the cost, keep, and loss on six animals, and the hire of two men for the trip which extends to four or five days, and the tear and wear of carts, it will be evident how greatly the carriage must add to the price of the coal. Yet it is sold here at $11.00; while the common kind, which requires a great draught, costs $8.00 per ton.

"At Pin-Su-Hoo there are seven mines worked by one Company. They employ about two thousand men in mining, bringing to the surface, weighing, loading, &c. Each of the coal-heavers brings to the surface two baskets containing about seventy catties each time, and in this cumbrous fashion they manage to get out about two hundred and fifty tons per day; but this lasts only during the cold season, or say four months each year. The pits are small, say from five to six feet thick and four to five feet wide, and the roof well shored up with piles. With larger cuttings, a steam donkey-engine, a tramway, cars, and a winch, the annual outcome could be so increased that they would fully supply the wants both of foreigners and natives. And as the heaviest element of price is the carriage to this port,

that also might be considerably lightened. Till better roads or
tramways, or a railroad (!) can be had, let the coal be conveyed
in winter to the side of the nearest creek and there stacked, and
when the rivers open let it be sent down here in flat boats, of
which there are many here. By this means the price might be
reduced to three-fourths or one-half of what it is at present.
All that is wanted is the authorization of the powers that be.
Capital could be easily got, and the rest would be easy work.

"At Lean Yang, about ninety or one hundred miles distant,
the mines produce bituminous coal. Iron ore is also abundant
in the neighbourhood, and much gold is said to exist in the
vicinity."

As coal is not used for domestic purposes, charcoal is in great
demand, and charcoal-burners are to be seen daily on the hills.
The hillsides of Pun-yu, Fa-yune, and Tsung-fa—districts of
Kwang-tung—are studded with their fires; and on the slopes of
the Lew-Shan range of mountains in Kiang-Si, the charcoal-
burners constitute the population of almost all the villages.
The houses of these labourers may be at once recognized by the
vast piles of charcoal in front of them.

In the island of Formosa there are numerous sulphur mines.
Large quantities of this combustible are brought to the mainland, where it meets with a ready sale, being much used by
the Chinese in bleaching, tanning, and dyeing, and in making
gunpowder and fire-crackers.

Amongst their most important minerals the Chinese place the
Yu-Shek or jadestone, which is regarded as of very great value.
It is chiefly used for decorations of dress. In one of the streets
of the western suburb of Canton lapidaries may be seen fashion-
ing this stone into earrings, finger-rings, hair-pins, bracelets,
brooches, and other ornaments. For such purposes the large
blocks of jade are cut into small pieces by means of wire-saws.

The country is also rich in metals. Mining operations, however, are not permitted to any great extent, as the government
entertain grave apprehensions that, if extensive discoveries were
made in this direction, large bands of robbers would at once
appear on the scene and prove a source of danger to the empire.
Government mines of gold and silver, however, exist, and are
evidently very productive, as both these metals are largely

circulated, not in the form of coins, but made into bars and shoes. The circulation of the precious metals is in a great measure confined to the governmental classes, as copper cash are especially the current coins of the realm. The Syae silver is considered superior to the silver of any other country in the world. The provinces of Yun-nan, Kwei-chow, and Sze-chuen are especially noted for their gold, silver, and copper mines. There is also an abundance of iron in the land. In 1862 I visited an iron mine in the neighbourhood of a village called Koo-teen, in the district or county of Tsung-fa. It was ninety English miles north-east from the provincial city of Canton. The mine, which is one hundred and twenty feet in depth, has been worked during a period of two centuries, but with no great diligence, as the mandarins restricted the proprietors to a certain quantity of iron ore annually. The present proprietor is an aged gentleman of the clan or family Soo. The mine, however, has not been worked for some time past in consequence of the principal local official having demanded a tax which the proprietor is either unwilling or unable to pay. With the view of extorting payment, the avaricious mandarin had put the son of Soo into prison. In close proximity are very extensive buildings containing all the necessary arrangements for the tedious processes by which the ore is rendered fit for use.

Before concluding this chapter I must say a few words on the climate. It has been very justly observed that it is remarkable for the singular excess in which heat and cold prevail in different parts of the empire at the opposite seasons of the year. The average of the thermometer is low for the latitude. Thus for example, although "Pekin is nearly a degree to the south of Naples, the latitude in the former place being 39° 54', of the latter, 40° 50', the mean temperature of Pekin is only 54° of Fahrenheit, while that of Naples is 63°. But, as the thermometer at the Chinese capital sinks much lower during the winter than at Naples, so in summer it rises somewhat higher. The rivers are frozen for three or four months together, from December to March, while, during the last embassy in September 1816, a heat of between 90° and 100° was experienced in the shade. It is well known that Naples and other countries in the extreme south of Europe are strangers to such a degree of long-continued cold, and are not often visited by such heats." In the southern provinces a fall of snow is almost unknown. It is nevertheless on record that in 1835 a snowstorm occurred at Canton. During my long residence at this port not a flake of snow fell, and very rarely indeed had we a shower of hail. As an illustration of a very severe winter in China, I may refer to that of 1871. So great was the cold at Canton on the 12th of December of that year, as to justify the conclusion that the tops of the mountains in the interior of the province were covered with snow. On several occasions during the same month, the many lotus and fish-ponds which are in the vicinity of the city were covered with sheets of ice of the thickness of a dollar. Many of the citizens in the humbler walks of life were to be seen entering the city in the morning with baskets on their shoulders containing ice for sale. The ice was readily purchased by the " upper ten thousand," and quickly deposited in earthen-ware jars, which were then hermetically sealed, ice-water being regarded by the Chinese as a certain specific in cases of fever of almost every kind. At Hongkong the winter of 1871 was, to judge from the description given of it in the *China Mail* of that date, certainly not less severe, and the oldest foreign residents there declared it to be the coldest season they had experienced in that city.

The mean annual temperature of Canton, which is just within the tropics, is what generally exists in the thirtieth parallel. The quantity of rain which falls throughout the year is generally very great, but it varies considerably. The average quantity which falls is, I believe, from sixty-eight to seventy-two inches. During the winter season, that is, from October to February, there is in the south an almost entire absence of rain. Towards the end of September, the north-east monsoon sets in, and continues until April. At this period, it is succeeded by the south-west monsoon, which is invariably accompanied by much rain. This, of course, is owing to the fact that the southern winds become impregnated with moisture in their course over tropical seas. On reaching the coast, the moisture assumes the form of thick fogs.

These are succeeded by heavy showers of rain, which of course
not only refresh the face of nature, but tend to some extent
to subdue the heat with which countries within and bordering
on the tropics are visited. At the summer solstice the sun at
Canton is almost vertical. The greatest heat of summer, however, is experienced during the months of July, August, and
September.

At the change of each monsoon thunderstorms are frequent.
They are not of long continuation, nor are they so severe as those
with which Great Britain is occasionally visited. During my
residence in the south of China, I remember one thunderstorm
only that was really terrific. A correspondent of the *Hongkong
Daily Press* of September 29, 1871, describes it in the following
terms :—

"On Friday night last, the 15th instant, this city (Canton)
was visited by a most violent thunderstorm. It continued
to rain throughout the greater part of the night, and so
long and heavy were the showers with which it was attended,
as to cause great destruction of household property. In the
Si-wa street of the Tartar quarter of the city, not to refer to
other places, ten houses were on this occasion destroyed. The
loss of life, however, in consequence of the falling of these
dwellings, was, I am glad to say, by no means great, one person
only, a Tartar youth of eight years of age, having been killed.
In many streets of the city and its suburbs, the water, in consequence of the heavy rains, rose to such a height as to inundate
the very houses. Moreover the streets being barricaded—as is
the case in all Chinese cities and towns by night—the water as
a matter of course, could not readily escape. During this same
thunderstorm, and also, in consequence of the heavy rains with
which it was accompanied, a portion of the large temple at
Honam fell to the earth with a great crash. The lightning,
however, as far as I can learn, does not appear to have done any
great amount of damage. It is reported, amongst other slight
casualties in this respect, that an old lady had the hair of her
head singed by the electric fluid. Whilst the storm lasted, it
appeared as if the four elements were at war with each other.
The roaring of the thunder was almost deafening, and the flashes
of lightning were so vivid and so uncomfortably near as to make
one apprehensive of danger. Towards its close there was a
strong wind from the north, which caused my house, and, I

suppose those of my neighbours, to rattle.   Such sudden squalls, however, have during the past few months been of so frequent occurrence as almost to accustom us and our houses to them. To Chinese boats they are oftentimes very fatal.   As, for example, the sudden blast of wind which I have just described, capsized, near the Dutch Folly, a boat in which were eight men and two women, of whom, it is said, nine were drowned."

Owing to the extreme rarefaction of the atmosphere throughout the course of the summer months, most violent storms of wind are of occasional occurrence.   One of the most terrible of these storms which I witnessed was that which occurred at Canton on the 27th of July, 1862.   On the 27th of September, 1871, Hong-kong and Macao were also visited by a typhoon, which almost equalled it in severity.   It is fortunate that such storms do not last longer than twenty-four hours.   These two storms were, if possible, surpassed in violence, and in the number of casualties which attended them, by a typhoon which visited Hongkong and Macao in the month of September, 1874.   According to the inhabitants this destructive cyclone was the greatest calamity which had befallen Hongkong and Macao within the memory of man.

INDEX.

INDEX.

A.

Abbot, the office of a Buddhist, i. 114; consecration of, 115—117; duties of, 117

Aborigines (Chap. XXXI.), subjugated by Yung-ching, ii. 302; slaughter of 40,000, 303; marriage customs, 303, 304; funeral rites, 305; a tribe offering human sacrifices, 306; a yearly festival, *ibid.*; bull-fights, 307; Nué-Koon, or woman-governed people, 307; employments of the aborigines, 308; tribes in Kwang-tung, 308, 309; in Formosa, 310; in Hai-nan, *ibid.*; regulations for the government of these, 311—313

Accoucheurs, i. 229 (*see* note)

Actors, low in the social scale, i. 378; their training, *ibid.*; how paid, 379

Adultery, a wife murdered on suspicion of, i. 223, 224; the law of summary vengeance in the case of, 224—226; other modes of punishing, 226—228

Adventures, personal; attacked at Tien-hshin, ii. 215; mobbed at Kow-hong, 228; visit to Kin-tee-ching in disguise, 234; mobbed at Shek-wan, 244; attacked at Yo-chow, 327; excursion in the north-west of Kwang-tung—captured by mountain robbers, 330—339

Aërolites, ii. 347

Aged men, of the class Fā-Koong, i. 215; respect paid to aged men, i. 272, 273; allowed to use walking-sticks, 376; use pipes with long stems for walking-sticks, ii. 149

Agricultural implements, ii. 114, 115

Agriculture: reclamation of waste lands, ii. 106; agricultural boards, 107; taxation, and sale of lands and houses, 108; farms and farmhouses, 111; agricultural implements, 114; festival in honour of spring, 115; festival in honour of Shin-Nung, 116; modes of irrigation, 118; manures, 121; ploughing and harrowing, 124; planting rice-shoots, 125; the rice harvest, 126; threshing, 127; winnowing, 128; granaries, 130; handmills, 131; crops of esculents, 132; tea-oil, 132; corn crops, 133; mill for grinding wheat, 134; millet, 134; grinding millet,135; bean farms, 135; pea farms, 137; pea-nuts, 137; the sugar-cane, 138; indigo, 140; cotton, 141; reeds, 143; cassia, 145; tobacco, 146; buffaloes, 151; the grunting ox, 152; milch cows, 153; Mongolian encampments, 155; treatment of cattle, 156; sheep, 159; goats, 164; swine, 165; horses, 170; mules and asses, 175; camels, 178; ducks, 180; geese, 185; hens, 187; pigeons, 188; fairs, 191

Agriculture, god of, ii. 116, 117

Agricultural boards, ii. 107

Alchemy, i. 98

Allied Commissioners at Canton, proclamation of, respecting torture, i. 37

Almanac, the official, ii. 14; prepared by the board of astrologers at Pekin, 15; distribution of copies, 16

Amusements and sports (Chap. XVI.): the stage, i. 377; marionettes, 382; musical entertainments, 383; pyrotechnic displays, 383; conjurors, athletes, ventriloquists, peep-shows, 384; gambling, various modes of, 385; cricket-fighting, 392; quail-fighting, 393; field sports, 395; athletics, 396; regattas, 397

Ancestors, worship of, i. 84, 85; consulted regarding a proposed marriage, 192, 193; titles of, carried in the marriage procession, 202; invoked to bless a newly-wedded couple, 209; worshipping at the tombs of, 320—322; repairing and decorating tombs of, 321; consulting spirits of, in time of trouble, 322.

Ancestral altars, funds connected with, i. 235; 274

Angling, ii. 296

Antiquity of Chinese Empire, i. 2

Shoo-King, ii. 141; early trade in, 142; cultivation of, introduced, 142; provinces in which it is grown, 142; mode of cultivation, 142, 143; harvest, 143; how separated from the seeds, 143; seed of, variously used, 143; processes to which it is subjected, 143; weaving, 143, 144; fabrics into which is made, 144; dyeing, 144

Counties, i. 5, 30

Cows, Chinese breed of, ii. 153; laws against slaughtering, 153; numerous in north of China and Mongolia, 155; treatment of sick, 157

Crane, the Mantchurian, ii. 316

Cremation, bodies of Buddhist priests usually disposed of by, i. 121; example of, 121, 122; history of, in China, 293, 294

Crickets, used in cricket-fighting, i. 392; how captured, 392; training of, 392; how matched, 393; successful fighters receive honourable interment, *ibid.;* cricket-pits, *ibid.;* stakes and prizes, *ibid.*

Crowns, placed on the dead, i. 281

D.

Days; lucky and unlucky, ii. 14, 15; regulating the direction in which one should go, 26; unlucky days, 26, 27

Dead-houses of prisons, i. 49

Deer, lucky animals, ii. 199

Deluge, in the reign of Yaou, i. 158

Detention, houses of, i. 53

Dinner, a Chinese, ii. 64, 65

District rulers, i. 29

Divorce, grounds of, i. 219; trial in an ancestral hall, 219, 220; fate of divorced wives, 220, 221; sometimes these are provided for, 221, 222; desertion on the part of a wife, 222; desertion on the part of a husband, 222, 223; a wife striking either of her parents-in-law, 223; unchastity, 223, 224; law of summary vengeance,224, 225; the working of this illustrated, 225, 226; other modes of punishing an adulterer and adulteress, 226, 227; adultery more heinous if committed between persons bearing the same surname, 228

Dogs, small black, used in exorcising, i. 336; used in hunting, 395; flesh of, eaten—how cooked, ii. 75; modes of killing, 76; flesh of, regarded as an antidote, *ibid.;* placards calling upon people not to eat the flesh of, 76, 77

Dogs' and cats' flesh restaurants, ii. 75, 76

Dreams, interpreters of, ii. 8; singular dream of Moo-ting, 8, 9; singular dream of Chow-man, 9, 10; dream of Confucius, 10; list of dreams, and their interpretations, 10–12; about articles of dress, 12; mode of averting the calamities betokened by a bad dream, 12, 13

Dress, of mandarins, i. 27—29; of Buddhist nuns, 132; of Buddhist priests, 368; of Taouist priests, 99, 368; of lamas, 134; of the upper classes, 364 —367; of literates, 367, 368; of οἱ πολλοί, 368, 369; of ladies, 369, 370

Ducks, worshippers of Hong-Yuen-Shuee refuse to eat or kill, ii. 180, 181; why sacred to this god, *ibid.;* breeds of, 181; mode of rearing, 181, 182, 183; establishments for artificially hatching the eggs of, 182, 183; boats for, 183; feeding on banks of rivers, 183, 184; establishments for salting, 184; mode of preserving eggs of, 184, 185

Dukes, i. 342

Dutch Auction, ii. 84

Dye-houses, ii. 144, 145

E.

Earls, i. 342, 343

Earthquakes, regarded with superstitious awe,ii.15, 351; the author's experience of, ii. 350, 351; earthquake at Chin-Kiang, 351, 352; violent earthquake at Bathang, 352, 353

Eclipses, record of ancient, i. 2; of the sun, i. 267, 268; of the moon, 268; regarded with superstitious feelings, 268; ii.15; official proclamations issued regarding, 16

Education, very general, i. 166; encouragement given to, by the state, 166; of women, 167; schools, 167, 168; children sent to school at the age of six, 168; choice of a schoolmaster, 168, 169; schoolboys, 169; schoolmasters, *ibid.;* course of instruction for school boys, 170; curriculum for the first or B.A. degree, 171; the B.A. examination, 172, 173; investing the successful competitors with their hoods and badges, 173, 174; great excitement on the publication of their names, 173, 174; visits of ceremony paid by them, 174; B.A.'s prepare at universities for the M.A. degree, *ibid.;* the M.A. examination, 174, 175; the clans of the successful competitors rejoice, 175; M.A.'s prepare at Pekin for the Han-lin, or LL.D. examination, 176; this is conducted in the Imperial Palace by the Emperor, *ibid.;* extraordinary interest taken in the double-first, 176, 177; conferring the Han-lin degree, 177; conditions with regard to the length of, and the mode of writing, examination papers, 177; the six modes of writing, 177; veneration for paper

END OF VOLUME II.

A CATALOG OF SELECTED
DOVER BOOKS
IN ALL FIELDS OF INTEREST

A CATALOG OF SELECTED DOVER
BOOKS IN ALL FIELDS OF INTEREST

CONCERNING THE SPIRITUAL IN ART, Wassily Kandinsky. Pioneering work by father of abstract art. Thoughts on color theory, nature of art. Analysis of earlier masters. 12 illustrations. 80pp. of text. 5⅜ x 8½. 23411-8

ANIMALS: 1,419 Copyright-Free Illustrations of Mammals, Birds, Fish, Insects, etc., Jim Harter (ed.). Clear wood engravings present, in extremely lifelike poses, over 1,000 species of animals. One of the most extensive pictorial sourcebooks of its kind. Captions. Index. 284pp. 9 x 12. 23766-4

CELTIC ART: The Methods of Construction, George Bain. Simple geometric techniques for making Celtic interlacements, spirals, Kells-type initials, animals, humans, etc. Over 500 illustrations. 160pp. 9 x 12. (Available in U.S. only.) 22923-8

AN ATLAS OF ANATOMY FOR ARTISTS, Fritz Schider. Most thorough reference work on art anatomy in the world. Hundreds of illustrations, including selections from works by Vesalius, Leonardo, Goya, Ingres, Michelangelo, others. 593 illustrations. 192pp. 7⅛ x 10¼. 20241-0

CELTIC HAND STROKE-BY-STROKE (Irish Half-Uncial from "The Book of Kells"): An Arthur Baker Calligraphy Manual, Arthur Baker. Complete guide to creating each letter of the alphabet in distinctive Celtic manner. Covers hand position, strokes, pens, inks, paper, more. Illustrated. 48pp. 8¼ x 11. 24336-2

EASY ORIGAMI, John Montroll. Charming collection of 32 projects (hat, cup, pelican, piano, swan, many more) specially designed for the novice origami hobbyist. Clearly illustrated easy-to-follow instructions insure that even beginning papercrafters will achieve successful results. 48pp. 8¼ x 11. 27298-2

THE COMPLETE BOOK OF BIRDHOUSE CONSTRUCTION FOR WOOD-WORKERS, Scott D. Campbell. Detailed instructions, illustrations, tables. Also data on bird habitat and instinct patterns. Bibliography. 3 tables. 63 illustrations in 15 figures. 48pp. 5¼ x 8½. 24407-5

BLOOMINGDALE'S ILLUSTRATED 1886 CATALOG: Fashions, Dry Goods and Housewares, Bloomingdale Brothers. Famed merchants' extremely rare catalog depicting about 1,700 products: clothing, housewares, firearms, dry goods, jewelry, more. Invaluable for dating, identifying vintage items. Also, copyright-free graphics for artists, designers. Co-published with Henry Ford Museum & Greenfield Village. 160pp. 8¼ x 11. 25780-0

HISTORIC COSTUME IN PICTURES, Braun & Schneider. Over 1,450 costumed figures in clearly detailed engravings–from dawn of civilization to end of 19th century. Captions. Many folk costumes. 256pp. 8⅜ x 11¾. 23150-X

FRANK LLOYD WRIGHT'S DANA HOUSE, Donald Hoffmann. Pictorial essay of residential masterpiece with over 160 interior and exterior photos, plans, elevations, sketches and studies. 128pp. 9¼ x 10¾. 29120-0

THE MALE AND FEMALE FIGURE IN MOTION: 60 Classic Photographic Sequences, Eadweard Muybridge. 60 true-action photographs of men and women walking, running, climbing, bending, turning, etc., reproduced from rare 19th-century masterpiece. vi + 121pp. 9 x 12. 24745-7

1001 QUESTIONS ANSWERED ABOUT THE SEASHORE, N. J. Berrill and Jacquelyn Berrill. Queries answered about dolphins, sea snails, sponges, starfish, fishes, shore birds, many others. Covers appearance, breeding, growth, feeding, much more. 305pp. 5¼ x 8¼. 23366-9

ATTRACTING BIRDS TO YOUR YARD, William J. Weber. Easy-to-follow guide offers advice on how to attract the greatest diversity of birds: birdhouses, feeders, water and waterers, much more. 96pp. 5³⁄₁₆ x 8¼. 28927-3

MEDICINAL AND OTHER USES OF NORTH AMERICAN PLANTS: A Historical Survey with Special Reference to the Eastern Indian Tribes, Charlotte Erichsen-Brown. Chronological historical citations document 500 years of usage of plants, trees, shrubs native to eastern Canada, northeastern U.S. Also complete identifying information. 343 illustrations. 544pp. 6½ x 9¼. 25951-X

STORYBOOK MAZES, Dave Phillips. 23 stories and mazes on two-page spreads: Wizard of Oz, Treasure Island, Robin Hood, etc. Solutions. 64pp. 8¼ x 11. 23628-5

AMERICAN NEGRO SONGS: 230 Folk Songs and Spirituals, Religious and Secular, John W. Work. This authoritative study traces the African influences of songs sung and played by black Americans at work, in church, and as entertainment. The author discusses the lyric significance of such songs as "Swing Low, Sweet Chariot," "John Henry," and others and offers the words and music for 230 songs. Bibliography. Index of Song Titles. 272pp. 6½ x 9¼. 40271-1

MOVIE-STAR PORTRAITS OF THE FORTIES, John Kobal (ed.). 163 glamor, studio photos of 106 stars of the 1940s: Rita Hayworth, Ava Gardner, Marlon Brando, Clark Gable, many more. 176pp. 8⅜ x 11¼. 23546-7

BENCHLEY LOST AND FOUND, Robert Benchley. Finest humor from early 30s, about pet peeves, child psychologists, post office and others. Mostly unavailable elsewhere. 73 illustrations by Peter Arno and others. 183pp. 5⅜ x 8½. 22410-4

YEKL and THE IMPORTED BRIDEGROOM AND OTHER STORIES OF YIDDISH NEW YORK, Abraham Cahan. Film Hester Street based on *Yekl* (1896). Novel, other stories among first about Jewish immigrants on N.Y.'s East Side. 240pp. 5⅜ x 8½. 22427-9

SELECTED POEMS, Walt Whitman. Generous sampling from *Leaves of Grass*. Twenty-four poems include "I Hear America Singing," "Song of the Open Road," "I Sing the Body Electric," "When Lilacs Last in the Dooryard Bloom'd," "O Captain! My Captain!"–all reprinted from an authoritative edition. Lists of titles and first lines. 128pp. 5³⁄₁₆ x 8¼. 26878-0

THE BEST TALES OF HOFFMANN, E. T. A. Hoffmann. 10 of Hoffmann's most important stories: "Nutcracker and the King of Mice," "The Golden Flowerpot," etc. 458pp. 5⅜ x 8½.   21793-0

FROM FETISH TO GOD IN ANCIENT EGYPT, E. A. Wallis Budge. Rich detailed survey of Egyptian conception of "God" and gods, magic, cult of animals, Osiris, more. Also, superb English translations of hymns and legends. 240 illustrations. 545pp. 5⅜ x 8½.   25803-3

FRENCH STORIES/CONTES FRANÇAIS: A Dual-Language Book, Wallace Fowlie. Ten stories by French masters, Voltaire to Camus: "Micromegas" by Voltaire; "The Atheist's Mass" by Balzac; "Minuet" by de Maupassant; "The Guest" by Camus, six more. Excellent English translations on facing pages. Also French-English vocabulary list, exercises, more. 352pp. 5⅜ x 8½.   26443-2

CHICAGO AT THE TURN OF THE CENTURY IN PHOTOGRAPHS: 122 Historic Views from the Collections of the Chicago Historical Society, Larry A. Viskochil. Rare large-format prints offer detailed views of City Hall, State Street, the Loop, Hull House, Union Station, many other landmarks, circa 1904-1913. Introduction. Captions. Maps. 144pp. 9⅜ x 12¼.   24656-6

OLD BROOKLYN IN EARLY PHOTOGRAPHS, 1865-1929, William Lee Younger. Luna Park, Gravesend race track, construction of Grand Army Plaza, moving of Hotel Brighton, etc. 157 previously unpublished photographs. 165pp. 8⅞ x 11¾.   23587-4

THE MYTHS OF THE NORTH AMERICAN INDIANS, Lewis Spence. Rich anthology of the myths and legends of the Algonquins, Iroquois, Pawnees and Sioux, prefaced by an extensive historical and ethnological commentary. 36 illustrations. 480pp. 5⅜ x 8½.   25967-6

AN ENCYCLOPEDIA OF BATTLES: Accounts of Over 1,560 Battles from 1479 B.C. to the Present, David Eggenberger. Essential details of every major battle in recorded history from the first battle of Megiddo in 1479 B.C. to Grenada in 1984. List of Battle Maps. New Appendix covering the years 1967-1984. Index. 99 illustrations. 544pp. 6½ x 9¼.   24913-1

SAILING ALONE AROUND THE WORLD, Captain Joshua Slocum. First man to sail around the world, alone, in small boat. One of great feats of seamanship told in delightful manner. 67 illustrations. 294pp. 5⅜ x 8½.   20326-3

ANARCHISM AND OTHER ESSAYS, Emma Goldman. Powerful, penetrating, prophetic essays on direct action, role of minorities, prison reform, puritan hypocrisy, violence, etc. 271pp. 5⅜ x 8½.   22484-8

MYTHS OF THE HINDUS AND BUDDHISTS, Ananda K. Coomaraswamy and Sister Nivedita. Great stories of the epics; deeds of Krishna, Shiva, taken from puranas, Vedas, folk tales; etc. 32 illustrations. 400pp. 5⅜ x 8½.   21759-0

THE TRAUMA OF BIRTH, Otto Rank. Rank's controversial thesis that anxiety neurosis is caused by profound psychological trauma which occurs at birth. 256pp. 5⅜ x 8½.   27974-X

A THEOLOGICO-POLITICAL TREATISE, Benedict Spinoza. Also contains unfinished Political Treatise. Great classic on religious liberty, theory of government on common consent. R. Elwes translation. Total of 421pp. 5⅜ x 8½.   20249-6

MY BONDAGE AND MY FREEDOM, Frederick Douglass. Born a slave, Douglass became outspoken force in antislavery movement. The best of Douglass' autobiographies. Graphic description of slave life. 464pp. 5⅜ x 8½. 22457-0

FOLLOWING THE EQUATOR: A Journey Around the World, Mark Twain. Fascinating humorous account of 1897 voyage to Hawaii, Australia, India, New Zealand, etc. Ironic, bemused reports on peoples, customs, climate, flora and fauna, politics, much more. 197 illustrations. 720pp. 5⅜ x 8½. 26113-1

THE PEOPLE CALLED SHAKERS, Edward D. Andrews. Definitive study of Shakers: origins, beliefs, practices, dances, social organization, furniture and crafts, etc. 33 illustrations. 351pp. 5⅜ x 8½. 21081-2

THE MYTHS OF GREECE AND ROME, H. A. Guerber. A classic of mythology, generously illustrated, long prized for its simple, graphic, accurate retelling of the principal myths of Greece and Rome, and for its commentary on their origins and significance. With 64 illustrations by Michelangelo, Raphael, Titian, Rubens, Canova, Bernini and others. 480pp. 5⅜ x 8½. 27584-1

PSYCHOLOGY OF MUSIC, Carl E. Seashore. Classic work discusses music as a medium from psychological viewpoint. Clear treatment of physical acoustics, auditory apparatus, sound perception, development of musical skills, nature of musical feeling, host of other topics. 88 figures. 408pp. 5⅜ x 8½. 21851-1

THE PHILOSOPHY OF HISTORY, Georg W. Hegel. Great classic of Western thought develops concept that history is not chance but rational process, the evolution of freedom. 457pp. 5⅜ x 8½. 20112-0

THE BOOK OF TEA, Kakuzo Okakura. Minor classic of the Orient: entertaining, charming explanation, interpretation of traditional Japanese culture in terms of tea ceremony. 94pp. 5⅜ x 8½. 20070-1

LIFE IN ANCIENT EGYPT, Adolf Erman. Fullest, most thorough, detailed older account with much not in more recent books, domestic life, religion, magic, medicine, commerce, much more. Many illustrations reproduce tomb paintings, carvings, hieroglyphs, etc. 597pp. 5⅜ x 8½. 22632-8

SUNDIALS, Their Theory and Construction, Albert Waugh. Far and away the best, most thorough coverage of ideas, mathematics concerned, types, construction, adjusting anywhere. Simple, nontechnical treatment allows even children to build several of these dials. Over 100 illustrations. 230pp. 5⅜ x 8½. 22947-5

THEORETICAL HYDRODYNAMICS, L. M. Milne-Thomson. Classic exposition of the mathematical theory of fluid motion, applicable to both hydrodynamics and aerodynamics. Over 600 exercises. 768pp. 6⅛ x 9¼. 68970-0

SONGS OF EXPERIENCE: Facsimile Reproduction with 26 Plates in Full Color, William Blake. 26 full-color plates from a rare 1826 edition. Includes "The Tyger," "London," "Holy Thursday," and other poems. Printed text of poems. 48pp. 5¼ x 7. 24636-1

OLD-TIME VIGNETTES IN FULL COLOR, Carol Belanger Grafton (ed.). Over 390 charming, often sentimental illustrations, selected from archives of Victorian graphics—pretty women posing, children playing, food, flowers, kittens and puppies, smiling cherubs, birds and butterflies, much more. All copyright-free. 48pp. 9¼ x 12¼. 27269-9

PERSPECTIVE FOR ARTISTS, Rex Vicat Cole. Depth, perspective of sky and sea, shadows, much more, not usually covered. 391 diagrams, 81 reproductions of drawings and paintings. 279pp. 5⅜ x 8½. 22487-2

DRAWING THE LIVING FIGURE, Joseph Sheppard. Innovative approach to artistic anatomy focuses on specifics of surface anatomy, rather than muscles and bones. Over 170 drawings of live models in front, back and side views, and in widely varying poses. Accompanying diagrams. 177 illustrations. Introduction. Index. 144pp. 8⅜ x11¼. 26723-7

GOTHIC AND OLD ENGLISH ALPHABETS: 100 Complete Fonts, Dan X. Solo. Add power, elegance to posters, signs, other graphics with 100 stunning copyright-free alphabets: Blackstone, Dolbey, Germania, 97 more–including many lower-case, numerals, punctuation marks. 104pp. 8⅛ x 11. 24695-7

HOW TO DO BEADWORK, Mary White. Fundamental book on craft from simple projects to five-bead chains and woven works. 106 illustrations. 142pp. 5⅜ x 8. 20697-1

THE BOOK OF WOOD CARVING, Charles Marshall Sayers. Finest book for beginners discusses fundamentals and offers 34 designs. "Absolutely first rate . . . well thought out and well executed."–E. J. Tangerman. 118pp. 7¾ x 10⅝. 23654-4

ILLUSTRATED CATALOG OF CIVIL WAR MILITARY GOODS: Union Army Weapons, Insignia, Uniform Accessories, and Other Equipment, Schuyler, Hartley, and Graham. Rare, profusely illustrated 1846 catalog includes Union Army uniform and dress regulations, arms and ammunition, coats, insignia, flags, swords, rifles, etc. 226 illustrations. 160pp. 9 x 12. 24939-5

WOMEN'S FASHIONS OF THE EARLY 1900s: An Unabridged Republication of "New York Fashions, 1909," National Cloak & Suit Co. Rare catalog of mail-order fashions documents women's and children's clothing styles shortly after the turn of the century. Captions offer full descriptions, prices. Invaluable resource for fashion, costume historians. Approximately 725 illustrations. 128pp. 8⅜ x 11¼. 27276-1

THE 1912 AND 1915 GUSTAV STICKLEY FURNITURE CATALOGS, Gustav Stickley. With over 200 detailed illustrations and descriptions, these two catalogs are essential reading and reference materials and identification guides for Stickley furniture. Captions cite materials, dimensions and prices. 112pp. 6½ x 9¼. 26676-1

EARLY AMERICAN LOCOMOTIVES, John H. White, Jr. Finest locomotive engravings from early 19th century: historical (1804–74), main-line (after 1870), special, foreign, etc. 147 plates. 142pp. 11⅜ x 8¼. 22772-3

THE TALL SHIPS OF TODAY IN PHOTOGRAPHS, Frank O. Braynard. Lavishly illustrated tribute to nearly 100 majestic contemporary sailing vessels: Amerigo Vespucci, Clearwater, Constitution, Eagle, Mayflower, Sea Cloud, Victory, many more. Authoritative captions provide statistics, background on each ship. 190 black-and-white photographs and illustrations. Introduction. 128pp. 8⅞ x 11¾. 27163-3

CATALOG OF DOVER BOOKS

THE STORY OF THE TITANIC AS TOLD BY ITS SURVIVORS, Jack Winocour (ed.). What it was really like. Panic, despair, shocking inefficiency, and a little heroism. More thrilling than any fictional account. 26 illustrations. 320pp. 5⅜ x 8½.
20610-6

FAIRY AND FOLK TALES OF THE IRISH PEASANTRY, William Butler Yeats (ed.). Treasury of 64 tales from the twilight world of Celtic myth and legend: "The Soul Cages," "The Kildare Pooka," "King O'Toole and his Goose," many more. Introduction and Notes by W. B. Yeats. 352pp. 5⅜ x 8½.
26941-8

BUDDHIST MAHAYANA TEXTS, E. B. Cowell and others (eds.). Superb, accurate translations of basic documents in Mahayana Buddhism, highly important in history of religions. The Buddha-karita of Asvaghosha, Larger Sukhavativyuha, more. 448pp. 5⅜ x 8½.
25552-2

ONE TWO THREE . . . INFINITY: Facts and Speculations of Science, George Gamow. Great physicist's fascinating, readable overview of contemporary science: number theory, relativity, fourth dimension, entropy, genes, atomic structure, much more. 128 illustrations. Index. 352pp. 5⅜ x 8½.
25664-2

EXPERIMENTATION AND MEASUREMENT, W. J. Youden. Introductory manual explains laws of measurement in simple terms and offers tips for achieving accuracy and minimizing errors. Mathematics of measurement, use of instruments, experimenting with machines. 1994 edition. Foreword. Preface. Introduction. Epilogue. Selected Readings. Glossary. Index. Tables and figures. 128pp. 5⅜ x 8½.   40451-X

DALÍ ON MODERN ART: The Cuckolds of Antiquated Modern Art, Salvador Dalí. Influential painter skewers modern art and its practitioners. Outrageous evaluations of Picasso, Cézanne, Turner, more. 15 renderings of paintings discussed. 44 calligraphic decorations by Dalí. 96pp. 5⅜ x 8½. (Available in U.S. only.)
29220-7

ANTIQUE PLAYING CARDS: A Pictorial History, Henry René D'Allemagne. Over 900 elaborate, decorative images from rare playing cards (14th–20th centuries): Bacchus, death, dancing dogs, hunting scenes, royal coats of arms, players cheating, much more. 96pp. 9¼ x 12¼.
29265-7

MAKING FURNITURE MASTERPIECES: 30 Projects with Measured Drawings, Franklin H. Gottshall. Step-by-step instructions, illustrations for constructing handsome, useful pieces, among them a Sheraton desk, Chippendale chair, Spanish desk, Queen Anne table and a William and Mary dressing mirror. 224pp. 8⅛ x 11¼.
29338-6

THE FOSSIL BOOK: A Record of Prehistoric Life, Patricia V. Rich et al. Profusely illustrated definitive guide covers everything from single-celled organisms and dinosaurs to birds and mammals and the interplay between climate and man. Over 1,500 illustrations. 760pp. 7½ x 10⅛.
29371-8